Published under the auspices of
The Center for Japanese Studies
University of California, Berkeley

Heritage of Endurance

HIROSHI WAGATSUMA
and GEORGE A. DE VOS

Heritage of Endurance

Family Patterns and Delinquency Formation in Urban Japan

UNIVERSITY OF CALIFORNIA PRESS
Berkeley · Los Angeles · London

University of California Press
Berkeley and Los Angeles, California

University of California Press, Ltd.
London, England

Printed in the United States of America

1 2 3 4 5 6 7 8 9

Library of Congress Cataloging in Publication Data

Wagatsuma, Hiroshi, 1927–
Heritage of endurance.
Family patterns and delinquency formation in urban Japan.

Bibliography: p.
Includes index.
1. Juvenile delinquency—Japan—Tokyo—Psychological aspects. 2. Family—Japan—Tokyo—Psychological aspects. 3. Personality and culture—Japan—Tokyo.
I. De Vos, George. II. Title.
HV9207.A5W33 1983 364.3′6′0952135 76-7770
ISBN 0-520-03222-5

Contents

Tables

Preface

Our fieldwork on delinquency in Japan began in 1962, the third year of a more general cross-cultural study involving a survey of the previous sociological and psychological studies in Japan. We then developed our own research plan, which sought to test specifically some of the conclusions of American and European research concerning the contribution of primary socialization and interpersonal relationships within the family to various forms of deviant behavior. Through an intensive contact with the parents of delinquent Japanese youth, as well as with the youths themselves, we hoped to gain substantiating or contradictory evidence concerning interpersonal family processes from outside a Western tradition. We set up an experimental design intensively investigating a group of fifty families, thirty with a son who gave evidence of what is considered antisocial behavior. These thirty cases were matched with a control sample of twenty families of similar socioeconomic backgrounds but with a nondelinquent son.

As the intensive work with the fifty families progressed, De Vos and Wagatsuma interviewed a large number of professional people, such as policemen, teachers, social workers, and merchants, in Arakawa Ward. They were most cooperative and helpful to us in more ways than we can say. Some, in turn, introduced us to other knowledgeable members of the community. We conducted subsequent interviews with members of special groups, such as volunteer probation personnel. We also did further interviews with artisans groups, such as those engaged in the production of pencils. In addition to such formal, purposeful interviewing, our sustained social contact and observation during parts of several years until 1968 contributed heavily to our gradual understanding of the way of life of the Arakawa people.

The authors owe gratitude to a large number of individuals, residents of Arakawa Ward in Tokyo, who agreed to have their life histories used by us as the major data on which this volume is based. They must remain anonymous. All the names of families that appear in our case studies are pseudonyms. Unavoidably, given the large number of households in a community of more than 250,000 people, some pseudonyms happen to be the names of others who live in Arakawa.

It is possible, however, to acknowledge by name some others who through their professional roles were especially helpful to us. We should like to apologize to others whose names should have received mention, but who may have been overlooked in the course of our more than ten years' work.

In setting up our project and organizing our team of interviewers, we owe a great deal to the generous help of the following: Judge Yorihiro Naito, then the Secretary to the Supreme Court of Japan; the late Judge Junshiro Udagawa, then the Director of the Research and Training Institute for Family Court Research Officers; Mr. Seiroku Tanaka, then the Director of the Tokyo Central Child Guidance Clinic; and the members of the Educational Commission of the Tokyo Municipal Government.

For organizing and supervising the interviewers for our family cases we are especially grateful to Professor Keiichi Mizushima of Rissho Women's College, then counseling psychologist at the Tokyo Central Guidance Clinic, who was responsible for much of the initial survey of research and initial organization of the project.

Tetsuo Okado at St. Luke's College of Nursing, then a staff member of the Research and Training Institute for Family Court Research Officers, helped in a supervisory capacity. For collecting family case materials, in addition to the authors' own efforts, the dedicated work of the following interviewers was invaluable: Sachiko Aiba (formerly Fujita), Hiroshi Akō, Yūko Baba, Tomoko Fujishiro, Kazuko Fukumitsu (formerly Kuchi), Tomoko Kinjo, Eiko Kojima, Atsuko Maejima, Rumiko Mukōmachi, Etsuko Nakamura, Kenzō Sorai, Shirō Takemasa, Hisako Tanemura (formerly Takano), Tokuhiro Tatezawa, and Kazuko Yamada.

During our data-gathering efforts, from 1961 to 1968, the authors and the interviewers were helped by the kindness and counsel of a number of professional workers who also resided in the community. Mrs. Kuni Hirayama and Toshiko Terashima introduced us to various community activities. We also appreciated the help rendered by Messrs. Nuinosuke Hayasaka, Shinichi Hironaka, Shigeru Ishiwara, Hoshio Itō, Eiichirō Kawazumi, Toshio Kobayashi, Naoyuki Kozu, Kanjiro Kudo, Tatsuzo Kushihashi, Shoichi Kuwana, Yasuhei Matsumoto, Mrs. Sen Miyamoto, Messrs. Takeji Muraoka, Shōtarō Nose, Takeo Ōtani, Hitisgu Saitō, Tokumatsu Sakurai, Kanjirō Sasaki, Yoshio Suzuki, Toshi Tabata, Koji Tateno, and Masao Yamamoto.

When the analysis of our fifty-family data was in progress at the Institute of Human Development at the University of California, Berkeley, from 1962 to 1965, we were assisted by our able research staff: Sachiko Aiba, Tōyō Ichikawa, Takao Murase, Pulin Garg, and Takako Sankawa. When our project was located at the Social Science Research Institute at the University of Hawaii in 1967, we had the assistance of Mrs. Bobbie Sandoz.

Both authors conducted a series of research seminars at the University of California with the graduate students at the School of Social Welfare, using part of our family case materials. These students contributed much to the analysis of the cases. In a 1962–1963 seminar conducted by De Vos, the students who worked on the data were Kenneth A. Abbott, Karen L. Dollings, David R.

Huerta, Deanna L. Lott, Margaret MacDonald, Gordon H. Nagai, Esther T. Sugg, George Turman, Mary Lou Valencia, Syed Waliuliah, Charles D. Whitchurch and Michiko Yamazaki. In 1963–1964 seminars conducted by Wagatsuma, the students were Barbara Bandfield, the late Judith Gold, and Sidney Goldstein, Maureen Grinnell, Dorothy Hoefer, Edward Hoshino, David Jensen, Hilda Kaplan, Margaret Knisely, Stratton Pierce, Alexandra Robbins, Robert Simon, Marie Skopal, Reiko True, and Barbara Ulery. In Wagatsuma's seminars in 1964–1965 the students were Lili Becker, Maureen Fisher, Bonnie Fugitt, Sabine Jospe, Anna Ofman, Syng Hyok Park, Cornelia Scovill, and La Verne Titus. In De Vos's 1964–1965 seminars the students were Joanne Backer, Madeline Berke, Carole Chanin, Hester Cohen, Karen Faircloth, Harriet Hailpern, Margaret Karn, and Patricia Snyder.

We should also mention the names of our assistants in various stages of our project: Jill Weyrauch, Carolyn Kohler, Suzanne Allen, Kathleen Wilson, Frances Hammond, Felicia Hance, Kim Johnson, Debbie Bilskey, Florence Cho, June Onodera, and Cynthia Cole, Virginia Enscoe, Janice Jastrebski, Frances Mavrodis, Josephine Stagno, Carol Walker, Donna Yakelis, and Miriam Warner. Mrs. Onodera with patience and goodwill performed the vital role of both preparing manuscript and coordinating the efforts of the authors, who were constrained to work at a distance from each other. We were fortunate to have Mrs. Ann Brower exert her considerable editorial talent to the improvement of the initial manuscript. Subsequently, Mrs. Grace Buzaljko, editor for the Department of Anthropology, University of California, Berkeley, was invaluable in later stages of preparation. Special thanks are due for the expert editorial assistance provided by Grant Barnes, Gladys Castor, and Phyllis Killen of the University of California Press.

Last but not least, we should like to express our gratitude to Mrs. Kiyoji Ichimura, Mrs. K. Tomono, and Mrs. Midori Wagatsuma, whose personal kindness and generosity enabled the authors to work together on the data in Tokyo and in Karuizawa in the summers of 1966 and 1968.

A note of gratitude to Karel Von Wolferen, gifted photographer and longtime observer of the Japanese scene, whose acute comments sharpened the theoretical discussions found in the various chapters.

The writing of this volume began in 1967 after the end of eight years of sponsorship by grant number MH 04087-07S1 of the National Institute of Mental Health, under which we conducted "Comparative Research on Delinquency" at the Institute of Human Development at the University of California, Berkeley from 1960 through 1967. After 1966 we received various additional sponsorship from the Social Science Research Institute of the University of Hawaii; the Center for Japanese and Korean Studies and the Institute of Personality Assessment and Research of the University of California, Berkeley; and the Center for East Asian Studies, University of Pittsburgh.

We wish to acknowledge, too, the support of The Japan Foundation of

Tokyo, which provided a subsidy toward the publication of this book. The Foundation, through its Publication Assistance Program, promotes the publication of works, in languages other than Japanese, that will contribute to a deeper understanding of Japan and its culture.

At one phase of our research, we had the intention to publish a work in two volumes: one on our specific family research and one that separately documented the life and social functions of the city ward we were studying, a community in transition. However, the exigencies of production costs in the contemporary publishing industry have forced us to cut back our primary research material on the community to that presentable in a single volume on both family life and community functioning. We hope that a need to delete documentation on a number of topics, as well as to delete some issues considered in our fieldwork efforts, will not reduce the cogency of our major contentions about community control of delinquency in contemporary Japan. We have kept our main focus on the fifty families in our study and on the intensive methods of observation and testing used, and we choose to give our case histories the full representation they deserve. Adequate demonstration of our results cannot be reduced to statistical tables. We wish to have our readers understand the "heritage of endurance" as well as possible by sharing with us the rich experience of our interviews.

Introduction

In approaching deviant behavior from a cross-cultural or an anthropological standpoint, two different forms of interdisciplinary research are possible. One approach is to attempt a form of comparative sociology in which the investigation is guided by a comparison of social-structural determinants as they influence behavior considered to be deviant within a given culture. A second possible form is "psychocultural"; that is, the anthropologist can examine psychological variables that influence the advent of deviant behavior. In effect, the anthropologist can bring to the comparative study of deviancy the controversies already found in American social sciences, in which professionals who place the cause of delinquency in general social conditions are frequently opposed to those who take a psychodynamic point of view.

In its present form this volume may seem to emphasize the latter approach. It is specifically concerned with intrafamily relationships and the genesis of deviant social attitudes within given youth in comparison with others who live in the same lower-class urban environment. It is a study of family influences on the genesis of delinquency as a form of deviant behavior, using Japan as a comparative instance. It might be interpreted by some, therefore, as an espousal of a psychodynamic approach over a sociological one, but this is not our intention. The fact that we are concerned with psychological determinants does not preclude our acknowledgment of the basic influence of adverse economic conditions or the effects of discrimination and other forms of oppression on impoverished segments of society as major determinants of what is considered to be criminal or other forms of deviant behavior.

For the sociologist, the determinants of delinquency are most frequently seen to emanate from the external situation with which one finds families attempting to cope. It is not surprising to find that a "situational" approach still characterizes many social science explanations in both Japan and the United States. Differences in the family life or in cultural traditions among those meeting with hardship or oppression are considered secondary to economic and social pressures. Indeed, such pressures have often been statistically correlated with the occurrence of delinquency in a particular class or in particular racial or ethnic segments of American society.

A psychocultural approach does not deny the determining influence of such social-structural factors. Indeed, it is concerned with social structure as part of cultural continuity in the appearance of both conforming and deviant behavior. However, it does emphasize that explanations for socially deviant behavior involve to some degree the particular psychological mechanisms and social attitudes resulting from the basic socialization process within given families of given cultures in contrast with others.

Psychoanalytically oriented psychotherapy has provided us with some intimate insights into how psychological defenses result from problems occurring in early socialization. A purely psychoanalytic approach, however, tends to emphasize the vicissitudes of the individual and neglects to perceive the family as a continuously interacting unit functioning with varying degrees of difficulty within a particular culture or subculture. It often also neglects the basic influence of peer groups and social conditions on socialization.

We contend that a more general psychocultural approach attempts to treat the family as part of a subcultural system in a complex society. It pays greater attention to the presence of sociological variables, such as class or minority status, as they interact with the psychological processes at work within the primary family.

The history of research on delinquency in Japan generally parallels that in America. In early psychiatric and psychological studies of family lineage done in the United States, such as the well-known studies of the Jukes and the Kallikaks, heredity was considered a principal factor in causing deviance. These studies and others had notable influence on early studies in Japan until World War II. In the postwar era, however, a more environmental approach to delinquency has come to have almost total ascendancy. Today, both Japanese and American social scientists generally accept the notion that the family as a social unit, rather than genetic endowment, serves as the principal agency of socialization. However, there is no consensus on how personality, normal or maladjusted, or social attitudes, deviant or conformist, are generated within the matrix of the family. There is a wide variety of possible psychological and sociological explanations in the published literature.

In their interpretation of the cause of delinquency, sociological theorists in Japan, like their American counterparts, have opposed both strongly psychological interpretations of family processes and the older concern with biological heredity. They have sought instead to demonstrate how adverse socioeconomic conditions are the principal cause of delinquency. The earlier sociological literature in Japan as well as in the United States focused heavily on poverty as the chief source of crime within society. In earlier studies, both psychological and sociological approaches often failed to examine the internal dynamics of family life itself.

We chose to work in Arakawa Ward as an integral part of Tokyo which reflects various community and family processes that contribute to the overall low rates of delinquency in Japan. These processes differ radically from those affecting patterns of delinquency in the American city. We have published elsewhere some of our specific findings on delinquency in Japan;[1] a brief history of Arakawa (Wagatsuma and De Vos, 1980); and a study of the attitudes of the artisans who constitute the bottom segment of Japan's dual economy (De Vos, 1973, pp. 201–219). We may yet write a more general work on the complex results obtained by Japanese social scientists who have been conducting research on delinquency in Japan with a wide panoply of methods and approaches, ranging from the measurement of individuals' brain waves to the recording of general statistics on crime and delinquency reported over the past fifty years.

The concentration in this book is narrowed down to our intensive research with fifty families in Arakawa Ward. Yet we feel impelled to put these results in a general community context. Hence Part One of this volume consists of a brief description of the ward and an overview of some of the social organizational forces at work that help explain the generally low delinquency rate found in Japan compared with any other industrial state. In Parts Two and Three we present our research findings, which document our evidence for the genesis of delinquent attitudes in Japanese family life. In Part Four we attempt to set these findings within a cross-cultural context as well as in the broader context of the forces of social control operative generally in the contemporary social life of Japan.

In our own study design, described in chapter 3, we have paid more attention to the parents of the delinquent boys and their interaction with each other than have most previous studies. In chapter 4, we examine the findings of our own intensive research in the context of previous family studies in Japan, Britain, and the United States in which various explanations have been used in attempts to trace the highly complex relation among factors in delinquency formation. In the subsequent chapters of Part Two we present a more detailed analysis of the salient features of family life that contribute to the selective appearance of delinquency in some children. We consider why personality variables per se are not the most salient explanation, and how and why family interaction patterns stimulate deviant social attitudes in some boys rather than others. In Part Three, in our detailed life-history materials on four selected families, we illustrate the interpersonal dynamics of these families, and we also illustrate indirectly some patterns of social control operative in the community.

In our detailed psychocultural analysis of fifty families in Parts Two and Three, we believe we have been able to substantiate in detail sufficient significant differences between the families of delinquent subjects and other families to make a contribution to present-day knowledge concerning the origins of deviant behavior in a cross-cultural perspective.

We found that people living in Arakawa have distinct social ideals and some unique traditions. These traditions have contributed to an integrative sense of special social belonging to an artisan and merchant subculture, which made it feasible to study the ward as a viable unit of analysis. In particular, atti-

1. See De Vos, 1973, especially chapters 10, 11, 12, and 13.

tudes of these people toward work and achievement are somewhat peculiarly Japanese. Though they are situated within what are considered to be the lower segments of a modern social-class structure, many of them are peculiarly "entrepreneurial" or capitalistic in attitude (De Vos, 1973, chapter 8). The life-history materials published in this volume provide rich data on culturally prevalent attitudes toward work, toward the acquisition of technological competence, and toward achievement. These data reflect motivational patterns influencing the direction and rate of social change occurring generally in Japan. In their descriptions of their parents and themselves, individuals provided us with much spontaneous material that went beyond that specifically relevant to delinquency.

In our conclusions in Part Four we come full circle. The amount and kind of delinquency appearing in Japan, as elsewhere, can be considered a social symptom. If it is, one reason for the low rate of delinquency in contemporary urban Japan is to be found in a continuity of culture. The patterning of Japanese culture is characterized by community cohesiveness and control of the individual within the group; but, even more, it is also characterized by a "heritage of endurance" that epitomizes Japanese family life.

Note that this work is written in the historical present: Arakawa Ward in the 1960s. The incomes of the Japanese have now reached the levels of those of the Americans; but the delinquency rates of Japan, while showing a slight increase, have not risen to any notable degree. Japanese culture has a continuity that validates today what we have described for a yesterday almost twenty years past.

PART I

The Urban Community

This first part looks at the city life of an urban ward as an historic community, a pattern of in-migration originating in the premodern past. Within the contemporary urban ward one finds a highly complex network that binds the community together and constrains both youth and adults to stay within the socially acceptable boundaries of behavior.

CHAPTER 1

Arakawa Ward and Its Culture

As a fragment of Japanese history, the growth of Arakawa Ward as part of metropolitan Tokyo typifies a number of historical and sociological processes evident in cities throughout Japan. The growth of the Japanese city differs in sociocultural terms from the growth of cities elsewhere.

Industrialization in Japan has had a culturally distinct evolution and has not been simply a replicate of the processes of industrialization and urbanization found in the United States or other Western nations. Despite many superficial resemblances, Osaka is not Chicago, and Tokyo is not New York. Urban migration from the countryside in Japan, swelling its city populations, is not at all similar to the mass foreign immigration that took place at the turn of the twentieth century into the expanding industrial complexes of the United States. Rather, there is a flow to Japanese urbanization that is continuous with its preindustrial past. The city existed before industry, and the life of the city in Japan still shows marked continuity with the life of the small town and the rural farm communities of preindustrial Japan. Patterns of land ownership, the buying and selling of land, radically affect the type of geographic and social mobility possible within Japanese urban culture. One cannot, then, study the Japanese city simply in the frame of reference developed by U.S. sociologists concerned with the city in the United States. In the Japanese city the cultural traditions of the past still play a vital role in shaping the present-day life of the people (Wagatsuma and De Vos, 1980).

To describe city life in Japan one must start with a basic examination of the city as a cultural environment. Urban centers in Japan, as elsewhere, developed to serve basic functions. First, they developed out of political and administrative centers, based either on the direct exercise of military power or on the less direct forms of control exercised through bureaucratic structures. Japanese social and family organization did not differ basically between city, town, and country, although patterns of interaction came to differ in some circumstances where individuals did not know one another through continuous face-to-face contacts.

As a second function, cities have, from their inception, been religious or ceremonial centers. They have been the foci of a symbolic relationship between sacred and secular rule found in any given culture. The cities of Tokyo (old Edo) and Kyoto (Heian) give evidence of their origins in two different periods of Japanese history that utilized two forms of religious and secular control. Along with the advent of literacy and the establishment of Buddhism under the guidance of Korean and Chinese influences, the royal court self-consciously modeled itself on the T'ang dynasty of China and developed permanent cities at Nara and later at Heian on formal grid patterns radiating from an imperial court. Given areas of the cities were allocated to the courtiers, to religious centers, to educational facilities (a third function of cities), and to merchants and artisans operating markets (a fourth function). Some religious institutions, for example, were established in the northeast direction, since in Chinese thought the northeast was a source of supernatural danger. In Heian a temple complex peopled with thousands of monks on Mount Hiei guarded the city from malevolent influences.

The formally constructed city plan changed with the advent of a more decentralized feudal political structure. Most Japanese cities, including Edo, evolved out of feudal bastions—castle towns with a central moated area. The areas surrounding the castle were laid out for protection as well as for governance. The samurai served dual political roles of warriors and relatively well educated administrators. Samurai social life in some aspects manifested an almost unique blend of administrative and military rule not to be found in other cultures. Religious or edifying arts were cultivated by warriors guided by priest specialists in architecture, landscaping, poetry, and aesthetic ceremonials derivative of the earlier imperial court traditions. Artistic activities as well as the martial arts were in some respects pursued as a legitimation of authority.

The castle towns, also serving as markets, developed some unique Japanese features. Specific districts of these towns were set aside for various social strata of merchants and artisans as well as for markets of agricultural and maritime produce. Some special artisan and entertainment areas were enclaves allocated to the hereditarily impure outcaste Eta and the more immediately "outcast" Hinin. The Eta were pariah artisans, some of whom, as cobblers and armorers, worked with leather. Others were specialists in making musical instruments and basketry. Besides slaughtering animals, they served as executioners of condemned criminals, and they handled the dead.

The ranks of Hinin were continually peopled by fallouts from proper social strata, either through commission of criminal acts or through active interest in the demimonde of entertainment or secular art. Many Hinin lived in entertainment areas in which various forms of gambling, sport, theater, and prostitution were to be found. These social outcasts could, under some circumstances, be symbolically cleansed by an *ashi arai*, a "foot-washing" ceremony, which could reinvest them with an acceptable role in proper society. The outcaste Eta were regarded as biologically subhuman and could never be cleansed.

Entertainment, we must note, is a fifth basic function of the cities of all civilizations. With economic surplus a culture can afford the embellishment of specialists in the production of art, sacred and secular, by the use of body and voice, painting and sculpture, the ornamentation of the living environment, and the enrichment of experience. The *chōnin*, or townsmen, during Japan's feudal period, cultivated forms of art and entertainment that we now consider "Japanese" in style. The special culture of the merchants and artisans evolved out of a way of life quite different from that followed by the dominant samurai. However, many samurai disguised themselves and temporarily gave up their special ranking when visiting the gay quarters, as they wanted to participate in their pleasures despite the constraints exercised by a strict and punitive governmental system.

The final basic function of cities lies in their role as centers of transportation and communication. They are vital nuclei of networks permitting the diffusion of political, religious, educational, economic, and cultural activities both outward and inward. To function, cities must allow for a fluidity and a mobility of population in and out, since the population of cities never remains static. How this pulsation of population occurs is related to the entire cultural life of a people. Japanese cities have been located where they form vital internal communication links. "Port" cities handling international trade have developed only within the modern period.

The city of Edo, now Tokyo, illustrates historically that city life in Japan must be viewed within the context of these six basic urban functions. Edo became important as an urban center when the seat of government was moved there in the early seventeenth century under the aegis of the Tokugawa shogunate. In setting up an administrative capital in Edo, the shoguns emulated some of the features that had existed in the ancient seat of secular and sacred power, Heian (later Kyoto).

One of the religious features of Heian, for example, was repeated in Edo when the shogunate established the Kanei temple northeast of their new capital, in what is now Arakawa Ward, to serve the same religious defensive function against malevolent supernatural forces as the temples to the northeast on Mount Hiei. Also located in a northeastern direction were the more proximate settlements of artisans and merchants, as well as the squalid hovels inhabited by Eta and Hinin, and the execution grounds they serviced for criminals and the politically disfavored. Records report over 200,000 executed here during the 250 years of the Tokugawa reign.

In Edo this *shitamachi* (literally "downtown") section was located partially on land filled in at the edge of Tokyo Bay. The samurai were settled upon higher ground spreading out to the west of the castle. These social segments of the premodern city were separated geographically, but the entertainment of the *chōnin* attracted many samurai to the night life of the Yoshiwara Yukaku, or gay quarters, memorialized in the woodblock prints illustrating the *ukiyo*, or "floating world."

Major roads united Edo with other regions. A series of way stations started at Senju to the north and northeast, Shinjuku to the west, and Shimbashi to the south, leading toward the Tōkaidō (Great Road to the Northeast), which ended in Edo from its start in the cities southwest of the great administrative barrier erected at Hakone, which denied easy access to the Tokugawa domains.

The demographic surplus of rural regions—second and third sons and younger daughters—have peopled the towns and cities of Japan from the Tokugawa period until the present. By placing them as apprentices to *chōnin*, parents sent out those considered an economic burden at home. Some boys were attached as youthful apprentices to the households of artisans or merchants.

Young rural girls often entered the city by being placed as maids to learn the better manners and domestic arts of the *chōnin* world. Less fortunate girls from impoverished families might be sold into careers as prostitutes in the many brothels of the gay quarters; serving first as *komuso*, or apprentice-maids, they cared for the needs of those who had already been formally inducted into adult status by an affluent customer who paid a heavy price to the brothel owner for their deflowering. Some apprentices would be married off or adopted by considerate mentors, who would arrange for their marriages on an appropriate status level. When circumstances permitted, young prostitutes were bought out of bondage to become wives or mistresses.

The population of Japanese urban centers in the premodern period was reportedly larger than their European or American counterparts. For example, during the Kan-ei era (1624–1643), the population of Edo was estimated at about 600,000, far larger than the estimated 200,000 of London in the middle of the seventeenth century.

The internal trade and transportation networks of Japan from a very early period established a bustling internal economy. Towns were settings in which the economic surplus could in many instances be better enjoyed by the wealthier townspeople than by the lower grades of samurai, who often were given status but relatively little in economic benefits. Wealthier farmers, as well as merchants and artisans, were motivated toward acquiring literacy and proficiency in the arts for various purposes, both practical and for prestige. Buddhist temples provided local places for learning, in both urban and rural areas.

Wealthier farmers also had their children taught at local *terakoya*, or temple schools. It is estimated by some that the literacy rate in premodern Japan must have been higher than that of most areas of premodern Europe. It was not only the samurai who were readers of fiction by such authors as Saikaku, but some townsmen themselves enjoyed literary offerings. Dramatic performances—dumb shows, puppet shows, dance plays—reached everyone, literate or not. Temples put on performances teaching Buddhist morals. Noh dramas were informative tracts as well as lyric poetic expressions. The puppet stage presented history as well as dance, and dramatized events of *chōnin* life.

The Japanese city, present and past, has perhaps had proportionately more inhabitants devoted to entertainment than has any other urbanized culture. As in all cultures, concepts of entertainment tended to range from the lofty down to forms that were considered risqué, improper, or obscene. Samurai were expected to attend the more edifying forms such as Noh. They were also prone to frequent, when they could, the entertainment found in the brothel areas, which were sequestered in particular sections of the city by puritanical administrators. These reckoned that if they could not stamp out prostitution generally, they could exercise forms of social control by maintaining an espionage network in these areas.

The emotional vitality and economic surplus of a merchant culture could best receive some expression within this "floating world," as it was termed. Its artist-artisans, as well as many performers, set social fashion. The female entertainers who lived there were ranked in various ways: the more talented geisha, who were specialists in various forms of "artistic" entertainment, would approximate in reputation and popularity the better singers and performers now seen on Japanese television. Prostitutes ranked from high-status *oiran*, who could be compared to the high-class courtesans of ancient Greece, down to the lowly prostitutes serving impecunious customers.

Gambling was popular. It was carried out by organized networks of gamblers, who operated within the entertainment areas of the cities as well as in the stage stops located along the chief transportation routes that united the capital of Edo with the older cities of Osaka and Kyoto. The tradition of these underworld figures, the *yakuza*, has been romanticized in some of the plays developed on the Kabuki stage and today in contemporary films and novels. Forms of sport were popular. Japanese sumo has maintained a popularity that extends back into premodern times.

Areas of entertainment were strung along the roadways of entry and exit to most Japanese cities. Usually located along these avenues, in addition to legitimate inns, were houses of prostitution and gambling, serving incoming and outgoing travelers, as well as the townsmen themselves, who would frequent them from within the city. These entertainment centers, though periodically restricted by the government, somehow always survived periodic crackdowns. Within the gay quarters there was a relaxation of the strict regard for formal rank to be found in the outside world. Commoners and samurai could mix freely. The modes of obtaining prestige were totally unrelated to those constraining the individual in his ordinary life. Successful entertainers, leaders of gambling gangs, and proprietors of unusually popular houses of prostitution were an informal elite within the demimonde which played a not-to-be-slighted role in the total fabric of Japanese feudal society. One found there also the various Hinin, "nonpeople," very often reduced to itinerant occupations. There were traveling monks and *Yamabushi* (mountain holy men), religious functionaries. *Rōnin* (lordless samurai), and those without permanent residence, were dropped out of ordinary society and assumed peripheral roles. Parts of Japanese cities, then, were gathering places for displaced individuals, as they were in medieval Europe.

THE MODERN CITY: SHITAMACHI CULTURE IN ARAKAWA WARD

Today, some centrally located artisan-merchant districts in each city are still inhabited by *chōnin*. Under a modern veneer one finds continuity of features of previous lifestyles and traditions, some of them transmuted and adapted into new molds. Although some sections of the original northeast *shitamachi* districts of Tokyo have been taken over by new commercial structures, the pattern of growth of the artisan sections of the city to the north and northeast has been marked by a tenacious hold onto center-city territory by the traditional occupational groups, so that the less successful are pushed farther out from the central areas. This pattern is totally different from the type of urban growth one finds in such American cities as Chicago, so well studied by sociologists. The merchants of Tokyo are giving way, with great reluctance, to modern economic pressures on land tenancy. We find, therefore, in central sections of Tokyo a pattern of growth totally unlike any to be found in the American city. It is a pattern determined by a way of merchant life still firmly rooted in the past, though viable in the present.

It is interesting to note how the cottage industries, or "home-factories," in this central area have retained some viability despite predictions by economists since the 1950s that the dual economy of Japan, with its giant manufacturing plants as well as small-scale factory units of less than five workers, would not survive. But the subcontracting from larger factories persists for a good percentage of the people living in the downtown areas. Inner cities are subsisting on small-scale production units.

In contrast, the so-called *yamanote*, or "foothill" sections of Tokyo, show a suburbanization to the west and southwest not unlike the patterns found in American cities. The modern so-called *sarariman* (salary-man), the middle-class bureaucrats, white-collar workers for commercial firms or government offices, are moving into high-rise apartment structures. They are also moving out into the suburbs that are growing out along the rail lines for considerable distances from the center city. This pattern of urban and suburban growth toward more space and better housing is recognizable to any American. By some estimates, nearly three million people flow in and out of the heart of Tokyo every day to commute up to two hours each way. The inhabitants of these newly suburbanized areas are the modern industrial, commercial, and service personnel of the Japanese economy. In this respect, they are the descendants of the samurai bureaucracy, who range in status through the various new forms and strata of the Japanese middle class. Here and there among the dwellers of *danchi* (ordinary apartment houses) as well as the "mansions," or higher-status apartment units, one occasionally finds some older-style wealthier merchants, still wedded in other ways to their past traditions. They have, however, compromised with modernization by no longer living at their place of business; they have moved to new residences built several stories above shopping centers.

Such men have in effect become managers in the American sense of the word, having chosen either a suburban way of life or apartment-house living, rather than continuing the life of the old-style, wealthy merchant who lives as a paterfamilias within his area of business.

At the same time, one still finds fairly large factory units in some central districts where the owner lives in a compound next to his factory. In the early 1970s in Arakawa Ward, Tokyo, for example, most resident merchants and artisans still ran enterprises with less than ten employees. Some of these enterprises are interconnected by a series of subcontracting operations that unite them into networks of families working out of their own houses. A typical home-factory has one room containing a few machines on which family members and one or two outsiders work long hours. The small-factory owners are petty entrepreneurs, who think of themselves in capitalist terms, producing on machines that they own, concerned not with wages and hours but with the maximization of profit on their machines. While the pressures of large-scale industry increase land values, they have not broken through into these neighborhood areas or driven out the small operators into the periphery of the Japanese city. There are evidently little-understood economic counterforces that help these individuals maintain their foothold in the center of the city.

These counterforces are strengthened by a sense of persistence of lifestyle that makes for psychological as well as economic difficulties which hamper changes in land ownership within the Japanese city. The economic base of an artisan-merchant Arakawa is represented by a significant segment of this type of Japanese lower middle class. The model economic and social unit of the individual family with one or three machines is a persisting element that finds modern functions within the totality of Japanese industry. The subcontracting system is indeed a cushion in the Japanese economy; the petty entrepreneurs are the relatively "inefficient," who will go bankrupt should there be slight fluctuations in demand. In Arakawa Ward, in a population of over 250,000 people, there were more than 5,000 official bankruptcies yearly over a several-year period reported in the statistics for the ward. One needs to draw on psychocultural explanations to ask why individuals will persist with optimism in a way of life in which many suffer failure and destitution.

A BRIEF ECONOMIC HISTORY OF ARAKAWA WARD

In spite of the introduction of big factories on the Arakawa River at the turn of the century, this northern section of Tokyo did not develop into a large-scale industrial district as did other wards to the south of central Tokyo.[1] Instead, the industrial age spawned tiny home-factories operated by subcontractors who cut wood, leather, paper, and metal products on small machines. The number of these small-scale factories and workshops multiplied rapidly in the years before World War II. With the colonizing of Manchuria after 1931, exports increased, stimulating industry in Arakawa. By 1935 there were 1,279 registered factories in Arakawa, the largest number in any Tokyo ward. The survival of the home-

1. Much of the following is based on *Arakawa ku no Seikatsu to Fukushi* (*Life and Welfare in Arakawa Ward*, a special volume produced by the Arakawa Ward Office, Tokyo, 1963).

factory depended on the cheap labor of neighborhood housewives doing *nai-shoku* (part-time work in their homes), and this resultant pattern of the interdependence of low-income families and the larger factories has persisted to the present.

Animal butchery was another early industry in the ward; the first large-scale slaughterhouse opened in 1871 on the site of the former Kozukappara execution grounds of the Tokugawa regime. The slaughterhouses of Arakawa prospered as the eating of meat, prohibited under the dietary restrictions of Buddhism, became popular—a symbol of modernity and Westernization. The widespread adoption of shoes instead of *zori* (straw sandals) added to the demand for leather, and the leather industry that the government had fostered in the Mikawashima central area of Arakawa with two factories—a fairly large one in 1883 and a second one in 1887—flourished. The presence of slaughterhouses made Arakawa a natural site for a new sewage-disposal plant, built in 1923. Thus, although Arakawa on the whole remained largely agricultural until the beginning of the twentieth century, after 1900 it rapidly took on its reputation as a "city dump," a place for processing the waste products of modern Tokyo.

THE DUMPING OF THE POOR INTO ARAKAWA

The prevalence of poverty and a low-income population in Arakawa began after the disastrous fire of 1907, when the government issued an order to move all the poor (then called *sai-min*, or small-income people) from their hovels in other parts of Tokyo into the western Nippori and south central Mikawashima districts of Arakawa. The city government built low-rent, cheap "apartment" units in long wooden buildings called *nagaya* (longhouses), and for more than a decade thereafter it continued to erect such housing in Arakawa. In 1909 *tonneru nagaya* (tunnel longhouses) were built throughout the northeastern Minami Senju district. In 1910 in Nippori the government began to build barracks, which came to be called *majinai nagaya* ("magic" longhouses), with some pejorative meaning. This program continued until the end of 1918. As the poor flowed into Arakawa from various parts of Tokyo to live in these "longhouses," the population rose at an ever-increasing rate.

Another, more sudden influx of low-income people followed the great earthquake and fire of 1923, which devastated large sections of Arakawa itself. To house the poor who had lost their homes in Arakawa as well as other parts of Tokyo, the municipal government constructed many more barracks, now known as the *kojiki nagaya* (the "beggars'" longhouses), in Mikawashima, and the *buta nagaya* (the "pigs'" longhouses) in the Ogu district. These public projects increased the immigration of rag-scrap pickers, tinkers, and repairers of shoes, umbrellas, and *geta* (wooden clogs). By 1926 Nippori, the western district of present Arakawa Ward, had become a large collecting and distributing point for waste materials, and a sizable quantity of paper and rags collected by the Nippori scrap-pickers was being exported to foreign countries. The 247 dealers who bought waste materials from pickers organized a cooperative and built a large disinfecting center to treat collected waste products. At present this industry is moving north out of Arakawa into Adachi, the ward most distant from central Tokyo.

In several ways the development of the present characteristics of Arakawa Ward may be traced to the 1923 disaster. Before the earthquake Arakawa's population had been more or less concentrated in Nippori and in Minami Senju, a district to the east of Nippori; after the earthquake, as Tokyo's poor arrived in ever greater numbers, the population spread north, more or less evenly over the entire district. The completion of the Arakawa Drainage Canal in 1924, by solving the age-old problem of sporadic flooding, opened up the possibility of new housing areas.

The Tokyo population, which by 1924 had reached the saturation point in the more central parts of the city, began flowing north in increasingly large numbers into Arakawa, causing a jump of more than 100,000 between 1923 and 1930 (from 173,000 to 280,000). In 1931, with a reorganization of administrative units, Arakawa was unified as a ward with its own headquarters, marking another epoch in its history.

Arakawa was heavily bombed during World War II. Nearly two-thirds of the residential and industrial areas were leveled in March and April 1945 by air raids and the resultant fires. Over the whole period that Tokyo was under attack, from November 1944 to August 1945, Arakawa suffered 926 people killed, 541 severely wounded, and 3,411 slightly wounded. Those residential areas that escaped bombing became extremely overcrowded. The prewar barracks in these surviving blocks were inhabited by the very poor, and the crime and delinquency rate quickly mounted. Immediately after the war Arakawa became known as an area of acute social disorganization with attendant deviancy and crime. After a fifteen-year increase in social problems, the prewar pattern of small-scale industry gradually reappeared, and there has been considerable economic recovery, a process that we documented while doing our family studies.

A VISUAL OVERVIEW

At present Arakawa is one of twenty-three wards, or *ku*, constituting Tokyo. Located about three and a half miles from the Imperial Palace, it covers 10.34 square kilometers and is ranked as the third smallest in area among the twenty-three wards of Tokyo. Its population in 1968, two years after we concluded our research, was 269,765 (72,155 households), fifteenth among the Tokyo wards. Arakawa ranked second in population density, with 25,216 people per square kilometer, almost twice the average density of the city as a whole. By 1976 the population of the ward had decreased to 207,890, making it eighteenth, rather than fifteenth, in population among the Tokyo wards. In density the ward ranked fifth, rather than second, with 20,105 people per square kilometer.

Viewed from the air, the Arakawa River, the largest river in the Tokyo area, winds eastward along the northeast side of the ward. Scattered along both sides of the Arakawa, large factories with tall smokestacks spew forth smoke into the generally leaden Tokyo sky. Occupying a wide, flat space on the south bank is the largest of Tokyo's three sewage-disposal plants, showing from the air as rectangles of bright bluish water in colorful contrast with the surrounding area.

Five bridges span the river to the north and east. They are continually crowded with traffic moving sluggishly across them from the several wide main streets that, like scars of light beige concrete, crisscross the lumpy masses of dark brown rooftops set in a network of tiny, crooked alleys. On the sides of the wider roads are the shopping districts, with here and there taller buildings of gray concrete.

Descending from this overview, we find a compact mass of small factories, apartments, and individual houses. In 1965 the stranger was certain to be impressed with the smallness and decrepitude of these wooden one- and two-story buildings, which stood so close to each other that virtually no air passed between them. Then more immediate sensations asserted and still assert themselves: There are various strange and strong smells—from the crematorium, the sewage plant, the leather factories, and piles of small industrial waste waiting for removal; the intensity and kinds of odors are determined by the district, the season, and the direction of the wind. Little children play in the narrow, winding alleys. Paper boxes and heaps of iron scrap are piled up in front of the houses. People move about in the midst of the harsh din of many small machines. The whole area is a spread-out factory zone, but it serves at the same time as the home of thousands of people who live and sleep in rooms they enter through other rooms occupied by machines that work wood, metal, and leather.

Higashi Ogu and Nishi Ogu districts to the northwest contain more than a fourth of the area of the Arakawa Ward. They are the most recently settled areas and still have some scattered plots of land that were used for marginal farming until quite recent times. Here a large electrical and chemical plant and some small metal and rubber factories face the south bank of the river. The houses in this area are like those found in Machiya, a central district of Arakawa Ward.

Scattered throughout the ward are six public kindergartens, twenty-seven primary schools, and fifteen junior high schools, each with its gravel and cement play area. There are also a small number of private schools, including one run by North Korean expatriates, and senior high schools, including a special navigation-training institute for air pilots. A number of small shrines and temples are maintained as family enterprises, affording a bit of greenery with their tiny surrounding gardens.

Here and there throughout the ward today, new, concrete, five-story walk-up apartments are making their appearance. The Tokyo municipal government is gradually razing the most dilapidated blocks. An interesting innovation in apartment-building construction is the provision made for small home-factories on the ground floor of most of these new structures; here, now in concrete, are the one-room factories and small shops with living space in the back. As elsewhere, the balconies of these apartments are used to dry laundry and to air bedding, and the sides of the buildings are continually covered with fluttering laundry.

Danchi, or apartment buildings, are becoming the dominant form of dwelling in denser parts of the city. Almost no single-family houses are now being built in Japanese cities. Most apartments have a tiny kitchen, usually Western-style. The rooms with their concrete floors are becoming more and more "Western," with chairs replacing the tatami mats on which one sat directly on the wooden floor. There is a transition going on from having most rooms prevailingly "Japanese" to having a single remaining tatami room, very often inhabited by an aged grandmother or older relative.

THE PATTERN OF LIFE IN SHITAMACHI

Unfortunately, we can give only a brief description of the economic, social, and recreational activities that flavor the *shitamachi* lifestyle of Arakawa. However, the life histories presented in Part Three do reflect some of these characteristics. Generally, our informants were much poorer than Dore's, although Arakawa is a newer section of Tokyo.

As Dore points out (1958), *shitamachi* life is determined to some extent by the close physical proximity due to the density of population. The *yamanote* resident has traditionally kept some distance from his neighbors by means of his small gardens and fences. The *shitamachi* residents, on the other hand, usually spill out much more directly into the tiny alleyways that serve as part of their living area. The housing is so close that there is very little privacy from neighbors.

It is in the more dense areas of Arakawa that one still finds scenes reminiscent of the past. One can still witness on a summer evening men wearing light, white "underwear," knee-length, under which there is a second, more intimate, garment. Many still wear a wool belly-band to keep the stomach warm (a surviving belief that a stomach kept warm will preserve one's health). Individuals may be sitting on benches brought out where some breeze comes through, using paper fans to cool themselves, perhaps with a mosquito coil burning beside them. There are groups playing either *go* or *shōgi*, Japanese chess. Mah-Jongg is played inside, as one can witness through some open windows. Indoors or out, adults may be watching television or half-listening to a blaring radio describing sports events or producing a miscellany of popular musical forms. One finds casual groups gathering in nearby noodle shops or bars to watch televised baseball games, sumo wrestling, or kick-boxing, while eating a snack or drinking beer.

On Saturday afternoon or Sunday, some families go out together, visiting the zoo or a public park. Few Japanese attend regular religious ceremonies of any kind. Religious traditions are marked most by attendance at memorials for the dead. In winter, on cold nights, individuals living in the old-style houses sit in *kotatsu*, a cut-out square in the floor furnished with an electric heater, covered by a blanket over which is set a square table on which one can play games or place tea cups and snacks.

Most families do not have much to spend on outside leisure activities. Whatever the budget, some money will go to the drinking of sake and hard liquor. Japanese males, generally speaking, drink a great deal of alcoholic beverages. Their beer consumption rivals that of the major drinking countries in Europe. Men in *shitamachi* enjoy getting drunk on Saturday night. The *shitamachi* resident will patronize a neighborhood bar now and then, but finds it cheaper to have his sake at home. Middle-class residents who must commute long distances are more likely to stop in bars at the various transportation ganglia that ring the center city than to do their drinking at home. One of the attractions of drinking at a bar is the attendance of professional waitresses who cajole and inflate the customer's ego. Sometimes it is more the ego boost than the alcohol that the man seeks out in drinking at a bar.

"Bar girls" are in effect a continuation of the female entertainers of the premodern period. Young girls entering the entertainment industry may do so as an alternative to marriage. A good proportion of them do not marry or have been divorced and no longer regard the role of wife and mother as one they wish to fulfill.

Perhaps the outstanding feature of present-day social life for middle-class Japanese are the commercial shopping and entertainment areas located around transportation connections. Shinjuku, the largest transportation hub, is now the largest night-life area in Tokyo, if not the world. It has countless establishments, large and small. In effect, these areas are the modern version of the staging areas located on the major arteries for the city of Edo. Now, instead of traveling the Tōkaidō, the weary, daily commuter arrives home late and leaves early. Except on weekends, he has very little contact with his wife and children. The absentee fathers are replaced in local social organizations by women who form various volunteer groups, creating some kind of neighborhood solidarity. In contrast, as we shall describe in Chapter 2, in the *shitamachi* area one still finds a very thick network of voluntary organizations related to business or to some form of public service.

In *shitamachi* on Sundays, there are periodic picnics held by families connected with one another in a complementary network of subcontractors; individuals doing directly competing work in the same area never meet in the same recreation group. Merchants and professional men form voluntary networks and also avoid bringing together direct competitors. For the middle class, "Kiwanis clubs," "Lions," and "Rotary" organizations function similarly in Japan and the United States. Members of the same company associate with one another socially much more than do their counterparts in the United States.

Sometimes marriages occur between young women who are working in a secretarial capacity and young men who are employees of the same company. Characteristically, the woman will quit her job to take up her domestic duties. Few women in Japan can find any long-lasting careers in commercial and industrial fields, whereas in the entertainment industry women can become very successful. Marriage and career are seen as totally exclusive categories by most Japanese. Few women can combine marriage and motherhood with a continuing career. This is not to say that many Japanese women do not work. On the contrary, in lower-class sections many women do piecework at home, which can be done alternately with their household tasks and at night when their children are asleep.

In the cities among young people today one sees a considerable amount of dating. Before the war it was considered unseemly for specific couples to have too much individual contact. The pattern of group recreation is still paramount; several young people of both sexes will go out together. Exclusive dating for a middle-class couple is still considered somewhat improper if there is no serious intent.

Home entertainment is perhaps the predominant form, with television set ownership being second only to that in the United States. Japanese go less frequently than Americans to movie houses. The number of films made has fallen off drastically from the postwar period, when Japan ranked first in the world in the number of films produced annually. Today, most films are specialized in nature. "Soft porn" movies are maintaining some popularity, the degree of explicitness being regulated only by the police. No sexual organs may be displayed, but simulated sexual activity may be fairly explicit.

Japanese television at the late hours is marked by a great deal of nudity, again with no revelation of pubic hair or sexual organs. Favorite evening programs include drama series, a number of quiz programs, comedies, popular songs, nostalgic programs about the old rural life, and sports. Professional wrestling matches between Japanese and foreigners and Thai-style kick-boxing matches are current popular modes, among both children and adults.

Japanese are conscious that the rate of serious reading has dropped and that there is a great increase of *manga* cartoon books catering to adults as well as children. Their content can be explicitly sexual or even sadomasochistic. There are acts of violence depicted which are not commonly found in their American counterparts. Japanese parents have as great difficulty in restricting the use of television as have their American counterparts. However, there are noted differences between the parents of those boys doing well in school, who insist upon shutting off the television, and those who are unable to exert this much authority over their children.

In *shitamachi*, much use is made of rental bookstores, whereas *yamanote* people are more inclined to buy the books they want to read and to display them in a library collection. Newsstands at every station carry a large variety of weekly magazines, and people riding trains or subways, whether sitting or standing or leaning against one another, read them avidly, along with the daily newspapers. *Shitamachi* residents, more than *yamanote* people, are apt to go to watch horse racing, bicycle racing, or motorbike racing. Income from gambling at the race-track can be a very important source of funds for some local social welfare programs. One reads periodically in the daily press of those whose gambling urges have gotten out of hand, who have impoverished their families by incurring debts, and who finally kill themselves.

Mah-Jongg is a very popular indoor form of gambling, less evident among middle-class Japanese than among their lower-class counterparts. Players are found in all walks of life. There are small Mah-Jongg parlors scattered throughout Japanese cities, where one pays a nominal fee per hour to play. What strikes a visitor much more forcefully, however, are the most visible *pachinko*, or pinball parlors, found in any commercial neighborhood. One sees hundreds of people standing or sitting in front of long rows of glass-fronted, upright pinball machines, incessantly flipping the metal bar that propels the ball up to the top of the forest of pins. The entire hall resounds with the metallic clinking and clanking of rolling steel balls and the blare of popular songs from the loudspeaker.

SHITAMACHI AND YAMANOTE: DIFFERENCES IN TEMPERAMENT

Reported differences in temperament and comportment between the *shitamachi* and the *yamanote* person, we find, are roughly valid. The *shitamachi* person is held to be more quick-tempered and at the same time more ingenuous and warmhearted, more frankly given to the seeking of pleasure, less calculating. These traits, of course, belie a concern with the future which governs present behavior, and which is, as we shall point out, very characteristic generally of the Japanese people. The *yamanote* person practices *enryo*, or reserve; he is not one to engage enthusiastically in shrine festivals and other demonstrative group activities. *Shitamachi* taste has been for the more exciting types of entertainment; the Kabuki was the townsman's entertainment, whereas the *yamanote* person was more concerned with the refinements of Noh drama. Sumo wrestling, *naniwabushi* or *rokyoku*, traditional forms of sentimental ballads, and geisha houses all grew out of the leisure time and pleasure seeking of the *shitamachi chōnin*. It was the *yamanote* person, in contrast, who was initially more attracted to Western culture—to foreign films, for example. As Dore points out, when *shitamachi* women wore Japanese dress, they had a distinctive way of wearing it, with the kimono collar cut lower and the obi worn lower on the hips than in the more "conservative" style of the *yamanote* woman.

In our interviews we found that a good number of Arakawa residents still self-consciously consider their ward to be part of *shitamachi* and like to identify themselves as "*shitamachi* people," as contrasted with "those people of *yama-*

note." For example, one community leader, who teaches in an Arakawa school, grew up in Arakawa, and would never think of moving elsewhere.

> *Shitamachi* people are frank, open-hearted, and warm, not like affected *yamanote* people. Children here are better equipped than *yamanote* children with a *seikatsu-no-chie* [wisdom of living]. I am teaching a special class of feebleminded children. When you compare these retarded children of *shitamachi* with those of *yamanote*, *shitamachi* children seem less "feebleminded" than their *yamanote* counterparts. You know why? Because they know better how to make a living. They have more *seikatsu-ryoku* [vitality] and practical knowledge for daily living. When you tell even these feebleminded children of *shitamachi* to do some shopping, they look for a store where the price is a little lower than elsewhere.

Another informant observes:

> In general, *shitamachi* ways are less formal than *yamanote* ways. In the formal occasion, therefore, you might say that *shitamachi* people adopt *yamanote* ways. Serving a guest a cup of tea on a tray and a cake on a small plate is a *yamanote* way, which we *shitamachi* people practice only with very formal guests. The *shitamachi* way of entertaining familiar guests is to bring out a teapot, a can of tea, and a kettle and serve as much tea as the guests like. Cakes are served in a large container so that each guest can take as many as he wants.

A middle-school teacher who had some experience of teaching at a school in a new *yamanote* district compared the *yamanote* and *shitamachi* children he has observed:

> In *yamanote* schools, it seems to me, both teachers and children are interested only in children's schoolwork and school records. They have a very strong orientation toward accomplishment and achievement. There is also a certain coldness in classroom atmosphere. In *shitamachi* schools like those here in Arakawa, children may not do so well at school as the *yamanote* children, but there is definitely a stronger human bond and more emotional interaction between teachers and children. They come into contact with each other more as humans. The atmosphere is definitely much warmer, though it is also much more informal.

A policeman who had been in charge of youth in Arakawa for more than ten years was temporarily transferred a few years ago to another station in a *yamanote* ward. In speaking of an easiness in his contact and rapport with youngsters and their parents in Arakawa and of a certain difficulty he experienced in his attempts with those in *yamanote*, he used an interesting metaphor:

> A *shitamachi* district such as Arakawa is like a house without much depth. You step into it and you can see everything inside the house. In *yamanote*, on the other hand, you step in and you see only an entryway. . . . In Arakawa there is no such need. It's wide open.

A ward officer who has lived in Arakawa for more than thirty-five years is very fond and proud of Arakawa:

> *Shitamachi* people are sensitive to *ninjō* [human emotions]. They are not concerned with *rikutsu* [logic]. *Yamanote* intellectuals like to speak of logic and give a clear-cut solution to emotional problems. Unlike *yamanote* people, *shitamachi* people of Arakawa live by emotions and feelings. They are *kiji-no-mama* ["unvarnished"]. They believe that "human nature" is basically good. They trust people. You might say they are simpleminded. The true human nature is exposed, so to speak, and is not covered. They directly express their joy, anger, sadness, and happiness. When they see someone in trouble, they are always ready to help. In turn, they are very sensitive to, and appreciative of, other people's kindness. You don't find such qualities among people in *yamanote*. They are aloof, indifferent, cold, and guarded.

The families of Arakawa we interviewed also reflected a pattern continuing from the premodern period wherein there is a secondary socialization of rural inhabitants into a *shitamachi* culture. Many came in as rural apprentices, still in their formative years. Imperceptibly, they were socialized into the modern version of the old *shitamachi* culture, although most of them were not born to it. They are, in effect, immigrants who have taken on the coloration of the neighborhood and the occupational groups into which they have been adopted. They are examples of urban migrants who did not consider themselves as having been forced to move into a slum. Rather they saw themselves as seeking to live in poor dwellings, which might be improved should they "make it financially." To the casual outsider this area might be considered a ghetto, but once one makes contact one finds a totally different attitude from that described in Oscar Lewis's writings on the "culture of poverty." The smells of Arakawa are not of garbage, decay, and disorder; rather, they are the smells emitted by tiny compressed industries dreaming of successful expansion.

In 1968 a new subway system opened up the ward, suddenly making access to it easier for the central part of the city. The ward is now considered extremely convenient for white-collar workers of the Tokyo central business district; entirely new groups of inhabitants are taking up residence in the ward. The last few years are a record of drastic ecological changes in this ward as elsewhere. We have not tried to keep up with all the changes. The historical present of our report is the late 1960s. We have not, for example, revised our description of the geographic profile of the ward. Accordingly, what is reported here in describing the economic conditions of our fifty families and house industries is the Arakawa that existed before 1968.

CHAPTER 2

Group Orientation in Arakawa Ward

Today, Japanese society is still characterized by stability and continuity. Underneath the dynamic, seemingly changing life of this highly industrialized and drastically urbanized nation, one can see the continuation of a basic value system and common psychological characteristics which motivate people to stay together and keep their society "intact." Despite environmental pollution, traffic congestion, housing shortages, a soaring cost of living, and overcrowded cities, one finds little evidence of any widespread social disruption or personal alienation in Japanese society.

SOCIAL COHESION AND ITS CONTINUITY

One of the apparent differences between modern city life and its premodern counterparts is the gradual diminution of concern with the extended patrilinial family and its name. Nevertheless, one finds that patterns of adoption are still very widespread as means of assuring some occupational as well as family continuity. In one small sample we found a 25 percent rate of formal or informal adoption of males as a means of assuring business continuity. Very often in Arakawa an adoption does not involve a change of names, which is still characteristic in middle-class professional groups. In Arakawa few individuals spontaneously state that the family name and its perpetuity is of primary importance to them. This does not indicate, however, a loosening of family obligations and of a sense of responsibility for other family members. These remain very much in evidence in urban as well as rural settings. The prevailing mode is still to accommodate older family members within the same residence. There is increasing reluctance among younger women, however, to marry men who are first sons when there is an explicit obligation to live with the mother-in-law. This pattern is one of great sensitivity, and younger women do not wish to carry out the role of bride vis-à-vis a nit-picking mother-in-law.

The divorce rate remains relatively low in spite of liberal divorce laws, and there is only one divorce for every ten new marriages yearly (in the United States there was one divorce for every two marriages in 1978). According to several studies by Japanese social scientists, there is no sign of increase in informal cohabitation. Premarital sexual intercourse is of frequent occurrence in Japan, but most youths still marry at the "right" ages (25–29 years for males and 20–24 for females), as social norms dictate. (In the United States "peak ages" for first marriages are 21–22 for males and 18–19 for females, but the ages of marriage are much more varied and widely distributed than they are in Japan.) In a 1969–1970 study, only 30 percent of male and female university students and young factory workers indicated that they would consider "love" the most important factor in marriage. More than 90 percent of the females and about 60 percent of the males said they would consider their parents' opinions when choosing their spouse. In a 1974 comparative study of moral attitudes by the Prime Minister's Office, 700 youths in Japan, the United States, and Germany were asked a variety of questions, including one regarding their attitudes toward "contract marriage." The Japanese were the least supportive of it (13% approving, 80% disapproving), and Germans were the most supportive of it (40% approving, 59% disapproving), while the Americans fell in between (27% approving, 69% disapproving) (Prime Minister's Youth Bureau, 1975).

Japan is the only industrialized nation in which there has been a recent steady decline in adult crime rates. As early as 1973, the number of murders per person in Japan was only one-fifth of that in the United States (1.9 in Japan and 9.3 in the United States for every 100,000 people). In the same year, Tokyo, with a population of 12 million, had only 196 murders, while the New York metropolitan area, with a population of just under 12 million, had 1,739 murders, nearly nine times that of Tokyo. In Japan, the incidence of rape is one-fifth that in the United States, and the rate of robbery with force or the threat of force is less than 1 percent of the American rate (in 1973, there were 1,876 robberies in Japan and 382,680 in the United States; 361 in Tokyo and 74,381 in New York City). Overall, there are four times as many *serious crimes* committed per person in the United States as there are *crimes of all sorts*, even the most petty, in Japan (Bayley, 1976).

Japanese society is basically stable, and such stability seems to be rooted in a strong interdependence characteristic of Japanese social relationships in family, community, and occupation.

THE FAMILY MATRIX

Japanese mother-child relationships and relationships among family members in general are characterized by physical and psychological closeness. Caudill and Schooler (1969) studied interaction patterns between mothers and their six-month-old babies in middle-class American and Japanese families. They found no significant differences in time spent by American and Japanese mothers in taking care of their babies' physical and biological needs (feeding, and changing diapers and clothes). However, the American mothers tended to leave their babies alone when the babies were asleep, whereas the Japanese mothers stayed with their babies, often holding or carrying them. American mothers talked to their babies frequently, whether the babies were happy or unhappy, whereas Japanese mothers, generally more reticent, spoke only when the babies were unhappy. In correspondence to these differences in mothers' attitudes, the American babies were much more active—moving their limbs about—and more vocal than the Japanese babies, who were more passive and quiet. American mothers seemed to encourage their babies to be active and vocally responsive, while Japanese mothers acted in ways which they believed would soothe and quiet their babies. The pace of American mothers in caring for their babies was much more lively; they were frequently in and out of the room. They also differentiated more sharply between kinds of vocalization by responding more quickly to unhappy sounds than to happy sounds. They appeared to be teaching the infants to make a more discriminating use of their voices. In contrast, the pace of Japanese mothers was more leisurely, and the overall period of direct caretaking tended to be longer.

From this study, it would appear that the American mother views her baby at least potentially as a separate and autonomous being who should learn to do and think for himself or herself. For the American mother, the baby is from birth a distinct personality with its own needs and desires, which she learns to recognize and respond to. She helps the baby learn how to express these needs and desires through an emphasis on vocal communication so that the baby can "tell" the mother what it wants and the mother can respond appropriately.

The American mother de-emphasizes the importance of physical contact, such as in carrying and rocking, and encourages her infant, through the use of her voice, to explore and learn to deal with its environment by itself. Psychologically speaking, here lie the beginnings of a greater separation between mother and child and the development of sharper ego-boundaries. The American mother also thinks of herself as a separate person, with her own needs and desires, which include time apart from her baby to pursue her own interests, and being a wife to her husband as well as a mother to her baby.

In contrast, the Japanese mother views her baby much more as an extension of herself, and psychologically the boundaries between mother and infant are blurred. The Japanese mother is likely to feel that she knows what is best for her baby and sees no particular need for the baby to tell her vocally what it wants, because mother and baby are virtually one. Accordingly, the Japanese mother places less importance on vocal communication and more on physical contact.

There is also a strong tendency for Japanese family members to sleep in the same room or adjacent ones, even though there may be other rooms in the house that are vacant. A number of Western as well as Japanese researchers have documented this tendency. An individual in Japan can expect to co-sleep in a two-generation group, first as a child and then as a parent, over approximately half his life. This pattern starts at birth and continues until about the time of menopause for the mother and occurs again for a few years in old age. According to

Caudill and Plath (1966), 48–68 percent of the 6–10-year-old children and 33–46 percent of the 11–15-year-olds sleep in the same room as their parents.

Family members often bathe together at home. Those who do not own a bath go to a public bathhouse in their neighborhood. Many factory workers bathe together after their day's work before going home. Children on their school excursions, friends, co-workers, and neighborhood association members on their group tours to a hot-spring resort co-bathe and co-sleep. The highly valued feature of such co-sleeping is the sociability it affords and the sense of belonging to a group. There is no assumption that anything improper will take place even in the co-bathing and co-sleeping of mixed-sex groups (although it sometimes does). Each participating individual gains comforting security, and a spirit of happy intimacy and solidarity pervades the group.

All these trends toward a "group life" among the Japanese indicate that the nature of their "ego boundaries" is very likely to be different from those of more "individualistic" Americans. The Japanese child grows up in an atmosphere of interdependence and collateral relations, so that it is a very real psychological struggle for the growing individual to separate his or her identity from what exists only in relation to others. For most Japanese such an attempt to separate one's identity is never completely carried out, and what one is in relation to others remains a fundamental part of that identity (Doi, 1966, 1971).

In Japanese society one is not simply an engineer, an accountant, or an anthropologist, but more specifically and concretely a member of the Toyota Automotive Company, the Mitsubishi Bank, or Tokyo University. The group to which one belongs takes precedence over one's special skills and training.

In conversational Japanese, kinship terms (like father, mother, elder brother, uncle) are used in place of first-person and second-person pronouns, as are occupational names (like president, professor, doctor, driver, fish peddler, greengrocer). These speech patterns constantly reaffirm the social roles of speaker and listener.

In contradistinction to the individual as conceived of in the Western tradition of moral philosophy, the individual in Japanese culture has never been conceptualized as an end in himself. Emphasis has always been placed on a network of particularistic obligations and responsibilities that an individual is expected to assume as a member of a family and a community. Living in accordance with one's prescribed role within the family and within a political and social hierarchy has been the ultimate basis of moral values. When one thinks of oneself, one's self-awareness tends to be fused with some conception of expected role behavior, which is often idealized in the mind as a set of internalized standards or directives. (Accordingly, one's ego-ideal is conceptualized in terms of some particular form of idealized role behavior.) The Japanese would feel uncomfortable in thinking of the "self" as something separable from his or her role. To actualize oneself is to fulfill one's role expectations, as a member both of a particular family and of a particular social group. In a traditionally oriented Japanese mind, to be "individualistic" in the Western moral sense would almost be equal to being "selfish" in the worst sense of the term. Japanese tend to equate "individualism" (*kojin-shugi*) with "selfishness" (*riko-shugi*). When a Japanese is "self-ish" (thinking only of the self), he or she fails to be an actualized person. To any ethical Japanese, a person cannot fully exist without performing a proper social role.

THE SOCIAL GROUP

Since every Japanese social group tends to be modeled after the family, a person in a superordinate position is expected to behave toward subordinates somewhat like a parent toward children. This gives a special quality the Japanese version of "paternalism" in that the connotation is essentially positive. Opinion surveys conducted repeatedly over a twenty-year period indicate that a majority of Japanese continue to prefer a supervisor who is interested in the general welfare of all the family members of those who work under him, even if this supervisor expects employees to work overtime without compensation when called upon. A more "rational" type who abides by fair rules but is not personally involved with the supervisees is not popular among the Japanese. The Western image of paternalism connotes an instrumental exploitative use of a contract-bound labor force, toward whom there is no real sense of personal involvement or belonging. In Japan, however, an employer is not psychologically free to dehumanize employees into faceless machine parts from which the maximum productive output is to be obtained. Ties between superordinates and subordinates in Japan often remain emotional, and a feeling of guilt can be generated in a subordinate who fails to repay the superordinate-benefactor, and also in the superordinate who fails to give proper care to the subordinate. Outside of business and industry, similar ties often develop between people in superordinate and subordinate positions in various areas of Japanese society.

Group orientation certainly works as a centripetal force for most Japanese. They do not casually leave their group behind and wander away from it: outside it they belong nowhere. One implication of this is that patterns of urban movement, geographic and social, do not show the centrifugal features found in American migration patterns. When Japanese become wealthier they usually do not move to another and better neighborhood, but remain in the same house, which they improve and enlarge. This makes Japanese neighborhoods much more "mixed" socioeconomically, although the heterogeneity is overridden by the homogeneity of shared residential history and community membership. Compared with those in Western societies, and especially those in the United States, a Japanese urban neighborhood remains more permanent, more "face-to-face" in daily contact. There is less anonymity even in prevailingly lower-income districts with a somewhat higher residential turnover. There is nothing in Japanese cities that comes close to patterns found in the large minority neighborhoods of American cities. Whereas Americans tend to live in a more impersonal human environment where people are "substitutable," Japanese live within stable networks of "named people." Urbanization processes are not personally or socially disruptive for the Japanese: they have not produced severe problems of personal and social disorganization in the city.

An urban community in Japan remains socially viable. In practically every urban neighborhood one finds the centuries-old institution of unofficial neighborhood governance (called *chōkai*, or "townspeople's association") in which every household has an almost automatic membership. In most places, notices from government are circulated to the heads of *chōkai* and from them throughout the community. Message boards are passed from house to house containing information of all kinds, such as "The fire season has arrived," or "Water will be stopped on the day after tomorrow." Households are obligated to participate in projects undertaken by the *chōkai* (for example, cleaning out the drains of the neighborhood). In rural areas the village as a natural social unit functions similarly. Townspeople's associations (and hamlet members' associations) are intertwined with crime prevention associations (*bōhan kyōkai*) composed of citizen volunteers led by their own chosen officials. Their activities vary, ranging from erecting signs ("Beware of pickpockets!") and distributing pamphlets about home protection to patrolling their neighborhood. Numerous other neighborhood associations and committees (for example, those for traffic safety, for protection of youths, and for continuing education of housewives) honeycomb Japanese society from the level of formal government (national and local) down to the level of informal neighborhood cooperation, each of which involves citizens in one way or another in collective efforts to keep their community "intact."

Everything discussed above, namely, group orientation and all its implications, works as a strong force toward social conformity among Japanese. Norms and rules are usually internalized—obeyed without much open resistance and without self-righteous questioning. The sight of a lone pedestrian in a large city, waiting patiently for the traffic light to change, with no cars in sight and no policeman around, is the rule rather than the exception.

VOLUNTARY ASSOCIATIONS IN ARAKAWA

The network of associations directly or indirectly involved with the problem of delinquency merits special consideration, for it is our conclusion that whatever the cause of the drop in delinquency rates for Tokyo as a whole in the 1960s, the increasing influence of such associations in Arakawa had some role in cutting down delinquency in this ward.

Their general effectiveness, at least in part, can be traced to the cultural preconditions particular to Japan which we have just discussed. In addition, one must not discount the effect of economic conditions on the rate of crime and delinquency in any industrial society, including Japan. The closeup perspective we gained by studying an individual ward revealed many instances of an indirect effect of recent prosperity in an increase in voluntary activities related to neighborhood betterment and social involvement. It was markedly apparent that Japanese small entrepreneurs over fifty years of age in Arakawa ward as elsewhere who had some leisure time were apt to devote it to some form of voluntary community activities. Such service is a recognized and compelling way to gain prestige within Japanese society. This type of community involvement, much more pervasive a phenomenon in Japan than in the United States, may be seen as a continuation of Japanese paternalistic responsibilities into a new social area. Whereas in the past the individually successful Japanese felt himself responsible to his employees for their well-being, he is now universalizing some of this energy into a feeling of responsibility for community service. Although for Westerners the word "paternalism" often has a negative connotation, for the Japanese paternalism is deeply expressive behavior—giving to others the nurturance that one had in one's own childhood. This interpenetration of affiliation and nurturance is clearly evident in the expected behavior in voluntary associations.[1]

The scope and vitality of these *shitamachi* associations in Japan are matched perhaps nowhere else in a modern culture. Although the large number of volunteer roles taken by Americans, as reported by Barker and his associates in comparing the United States and England, attests to the density of voluntary activity in American culture (Barker, 1968), it is our impression that the social networks (related usually to occupation) operative in Japan far exceed in complexity the voluntary social-organization patterns of middle-class America. They also include more individuals farther down the economic status ladder of the society.

Rather than discussing the interaction of social, economic, and political associations in Japan—a subject worthy of intensive study in itself—we shall first briefly allude to the formal structure of the ward as it is organized politically and to the type of voluntary organizations that organize activities. We shall then illustrate the social networks related specifically to the prevention of delinquency. By using this one illustration we believe we can make it sufficiently clear that there is considerable voluntary local community involvement and that this involvement is sufficiently intense to have some effect.

Arakawa Ward Government

Three cities in Japan—Tokyo, Osaka, and Kyoto—rank administratively on an equal basis with the prefectures, or *ken*, into which the country is divided. This gives the twenty-three wards of Tokyo a status comparable in certain respects to that of city units in other prefectures—or at least somewhat more autonomy than have the ward subdivisions of other cities. The postwar decentralization policy, especially the recent revision of the national "local self-

1. The subject of affiliation and nurturance in Japanese society is discussed from several aspects in De Vos, 1973.

government body law," has curtailed the considerable local political autonomy once enjoyed by Tokyo ward offices. Nevertheless, the ward office remains a semiautonomous part of the administrative network centered at the Tokyo Municipal Office.

Thus the Arakawa Ward Office independently administers welfare programs, for which the ward receives a yearly budget, and makes local decisions concerning health, parks, building programs, and the like. Although control of other Arakawa affairs is retained under the official jurisdiction of the central Tokyo Municipal Office, de facto administration often takes place at the ward level. A large number of Arakawa Ward staff members, while officially employees of the central Tokyo office, are assigned directly to the ward office and work directly with other staff members there. Their principal contacts are with residents in a number of different contexts. These employees soon begin to think of themselves as part of the local establishment rather than part of the central office.

In its basic structure the government of the ward represents an amalgam of a number of public and private agencies surrounding an official legal core made up of the ward headman's executive office, the ward assembly, and a bureaucracy of six divisions. The ward headman (*ku-chō*) is elected by the local ward assembly with the consent of the governor of Tokyo for a term of four years (successive terms are permissible) and appoints his own assistant headman (*jo-yaku*) and treasurer (*shūnyū-yaku*).[2] The ward assembly (*ku-gikai*), an elected legislative body, has forty-four assemblymen drawn from local groups.

Attached to the ward headman's executive office are three administrative committees, each with some citizen members. Auxiliary executive committees (a total of ten at the time of our inquiry) are appointed by the ward headman from among assemblymen, ward office staff, and community leaders to organize the block associations (*chōkai*) and retail store associations (*shōten kai*, to be discussed below) into larger units for specific purposes—for example, cooperation with the ward in the planning of youth programs or the management of ward facilities. In addition to these committees, a secretary is appointed to act as liaison with the various ward sections of bureaucrats within the ward office.

To provide office space for the ward office and the six bureaucratic divisions, the ward operates three main buildings, near the central Arakawa police station, and eight branch offices. All of these offices receive a constant stream of residents, who come for various purposes closely connected with their daily life. Every Japanese citizen needs a copy of his family registry (*koseki*) or a residential registry (*kyojū shōmei* or *jūmin tōroku*) for identification and certification when entering school, when applying for a job, a driver's license, or a passport, and when dealing with officials in many similar matters. It is in the ward office that a citizen's family or residential registry record is kept, and there that all marriages, births, and deaths must be registered. Pregnant women come to the ward office

2. There is no residency requirement. In 1966 the ward headman was from Arakawa Ward, but the assistant headman lived in Adachi Ward, and the treasurer in Chiba Prefecture.

to receive a mother-and-child card in order to receive maternal and child welfare services (such as health checkups at a public clinic). The ward office is where people come to complain about the inadequacy of playground facilities, to ask for the repair of a street, to pay their national health insurance, to consult about their national old age pensions. They come to receive permission to build or expand their houses, to register their dogs, and to receive various welfare services. A foreigner who wants to live in the ward must appear at the ward office at least once to receive an alien registration certificate.

We do not consider questions of informal political functioning germane to our present research, and we cannot, therefore, describe how decisions are negotiated within the ward's official complex administrative structure; we can only say that the local political-administrative structure allows for some considerable exercise of decision making by bureaucrats, interacting within a social prestige network involving the better-placed business, commercial, and professional residents of the ward.

The yearly list of activities in which both elected and appointed ward officials themselves not only participate but also seek participation by ward citizens is impressive. In this yearly cycle of activities each section vies with others to demonstrate its continual involvement with the health and welfare of Arakawa residents.

Town Block Associations (chōkai)

The basic unit of Japanese urban social organization is the town block association, the *chōkai* (colloquially called *chōnaikai*). The *chōkai* provides a sense of community membership and solidarity. It is through the *chōkai* that city dwellers are mobilized for various recreational and cooperative activities, for social education, for environmental improvement, and for community maintenance—which are often initiated (or encouraged) by the ward, municipal, or even national administration and its auxiliary organs. Various councils and cooperating committees for education, health, welfare, and other social programs at the ward level are composed mostly of *chōkai* presidents. Such committees are the chief means of communication from the people upward to the ward, municipal, and national administrative bodies as well as downward from the government to the ordinary *chōkai* member.

The *chōkai* came into existence in the Tokugawa era, when the *shitamachi* townsmen in the capital were rigidly organized into neighborhood groups whose members were collectively held responsible for tax payment and for criminal activity on the part of members. During World War II, each *chōkai* was divided into a number of smaller neighborhood associations (*tonari gumi*), which played an important functional role in mobilizing Japan for the national war effort. At the end of the war, both *tonari gumi* and *chōkai* were dissolved by order of the Occupation authorities, but *chōkai* were revived in 1951 and resumed their local organizational functions.

There were at the time of our research a total of 109 *chōkai* in Arakawa

Ward, averaging about 400 households each. Membership is voluntary, in principle, but in a *shitamachi* area such as Arakawa social pressure can be very strong, and practically every household joins the *chōkai*, paying a monthly membership fee of 30 to 50 yen (10 to 17 cents). The members elect a president (*kaichō*), who in turn appoints two vice-presidents (*fukukaichō*), two treasurers (*kaikei*), and two supervisors (*kansa*). *Chōkai* have various sections—such as a general affairs section (*sōmubu*), a women's section (*fujinbu*), a traffic section (*kōtsūbu*), a crime prevention section (*bōhanbu*), a fire prevention section (*bōkabu*), a welfare section (*kōseibu*), a youth section (*seinenbu*)—and each section is headed by an elected director. The important officials of a *chōkai* hold a regular meeting once a month to discuss and decide on activities. Once a year, a general meeting of all members is held (in the ward hall auditorium in the case of Arakawa). Larger and wealthier *chōkai* may own their own building and use it for various small meetings of officials and members, and some employ a part-time or a full-time secretary. Usually, however, the *chōkai* office is located in the store or the house of the *chōkai* president, and clerical work is done by his family members and neighbors on a voluntary basis.

We observed the typical activities of the ward in five major areas: adult education, youth programs, environmental improvement, public safety, and cooperation with public administrators. We will not report on how the *chōkai* functions, but we can say that in each instance a very large network of individuals are given tasks and titles related to the activities at hand.

For example, club committees of the *chōkai* take the initiative in maintaining a clean and neat neighborhood, encouraging people to sweep the streets, supervising local garbage collection by the ward, and campaigning for the use of disinfectants. The *chōkai* may also file petitions with the ward office and municipal government for the repair and improvement of streets and bridges and the installation of traffic lights and street signs.

For public safety, in cooperation with the police and fire stations, the *chōkai* assumes responsibility for maintaining order and safety in its neighborhood—for example, organizing the *keibō dan* (a vigilance corps of civilian guards), whose members take turns making the rounds on winter nights, typically beating wooden clappers or calling *hi no yōjin* ("Take precaution against fire"). Another regular function of the *keibō dan* is to help children cross streets in heavy traffic.

Supraneighborhood committees may proliferate wherever a new approach to a problem is needed—and almost no community problem is beyond their scope. Little purpose would be served by a list of the many ad hoc organizations to be found in Arakawa Ward at any given moment, but some idea of their interrelation and usefulness may be gained from the following description of the principal committees concerned with preventing delinquency and coordinating efforts toward this goal by *chōkai*, the Education Committee in the ward office, and the correctional authorities of the national government.

District Committees for Youth Guidance (Chiku Hodō Renraku Iinkai): Central Arakawa District, 68 members; Machiya, 31; Ogu, 78; Nippori, 63; and

Minami Senju, 76. These district committees—composed of volunteer supervisors (*hogoshi*), policemen, schoolteachers, staff members of the Child Guidance Clinic (located in Kita Ward), and family-court probation officers—organize various programs to prevent delinquency and also to help in the rehabilitation of delinquents.

District Committees for Youth Problems (Seinen Taisaku Chiku Iinkai): Arakawa Central District, 72 members; Machiya, 49; Ogu, 64; Nippori, 75; and Minami Senju, 55. The membership of the committees on "youth problems" and on "youth guidance" largely overlaps, although the former also include people who are not directly involved with delinquents. Activities are directed toward youth problems in general rather than toward the prevention of delinquency or the rehabilitation of delinquents. In their concern for better education, recreation, and health for youth in the ward, these committees sponsor athletic events, organize outings, award good-conduct citations, and in other ways try to improve the social environment.

The Youth Committee membership (Seishōnen Iin) comprised 49 individuals—schoolteachers and civilian leaders. Again, the membership partly overlaps that of the district committees on youth problems as well as that of several smaller groups.

To an outsider interested only in the instrumental solution of a particular task, such as "youth problems," the presence of so many different committees might seem a waste of time and effort. This would be a superficial conclusion showing lack of understanding of the underlying functions of Japanese voluntary organizations. There are actually a number of social benefits. First, the existence of many committees, even with some overlapping membership, increases the number of people involved. Second, voluntary associations provide group reinforcement of the need to donate service and time and effort to community problems. Third, more "community leaders" can receive the psychological rewards of prestige and the gratification of social status. Fourth, the communication network is broadened to include other segments of the community. Fifth, those in whose interest the committees are set up are aware of widespread community concern and involvement—someone "cares." People feel themselves part of a community that cares for its members, paternally and maternally, in a diffusion of traditional familism that supplants the disappearing lineage structures of Japanese society.

Retail Store Associations (shōtenkai)

The functions of *chōkai*, as we have described them, are both instrumental and expressive. Somewhat similar but with more limited occupational membership and with more specific instrumental purposes are the many *shōtenkai*, or retail store associations, which unite local people and continually bring them in contact with one another. They cut across the block organizations. *Shōtenkai* are associations of all the owners of shops, restaurants, and other retail businesses in the same neighborhood regardless of the nature of their services, to be distinguished from still other associations of all those in the ward engaged in a particular occupation or profession. The criterion of locality is absolute; for instance, a shopkeeper whose store is in one neighborhood and whose residence is in another will belong to the *shōtenkai* of the one and the *chōkai* of the other. At the time of our research there were fifty-five *shōtenkai* in Arakawa Ward, of which forty-four belonged to the inclusive Arakawa Stores Associations League (Arakawa Shōtenkai Rengōkai). The reason for the independence of the remaining eleven *shōtenkai* could not be determined. Internal organization is much the same as in the *chōkai*: an elected president, vice-presidents, treasurer(s), directors, and supervisors. The main function of *shōtenkai* is to facilitate the business of its members by cooperative action, such as holding special sale days, decorating the stores and streets for special seasonal events such as the New Year, and issuing raffle tickets to their customers.

Court Procedures: Parole and Probation

Much of Japan's administration of justice—arrest practices, investigation, indictment by the public prosecutor's office, court trial—is essentially the same as in the United States, with the one important and fundamental difference that in Japan the courts are organized on a national basis and are not under local control.

The courts deal with delinquents on the basis of a juvenile code that classifies "problem juveniles" into three categories: (1) criminal juveniles (*hanzai shōnen*), those age fourteen to nineteen who have committed a crime; (2) lawbreaking juveniles (*shokuhō shōnen*), those under fourteen years of age who have committed a crime but because of their age are not held to be criminal; and (3) crime-prone juveniles (*guhan shōnen*), those who, while innocent of any actual crime, are considered prone to future criminal activity because of bad character, bad environment, or such bad behavior as rebelling against the proper guidance and supervision of a guardian, vagrancy, or the frequenting of undesirable places. All three types of youths are collectively referred to as delinquent juveniles, *hikō shōnen*.

Their ultimate treatment depends not only on the courts but on a complex network of agencies whose various and overlapping functions attest to the problems of classification and administration that accrue in modern bureaucracies.

If at a time of arrest a juvenile is over fourteen and considered sufficiently delinquent, he is usually turned over to a family court. A juvenile may come before family court at the request of parents or other people or as the result of a report by a family-court research officer (*chōsa kan*). A family-court judge determines whether the juvenile will be allowed to return home or will be detained at a juvenile classification center (*shōnen kanbetsu sho*). Those who are detained receive physical and psychological examinations whose results are presented to the court, and the judge orders a family-court research officer to prepare a report on the juvenile's life history, character, behavior tendencies, attitudes, lifestyle, family relations, friends, school or work environment, and community circumstances. The research officer does this by calling parents to the family court for interviews, visiting the juvenile's home and school or working place, and sometimes administering diagnostic psychological tests. After studying the background reports and test results, the judge again interviews the juvenile and talks with other people concerned. At this point the judge decides what action the court should take. His alternatives include trial, acquittal, protective treatment (usually probation), or referral to a public prosecutor.

A juvenile turned over to a family court by the police may also be put on tentative probation (*shiken kansatsu*) by a family-court research officer, who with the help of a volunteer layman, or *hogoshi*, will observe and supervise the juvenile's life for awhile before the judge, taking into account probationary behavior, decides on the disposition of the case.

We shall not deal here with the procedures of professional custodial institutions, to which only a small proportion of juvenile offenders are sent, but rather we shall touch upon how voluntary organizations within the community participate in the special surveillance of juveniles who have been put under what is called "rehabilitative protection" (*kōsei hogo*), a concept somewhat more paternalistic and nurturant than the English terms "probation" and "parole."[3]

The two main categories of rehabilitative protection are "protective observation" (*hogo kansatsu*) and "rehabilitative emergency protection" (*kōsei kinkyū hogo*). Protective observation includes a supervisory-disciplinary aspect and a guidance-protective aspect, labeled by the Japanese "directional supervision" (*shidō kantoku*) and "guidance aid" (*hodō engo*), respectively. Those individuals put under directional supervision have voluntary supervisors called *hogoshi*. Others put under guidance aid are referred to professionals working in technical training centers or medical facilities and may receive assistance from social workers in finding a place of residence or a job or in improving their general social environment.

The second major category of rehabilitative protection, "rehabilitative emergency protection," applies to those who have completed a prison term, those who have received suspended sentences, and those for whom the court has postponed sentence pending further examination.[4]

The Hogoshi *System*

The most important voluntary program, and one which is indispensable for the adequate functioning of probation and parole in Japan, is carried on by the voluntary supervisors (*hogoshi*). Their work warrants detailed study not only

3. The Japanese legal term corresponding to probation and parole is *hogo kansatsu*, literally translated "protection-observation." The English word "probation" has the connotation of "examination" or "testing," and the word "parole" derives from "word of honor," an individual's pledge of good behavior. Probation requirements in Japan, as described in the official manuals, are divided into categories according to the classifications of the delinquents.

4. Individuals who cannot obtain immediate aid and protection from responsible relatives or friends or from some public health or welfare facility in their area are given emergency protection,

because it bears so directly on the control of delinquency but also because it reveals some basic features of why and how voluntary dedication of time to public service flourishes within the Japanese social system.

The *hogoshi* are civilian volunteers commissioned by the Ministry of Justice to work for rehabilitative protection, their status being that of part-time, unpaid, national public servants. The *hogoshi* system is a unique institution rooted in Japanese traditions of paternalism and community commitment to the protection and rehabilitation of troubled members. It grew out of the government's Ex-convicts' Protection System of the early 1900s under which volunteers, mostly Buddhist monks, were called on to help rehabilitate ex-convicts under government sponsorship. In 1939 the system was taken over by the public prosecutor's office and reorganized as the Judicial Protection Activities System. At that time a committee of civilian volunteers was formed to assist local groups interested in this work to set up the proper administrative machinery. The postwar Criminal Protection Law (Hanzai Hogo Hō) made juvenile delinquents a special category under this system.

At present the procedure for the appointment of a *hogoshi* begins with an informal recommendation by the local *hogoshi* association or by the ward head to the director of the local parole and probation bureau. Appointments are for two years and are renewable. The major requirements for appointment as a *hogoshi* are financial security, community trust and confidence, sufficient free time, and evidence of definite commitment. Furthermore, the candidate should have an unsullied past, that is, should never have been considered legally incompetent, jailed for illegal activity, or involved in any form of subversive political activity. Old age, failing health, change of residence, and too pressing business concerns are among the reasons a *hogoshi* may be denied reappointment. Despite these stringent qualifications, there were a reported 52,500 *hogoshi* in 1968 working throughout Japan.

However, in Tokyo there is considerable difficulty in filling the number of

---

which may involve aid in finding a place to live, provision of room and board, medical care, and sometimes a small amount of money.

Rehabilitative protection is provided by a bewildering array of agencies, some working through a bureau of the Ministry of Justice, some through district councils, some through parole and probation bureaus connected with district courts. The efforts of such agencies are augmented by "protective observation" officers, specially trained case workers with at least some undergraduate training in social work, who are assigned to a regional council for rehabilitative protection. In addition, there are national organizations of civilian volunteers which operate facilities providing those on parole and probation with room and board, education, vocational training, medical care, and other aid. There are also neighborhood groups, called protective observation associations (*hogo kansatsu kyōkai*), composed mostly of women, which attempt to rehabilitate ex-convicts. For example, the nationwide Woman's Rehabilitative Protection Association, with 843 local chapters and a membership of about 570,000 (in 1968), helps with the rehabilitation of former prostitutes. There are also the so-called BBS (Big Brother and Sister Associations), with 539 chapters and a total membership of about 10,000, concerned principally with delinquents; and a Cooperative Employers Association (Kyōryoku Koyō Shu Kyō Kai), numbering about 1,600 members, who have pledged to employ ex-convicts in their businesses.

possible appointments; the fixed quota for the city is 4,450, but the number of functioning *hogoshi* rarely exceeds 3,500. It is obviously not easy to find enough good candidates. Younger people are too busy in their own occupations, and since a *hogoshi* is expected to have considerable wisdom and experience, there is probably a tendency not to consider younger candidates seriously. Most applicants who have the time and necessary commitment are at least fifty years old, and those over sixty-five are considered to be too old to function well with their somewhat trying charges.

According to our interview at the Tokyo Parole and Probation Bureau in 1966, the usual case load for each *hogoshi* is four individuals. The *hogoshi* makes contact with his charges approximately twice a month for about an hour and writes a monthly report, which he submits to the probation and parole bureau. For each case undertaken the government gives the *hogoshi* a small stipend (about 400 to 600 yen monthly) to cover some of his actual costs.

Police and ward officials who work with *hogoshi* perceive the assets of the system to be these: (1) *Hogoshi*, being community leaders, in most instances men, but sometimes professional women, know the community network thoroughly and can help ex-convicts or repentant juveniles return to normal society better than professional government officers can. (2) Though technically public servants, the *hogoshi* function as unpaid volunteers and are therefore in a better position to establish rapport with delinquents or ex-convicts, who tend to regard government officials as a form of authority. (3) As civil leaders, *hogoshi* can be expected to have wider views of society than government employees concerned with their immediate job. Officials see as liabilities of the *hogoshi* system these facts: (1) Levels of intelligence, ability, personal maturity, and education vary among *hogoshi*, and few fulfill the ideal. The pressing need to fill openings sometimes leads to the selection of individuals who are less than adequate. (2) It is difficult to find good *hogoshi* in areas with high delinquency rates. (3) Some *hogoshi* are hopelessly out of touch with the changing needs and concerns of youth. (4) Because of pressing business activities or illnesses or necessary trips, *hogoshi* may spend too little time with their charges or even leave individuals unsupervised at critical periods. (5) Some *hogoshi* are old-fashioned and authoritarian, refusing to adapt to the more "scientific" and "rational" approaches that have become policy in professional agencies. (6) Many of the less educated *hogoshi*, though very effective in face-to-face contact with ex-convicts or delinquents, do not know how to write good reports. This can create serious problems for probation officers, who must keep meticulous records.

In 1966 there were 115 *hogoshi* in Arakawa, all members of the Arakawa *hogoshi* association, distributed fairly equally among the various districts of the ward. More so than most other ward offices in Tokyo, the Arakawa Ward Office had in the 1960s a very positive and close relationship with the *hogoshi* association, a relationship which seemingly accounts, to some degree at least, for Arakawa's relative success in cutting down delinquency. That the ward headman was himself a *hogoshi* had decisive effect. Administratively speaking, the ward office and the *hogoshi* association have no formal relationship, but it is customary in Arakawa, as elsewhere, for ward offices to allocate some funds—usually about 150,000 yen—to the *hogoshi* association. The Arakawa *hogoshi* received as much as 4,000 yen annually from the ward office during these years. Both ward officers and members of the association liked to talk about their close and harmonious relationship.

Social Status of Arakawa Hogoshi

We were curious about the social status of those appointed *hogoshi* in Arakawa. The Arakawa association's membership directory was quite explicit as to their occupational background and community activities. Predictably, most members were relatively well-off and of considerable social influence in the community, typically belonging to a large number of voluntary associations. The occupational distribution of the *hogoshi* indirectly revealed a dual prestige network in the ward, with some occupations having high status owing to their past history and others having become important in more recent times, but the "professions" predominated.

Representing the traditional professions were thirteen individuals classified as physicians, dentists, midwives, and pharmacists.[5] It was not surprising to find eight priests and monks among the *hogoshi* in Arakawa, but, interestingly, there were no leaders of "new" religious groups. Although Sōka Gakkai, one of the most successful of those groups, is quite active in the ward, no Sōka Gakkai leader has been recommended for appointment as a *hogoshi*. This attests that membership in Sōka Gakkai cannot yet be translated into generally acceptable social prestige in Arakawa Ward.

Those engaged in education would seem to make natural candidates for the role of *hogoshi*, and one might wonder why only six such individuals were working as volunteers. According to one of our better informants, schoolteachers either are too busy with their own work or are not sufficiently well-off financially to be considered. Here one finds rather direct testimony that the status of the schoolteacher today is not as high as it once was. This lowering of social status has come about both because there are now proportionately more

5. In the older Japanese society, experienced midwives played a role very similar to that of physicians. Most births took place at home, and the old midwife of a village was accorded special status as a "mother" of the village. Today, as increasing numbers of women choose maternity clinics or hospitals, midwives are being trained to assist at births in hospitals under the supervision of a physician, who intercedes only when there is an emergency. Older people in times of crisis sometimes still turn to their midwife; younger people have learned to expect personal instruction from her in the proper use of contraceptive devices and drugs, which often puts the midwife in the position of a teacher-confidante. Of somewhat more recent origin is the high community status of the pharmacist. In Japan, where many medicines may be purchased without a doctor's prescription, the pharmacist serves as a kind of auxiliary doctor. Pharmacists as well as general practitioners live in the back of their professional offices and tend to be very knowledgeable about their community.

teachers and because teachers' salaries in recent years have declined in comparison with pay scales in other fields.

The continued high status of four *hogoshi* who were dealers in coal, oil, fuel, rice, soy sauce, and sake is of some anthropological significance. During the Tokugawa period a single merchant might hold a monopoly on rice, *miso* (bean paste), soy sauce, sake, and firewood in his village or rural town and also act as moneylender, at a very high interest rate, to poorer neighbors. Such a merchant was likely to be the richest tradesman in the community. Today one still finds, especially in rural communities, a residue of deference paid to individuals running a basic supply store.

A more or less similar monopoly is held by the owners of pawnshops and bathhouses, of whom three were represented among the *hogoshi*. The owner of the bathhouse, who customarily sits at the entrance and collects fees, is a well-known person in his local community. In Arakawa there still were few private bathing facilities in the 1960s, and the public bathhouse remained an important meeting place for *shitamachi* people.

As might be expected, a large proportion of *hogoshi* in Arakawa were drawn from the more successful small manufacturers (14), retail store owners (17), workshop owners (14), wholesale dealers (5), and contractors (3), reflecting the occupational distribution noted in our statistics on demography. There were also seven individuals with bureaucratic positions, all in the upper areas of the bureaucracy. In fact, *hogoshi* are quite likely to be active in local politics, whether directly running for office or indirectly helping to elect others. Obviously, most *hogoshi* in Arakawa are people of relatively high social standing, influence, and prestige. Their previous social background is an important consideration, and membership in this association is a desired symbolic recognition of status, making it truly "a privilege" to serve. Work as a *hogoshi* is, in effect, a Japanese analogue of the service expected of upper-middle-class individuals in the United States as affirmation of high social status and social acceptability—a modern form of noblesse oblige.

Other Voluntary Efforts toward Delinquency Control

Complementing the rehabilitative work of the *hogoshi* associations and their auxiliary organizations are periodic campaigns to prevent delinquency, which are conducted in cooperation with such voluntary advisory groups as the Seishōnen Mondai Kyōgi Kai (Council for Youth Problems). This council, an adjunct of the headman's office, is a local counterpart of the Tokyo Municipal Council for Youth Problems, which acts as a committee to advise the governor of Tokyo, and the national Council for Youth Problems attached to the office of the prime minister. The Arakawa council was established in February 1955.

At the time of our study, its executive committee was composed of ward department heads (general affairs, civic affairs, welfare, and construction), the chief of the general affairs department of the ward clinic, the police chiefs in charge of youth at the three Arakawa police stations, the deputy principals of primary and middle schools, a case worker from the child guidance clinic that services the ward, the head of the department of vocational education at the Adachi Public Employment Security Office, and the chiefs of the departments of school education and social education of the Arakawa education commission. Beneath this top executive committee were a liaison committee for guidance and district committees in Nippori, Central Arakawa, Machiya, Minami Senju, and Ogu districts. The liaison committee was concerned with case work involving problem youth and drew its membership from among *hogoshi*, policemen in charge of youth, social welfare workers, child-case workers, schoolteachers in charge of family-life courses, members of Big Brothers and Sisters, and so on. The district committees, oriented toward community problems, consisted of representatives from the district youth committee, the PTA, the district educational commission, the district merchants' association, youth and women's associations, and similar community organizations. Their main stated activities and interests were to (1) improve the social and cultural environment of youth, (2) furnish out-of-school guidance for school youth and special guidance for working youth, (3) encourage the development of voluntary organizations among youth, (4) promote education for parents, and (5) reinforce welfare programs for children.

To illustrate: In 1965 the council decided to make an all-out campaign for the "improvement of the social environment of youth" during the months of September and October. An executive committee for the campaign was organized and divided into subcommittees for "publicity activities," "environment," and "healthy sports." The subcommittee for publicity activities prepared fifty placards with two slogans—*seishōnen ni ai no hito koe o* ("Give a word of love to youngsters") and *kenzen na yoi kankyo o tsukurimashō* ("Let us create a healthy and good environment")—which schoolchildren in each district carried in a parade along the street, following their own fife-and-drum band; each child who participated received a small gift. The subcommittee also prepared for display throughout the ward 350 standing signboards with the same slogans and 3,000 posters reading "Let us protect our youth!" as well as 40,000 handouts for schoolchildren to take home to their parents. Further publicity was generated by talks over a loudspeaker (borrowed from the ward office) blaring from a car that cruised the streets, a series of lectures in which four speakers from outside the ward showed films on parent-child relationships, and a number of public forums on youth problems.

Less visible but just as ambitious were the activities of the subcommittee for environment, which marshaled a force including police and *hogoshi* to comb the streets and entertainment areas for children engaged in questionable activities; the children were given a lecture and sent home. The subcommittee for sports held a ping-pong tournament and kendo and judo contests, in which about 1,300 youths participated. This and similar campaigns have the full support of community leaders in Arakawa, who firmly believe that such efforts can help reduce the delinquency rate.

An example of field notes, made when Wagatsuma was invited to join twelve *hogoshi* at an informal lunch in Minami Senju on July 20, 1966:

> The twelve included a pharmacist, a bathhouse owner, a sake dealer, a building contractor, a coal dealer, a cloth manufacturer, a pencil manufacturer, a Buddhist monk, a restaurant owner, and three furniture manufacturers. The *hogoshi* all agreed that the delinquency rate in Arakawa was decreasing and felt the decline had been due mostly to total community involvement in the campaigns for improvement of the social environment in the previous three years, in which children's groups, mothers' groups, every kind of group had taken part.
>
> According to one *hogoshi*, the area around the Jōban railroad tracks used to be frequented by delinquents because the area had no residences and was occupied mostly by storehouses. The community leaders asked parents to pay special attention to this area, and parents told their children not to go there. Policemen, at the community's request, began frequent patrolling. "Now the place is no longer a blind spot in the adults' minds, and so the children have stopped using it for dubious gatherings."
>
> [Wagatsuma asked whether the real delinquents are actually affected by such community campaigns.] "Suppose you hold an athletic meeting for boys or provide the boys with a library or offer them a room for their activities. I wonder if the delinquent boys would not say 'I'm not interested in such kid stuff.'" Some *hogoshi* agreed that such attitudes could be a real problem, and they believed that the community's efforts to provide youngsters with healthy outlets for their energy and to increase adult supervision did in fact help many boys who otherwise might follow the lead of those with more extreme delinquent attitudes. They declared that most delinquents are of the "follower type," and if they are prevented from becoming too involved with the smaller number of "hard-core bad ones," their problems can generally be solved. It was also their opinion that in more than 80 percent of the cases the children's delinquency is a direct fault of the parents. "They leave their children's education completely to the school and do not supervise or discipline their own children," said one elderly *hogoshi*.
>
> Others commented:
>
> "They say 'I did not ask you to arrest my child; now what do you want from me?' They do not realize that their children have done wrong and therefore have been arrested."
>
> "You will be surprised to learn that in Arakawa not a few parents take what their children have stolen to a pawnshop and make money that way."
>
> "In a group crime I have never met any parents of the leader who did not defend their child by saying that somebody else was really responsible and it was not fair that their child was caught while the real bad ones got away."
>
> These community leaders were convinced that campaigns for the

prevention of delinquency were effective in "awakening" the parents of delinquents and so were helping to remove one cause of the problem.

After lunch Wagatsuma accompanied the *hogoshi* on a trip through the neighborhood in behalf of the "campaign to brighten the society" (*shakaio akaruku suru undō*) then being conducted by the Arakawa Council for Youth Problems. Here are excerpts from his field notes:

> The fleet of three cars moved slowly along a winding road. It would stop occasionally. The *hogoshi* would get out of their cars. One of the speakers on top of the car of the public relations department would broadcast a tape-recorded talk by the president of the Arakawa Hogoshi Association, a distinguished-looking man of sixty-eight years, who had lived in Arakawa for more than forty years of his life: "Ladies and gentlemen on the street and at home, now the campaign to 'brighten the society' is being made all over the country. This is a national campaign to remove crime from society with everyone's cooperation. In order to protect our youth from crime and delinquency we need bright homes and a bright society. Crimes are our own concern, not someone else's. For those who have made mistakes and now want to better themselves, society is not always warm and kind. Let us help them warmly. Let us unite our efforts to protect our youth and children from crime." This speech lasted for four minutes; meanwhile, the *hogoshi* and BBS members began to pass out balloons of various colors and pencils on which were printed the slogan "The movement to brighten the society." Numerous children came to the cars to receive their free balloons and pencils. When children were accompanied by parents the *hogoshi* handed each parent a piece of paper containing a copy of the Hogoshi Association president's four-minute speech. There were eighteen stops in over two hours—among the ragpickers' shacks next to the stadium, in the slums near Tokyo Municipal Sewage Disposal Plant, and amid the strong stench of a leather tannery.
>
> Children were eager to receive the balloons and pencils. Adults, however, were generally indifferent. I did not notice anyone who looked as if he were really listening to the speech. Some mothers eagerly came to the *hogoshi* in order to receive balloons for the children, but then they hurried away even before any *hogoshi* could hand them a printed copy of the speech. The sound of the loudspeaker did cause many faces to peer out of windows and doors, but the faces most often disappeared long before the taped speech came to the end.
>
> I saw many adults bowing to the *hogoshi* and reentering their rooms. Some came up to a *hogoshi* and greeted him politely and then walked away, and I had an impression that it was important for them to make a personal greeting to given persons among the *hogoshi*, saying, "*Gokurō sama de gozaimasu*" ("Your arduous efforts are much appreciated") or reporting briefly that things were going well thanks to the *hogoshi's* kind efforts.
>
> I commented to myself that, although no one really listened to the speech, and perhaps only a few would read it on the piece of paper handed out, for residents it was clear that these influential community leaders (to

whom many residents owed particular obligation) were busy at something, something connected with bad boys or with the prevention of crime. Perhaps this in itself was enough. People saw community leaders doing something, sacrificing their time. Wealthy and influential old men walking around in the hot summer day's sun, perspiring and handing out balloons to children—by giving people an impression that their leaders were exerting efforts toward something which seemed related to the improvement of their community, a form of social pressure was being exerted.

THE SOCIAL ATTITUDES OF DELINQUENTS

In the course of our contacts with both adults and youths in Arakawa, we were able to gain some ethnographic impressions of the attitudes and practices of youths in respect to what would be considered "delinquent" behavior. Our information came from many sources, the most relevant being teachers working in the Arakawa schools, police officials dealing specifically with youth problems, *hogoshi*, some special interviews with delinquent and nondelinquent youths, and, of course, our intensively studied sample of fifty families in the ward. The composite picture we obtained from these various sources cannot be presented here except in brief anecdotes, but we believe it reflects with reasonable accuracy adolescent attitudes and activities in Arakawa in the 1960s.

A number of our informants in Arakawa Ward defined delinquency as we do, as basically a social attitude marked by a flouting of socially acceptable behavior in regard to persons and property. Among the delinquents themselves what is very often symbolically displayed is some form of hostility toward constituted authority. A police officer concerned with delinquency in Arakawa estimated that in the mid-1960s there was a hard core of about 3 percent of the boys in the middle schools who manifested basically delinquent attitudes. Around this group were a coterie of followers who often found themselves involved in delinquent behavior as part of group activity.

A very perceptive probation worker, who had dealt with delinquent boys in Arakawa Ward over a period of years, made a number of cogent statements about their social attitudes: "Delinquent boys feel they are on one side of the river and all the others are on the other side. Normal boys, teachers, parents, adults—all are on one side, while they look at them from across the river. They will not come to us. We must somehow build a bridge over to their side. Then we can talk. They might even agree thereafter to join us."

Attitudes toward Sex

In special segments of a population, covert behavior that deviates from legal or dominant social mores, but is generally condoned, usually shades into overt behavior that expresses defiance of authority in such a way as to be quickly judged "delinquent" both by police and by the community generally. Difficulties in defining the subtleties that often distinguish the two are particularly apparent in respect to sexual behavior. Although our data from Arakawa Ward do not include detailed or systematic knowledge concerning the actual patterns of sexual experience among youth, the sexual histories as reported by the parents in our fifty families suggested middle-class patterns of delayed heterosexual experience, especially among the women. Those of our informants who were community leaders also expressed essentially middle-class values, and we sensed in some of them a negative evaluation of what might be seen as lower-class sexual behavior. These patterns were in line with the typical Japanese double standard, stressing continence in women while condoning premarital sexuality with prostitutes on the part of young men. There was little revelation of premarital sexual behavior on the part of the mothers, and most of the boys, when interviewed at thirteen to fifteen years of age, were not yet involved in sexual activities. In some of the families in our sample, we did gain the distinct impression that the wife had had sexual liaisons prior to her official marriage, but there was no way to determine from our interviews the extent of such behavior. Marital irregularities were found to be especially prevalent in the delinquent subsample, but again, we have no basis for evaluating the specific material of our sample against the total community.

Less representative of what was reported to us in our family interviews and perhaps more representative of attitudes among present-day Arakawa youth was a pattern of sexual license that allows a couple to live together on a temporary basis, which may or may not result in official marriage. Very often such a relationship is formalized only after the appearance of a child, who needs registration in order to attend school and to participate in any kind of formal community activity. Sometimes these living-together arrangements exist in spite of parental opposition. One informant mentioned a case involving a nineteen-year-old boy and a seventeen-year-old girl. The girl was known for her somewhat promiscuous behavior, but the boy was not considered a delinquent even though he had come into contact with the police. The parents were very much opposed to their living together and to their marrying, but the boy and girl proceeded to declare themselves married, although there was no official registry of any kind. He began to work and showed a seriousness of intent that had not been apparent in his behavior before, and the parents were finally forced to accept the situation. It is interesting to note that our informant, while quite aware that the couple were not married in any legal sense, spontaneously used the word "marriage" to describe the arrangement they had worked out, attesting to a still-prevalent Japanese attitude about the value of "marriage." The concern with official registration in the past generally focused more on registering children for family continuity than on legalizing sexual behavior between two individuals. In the middle class, where informal liaisons are rare—for girls at least—there would be more concern with legalization through registration.

There is a class of individuals in Arakawa Ward, principally among the day laborers, who lack all concern about the registration of their marriages or of their children's births. Children of these people often have names obviously different in one way or another from their parents, and where secondary liaisons occur, there is no attempt to straighten out official parental responsibility. According to a schoolteacher-informant, one or two out of every hundred children in Arakawa have some kind of irregular situation at home.

The police do not usually interfere with private youthful sexuality, taking action only to stop overt amorous displays by youths or to question very young adolescents found together on the street late at night. Nor do the Japanese have any legal category of statutory rape. Arrests, however, are made under a category called "bad behavior," which includes drinking, smoking, fighting, truancy, stealing from parents, use of drugs, and "obscenity" (*fujun isei kōyū*).[6] Such arrests usually involve youths found sitting together at late hours in coffee shops or loitering on the street. Few of these cases ever result in adjudication before a court, and many, when brought to court, are dismissed. Court action ensues only for individuals who have been picked up with considerable frequency, and these are most often promiscuous young girls. According to one policeman, only 10 percent of those picked up (not necessarily adjudicated) by the police are involved in actual sexual intercourse; most of the young girls engage only in necking or petting.

One *hogoshi* reported to us that many delinquent boys whom she had interviewed confided that they had had their first sexual intercourse in about the sixth grade. Such first experience sometimes takes place in an empty classroom, when the rest of the class are out in the schoolyard for physical education or some such activity.

This same *hogoshi* described a few instances of sexual delinquency that had come to her attention. One involved a group of three girls, two ninth-graders and one eighth-grader, who had absented themselves from school for a number of days. Upon inquiry, their parents told her that the girls had been away from home and vaguely suggested they were working at a restaurant somewhere. The *hogoshi* persisted and finally tracked down the girls at a coffee shop in a neighboring ward. After forcing the girls to return home, she warned the woman manager of the shop that she could be arrested for violation of the law against child labor. The woman claimed that because the girls had never told her that they were still in junior high school, and were so "physically mature," she had never thought of them as minors. But the girls told the *hogoshi* that other middle-school girls had worked there, and it seemed certain that the coffee shop had a regular policy of using very young waitresses to attract male customers. The *hogoshi* discovered that the three girls had been having fairly frequent sexual relations with members of a criminal gang operating out of Adachi Ward. In spite of their sexual behavior, these girls—like many others their age—were remarkably uninformed about sexual matters. When one girl suddenly, somewhat hyster-

6. In 1967, the police statistics for the entire city of Tokyo included 61,463 contacts with juveniles for "bad behavior," of which 3,873 were specified as involving "illicit sexual activity."

ically reported to the others that she "felt" pregnant, the others quickly concluded they too must be pregnant and all three decided to visit a doctor, going to a clinic some distance from Arakawa. The doctor examined the first girl and said she was not pregnant, whereupon the other two said, "Well, if she's not, then we must not be either," and promptly left.

A policeman reported to us a number of cases coming to police attention, from which we can draw a few illustrations. A boy, about fifteen years old, explained to a policeman upon being apprehended that he had initiated intercourse with his younger sister, about twelve years of age, after watching the sexual activities of his parents in their one-room dwelling and becoming "obsessed" with sex. Even before the incest with his sister, he had started to steal women's underthings—the impulse that led to his finally being caught late one afternoon when he visited an apartment house to deliver the evening papers on his newspaper route. The residents of this apartment house were mostly women who worked in bars or cabarets. Finding a number of women's panties hung out to dry, he became excited sexually and, breaking into one of the apartments, took off his own clothes, took out the woman's clothes, and put on panties and brassiere. The manager discover the boy as he entered another apartment to put on more underwear, and turned him over to the police. At the time of his arrest, he was wearing, one on top of another, seven pairs of women's panties.

The police officer, like our *hogoshi*-informant, found very curious the extent of misinformation among sexually promiscuous girl delinquents. Very often they are totally ignorant both about how they may become impregnated and about the problem of venereal disease. Another officer estimated that about eight out of ten of the more promiscuous girls picked up by the police have gonorrhea and that this disease has been in rapid increase. A common belief among these girls is that they will not become pregnant if they have sexual relationships with more than one man. One of our police informants remarked, "I don't know whether it's true, but many girls say that this belief is based on accurate observation." The policeman indicated that many boys share this belief and give this as an excuse when caught in the group rape of a girl. We found another informant, a schoolteacher, who also attested to this belief: "It is true. It has a scientific basis. When a woman sleeps with more than one man, their semen is mixed and there is a neutralization so that it loses its impregnating potential." Many of the younger girls have no idea how to use contraceptives; only those over eighteen, according to our informant, have any general knowledge about contraceptive devices, and sexually active girls of this age are quite likely to carry condoms with them.

Another probation worker noted that in illegitimate births it is sometimes very difficult to determine paternity because the mother was having intercourse with a number of boys. In some cases coming to her attention, the pregnancy resulted from an incestuous act. She told us of a pregnant twelve-year-old girl who lived with her family of seven in a nine-by-nine-foot room and reported having had sexual intercourse with both her father and her brother. The girl had no idea who was the father of her baby.

Sometimes a pregnant girl's friends will collect money to help pay for an abortion. The names of doctors willing to perform illegal abortions are passed around secretly, but are rarely divulged to the police, probation supervisors, or any other outsider.

Acts of sexual violence such as rape are considered rare among early adolescents. One police officer familiar with the statistics of the district could recall only two cases of middle-school boys raping girls in the past ten years. Rape appears to be more frequent among senior high school students and young workers of similar age. Also there are very few reported cases in which a middle-school girl was the victim of rape; this same officer could only recall six or seven such instances. The victims of sexual attack are usually over sixteen years of age.

Some young girls make a deliberate choice of going into prostitution for the money. Such a girl will find out from older girls where to go in the Asakusa amusement area to make contact with a pimp. He will ask her if she's "ready"; if not, that is, if she is still a virgin, as occasionally happens, the pimp will attempt to find a special client, for there are apparently a number of men, usually in their fifties, who will pay extra to have a virgin. The going rate in the lower-class section as of 1967 was between ¥10,000 to ¥20,000, which the girl and the pimp split equally. According to our policeman-informant, young girls cashing in on their virginity this way seem to have no sense of guilt: "They don't even know that they did something wrong."

In Arakawa Ward almost all the sexually delinquent juvenile girls apprehended are locals, including those who work in bars or cabarets and practice prostitution. But the ward is not noted as an entertainment place, and a number of the local girls spurn Arakawa, as do girls coming from the country, in favor of entertainment areas like nearby Asakusa or the more "glamorous" areas of Shinjuku, Ginza, or Shinbashi. A juvenile police officer at the Arakawa station explained that local bar and cabaret girls or semiprostitutes tend to remain in the entertainment world and do not expect to marry ordinary men. The man without a police record will seldom make a permanent liaison with a girl of this kind, although occasionally a cabaret or bar girl will marry a man who has lost his wife or has been deserted. Sometimes such a man will have children whom the girl is supposed to take care of, but the policeman reported that these children are quite likely to be neglected or abused by the stepmother because she has very little interest in assuming a maternal role.

A fairly typical career line for a cabaret girl is to start living with a man when she is about fifteen or sixteen years old. By age twenty-four or twenty-five the girl may have had fairly long-term liaisons with two or three different men. It is not infrequent that a baby results from such a liaison, in which case the man usually disappears, the baby is taken to the woman's parents, and the mother goes to work in a bar or a cabaret. A large number of cabaret girls known to our policeman-informant are helping support a child.

Rather hard and callous attitudes toward sex characterize these prostitutes, seemingly from an early age. This same police officer recalled, for example, one girl who at age twelve had been caught by a patrolman in the act of having sexual intercourse with five boys fifteen to seventeen years old in an empty house late at night. As reported to the police at that time, the girl had had her first menstrual period when she was nine years old and had engaged in sexual activities ever since. At the police station, in front of her parents, the girl blurted out, "Why shouldn't I do the same thing that my parents do? Why can they do it and I can't?" Upon graduation from junior high school, she began work in a nearby cabaret in Ueno Park, concealing her age. She was considered quite attractive and quickly became popular, but she spent money as fast as she received it and was frequently in debt. After work at night, returning home on one of the rail lines, she would approach a man and invite him to her apartment. Her next encounter with the police came because she not only practiced prostitution but also would sometimes take a man to a hotel, then take his wallet and leave while he was taking his bath. At the same time the policeman told us this story the girl, then nineteen, was serving a term in prison for theft.

Attitudes toward Drinking

Although the Arakawa police do not regard drinking as a major problem among youth, it may occur as a secondary problem among a few delinquency-oriented boys. Drinking by older men is mentioned in case histories taken by both police and voluntary probation workers as it relates to the men's meager incomes; however, it is noticeably absent from official police records. In Japan heavy drinking itself is not ordinarily viewed as a social, medical, or psychiatric problem. The individual who becomes violent when drunk is termed *shu-ran* (alcohol-crazed) and is a special focus of concern, but, generally speaking, Japanese do not become aggressive when drinking. As has often been described, the drunken behavior most characteristically observed is a maudlin or affectionate childishness.

Our informants voiced the rather general feeling among Japanese that alcoholism is not so much a problem in Japan as it is in America or Europe, partly because sake has a lower percentage of alcohol than whiskey and so is less addictive. It is our impression that this notion is by no means accurate and that the number of adults in Arakawa with a serious drinking problem is probably considerable. For example, within only a few months of our inquiry the Educational Guidance Center had handled four cases in which wives had left their drunken husbands and begun working as day laborers. These cases were called to the attention of the center because in each instance their sons had initiated some form of delinquent activity. Another case arising from excessive drinking by a parent was that of an eighth-grade girl whose widower father forced her to work in a store for approximately ¥800 a day and then spent almost all her wages for drink. One day, having stayed home during the morning to do laundry and clean the rooms, the girl brought back from the store only ¥400 and became so frightened by her father's wrath that she went out and somehow stole ¥400. The police caught her after several subsequent thefts.

Another case reported to us by a voluntary probation worker illustrates a type of problem drinking not infrequently found in Arakawa, and it is also an instance of successful surrogate mothering of a delinquent youth by a *hogoshi*. Mrs. Hirayama, an experienced worker, told us of Masao, whose mother had died when he was about fourteen and in middle school. He had two younger brothers, one in primary school and the other of preschool age. After his mother's death, his father sank into heavy drinking and gave up all attempts to maintain a home. Before leaving for work in the morning, the father would give each child ¥30 (about 10 cents) to buy three pieces of bread for "lunch." By late afternoon the children were always very hungry, and so Masao, leaving his youngest brother with a neighbor, would take his other brother and go look for their father. They knew just where to find him, for his habit, after finishing the day's work, was to go to one of the small, cheap drinking places that lined a nearby street. He was invariably drunk by the time they found him, and would often fall on the street in a stupor on the way home. The boys would shake him, trying to arouse him sufficiently to get him the rest of the distance. Little would be left of his daily wage.

Day after day the scene was repeated. When this state of affairs became known at school, the principal asked Mrs. Hirayama to help. She discovered that the boys had a married sister, and with the sister's cooperation she was able to arrange care for the two youngest boys, but the eldest wanted to stay with his father. However, he soon turned to delinquent behavior. While in the second year of middle school he started smoking and struck a teacher who tried to stop him; he committed several thefts; and finally he participated in a group rape. The court put him in charge of Mrs. Hirayama under the formal supervision of a probation official.

An old friend of Masao's father, who felt sorry for the boy, gave him a job at his small factory and took him into his home to live with his family. Just about this time Masao's father was hospitalized with tuberculosis and, finding that his son now had a small income, began demanding that he send money. The son started to drink and quickly became a heavy drinker, behaving violently when drunk. The culmination came one evening when he was about eighteen years old. Having become quite drunk at a nearby snack shop—staggering around, talking loudly, and upsetting chairs—Masao went home to his employer, shouting abusive language, and left the house again with a butcher knife in his hand. The employer called the police and also phoned Mrs. Hirayama. Very early the next morning Masao suddenly appeared at Mrs. Hirayama's house, his clothes torn and muddy, and upon seeing her worried face he suddenly started crying. She said to him, "Now I'll give you a glass of warm milk. Drink it and take a rest. I'll take you to your employer and apologize for you so that you can work at his place again." She went to a doctor in a nearby clinic and asked him to talk to the boy, to let him know that unless he quit drinking he would ruin his health, adding, "I don't care how you say it. Please exaggerate if necessary and scare him out of drinking." Then Mrs. Hirayama sent her charge to the doctor to have his cuts and bruises treated.

The doctor apparently was quite successful in his lecture, for Masao quit drinking and began working very hard. Mrs. Hirayama induced the boy's hospitalized father to stop bothering him for money, and she also apologized for Masao to the teacher whom he had struck. She asked the school principal to issue a graduation certificate and give it to the boy "ceremoniously." The principal had a platform built in his own office and handed the certificate to the boy in the presence of his employer, who had dressed up just as he would have for a formal graduation. When Masao came to show Mrs. Hirayama the certificate, he shed tears of joy and gratitude. Recently, Mrs. Hirayama told Masao that she would be willing to recommend the termination of his period of probation, which otherwise would last for another year. But Masao said he wanted to keep the relationship with Mrs. Hirayama and asked her not to recommend early termination. This nurturant relationship, so Japanese in tone, exemplifies the type of relationship that can spring up between *hogoshi* and charge.

Attitudes toward Gambling

Gambling is rather rare among Arakawa delinquents, by all reports, with only seven or eight arrests in a typical year. Mr. Itō, an experienced youth officer, suggested several reasons why this is so: first, gambling has been illegal for a long time; second, Arakawa boys do not have enough money for serious gambling; and, third, it is easier to steal money than to go through the more arduous procedure of playing the odds.[7] This is not to say that there is not considerable gambling, even addictive gambling, among adults, but children or young adolescents do not seem to be similarly inclined.

Mr. Itō cited one exception that involved police action. Five boys gathered frequently to gamble in the room of the son of a respectable family, whose parents thought the boys had come together for study and were rather pleased. The son of this family lost approximately ¥120,000 over a period of time and thereupon stole his parents' bankbook and withdrew a covering sum from his parents' account. The parents found out, brought the son to the police station, and all five boys were booked for illegal gambling. "It is the parents' fault," Mr. Itō commented. "They should have checked what the boys were doing."

Attitudes toward Drugs

Drug abuse has not been a severe problem in Japan. Nevertheless, some fads have appeared periodically. From about 1950 to 1954, for example, the use of a very popular form of intravenous stimulant called *hiropon* appeared as a

7. Such explanations do not altogether satisfy us, but we have no concrete alternatives to offer except to suggest differences between psychocultural traditions and hence differences in the personalities of Japanese adolescents. Gambling behavior seems to be more prevalent in Japanese outcaste communities than in the Arakawa lower-class district (De Vos and Wagatsuma, 1966). Japanese Thematic Apperception Test responses seldom refer to luck or external circumstances as governing the destiny of individuals.

juvenile craze in many of the larger cities, and Arakawa seems to have had a particularly high rate of reported cases. Stringent government control of the manufacture of the Methedrine-like substance was finally imposed to end the practice. Evidently the smuggling of drugs such as "speed" does not pay off sufficiently to make such drug traffic a serious concern. There is a reported increase in the use of heroin, but this involves a very minor portion of the Japanese public. LSD, which was quickly declared illegal by the government, is hard to come by and rather expensive. Marijuana is talked about considerably but in reality is not much in use among the Japanese.

A fad among very youthful adolescents in the 1960s, even thirteen- and fourteen-year-olds, was so-called sleeping-pill play (*suimin yaku asobi*), which almost invariably took place in a group. The challenge was to fight back the drowsiness that occurred when the drug's effect began to be felt. Government regulations were tightened to prevent the sale of sleeping pills to minors and those without a recognized medical certificate or identification, and pharmacists were cautioned to be more careful about selling pills to all persons. For these reasons, according to the police, sleeping-pill play with the use of regular barbiturates has been almost stopped in Arakawa.

Adolescents quickly found a substitute, a drug with the brand name Nalon, intended to ease menstrual pain. There is, thus far, no established way for legally controlling its use. The drug was routinely kept for young girls in the dispensaries of Arakawa schools and was regularly stolen until it was locked up. One gains the distinct impression that this type of play with barbituates is a form of experimental rebelliousness on the part of the youngsters.

Of more serious concern, since the brain-damaging effect is known, is the more recent glue-sniffing and paint-thinner-sniffing, which has appeared in Arakawa Ward as elsewhere. No action has yet been taken, to our knowledge. Several deaths related to glue-sniffing have been reported periodically in the Tokyo newspapers, a few caused by suffocation after youths put their heads in plastic bags to increase the effect. The schools issue warnings about the brain damage that may result from glue- or thinner-sniffing, but cases still occur.

Delinquent Group Formation

Over the period of our study there was some diminution of so-called gang behavior in Arakawa Ward, probably because of coordinated efforts by the schools, the police, and such groups as the PTA and the voluntary probation workers to rid the middle schools of the institution known as the *banchō* (the tough leader of a juvenile gang). Their efforts did not eliminate all juvenile gang behavior in Arakawa, nor did they have any effect on the adult underworld gangs that are found in Arakawa as in other areas of Japaneses cities, but the focus of their attack on the problem is significant.

During the first days of our study in Arakawa Ward we gathered a great deal of information concerning the way the *banchō* functioned to control peer groups in the Arakawa junior high schools. Every year in September or October—about six months before the graduation of the seniors—a secret election was held to choose the *banchō* for the next school year. In preparation for the election, the retiring *banchō* would incite likely candidates to fight on the school grounds to test their relative strength. The strongest and most skillful usually won the election, and four or five others who had also fought well became his lieutenants. Sometimes a boy from a lower grade, if exceptionally aggressive, might become a sub-*banchō* and so be in a better position to win the next election for himself.

When a school acquired a particularly strong *banchō*, his supporting group grew in size and caused increasing problems within the school. There was also an associated tendency for increased violence in relation to rival gangs from neighboring schools. The graduation of a strong *banchō* meant a relative lull in the gang activity until another strong *banchō* emerged. In the memory of the older teachers, there was a continual alternation of these patterns over the years. The central core of a gang fluctuated accordingly from as few as twenty to as many as forty members drawn from all three grade levels of the school (total school enrollments vary from 700 to 1,000).

Shortly before our investigation the membership of one of the juvenile gangs jumped from thirty to sixty, according to the estimates of the teachers, as the result of an amalgamation of two groups from different schools. This interschool gang soon became involved in stealing, intimidation, and the like, and at least some of the members spent considerable time at nearby amusement centers. The group included, to the knowledge of the informants, a couple of boys who had already graduated from junior high school and joined a gang of mixed adolescents and adults. One of these boys, who was also indirectly associated with a group of adult *yakuza*, took over as the actual leader of the enlarged juvenile gang.

Juvenile gang members adopted unique haircuts or dress styles, to distinguish themselves from ordinary nondelinquent pupils, and developed special speech patterns to demonstrate their toughness. (Their way of speaking and their language, used especially when bullying other boys, apparently did not derive as directly from the traditional adult *yakuza* jargon as from gang stories depicted in the mass media.) The most characteristic activity of the gang was some form of violence or threat of violence, which was most often connected with establishing an order of domination, whether within the gang or over boys outside a gang. Moreover, threats of violence accompany acts of intimidation or robbery. Some time before our study a fairly well organized campaign of intimidation was carried on by a *banchō* and a sub-*banchō*, who, in order to obtain a large amount of money for a project of some sort, demanded a specified sum from each of their subordinates. To meet this demand, the subordinates forced other boys in the gang to go out and extract the money from the ordinary pupils of the school.

In one of the schools where truancy remained quite low, gang activity took the form of symbolic rebellious acts directed against teachers, especially those who were perceived as weak. Members of this gang also showed off by smoking and drinking, and some were reported to be involved in sleeping-pill play.

The *banchō* was a kind of hero among delinquency-prone youth of both sexes. One of our police informants remarked, "The *banchō* used to be very popular with girls. There were always some girls around who were willing to sleep with the major *banchō*." As to boys, a probation worker who owns a bathhouse informed us that whenever a *banchō* came to his bathhouse the boys accompanying him eagerly served him, offering him soap, washing his back, and so forth.

Mrs. Hirayama remembered when a boy would pay as much as ¥1,000 to have his picture taken standing beside a *banchō*, this photo serving as a certificate that the *banchō* was his "close friend." Boys counted on such pictures both for greater prestige among other children and for protection from gang bullies. "There was a time," Mrs. Hirayama recalled, "when I saw many children proudly showing pictures taken with the same *banchō*. His income from such picture-taking must have been quite large."

In fights at school, boys generally used only their fists, but in "battles" between schools wooden swords, bicycle chains, and pieces of steel would appear. A favorite spot for these battles was the river bank of Arakawa, and although skirmishes of an impromptu nature had occurred there over the previous ten years, the teachers and police prided themselves on having thwarted several attempts to stage large-scale interschool fights. The most common motive for a gang fight was retaliation for an attack on one of its members by another school gang. The *banchō* of one school who has been defeated by the *banchō* of another school may on occasion become a *kobun* (disciple) for the stronger *banchō*. Frequently, a member of a *gurentai* or *yakuza* group was seen acting as an *aniki-bun*, or "big brother," to the younger *banchō* leaders in junior high school, furnishing them with meals and lodging for several nights.

It was reported to us that some Arakawa delinquents regularly shared a taxi ride to Ueno or Asakusa to gather on the roof of a department store or a coffee shop or to spend the night at a cheap inn. These excursions were often financed by money stolen from their parents.

One of the major activities of a gang of older delinquent boys in Arakawa was to sell "party" tickets. Holding "parties" at some park or beach was most characteristic of eighteen- or nineteen-year-olds, but sometimes younger gang members would also organize them. Tickets to the "parties" were priced at about ¥130 (slightly less than 50 cents). In order to evade government taxes (applied to gatherings of more than 200), only 200 would be reported, whereas up to 500 would actually be printed. There would be chartered cars or buses to take everyone out to the picnic area. What finally evoked police investigation was not so much the tax evasion, or even the occasional complaints of intimidation from ticket buyers, but the outright fraud by some gangs who sold *o-bake*, or "ghost" tickets, to parties that never came off.

Later Careers of Former Delinquents

Most juvenile delinquents do not become "professional" but instead somehow find their way back into ordinary lower-class society. The answers obtained to our questions about the occupational careers of delinquents after their release from probation gave us the general impression that most of them go into construction work or do some form of physical labor in or about Arakawa.

Mrs. Terashima, one of our principal informants and herself once a governmental probation officer assigned to Arakawa, said her experience led her to believe that delinquent youth have great difficulty in adjusting psychologically to a sustained kind of ordinary occupation. Their typical restlessness and inability to concentrate on any one thing for very long makes their ideal of a job one that involves movement and minimal responsibility. Work as an assistant to a truck driver, riding around and helping him load and unload his vehicle, is a popular choice. After working as an assistant, many aspire to become drivers themselves, but Mrs. Terashima could remember only a few with enough perseverance to finish preparation for the driver's test and acquire the knowledge of automotive mechanics needed to meet the technical driving-law requirements.

Mr. Itō, a policeman, made a similar observation, saying that a very common occupation for former delinquents is as a *bōsui-ya* (literally "waterproofer"). Working in groups of four or five, *bōsui-ya* apply a cement-like substance (similar to stucco) to the walls of a house to seal out moisture. This work, which pays approximately ¥2,000 a day, requires a considerable exercise of muscle but little in the way of intellectual activity, and because this waterproofing can be done only in dry weather the workers have a number of days off each month and so do not feel constricted to a steady job.

Mrs. Hirayama, another of our principal informants, cited similar cases of former delinquents who, as she termed it, "found it difficult to sit still." One of her charges, for example, became a driver's helper on a dump car used to transport dirt and gravel. Eventually, he became a driver himself and seemed to take great pleasure in driving a huge, powerful vehicle.

Attitudes about Peers, Authority, and Society

The following are brief selections of material from informal tape interviews with several teenage informants in Arakawa between 1960 and 1965, including some with reformed or former delinquents. The interviews were directed at learning about their sense of peer-group membership, their activities at school and in the neighborhood, their sexual interests and attitudes toward the opposite sex, and their view of authority and society in general. Although we were not always successful in eliciting what we wanted, these interviews were of considerable value as a supplement to our formal case materials.

Hideo. A fourteen-year-old in the second-year class of a junior high school (eighth grade), Hideo had some "delinquent" background, although the nature of his past delinquency was not clear from our data. There were about fifteen boys with an age range from thirteen to seventeen in the group that Hideo considered his *nakama* (peer group), a group seemingly consisting mainly of tough boys, some with records of police contact. Unlike many "clubs" of delinquent boys, his group had no special name nor, apparently, anyone in a clearly defined role of leader, although the hierarchical order of toughness of the members seemed well established. The group was not affiliated with criminal adults and had no special initiation rites for newcomers and no particular rules, except that the younger boys were expected to bow to the older boys on the street, the polite Japanese custom for a person of lower status when meeting someone of higher status. Hideo said that "things occurring between two people are straightened out between the two," a statement we took to mean that conflicts within this group were settled by some form of duel.

Four or five boys belonging to the group hung around together at school between classes and very often, after going home about three o'clock, rejoined on the street. Group members occasionally engaged in secret cigarette smoking or in sleeping-pill play. Although Hideo did not drink, he told of once trying sake with his group in a car at a junkyard. He said his group never mixed with girls; nobody played tricks on girls or wrote love letters to them. He himself had no girl friends, and he claimed he was simply not interested.

His group seemed to have acted periodically—it was not clear how often—in antisocial ways; Hideo mentioned shoplifting, stealing from storehouses, and obtaining money from other boys by threatening them. Very often "money taking" was described as "money borrowing": "We don't take money away from the boys. We borrow it." On being asked if he or his friends ever paid back the money, Hideo laughed: "Yeah, a little bit of the total sum, like ¥10 when we borrow ¥1,000." If someone in his group happened to get some money, the boys shared it and bought food (usually *o-konomi-yaki*, a Japanese pancake, a cultural equivalent to the hot dog). Hideo felt that his major benefit in being a member of this group was that he was treated by the group to food; however, he was expected to take his turn in treating the rest.

He knew at least the names of the *banchō* of all four junior high schools in Arakawa Ward (in 1963) as well as their rank order of toughness.

A typical day for Hideo was as follows. He got up at 6:30 A.M., even on weekends, because his father went to work early on Sunday too. (We were not informed about the occupation of the boy's father.) After breakfast on Sundays and holidays he watched singing programs and news on TV for about thirty minutes beginning about 7:30, then read the newspaper, principally the *sanmen kiji* (a gossip weekly about crime, accidents, personal affairs of celebrities, etc.); he said he usually followed with interest the news of criminal cases such as kidnappings. He never exchanged opinions with his parents or even got into casual talk with them about news or TV programs. Still early in the morning he would go to friends' homes, or his friends would drop in, and together the boys would go to school on weekdays or out to play on Sundays and holidays. On weekdays Hideo usually went home after school and then went out again to join his group, ordinarily returning in time for supper with his family. After supper, especially if his father had not come home early, he would go out again and hang around with his group, returning home at 9:00 or 9:30 P.M. and watching TV in bed until he became sleepy.

One member of his group had a relative in an adult gang organization, and from this boy he occasionally heard about gang activities. He admitted that hearing about such "action" was interesting, but he added quickly that he had never thought of becoming a gang member.

The peer group put certain conformist pressures on the appearance of its members in regard to their attire and hair style. Hideo used to have his hair cut short, before he joined the group, but afterward he started growing his hair long: "When we get together, if your hair is cut short, they say your hair looks awful. You feel ashamed and you change it to look like the rest of the boys."

An interesting episode, indicative of his emotional tie to his peers, occurred when one of his friends and another boy escaped from a correctional institution and came back to the neighborhood. His friends asked Hideo to "be with him" and so, leaving home without telling his parents, Hideo wandered around with the two boys, sleeping at night in a lumberyard and eating food supplied by other members of the group. After two days the two escapees were found by a policeman and taken back to the institution.

Hideo did not particularly care for schoolwork and complained that the teachers at his school usually resorted to physical punishment (hitting a boy on the head with their hands or slapping him on the cheek) of those who began fighting with each other or otherwise caused disruption. Moreover, if one of the boys happened to be "a marked boy" (having a bad reputation among the teachers), the teacher did not take the trouble to find out how the fight started but simply punished that boy.

As for high school, Hideo had no intention of going and said that in any case his family could not afford to send him. He believed he would do about average in school "if I really tried," but he said he had never done so.

Three Eighteen-Year-Olds' Retrospect. Once considered the toughest boys at their middle school, X, Y, and Z seemed to have changed from troublemakers to stable young adults. X, a former *banchō*, was helping his father run a tiny metalwork shop; Y was supervisor of a construction work gang; Z was working at his father's furniture store. We reached them through one of their former teachers with whom they were on good terms, and interviewed them together.

X spoke about marriage customs in Arakawa:

> Our generation is no longer concerned with the old family system. When a man and a woman like each other they find a room to live in and live together. They don't bother to register their marriage. But when a baby comes they have to register their marriage. They usually stick together, especially after the baby comes. Their parents more or less accept such a marriage and especially when a baby comes; they cannot resist loving their grandchild. They've got to accept their children's marriage.

X said that both the woman and the man usually work these days.

All three had comments on the generation gap. According to X, parental authority has weakened and is no longer respected: "In most homes the phrase 'parental authority' is disliked. Things are no longer the way they used to be." Y added that mothers are more nagging toward their children and husbands, and fathers occasionally resort to violence toward their wives and children. X noted:

> Recently democracy has developed, and thanks to it children can talk frankly with their parents without being afraid of parental authority. Children assert themselves and express their opinions. Parents may not like this kind of democratic relationship between parents and children, but as the children grow up parents have to accept such relationships. They have to give in.

Z agreed, and Y added that the older generation cannot understand the younger generation and vice versa; the younger generation is stronger in their self-assertion, and the older ones must give in.

These boys said their parents were not looking for candidates for their future wives, but had left it to them to find suitable girls, and they thought this was the general tendency in the homes they knew. Arranged marriage was no longer an issue.

Y says he had had a wonderful time at school.

> I did everything I wanted. I have nothing to regret. I could do whatever I wanted and I really did all I wanted. I ignored teachers completely, for instance. I don't think I was always acting as I liked, but when I wanted to do something, I did it without hesitation and without hindrance. I didn't like English class, so I cut the class and played in the schoolyard. The teachers let me do whatever I wanted to do as long as I didn't bother other children. My father told me not to bother other children without reason. He said I should not hit or kick the other kids who had not done anything to me. But when other kids attacked me, my father always told me, I should be strong, though I should never bother weak ones. Therefore I never beat the kids who did not do anything to me. When I fought, it was with good reason. I fought only with those who attacked me. Therefore when I was picked up by policemen for fighting I never felt guilty.

According to Y, all three boys were in the volleyball club at their school. At the time of interschool matches boys of the two schools used to fight with each other, and at these fights X, Y, and Z, even while still in the first-year class, proved themselves to be strong fighters. The news spread among the Arakawa boys, and many boys were afraid of them. They said that they did not have to defeat all the strong boys to establish their power; X said he was not aware of his being a *banchō*. All three felt they had been very popular among the other boys at school "because we never bothered them as long as they did no harm to us."

None had ever wanted to have anything to do with *yakuza* and *gurentai*, although an invitation did come to them to join an adult *gurentai* band. Just before graduation they made a special effort to avoid meeting members of the band as the invitation became more persistent: "We could not ignore them. We greeted them but tried not to get into any conversation with them. We tried to avoid running into them on streets, too."

All three claimed never to have been interested in going to places like Asakusa. They liked playing volleyball so much that they spent most of their free time on the school grounds. "Even during school hours we put up the net and played volleyball," Y said. They agreed that only "those really bad ones" went to places like Asakusa and Ueno. "We were kind of afraid of going to these places. Perhaps we were *uchi-benkei* (a lion at home, a mouse abroad)," Z mused, but X pointed out that they generally played volleyball until six or seven in the evening. Y recalled that after volleyball eight friends used to go to a public bathhouse together:

> It was real fun. We used to have a great time taking baths and talking together. I used to hate coming home. When I returned home early I often took a streetcar to go to a bathhouse in my friend's neighborhood so that I could get together with some of my friends. Even on Sunday we went to school to play volleyball. It was against the regulations to use the school's sport facilities on Sundays, but our physical education teachers were all nice to us and let us play.

The eight boys from the volleyball club more or less stuck together and did not mix with many other boys. Six were especially close, spending a lot of their time talking about cars, teachers, and girls.

Sleeping-pill play had just become popular when they were at school, but they did not approve of it and used to beat up those who played with sleeping pills, to stop them. Z commented, "The boys who played with sleeping pills were those who did not belong to our honest, diligent boys' group on the one hand, or to 'bad' groups on the other. They were sort of in-between. Real weak ones."

Y said that tattooing with only black or blue lines in the design cost as much as ¥30,000 ($100) and tattooing with various colors more than ¥100,000 ($300): "One cannot afford to pay the price at once, nor can anyone bear the pain of tattooing all at once. The delinquents who want to be tattooed earn money or obtain it by extortion. When they have collected about ¥3,000 they go to a tattooer and receive partial tattooing for that sum. It takes a guy half a year or one full year to get his tattoo finished." All three deplored the practice, Z saying, "It's a silly thing to do, smearing up the skin which one received pure from one's parents." These postwar youths were expressing, without knowing it, the traditional Confucian notion that "the first step of filial piety is to protect and not to do harm to one's body and limbs that one received from one's parents."

X said that at the time he was at school boys were "wilder" (*yaseimi ga aru*). The boys at present are "easy to handle" (*guai yoku chiisaku matomatte iru*). "They are smaller. Even the bad ones at most simply make noise in the classroom. Nobody really acts wild or gets into fist fights with a teacher." X himself was known to have beaten a schoolteacher when he was in the second year of middle school. He told us this story:

> At the school festival Y was walking along the corridor wearing leather shoes. A schoolteacher noticed it and told Y not to enter the school building with outside shoes. Y said he would take off his shoes and starting walking to the entrance hall. [He did not take off the shoes on the spot. Probably the teacher expected him to take more prompt action.] The teacher angrily told Y to take off the shoes. I came alone and said to the teacher, "Don't press him. He said he would take off his shoes, didn't he?" The teacher got angry when I told him to stop nagging Y as Y was going to take off his shoes. The teacher hit me, which he never should have done. I got angry and beat and kicked him.

Three stitches were needed to close a wound above the teacher's eye. X obviously enjoyed recollecting this incident. Y repeatedly said, "He [the teacher] should not have struck X. He would not have got into the trouble if he had not struck X." X said, "As I was attacked, I had to strike back." The physical education teacher supplemented the story by saying that previous to this incident the same teacher had hit X in the classroom when he found X wearing a chain necklace (probably a *gurentai*-type accessory). This must have made X angry at the teacher, and perhaps X was waiting for the time to retaliate. Z said again happily, "That was a great incident anyway. Such fun!" Y said, "After that the other teachers were afraid of us. They were afraid that they would be beaten up also if they said something to us. They feigned a smile when they saw us, though they must have been boiling with anger inside." The three boys laughed. When asked if he went to the teacher to apologize, X answered flatly: "No, I didn't apologize, because I didn't think I had been wrong."

The three boys seemed to enjoy talking about the teachers:

> X: Some teachers try to put too much pressure on the boys. They want to maintain the appearance of being a teacher by putting on too much pressure. The boys naturally begin to hate them.
>
> Y: There are two types of teachers: One group of teachers is understanding toward the kids; the other group is old-fashioned and rigid. The former is popular among the kids, the latter is hated. A schoolteacher must be willing to talk frankly with his boys. Some teachers give themselves airs as if to emphasize that teachers are a different form of existence from school kids.
>
> Z: These guys should be punished. Otherwise they do harm to less aggressive kids. (He made it sound as if beating up a teacher had the effect of threatening other "bad" teachers and thereby protecting other kids.)
>
> Y: Some teachers are really obnoxious. They don't even let us talk frankly with them. They quickly say, "Is that the proper way for a boy to talk to his teacher?" When some boys don't behave well in the classroom perhaps they [the teachers] want to show off their authority to other kids. They say, "Come outside. I will punish you." Young teachers, fresh out of college, don't want to be beaten up by the boys, and in order to avoid such

> problems, they decide to scare the boys first. They act strictly. They are making a great mistake. Their efforts simply make the boys more rebellious against them. . . . When someone did something wrong and was told by a teacher to stand up [as punishment], we used to say, "Don't stand up. There is no need for it." Teachers get paid as long as there are students to teach.
>
> X: I used to, and still do, associate myself with my teachers as I do with my friends. Those teachers who are disliked by the boys are poor teachers, who do not know how to handle the boys properly. The kids are all very simple-minded, after all. Therefore, if the teachers can communicate with them, soul to soul, person to person, the kids will all obey them. If the teachers always relate well to the boys, the boys understand them, and when they tell the boys to do or not to do certain things, the boys understand why they say so and therefore the boys all obey. If they don't associate themselves well with the boys, the boys don't understand them, and when they tell the boys to do something the boys won't do it.

X went on to make a rather remarkable comment: "But now I am grateful to those stubborn, rigid, and bad teachers because they taught me that the world is not made up of my friends. Thanks to them I learned that there are enemies, as well as friends, in this world."

X had become a member of Sōka Gakkai (see his case history in chapter 12). He was a *banchō* (youth leader) in charge of sixty members and had obtained the rank of lecturer. What attracted him to the Gakkai, X explained, was the fact that so many young people like himself—the boys put the Youth Group membership of Sōka Gakkai at six million—had enthusiastically embraced its teachings: "By following the Gakkai's teacher one can establish one's life, and through establishing one's life one can contribute to the establishment of a new world." For a year and a half after he had left school X had felt depressed, lonely, and apathetic. He used to spend evenings watching TV, terribly homesick for his former school days. Then he went to a meeting of Sōka Gakkai youth and was impressed by their conversation, which was concerned with the improvement of one's own life and with the society and the world in general.

CHAPTER 3

Research in Arakawa Ward

We selected Arakawa Ward because a previous ecological study of delinquency in Tokyo by Japanese in 1960 had indicated that Arakawa was one of the few wards in Tokyo in which the delinquency rate had remained consistently high since World War II. Japanese cities generally show a different pattern from that of the United States. Delinquent acts are usually committed in amusement/shopping areas outside the poorer residential districts where the delinquent boys actually live. Delinquents usually "commute" by train or bus to these amusement centers. Arakawa Ward was one of a few exceptions in Tokyo in this respect. Arakawa delinquents did commute to nearby amusement/shopping areas such as Asakusa and Ueno; however, more than in most wards, the reported arrests of delinquents in Arakawa were of local youths who had committed delinquent acts in the local area.

All in all, Arakawa seemed to qualify best as an area where family patterns could be studied in the context of a neighborhood exhibiting some features that bore comparison with neighborhoods in American cities also reporting relatively high rates of delinquency.

Delinquent Activities in Arakawa

The Arakawa statistics for the early 1960s on what might be considered serious delinquency among residents under twenty years of age reveal that there were a proportionately lower number of thefts and a higher number of acts of violence and intimidation than for adults (those twenty years of age and older). The local ward statistics attested to an increase in delinquency between 1955 and 1963, with an almost threefold increase in the arrest rate for serious offenses. There was no question, therefore, that delinquent behavior had increased over the period immediately before our investigation. It was also clear from the informal impressions of police officers as well as from the statistics that a major proportion of the increase at that time was in the younger age brackets. Subsequent to our study, however, arrest rates for delinquent activities in the ward, as elsewhere in Japan, declined until about 1969. A very gradual increase has been reported since then.

The statistics specific to Arakawa junior high groups (ages 12–15) showed a peak in arrest rates in 1964 and an abrupt drop in 1965. In 1964, junior high school students made up almost 40 percent of the delinquents arrested, but the figure dropped to approximately 33 percent in the following year. In our opinion these downward trends were related to the collaborative action taken about this time by the police, the schools, and the community, which led to the disappearance of the more or less organized youth gangs from most of the junior high schools of Arakawa. If we examine the Japanese statistics of those arrested in 1964–1965 for serious delinquent acts, we find evidence supporting the police impression in Arakawa that an increasing number of 14- and 15-year-olds were then committing "delinquent acts," principally stealing and forms of intimidation for money. This age group was recorded as having as high a rate of delinquency as that reported for the 16- and 17- or the 18- and 19-year-olds. In Arakawa at that time, junior high school students had a much higher arrest rate than senior high school students, reflecting the fact that junior high school is compulsory and senior high school is elective. Most of those who are delinquency-prone have negative attitudes toward school and do not voluntarily continue into senior high. Therefore, delinquency-prone individuals beyond junior high school age are usually recorded in the "worker" or "unemployed" categories rather than as "students" of a senior high school.

In the "delinquency-prone" category a large number of arrests were made for smoking in public or frequenting places off-limits to minors. These arrests were principally of 16–19-year-olds classified as workers (actually in many instances apprentices) rather than senior high school students. They were a police attempt to enforce laws keeping apprentices in a subadult status as far as society was concerned, even though most apprentices thought of themselves as adult, since they had quit school. These arrest figures might also have reflected some implicit understanding between the police and small-factory owners, who used the police to enforce some of the restrictions they imposed upon their minor apprentices.

Of the delinquent acts committed by the thirty-one delinquents in our own sample, stealing was the most common; five boys had tried intimidation and extortion, usually as a member of a gang putting pressure on another juvenile; one boy had committed rape. In number and kind, these acts were typical of those performed by younger delinquents in Arakawa in the early sixties.

SELECTION OF FAMILIES FOR STUDY

The specific objective of our intensive study of fifty lower-class families in Arakawa was to test if and how personality factors in the parents, and intrafamily dynamics, influenced the formation of behavioral problems on the part of given children. For this purpose we collected intensive interview and psychological test materials to assess (1) the parents' own childhood experiences and the processes involved in their personality formation; (2) the interaction among members of given families; and (3) the relationship between family interaction and given behavior by the member of the family who was designated as delinquent by society.

The rationale behind the psychological aspects of our study developed out of previous experiences with psychological test materials of Japanese delinquents, which were collected during the summer of 1959. George De Vos and two Japanese psychologists, Professors Eiji Murakami (1959 and 1962) and Keiichi Mizushima (1964), cooperated in analyzing these data and comparing them with materials collected from some samples of delinquency in the United States. As this work proceeded, it became increasingly clear that, for a fuller understanding of the personality structure of delinquent children, as well as of the particular interpersonal configurations contributing to delinquency formation, the analysis of test materials alone was insufficient. We determined that further intensive interview materials on the developmental history of the delinquents and of their parents would be necessary. By 1961 it was decided to try out an intensive study of family units, including delinquent boys and also their parents, using a matched control sample of nondelinquent children and their parents.

We concluded that our main study should consist of intensive and qualitative, though controlled, interviews of a small number of families rather than highly structured interviews of a larger number with standardized questions.

Criteria for Selection of a Sample

Delinquency in Japan, as elsewhere, is largely a "lower-class" phenomenon. We were also aware, however, of the increase of the delinquency rate in the late 1950s and early 1960s among younger Japanese adolescents and among middle-class children, seemingly a worldwide phenomenon. At the beginning we thought we might obtain a sample of "problem boys" for the last year of primary school, but we decided that this was not feasible. We found that cooperation and interest was greatest among teachers in the junior high schools of Arakawa.

We decided to choose junior high school boys from lower-class families as the subjects of our study, for several reasons. It is usually in the junior high age group, twelve to fifteen, that the preceding personality disturbances and maladjustments of childhood begin to take the more manifest forms of socially disturbing behavior. Attendance at junior high schools is compulsory, and by working through the schools we could obtain a more representative sample of youth. Our exclusion of older boys had the practical reason that after junior high school, which is the end of compulsory education in Japan, many lower-class children, and most delinquents, drop out of the formal educational system. We would find it difficult to reach such samples and match appropriate control samples. It was easier to reach subjects and their families through schoolteachers, who became our major liaison. Subsequently, we also established contact with some families of delinquents through agencies of the Tokyo Family Court system.

Our major criterion for judging a child to be delinquent was his history of contact with the police. Generally, this major criterion worked well as a means of differentiation. We originally planned to select our subjects in such a way that they would fall into four different categories of behavioral characteristics: (1) socialized delinquents, (2) isolate delinquents, (3) socialized "normals," and (4) isolate nondelinquents. The distinction between "social" and "isolate" delinquents was made on the basis of the following criteria.

Criteria Designating a "Social" Delinquent

1. He associates with those who have had police contacts.
2. He is mischievous or is truant, together with others.
3. He has known contact with delinquent gangs.
4. He plays an active role in a delinquent gang.
5. He has been involved in group stealing.
6. He speaks and dresses like a delinquent.
7. He frequents amusement quarters.
8. He, together with others, has intimidated another individual.

A high score (five or more items) connoted a social delinquent. A low score (two or fewer items) connoted an isolate delinquent. No individuals scoring three or four items were included in our sample.

Criteria Designating an Isolate, either Delinquent or Nondelinquent

1. He appears to be isolated from friends.
2. He seems fond of doing things by himself.
3. He is reluctant to join any group activity.
4. He appears to have no intimate friends.
5. He is shy and withdrawn.
6. He is not popular among his peers.
7. He is not a leader among his friends.
8. He is not seen as spirited and active.

A high score of five or more items in this rating suggested isolation in either delinquents or nondelinquents. For isolate delinquents, a high score in this rating could be double-checked against a low score in the previous rating.

Criteria for Lower-Class Status

To define "lower-class" families was not easy. Our attempts to give precise criteria by which the teachers could eliminate the minority of middle-class students in the Arakawa schools were not completely successful (see chapter 6). We set up rather broad indices applicable to the parents of lower-class delinquents insofar as the teachers had information on them.

Education: Father's education should be not more than six to eight years.

(In prewar Japan, six years of primary school was the compulsory and therefore the minimum education.)

Occupation: Exclude owners of large stores, etc.; consider those culturally designated as "low" status, such as peddlers, unskilled small-factory workers, day laborers, operators of tiny shops, semiskilled workers, janitors, unskilled clerks, and the like.

Income: Estimate an income of less than ¥36,000 ($120) per month.

Living conditions: Should be no better than one or two rented rooms or a one-room owned house.

We sought the cooperation of teachers in the four public junior high schools in Arakawa in selecting students known to have been in trouble with police, and supplied them with our lists of criteria for social delinquency, isolation, and status. We also asked the teachers' assistance in selecting control families matched with the delinquent families from the same second- and third-year junior high classes, in which the boys were usually fourteen and fifteen years of age.

Changes in Procedure: Problems of Bias

Soon after the project began, we found that it would be difficult to fill our "isolate nondelinquent" category because the teachers could not seem to locate many boys falling into this category, and some boys who had been selected by their teachers as "isolate" turned out, when their interview materials were analyzed, to be not quite so isolated as their teachers perceived them to be. Accordingly, we eventually abandoned this category and proceeded with three categories: socialized nondelinquent, socialized delinquent, and isolate delinquent. As the result of this change in classification, our nineteen socialized normals now include two boys who originally belonged to the abandoned "isolate nondelinquent" category and, therefore, show more "isolate" traits than do the rest of the boys in that category.

Our original plan was to have a total of sixty cases, fifteen in each of the four categories. With the abandonment of one category, however, we decided to get materials from a total of fifty cases: twenty normals, twenty socialized delinquents, and ten isolate delinquents—since this group too was difficult to fill. As the analysis of our early cases suggested, those considered "isolate" delinquents were among the most emotionally disturbed boys, and the teachers could not find many of them in their classes; "social" delinquents were much easier to find.

The families thus selected and approached were remarkably cooperative, especially if we consider that the parents of delinquents might be somewhat defensive in talking about their problems with their boys. The fact that the research was defined as a University of California research project that had no connection with any Japanese agency seems to have helped in some instances. Only ten families refused to cooperate with the researchers. Among the seven families that entirely refused to cooperate when first approached, there were one social nondelinquent, three social delinquent, and three isolate delinquent families. Among three families in which the husband refused to continue after the beginning of the initial interview, there was one social nondelinquent, one social delinquent, and one isolate delinquent family. One additional interview sequence in an isolate delinquent family had to be terminated because of serious illness in the family.

This very cooperativeness on the part of our Arakawa families may very well limit the degree to which they are truly random and representative. The teachers, in choosing boys from their classes, may have selected some boys whose parents could be expected to cooperate. The normal control boys they selected, as it turned out, included a few class leaders and boys who had received community citations for their diligence or other "good" behavior. The selection process may have excluded some delinquents, both social and isolate, whose parents may have been known to be more overtly antagonistic toward the teachers.

Another "built-in" bias of our subjects—particularly the delinquents—derives from the fact that from the beginning we wanted only "intact" families, simply because we wanted to interview the boys and *both* parents. Our sample does include several families in which one parent, most frequently the mother, is a stepparent for the boy, but it does not include any permanently "broken" family in which either a father figure or a mother figure is lacking. Japanese statistics show, however, that in present-day Japan a good percentage of delinquent boys come from "broken families," and by excluding such boys we probably biased our sample of delinquent subjects toward more "intact" families. The design of our research project—the necessity to interview both parents in order to study their patterns of interaction—made such a bias unavoidable. It must be noted, however, that the nature of our generalizations about lack of cohesion as a large factor in delinquency were strengthened by this more severe test.

In the selection of subjects, teachers did not always apply our criteria accurately. As was mentioned above, some boys who had originally been selected by the teachers as "isolate" did not seem to us characteristically "isolate," and on the basis of further evidence we reclassified them as "social." This was true both for delinquents and for nondelinquents. One boy, who had been selected by the teachers as a "social nondelinquent," revealed to the interviewer that he had had a police contact, although his teacher had never been so informed, and thus he had to be reclassified as a "social delinquent." Another boy, whom his teacher had classified as an "isolate nondelinquent," turned out to be a delinquent boy with many delinquent friends outside school, although he remained isolated from his classmates at school and never bothered the teacher. He was also reclassified as "social delinquent."

Toward the latter half of our seven years of data gathering, we employed other techniques to find seven additional delinquent boys. We solicited cooperation from the Tokyo family court as well as from teachers; and an officer in charge of "intake" of delinquent cases selected boys who were students of the public schools already selected. The interviews with these seven delinquent boys and their parents had to be conducted by the family court research officers. It is our impression that while the material was satisfactory, it was not as rich as that obtained directly in the homes by interviewers who had no official agency role.

At one point in our research we began working with a sample of delinquents, including girls, in Sapporo City in Hokkaido with the cooperation of the family court in that city. We were not able to carry out this research, for lack of personnel, and we abandoned it after collecting seven cases. These cases have been examined clinically, and are in line with our general conclusions, but are not included in any of the reported research in this volume.

We also obtained a number of additional cases through child guidance clinics in Tokyo, which provided us with considerable clinical insight. We gave some of these cases intensive analysis, but we decided that it would be somewhat confusing to include such material along with that of our regular sample. Since all these cases supported our findings but added nothing to what we have reported, we have excluded them from any consideration here.

The Research Data

The research materials we gathered from the father, mother, and selected youthful subjects in each of our fifty families consisted of (1) Rorschach Test responses (see Appendix A) (2) Thematic Apperception Test (TAT) responses (see Appendix B), and (3) a minimum of six hours of life-history interviews. For the Rorschach responses each person was individually tested with the ten standard Rorschach cards in a standard fashion. For the TAT responses each subject was individually tested with twelve pictures from the set that had been developed by George De Vos and Fumio Marui at Nagoya National University. This set included eight standard Murray TAT pictures modified in face and dress for use in Japan (De Vos, 1973). The responses were tape-recorded and transcribed verbatim. For the life-history materials, we developed a manual, adapted from Kimball Young's "An Outline for Writing a Case History" (1947), mainly to provide our interviewers with guidelines to help them make sure they acquired enough data covering major areas in the life history, including the current interaction between parents. The interview sessions were kept as open and unstructured as possible. All the sessions were tape-recorded and later transcribed verbatim. In addition to the boys and their parents, the boys' teachers and siblings were also interviewed when we felt it was necessary or helpful.

Brief History of Data Gathering

In the summer of 1961 Keiichi Mizushima (since 1970 Professor of Counseling Psychology at Rissho Women's College in Tokyo) returned to Tokyo after working on psychological test materials of Japanese delinquents with George De Vos at the Institute of Human Development, University of California, Berkeley.

De Vos and Mizushima had discussed the plan of the new research project in Berkeley, and after returning to his position as a psychologist at the Central Child Guidance Clinic in Tokyo, Mizushima discussed the plan further with Hiroshi Wagatsuma, then at the Research and Training Institute for Family Court Research Officers. With support from the Director of the Central Child Guidance Clinic, the Secretary of the Supreme Court, and the Director of the Research and Training Institute for Family Court Research Officers, Mizushima and Wagatsuma organized the group of interviewers and trained them for the interviews and testing. Meanwhile, they approached the Educational Commission of Tokyo Municipality and that of Arakawa Ward, and finally the schools, and solicited the teachers' cooperation in selecting the subjects. The interviewers, hired for the project, totaling sixteen over the entire period of data gathering, were in a variety of occupations, although almost everyone had had undergraduate or graduate training in psychology. There were seven family-court research officers, two psychological diagnosticians at the Tokyo Juvenile Classification Center, one psychologist at the National Police Science Research Institute, one psychologist at the Tokyo Municipal Educational Research Institute, and five psychology graduate students in several universities in Tokyo.

Actual interviewing and testing began in January 1962 and continued intermittently for five years, until November 1966. Data gathering was very slow, mainly because our interviewers had their own jobs and could participate in the project only on a part-time basis, using their evenings and weekends. The work was intermittent also because some of the interviewers had to leave the project owing to occupational circumstances such as transfer, promotion, or change to another position, and new people had to be found and trained. During the summers of 1962 and 1966 De Vos went to Japan, where he supervised the data gathering and participated in it. Mizushima supervised the interviewers in 1962, 1963, and 1964 while Wagatsuma was engaged in data analysis at the Institute of Human Development in Berkeley. During 1965 and 1966, Wagatsuma, back in Tokyo, participated in and supervised the interviewing. As was mentioned before, seven delinquent cases were obtained directly from the Tokyo family court. Two family-court research officers, one of whom had been with our project from the beginning, interviewed and tested these subjects.

Brief History of Data Analysis

With Wagatsuma's arrival at the Institute of Human Development in the summer of 1962 with two Japanese research staff members, the analysis of the materials began in earnest. Both De Vos and Wagatsuma began yearly seminars in the School of Social Welfare at the University of California, which resulted in a series of group research projects, each with twelve graduate students in social work participating in analyzing the intensive case materials. The interviewers had written a detailed case summary of each family, based upon the results of the interviews of family members. Case summaries and selected translations of verbatim transcriptions of tape-recorded interview materials and psychological test data were sent to Berkeley from Tokyo as they were collected. In Berkeley, additional case summaries and test responses from the tapes were translated into English by several Japanese graduate students on the campus.

Wagatsuma read transcribed interview materials and took careful notes in English to recover necessary information not included in the English case summary but of sufficient importance to be taken into consideration in the analysis of each case. De Vos and Wagatsuma also interpreted the Rorschach and TAT responses of each individual and made independent written diagnoses of the personality structure and social attitudes of each individual.

For each family, a case summary in English notes taken from interview materials, and the psychological test analysis, were given to a graduate student in the research seminars. De Vos and Wagatsuma, with the Japanese assistants, had case-analysis conferences with each student on the family assigned to that student. The group dissertations (1962–1965) are on file at the School of Social Welfare, University of California at Berkeley.

An Operational Framework of Instrumental and Expressive Role Behavior

To better order our understanding of the functioning of Japanese role behavior and social attitudes in the following chapters, we have made a comparison of the instrumental and expressive components of the three generational and the two sex-role positions found within our Arakawa delinquent and control samples. In so doing, it has been possible for us, first, to show the general continuities from past to present that are still operative in modern Japanese interpersonal behavior and, second, to record how differences in expected role functions operate selectively within families with delinquents. We examined the social attitudes governing Japanese role behavior in terms of ten basic motivational concerns. Five of these concerns are primarily "instrumental" in nature, and five are basically "expressive." In instrumental role behavior, action is motivated to achieve a goal or to meet a standard by which behavior is judged. Such behavior is a means to an end rather than for the immediate satisfaction inherent in the action itself.

Our five basic instrumental categories are (1) "achievement"—a behavior motivated by the desire to attain a future goal, within a given set of standards of social codes, or negatively, through what is socially defined as "criminal" behavior (see chapter 6); (2) "competence"—a concern with actualizing personal adequacy or capacity, or a need to acquire a mastery or competence (see chapter 6); (3) "responsibility"—behavior motivated by a sense of duty or obligation to internalized social directives, or the opposite, avoidance of or flight from responsibility into profligacy (chapter 7); (4) "social control"—behavior directed toward the actualization of power, authority, or control in social relationships, or toward autonomy, compliance, or rebellion (chapter 7); (5) "mutuality"—the phrasing of instrumental behavior in cooperative or competitive terms, whether within socially prescribed norms or outside them (chapter 8).

By contrast, we consider "expressive" behavior to be primarily the attempt to resolve an internal feeling rather than being concerned with goals and objectives. An inherent sense of satisfaction may be gained from the act itself or from the relationship in which the behavior is expressed. The five expressive categories are (6) "harmony/hostility"—behavior maintaining peacefulness or harmony or the sense of disharmony, discord, or even violence and destructiveness in human relationships (see chapter 8); (7) "affiliation/isolation"—behavior related to feelings of closeness and intimacy (in a horizontal relationship) or to their opposites, isolation, rejection, or avoidance (chapter 9); (8) "nurturance"—behavior demonstrating care, help, comfort, and succor (in vertical relationships), or their opposites, personal, social, or economic deprivation (chapters 7 and 9); (9) "appreciation/abasement"—an expressive concern with needed recognition and responsiveness from others (see chapter 6). This is the expressive counterpart to the instrumental concern with adequacy and competence. Negatively perceived, it is a feeling of being ignored, depreciated, or degraded by others (chapters 8 and 9). The last expressive category is (10) "pleasure/pain"—behavior generally governed by a direct experience of satisfaction or pleasure, or by suffering or endurance of hardships (chapter 9).

In general, delinquent subjects, as we shall demonstrate in the following chapters, are particularly concerned with negative expressive behavior in family relationships: discord, rejection, neglect, deprivation, depreciation, boredom, or intolerance of frustration. They compensate by emphasizing concern with immediate pleasure rather than by guiding their behavior instrumentally in terms of long-range goals. They do not internalize responsibility very well nor respond compliantly to authority.

When one goes beneath the surface appearance of the family in Japan to understand the motivations underlying the observable patterns of interaction, one finds a complexity in which various instrumental and expressive motives are inextricably intertwined, as our case histories clearly demonstrate. There are culturally consistent variations in the strength of and the direction taken by the particular role-interaction variables characteristic of the various positions in the family. These consistencies can be defined in formulating an ideal normative picture of Japanese life. In the following chapters variables in attitudinal vectors will be examined as they shed light on the nature of family role patterns in families with delinquent sons as compared with those with nondelinquent sons. We were particularly concerned with the way family and occupational roles are actualized in individual families in Arakawa Ward. The manner in which role behavior is carried out is significantly related to the appearance of delinquency in our experimental sample.

Quantitative Measures of Family Cohesion and Parenting

As will be discussed briefly in the following chapter, our survey of the considerable literature on delinquency in both Japan and the United States reviewed numerous studies that have focused on one or another set of variables. The realities of parental interaction with children are very complex, and it is difficult to order possible variables in any unilinear fashion. We have found it expedient in presenting our results to start out from our application of the Gluecks' relatively successful construction of a prediction scale with five variables. Their work, still subject to considerable controversy, does not give the most cogent psychohistorical analysis of the particular variables considered. It is, however, an excellent attempt to consider the major dimensions of family life as related to conformity and deviancy in children and adolescents.

Sheldon and Eleanor Glueck, in their large-scale work on the prediction of delinquency, attempted to consider statistically a number of social factors that were considered to be present in delinquent youth to a much greater degree than in nondelinquent youth. The items included were based upon their previous observations of delinquent youth, detailed perusal of case histories, and the advice of their associations. They tested items with multiple raters. Items were added, dropped, and qualified. A semifinal list of forty-four items was then evaluated by interviewing and gathering social histories on 500 delinquent and 500 nondelinquent youths. These forty-four items were reduced to five factors that showed the greatest predictability in differentiating predelinquent and nondelinquent groups at the time of first school entry. These five factors were used to build a prediction table (Glueck and Glueck, 1950). Briefly, the criteria for rating the family's social factors were as follows:

1. Discipline of Boy by Father

Criteria	*Description*	*Score*
Overstrict or erratic	Father is harsh, unreasonable, demands obedience through fear. ("Erratic" means inconsistent in control.)	72
Lax	Father is negligent, indifferent; lets boy do what he likes.	60
Firm	Discipline is based on sound reasons.	9

2. Supervision of Boy by Mother

Unsuitable	Mother is careless in her supervision, leaving boy to his own devices.	83
Fairly good	Mother gives only partial supervision.	58
Suitable	Mother personally keeps close watch on boy or provides for his leisure hours in clubs or playgrounds, or sees that another responsible adult is in charge if she cannot do it herself.	10

3. Affection of Father for Boy

Indifferent or hostile	Father does not pay much attention to boy. He is "hostile," rejects boy.	76

Warm (including overprotective)	Father is sympathetic, kind, attached, sometimes even overprotective.	34
4. Affection of Mother for Boy		
Indifferent or hostile	Definition same as above.	86
Warm (including overprotective)	Definition same as above.	43
5. Cohesiveness of Family		
Unintegrated	Home is just a place to "hang your hat." Self-interest of members exceeds group family interest.	97
Some elements of cohesion	Even if the family group is not entirely intact, the remaining group has some of the characteristics of the cohesive family.	61
Cohesive	Strong "we" feeling among members of the immediate family, as evidenced by cooperativeness, group interests, pride in the home, affection for each other.	21

A low score indicated those boys least likely to become delinquents, and a high score indicated those most likely to. The total score of each boy was then compared with a table that showed the probability of his delinquency. Subsequent studies in New York and elsewhere have attested to high predictability in using this system of relatively simple forced ratings. This has been true in spite of the possible problems of validity related to a need to make a forced simple judgment of complex life histories. Our quantitative results with the Glueck scale are reported in the following chapter in a more general context of other research and theory.[1]

1. Our ratings were made with prior knowledge of which families were delinquent. However, we rated the families independently and found no disparities in our overall ratings.

PART II

Comparison of Families

We begin by a consideration of the theoretical contentions and conclusions forwarded by a number of researchers in the United States, England, and Japan. By using the Glueck scale as a point of departure, we test out the contention that family cohesion, expressions of affection, supervision, and discipline on the part of the parents are the most salient demonstrable differences found between families with a delinquent child and those of similar social and economic background whose children do not evidence delinquent behavior.

However, if our presentation stopped at this more general level, our evidence would not suffice to convince a critical audience. We believe that is far more compelling to present anecdotal material that illustrates the evidence on which we based our judgments. The interactional genesis of delinquency within the family is quickly manifest in case history material. In each subsequent chapter we examine these patterns in detail: the relationship to status and occupational inadequacy; role playing vs. depreciation and dissatisfaction; problems of neglect and isolation; feelings of unfairness and deprivation—as they were recounted to us by given families.

We contend, therefore, that to better understand the genesis of delinquency in particular families, the reader should examine clinically and critically the case material excerpts, one by one, as well as refer to our quantitative summaries. Both methods of presentation and documentation are valid and necessary. It is more difficult, however, to publish extensive case material, since sheer volume is needed in order to provide the reader with sufficient evidence to make a judgment. Unfortunately, all studies, clinical or not, tend to be reduced to some form of quantification because of economic considerations. Nevertheless, only illustrative case material can convey to others the interaction patterns and personality variables in operation. Therefore, reports such as those which follow are few in number. The reader, we hope, will find that Japanese families reflect some of the same universals found in family life in other modern industrial societies.

CHAPTER 4

Perspectives on Family Life and Delinquency

One cannot hope to tie together satisfactorily in any brief statement all the implications and suggestions found in Japanese studies of delinquency. Nevertheless, we offer here some impressions arrived at as a result of surveying the extant published material.[1]

Japanese research on delinquency takes into account a variety of selective factors, social as well as psychological, that one finds in research conducted in the United States, but there is little agreement in either country as to the relative weight or manner of interrelationship of these sociological and psychological determinants.

Over the years we noted in our survey of Japanese material a complete turn away from earlier biological explanations as knowledge of both the social and the psychological dynamics increased. It is our impression that although psychoanalytic or some other forms of psychodynamic theory are often discussed, these discussions are seldom based on detailed clinical evidence. Specialists publishing the present literature on delinquency lack direct experience in using psychoanalytically oriented methods. Such a lack reflects a more general absence of this framework in the fields of psychiatry, clinical psychology, and social work in Japan generally. Arguments dismissing psychoanalytic conceptualizations of delinquent character development are frequently no more cogent than those brief asides found in many American psychological or sociological texts written for the easy comprehension of the college undergraduate.

In most recent books one finds much more emphasis on environmental approaches organized around some form of what can be termed ego psychology or field theory. On the other hand, discussions of the influence of Japanese culture and changes in its economic and social institutions on the incidence of delinquency also leave much to be desired. Nevertheless, sociological theory in Japan generally seems much better integrated than are psychodynamic formulations related to psychosexual development.

Studies of the broad environmental influence on criminal and delinquent behavior considered in Japan are in the main concerned with four principal

1. Parts of the present chapter first appeared in modified form in W. Lebra, ed., *Transcultural Research in Mental Health*, 1972, and are reprinted by permission.

themes: (1) group processes in delinquent formation, including gang behavior; (2) the effect of culture and social change on patterns of deviant behavior; (3) postwar trends in crime in Japan; and (4) ecological studies of crime in various regions of Japan as well as in the modern industrial urban environment.[2]

The shift in Japan toward environmental explanations has been due less to some definitive ruling out of physiological predispositions than to the discovery of other forces of sufficient causality. Some measures of physiological as well as psychosocial maturation indeed are cogently suggested by studies of social maturation as a significant variable. These are studies that indicate, for example, that delinquent subjects manifest immaturity of personality or lack impulse control or frustration tolerance on some psychological tests. (See Ono, 1958.) There are also a series of studies that find immaturity in physiological functioning of the brain on the electroencephalogram.[3]

In spite of the attention paid to the influence of the parent on delinquents, there have been almost no direct studies of the parents themselves, nor have there been any studies that satisfactorily trace the direct effects of very early trauma on delinquency formation.

Comparative studies of recidivists and nonrecidivists tend to suggest some differentials in degree of early motivation toward deviant behavior related to difficulties in the primary family prior to the problem period of adolescence. A number of the Japanese studies show the individuals already truanting from school during the earlier school period and running away from home. Earlier acts of stealing are sometimes committed against parents.

Contrary to some sociological theorists, we cannot attribute such early predelinquent behavior to "differential association" with a delinquent gang, nor to quasi-rational decisions on a course of behavior caused by one's being deprived by society of the opportunities for success and achievement. What is suggested by cases of earlier delinquency and more pronounced recidivism are the types of emotional deprivation and disadvantages involved in the formation of basic social attitudes that exist prior to more direct experience of social inequities or situational inducements toward goals reachable only by illegal means. It is in the institutionalized recidivist in Japan as well as in the United States that one very often finds the greatest differences from the norm in physiological as well as psychological measurements of egocentricity, and immaturity in ego integration.

There are repeated reports of intolerance of tension or frustration, and in a number of instances, reports of lack of internalization of a generally accepted social as well as personal conscience. Although few delinquents would meet all such personality criteria, it is obvious that any specific delinquent is apt to manifest a number of social and personal traits related to inadequate personality development. Studies of individual cases indicate that certain types of maladjust-

2. See De Vos, 1973, pp. 327–368.

3. For example, see Satake, et al., 1957, pp. 111–186; and also Makino, 1953, pp. 1–11.

ment seem to be more closely related to delinquent "acting out" than do others. From the sociological point of view, however, the number of cases studied in which psychosexual maladjustment and problems of superego internalization are demonstrably involved are few, and their statistical incidence in the entire population of delinquents is not recorded. No matter how committed one is to an understanding of human behavior in terms of developmental determinants, it is obvious that certain types of delinquency occur characteristically within certain propitious social environments, whether in the United States or in Japan. Certain specific environmental correlates appear repeatedly in the numerous studies that control for social variables. Delinquency rates are high for certain definable local areas, low for others. The possibility of becoming delinquent seems to require much less psychological motivation for individuals in certain environments than for those in others.

That these social determinants work over more than one generation cannot be overlooked. Here the focus devolves upon the field of the psychologically oriented theorist. Certain neighborhoods are selected by certain types of parents, who are prone, by fact of social position or personality propensities, to produce delinquent offspring. Therefore, one must consider that there is some parental selectivity of neighborhood, as well as direct influence of the neighborhood on the child, in delinquency formation. Certain types of antisocial identification are more prone to occur in the disaffected or lower echelons of a society than they are in the more responsible and successful groups. There are obvious differences of economic opportunity in any society. Nevertheless, opportunity itself is not the only variable to explain the individual's resorting to delinquent behavior to gain social ends. The general attitude and types of self-control practiced by the parents are essential elements, as we shall document in the following chapters. Before going into our own material in detail, let us turn to some conclusions of previous studies on family and delinquency in Japan and elsewhere, and in this context present some of our own quantitative findings on certain family interaction variables, first reported by Sheldon and Eleanor Glueck in 1950 as being crucial in distinguishing families that produce delinquent children.

Studies of Family Patterns and Delinquency

A number of Japanese studies make conscious mention, in their theoretical statements, of recent changes in role and status relationships between married men and women in Japanese society. However, there has been no controlled research linking such changes directly to changes in the incidence of delinquency. Although changes in the statistical incidence of crime rate in adolescent individuals are noted, there is very little direct theoretical discussion of the broader influences of modern industrial changes on the social role of the adolescent within Japanese society.

In viewing research literature on families studied in Japan as well as in the

United States, we note that a number of authors made serious attempts to trace the highly complex relationships among various factors regarded as determinants in delinquency formation. We have classified these studies of the family into categories in which the principal focii of attention are these: (1) the family as a social environment; (2) problems of parent-child separation and consequent deprivation; (3) types of discipline and appropriate expressions of affection in relation to personality development; (4) relative fairness in the treatment of sibs; and (5) "induction theories" of intrafamilial processes. Among "induction theories" are, first, those mainly concerned with direct social learning and, second, those based on the relationship of conscious and unconscious motives in the parental generation as they related to delinquency formation in children.

In our own intensive research in Arakawa Ward, we have examined our results in the context of such previous studies in Japan and the United States. In our own studies we have paid more explicit attention to the parents of the delinquents than is found in previous work. From this standpoint, our work is innovative and strengthens some conclusions and interpretations. In this chapter we shall briefly report some of our specific quantitative results that support the earlier research of the Gluecks. In the subsequent chapters we shall examine more detailed findings, which resulted from intensive interviewing and psychological testing.

THE FAMILY AS A SOCIAL ENVIRONMENT

The Influence of Poverty

The assumption of many of the earliest studies reported was that the impoverished condition of a family was itself a principal cause of crime and delinquency. One very early study by Breckinridge and Abbott (1912) in Chicago reported that 89 percent of delinquent girls and 76 percent of delinquent boys were from poor and impoverished families. There were a number of subsequent studies of this kind to be found in the early literature on delinquency. The Gluecks in their 1950 study in Boston contrasted the economic factors in their delinquent and control samples (pp. 84–94). They found that whereas 5 percent of delinquents came from families with some economic stability, nearly 29 percent came from families who were in need of public welfare support in one form or another. In the nondelinquent controls, in contrast, 12 percent were economically stable and 12 percent were in need of public assistance. Comparing the family incomes in their matched groups, the Gluecks found that the delinquent groups had more families with extremely low incomes. Nevertheless, the Gluecks did not contend that it was poverty per se that was a contributing factor in the delinquent development of the children. Poverty, rather, was seen in some families as related to the unstable work-record of the father, or the lack of stability in the family relationship itself, or the lack of planning and resourcefulness in the use of money on the part of the parents.

Healy and Bronner, in a classic early study (1926) based on detailed clinical material, came early on to disregard poverty per se as an important factor in the genesis of delinquency. Although there are still some sociologists who would rank impoverishment as an important contributory factor, there are fewer today who would seriously place poverty itself as a direct determinant of the high delinquency rates found in urban settings. Unemployment of youth takes place in a total environment involving other forms of social disparagement and family disorganization.

One can quote, from the Japanese research literature, studies that parallel those done in the United States. A number of these studies suffer from inadequate methods of control, however. For example, Takemura attempted to demonstrate that after World War II the middle-income groups were more stable and had a generally lower incidence of delinquency than did either high-income groups or poor families (Takemura, 1953). He sought to demonstrate this differential by obtaining from a number of prisons the relative incidence of individuals within certain stated family incomes. He found that 3 percent of delinquents came from what could be considered wealthy families, whereas 21 percent came from families that were characterized by a day-by-day work income of government welfare support. In contrast, in a particular high school that he studied, he found that only 0.7 percent of the delinquents represented the wealthier group, and only 3.2 percent represented students from very poor families. He therefore came to the conclusion that in the prison both the very wealthy and the very poor are overrepresented. But such a study does not take into account the lack of representativeness of one high school (which is compounded by the fact that students select high schools on the basis of their perceived social status), nor the various factors that lead to differences in institutionalization versus probation in Japanese adjudication of juvenile cases.

In slightly later studies that were concerned with other factors besides poverty in the family and were at the same time more carefully controlled, no such remarkable differences are obtained. Tatezawa reported that poor families were somewhat overrepresented in delinquent groups when compared with nondelinquent controls (Tatezawa, 1953). Ushikubo also found that there were more boys from impoverished families in delinquent groups than in nondelinquent control samples. However, the differences he reported were not very great (Ushikubo, 1956). In such studies by the Japanese, when poverty is stressed, the position usually taken is that poverty has an indirect rather than a direct influence, or that poverty is a consequence of family instability as well as a direct cause of delinquency per se. Poverty, for example, may induce the mother to leave the home to work, and to neglect children as a result. Poverty may force families to seek residence in neighborhoods where the social inducement to delinquent activity is high. Poverty may also cause conflict between family members. However, conditions in Japan at certain postwar periods showed an increasing rate of delinquency in spite of the total increase in the national average income and in spite of the fact that there has been no radical unemployment.

However, the impoverished condition of the country shortly after the war probably contributed to the very high rate of stealing and other offenses against property. It is notable that at that time stealing and such crimes contributed toward high crime figures among adults as well as juveniles.[4] The Research Institute of the Ministry of Justice in 1960 suggested that juvenile delinquency at that time showed a notable increase among individuals from middle-income families. We may raise the question whether this demonstrates an increase in juvenile crime among those families previously classified as middle-income, or whether, with increasing prosperity, a number of families that were previously classified in a lower income bracket have moved up into the middle-income classification in the Japanese statistics without improving their relative economic status. The statistics, therefore, may not show as radical an increase in middle-income delinquents per se as the fact that there has been a general shift in the prosperity of the country at large.[5]

Another aspect of family living that is often compared with incidence of delinquency is the living conditions of the household. In the United States, resident space does show some correlation with delinquency, although the interpretations differ. In Japan the space available per individual is radically less than in the United States, but Tatezawa (1953) reported that there was some slight inverse correlation between residence size and delinquency. By contrast, Ono (1958: 103) in his statistical comparisons found less area of living space for boys in delinquent groups than for his control sample. He also found that institutionalized delinquents were likely to come from homes with less space per individual than were noninstitutionalized delinquents on probation. But, as Ono suggests, this difference may have been due to selectivity in the courts' adjudication. Judges probably took living conditions and the presence of an intact home into account when they decided whether to put an individual on probation or to send him to an institution. Therefore, studies based only on comparison of institutionalized delinquents with unmatched normal controls are apt to be spurious. Furthermore, this study in no way demonstrates that living space is correlated with delinquency independently of family income. In our own research with matched samples of fifty families, there was actually slightly less space per person in the families without delinquents than in those with delinquents (see chapter 5).

The Gluecks stressed the interpretation that the poorer home conditions of delinquents with the same economic circumstances as nondelinquents were an indirect reflection of the general attitudes of the parents toward family life (1950: 106–108). That is, in economically stressful situations, families that produce delinquents put a smaller proportion of their income into trying to main-

4. It is possible that the importance of poverty for delinquency is actually decreasing with time. After World War II, many boys committed theft as a means of survival in a very difficult economic situation, but such cases are now rare.

5. There is some tendency among Japanese statisticians to define class affiliation simply by income classification. This same oversimplification is also very common in American statistics.

tain home standards. The suggestion is that in a number of families where drunkenness or other conditions of emotional difficulty occur, money that would be otherwise available to better the somewhat impoverished living standard is used to buy liquor or is spent on other interests.

The Effects of Broken or Disrupted Homes

Perhaps of all the factors in family life, that of broken homes has historically received the most detailed statistical examination in attempts to understand the genesis of delinquency. Numerous studies identified the broken home itself, whether broken by desertion, divorce, or death, as a condition which, without other explanations or psychodynamic interpretations, could cause delinquency. More recent studies tend to see the broken home as symptomatic of the types of relationships occurring within the family; the authors of these studies state that only when certain patterns of interpersonal relations exist in the family will a broken home lead to delinquency. A 1925 study by Burt in London (Burt, 1944), which is much quoted in Japan, found that 60 percent of juvenile delinquents examined were from broken homes. Slawson (1926), replicating the Burt study in New York, found that 45 percent of boys in correctional institutions were from broken homes, whereas in his control groups only 19 percent were from nonintact families. Shaw and McKay in their Chicago studies (1931) did not consider broken homes per se an important factor in the genesis of delinquency. They found that 42 percent of their delinquents came from broken homes, and that 36 percent of normal control groups obtained from the same neighborhood areas also had broken homes. The differences, therefore, were considerably less than those found in the previous reports where adequate matched samples were lacking. A number of other studies followed, seeking to disprove the broken-home theory (e.g., Carr-Saunders, Mannheim, and Rhodes, 1942) or considering the broken home to have only a temporarily traumatic effect (Campbell, 1932:44). More lasting criticisms were established by Ashley Weeks (Weeks and Smith, 1939; Weeks, 1940), who found that children from broken homes were more likely to be brought to court or institutionalized than were those coming from intact homes, for whom informal adjustments between parents and professional personnel were more common than formal adjudication. Such simple administrative factors create a differential rate between the institutionalized delinquents and normal controls, since the individual on probation is usually not considered in such studies. Ono's careful work in Japan (1958:104) amply replicates the findings of Weeks and shows how important such factors are in assessing the principal determinants of delinquency in prewar Japanese studies of broken homes.

One of the earlier studies in Japan on the question of broken homes was by Yoshimasu between 1927 and 1929 (Yoshimasu, 1952). Although his general theoretical orientation was that of a psychiatrist interested in heredity, Yoshimasu nevertheless attempted careful empirical work which considered the environmental differences of delinquents. In this early study he found that 62 percent of the delinquents in institutions were from broken homes. He replicated the same study over a second two-year period, 1931–1933, in which he studied 100 juvenile prisoners and found similar results: that 65 were from broken homes. Higuchi (1953), doing a postwar follow-up on Yoshimasu's work, compared his own results with those of Yoshimasu and of Teishin Tani, using Tani's study (1929) rather than Yoshimasu's, since Yoshimasu's had no control for age and the individuals in his study in fact tended to be of an older age group. Higuchi found in his own survey of younger institutionalized delinquents that 48 percent were from broken homes, a rate considerably lower than that reported by either Tani or Yoshimasu. Nevertheless, the rate of broken homes that Higuchi found was higher than that of a secondary school sample he used as a control, in which only 24 percent came from broken homes. Higuchi also used a noninstitutionalized delinquent sample as a control and found that among them 37 percent were from broken homes, which made this sample intermediate between the other two. It would be anticipated that a high rate of broken homes would exist in Japan with the large-scale dislocation and the many casualties of the war. That these studies show an overall lower rate of broken homes than do prewar studies might bring into question the accuracy of the earlier statistics or might attest to a higher incidence of broken families in the past than would be suspected from the generally held attitude that Japanese family ties are weakening. Higuchi does not relate the differences between institutionalized and noninstitutionalized delinquents to questions of administrative policy as Ono does. Rather, he sees the differences as related to degrees of severity of disturbances of both an emotional and a delinquent nature.

Mizushima in a similar study (1956) did not find as great a difference between recidivists and nonrecidivists with regard to the incidence of broken homes as did Higuchi. Oura (1957) carefully pointed out that the question of broken homes versus unbroken homes was not simply a question of intact families, but that delinquents actually had more cases of stepparents or parent-surrogates in the so-called intact families than was true for the nondelinquent controls he used. Therefore, it must also be considered that nondelinquent youths are more likely to be living with their natural parents than are delinquent youths. Ono (1958:412) pointed out that there was only a slight difference between boys on probation and normal controls in respect to the incidence of broken homes, while the institutionalized delinquents differed significantly from both. The overall results, therefore, would indicate some selectivity in adjudication among delinquents, resulting in higher rates of commitment to institutions for those coming from broken homes. It may also indicate, however, greater frequency of occurrence, severity of problems, or greater visibility among those coming from broken homes.

Some studies attempted to test whether broken homes had a differential effect according to the sex of the young delinquent. In Healy's and Bronner's

(1926) early survey of 4,000 delinquents in Boston and New York, approximately half came from broken homes. The greatest incidence of broken homes was found among delinquent girls. Several other early studies had similar results. For example, Mabel Eliot, in her study (1928) of delinquent girls in Pennsylvania, stressed the prevalence of broken homes among them. Studies in Japan, however, show no such differential between young male and female delinquents, according to Takemura (1953:95).

A number of studies concerned with the age of delinquents have found that among individuals who start their delinquent activities earlier, the rate of broken homes is greater. Shaw and McKay (1931) and Reckless and Smith (1932) illustrate this differential. The Gluecks' study (1950:122) also suggests that the effect of a broken home is more serious with younger delinquents. Similar results were obtained in several Japanese studies explicitly concerned with age. Takemura (1953:223) compared the rate of broken homes of delinquents in a children's training school, a juvenile reform training school, and a juvenile prison. The average age of the inmates was lowest in the children's training school, medium in the juvenile reform school, and highest in the juvenile prison. The rate of broken homes was 76 percent in the children's training school, 58 percent in the juvenile reformatory, and 48 percent in the juvenile prison. This study did not ask the question whether the adjudication that led to placement at early ages was influenced by the absence of one or both parents. Therefore, the conclusion that the effect of broken homes shows up in earlier delinquency is as yet unsupported.

Other studies of broken homes have attempted to ascertain whether the absence of a father or of a mother is the more consequential in delinquency formation. The Gluecks' large-scale study finds no such differentiation (p. 124). However, some of the earlier studies—for example, that of Healy and Bronner (1926:101)—cite contradictory evidence.

In Japan, there were several studies related to this problem. Yoshimasu (1952:145) cites statistical research from which he concludes that homes broken when the child is less than five years old produce a higher incidence of delinquency later, when the mother is not present, whereas homes broken when the child is more than five years old show a subsequent higher incidence of delinquency when there is no father.

Similar results to those of Yoshimasu are reported by Higuchi (1953:44). It is interesting to note that these materials are presented by psychiatrists who are somewhat antagonistic to psychoanalytic interpretations of child development; however, the material immediately becomes suggestive to individuals thinking in a psychoanalytic framework. More psychodynamically oriented researchers go beyond the mere assessment of the physical presence of a parent and are concerned with the psychological effects of separation from the parents. Some put heavy emphasis on the effect of early separation. Bowlby (1947:55), in the study of forty-four juvenile thieves from the London Child Guidance

Clinic, found that early separation from the mother was very important, occurring in 17 out of 44 delinquent cases, but in only 2 out of 44 cases in the control group of unselected emotionally disturbed nondelinquents from the same clinic.

Bowlby also notes that hostile or rejecting parents are as important in the genesis of delinquency as is the fact of early separation. Of the 27 thieves who had not suffered early separation, 17 had mothers who were either extremely anxious, irritable, and fussy, or else rigid, domineering, and oppressive, traits which in all cases mask much unconscious hostility. Five of the 27 had fathers who hated them and expressed their hatred openly. In these respects, however, the thieves do not differ from the neurotic controls, although both groups would probably differ substantially from a group of normal children. Unfortunately, Bowlby used no normal groups for comparison.

Bowlby discussed the pathological effects of prolonged maternal separation and the psychopathology of the affectionless thief. He drew attention to the strong libidinal and aggressive components in stealing, and to the failure of superego development in these individuals following the failure to develop a capacity for object-love. The latter deficiency was traced by Bowlby to a lack of opportunity to develop inhibitions resulting from early rage over deprivation and an inability to develop fantasy as an internal control. Stating that a normal conscience cannot develop in the context of deprivation, he saw a psychopathic lack of affection in children having such experiences. Such character traits are apparent to some degree in many thieves and prostitutes, according to Bowlby.

The later, psychoanalytically oriented study by Ivy Lee Bennett (1960:35) in England compares, among a number of other factors, types of family disruption, including broken homes, that she found in her fifty delinquents and fifty neurotic subjects. She indicates that as far as the appearance of stability goes, her neurotic subjects came from apparently more "stable" homes, in contrast to the manifestly more unstable home environments of the delinquents in her sample. Her findings are in full accord with previous statements by Friedlander (1949:424) that the homes of neurotic children are more often unbroken, but that the home environment has certain unhealthy features that contribute to neurotic disturbances. Banister and Ravden (1944) also say that their findings in Britain demonstrate that delinquent and aggressive children come from "broken" homes, and "nervous" children tend to come from homes with at least surface stability.

We have no statistics in Arakawa on the relationship to delinquency of broken and of intact families. By design our Arakawa Ward sample consisted only of families that were then intact. We could make no direct comparison, therefore, of the immediate effects of a broken home and of an intact home. Nevertheless, among our subjects, we were able to obtain some previous evidence of the differential occurrence of family disruption. Of the parents of our delinquents, 58 percent had a previous marriage, in contrast to 26 percent among the parents of nondelinquents—over twice the rate. Many of the disruptions were caused by war deaths in both groups; however, considerably more disruptions were due to divorce or separation in the delinquent sample.

This finding is related to that of Oura, (1957 : 414) who found that in comparing delinquents who had good prognosis with those who had bad prognosis, those with poor prognosis came more often from families in which the parental home was broken by divorce or desertion. There was no difference between delinquents and nondelinquents concerning homes broken through death. Other studies indicate that stepparents are found more frequently in delinquents' homes than in those of nondelinquents (Suzuki, 1957; Tsubota, 1955). Some authors are unfortunately prone to relate such results to stereotypes of wicked or unfeeling stepparents rather than to more complex factors arising from attitudes held by the child in situations of parental loss at given periods of psychosexual development.

The influence of family disruption is not limited to the immediate parental generation. The personality and attitudes of Arakawa parents were shaped by their own experiences as children, which are indirectly passed on when they in turn become parents. According to the retrospective reports of parents, there were many more disruptions in the grandparental generation of the delinquent subjects of our Arakawa familes than for the grandparents of the nondelinquent controls. Only two, or 6.5 percent, of the families of delinquents were intact for two generations, contrasted with 44 percent of the nondelinquent families, whose grandparents on both sides remained together at least until the given parent interviewed was twelve years of age or older. There were six common-law liaisons in five different family histories of the thirty-one families in the delinquent sample. Only one such common-law liaison was reported in the nondelinquent sample. Our small-scale data would therefore support the contention that a history of family disruption is related to the appearance of delinquency in children, even when the present family circumstances show an intact family unit.

From a cross-cultural perspective, many studies in both the United States and Japan provide a rather mechanical juxtaposition of events, limited to simplistic surface interpretations that do not consider possible differences in cultural patterns. One cannot simply look at direct statistical comparisons of two cultures. For example, studies reporting the effects of divorce as related to delinquency in Japan seem to be more conclusive than similar studies in the United States, where there seems to be less difference between the effects of broken homes caused by separation and those caused by death.

In attempting to compare results in this matter, one must note that divorce is much more common in the United States and hence is possibly much less indicative of extreme difficulties between parents than in Japan. Similarly, when we later report the positive relationship between bottle-feeding and delinquency in Japan (chapter 9), it must be noted that the rate of bottle-feeding in Japan is much lower than that in the United States. Hence, bottle-feeding is more apt to be a symptom of maternal rejection in Japan than in the United

States. In any comparative cultural context, the meaning of any statistical correlation between one form of social behavior and another must be interpreted in the light of the overall frequency or social expectancy of either pattern. Once a certain degree of frequency of behavior is reached by a population, behavior such as divorce or bottle-feeding is no longer "deviant" in the sense of requiring a strong motivation to go counter to expected role patterns.

Similarly, one must guard against the supposition that more recent studies can be interpreted as "disproving" previous ones when results are different. It may well be that the more recent American studies are more careful and critical, and therefore have found less correlation between factors than those of the past. Or it may be that the social situation is gradually shifting, and that at the turn of the twentieth century questions of poverty and broken homes in both the United States and Japan may have shown some mechanically higher intercorrelation than they do today. Nor can we rule out the possibility that the nature of delinquency is gradually changing, and that such factors play less important roles among delinquents today than they did in the past. The generalization we would make from the foregoing material is that a simple correlational juxtaposition does not solve the issue of understanding causative factors in delinquency; it merely indicates the direction in which one must look. Evidence of poverty or overt family disruption may be secondary to the personalities and basic attitudes of parents as experienced by children who become delinquent. To resolve such issues, more intensive studies are necessary. Finding statistical relationships is only one step in scientific inquiry.

Parental Relationships: Love, Discipline, and Family Cohesion

Among those authors considering how parental attitudes relate to delinquency formation there is general unanimity that among the key factors to be considered are, first, whether and how love is expressed, and, second, how parents maintain discipline and supervision in their upbringing of the child. Family disruptions growing out of parental discord or overt separation are generally accepted as causative factors. However, one finds among researchers considerable difference in their assessment of the relative weight to be given to maternal and paternal care and family cohesiveness. There is also considerable difference of opinion as to whether delinquent attitudes arise from direct conscious experiences or from more unconscious layers of personality as shaped by family patterns.

In surveying the considerable literature on delinquency in both Japan and the United States, one finds studies that attend to one or another set of variables. The realities of parental interaction with children are very complex, and it is difficult to order the variables in any unilinear fashion for presentation. We have found it expedient in the following discussion to start out considering the five variables of the Gluecks' (1950) prediction scale. As was noted above, the items included were based upon their previous observations of delinquent youth, and detailed perusal of case histories.

In Japan, Tatezawa (1953) has replicated the Gluecks' study on a much smaller number of individuals with amazing similarity of results. According to his sample, 77.3 percent of nondelinquent parents were regarded as manifesting adequate supervision on the part of the mothers, whereas only 13.2 percent of delinquents could be so considered. The discipline of the father was considered adequate in 51 percent of families with no delinquents, but in only 2 percent of the delinquent subjects in Tatezawa's study. The affection of the mother toward the boy was considered good for 77.3 percent of nondelinquents, contrasted with only 32.1 percent for delinquents. Affection expressed by the father toward the boy was good for 64 percent of nondelinquents, but for only 20 percent of delinquents. Cohesiveness of the family was positive in 85 percent of families of nondelinquents, but was considered adequate in only. 38 percent of the delinquent sample.

Ushikubo (1956), using the same factors as the Gluecks, matched 121 delinquents and 120 controls. Comparing delinquents and controls, he found that the rate of broken homes, the educational level of the family, and the occupation of the parents did not differ in normals and delinquents. However, disciplinary attitudes and behavior indicative of lack of family cohesiveness clearly differed in the two groups. He found that both parents had generally punitive attitudes toward delinquent children. Frequent changes of residence, economic instability, emotional conflict, tension within the family, and the lack of joint activities of a pleasant sort by family members were significantly more common in the families of delinquents than in those of the nondelinquent group.

Our own intensive study of fifty Japanese families produced very apparent differences between delinquent and nondelinquent samples when we rated our cases in accord with the Glueck criteria. In respect to the fathers' discipline, we concluded that 58 percent of the fathers in our nondelinquent sample of 19 showed adequate consistent discipline, and none of the fathers of delinquents did (see table 4.1). Conversely, 18 out of 31 fathers (58 percent) of delinquents evidenced withdrawal or laxity in their discipline. Only 1 father of nondelinquents (3 percent) was so categorized.

In respect to the supervision of the mother, only 2 mothers of delinquents (6 percent) obtained an optimal rating; 15 (48 percent) showed unsuitable maternal supervision. Of the mothers of nondelinquents, 18 out of 19 (94 percent) were rated as "good" in this respect.

On the ratings of affection or love, only 2 of the nondelinquent fathers were rated unsatisfactory, as were 16, or over half, of the delinquent fathers. No mothers of nondelinquents were rated unsatisfactory in this regard; 19 (63 percent) of the mothers of delinquents were considered by us to show insufficient maternal affection in one way or another.

In respect to family cohesion, no nondelinquent families were rated as un-

TABLE 4.1
Glueck Scores of Fifty Arakawa Families

	Japanese Normals (N=19)	*Japanese Delinquents (N=31)*	*Fisher's Exact Test*
I. Discipline by father			
A. Suitable	11	0	A−B ($P<.001$)
B. Lax	1	18	A−C ($P<.001$)
C. Overly strict or erratic	7	13	B−C ($P<.05$)
II. Supervision by mother			
A. Suitable	18	2	
B. Fair	1	14	A−BC ($P<.001$)
C. Unsuitable	0	15	
III. Affection of father			
A. Positive	17	15	A−B ($P<.005$)
B. Basically negative	2	16	
IV. Affection of mother			
A. Positive	19	12	A−B ($P<.001$)
B. Basically negative	0	19	
V. Cohesion of family			
A. Good	12	1	
B. Some	7	19	A−BC ($P<.001$)
C. None	0	11	
High–Low Score Range			*Chance of Delinquency (per hundred) according to Glueck*
117–150	10	0	2.9
150–199	3	0	15.7
200–249	3	2	37.0
250–299	3	7	63.5
300–349	0	12	86.0
350–399	0	6	90.1
400–414	0	4	98.1
Mean Scores	164.5	327.9	

integrated or totally lacking in cohesion, whereas we rated 11 (35 percent) of the families of delinquents as totally unsatisfactory in this regard. Conversely, 12 families (63 percent) of nondelinquents were considered to show sufficient evidence of cohesiveness, and only 1 such family among those of delinquent children.

There is no question in our minds that in spite of the obvious rigidities entailed in rating families on either a trichotomous or a dichotomous scale in respect to these criteria, they do strongly point up significant differences between the families of our delinquent and nondelinquent subjects.

The variables included in the Glueck scale for predicting delinquency (see chapter 3 above) were considered qualitatively and quantitatively in a number of noteworthy studies that both preceded and followed their work.

Hewitt and Jenkins (1946) were concerned not only with delinquency but with types of delinquents. They sought to characterize differences in parental attitudes and behavior related to each of three behavioral patterns found in lower-class delinquent children in Chicago. In the first pattern, one of "neurotic behavior," they found the father's discipline to be inconsistent. The father tended to be at times hypocritical and somewhat unsocial. The mother also tended to be socially isolated, but was dominating at home, and used controlling behavior, compensating for a tendency to reject the child. Sibling rivalry was also very often observed in this pattern of family. Here the father's inconsistent discipline was related not so much to delinquency as to overinhibited or neurotic behavior on the part of the children.

Parental behavior related to "antisocial" aggressive children involved more severe forms of early rejection. Some of these families were characterized by a premarital pregnancy that was unwanted by the father or the mother. Sometimes there was a postdelivery rejecting reaction by the mother or by the father; many of the mothers demonstrated a general unwillingness to assume the parental role and expressed open hostility to their children. In a number of these cases, the mother's sexual behavior was somewhat unconventional. These children in some instances had later lost contact with both natural parents.

The "socialized" delinquent, in contrast, was characterized more by a negligent attitude on the part of the parents, reflected in the mother's lack of interest in homekeeping, a lack of regularity in the home routine, lack of supervision, and rather lax discipline by both mother and father. Some of the mothers showed mental inadequacies. There were other cases in which the converse to laxity was overly harsh discipline on the part of one or both parents. Sometimes the mother attempted to protect the child from the father's physical attacks. Often more than one of the children in the family became delinquent, and this pattern was found related to individuals living in urban, deteriorated areas.

Hewitt and Jenkins found that there was no simple correlation between the three attitudinal and behavioral categories of rejection, neglect, and repressive discipline. They concluded that severe, active parental rejection, especially in the early ages, produces the type of antisocial, aggressive delinquency based on faulty internalization and a lack of capacity to have feelings for others. Parental neglect, either by inadequate or by disorganized parents, tended to induce the child toward some socialized form of delinquency. However, a number of cases in the study showed a mixed type of delinquency in which there was evidence of both rejection and neglect in the child's background.

A similar study based on the criteria set up by Hewitt and Jenkins was tried in Japan. Sasaki (1962) investigated the family patterns of 81 delinquent boys encountered in the Kobe family court, classifying them basically "rejecting," "neglecting," or "other." Boys from rejecting families tended to act in lone offenses, while those who had neglecting families tended toward group or cooperative offenses. Kobayashi found evidence suggesting the same three types of problem children by observing cases referred to a child guidance center in Tokyo (Kobayashi et al., 1963 : 404). Although the family background material available was sometimes limited, in their judgment they found definite tendencies for socialized delinquents to have neglecting (or rejecting) parents, more aggressive children to have rejecting parents, and overinhibited, neurotic children to have strict or overanxious parents.

In the United States Nye conducted a study (1958) of the role of punishment in delinquent behavior. He found that if discipline involves partiality, unfairness, or rejection, it not only may be ineffective as direct control but may tend to reduce both indirect and internalized controls in the child. He found that nagging, scolding, and withdrawal of love in his sample were significantly related to delinquency when these types of delinquency were related to a basically rejecting attitude on the part of parents. The technique of discipline through withdrawal of affection is related to delinquency only when it is part of a general pattern of rejection. When it is part of a pattern in which the child usually feels loved by the parents, then it leads to a rather strong superego development. In Nye's sample, the disciplinary role of the father was more closely related to delinquent behavior than was that of the mother. The disciplinary role of the mother appears to bear a stronger relationship to delinquency in girls than in boys. Nye found that complete laxity of discipline deprives the adolescent of the necessary controls to assist him in achieving social conformity. On the other hand, overstrictness deprives children of recreational opportunities and companionship with peer groups, which also causes difficulty in assuming later adult status. The individual may become alienated from parents if either extreme of discipline is exercised. Nye tried to judge whether lack of congruence between parental and adolescent attitudes was related to delinquency. He attempted to demonstrate that it was *not* the lack of internalization of conforming variables that was related to delinquency, but the lack of congruence with parental attitudes. This type of approach shows a basic superficiality in Nye's work, for, as we will indicate later in the study of social attitudes, attitudes are sometimes secondary reflections of the nature of internalization, rather than something basic in themselves.

Many of the American studies of parental discipline attest to the difficulties encountered in obtaining accurate information about the influence of discipline. Many of these studies depend upon retrospective interviews or upon reports of investigators who already knew that the child was delinquent or nondelinquent. This is usually an unavoidable condition in delinquency research. From this point of view, the study of William and Joan McCord (1959) is of considerable value. They did a follow-up study of the well-known Cambridge-Somerville youth project, having their social workers and counselors investigate home situations over a period of at least two years.

A strong virtue in the structure of the McCord study is found in the clear distinction maintained between punitiveness and affection. The McCords made an examination combining love and discipline, to see how they were interrelated in their subjects. As in the Glueck study, the McCords found that a significantly lower proportion of delinquents were from cohesive homes than from other types of homes. However, they found that this factor is largely related to parental discipline. Cohesive homes emphasized love-oriented techniques, and those in which there was discord seemed to be more characterized by erratically applied punitive methods. Holding either discipline or home atmosphere constant, the McCords found that boys who had been disciplined by a love-oriented technique had a generally lower crime rate than their counterparts who had been disciplined by lax or punitive measures. Only for normal or neglecting homes was this difference statistically significant, however. They found that nearly every boy with a background of both lax discipline and a quarrelsome, neglecting home had a criminal record. The crime rate for this combination was decidedly greater than that for lax discipline in combination with any other types of home atmosphere.

In another analysis, the McCords found that the type of father appeared to be related to the proportion of children who later became criminals (pp. 91–100). A cruel and neglecting father, a dead father, or an absent father contributed significantly to delinquency. The type of father was related to the general disciplinary patterns of the parents. Families with warm fathers tended to use more consistently love-oriented techniques. Families with passive or absent fathers showed no particular form of discipline. It was not surprising that boys with cruel fathers were subjected to harsh discipline, and those with neglecting fathers were usually completely undisciplined. By holding constant either the father's personality or the type of discipline, the McCords found that in the loving—that is, the warm and passive—father groups who nevertheless used erratic discipline, there were fewer delinquents than among the families with nonloving fathers (including cruel, absent, and neglecting fathers) who used erratic discipline. They concluded, "The importance of discipline can best be seen in relation to other conditions within the home. Consistent and kindly methods of control are most important when other factors are conducive to rebellion" (p. 95). Similarly, in respect to mothers, the McCords found that "loving mothers, regardless of other personality characteristics, apparently gave the children enough emotional security for the internalization of moral controls" (p. 98). The most controversial of the McCords' finds from a psychodynamic standpoint is that according to their criteria passive mothers produced a higher proportion of criminal sons, whereas passive fathers tended to produce a lower incidence of crime (p. 100). According to their interpretation, the contrast in influence of maternal and paternal passivity may be due to different expectations which the child has concerning each parent. This finding is difficult to understand from a psychodynamic standpoint. Since the McCords, throughout their studies, neglect to relate intercorrelations to dynamic patterns, these studies show a general weakness in suggesting the psychological mechanism whereby these various categories induce or do not induce delinquent behavior.

Summing up various interrelationships between love and discipline, they concluded that "a combination of lax or laxly punitive discipline, with a lack of maternal affection greatly increases a tendency toward criminality. On the other hand, consistent discipline, coupled with maternal love greatly reduces chances of criminality" (p. 102).

In Bennett's intensive comparison of 50 delinquents and 50 neurotics (1960: 47), she found a number of statistical associations which she carefully avoids regarding as causes, for she states that such occurrences as broken homes are probably related to instability in the parents rather than having a direct intercausal relationship with delinquency. In addition to findings positively relating broken homes and delinquency she found antisocial tendencies in a number of parents of delinquents, in contrast with the neurotic children's parents. She stresses, however, that the category "delinquent" is a heterogenous one rather than one that points to a specific personality syndrome. Inconsistency in discipline, in contrast with overstrict or normal discipline, characterized the parents of delinquents. A very high proportion of the delinquent children she studied had consciously disturbed relationships with one or both parents or a quarrelsome, aggressive and sadomasochistic type of relationship, according to her description. Similarly, the relationship of the parents of delinquents to each other was of an outspoken, quarrelsome nature and had sadomasochistic features. There was considerable evidence of immaturity, instability, and mutual incompatibility. In addition to permanently broken homes, the delinquent-family histories were marked by breaks and interruptions in the parental relationship at all ages. Bennett stresses that the most significant age in her sample for a break in mother-child relationship seems to be the second year, supporting some of the conclusions of Burlingham and Anna Freud (1942). However, the delinquent children appeared to suffer from repeated separation or disruption rather than from any single traumatic occurrence. Bennett found that the descriptions of many delinquents stressed willful, impulsive behavior, inability to bear frustration, and shameless and greedy demanding attitudes. She found, interestingly enough, that there was some tendency for delinquents to come from larger families than neurotics, but she had no control data for the group at large from which her samples were drawn.

Sib Position and the Manifestation of Delinquency

In our Arakawa study we were interested in family size and sib positions as being possibly relevant to delinquency, considering these factors as sources of relative neglect or rejection which could be experienced by some children in growing up.

In Japan it is a common observation that the eldest son has been treated differently from other children in the family. It has been said also that in the patterns of urban in-migration, it is more often the second sons of rural families who go to the city. We therefore explored the sibling position of both the parents and the children in our sample (see chapter 5). We found some differences that were significant even for our small sample. We found a lower average number of children (2.95) for our normal controls, compared with either the isolate (3.45) or the social (3.75) delinquent groups. Among delinquent subjects, we found the position of middle or second son overrepresented. Eleven out of 31 of our delinquent subjects were in this sib position, compared with 1 out of 19 of our normal subjects. Among the normals, the subjects tended to be either oldest child, oldest son, or youngest child, in contrast to the social and isolate delinquent subjects.

Going back one generation and examining the sib position of the parents, we found that it was less important to examine sib position of the children regardless of sex, but highly relevant to examine the sib position of the parents with their sibs of the same sex. Nine out of 19 of the fathers of our normal subjects were first sons, compared with 8 out of 31 of the fathers of delinquents. Three out of 19 fathers (16 percent) of normals were second sons, compared with 18 out of 31 fathers of delinquents, or 58 percent. This would appear to be a highly significant difference.

Turning to the mothers, we also found some significant differences. Eleven out of 31 of the mothers of delinquents were third or later-born daughters in their own families. This is over 35 percent of the mothers or stepmothers of delinquents, compared with 2, or about 10 percent, of the mothers of the nondelinquent sample. What these figures suggest is perhaps a position of relative neglect found in the parents of delinquent subjects, which may in turn contribute to the relative neglect of one or more of their own children. In a sense it may be a passing on of a pattern of experience which contributes to delinquency, in some degree at least, given other convergences of experience.

In our study of Arakawa families, we gathered materials from each of the parents in regard to attitudes about mothering and the problems they encountered in bringing up their children. From this material two very clear patterns appear, which differentiate statistically the delinquent children from the nondelinquent controls.

One pattern related to feeding (see chapter 9 for further details). Nearly half the delinquent sample were bottle-fed, whereas only 2 of 19 nondelinquents were bottle-fed. This is in keeping with the cultural norm in Japan, where over 85 percent of children are breast-fed. Thumb-sucking or nail-biting was reported in almost one-third of the delinquent children; no such problem was reported among the nondelinquent controls. This finding agrees with the case findings of the intensive comparative study of Ivy Lee Bennett (1960:176–178) in England, and also with previous findings that she reports for Australia.

It is not necessary for us here to recapitulate psychoanalytic theories about the possibilities of problems arising from the early mother-child relationship.

Such problems are not limited to humans. Levy (1934) observed how difficulty gaining satisfaction in sucking related in puppies to aggressive behavior in some and excessive submissive behavior in others.

In all probability, however, findings relating back to breast-feeding and delinquency would not usually be applicable to the United States, where the cultural mode is recent years is bottle-feeding. Therefore, one cannot assume the same degree of motivational and attitudinal differences in bottle-feeding American mothers as is true for bottle-feeding Japanese mothers, since the mode in Japan still remains breast-feeding, especially in lower-class and traditional segments of the population.

The second striking difference in our sample was in the reporting of enuresis. Only 2 normal families reported bed-wetting into the school period, as contrasted with such reports for 13 out of 31 delinquents.

This finding of the relationship between enuresis and delinquency has been reported previously in the psychiatric literature. Michaels (1938, 1961), and Michaels and Goodman (1939) report that the highest percentage of enuresis in their studies is found in rejected or neglected children, including delinquents, and the lowest number in "overprotected" children. There are numerous interpretations given for the continuance of enuresis in children. Generally, it is considered to be a sign that certain emotional needs do not have appropriate gratification. It is sometimes interpreted as a substitutive form of gratification, or passive sexuality of a repressed nature. It is sometimes related to sibling rivalry or to deep-seated fears or anxieties. It is often seen as a disguised expression of repressed hostility toward the parents. It often seems to be a masked form of masturbation, and allied with a high degree of covert aggression. Karpman (1948) presents a configuration suggesting that enuresis in delinquents is part of a general syndrome of immaturity and insecurity. It is highly correlated with other symptoms, such as poor sleeping habits, thumb-sucking, nail-biting, and temper tantrums. These all suggest some common fundamental disorder of personality.

General Family Atmosphere

The Gluecks' large-scale study concerned itself with a large number of other variables which we also considered under the rubric of general family atmosphere and organization. They found the following significant differences between delinquent and nondelinquent families: there was less planning of household routines, less concern with cultural matters in families of delinquents; these families were less self-respecting than the families of nondelinquents, and less ambitious about improving their status and that of their children. Standards of conduct were lower in homes of delinquents generally, and the quality of family life was less positive and less concerned with the children's welfare. Also, in their conclusions the Gluecks found that parents of delinquents, although stemming from backgrounds similar to the nondelinquents in size of family and other economic considerations, showed a larger number of cases of "forced" marriages, mental retardation, emotional disturbance, drunkenness, and criminality in previous family members. No such tendencies showed up in our Arakawa material except drunkenness, and that tendency in parents and grandparents did not reach significance. Regardless of whether attributes found by the Gluecks were hereditary or environmental in origin, they must be seen as having had some adverse influence upon the parents of the boys, who, in their turn had to assume the responsibilities of marriage and children. In the Gluecks' sample there was no difference between delinquents and nondelinquents in age of parents at marriage, nor disparity of ages between parents, and there were no significant differences in these factors in our Arakawa sample.

The nature of the marital relationship of father and mother showed significant differences between delinquent and nondelinquent families in Japan as well as in the United States. Although the type of recreational activities within families was important as a discriminator in the Gluecks' study, it was not so among the Arakawa families, as might be expected from the different nature of the customs of togetherness in Japan and the United States. It is very unusual for Japanese fathers to spend much time in recreation with their families. The work habits of the father in Japan also had less importance, although there was some tendency noted in the expected direction. Our Arakawa study also concurred that the fathers of delinquents were less positive in relating to their children. (This evidence is included under our general scoring of discipline and affection in table 4.1 and also in chapters 7 and 9.)

A number of the early studies of delinquency investigated the influence of "immoral" homes or "immoral" atmospheres or "immoral" individuals in the family. Healy and Bronner reported in their studies in Chicago and Boston (1926: 75) that 21 percent of families of delinquents had someone either alcoholic, criminal, or sexually deviant. Breckinridge and Abbott (1912: 79) found in Chicago, 1903–1904, that 20 percent of delinquent boys came from families with problem drinkers, and also that 20 percent of juvenile delinquent girls had alcoholic fathers; of these girls, 6 percent also had an alcoholic mother. In addition, 13 percent of both the boys and the girls had a criminal father, and 10 percent a mother who had been adjudicated for some form of illegal activity; 7 percent had living with the family some other person who had a criminal career. In their study among inmates of the Massachusetts Reformatory the Gluecks found that 85 percent had other criminals in the family (p. 101). In a postwar study in Japan by Higuchi (1953), among 73 reformatory inmates whose families' mental condition was carefully examined, 17 percent had criminal members and 7 percent had alcoholics. Of another 214 delinquents in a medical reformatory, 14 had criminal fathers; 2 had criminal fathers *and* mothers; 20 had criminal siblings; 39 had alcoholic fathers; 2 had alcoholic mothers; 11 had alcoholic fathers *and* mothers. In addition, 50 individuals had family members whose conduct was considered in some way reprehensible. The parents probably do not actively seek to have their children follow their way of life; but in an atmosphere in which parents have trouble with the law there are bound to be other types of conflict among family members as well.

Higuchi's interpretation of his data was based somewhat upon his belief in hereditary influences on delinquency. The study by the McCords (1959) was somewhat more elaborate in that they considered the role model of the father in relation to the discipline of and affection expressed toward the child. If the father's criminality is combined with lack of affection, cruelty, or neglect, it is more likely that a child will turn to criminal activities. If there is affection within the home situation, however, the child does not tend to follow in the father's footsteps as far as crime is concerned. Similar results are related to the mother. Whereas there were a high number of criminal fathers (45 out of 253 subjects), there were only 15 cases of a mother with a criminal career. However, there were an additional 30 cases of an alcoholic or sexually promiscuous mother, as compared with 206 nondeviant mothers. The McCords noted a tendency for a son to become criminal when the mother was deviant; they found, however, that when the mother was nonloving in addition, the boy's chances of becoming delinquent increased significantly. If the mother, even though deviant, takes a loving role toward her son, the chances of his becoming criminal are reduced. The most apparent combination that induced criminality was a deviant mother and an erratically exercised discipline.

In our examination of Arakawa family background, no evidence other than the number of broken families in the delinquent groups became significant. There was proportionately greater evidence of drinking problems and of black-market activity in the immediate postwar period in the delinquent sample, but these were trends that did not reach significance.

We therefore do not interpret the influence of "immoral" parents as directly producing delinquency simply through imitation. What seems to be necessary in the interpretation is some further consideration in the relationship between parent and child. It seems that the introduction of a son into a professional criminal career by the father is a very rare phenomenon; even when the father is a criminal, identification or imitation on the part of the son occurs only through some father-son conflict, so that it is the negative aspects of the identification that may cause the continuity from one generation to the next in criminal careers.

However, latent negative attitudes toward authority may be as important as manifest behavior. Adelaide Johnson (1949) in her work with Szurek (1952) and with Robinson (1957) has produced very striking material suggesting how the mechanism of "induction" into delinquency operates within certain families at both a conscious and an unconscious level. (See also Falstein, 1958; Giffin, Johnson, and Litin, 1954; Rexford et al., 1957; Jacobson, 1957.) Johnson's work points out how parents may find various forms of gratification for their own poorly integrated forbidden impulses in the acting-out behavior of one or more of their children, which is induced through some form of unconscious permissiveness or inconsistency toward the child. The child's "superego lacunae" corresponds to similar defects in the parents' parental superego, which in turn is often derived from conscious or unconscious permissiveness on the part of their own parents. The neurotic needs of the parents, whether of an excessively dominating, dependent, or erotic character, are vicariously gratified by the behavior of the child or by the parents' relations with the child. Such needs of the parents persist, either because of some current inability to satisfy them in the world of adults, or because of stunting experiences in the parents, or more commonly because of a combination of these factors. Because the parents' needs are unintegrated, unconscious, and unacceptable to the parents themselves, the child's behavior is not consciously condoned but is "punished." However, discipline is often administrated with guilt and ambivalence, so that the child may learn to exploit the parents and subsequently to blackmail them emotionally. Especially illuminating are the case history materials reflecting parent-child emotional and behavioral involvements.

Japanese studies related to any form of unconscious parental induction theory are lacking. We could not quantify any of our Arakawa materials to support the induction theory of delinquency, but we did find interview material in several of our cases from Arakawa and in others from the Sapporo family court and clinics in Tokyo, which supported the presence of such features in some delinquent families. In presenting some of our case history material from Arakawa we illustrate instances of what we consider to be "induced" delinquent behavior. It is useful to have an awareness of the presence of such mechanisms in understanding patterns of family interaction. It is doubtful, however, that such patterns can be quantified in such a way as to lead one to see induction as a necessary occurrence in the appearance of delinquency; rather, we must consider induction to be part of socially inherited patterns that manifest themselves over the generations in the same families.

CONCLUSIONS

As we shall demonstrate in more detail in the following chapters, our cross-cultural research on delinquency tends to confirm a number of previous conclusions about the influences of family life and delinquency. According to research in Japan, similar social and psychological factors are at work there, as in the United States. In both cultures, social deviancy in youth is more likely to occur among those suffering neglect or deprivation in their formative years. In our specific research with Arakawa families, we found indirect indices supporting these conclusions. We were also able to find by use of indirect indices a relationship between the interpersonal attitudes of parents toward each other and the appearance of delinquent behavior in at least one child.

Our study has little new to offer in respect to psychodynamic theory as applied to delinquency. Its chief virtue is that it examines generational continuities in familial patterns. The karma of delinquency does not start and end within one generation; it results from a number of factors influencing the grandparents as well as the parents of delinquents. The fact that the grandparental generation in our sample gives such striking evidence of interpersonal disruptions is indicative.

We were also able to find evidence relating delinquency to specific features of family life associated with sibling position. This find relates to the evidence reported by Caudill (1963) of the more frequent appearance of mental illness in the eldest son and the youngest daughter within Japanese families. Our results therefore further the contention that the total psychocultural environment of the family needs a more intensive investigation in studying the psychosocial problems occurring within the individual.

CHAPTER 5

Social Status Characteristics

We turn now to a detailed description of the status characteristics of the fifty families sampled: their origins, educational level, present occupations, family role positions, the relative size of the family units, and their living conditions. These demographic and social facts form a background for an interpretation of results related to motivational attitudes and interaction patterns in the subsequent chapters.

PLACES OF ORIGIN

The general statistics on Arakawa Ward indicate that the largest number of inhabitants are in-migrants who have come from other sections of Tokyo. The neighboring prefectures of the Kanto Plain—Chiba, Tochigi, Saitama, and Ibaragi—are the next most important source of migration, followed by the northeast section of the main island of Honshū, known as Tōhoku. The geographical background of our 50 families more or less fits this general pattern. In our sample, there are fewer individuals who have moved into Arakawa Ward from other parts of Tokyo. Nevertheless, of the 100 parents in our sample, only 10 were born in Arakawa Ward itself. Twenty-six others were born in other parts of Tokyo, mostly in places included in the old *shitamachi*, the merchant areas (Asakusa, Shitaya, and Kyobashi), and the new *shitamachi* (Honjo, Kameido, and Kameari). No one in our sample came from a Tokyo ward that could be defined as *yamanote*, the modern middle-class districts in Tokyo. Twenty-seven of our sample originated somewhere in the Kanto Plain: 17 individuals came from the northeast prefectures, another 9 came from rural parts of central Japan; 1 man was born in Manchuria. The remaining 10 individuals came from other cities (Hakodate, Kyoto, Osaka, Kobe, and Sendai).

Roughly half of the individuals studied had an urban background: 24 husbands and 22 wives. There appeared to be no radical differences in point of origin of husband and wife except that 7 of the husbands but only 3 of the wives were natives of Arakawa itself. Among the fathers there was a discrepant trend, 7 fathers of delinquents coming from the northeast area of Honshū as compared with 1 father of a nondelinquent.

We found no cases of marital maladjustment in which a difference between rural and urban background seemed a relevant factor, but in fact marriages between individuals of rural and of urban origin were relatively rare.

AGE AND PURPOSE OF IN-MIGRATION

Most of the in-migrating men came to Tokyo by age sixteen; the women tended to be slightly older at the time of arrival. The age distribution of in-migration is related to vocational training, since many (17 of the 31) male migrants (7 fathers out of 11 controls, and 10 out of 21 fathers of delinquents) came to obtain a job or an apprenticeship. There were more in-migrants coming in specifically for an apprenticeship among the fathers of the delinquents (10 of 21, as against 2 of 11 controls). Of the women migrants, 14 of 32 came to work as domestics or maids (6 of 12 controls; 8 of 20 mothers of delinquents), but more mothers of the control sample came for marriage (4) or to join families, as compared with the delinquent sample (1). Six mothers of the delinquent sample reported coming to Tokyo specifically to get a job and live independently, whereas no mothers in the normal families came for this specific purpose.

Looking at this distribution, there did not seem to be any obvious pattern related to delinquency except perhaps that more of the mothers of delinquents had taken the initiative in obtaining an independent livelihood in their youth, perhaps reflecting an unwillingness to take a more traditional woman's role.

FORMAL EDUCATION IN THE PARENTS

There are some suggestive, though not significant, differences in respect to educational background between the delinquent and the nondelinquent samples of Arakawa parents. Proportionately more fathers of delinquents than of controls failed to finish school or barely met the obligatory schooling period (17 of 31 fathers of delinquents; 7 of 19 controls). There was also a tendency, in the families of social (nonisolate) delinquents at least, for the wives to have reached or surpassed the educational level of their husbands. This was true for 24 of the total of 31 mothers of delinquents and for 11 of 19 mothers of controls; 12 of 20 mothers of social delinquents surpassed their husbands in education. Only 3 of 20 husbands in the social delinquent sample and 8 of 19 fathers of normals, had had more education than their wives.

One might infer from this that the educational careers of the fathers of delinquent subjects were somewhat less positive than those of the fathers of normal subjects, although the backgrounds of these individuals are fairly comparable. A number of fathers of social delinquents report that they quit school to seek an apprenticeship in the city. In comparing overall social status below, we find greater discrepancy between educational level and stated occupation in the delinquent sample than in the nondelinquent one.

Putting these findings in the total context of education in prewar Japan, we must stress that at the time there was only a six-year compulsory primary school education program. One might, therefore, expect to find the majority of individuals in a lower-class sample to have had a minimum education. Surprisingly enough, a fairly large proportion of our sample had more than the minimum education. Seventeen husbands and 22 wives had seven or eight years of schooling, and some individuals had up to twelve years. Only 5 of the total sample had less than the minimum requirement. One suspects that this is fair evidence that the pressure in Arakawa Ward as elsewhere was to have more education than was required. This finding attests to the achievement-through-education motive that was apparent throughout Japan.

OCCUPATIONAL DISTRIBUTION OF THE ARAKAWA SAMPLE

It was our purpose, so far as possible, to select individuals for our sample who were in the lower-class end of the occupational spectrum, and our initial criteria for selection were related to occupation as well as to the nature of the area lived in. As it turns out, there are 3 families in the delinquent sample that might be considered to have middle-class occupational status; there is only 1 such family in our normal sample. (Other criteria eventually led us to classify 11 families in our sample as middle class in some respects.) Of the 50 fathers in our sample, there are 12 factory workers, 5 construction workers, 5 carpenters, 5 metalsmiths, 4 clerks, 4 artisans manufacturing toys and other commodities, 3 tailors, 2 waste-material dealers, and 2 peddlers. There is 1 barber, 1 bus driver, 1 eel baker, and 1 repairman. As we shall discuss later, in a number of families the present occupation of the husbands is somewhat lower than it was in the past, and several of these families have had a history of bankruptcy or occupational failure.

OCCUPATIONAL CATEGORIES USED IN CODING OUR SAMPLE

To classify the occupations of our sample, we devised a coding system that took into account the size of the operation in which the husband was employed, the nature of acquired skills, occupational types, employment status, and income level. The distribution of occupations in our special sample reflects the lower-class composition of Arakawa Ward generally. There are no significant differences between the occupations of the fathers of nondelinquents and those of the fathers of delinquents in our total sample. Half of our sample is self-employed and would be listed technically, in Japanese usage, as "entrepreneurs."[1]

1. The term "entrepreneur" to Western readers may mean only those who own and operate relatively large business enterprises. In Japan, however, anyone who owns and operates his own business enterprise—however small its capital may be—is designated an entrepreneur.

Working Wives

It is characteristic for the wives of Arakawa to be gainfully employed, usually at home; in our sample, 23 of the 50 women report doing paid work at home in one capacity or another. An additional 14 women have some form of outside work, so that two-thirds of the women of our sample bring in additional income for the family. But of the 19 women in our control families, only 3 work outside the home. There is a significant differential tendency shown for women in the delinquent sample either to work outside (11 of 31) or not to work at all (10 of 31), whereas women in the normal sample tend to aid family income by some form of work at home (13 of 19), either as a seamstress doing various forms of cottage-industry work (*naishoku*) or as a helper to the husband in his house-factory operation (Fisher's exact test at the 5 percent level).

The incomes earned by women at home in *naishoku* were generally quite low at the time of our research, and long hours were necessary to bring in more than $50 a month at such work. The women often stayed up until midnight, and sometimes their children joined them in their work. When financial need was sufficiently pressing, the entire family would sit down and eke out additional income in the evenings at such tasks. Seven women do outside work in nearby factories; 3 women work as night janitors, 2 do some form of common daily labor, 1 works in a barbershop, and 1 peddles from door to door. In our particular sample the occupation that is poorly represented among the women is the fairly common one of running a small shop in the front of the home; there is only one such shop, a tobacco shop.

The distribution of women's work among our sample, we believe, is related to attitudes toward the home and the wife's role. Some women who work outside the home seem to be doing so as a means of avoiding interpersonal contacts within the home itself.

The amounts the wives earn by *naishoku* (work at home), according to our reports, range from an exceptional high of approximately $116 per month, by an extremely hardworking seamstress, to an average of about $74 (at the 1960s rate of exchange) by women who are occupied at such tasks as assembling toys or some other form of piecework. Among those who work outside, the monthly income ranges from about $26 per month, earned by the peddler, to about $41 per month, earned by the home-factory workers.

There is a trend for the mothers in the isolate delinquent families not to work at all, as reported by 6 out of the 11 in this group, so that although the husbands' income is slightly higher in the families of isolate delinquents, the average family income in this group approximates that of the normal or the social delinquent subsamples. With this exception, no trend of difference is noticeable among the 3 subsamples in either the husband's income or the total family income. In only 5 families is there an additional source of income from the renting of rooms, 3 of these in the nondelinquent subsample. In 10 of the 50 families, adult children contribute income to the total family budget.

The modal monthly income of the husband alone in 1964–1965 in our sample was somewhere between $60 and $108 a month, and the total modal family income was somewhere between $100 and $180 a month at the time of reporting. (We did not ask for exact income but asked the subjects to report income between two figures on a range.) There were 8 husbands who made less than $60 a month; of these, 3 families had a total family income of less than $60 a month. Seven families reported an income in excess of $180 a month, and only 2 reported incomes above $300 a month. When we compare these income distributions with other statistical materials available on Arakawa Ward, it is our impression that our sample was quite representative of the total community in the early 1960s.

LIVING CONDITIONS OF THE ARAKAWA FAMILIES

Since we intended to do a status rating of the Arakawa families that would be comparable insofar as possible to the studies by Lloyd Warner in the United States (1963), we were concerned with finding some quantifiable measures of living conditions that would allow us to use a form of scaled scoring. We settled on three criteria from which we attempted to derive an overall rating of living conditions: the first, ownership or rental of a house; second, the number of rooms per family; and third, the number of *tatami* mats covering floor space per person. These criteria allowed us to define living space per person. The area of the city could be rated generally as lower class, but, as we have indicated in discussing the heterogeneity of the Japanese ward, this is not so valid a measure in Japan as it would be in the United States, where areas are more socially homogeneous.

Most of the Arakawa homes are extremely crowded, even when judged by the usual crowded conditions of Tokyo. The amount of living space per person for our sample would be considered an extreme condition of crowding even for the most horrendous slums in eastern American cities. One available statistic generally used in Japanese demography is the number of the tatami mats per person in a household. Most Japanese homes are standardized in living space in respect to the number of tatami mats covering the interior floor space. One tatami measures approximately 3 by 6 feet.[2]

In our sample the largest room in a home was usually six mats, or 9 by 12 feet; eight-mat rooms were quite rare. As is shown in table 5.1, the modal amount of living space available per person in our Arakawa families was between

2. It is a noteworthy indication of the greater crowding of the Tokyo area that the overall area covered by a "standard" tatami mat in Tokyo is slightly smaller than the standard 3′ x 6′ found in such cities as Osaka or Kyoto. One can quickly determine the size of rooms, which will be 6′ x 6′ (two mats), 6′ x 9′ (three mats), 9′ x 9′ (four-and-one-half mats), 9′ x 12′ (six mats), and (very large rooms by Japanese standards) 12′ x 12′ (eight mats) or 12′ x 15′ (ten mats). The ten-mat rooms are most infrequent and are usually found only in the wealthier homes.

TABLE 5.1
Living Conditions of Arakawa Families

	Normals (19)	*Social Delinquents (20)*	*Isolate Delinquents (11)*	*Total (50)*
NUMBER OF ROOMS PER FAMILY				
One	4	7	2	13
Two	8	6	4	18
Three	4	1	3	8
Four	3	4	2	9
Five	0	2	0	2
NUMBER OF MATS PER PERSON				
0–1.49	2	6	2	10
1.5–2.49	10	8	6	24
2.5–3.49	2	0	0	2
3.5–4.49	2	4	2	8
4.5 +	3	1	0	4
Unknown	0	1	1	2
OWNERSHIP OR RENTAL OF HOMES				
Own	11	7	5	23
Rent	8	13	6	27
SLEEPING ARRANGEMENTS				
All family members sleep in one room	4	7	2	13
Husband and wife do not sleep in their own separate room, although there is more than one room in the house	8	3	4	15
Husband and wife sleep in their own separate room	3	1	5	9
Information lacking	4	9	0	13

1.5 and 2.5 mats per person. Compared with the average for Tokyo in 1965, which was 3.87 mats per person, our Arakawa sample figures show a greater density. The modal number of rooms per family was two, with 31 out of the 50 families, regardless of the number in the family, having two or fewer rooms, and only 2 having more than four.

Home Ownership

Home ownership in Japan is separate from land ownership; a person can own a home yet not own the land on which it has been built. In our interview materials, unfortunately, we did not distinguish between these two factors. We know that only 23 out of our 50 families reported owning their homes, and that a slightly larger proportion of the control sample reported that they owned rather than rented their living accommodations (see table 5.1). We had an impression, which we could not confirm, since it was not systematically observed, that the care of the homes themselves was slightly better in our nondelinquent subjects.

Sleeping Arrangements

Caudill and Plath (1966) as well as Vogel (1963) have emphasized the importance of close physical proximity among members of Japanese families. It is the rule in Japan, in the middle class and, from our evidence, in the lower class, for family members, including husband and wife and children, to sleep together in the same room. We were interested to determine as well as we could within our families whether such patterns existed even when other rooms were available. It is characteristic, especially in the United States, for Western married couples to guard the privacy of their own bedrooms. Such a trend has not appeared in present-day Japan. The parents often sleep in the same room with their small children until the children are well into grade school. Where there are several children, it is not unusual for the father to sleep on one side of the room with the boys, and the mother on the other side with the girls. There is a Japanese expression for a sleeping pattern, *kawa no ji ni neru*: sleeping in the form of the ideograph for river, which is composed of two longer outside lines and a short line in the middle; that is, the child sleeps between the mother and the father.

A common explanation for such familial sleeping patterns is the limited space available in the Japanese home. Where there is more than one child, the reason is often given that the older children need a study room of their own and hence the younger children sleep with their parents; the value of children's school achievement is placed ahead of the importance of privacy for the parental bed. However, this rationalization does not seem to offer a satisfactory explanation of the actuality, and we believe it more probable that there is a positive feeling and gratification from communal sleeping in Japan. Of those 37 of our Arakawa families for which we have information, 13 had only a single room, so they had no possibility of alternative sleeping arrangements (see table 5.1); according to our records the remaining 24 families had more than one room available, so it was technically possible for the parents to sleep apart from the children, but in only 9 of the 24 families did they do so. It is interesting to note that it is among the isolate deliquents' families that husbands and wives show the greatest preference for sleeping privately. Of the 9 in the entire sample who slept privately, 5 were in the isolate group, and these 5 were nearly half the total considered in that group for this factor. For the social delinquent group, even in those families with a single room, the parental couple were not sufficiently motivated to seek out quarters in which they could obtain some privacy.

This familial type of sleeping arrangement must undoubtedly influence the sexual practices that occur and also the psychosexual development processes of the children growing up in the household. It is remarkable, given the type of sleeping arrangement in Japan, that one finds, impressionistically at least, a type of latency period—a supposed lack of knowledge of parental sexuality—similar to that characteristic for a middle-class individual in the West. We did not probe this in our study, but our impression is that the restriction of sexual knowledge is evident. The psychological mechanisms that allow for a desexualized image of the mother seemed to operate fairly well in most of our subjects. There were only a few indications in our case materials of concern either with seductiveness or with sexual acting out on the part of the mother in the psychological material of the adolescent subject. Our general impression is that there is much less "sexualization" of the subjects by overt sexuality of parents in the Japanese delinquent families than there would be of lower-class American subjects.

OVERALL RATINGS OF SOCIAL STATUS

To establish overall estimates of the present social status of a family,[3] we initially decided on five criteria: education, occupation, income level, income source, and living conditions. Each of these criteria was divided into a six-point scale of which the top category was in no instance appropriate to Arakawa Ward. In the course of our work we decided to abandon the income-source criterion as too unreliable and to use the four remaining criteria in combination to arrive at an overall rating of each of the families.

In rating the families according to financial status and occupation, we had to depend on impressionistic language rather than on absolute monetary values; for example, "He was very successful and we were very well off," or "We often felt hungry and did not have enough to eat."

To gain perspective on at least subjective conceptions of social mobility, we attempted to rate retrospectively the status of both the maternal and the paternal grandparents. Only education and occupation seemed to have any degree of validity as far as these retrospective ratings were concerned, although we found that occupation very often was intermingled with some kind of evaluative conception of the relative prestige of the family from which the husband and wife came.

Splitting both the lower class and the middle class into an upper and a lower section (table 5.2), as is done in Warner's six-class system, we rated our sample as follows: 1 family as middle-middle or upper-middle, 10 as lower-middle, 30 as upper-lower, and 8 as lower-lower class (there was 1 case where the available materials were insufficient for accurate classification). According to our ratings, therefore, at least 20 percent of our families would be reckoned as at least of middle-class status. It is interesting to note the difference in the pat-

3. These criteria were used in our previous research in Nagoya and elsewhere. See E. Murakami (in Muramatsu, 1962). We made a previous attempt at modifying the Index of Status Characteristics developed by W. Lloyd Warner and his associates in their study of American social class in Warner, et al., 1963.

TABLE 5.2
Status Ratings of Arakawa Families

	Normals (19)	*Social Delinquents (20)*	*Isolate Delinquents (11)*	*Total Delinquents (31)*	*Grand Total (50)*
OVERALL RATING					
Middle	0	0	1	1	1
Lower-middle	3	5	2	7	10
Upper-lower	15	9	6	15	30
Lower-lower	1	5	2	7	8
Unknown	0	1	0	1	1
STATUS CONSISTENCY (rated on the same level in respect to education, occupation, living conditions)					
Rated as consistently:					
Lower-middle	2	3	1	4	6
Upper-lower	15	5	3	8	23
Lower-lower	1	2	2	4	5
Inconsistent in one or more status ratings	1	10	5	15	16

Control Sample: status consistency significant at 1% level.

terns of status characteristics between the normal and the delinquent subjects. There is much greater consistency in the ratings between levels of education, occupation, and living conditions in the normal family homes than in the homes of delinquent subjects. Fifteen out of the 19 normal families rated consistently upper-lower, with 3 listed as lower-middle and only 1 as lower-lower. A greater proportion (7 families of the 31) of the delinquent group were lower-lower, and 8 families were at least middle class but with considerable discrepancies among them in level of education, occupation, and source of income. One could state, therefore, that the status ratings of the normal subjects were more solidly upper-lower class than were those of the delinquent group. Furthermore, this material suggests some inconsistencies in what constitutes the social status of the families of the delinquent subjects. These inconsistencies must reflect some incongruities in self-concepts and living patterns; the degree to which this is determinative of or reflective of other forms of interpersonal tension remains open to conjecture.

Occupations in the Grandparental Generation

The reported occupations of the parents of the husbands and wives in our 50 families range quite widely, from large landowner to fish peddler. It is noted that there were more self-employed in the grandparental generation than in the present generation, obviously because ther were far fewer individuals working in urban factories in the previous generation. Of those we could classify, a large number (18 of 100) of grandparents had a poor rural background as tenant farmers of one kind or another; another 17 owned small to moderate holdings. In the older generation the proportionate number of artisans is lower (13) than in the present (17); there were, however, 21 independent merchants (only 1, a woman, in our current sample). There was 1 small-factory owner and a variety of laborers and peddlers (21) (5 construction workers and 2 peddlers today).

There are no farmers among the husbands in the present-day Arakawa families, although 35, or one-third, of our parents reported coming from farming families of various degrees of financial status, ranging from 1 large-farm owner to 18 tenant farmers. More wives (21) than husbands (14) are from farming families, and 5 women reported coming from fairly wealthy farm families.

Occupational Mobility

One of the chief purposes of attempting some retrospective classification of the older generation was to gain some impression of the subjective perceptions of mobility held by our families, both in comparing the husbands with their own fathers and in comparing the wives' status background with that of their husbands. In chapter 8 we report the relationship between the social mobility patterns as perceived by families and their ratings of marital satisfaction and dissatisfaction.

Occupational Continuity

There is a great deal written about Japanese occupational continuity from one generation to the next, but in our sample only ten, or one-fifth, of the husbands showed any direct occupational continuity with the work done by their own fathers. The others entered apprenticeships, most of which did not train them to continue the same kind of work as the fathers. The lack of merchant continuity has been noted above and attributed to the selective residence pattern we used in gaining our Arakawa materials. Naturally, a continuity in farming is impossible in the urban environment. Close to half of the husbands had fathers who had been in either merchant activity or farming. The artisan workers do manifest continuity but not in as great a proportion as might be expected, given the social ideology of direct inheritance of occupation. The following chapter, in which we discuss occupational vicissitudes, will demonstrate how some individuals go rather far afield from the occupation of their parents in an attempt to find a satisfactory occupation for themselves.

Generational Mobility in Occupational Ratings of Husbands

In table 5.3 we report our assessment, from descriptive materials, of how the husbands in the Arakawa sample seem ot rate themselves vis-à-vis the apparent social status of their own fathers. Of the 50 fathers, 10 seemed to rate them-

TABLE 5.3
Two-Generational Mobility in Occupational Ratings for Husbands

	Normals (19)	*Social Delinquents* (20)	*Isolate Delinquents* (11)
Husband 2 steps higher than his father	1	0	0
Husband 1 step higher than his father	2	5	2
Husband equal to his father (no mobility)	7	9	4
Husband 1 step lower than his father	5	3	3
Husband 2 or more steps lower than his father	4	3	2

	Normals (19)	*Social Delinquents* (20)	*Isolate Delinquents* (11)	*Total Delinquents* (31)	*Grand Total* (50)
Upward mobility	3	5	2	7	10
No mobility	7	9	4	13	20
Downward mobility	9	6	5	11	20

selves as having done better occupationally than their own fathers, and conversely, 20 apparently rate their present occupation as somewhat lower than that of their fathers. Proportionately more of the normal control fathers than fathers in the delinquent group rate themselves as having suffered some form of downward mobility. It is difficult to extract from these subjective ratings the degree to which individuals compensate for their present situation by clinging to pride in past family status. We have the impression that compensatory mechanisms are present, but we cannot check the objectivity of the evaluations given us.

In table 5.4 we attempt to make a comparison between the background of the husband's parents and that of the wife's parents as they were described to us. It is noteworthy that among the social delinquents the wife's background is rated higher than the husband's in eleven instances, and in only four instances is the husband's background rated higher than the wife's. The normal group is intermediate in this regard, with 8 families rating the wife's background higher, and 6 the husband's background higher. In the isolate delinquent group only 2 rate the wife's background higher, whereas 6 out of the total of 11 rate the husband's background higher.

By comparing the husband's present status with that of his wife's father (see table 5.5), we gain some impression of the wife's perception of herself as having gone either up or down socially through marriage. The results are rather striking in that 28 out of the 50 wives in our sample seem to perceive themselves as having gone downward, the strongest trend in this perception being found in

TABLE 5.4
Background Occupational Ratings of the Parents of Husband and Wife

	Normals (19)	*Social Delinquents (20)*	*Isolate Delinquents (11)*	*Total Delinquents (31)*	*Grand Total (50)*
Husband's father 2 steps higher than wife's father	4	0	3	3	7
Husband's father 1 step higher than wife's father	2	4	3	7	9
Husband's father equal to wife's father	5	5	3	8	13
Wife's father 1 step higher than husband's father	4	6	1	7	11
Wife's father 2 steps higher than husband's father	4	5	1	6	10

TABLE 5.5
Two-Generational Mobility in Occupational Ratings for Wives

	Normals (19)	*Social Delinquents (20)*	*Isolate Delinquents (11)*	*Total Delinquents (31)*	*Grand Total (50)*
Husband 2 steps higher than his wife's father	0	1	0	1	1
Husband 1 step higher than his wife's father	4	2	4	6	10
Husband equal to his wife's father (no mobility)	7	3	1	4	11
Husband 1 step lower than his wife's father	1	9	6	15	16
Husband 2 or more steps lower than his wife's father	7	5	0	5	12

the social delinquent families, where 14 out of 20 women, by their own criteria, have suffered downward mobility. In comparing their husband's present status with that of their father, only 3 of these wives see their status as improved.

In chapter 8 we shall relate these perceptions to both husband's and wife's attitudes of satisfaction and dissatisfaction in the marriage. We shall then discuss how the perception of status may be related to marital maladjustment and conflict, which in turn bear some relationship to the appearance of delinquency in a child. As in the overall rating of status, there is less internal inconsistency in the normal sample compared with the delinquent sample, but the results are by no means clear-cut or highly differentiating. In discussing occupational vicissitudes, many wives emphasize the decline of the "once very respected family." Such stories of a possibly romanticized past status seem to be common in our Arakawa material, and it is difficult to judge how much is fantasy and how much reflects an accurate estimate of the past. The following are a few illustrative examples of a perception of status loss in Arakawa families.

Examples of Perceived Social Decline

In some of our case history material, a sense of decline in social status goes back more than one or two generations. It is often attributed to the inadequate behavior of either the wife's or the husband's father. For example, in case D-19, the Tozori family, the husband's grandfather was described as having been a doctor. However, the husband's own father ran away from home at an early age and lived an irregular life; he was subsequently adopted into another family of meager circumstances and was constrained to spend most of his early life as a food peddler to daily laborers. The husband describes his father as a very heavy drinker, who became fierce and uncontrolled in his frequent bouts of drunkenness. His father, according to the husband, died when the boy was about six years old, so that the reported memory reflects information given to him by others in his family. The husband in this case continually refers back to his own grandfather, whom he does not remember, as the image against which he measures his own lack of status. The reported social degradation of his own father is considered an inherited, negative destiny. Further status sensitivity is noted in the fact that he stressed the high social status of his brother's friend, the *baishakunin* (go-between), in his arranged marriage. The status was significant, in this instance, in that he felt he could not refuse the services of this man on his behalf, although he was not satisfied with the wife chosen for him. The only way he could avoid the marriage was to move away from his job and to take up with another woman after the marriage was consummated (see the description of his common-law wife's fear of desertion in the anecdotal material in chapter 8). This man now works as a construction laborer, but he is very skillful and is used in special jobs, so his income is higher than most in this occupation. His sense of his present self is obviously at variance with his sense of what he could have been if his father had only been a more steadfast person.

In case I-11 Mr. Ihashi describes the downward mobility of his family as being due more to his grandfather than to his own father, who was victimized by the grandfather, a large landowner. He has cousins who have achieved high status in manufacturing companies because their father was given more education than his father. As Mr. Ihashi describes it, the father was deprived of sufficient education because his mother was ill and could not take the children's part against the irascible, obstinate grandfather, who did not believe in education, although he advocated strict training for his children. The children were supposed to work diligently rather than go to school. Although case I-11 is not representative, it does indicate in another form how relative educational deprivation in a past generation is offered as the reason for a lowly present status position.

Some of our cases give evidence of childhood memories in which there was a crisis resulting in loss of wealth and property. In case N-12, Mrs. Sayama remembers a situation in which her father was the assistant village head with large landownings, considerable wealth, and a long-standing history of status in his community. In 1920, when she was about five years old, the family lost its holdings for reasons that she herself does not understand. She remembers that the big house in which she had lived was sold and the family was forced to move into tiny, poor quarters. She remembers being reared, until that time, as a child of a wealthy family, with a nurse hovering about her with a protective parasol (high-status children were protected from exposure to sunlight, which was considered "bad"; for one thing, it darkened the skin, and light skin was a symbol of high status). Since that time of crisis, as she looks back, her life has been one of continual hardship and suffering. She remembers her father as a silent and gentle man, who, however, became either quick-tempered or gay when drunk. Her mother was the daughter of an inn-owner, a woman of firm character who carried on in spite of the status degradation the family had suffered. Her mother's endurance and suffering is equated with her own present role behavior as the wife in an impoverished family. She sees some direct continuity between the pattern taken by her mother and her own present behavior. But she harkens back to the time of childhood, when she tasted a higher status.

RELATIVE SOCIAL STATUS WITHIN THE FAMILY IN MARRIAGE AND ADOPTION

A traditionally difficult status position within the Japanese family was that of the *muko-yōshi*, or in-marrying husband, who was adopted and assumed the family name of the wife and the responsibility for continuing the wife's family lineage where there was no eligible male heir present. In the previous generation in Arakawa but not in the present one, there were proportionately a much greater number of in-marrying adoptions reported for the normal sample than for families of delinquents. The husband in 9 out of 38 of the normal marriages in the grandparent generation was *muko-yōshi*, indicating an almost 25 percent occurrence of this practice, whereas in the grandparent generation of the delinquent sample, only 3 out of 62 (5 percent) report such a situation. We have no ready explanation for this difference. In the present generation no *muko-yōshi* are reported in the normal sample, although matrilocal residence and an implicit kind of continuity of the wife's family occurred in 2 cases. In the delinquent subgroups, there were 5 instances out of 31 of *muko-yōshi* and 2 cases of matrilocal residence. If there is some relationship between these patterns and deliquency, it is not apparent to either author.

There seems to be a change of attitude among our informants about attempting to continue "family" business today, at least in the lower class, by some form of adoption for inheritance. Fewer small, family merchant-shops are being inherited (or passed along to the younger generation). There is greater individual freedom for youngsters to follow new and different vocational pursuits. Moreover, the practice of *muko-yōshi* has no longer much economic or ideological support. Although it seems to be disappearing in the recent lower-class generation, it may be continuing in some professional middle-class families. In one of our cases, D-8, Mr. Fukuhara is rather better off financially than most. He reports some ambivalence in relation to the possible use of adoption for inheritance. He states:

> Since my only son, from the time he was small, has been very weak in health, I have considered the possibility of having someone coming in as heir to my factory. I thought that, therefore, I would have my daughters study bookkeeping and accounting and learn such women's arts as flower arrangement, sewing, and knitting so as to be better able to marry a man who could take over my business and my family name. Since she should prepare for such a marriage, one of my daughters should be very well educated for the role of wife.

Subsequently, however, he abandoned his original thinking; since he has retired from business and is now renting his building to someone else for an apartment, he has given up the idea of maintaining such continuity in his business life. He says, "Times have changed and children are supposed to be more independent from their parents." He is well aware that the old patterns are passing and says that his children should continue the course of their own lives as they choose for themselves.

In the same case, D-8, Mrs. Fukuhara tells that her husband's eldest brother wanted to adopt one of their two daughters so that he might have an in-marrying *muko-yōshi* himself. What is interesting about this anecdotal material is the degree to which the mother resisted losing her child. She states that her husband approved of his brother's plan and wanted to send their second daughter to the uncle's house, but Mrs. Fukuhara objected to the idea and sought various reasons to prevent it. She said:

> I was opposed to the plan especially because our daughter had grown up in the city and would not be able to adjust herself to farm life. My brother-in-law and my husband said she would not have to be engaged in

farming if she didn't like it. I argued it would be simply impossible for my daughter to stay away from the farm while everyone else was working energetically on it. My husband was very angry with me and with our daughter, who didn't want to leave our house. He hit me in anger. It was about four or five years ago. Our daughter told me she would run away from home if she were to go to her uncle's house. I couldn't persuade my husband, and without knowing what to do I suddenly went back to my brother's home. He was surprised to see me visiting after five or six years of silence. I told him everything. I said that one cannot give away one's child like a puppy or a kitten. Although he was too busy to come with me to talk to my husband, he promised to come as soon as he could.

Mrs. Fukuhara also resorted to the use of a religious oracle to help build her case against adoption (see chapter 9 on the uses of religion). On her way home from her brother's, she stopped over with a nephew who thought it would be helpful if she could consult with *Kami*[4] about the matter. She was taken to what Mrs. Fukuhara describes as a "wise man" for consultation, who said he would consult with his *Kami*. The mother does not describe the nature of the magical practices that ensued, but according to the *Kami*, she was told that if the daughter was forcibly taken she would kill herself either by drowning in the sea or by throwing herself in front of a locomotive. The mother said, "I returned to my husband, who had become much calmer than when I left for my brother's house. I told him what I had been told by the god, and my husband gave up the idea of giving our second daughter to his brother." Mrs. Fukuhara obviously used the implicit threat of leaving and going to her relatives as well as divine sanctions to bolster her case against adoption.

Adoption patterns are sometimes used in conjunction with apprenticeships. For example, in case D-17, Mr. Torihashi, after graduation at age fifteen, was apprenticed as a barber in a place where conditions were extremely exploitative. He continued his apprenticeship passively, although hating his situation. At this time he was turned down by the army, which classified him as ineligible for service because he had stomach trouble. One gains the impression from the way he tells the story that he had hopes of being rescued from his apprenticeship by going into army service, but when this plan failed, he used what seems to have been a psychosomatic stomach complaint to interrupt his apprenticeship.

Mr. Torihashi shifted several times from one barbershop to another until he went to work for a widow who was running her own shop. From the way the story was told to our interviewer, we have the impression that Mr. Torihashi is a rather passive though deeply resistive person. While working for the widow he made some attempts to learn another trade but found that barbering, after all, was better than working with machines. In the meantime the widow had found a young woman to come to work in her shop, and so she arranged a marriage between the two young people, adopting both of them. However, the young woman was herself an extremely strong-willed person, and the widow ended up

4. The vague Shinto concept of deity, not defined as singular or plural.

losing both her adopted son and the daughter, who left the widow's shop and set up a business on their own. The widow's story is not available, but we might assume that she was trying to assure herself of a situation in which she would be taken care of financially and otherwise by her two heirs.

In our case histories, the relatively powerless position of the *muko-yōshi* in a family is borne out by the decriptions some women give of their fathers who had this role. For example, in case I-4, Mrs. Iida reports that her father was extremely quiet, never making any decisions on his own but always following the lead of his wife. She has no memory of her parents ever quarreling nor of her father ever asserting himself against her mother. Her maternal grandfather, as she remembers him, was also a very quiet person, while her grandmother was noted for her "strong character." Her grandmother made decisions inside the house, and her mother took the intiative in running the farm. Together both women ruled their home very firmly, a type of matriarchal patterning not infrequent in Japan.

Now and then the *muko-yōshi*, to everyone's surprise, seems to have developed some independence. In case N-10, Mr. Seki describes his father, a *muko-yōshi*, as being so fed up with the situation at home that he eventually left for Shizuoka. While he was still in the home, however, he remained a quiet, gentle person who could not directly take on his wife, Mr. Seki's mother, whom he describes as a person of strong character, the only daughter of the house, over which she ruled with no opposition.

Not all cases of adoption of a child or a young man as a *muko-yōshi* are for inheritance. In our case D-20, Mrs. Tayama decided to adopt a child because her husband was drafted into the army; thinking he would never return from the war alive, she wanted a child, to avoid the anticipated pain of loneliness. She adopted an illegitimate child, five or six weeks old, without going through legal adoption procedures but simply registering the baby as her own, a customary practice in Japan. The case became complicated; Mrs. Tayama became pregnant without knowing it, shortly before the registration of the child. Since the timing for two children was impossible, she waited several months after the birth of her own child and falsified the date of that birth so that the official documents looked more plausible.

In general, none of our material on adoption is systematically related in any way to the appearance of delinquency in particular families, as far as we can determine. Adoption is such a common experience in Japan that it is not conceived of in any ways as aberrant or abnormal. It would therefore have been strange indeed had we found some evidence suggesting patterns of neglect or favoritism related specifically to adoption situations.

FAMILY STATUS: SIB POSITION AND DELINQUENCY

In anthropological discussions of the Japanese family it has been traditional to stress the status discrepancies between the first son, sons generally, and

Table 5.6
Distribution of the Number of Children in Two Generations

Number of children	*1*	*2*	*3*	*4*	*5*	*6*	*7*	*8*	*9*	*10*	*11*	*12*
NORMAL CONTROL												
Present family	2	6	5	3	3							
Father's family	3	2	1		3	4	1	3	2			
Mother's family	1	2	3		4	2	1	1	4	1		
SOCIAL DELINQUENT												
Present family	2	4	3	6	4							1
Father's family	2	4	3	2	5	1	3					
Mother's family	1			8	2	2	5	1	1			
ISOLATE DELINQUENT												
Present family	1	1	5	3				1				
Father's family		2	1	3	2	1	1				1	
Mother's family	1			1	2	2	2	1	1			1

	Normals	*Social Delinquents*	*Isolate Delinquents*	*Average*
AVERAGE NUMBER OF CHILDREN				
Present family	2.95	3.75	3.45	3.38
Father's family	4.10	3.95	4.90	4.32
Mother's family	5.63	5.35	6.35	5.78

daughters in the family. Despite the formal indications that there is an experience of relative neglect of second sons or middle children of both sexes in the Japanese family, we were not prepared for the significant distributions we obtained relating to sib positions of the parents and the appearance of delinquency in at least one child. As we shall discuss further in chapter 9, one must consider the psychological effects of relative neglect experienced by middle children in multisibling families in Japan as these effects influence the taking on of a parental role.

First, looking at the overall number of children in the past generation listed in table 5.6, we find the normal sample intermediate to the social delinquent and isolate delinquent groups. The number of children in both the paternal and the maternal families of the isolate delinquents exceeds the average number in the other two samples.

In the present generation, the nondelinquent families have the lowest average number of children. Our sample dramatizes the general trend toward smaller families in Japan. Although it was not uncommon to have four or more children in the previous generation, there are relatively few such large families in the present generation.

Regardless of differences in overall size, a consistent pattern appears in both generations of a greater incidence of deliquency in middle sons and in the sons of younger daughters in large families (see table 5.7). The fathers of delin-

Table 5.7
Sib Positions of Parents and Subjects

SIB POSITION OF NORMAL AND DELINQUENT CHILDREN

	Normals (19)	*Delinquents (31)*
Oldest or only son	13	17
Middle son	1	11
Youngest child with older sibs	5	3

Non-middle son vs. middle son, $P < .025$, Fisher's exact test significance level.

SIB POSITION OF PARENTS OF NORMAL AND DELINQUENT CHILDREN

	Normals (19)				*Delinquents (31)*			
	Father		*Mother*		*Father*		*Mother*	
	Child*	Son	Child	Dau	Child	Son	Child	Dau
First	6	9	7	10	6	8	9	12
Second	5	3	4	7	10	18	8	8
Third	1	2	0	1	8	3	4	7
Fourth or more	7	5	8	1	7	2	10	4

	Not second son	Second son
Fathers of nondelinquents	16	3
Fathers of delinquents	13	18

$P < .005$, Fisher's exact test.

	1st or 2nd daughter	3rd or later daughter
Mothers of nondelinquents	17	2
Mothers of delinquents	20	11

$P < .05$, Fisher's exact test.

*Sib position regardless of sex; for example, a father may have been a second child but eldest son.
†This category includes second sons whether they are middle or not. It includes some youngest sons (2nd of 2 sons) and excludes some middle sons (3rd of 4, etc.). The correlation is therefore all the more striking.

quents are significantly found to be second or third sons in 21 out of 31 cases; 5 out of 19 second or third sons were found in the normal sample. Eleven out of 31 delinquent subjects were the sons of third or later daughters in larger families; there were 2 out of 19 in the families of nondelinquents. Since our sample of 50 families is a fairly small one, this particular result is highly suggestive and should be investigated in larger samples of Japanese delinquents. There are 4 families of delinquents in which children of a previous marriage are present, and no such families in our normal sample, a situation that indirectly reflects the lack of marital disruption in the normal group compared with the delinquent group, a topic we shall discuss in chapter 8.

In Japan the eldest son commonly has been treated differently from the other children in the family, and in urban in-migration it is more often the second son in rural families who goes to the city. In our sample we did not find this pattern of in-migration, but we did find the middle son overrepresented in both the present and the parental generation in families of delinquents. It is less important, as far as our limited statistics are concerned, to examine the sib position of all children regardless of sex than to consider the birth order of children of the same sex. In sum, the two-generation patterns suggest a passing on of experiences of neglect or favoritism toward other siblings which contributes in some degree, at least, to delinquency (see especially chapter 9).

Our anecdotal, illustrative material provides examples of resentment of neglect or rejection in both the parental generation and in the subjects themselves related to an unfavored sib position—for example, as a last girl child. In other instances, informants report indirect favoritism given a brother or a sister. In yet other instances, tensions arise when an eldest son takes over a disciplinary or supervisory role in his relations with his younger siblings as part of his assumed responsibility toward them.

In case D-20, for instance, both parents in the Tayama household describe frequent fights occurring between their eldest son and the delinquent subject in our sample. The eldest son is interested only in discipline, though he is described as generous to his younger siblings, buying them things out of money he receives from a milk-delivery route. But the siblings, especially the delinquent subject, bitterly resent the elder brother's attempts to boss them around. Fighting of a physical kind sometimes breaks out. The girls in the family seem to be able to resist the eldest brother's attempts at bossiness without getting into the same kind of crisis situation that the youngest brother creates. One sister is quite vocal with her older brother and is able to best him verbally at times; when she does so he loses all control and throws things at her. His father tends to support his firstborn son, expressing the attitude that it is wrong for a woman to talk back and it is natural for a man to use violence when women do not obey. The older brother forces his younger brother to lay out his *futon* (bedding) at night, under such duress that he sometimes obeys with tears in his eyes, according to Mrs. Tayama's description.

In one of our cases where the delinquent subject himself is the eldest son, we see some partial identification, in an inconsistent way, with his responbilities in the role of eldest son. In case D-6 the Funahashi boy shows considerable ambivalence in relating to his younger siblings. He himself, in his interviews, expresses no consistent attitude of liking or disliking them. When he is asked to express an opinion, he avoids committing himself. Nevertheless, from the parents' interviews, we gained the impression that he likes to boss his younger brother, who in his behavior is reported to be more like his father than is the delinquent subject. The father plays a very compliant role in the family, taking no disciplinary action but remaining lax and letting a schoolteacher, in effect, take over some of the parental supervision of the younger son (see further description of case material on D-6 in chapter 7).

Traditionally, the least desirable sibling position is that of a twin. Some of the rejection of twins in line with traditional thinking is well represented in case D-8. When his twin sons were born, Mr. Fukuhara, according to his wife, said that there was "one child too many." He himself says, in his interview, "One male child was enough. It is hard to raise twins. And also in the past twins were detested." In traditional Japanese culture, the womb producing twin births was called a *chikushō-bara* (bestial belly). Twins, especially when they were a boy and a girl, were often believed to be the rebirth of a couple who had committed suicide together. Accordingly, they were greatly detested as the reincarnation of individuals whose death was caused by some antisocial pattern.

Judging from the father's description of the feeling he had at the time of his twins' birth, one can judge that the emotional shock to him was extremely strong. "People say it is not good to have twins—there are many people who have twins or triplets or even quadruplets. I was certainly surprised and appalled. Then after awhile I felt all right." The father actually had very little contact with his twin children until they were more than four years old. He admitted, for example, that he never dined with them until then; he never helped his wife to discipline the children or take them to a public bathhouse; he never helped them dress.

One gains the overall picture of severe rejection of our delinquent subjects by both parents. The husband states that his wife also had "little time" to take care of her children because she was working hard. He recognizes that his wife feels a strong dissatisfaction with the attitude he has taken toward his twins since their birth. He says, "Seen from the standpoint of my wife, I may not be a very good father or there may have been times again when my wife thought that I was not much of a father. I can't recall well, but generally speaking, I never took my children to a bathhouse. I took them hiking only once."

The mother shows some similar attitudes about being responsible for giving birth to twins.

> Looking at our babies, people would say they were twins. Every time I heard the word "twin" I felt ashamed. A little after they were born I remember that my husband and I used to talk about it, and he used to say it was my fault that we had twins. I would answer that it was not my fault. My husband used to tell me not to use the actual word "twin" [*futago*] because he felt ashamed. People often asked us if our twin children were different ages. I would answer that they were twins. My husband would tell me afterwards not to correct them (laughs). He doesn't seem to be much concerned with it any longer. I feel that my children themselves do not like being twins. I somehow feel that way, too. I don't remember how long I felt ashamed, but gradually the feeling disappeared, especially as we saw other twins becoming famous people. I came to think that there was nothing to be ashamed of in giving birth to twins. [The wife's reference is to a famous set of twins who sing frequently on television.] These days in a joking way I say to them, "It is too bad you were not identical." One can sing now, but the other is always completely out of tune.

In other contexts, she describes the difficulties she had in bringing up two children at the same time. "Without knowing how to raise them, I often cried until my eyes were swollen."

There are a number of features of status and role behavior that will be further considered in the following chapters in the context of discussions of responsibility or authority, in chapter 7, and in respect to patterns of nurturance and affiliation, in chapter 9, which seem to distinguish our deliquent from our nondelinquent subjects. Perhaps the best indication of how status and role are related to the appearance of deliquency in some families is to be found in the material presented in our discussion of harmony and discord in chapter 8, and in sibling position and delinquency in chapter 9.

Before going further into this type of material, however, we shall first look at the patterns of achievement motivation represented in our case histories in chapter 6. As far as we can ascertain, poverty or patterns of occupational failure themselves are in no way directly related to delinquency formation. Nevertheless, looked at from the ethnographic standpoint, our material on occupational vicissitudes and on individual concern with adequacy is of considerable pertinence to an understanding of social change and the nature of urbanization in Arakawa Ward.

CHAPTER 6

Achievement and Inadequacy

In this chapter we shall present illustrative materials supporting our generalizations about the entrepreneurial attitudes of the lower-class Japanese. Some of these anecdotes dramatize the ups and downs of typical careers in Arakawa. Many of the husbands in our sample have stayed in one or a few jobs of a similar kind all their lives, but others have gone through a variety of jobs in their attempt to "make it."[1]

The economic base of life in Arakawa Ward is representative of a significant segment of the Japanese urban lower class. In studying this ward in detail, we gain some insight into one of the seeming enigmas of Japan that have baffled Western economists. Many questions concerning the source of the viability of the Japanese economy have defied an easy answer. For example, how were the Japanese able to launch a large-scale industrialized war effort against the United States and maintain it so long without the extensive plant facilities considered necessary by any Western industrial nation? Where were the machines? Where were the skilled laborers? Could the tiny workshops forming part of the individual homes housed in flimsy wooden structures possibly compete with the large, developed factories of the United States in mounting a significant war effort? Obviously they did, but how?

What we found in our investigation of Arakawa Ward was a prototype of an economic system: an individual family owned from one to three machines placed in one room; characteristically, the family lived in one or two additional rooms of a small frame-and-paper dwelling. These home-factories were found along narrow, irregular streets that are cut through at intervals by major traffic arteries with more modern stores, sidewalks, and larger buildings built of concrete. Only here and there in Arakawa Ward was there a factory of any significant size.

1. See the detailed description of achievement motivation and entrepreneurial mentality in De Vos, 1973, chapters 6–9.

APPRENTICESHIP AND ENTREPRENEURSHIP: OCCUPATIONAL VICISSITUDES IN ARAKAWA FAMILIES

Looked at anthropologically, these home-factories developed out of particular Japanese premodern cultural traditions, so called feudal social-structural elements that carried over into Japanese industrialization. Thus, Japan was transformed into a modern industrial state with relatively little major disruption of the total social fabric. It is our contention that this successful transformation was brought about not only by certain social-structural elements but also by persisting psychological continuities in Japanese culture. Semiautonomous socialization patterns must be considered, if we are to understand the peculiarities of the way motivation for achievement was, and is, structured in the Japanese national character.[2]

Our intensive examinations of fifty family units in Arakawa Ward has helped us understand why and how traditional patterns of thinking continue and remain adaptive. For example, we found that farm youths who come from isolated rural areas were treated in ways familiar to them when they came to find jobs in the city. Ties with the family often remained unbroken, and even when they were ruptured, many city employers acted *in loco parentis* as part of a tradition of responsible paternalism. Among the country employees in our sample, some who had ambitions to stay in the city and establish an "independent house" were encouraged to do so by their city mentors, who sometimes helped them find a wife as well.

Urban migration was a feature of Japanese culture even during the Tokugawa period, especially from the late eighteenth century onward. It was not unusual for second sons of farmers, petty merchants, and artisans to be sent as apprentices to a wealthier artisan or merchant family in the vicinity of Tokyo. The social arrangements for in-migration today remain, under the surface, much the same in many respects as they were in the past.

Within our particular sample of households, numerous farm youths eventually established themselves in business, usually by purchasing one or two machines and, with a wife, setting up a household economic unit, which was readily incorporated into an already existing organizational network. This assumption of an entrepreneurial role depended heavily on traditional forms of mutual expectations and responsibilities between a master artisan or merchant and a former apprentice.

Many of the studies of urbanization reported in the sociological literature are based on experience within the United States. Urban "in-migration" into the United States from a foreign country meant virtually a complete split with the immigrants' place of birth because of the great difficulties in transportation back and forth to the old home. This was not true in Japan, where if the urban

2. This subject has been discussed in detail in De Vos, 1973, chapters 5 and 7.

in-migrant encountered economic or other difficulties, he could always go back to his rural relatives. In fact, a great deal of movement between the city and country occurred in Japan with fluctuations in economic conditions within the city.[3] These two features of Japanese urbanization—the pattern of occupational paternalism and the capacity to maintain some continuity with the family network—meant that the change to city life could be accomplished without a great deal of psychological insecurity or anomic disorientation.[4] Today, however, in an ever more rapidly urbanizing and industrializing Japan, such continuity between rural and urban lives is beginning to disappear.

The traditional relationship of apprentice to master artisan or merchant defined expectations of dependency toward an employer and of his responsibility toward his employees. No matter how often this latter expectation was breached in practice, there were a sufficient number of employers who took seriously this moral paternalistic directive to meet, to some degree at least, the expectations of their dependent workers. It was mutually understood that hiring involved a long-term commitment by both parties. Traditionally in Japan, learning a skill meant that a young employee or apprentice would work a good number of years for food, shelter, and low pay toward the day when he would be recognized as worthy of sponsorship in a semi-independent role, very often in a subsidiary shop, while still drawing on the continuing sponsorship of his former employer. In more modern times this sponsorship has taken the form of a loan to enable the former employee to invest capital in his own machinery, even if only one or two simple machines. The employee expected to be rewarded for his past loyalty by benevolent support as he embarked on his own increasingly independent occupational career, as either a *shokunin* (artisan) or a *shōnin* (merchant).

The traditional Japanese economic-occupational models of artisan, merchant, and farmer blended readily into the newer machine industries developed for trade. For example, in textiles, the manufacturing of cotton products by large-scale factory units was one of the early big export industries developed in Japan, but the silk industry, which was still important, remained essentially small-scale and rural in character. The Japanese type of familism and paternalism were as adaptive to industrialization as were the more individualistically oriented patterns of socioeconomic relationships found in northern European countries and the United States. It is a fallacy to assume that only Western psychocultural conditions can be readily transmuted into a modern industrial system. On a more strictly psychological level, also, there are alternative modes of

3. A number of times Japan's young capitalist economy survived a crisis by laying off many factory workers, who then returned to live with relatives. Rejoining their families, although impoverished, kept the workers from starving or from participating in movements of social unrest, and disguised the seriousness of the economic fluctuations.

4. A. Inkeles (in De Vos, 1976), in a comparison of patterns of urbanization in six different cultures, and E. Bruner (in De Vos, 1976), in Indonesia, cite other examples of patterns of urbanization that take place without the anomic dislocation often assumed to be an essential part of the experience of urbanization.

achievement motivation in Japan that have contributed to the energy and drive that have made the modern transformation such a relative success. Family and pseudo-kinship ties kept a firm hold on most individuals both socially and motivationally as the Japanese gradually shifted into newer forms of commercial and industrial life.

Warner and Abegglen (1955), in their study of business leaders in the United States, pointed out that in order to move upward occupationally and socially in American culture, one must be able to cut oneself off easily from the primary group, from peer groups and friends and relatives, and also from former colleagues left behind as one moves alone up the social ladder. Those with strong need for affiliation, who find it hard to cut themselves off from their old ties, will very likely not "make it." This, as our discussion indicates, hardly applies to the Japanese scene. A Japanese individual more characteristically achieves for the sake of and on behalf of the family. Those who move upward take along their families, their own parents at least, if not all their relatives. It is a common expectation that when the son of lower-class parents becomes successful and wealthy, he will see to it that his parents spend the rest of their lives in physical comfort and emotional satisfaction. "Need achievement" and "need affiliation," so to speak, go hand in hand in Japan, rather than tending to be contradictory or incompatible as in the West (De Vos, 1973).

Bennett and Ishino (1963), see two general features characterizing paternalistic economic organization. The first feature is a degree of hierarchy that is not purely a matter of instrumental necessity but contains a cultural or ideological element suggesting that the employer is more than just an employer. In a terminology we prefer to use, on a psychological level there are "expressive" elements to the relationship which serve as major determinants of behavior, in addition to the direct power and economic elements. The second characteristic is an institutionalized concern shown by the employer for aspects of the personal lives of his employees which has nothing to do with the actual work performed or the organization for which it is performed; that is, the employer's responsibility extends beyond the immediate economic sphere, even extending to helping the families of employees. A great deal of Japanese economic as well as social history is to be understood in terms of such paternalistic structures as they permeate the entire culture and characterize many relationships throughout Japanese society today. In the past they were not confined to apprenticeship structures and *dōzōku* (stem-and-branch family organizations of merchants and artisans). The hierarchical loyalty and responsible paternalism often cited as part of the code of the samurai existed even in outlaw organizations and in the entertainment industries that operated and still operate on the peripheries of the regular social organization (De Vos and Mizushima, 1973; De Vos, 1973). Such paternalism is an integral part even of the Japanese outcaste communities (De Vos and Wagatsuma, 1966).

One has to note the difference between the use of the term "entrepreneur" in Japan and its use in Europe or the United States. In its Western usage, the term connotes a degree of independence and "middle-class" well-being associated with owning and controlling one's own business. The Japanese, however, use the term more broadly and include individuals whom Westerners would consider of lower-class status. These individuals are motivationally what we term "lower-class capitalists," whose economic status may not be any higher than that of unskilled factory workers and who have only the barest capital resources or skills; nevertheless, according to our evidence, they maintain attitudes and social self-identities that motivate behavior far different from that of a simple employed factory worker in the United States or Europe.

The entrepreneurial mentality—as we found it in Arakawa Ward—includes those at the very bottom of the social hierarchy of Japan. Our contention is that Japanese entrepreneurs of the lower and middle class share, psychologically at least, many motivational features characteristic of only the middle class in the West.

The Actualization of Competence or Adequacy

The importance of the apprenticeship of youth during premarital years in traditional Japanese culture has perhaps not been given the close attention it deserves as an essential part of socialization toward adulthood. To understand adult Japanese it is necessary to understand the work mentality as it is developed around some form of apprenticeship experience. The intensity of dedication to the adult role in both men and women receives strong reinforcement during this formative period. The anecdotal material presented in this and the following chapters bears this out.

The Japanese, whether samurai, merchant, or artisan, was expected from about age twelve to undergo rigorous training under an adept master as a means of acquiring the technical competence necessary for adult performance. Even when a boy was to inherit his father's craft or business, he was very often sent out because it was considered more rigorous, and hence better, training to be apprenticed to someone other than the father. Second sons of farm families were encouraged to seek apprenticeships in an urban setting, most often with an artisan but sometimes with a merchant. There was no easy acceptance of incompetence or lack of application to the task of learning. Standards were exacting in every field of endeavor. The apprentice had no time for "selfish pleasures" and interests, but had to put such thoughts out of his mind or limit himself to fantasies about the future day when he would enjoy the pleasures allowed a person of recognized status.

Such an apprenticeship period was not limited to the male vocational role. There were many apprentice-like equivalents for women during their premarital period. Just as many boys were sent out of their own homes to work under someone other than their fathers, girls were frequently sent out to work as maids in the homes of wealthier folk of higher status to learn proper marital-housewife behavior. If not, they were required to perform some service for their parents and to train themselves for future performance.

For girls from wealthier families, there was required attendance at a special school to train them in the polite arts so necessary for brides marrying into a respectable lineage. A lineage kept its pride by expecting refined behavior of its in-marrying women.

The prewar discrimination in patterns of formal education between men and women is still somewhat in evidence today, although all the major universities, including the University of Tokyo, admit qualified women on an informal quota basis. Any determined woman, if she so chooses, can seriously consider a professional career. Many educated women in Japan, like some in the United States, forego their careers when they marry. Some Japanese women choose to return to a professional career after the death of a husband.

One of the real changes in socialization occurring in today's Japan is in respect to the type of vocational "imprinting" preceding marriage. The traditional forms of apprenticeship described above are being replaced by formal education, on the one hand, and by the mass communication media, on the other. This change is especially evident as it influences the woman's role. Mass media have almost entirely supplanted the direct first-hand experience of the preparatory "maid" period for women as a means of acquiring knowledge concerning the expected role of the housewife. The traditional Japanese definition of a "maid" has now shifted toward its Western concept of a lifelong occupational role rather than what it was in the past—a learning role through which one acquired desirable adult skills.[5] As a consequence, role emulation of domestic patterns of higher-status households by lower-status women no longer occurs through direct experience. Young girls instead turn to popular magazines and television for inspiration and instruction in homemaking. The "Westernization" of Japanese women is going on at a rapid pace in inculcating a mass-media conception of what a home should be.

Apartment-house dwelling is becoming increasingly prevalent in congested urban areas.[6] The young bride learns to make the most of a small living space in which many of the domestic refinements of the old culture no longer have any pertinence. There is widespread use of the recently developed convenience foods such as "instant noodles" and soups. The small Japanese home kitchen has become mechanized with such devices as toasters and electric rice-

5. De Vos noted in 1954 that American families in Japan had many difficulties with Japanese "maids." Americans wanted to pay them more than they expected, as they considered the Japanese salary "exploitative" (about $15 a month in 1954). But many maids, although highly paid by Japanese standards, would leave when they discovered that the American housewives for whom they worked assumed no responsibility for "training" them in the English language or in European cooking, which had been the major reasons many young girls sought service in American households.

6. A detailed description of personality and social change in Japanese apartment houses has been made by Kiefer, 1967.

cookers. The complicated and time-consuming skills needed for food preparation in the past are rapidly dropping off. For most housewives there remain the necessary daily purchases in neighborhood shops, since the buying of large quantities is difficult for those shopping on foot. Increasingly, however, those with cars do stock up refrigerators, which are continually growing in size and capacity. More housewives are buying at large food centers and department store basements. Western cooking is demonstrated on daytime television and is very popular as a home diversion for the housewife, who finds herself with increasingly longer periods of leisure.

For men the apprenticeship pattern still has considerable vitality as a means of vocational socialization, in spite of the rapid inroads into this pattern made by increasingly large-scale factories in the postwar period. Nevertheless, young men are no longer tolerant of the psychological dependence, the hard work, and the harshness of a formal apprenticeship. After graduating from nine years of compulsory school, many prefer to find, as quickly as possible, some position in a large factory which will afford them both security and wages that will increase steadily with seniority. The focus of vocational concern is shifting from acquiring special skills mastered with difficulty to finding positions with shorter hours and higher pay—attitudes that have been primary for years in Western blue-collar workers.

Japanese youth wish to have time free for after-hours recreation. A variety of such recreation is afforded by the many places of amusement now accessible through the transportation ganglia of modern Japanese urban areas. The virtue of loyalty and the network of associations related to the apprentice-master structure of the past are beginning to disappear, for urban workers at least. In professional, clerical, and managerial positions, however, the network of expectations is likely to endure for some time, since there is still considerable emphasis on loyalty of service in the middle-class segment of the population.

It must be pointed out, of course, that the ongoing process of change does not terminate the many continuities in Japanese personality configurations and role performance related to the concern with competence and adequacy. The culture continues to be a demanding one in its definition of the adequate performance of adult social roles. Even today it is no mean task for most Japanese to actualize the adult role, to have a sense of achievement or success. In various studies made since 1960 with the Thematic Apperception Test in Japan (De Vos, 1973, chapters 2–5), we have consistently found evidence of very strong achievement motivation related to family responsibility and interdependent nurturance, in both young and middle-aged Japanese. These concerns are almost invariably expressed in the context of potential incapacity to realize one's own internalized standards. It is interesting to note that concern with adequacy has not diminished as far as TAT responses from Arakawa Ward show, either among adults or among fifteen-year-olds.

No field of endeavor in Japan has escaped concern with refinement and finesse. During the traditional apprenticeship period, an individual, whether he was treated gently or harshly, was required to continue until he showed himself to be sufficiently aware of what was expected of him in the way of proper standards. Only then would he be considered worthy of independence. And in marrying an eldest son, a young bride coming into a new household was in a sense entering her second period of apprenticeship, under the severe and sometimes jealous tutelage of her husband's mother. If she failed in any way to meet the exacting requirements or showed herself to be inept, she could be sent back to her family as a "failure."

It is no wonder, therefore, that the pressures of the past still make becoming "adequate" a difficult and problematical process. It demands of the individual a strong endurance and a capacity to maintain oneself in submissive and subordinate positions until society deems one capable of independent assertion. For a man, ideally achieved social status was that of master merchant or artisan or of a successful bureaucrat in the premodern samurai hierarchy. Similarly, a farmer prided himself on his proficiency and diligence in producing the maximum crop from a very limited acreage. For a wife and mother, endurance continued until her children showed to the world their capacities, attesting to the mother's years of careful nurture and training and preparation. Much of what Freud (1955) and Reik (1941) have described as "moral masochism" applies directly to the apprentice mentality maintained by Japanese throughout their preparatory years of training. One must not overlook the fact that submissiveness in the young was and is related to a sense of the future long-term goal of acquiring competence so as to become independent or dominant in relation to others.

It is a general comment often heard in present-day Japan that among artisans concern with standards is disappearing in direct proportion to the increasing presence of mechanically standardized products, which are displacing the various handicrafts in the marketplace. However, Japanese concerns with success or failure remain, on a conscious level at least, focused on problems of personal adequacy. Japanese still see themselves as needing to meet expectations, and their concern with their own individualized motivation or lack of motivation is less evident than it is in comparable material obtained from American subjects. Even though choice of vocation may have been decided by their families rather than by themselves, most Japanese do not have leeway for conscious awareness of any motivational ambivalence on their own part. There are many Japanese for whom it is still psychologically impossible to consider directly their own unwillingness to perform an expected vocational role. One can be excused to some degree for lack of performance only if one is simply not capable either physically or mentally of performing in an expected role. This enduring cultural characteristic is related to the fact that in traditional Japan the assertion of an individual's will, in terms of either willingness or unwillingness, was considered destructive to the harmony of a cooperative community and, from a psychodynamic standpoint, even more basically destructive to one's own parents (De Vos, 1973, chapter 6). Feelings of unwillingness, therefore, can give rise to a very strong sense of guilt, and such guilt is still to be found deeply motivating the behavior of modern Japanese. We include here occupational and vocational histories, stories of failure as well as success, reported to us by numbers of our Arakawa sample, which will illustrate these generalizations.

Apprenticeship in Life History Materials

In Arakawa, individuals first gain occupational "know-how" and learn basic skills in relatively small operations, such as tiny factories, small restaurants, and retail stores. This pattern of apprenticeship was described to us by a number of our Arakawa subjects.

A shift from rural to urban life is part of the occupational and social adjustment for many individuals in our sample. As was reported in chapter 5, of the wives and husbands in our 50 families, 18 husbands and 18 wives were born in Tokyo, and the remaining 64 individuals came to Tokyo at varying times in their lives, most of them from rural areas. We noted that 23 men and 14 women came to Tokyo under the age of sixteen. The purpose of their coming varied, but 12 men and 4 women stated that they came with the specific purpose of becoming apprenticed. In addition, 14 women came to Tokyo in their adolescence to work as maids or domestics.

The husband in N-2, Mr. Sakiyama, had a typical apprenticeship, although he came to Tokyo fairly late, at age seventeen. Apprenticed to a paternal cousin's husband, who was a carpenter, he underwent rigid training, working thirteen hours a day, from 8:00 in the morning to 9:00 at night. During a busy period he would work until midnight. Though he was periodically angry with his boss, he reported to us that he knew he had to submit in order to learn necessary skills. He was apprenticed for approximately two and a half years, and at about age twenty-one he set up his own carpentry shop, a business in which he has continued in one way or another until the present day.

The husband in case D-1, Mr. Fukui, was apprenticed at age sixteen for three years to a tailor, learning how to make trousers. Part of the arrangement, mutually understood, was that his master would help him start his own business, and when the master did so, Mr. Fukui made a promise that for the next four years he would only make trousers ordered through his master. This is an example of the kind of implicit or explicit understanding between master and apprentice which enables the master to receive some continuing benefit, even after assisting in the so-called independence of his former charge. The apprenticeship period is considered to have tested the loyalty as well as the capacity of the youth, and the master therefore feels safe in investing in his former apprentice.

Case I-7 illustrates a pattern of apprenticeship in which the youth is sent to Tokyo to a relative or a person who is somehow connected with the father's business located in the rural area. Mr. Ishisaka, the husband, was sent to Tokyo to work at another store instead of remaining to work in his father's, but when his grandfather died he was called back to help at home. Later he was again sent to Tokyo, where he began to set up his own small business, but he was called back home once more to help out with his father's now failing business. While attempting to help his father, he also did extra work at a nearby factory to supplement the family income. After these varied transfers back and forth, according to his own report, he finally ended up as a day laborer in Tokyo. (He admits to being a heavy drinker.) Throughout his interviews he reverted to discussing his youthful apprenticeship and his earlier attempts to better himself, referring with some nostalgia to his efforts to be a dutiful son and fulfill his filial piety to his parents. Such a self-conscious discussion of "filial piety" as Mr. Ishisaka's did not come up as frequently in our sample as might have been expected, considering the very strong social emphasis usually given this virtue. The occupational activity of our families is more often expressed simply as a necessary reality of family life rather than as the acting out of filial piety.

Sometimes the apprenticeship is to a relative who has previously left his rural business to go to the city and attempt to establish a similar family business there. Mr. Sorai, in case N-11, after finishing the eighth grade, took an entrance examination for a commercial school, but he failed, and at age sixteen he was sent to Tokyo to work in a bakery his grandfather had started some time earlier. The grandfather had left his own rural bakery business in the hands of his eldest son (Mr. Sorai's father) and had gone to Tokyo to establish a new business. In our lower-class sample, it is not unusual for a father to give an established business to his son and his son's new wife, and for the father, with his considerable experience, to try to start a new business elsewhere. (This is a pattern that should be checked in other areas of Japan; it came up with considerable frequency in our material.) Mr. Sorai was apprenticed to his grandfather, for whom he worked for seven years. A marriage was then arranged for him, and at that time he was also set up in an independent business. His father came to Tokyo to join him, and the father and son ran the business venture. In this case one notes a leapfrogging method of transferring a family business from a rural region to Tokyo. The business shared by Mr. Sorai and his father thrived, and at one point they employed as many as thirty women selling cakes that were distributed throughout Tokyo. However, about seven years before our interview, Mr. Sorai's business failed and the bakery was closed.

We could get no information about the reason for the failure other than that Mr. Sorai had a "stuttering problem" (he had been stuttering since childhood). One would suspect that there were reasons related to the aging of his own father, whose retirement left him alone and inadequate to cope with the problems of running a business. It is not unusual among Japanese for business failure to be attributed to some weakness of the body, at least when one is discussing failure with outsiders.

The situation of the husband in case I-11, Mr. Ihashi, illustrates the way in which siblings sometimes support one another during apprenticeship programs. Mr. Ihashi worked in a metal-plating business with his older brother, and after four years under the tutelage of his brother, he set up an independent establishment and, in turn, taught metal-plating to his younger brother and to his younger sister's husband.

Some individuals who suffered occupational failure describe a sense of deprivation in terms of unrewarding present environment, but beneath this one senses the deeper deprivations of essentially unhappy childhood relationships with their own parents. We might cite, as one example, some background materials from case I-10. Mr. Imura was the eldest son in an extremely poor family, as he describes it, who was not really loved and was treated harshly by both parents. What love he received came from his paternal grandmother, who taught him strict Confucian ethics, which he was able to accept without ambivalence because the teaching came from her. His two older sisters were apprenticed at very early ages, and he accepted as a matter of course his own apprenticeship at eleven years of age to a metalworker in Tokyo, who was his distant uncle. Mr. Imura found the work hard and unsatisfying, and felt thoroughly isolated on the deaths of his mother and grandmother when he was twelve years old. Finally, at age fifteen, he could no longer take the treatment given him, and running away from the shop, he returned home to his father. What he found there was no better; his father had remarried, and his stepmother saw to it that Mr. Imura was immediately sent back to his apprentice position in Tokyo. Interestingly enough, he reacted to the rejection by his father by resigning himself to work from then on, putting his energy into achieving skill and gaining satisfaction from the work, to which he could see no alternative. He worked for the next ten years, finishing his apprenticeship at age twenty-six. By that time he took considerable pride in being one of the best metalworkers making ornaments for Buddhist altars.

During these years Mr. Imura led a very restricted life; he reports in his interviews that in all this time he visited a house of prostitution only once and had no other contact with women. He ordered his life around the thought of his eventual independence and the financial gain that would come as a just reward for his ten years of hard work and self-deprivation. He saved out of the meager allowance given him, and he borrowed more in order to open his own shop, which started off well. But only two years later, in 1927, a financial panic swept Japan, and all his savings, as well as the money he had borrowed from others, were wiped out. He was forced to take a job as a daily laborer, and when economic conditions improved he found that his particular skills had become almost obsolete. He had had a marriage arranged at the time he opened his shop—the usual procedure in the tradition of apprenticeship, since it is at this time that a merchant or an artisan is first considered "mature" socially. The marriage was described as basically unsatisfactory. There were five children, three of whom died, and after ten years of marriage his wife died as well. He married again, and his second marriage was no more satisfactory than the first.

Mr. Imura is now working as a repairman, having given up all hope of an independent entrepreneurial existence. Listening to him discuss his past with bitterness, one senses that he feels he was poorly rewarded for his efforts, and yet he does not in any way place the blame for his failure on impersonal economic forces. Rather, he seems to see his lack of success as somehow related to personal inadequacy and to the built-in unhappiness of the family in which he was born and through which he made his economic and vocational contacts. One could describe his attitude as one of fatalistic resignation, but this would entirely miss the point that (at least as he tells it) he had indeed mobilized considerable energy in attempting to achieve a goal.

In Mr. Imura's case it appears valid to assume that outside economic forces had more to do with his failure than did internal difficulties in psychological adjustment. And yet we can never know. Certainly, in assessing how Adam Smith's concepts of relative efficiency and competition work in a free market society, one must conclude that those who are in some way or another psychologically disadvantaged in comparison with others are more likely to end up as failures.

One must not, however, overstress personal psychological inadequacy as the prime determinant of occupational failure in an economic structure that averages close to 5,000 business failures a year in a ward of 265,000 people. In the Japanese dual economy large factories and traditional small enterprises continue to coexist. A great number of persons try their hand at independent business ventures, though many of them fail sometime in their lives as a result of vicissitudes of the marketplace, which have little relevance to personal failings. It is interesting to note that individuals in our sample seldom direct the blame for failure at the market only, and that the sense of guilt for failure seeks a more personal explanation within the individual.

A few men and women describe their apprenticeship as having been exceedingly harsh. The wife in case D-8, Mrs. Fukuhara, for example, says that the wife and family to whom she was apprenticed as a maid were very harsh and mean to her, sometimes hitting or pinching her when she made a mistake. She said she didn't want to bear such treatment, and tried to go home, asking permission to do so of the wife of the house, who told her that it would be to her shame if she returned from Tokyo without being able to endure the hardship of her work as a maid. She was told that the people of her village would all laugh at her, and would say sarcastically that she only went to Tokyo to urinate. Mrs. Fukuhara then decided that probably her mistress was right and that she did not want to go home to be the laughingstock of the village, so she made up her mind to endure the hardship she was experiencing in Tokyo. This is an example in which the shame phenomenon often described in Japanese culture seemed to operate to keep a young person in a painful apprentice program, although it must be pointed out that this is not a usual description.

For one reason or another, some young women who start out in an apprentice role shift over to factory work or to other situations in which they can be self-employed. A number of these women expressed a carefree and happy feeling about having been on their own, as they view it retrospectively. In case I-4, Mrs. Iida, who is the second wife of a widower, initially came to Tokyo to work as a nursemaid in a family, where she was taught dressmaking as part of her apprenticeship and was well treated by the master of the house, who was bedridden with tuberculosis. When he died, Mrs. Iida returned home to her family, but she did not enjoy her home and found an opportunity to go to Tokyo again, where she got a job as a kitchen aide in an army hospital. She rented a room on her own and cooked her own food, and she recalls this period as a very enjoyable part of her past. During this time she made a love marriage in spite of the opposition of her parents. What we see in this woman is an independent spirit which she could actualize to some degree. The independence that she asserted in carrying off a love marriage in spite of parental opposition did not extend to an ability to be free of her husband's mother. What she remembers fondly about the past with her husband, however, is that he was gentle with her and acted as a buffer not only between her and her mother-in-law but between her and her sisters-in-law as well.

In some of the traditional occupations, the expectations of entrepreneurial independence can no longer be realized today. In case N-12, Mr. Sayama is now working as an eel-baker. Today eels are cultivated and raised in large quantities and no longer represent the luxury they did in the past, when little eel-shops were scattered about old Edo as places where one periodically indulged in a luxury. The eel-baker would kill the eel and begin cooking it after he saw the customer coming to his restaurant, which was not crowded and where there was a generally relaxed atmosphere—quite different from the harassed atmosphere of eel-restaurants today. In this changed situation, one even sees a reflection of the change in status of men and women; in the past eels were considered a luxury that was not available to women. Now cooks work on a mass-production basis from 7:30 in the morning, preparing eels for the daily flow of impatient customers of both sexes.

The "modernization" of eel-restaurants is quite complete as far as the customers are concerned, but the employees' system is still in a state of transition. In the old, extended-family system that existed among merchants, eel-shops had a tradition of *noren-wake*,[7] that is, when an apprentice had served sufficient time, his master would give him permission to use the store's symbol printed on a *noren* cloth to hang over the entry of a branch shop, and would help set him up in another district. Times have changed, and the *noren-wake* system and its familism have disappeared from the eel-restaurant business. The restaurant in which Mr. Sayama now works is a joint stock corporation; the situation was different when his own father worked as an eel-baker.

Entrepreneurial Innovation in Life History Materials

One of the remarkable findings in our case material is the large number of reported instances, whether true or fanciful, of individualized entrepreneurial activities and attempts at inventiveness directed at breaking into success through some novel activity that no one else had thought of before.

The following experiences of the husband in case N-5, Mr. Sonotani,

7. A "split off" of the *noren*. The *noren* is a split cloth hanging across a shop entrance and imprinted with the shop emblem or name. These trademarks attest to the owner's pride in his store or trade. One ducks one's head through the *noren* when going into a traditional restaurant or shop.

demonstrate such attempts. Mr. Sonotani comes from a family that ran a Western-style restaurant when such shops were still relatively rare. After the great earthquake and fire in Tokyo in 1923, Mr. Sonotani's father opened what was called a "cafe," a type of restaurant that was to become very fashionable in the early 1930s, a small tavern with several waitresses, who usually wore white aprons. The business thrived, catering primarily to the carpenters, painters, and plumbers who were receiving a considerable income working on the reconstruction of destroyed sections of Tokyo.

Mr. Sonotani finished primary school in 1927 and went to work in a camera shop in Tokyo. He had taken it for granted that he and all his brothers would work after primary school, so he did not feel it unfair that he could not go on to middle school. He worked for the store owner as an art photographer, and during his apprenticeship he learned the special techniques of development and enlargement used in custom photography. The work suited his aesthetic tastes and interests, and he was quite contented. After two years, however, he was forced to leave because, as he explains it to the interviewer,

> the child of the camera-store owner was very naughty and disobedient, and one time I became angry at him and said that the child's disobedience was his mother's fault, since she had failed to discipline the child properly. The child's mother overheard me and became very angry. The store owner told me that I had to go because he could not afford to lose his own wife.

Mr. Sonotani then found a job with a trading company that imported foreign cameras. He became a very capable salesman and was well liked by his employer. Although still in his late teens, he was given a car and a large salary, at least according to his own story, and he led a very good life, enjoying good food and tailored suits. He soon was the number-one employee in the company, but the war in China began, and the trade in imported cameras suffered a severe slump. At this time someone he knew in an optical company suggested that Mr. Sonotani go into the camera-manufacturing business himself. Shiseidō, now a well-known producer of cosmetics with a nationwide chain-store system, agreed to accept the merchandise. Mr. Sonotani did not have enough money for the capital investment, however, and the optical company mentioned above was unwilling to back him financially. Mr. Sonotani tried to convince the owner of the trading company he had worked for to join him in starting their own camera manufacturing, but he could not be persuaded. Mr. Sonotani did not give up and finally gathered together a group of camera-store owners in Tokyo who were willing to back him. They hoped that the Mitsui Trust Bank would finance their venture, but their optimism was unfounded; the bank refused to lend them the money.

The person in the optical company who initially had suggested that Mr. Sonotani go into camera manufacturing felt sorry for him and recommended him to another trading company dealing with photographic equipment in Shanghai. (Mr. Sonotani was then twenty-three years of age.) When he arrived in Shanghai, he was given a car and a Chinese interpreter; he began working as a salesman and was very successful. He could not, however, give up his idea of manufacturing his own cameras, and he quit his new job after ten months. After his return to Japan, in the summer of 1939, Mr. Sonotani made his living by ordering lenses from small factories and selling them to camera makers.

About this time rice was made subject to rationing, and the rice retailers were organized into a cooperative, leading the owner of one rice retail store to seek to transfer his capital investment to some other business. Mr. Sonotani talked him into backing a small enterprise manufacturing camera shutters. Hattori, at present a well-known watchmaker, was also producing cameras at that time, and Mr. Sonotani and his business associates were able to sell their products through Hattori. The business was successful, and Mr. Sonotani enjoyed a good, stable monthly income until 1942, when, at the age of twenty-eight, he was drafted into an airplane factory for wartime service. Then the navy drafted him, but he had sciatica and was soon discharged. Until the end of the war, he worked as a leader of his neighborhood group in charge of rationing food and of supervising fire-fighting, also working occasionally as a volunteer in a steel factory.

After the war, Mr. Sonotani, like so many others, survived by going into illegal dealings in the black market that was located in front of Shimbashi station, one of the largest such markets in Tokyo. Mr. Sonotani liked us to see him as a clever black-market dealer who could escape police arrest. He recalls:

> Eventually most of the illegal black-market dealers in cigarettes were arrested, and I was the last to survive. I was smart. I used to display only one or two boxes of cigarettes among other merchandise, like dried food. A plain-clothes detective would come to my store and say, "You should not sell cigarettes in such a place." Then I would say, "They're not for sale; I smoke them." The cop would say, "You are a liar. You must be selling them." I would answer, "Of course not. I have only one or two boxes here like this, and what is the point of selling such a few boxes? I could not make much money." Then the cop would search inside my store but could not find any cigarettes because I used to keep them elsewhere.

But Mr. Sonotani was finally arrested when a policeman observed him selling cigarettes to a customer.

Shortly after he quit his black-market activities, he was married, in the spring of 1946, when he was thirty-two and his wife was twenty-six. Joined by his wife, Mr. Sonotani again attempted to make a breakthrough into some kind of successful business enterprise. The couple began to make *korokke*, a Japanese deep-fried mashed potato (the word comes from the French *croquette*), which they sold to restaurants catering to those who took their food-ration coupons to specified restaurants. Mr. and Mrs. Sonotani were kept very busy. They had to get up at two o'clock in the morning to start cooking, because they had to finish their *korokke* by seven o'clock in order to deliver them to the various restaurants on time. They would finish their delivery by noon and then would go to buy the raw materials for the next day. Mr. Sonotani could sleep from early evening to recover from the fatigue of the previous day, but Mrs. Sonotani had to take care of their baby, who was born the first year of their marriage, and she soon became pregnant again. Once she became so exhausted that she fell down and slept for three days. Mr. Sonotani was shocked by this incident; as he recalls, "I wondered which was more important, my wife or my work. I thought I could certainly change my work but hardly my wife. I stopped cooking food."

Mr. Sonotani visited individual homes and bought the rationed sugar and starch that had been distributed but not consumed. (Food was very scarce in Japan at this time, and it does not seem likely that people would not have used up all their rationed sugar and starch, but this is what Mr. Sonotani told us.) He resold the sugar and starch to a man who made candy. One day someone told Mr. Sonotani that he might be able to buy a larger quantity of starch directly from the manufacturer. He went to such a manufacturer, who told Mr. Sonotani that he could not give him any rationed starch, but that he could give him the refuse that was left after the process of refining and that this could be further processed so that starch of lower quality could be obtained. Mr. Sonotani was interested and tried to make candy out of low-quality starch, but found the process too expensive. He experimented with a variety of different methods and finally succeeded in making a sweet material that he called "*anko* substitute" (*anko* is sweet, thick, bean paste used for the filling in Japanese *kashi* cakes). Mr. Sonotani tried to sell his invention to the food section of a department store, but was told that the texture of his sweet paste needed improvement. His attempts to improve the textural quality of the paste all ended unsuccessfully, so he began to sell his sweet paste to a bread factory for making *anpan* (a cheap round bread with sweet bean paste inside).

A liquor store owner told Mr. Sonotani that people would drink more *shōchū* (something like a potato brandy) if some wine were added to it. Ordinary wine was very expensive and *shōchū* was cheap, so one would need to find an inexpensive wine for this purpose. (This was at the time of relative social chaos in American-occupied Japan, when many people drank low-quality alcoholic beverages as one of the few forms of recreation and escape.) Mr. Sonotani was interested and began looking for a way to make what he called "substitute wine."

The Sonotani family was in the meantime living solely by selling the "substitute *anko*" that Mr. Sonotani had invented. However, they were becoming increasingly poor, especially since Mr. Sonotani needed both time and money for his experimentations with substitute wine. By 1949, when Mrs. Sonotani was pregnant with their last child, the family was destitute. Mr. Sonotani's well-to-do brother refused to lend them money, and Mr. and Mrs. Sonotani seriously considered "committing family suicide" (*ikka shinjū*). By that time, however, Mr. Sonotani had discovered a way to make something that might serve as "substitute wine," although he was not sure he could sell it. It was Mrs. Sonotani who kept the family from suicide, saying:

> It is easy to die, but I do not want to die before finding out if your effort was after all worthless. Let us try to sell the stuff you made. Let the people decide if it is good or bad. If they do not like what you have made, then you have failed. Let us kill ourselves then. But let us try to sell it first.

The Sonotanis were able to sell their product, and by the summer of 1950 they had risen gradually out of their utter poverty. Mr. Sonotani says:

> My bicycle had been stolen. I went to a nearby bicycle store and asked the man to sell me a bicycle on a daily payment basis. It cost 25,000 yen. I began selling my new substitute wine, using my new bicycle. I paid back every day 1,000 yen, and I finished the payments within twenty-five days. Soon I needed more than a bicycle. I bought a *riya-ka* [rear car pulled by a bicycle] for 15,000 yen. I began depositing 1,000 yen every day in a bank account. Our entire life changed. I soon needed something better and faster than a bicycle and rear-car, so I bought a motor tricycle. Then I bought another. Eventually as many as thirty people were working for me.

Mr. Sonotani's friend, the owner of the liquor store, who had been his business partner in substitute-wine manufacturing, schemed to take over the business for himself. Mr. Sonotani says that his partner had used him in testing the product, then, when the test was successful, the partner wanted to monopolize the business.

"Betrayed" by first one and then another business partner, Mr. Sonotani wanted to start his own business all by himself. This time he had the idea of selling his substitute wine in an automatic juice-vending machine. One of his primary school classmates had an elder sister married to a lawyer, a member of the House of Councillors, who introduced him to the president of a finance company. Mr. Sonotani borrowed ¥1,000,000 from this company, and with this considerable loan he went into his new business. He had automatic juice-vending machines manufactured and used them to sell his substitute wine, cutting down the cost of labor so that he could sell his product with half the previous overhead. However, after less than a half a year, a minor economic crisis wiped out his business, together with hundreds of other small-scale industries in Arakawa Ward.

By this time Mr. Sonotani had begun working on a portable, plastic juice-cooler, and he tried to start again with this new invention. Someone in ice-cream manufacturing became interested in Mr. Sonotani's invention and promised to give him ¥15,000 a month until he finished designing the cooler, which was to be used for selling "soft" ice cream and tea at railway stations. The money was not enough for Mr. Sonotani to support his family, and his debts increased. It became impossible for the man in the ice-cream industry to continue subsidizing Mr. Sonotani, and so his attempt to start another business failed.

Then Mr. Sonotani was introduced to someone who gave him a job making and selling plaster dolls and wall hangers. Reduced to this present rather insignificant occupation, Mr. Sonotani tells us he has not yet completely given up and still hopes to start again in business for himself, making a new kind of wall hanger.

Although probably much exaggerated and glorified in a series of wishful reminiscences, Mr. Sonotani's life history, as he told it, still attests to the man's remarkable resilience and the determination with which he tried time and time again to come out of his failures and to make it again on his own. Speaking of his almost continual preoccupation with entrepreneurial independence, Mr. Sonotani has this to say: "I dislike being employed by someone else. I dislike having someone over my head pressing me down and telling me what to do. I always want to be on my own; that is why I have been trying so hard throughout my life."

Though much less dramatic than Mr. Sonotani's story, accounts from many others reported their continuous efforts to improve their living standards, and most of these persons seemed to like telling us how hard they have been trying. This drive for improvement is also apparent, for instance, in people's efforts to build and improve their own houses. Many people have put in extra work and effort to "buy" their own tiny houses built on miniscule lots.

For example, the Sekis, in case N-10, moved into Arakawa in 1951. They built a shack with one six-mat room (9′ × 12′) where six people all lived together: husband and wife, husband's two sons, and wife's son and daughter. Since then they have been gradually remodeling their house, expanding and rebuilding it. Their lot now houses a structure with a factory and two rooms on the first floor (9′ × 9′ and 12′ × 12′), and a second floor, added five years ago, with another three rooms. They borrowed money from the ward office and from a housing finance corporation in order to do this building. In order to repay the loan, Mrs. Seki worked days and nights as a seamstress; she says that on some nights she slept only a few hours so that she could manage to earn as much as ¥35,000 ($116) a month. She now makes a maximum of ¥24,000, but she recalls vividly her days and nights of continual hard work in order to help with their building.

In emphasizing our findings of such a prevalence of entrepreneurial attitudes, it would be erroneous to create the impression that entrepreneurial ambitions are characteristic of all our sample. This is obviously not true. A number of individuals in the sample seem to have made an adjustment of compliant dependence through which they have found relative satisfaction. The father of a social delinquent in case D-5 is an example. As Mr. Fuchitani describes his background, he was a compliant son who had a traditional patriarchal father and a solicitous, overprotective mother. He describes his own educational background as average. He was considered a neat, proper, "middle-of-the-road" person, well behaved both at home and at school. Transferring at an early age to a vocational school, he learned electrical work as a technical skill. This was not his favorite subject, but he was obedient to his father's decision and graduated from the vocational school with average grades. When he was sixteen, he got a temporary job with a friend doing metalwork and continued to live at home. At the age of eighteen, he became a formal apprentice in an electric shop, where he lived with his master's family and worked for three years. Mr. Fuchitani then became an employee of a company manufacturing electrical appliances, and, as he describes it, he "formally entered the company two years later" and has been a loyal employee ever since. Thus he did not complete a formal apprenticeship, going to work in a more untraditional factory, but even so he became a traditionally loyal employee who was satisfied with his subordinate role. He is particularly pleased to have his hours of work defined for him so that he has time to pursue leisure activities—going to baseball games and playing *go* and *shōgi* (Japanese chess) with friends. He married at age twenty-seven, four years after his "formal" entry as a worker in the factory.

At one period he appears to have developed some psychosomatic difficulties; he did not eat or sleep well and suffered from a "weak stomach," becoming so ill that he was hospitalized. Throughout this period the company for which he worked continued to pay his regular salary. When asked whether this was owing to a union policy in the factory, Mr. Fuchitani indicated that there was a kind of company union, but that it was the boss's decision that loyal employees would be supported whenever they were ill.

ATTITUDES TOWARD EDUCATION AND THE ASPIRATIONS HELD FOR CHILDREN

The general Japanese emphasis on children's education is a pervasive social attitude to be found everywhere and at all class levels. However, some of the lower-class children in Arakawa Ward were not oriented strongly toward dedicated school performance, and some parents, especially in our delinquent sample, were somewhat indifferent. The delinquent subjects themselves, as might be expected, generally have negative attitudes toward school. From the parents of delinquents, as well as from our control parents, we elicited a wide variety of attitudes about school, about future jobs, and about the desirable character traits that would be most adaptive for the future well-being of their children.

Mr. Sonotani, in case N-5, whose varied occupational history we have just recounted, emphasized not only the necessity for education but also the need to develop a "spirit of independence" in his children, the independence he considered so important for himself. He says:

> At the time when we lost our war with America I thought that now we Japanese have to learn many good things from the Americans. We should no longer spoil our children as we used to but raise independent individuals. I thought we should raise our children in an American style, so to speak. For instance, when a child falls down, if you do not help the child but watch him he will give up expecting to be helped, and will soon learn to stand up for himself. I did not want my children to get into a habit of wanting to be carried always; therefore, I told my wife not to carry the baby except at time of nursing.

We found that a number of parents had been taken out of school as young children to work or had been sent away to ease the economic burden of the family. Many of these parents, as they described the situation to us, saw themselves as being forced by circumstances to leave school against their own desire to continue. It was seldom directly reported to us that the informant himself had actually quit. In some instances, however, it was obvious that an informant had avoided schooling as soon as it was possible for him or her to do so.

In case I-11, for example, the husband, Mr. Ihashi, reports going as far as the eighth grade by 1932; he says he enjoyed study and ranked somewhere in the middle of his class. During the busy farm season, however, his father forced him to work on the farm, since his mother was unable to help because of illness. Thus, when he was a boy he missed at least half his classes. On completion of the higher primary in 1932, in perhaps the eighth grade, he was sent to Tokyo as an apprentice in a small cake-making store, where, as he remembers it, he worked continuously for five years from five in the morning until eleven at night. During this employment, Mr. Ihashi wished to attend night school but was unable to do so because he was kept too busy.

There was nothing systematic in our evidence to enable us to correlate the educational attainment of parents with their desire for the education of their own children. Generally, education is seen as a means for a child to better himself beyond the present circumstances of his family.

Although some parents state that they leave the matter of the child's educational aspirations to the child himself, one sometimes gains the opposite impression in the course of interviews. In case I-3, the father, Mr. Itahashi, stated several times that he "leaves the matter to the boy's wishes." However, other information affords the impression that he is putting continued pressure to excel in school on an inadequate and fairly dull son, who cannot take the pressure very well. Mr. Itahashi, as a father, is perhaps unaware of what he is doing. He himself is completely preoccupied with his work, so that he puts continual implicit pressure on his children, but his projective tests, as well as the attitudes expressed in the interviews, demonstrate that he cannot realize any inner sense of accomplishment. What comes through instead is the impression of a man in a state of chronic fatigue and frustration. His work activity shows an obsessive quality, suggesting that it serves as an outlet for a man who has inadequate avenues of expression in other areas. Whatever the inner attitudes of his father, they are not acted upon with any measures of discipline or encouragement of the child. Giving little time or attention to his son, Mr. Itahashi leaves actual matters of discipline to the mother, who feels helpless in coping with her son's delinquency.

Competition for better grades is generally, albeit covertly, emphasized in Japanese schools, and parents in Arakawa, as elsewhere, are usually concerned with their children's grades. The parents of many of our subjects had to resign themselves to the relatively mediocre performance of their children, though that did not necessarily dampen high parental aspirations.

Other parents tried to trim their hopes to fit performance. In case N-11, for example, Mrs. Sorai said that her son does not like to study and she does not want to push him. "He is not interested in studying; he does not want to go to high school. It is OK. He will learn to be a merchant working at his aunt's market." Mrs. Sorai nevertheless expects him to be a "filial" son. When she gave birth to him, serious bleeding took place. "I bled so much that my body became cold. I thought I would die. So I tell him that, as I almost lost my life for his sake, he owes me special *oya-kōkō* [filial piety]" (she laughs). Her son is considered a "good boy." We gain the impression that in some families with delinquent children what the parents are hoping to settle for is that their child will achieve "some kind of average mediocrity." In other words, they hope that he will eventually conform to society rather than continue to be a deviant. The husband in case D-8, Mr. Fukuhara, for example, keeps using the word *heibon* when he describes what he expects of his children. This word translates as "mediocre" or "ordinary," and is also used to describe eventless situations. What he wants his son to be is a salary man working for some steady business, receiving not too little but not too much, and leading a safe and peaceful life. He says:

> I never tell them to live in any particular active fashion. I know education is important, especially for a man, but I myself do not like to study, so I cannot force it on him. Also, higher education is not the only thing necessary for a man to survive in this world. As long as one develops a way to see things properly and wisely, I think that's enough.

Mrs. Fukuhara, the mother, also is limited in her aspirations for her children:

> I tell them that they should improve their school records by studying more. I tell them so, but nowadays a characteristic of our recent education is to discourage one or not to force something on one's children. So I feel there is no point in pressing them too hard.

One gains here the impression that the mother is blaming recent trends in education for her own obvious lack of involvement with the educational activities of her children. She says also:

> My son wants to enter the Japanese Defense to be trained as a pilot rather than going to high school. He wants to study airplanes. Of course, it's up to him. No matter what a parent wants a child to do, if the child is not willing you can't do anything about it. You can't force your child to enter something if he doesn't like it.

Compared with such parents of delinquent boys, who place little emphasis on the merit of educational achievement and tend to be "lax" in their attitude toward their children, a number of the fathers of nondelinquents are characterized by a sense of involvement in the educational future of their children. They exhibit this interest with a considerable degree of intellectual pretentiousness, which seems to us part of a compensatory defense against their deep sense of inadequacy. This pretentiousness in the fathers of nondelinquents, contrasted with those of delinquents, takes place in the context of a generally compliant and dependent attitude toward formal authority. Part of their pretentiousness is expressed through language in the projective tests, as well as through the perception of status or authority symbols. Some give such responses to the Rorschach cards as "crowns," "medals of merit," and other symbols of prowess and social status. Some of these fathers emphasize a need to be strict with their children. There is in them a type of "authoritarian" attitude that tends to counter any appearance of delinquency.

There are fathers who try very hard, despite obvious personal limitations, to be involved with the supervision and direction of their children. We must note in this context, however, that the Rorschach findings do indicate less rigidity in the personality structure of fathers of nondelinquents than in the fathers of delinquents. Even though the fathers of the nondelinquents avow "strictness," their attitudinal affirmation is coupled with a more flexible personality and a more positive attitude toward authority generally. Appropriately enough, in our sample at least, more socially rebellious attitudes are found in the fathers of delinquents, who are, as far as personality is concerned, significantly more rigid and constricted. These more rigid fathers of delinquents actually tend toward behavioral inconsistency related to their less well resolved attitudes toward authority. While we also find submerged in some of the nondelinquent fathers a residual rebellious attitude, it is usually well sublimated and does not appear close to the surface.

FAILURE AND INADEQUACY

Along with the rather remarkable displays of entrepreneurial spirit and dauntless efforts recounted to us in the life histories of the lower-class men of Arakawa, our materials also include acknowledgments of failure and confessions of inadequacy.

A majority describe "failure" as occurring only after repeated attempts to "make it," like Mr. Sonotani of case N-5 and Mr. Imura of case I-10, whom we described above. A few men attribute their failures to external events rather than to personality problems. The effect of war and destruction, bad timing in the economic development of postwar Japan, and financial depression, over which these men of small capital had no control, are the causes of failure stated most often. Granted that the war economy, destruction from air raids, and postwar confusion were indeed the actual cause of economic failure for many, as described to us, those who emphasize wartime disorganization the most seem to exhibit more personal reasons for failure as well. We get a strong impression that, in spite of their avowals of hard work and continuous efforts, such individuals were more often than not psychologically "unfit" to be successful. The husband in case I-7, Mr. Ishisaka, sees himself as a victim of wartime disruption, and blames social change for his occupational failure. He tries, somewhat feebly, to justify what he is doing now:

> Everything went wrong, and I became a victim of war and of the Japanese government. I worked hard for the sake of our country, but the war ended and suddenly everything lost meaning. I got disgusted. After all, being in an inferior position, I had no luck. I didn't bear a grudge, but I felt that life was absurd. I felt fed up; therefore I became a daily laborer living from hand to mouth, one day after another. But this is OK. I can say whatever I want. I don't have to be afraid of anyone, no company president, no boss.

He is a day laborer who registers with the public employment security office, a government program to help the unemployed and give them a minimum income by putting them into various temporary jobs like cleaning up, working in construction, repairing roads, and maintaining parks.

A sense of personal inadequacy sometimes involves identification with the inadequacies of one's own father. This was quite apparent in the case of Mr. Fudasaka, case D-7. His own father, a person without much education, was a man he remembers as always drinking. He states that his father moved to Tokyo after failing in a "business" (unspecified) elsewhere. The mother was in full control of educating the children. The father, Mr. Fudasaka recalls, was totally lacking in self-control, had a short temper, and was given to beating his children or throwing cups about the house when upset. Throughout the interview, Mr. Fudasaka describes women as being much stronger than men. He saw his sisters as bright and capable, whereas he saw himself as rather mediocre in his educational attainments. He remembers very clearly his feeling of social inferiority in school because his clothes were poor and shabby. His father is described as drinking up most of the income he brought into the house.

His own occupational history is of a more "modern" type. His first employment was in a large factory, where he was at first given hard jobs and was sometimes beaten by the older workers. However, he says, "Fortunately, I had a nice boss who paid me some attention." After a few years he came to enjoy his routine job and found that his earnings were comparatively high for those in his neighborhood. Again, one notes that those who work for factory wages make more mention of their recreational activities. Mr. Fudasaka responded to questions about recreation by saying that he liked buying books and playing the violin, and he belonged to a group of harmonica players. He also "played cards" with some of his friends and was an avid movie-goer, going to movies about three times a week. With other youthful companions he used to spend time in the nearby Yoshiwara prostitution area, and he related this naturally without exhibiting any feeling that this was unusual behavior. He admits to drinking, although "not as much as my father." The material gathered from his present wife points up a serious failing that has kept his family financially destitute. In his interviews with us, Mr. Fudasaka did not mention his need to gamble, but his present wife reports that his first marriage was dissolved because he was an obsessive gambler. Less than a month after the marriage, when she found out about his gambling, his first wife went home to her family, who, in Japanese style, refused to take her back and ordered her to return to her husband and apologize, which she did. She remained for two weeks, then left again, and this time was brought back by her own relatives. Mr. Fudasaka refused to take her back; in a later interview, when the history of his former wife's leaving him was mentioned, Mr. Fudasaka said, "A wife should not desert her husband for such a cause, even though the wife recognized the husband's faults." His present wife seems to maintain stronger control and supervision over her husband, and she has fewer complaints about his gambling activities.

There is evidence in some of our materials of what can be termed anomic reactions to success and failure. There were among our sample a number of persons who attempted an entrepreneurial career and found it difficult to "set limits" on involvement, suffering from economic vertigo of one form or another. Such people don't seem to know where to stop in order to prevent exhausting the capacities of their own bodies, and for many, like Mr. Shiratori, case N-8, stress results in a flare-up of some type of somatic complaint, such as stomach trouble. As Mr. Shiratori describes his vocational history, he repeatedly exhausted himself both physically and financially and had to declare himself bankrupt. The obvious interpretation is that his own ego ideal, the individual need to meet entrepreneurial expectations of success, is so strong that he pushed himself beyond his capacities. Japanese achievement is often gained at such a physical cost; the individual can become almost self-destructive in his desire to reach a goal. If there is failure, it may be easily explained in terms of physical exhaustion. Most Japanese cannot admit to themselves that they are incapable of running a business, and so physical exhaustion or a somatic complaint becomes the excuse for failure.

As we have pointed out, a number of men in our sample have gone through a considerable series of "ups and downs" in their occupational achievement. The case of Mr. Sonotani (N-5 above) and others demonstrate that many men "bounced back" with remarkable resilience and perseverance from occupational failure and financial catastrophe to at least a temporary success. We do notice, however, that in a series of such efforts to recuperate, many men gradually, or suddenly, lose their sense of reality to such a degree that their behavior becomes "reckless" or "desperate." One gets the impression that their behavior is then not so much a realistic effort to improve their situation as what might be called an anomic reaction to economic disaster.

Some such men in our sample took to gambling in the hope of changing their financial status. An example is case D-7, mentioned above: At one point Mr. Fudasaka attempted to run a small store. When it began to fail his brother, who had been making deliveries to a race track, suggested in desperation that if they had an organized scheme they could make a profit betting on the bicycle races. They tried what they thought was a sure plan to recoup their losses by betting systematically. Although Mr. Fudasaka's wife strenuously objected to the idea, she went along finally when they assured her they had a sure-fire scheme. They started very conservatively on their betting system, but ended with all their investment lost. Then they borrowed a large amount and continued to bet on the races for another three months, losing all the money they had borrowed.

This is an apt example of the kind of anomic breakdown that occurs either with threat of failure or, conversely, with unusual success. In such cases, men seek by some kind of magical means to increase their money, losing all the constraints and cautions that their culture teaches them are the gradual means to success.

Some of the fathers of delinquents see their failure as related to some problem of "overconfidence"; with initial success they obviously lacked any self-control. For example, Mr. Fuchino in case D-9 quit his job at his uncle's rubber factory, and with the retirement fund he had accumulated, he began his own little business, borrowing additional money with a friend who put up most of the capital. Mr. Fuchino contributed his experience, and the business thrived; they were eventually employing four or five girls and could not keep up with the demand for rubber shoes. However, as Mr. Fuchino put it, "This success invited evil" (*tonton byōshi ga wazawai shita*). He became "overconfident" at his unexpected success and began to play in the stock market with speculative stock which, he asserts, "even the most experienced speculators are afraid of touching." He lost his money very quickly and, becoming despondent, sold his factory equipment as "scraps for pennies," and returned to his uncle's factory. His entrepreneurial dream had lasted only a year. The uncle was angry because Mr. Fuchino had previously left that job, disregarding opposition, and was now returning simply because his own business had failed. The relationship never improved much after that, and although he was forced to live in his uncle's house because of his impoverishment, he finally left and rented a room with his wife and two children. During a depressed period of the economy, the uncle was working in another small rubber factory and was living in a corner of the warehouse with his family. Mr. Fuchino subsequently took a job as a laborer.

There are some people in our sample who admit to being addicted to taking chances and gambling as a means to success. In case D-20, for example, Mr. Tayama describes his attitudes about gambling and relates them to attitudes he saw in his own father, whom he describes as also having been addicted to gambling. Mr. Tayama spends considerable time and money betting on horses and on bicycle races, and he plays Mah-Jongg far into the night. When his boy entered primary school, he did not have enough money to equip him with the barest necessities, such as notebooks, a school uniform, shoes, and the like, and so Mr. Tayama went to the cycle race. As he reports it, he bet ¥800 and won ¥4,000, which he spent on his son.

It is likely that Mr. Tayama's occupational vicissitudes were indeed sometimes related to gambling, although some of his stories are almost incoherent or are unfinished as he moves to another topic. He describes having once been hired by a coal dealer to carry coal and eventually becoming a salesman and working hard selling coal for about a year and a half, but he did not stay on this job. He says:

> I became fed up with my employer who, after all, did not recognize my ability. I was working for him as a manager. I should have stayed there. He was a nice man. It was a nice job. I usually was very lucky and could find a

> good place to work. Once I asked my employer to give me an advance of salary of ¥5,000 because I needed money badly. I had been fond of cycle racing. I had been lucky with it also. While I was riding a tram car I took out of my pocket a newspaper which reported all the results of the races. I had put the envelope containing my advance salary in the same pocket. When I took out the newspaper the envelope fell out of my pocket and was lost.

Mr. Tayama did not continue telling the story, although he seemed to have started it as an explanation of why he had quit work with the charcoal dealer. He seems to have left a subsequent job as a furniture dealer because, as he claims, he was not put on a regular monthly salary. Some of his jobs as he describes them seem to be of dubious honesty. At one point he and someone else were selling concrete garbage containers for a group who pretended that they had been sent as distributors by the Tokyo city office and that the containers were to be officially adopted to hold garbage. This approach made people feel obligated to buy. He claims that he worked at this business for two years, making a very easy profit. Sometimes he took days off and spent them at the races because he did so well on other days. Mr. Tayama finally decided to get out of this business because he didn't want trouble with the police nor did he want his children to "feel ashamed of their father" for working in a "shady business." In one sense, one might say that this man's ambivalence about regular work and self-regulation is reflected in the delinquency of his own son.

Attitudes about regularity in work are related to attitudes about authority. Mr. Fukuhara's gambling attitude (D-8) is evident in other sections of his interviews. He has had a very spotty occupational career with a number of changes of jobs, which he accounts for in terms of his ambitions:

> It is not that I can't stick to one thing. Probably I am an ambitious man. I have always had a wish to "hit the jackpot" [*hitoyama ateru*]. When my wife complained, I used to tell her that at least once or twice everybody can grab an opportunity; there is no way to see ahead or to find out when the chance will come. We must keep trying.

In the course of the interviews we found that at one time he did try some kind of entrepreneurial activity in which he lost from ¥500,000 to ¥600,000, a failure he describes as "not having caused too much unhappiness to others." The impression one gains is that he borrowed and lost other people's money as well as his own, but he says, "I didn't cause much trouble to others. After all, I think I am not a very lucky person."

This case is cited not because it is representative of the attitude about chance and gambling, but to stress that most Japanese do not emphasize the gambling aspect of their entrepreneurial activities. Although Mr. Fukuhara tells us about his entrepreneurial attempt as if it were a kind of blind gamble with fate in which he was unsuccessful, such attitudes do not seem to characterize Japanese small entrepreneurs generally, but indicate a deviancy in social attitudes.

As was already indicated, a number of men reacted to a financial crisis, not by gambling of one kind or another, but by becoming emotionally depressed or apathetic. Others reacted "psychosomatically," becoming physically ill, and one gets the impression that their physical ailment gave them a final excuse to give up lifelong efforts to "make it."

CHAPTER 7

Attitudes toward Responsibility and Authority

Social role obligations are the essential components of the Japanese sense of responsibility. The word "responsibility" (*sekinin*) in Japanese often has negative emotional connotations that are not felt quite similarly in the West. Japanese have learned to avoid committing themselves to responsibility unnecessarily, since a person who is responsible assumes all the blame when anything goes wrong, no matter what his own culpability may have been. Japanese internalize social control. Social hierarchy for them does not signify external constraint or domination. They see the police not as an extraneous force imposed on them but as symbols of legitimate authority.

RESPONSIBILITY AND OBLIGATION IN JAPANESE CULTURE

This sense of responsibility in Japan is the residue of the familism of the past in which the individual ego was not differentiated from an intense sense of family belonging shared by each person, whatever his particular position within the family or organization. In employment relationships also, workers in Arakawa today still tend to identify in a familial sense with the boss, assuming the operation of a reciprocal relationship that goes far beyond that found in Western "paternalistic" practices. The boss is not an oppressor but a means of livelihood sometimes unrealistically perceived as a benefactor.

In the Japanese family it has been and still is the mother who is "responsible" for bringing up the children. Traditionally, this has meant that when children acted in an improper way or committed some delinquent act, it was the mother who made apology to others for the behavior of the child. Often, when the perpetrator of some shocking crime, such as murder or a bank robbery, is apprehended, the mother of the criminal (more frequently than the father) is quoted in the newspaper as saying that she feels very sorry (*mōshiwake ga nai*) for her son's behavior. A mother may feel impelled to make a public apology, taking full responsibility for her son.

Japanese children know implicitly that they can cause their mother pain through her sharp sense of responsibility. Such knowledge often leads in consciously explicit terms to the inhibition of improper behavior outside the family.

However, some of the case history material from families with delinquents documents that there are mothers who do not feel compelled to be thoroughly vigilant and responsible for their children.

Self-Control as Responsibility

Traditional sex roles differed in the degree of "self-control" that was expected. A few men in our sample are impulsive to the point of violence with members of their own family. However prevalent such behavior within the family may have been in the traditional culture, it was not matched by freedom to behave impulsively in outside relationships, and women were expected to restrain their feelings of anger or discord in their relations with both husband and children. As a whole, role requirements of both male and female put strong emphasis on maintaining self-control so as not to bring any injury from the outside upon one's family.

The practice of self-control in role behavior in Japan differs from that in the West in that Japanese depend heavily on mechanisms of *suppression*, whereas Western Europeans and Americans tend to practice *repression*. That is to say, Japanese are often totally aware of their underlying emotional stress when these emotions are not appropriate to expected role behavior, but they choose to suppress them. In certain circumstances, Westerners control emotions by modes of unconscious repression buttressed by a strong value placed on the maintenance of "rational" behavior. Japanese in similar circumstances are often painfully aware of their own inner feelings and highly sensitive to the feelings of others, but the "self-control" demanded by the expected role requires them to maintain a blandness of surface behavior that Westerners often consider "inscrutable." Westerners expect behavior to be more or less in accord with underlying spontaneous feelings and consider that to behave otherwise is insincere. The Japanese concept of sincerity, in contrast, is the maintenance of behavior that is fully in accord with what is required by the individual's role. Needless to say, the Japanese understand and are aware of one another's covert attitudes in spite of the surface control, whether the hidden feelings are intense anger or profound sorrow. They often refer to the surface role behavior as *tatemae* and to the hidden feelings as *honne*. In order to cope successfully with others in Japanese society, one must be capable of differentiating between *tatemae* and *honne*.

Covert patterns are hard to document; nevertheless, in our life histories we believe we can demonstrate critical differences in the exercise of authority related to delinquency formation.

Authority and Control in the Japanese Family

Many who read about Japanese authoritarianism assume simply that Japan was traditionally a hierarchical society in which the individual on top made the decisions and took the initiative. Both in the external political sphere and within the family or household, this is rarely true. Decisions are very often collective efforts "on behalf of" the family or the company head. If a person in such a head position too often counters the collective will of his subordinates, who in many circumstances take initiatives that would not be acceptable in the West, he may lose his power base entirely through the withdrawal of active support by his subordinates or through some sort of silent resistance that makes it difficult to continue functioning. In actuality, therefore, the distribution of power in Japanese society is a complex matter. It is well known in Japanese political history that the person in the official role was very often controlled by his "advisers" or by "retired" individuals who continued to manipulate events. Much as in the performance of a drama, the actual direction took place behind the scenes while the audience observed only the role performances on stage.

It is often thought that Japanese women generally were relegated to servile subordinate roles in which their behavior continually symbolized their inferior social positions vis-à-vis men. What is overlooked when only overt behavior is observed is the operation of actual control of the family by women within the household. No matter what the real dynamics of the family, women always carefully deferred to men in accordance with role requirements, just as a powerful regent defers to the royal figurehead on the throne.

Recent trends toward a more overt expression of latent dominance on the part of women are more apt to appear in urban lower-class families, as is well illustrated in the case histories herein reported, in which women as well as men are less restricted by status considerations than in middle-class families, and therefore are more likely to give freer vent to emotional expressions, whether of a sexual or an aggressive nature. The surface appearance of strong-willed wives and dependent husbands is not, however, entirely a product of any postwar "emancipation" of Japanese women or of any such sociological factor as the effect of industrialization on the whole society. One can find in the traditional culture many comic stories and anecdotes (called *rakugo*) about the common people's life in the Tokugawa period which describe an impulsive and somewhat careless husband as a foil to his more realistic, practical, and dependable wife. It is clear in all these anecdotes that the so-called boss is, in actuality, the "dependent" marital partner.

Dominant or submissive role behavior and dominant or submissive personality structure are independent of each other. A sample of 800 records of Rorschach tests administered in both rural and urban communities in Japan by De Vos and others (Muramatsu, 1962; Murakami, 1959) revealed no basic, significant, consistent structural differences in personality between Japanese men and women. The general results would indicate that the distribution of personality traits through processes of socialization, including identification, does not lead to obvious personality differences corresponding to the obvious Japanese dichotomy in observed social sex-role behavior. Hence we would assume that in the past, as in the present, there was no significant difference between men and women in Japan in the incidence or distribution of structural traits of personality, in basic active or passive attitudes, dominant and submissive needs, and the like. Hence, while a dominant man can directly assert himself readily within the behavioral prerogatives of the male role, a potentially dominant woman has to find some indirect means of self-expression of dominance within the narrow strictures of acceptable female role behavior. A potentially dominant woman learns to manipulate susceptible men in such a way that they are often totally unaware they are "deciding" in accordance with the woman's wishes. A dependent male child naturally is most susceptible to the exercise of a nurturant control on the part of a mother.

The role of the paternal grandmother is one of the key points of tension in traditional Japanese family life. Tensions arise out of the harsh dominance with which a mother-in-law very often exercises control over a powerless in-marrying daughter-in-law, and also arise out of the way she manipulates the dependent-nurturant ties that are maintained between herself as mother and her favorite adult son. There is, in essence, a competition for the husband that even today is only infrequently won by the wife, and then only in situations in which the mother no longer lives with the nuclear family. The defeated wife in turn learns quickly to play the game when she herself has propensities for dominance; she shifts her affective needs and emotional requirements from her husband to her growing children. The inherent power of the role of the mother-in-law, therefore, is such that many major decisions within the family and sometimes even outside the family are subject to her control.

The paternal grandfather, conversely, plays a minor, somewhat withdrawn role in many families. In some he may express an almost maternal kind of nurturance toward the young. If he is a sufficiently dominant personality, however, he will continue to exercise control in business matters even after his "retirement."

The power exercised within the Japanese family in the past was always in the name of the preservation of lineage and the enhancement of family status. Therefore, the family head was never considered to be in a position of true personal power but was regarded more as an inheritor of a role through which power was exercised for family benefit. A family head who was a dominant person would exercise personal direction of the other members of his family, whereas a more passive person, if not totally inadequate, would heed "suggestions" made directly to him.

QUANTITATIVE RATINGS OF PARENTAL DISCIPLINE AND RESPONSIBILITY

The families of delinquents show some significant differences from the nondelinquent controls in respect to patterns of role expectations related both to parental responsibility and to the exercise of authority and control.

Table 4.2 demonstrated that overall ratings on the Glueck variables were strikingly different for the three groups. We shall elaborate here how the quantitative findings specifically related to parental discipline, supervision, and re-

TABLE 7.1
Ratings of Parental Discipline and Responsibility

	Normals		Social Delinquents		Isolate Delinquents		Total Delinquents	
	Fa (19)	Mo (19)	Fa (20)	Mo (20)	Fa (11)	Mo (11)	Fa (31)	Mo (31)
RIGIDITY								
OK or not reported	13	16	17	16	9	4	26	20
Negative	4	3	3	3	1	5	4	8
Very negative	2	0	0	1	1	2	1	3
LAXITY								
OK or not reported	15	16	6	10	5	7	11	17
Negative	3	3	10	3	5	3	15	9
Very negative	1	0	4	4	1	1	5	5
PHYSICAL ABUSE								
OK or not reported	12	17	11	11	5	6	16	17
Negative	6	2	4	7	3	3	7	10
Very negative	1	0	5	2	3	2	8	4
INCONSISTENCY OR FAVORITISM								
OK or not reported	16	19	14	12	8	7	22	19
Negative	3	0	5	5	3	2	8	7
Very negative	0	0	1	3	0	2	1	5
TOTAL ONE OR MORE ADVERSE TRAITS PRESENT PER PARENT								
None reported	11	15	0	1	1	1	1	2
One present	5	4	7	8	3	1	10	9
Two or more present	3	0	13	11	7	9	20	20

X^2 (Yates correction):

N Fa. vs. Total Del. Fa.
Laxity $P < .01$
Lt. trait $P < .001$

N Mo. vs. Total Del. Mo.
Laxity $P < .05$
Phys. $P < .02$
Favor. $P < .001$
Lt. trait $P < .001$

Total Del Fa vs. Total Del. Mo.
Laxity $P < .05$

sponsibility compared in our samples. Then we shall give illustrative material from the case histories.

The overall Glueck scores of maternal supervision and parental discipline reported in table 4.2 were derived from the more specific ratings reported in tables 7.1, 7.2, and 7.3 in this chapter. In attempting to arrive at overall quantitative ratings of paternal discipline and maternal supervision, we first separately considered four variables and rated each parent in relation to them: rigid attitudes related to discipline; laxity of discipline or supervision; physical punishment or abuse in the discipline of a child by either parent; and inconsistency and favoritism in the treatment of the delinquent subject and his siblings (see table 7.1).

In addition to those four variables, we noted boys' complaints about the

TABLE 7.2
Boys' Complaints about "Nagging" Parents or Presence of Negative Attitude toward Parental Discipline

	Normals		*Social Delinquents*		*Isolate Delinquents*		*Total Delinquents*	
	Fa (19)	Mo (19)	Fa (20)	Mo (20)	Fa (11)	Mo (11)	Fa (31)	Mo (31)
OK or not reported	17	16	15	11	7	4	22	15
Negative	1	3	4	7	3	4	7	11
Very negative	1	0	1	2	1	3	2	5

Yates correction:
N Mo. vs. Total Del. Mo.: $P < .01$

TABLE 7.3
Ratings of Possible Presence of "Superego Lacunae" in Regard to Parents' Rebelliousness, Sexual Irregularities, and Legal Irregularities

	Normals		*Social Delinquents*		*Isolate Delinquents*		*Total Delinquents*	
Traits Present in Parent	Fa (19)	Mo (19)	Fa (20)	Mo (20)	Fa (11)	Mo (11)	Fa (31)	Mo (31)
REBELLION								
None reported	18	17	13	14	8	8	21	22
Present	1	2	7	6	3	3	10	9
SEXUAL IRREGULARITIES								
None reported	18	19	19	17	11	7	30	24
Present	1	0	1	3	0	4	1	7
LEGAL IRREGULARITIES								
None reported	17	19	17	17	10	10	27	27
Present	2	0	3	3	1	1	4	4
TOTALS								
None reported	16	17	8	9	8	6	16	15
Present	3	2	12	11	3	5	15	16

X^2 (Yates correction):

N. Fa. vs. Total Fa.		N Mo. vs. Total Del. Fa.	
Reb.	$P < .05$	Sex	$P < .05$
Lt. trait	$P < .05$	Lt. trait	$P < .01$

"nagging" of parents (see table 7.2). (No other attitude expressed in the interviews came out consistently enough to have us attempt quantitative comparison.) We therefore assessed the manner and content of parental supervision, as seen through the eyes of the subjects, only in regard to their dislike of what in various ways was described as "nagging."

Finally, in regard to supervision and discipline, we attempted to assess "superego lacunae" (Johnson, 1949; Johnson and Szurek, 1952) by using either the reports of parents about their previous behavior or our judgments of their implicit attitudes toward authority as expressed in the course of the interviews. We tried to assess both parents as to the possible presence of underlying as well as overt rebellious attitudes that could in one way or another be communicated in child-parent relationships. We also noted all reports of possible irregular sexual behavior and illegal activities in occupational or financial dealings (see table 7.3). In all three of these tables the differences between the nondelinquent and the delinquent sample are striking.

Differences in Rigidity or Laxity

In comparing the ratings we gave the fathers in our judgment of their rigid or lax behavior toward their sons, we found no significant differences between the fathers of the nondelinquent subjects and those of delinquents. However, our assessment of "rigidity" scores obtained from the Rorschach records showed significantly higher scores for the delinquent samples. The Rorschach test results (see Appendix A) contrasted with our ratings based on interview data, which tended (nonsignificantly) to assess a higher proportion of fathers of the normal subjects as strict or even rigid in their discipline, compared with the fathers of delinquents. Conversely, our personal ratings for laxity of the fathers of delinquents were higher than from the Rorschach tests. We rated 20 of the total of 30 fathers of delinquents as lax in discipline, compared with 4 out of 19 of the fathers of nondelinquents. In assessing our own ratings of rigidity and laxity, we must note that we rated inconsistent or abusive behavior as counterindicative of rigidity. We now question these criteria. Nevertheless, generally speaking, our ratings show that the fathers of delinquent subjects paid less steady attention and gave less sustained supervision to their sons than did the fathers of nondelinquents.

The mothers of isolate delinquents manifested the highest of our ratings for rigidity, whereas the mothers of social delinquents and the normal controls did not differ significantly from each other. The mothers of social delinquents in half the cases (10 out of 20) were rated by us as revealing inappropriate laxity of supervision compared with 4 out of 11 in the isolate delinquent cases and 3 out of 19 in the normal controls. Our assessment of "laxity" overlapped considerably with our criteria for "rejection" and "neglect," which we shall discuss in chapter 9. Indeed, it is impossible to separate our ratings for "laxity" from what we considered indicative of some form of neglect or rejection.

Ratings of Physical Abuse, Inconsistency, and Favoritism

Contrary to the general impression that avoidance of "physical" discipline is characteristic for Japanese mothers, there were reported to us, in our total of 50 families, 16 mothers who admitted to periodically striking their children as a means of discipline, and it is significant that 14 of these 16 were the mothers of delinquents. Twenty-two of 50 fathers said they struck their children at one time or another; 7 out of 19 were fathers of nondelinquents, and 15 out of 31 were fathers of delinquents. There is no significant difference, therefore, between the two groups of fathers in this regard, whereas there is a strong significant difference between the delinquent and nondelinquent samples in the number of mothers who struck their sons. Although one must consider the possibility that physical abuse from a mother may be an act of desperation in response to a prior delinquent attitude in a boy, it is nevertheless safe to assume that often the use of physical punishment attests to the mother's incapacity to use other means of asserting authority effectively. In the individual cases, as we assessed them, the use of physical punishment was often linked to inconsistent discipline on the part of a parent who was somewhat lax, but who, at a point of crisis, sought to assert authority by physical dominance over a child.

We rated 9 fathers and 12 mothers of the 30 families of delinquents as showing inconsistent behavior or blatant favoritism toward other children, and only 3 fathers and no mothers in the nondelinquent sample of 19. The illustrative cases cited below dramatize the various types of inconsistent attitudes toward the exercise of authority. They are in some respects the opposite side of the same coin shown in table 7.3, which tabulates problems of internalizing authority as evidenced in the ratings of unresolved rebelliousness in particular parents. As the totals in table 7.1 indicate, only 1 father and 2 mothers of delinquent subjects were not rated adversely in some manner, whereas over half the parents of nondelinquents (according to reported evidence) showed no signs of inappropriate discipline or supervision.

Ratings of "Nagging"

We used the boys' description of the disciplinary attitudes of their parents to rate the use of physical punishment. (Some boys did not report physical punishment, whereas their parents did.) The only other consistent descriptions in the boys' records were vaguely defined statements or complaints about the nagging of a father or a mother. We found that such statements occurred significantly more frequently in the delinquent subjects (see table 7.2). Nine out of 31 fathers were accused somewhere in the delinquent boys' interviews of some form of nagging or harrassment about behavior, and only 2 out of 19 fathers in the nondelinquent group. Sixteen out of 31 mothers of delinquents were accused of some form of nagging, and only 3 out of 19 mothers in the nondelinquent sample. These complaints by the boys were very diffuse and reflected a feeling of dissatisfaction with the adequacy of parental discipline.

Evidence of "Superego Lacunae"

As table 7.3 demonstrates, approximately one-third of the fathers of delinquent subjects showed some form of rebellious attitude toward authority, whereas only one father was similarly rated in the nondelinquent group. Two mothers of nondelinquents out of 19, and 9 mothers of delinquents out of 31, showed rebellious attitudes either in their previous behavior or in their current statements.

Our ratings of what is socially unsanctioned sexual behavior of one kind or another is influenced by the prevailing Japanese double standard. We did not rate youthful visits to prostitutes or premarital sexuality as irregular on the part of males. Our rating of "irregular" sexual behavior for men is thus quite low. We show only 1 father of a nondelinquent and 1 of a delinquent as exhibiting irregular forms of sexual behavior. Seven out of 31 mothers of delinquents and no mothers of nondelinquents have demonstrated some form of irregular sexuality, by Japanese standards. It is noteworthy that 4 of 11 mothers of isolate delinquents have reported such activities.

Totaling the evidence of one or more "superego lacunae" as we defined it, we found that approximately half the parents of delinquents showed one or another sign, compared with only 3 out of 19 fathers and 2 out of 19 mothers of delinquents. This difference is highly significant. The various subcategories of "superego lacunae," we believe, are symbolically indicative of basic attitudes toward external authority; they are evidence of a lack of complete internalization of the superego in line with usual standards of conformity to Japanese norms.

Ratings on "illegal" activity are, as we have said, governed by Japanese standards. We did not include simple postwar black-market activities, but we took note of any other kind of shady illegal transaction reported to us. We found no significant differences in our groups in this respect, though obviously individuals tend to be self-protective in revealing activities of this nature.

We initially attempted to record any reported involvement in crime by extended family members, but the facts as reported to us did not permit any satisfactory judgments in this regard. Aside from a few cases of black-market activities, no cases of criminal acts were reported by the nondelinquent group. Only four cases of criminal behavior on the part of the parents' brothers, their spouses, and other close relatives were reported in this delinquent sample. The few cases of black-market involvement were reported equally by delinquent and nondelinquent families. In the postwar social disorganization, black-market activities were a semilegal means of survival for many lower-class people.

We noted several cases of habitual gambling in the records of families of delinquents, but the numbers were too small for statistical treatment. Alcoholism in Japan does not constitute a social problem that draws psychiatric and public attention to the degree that it does in American society. However, we did find a considerable number of cases of heavy drinking in our sample, most of them among the families of delinquent children (see table 7.4). The consequence of heavy drinking in some of these families was the economic breakdown of the family, and in some, family dissolution. The evidence in some cases shows that excessive drinking was symptomatic of lack of proper discipline or supervision of children.

TABLE 7.4
Incidence of Excessive Drinking

	Normals	*Social Delinquents*	*Isolate Delinquents*
Excessive Drinking within Families	(19)	(20)	(11)
Total number of families reporting excessive drinking of a member	10	16	7
Total number of families reporting excessive drinking in both paternal and maternal grandparents	0	5	0
Excessive Drinking by Individuals			
Husband's father (HF)	2	10	2
Husband (H)	5	8	4
Wife's father (WF)	6	8	4
Wife's mother (WM)	0	1	0
Wife (W)	0	1	0
Generational Continuity of Drinking			
	2 HF-H	1 HF-WF-H-W	1 HF-H
		1 HF-WF-H	2 WF-H
	1 WF-H	2 HF-H	
		1 WF-H	

ATTITUDES TOWARD RESPONSIBILITY AND AUTHORITY: ILLUSTRATIVE ANECDOTES

We find it relatively easy to demonstrate the considerable ambivalence in some of the women interviewed toward accepting the roles of wife and mother. It may be assumed that their expressed attitudes had considerable influence on how they exercised supervisory functions with their children. Problems of inadequate discipline on the part of fathers, again, seem to be related directly to unresolved difficulties over the meaning of the authority role. There are a few cases in which negative attitudes toward authority and parental constraint on the part of both parents possibly served as covert inducements to delinquent behavior on the part of a child.

Sexual acting-out can be indicative of unresolved attitudes about responsibility and authority. There are more frequent family disruptions related to impulsive behavior in the parents of the delinquent group than in the nondelinquent group. Episodes of irregular sexuality and deviant behavior are not only relevant in the present context of unresolved attitudes about responsibility and authority, but must also be considered in the context of family cohesiveness or discord, discussed in the following chapter. Sexual irregularities and chronic drunken behavior also relate to feelings of neglect and deprivation experienced by children. We can, it seems, separate these topics for presentation only artificially. The various topics of authority and responsibility, harmony and discord, affiliation and nurturance, neglect and deprivation are all interrelated in the following anecdotes.

Continuities in Problems with "Superego Lacunae"

Some parents recognize that there is a relationship between their difficulties with their own parents and the fact that they somehow seem unable to control their children or to discipline them properly. For example, in case D-7, Mrs. Fudasaka told the interviewer several times that she "deserved to have a son" like the subject, since she herself had not behaved properly toward her parents. She kept reiterating how "bad" she had been to them when she was young, but she did not make clear what this bad behavior had been. In giving her life history, however, she indicated that she had run away from home to stay with her elder sister for more than a year and a half. She also described herself as a "naughty child," and some material she offered could imply sexual irregularities during adolescence. Her record, in any case, shows her continuing ambivalence between rebellion and conformity and her concern with lack of internalized standards. She herself relates her own trouble with her parents to her function as a mother, and her ambivalence about authority relates also to her expressed dissatisfaction in marriage. (See other examples in the section on role rejection, below.)

There is ample evidence in our case history material, as well as some indirect evidence in the projective tests, that a principal discrimination between the families producing delinquent children and those producing nondelinquents can be made in terms of basic attitudes toward authority and the general acceptance of social constraints. These are differences recognizable in patterns of internalization or in readiness to conform. It is obvious in our sample that parents who have not resolved their attitudes toward some acceptance of authority are extremely poor in disciplining and supervising their children. Some parents frankly admit that their children's problems are related to their own deviant behavior. In other families we find no direct evidence of deviancy in the parental case histories; nevertheless, the parents manifest difficulties in disciplining their children.

Family Continuity in Antisocial Attitudes

Case D-20, the Tayama family, well illustrates the continuity of negative attitudes and behavior from parent to child. The father and mother in this case were frank in discussing their own antisocial attitudes. We found an explicit continuity in enuresis between father and son. (Enuresis is a condition frequently found in delinquent subjects; see chapter 9). Mr. Tayama, in talking about the fact that his son was enuretic until he was a fifth-grader, mentioned that as a child he himself had wet his bed until he was in the sixth grade. He seems to have had considerable conflict with his mother over this problem. He remembers that as a child he used to feel closer to his father than to his mother, who was strict and often nagged her children when they failed to keep themselves neat and clean. He says that his own present preoccupation with neatness and cleanliness comes from his mother. However, his attitude toward his son about bed-wetting is more tolerant than that of his wife, who says, "In order to prevent the boy from wetting the bed I used to wake him up several times during the night and take him to the toilet." The father says:

> My wife woke up my child very frequently, but I told her that if she had our boy urinate frequently and a little at a time his bladder would not develop and enuresis would continue. My mother did the same to me, which I don't think helped the situation, because the habit developed of urinating a little at a time and frequently. I often told my wife not to be strict about it. After all, a child is a child. It can't be helped. As I had the same experience in bed-wetting myself, I am more understanding than my wife.

Mr. Tayama very frankly discusses his love of gambling, his frequent job changes, his difficulties with authorities—which he usually rationalizes as their being "inconsiderate" of him in one way or another. He obviously has had a very labile work record, frequently changing jobs, and he has participated in some shady dealings. Yet, as he describes what he does, he often stresses that he is well aware of the example he must set for his child. He tells that he was a wild, aggressive child who fought other children, and, with a certain relish, that his relatives always considered him hard to control. In one interview he sees himself as having always been self-assertive and never hesitating to say what he thought, but in a subsequent interview he says he never was able to assert himself very much or carry through his opinions in the presence of others.

A series of interviews with this man revealed continual inconsistencies in self-image and in his descriptions of his disciplining of his children. He saw his own father as a physically violent man who sometimes hit his mother with a bamboo stick, and who once hit him when he was being carried by his mother on her back. And yet, at other times he tells how his father loved him and showed his love by concern for his welfare, describing in emotional terms how his father once put his feet in lukewarm water when he came home from school with frozen feet. He remembers a number of instances in his childhood when he stole from others or went against authority, sometimes at the implicit request of his mother or father. He describes his own childhood as one of extreme impoverishment. It is obvious from his description of his parents that he considered them somewhat loose in their concepts of legality.

> When I was in the first grade people were building a house right near ours, and there was much lumber and pieces of wood piled up. Our family was very poor. At night I went and collected scrap pieces of wood for firewood, climbing around the partly finished building. I made some noise and a supervisor came out to question what was going on. Hearing his shouting, I became upset and jumped down to the ground in the darkness, hitting my chest badly. I was sick for quite a while afterward. It had been suggested implicitly by my mother (she did not tell me openly) to go there and pick up wood. She would repeat often, as if talking to no one, that nobody would use those pieces of wood anyway and yet, for such a poor family as ours, having a day's supply of firewood free of charge would make a lot of difference. I thought that Mother was actually wanting me to go out and collect wood.

Describing the discipline of his own son, he says:

> When he was a child I often hit him. I often lifted him and dropped him [laughs]. I treated him fairly harshly, but he never got hurt. Once I hit him on the head with a piece of wood and made a cut on his forehead. This happened twice, if I remember correctly. . . . But since he started going to junior high school I have not scolded him at all. He is already in the stage where he understands. If I would stand up to him, he would stop fighting with his sister; however, he is no longer at the stage where parents can scare a child. It was the same with me and my parents. I was small, I was often scolded, although I do not remember being hit. But after I finished sixth grade, my parents never complained about me at all because I was already at the stage where I could make my own judgment.

Mrs. Tayama also says that her husband used to be much more punitive toward his children than he is at the present time. When he came home from a job or from job-hunting in a bad mood and found his children asleep with unclean hands or legs, he would become furious and wake them all up by smacking them and order them to wash themselves. The husband states that after spending several years in the army, he could not tolerate "sloppiness." Recently he has simply ignored the children's bad behavior, and even when his son fights violently with the elder sister, and the mother vainly tries to stop them, he does not bother to interrupt the fight. The daughter's version of the family situation is this:

> It's not quite that we obey my father because we're afraid of him. After all, he understands us; he scolds us, but he also does many things for us. We can't obey somebody who simply nags and doesn't do anything for us [the mother]. Although my father nags and scolds us, he always does things, so we feel he is right.

This daughter seems to imply that her mother doesn't set a good example and that she and her sister can't willingly obey her, since she is inconsistent and nagging. All the children seem to be more positive toward their father than toward their mother. It must be noted that the subject in our case is not the only one in the family who steals; a younger brother, ten years old, has already stolen money and has had a number of police contacts. The father's mixed attitude about stealing is apparent in the following:

> There's nothing to worry about Ichirō [the teenage delinquent]. But we have a headache with our second son. As he is the youngest child, nobody paid much attention to him and left him alone to do what he wanted. Maybe he was spoiled that way. The other day I received a telephone call from the Asakusa police station. I was told they had my boy in custody. I went to take him home.
>
> He had been playing with a boy who was younger than he; this boy's parents completely neglected this child. Anyway, they went into the toy store where there was a box containing some money. My son grabbed a hundred yen out of the money chest and escaped. The younger friend also wanted to have some money. My son told him to go into the store and help himself, so this younger boy went into the store and came back with all the money he found in the money chest, about ¥8,000. That was too much, but they reasoned that if he returned the money to the store he would be caught, so they decided to split the money. Hiding most of the money under a garbage box, they spent some every day on toys. They finally managed to spend it all. Then they went back again to the store to get some more money. This time the storekeeper was alert, and they were caught. Our son said it was not he who took all the money, thereby revealing his own deed. He should have kept his mouth shut; by talking he was found out. It's almost like a joke. He should've kept his mouth shut when he was caught. After all, he's just a kid.

One notes here the "superego lacunae" of the father in describing the incident. He also went on to say that both he and his wife had noticed the son's expensive toys and wondered where he got them, but they never pressed him to explain. The mother's attitude is full of rejection and indifference. She tries to sound supportive about her son's finishing school, but at the same time she reveals doubt about what good it would do.

> As he is a boy, I would like to let him finish his high school education, however financially hard it may be for us. Even if I wished more concretely for my son to go into a particular occupation, it is not at all clear how much ability he has. As long as he can live like an ordinary person and he can make a salary as an average person, I wouldn't expect more than that.

The mother admits that she can't make her children obey her.

> They don't listen to me. When they were small children, my husband used to give them very harsh physical punishment. Therefore, they

> listened to him and obeyed him, but I rarely punished them physically but only scolded them by words. As they knew that I would not punish them physically, I cannot now make them obey me. My husband has recently stopped scolding them, so I have to tell them what to do and what not to do, but they rarely listen to me. I wish my husband would scold them at least occasionally. . . .
>
> When he was a small child our boy rarely hit others, but recently he has been hitting others with a wooden stick. He doesn't listen when I stop him and I have even tried to hit him a few times; I couldn't control myself. When he gets into an argument with his sister, his sister gets the better of him, so he gets mad, hits her on the head, on the leg, or anywhere with whatever he has in his hands at the moment. His sister fights back, and a real fight starts in our small house.
>
> I don't know why they have to fight. I have no experience, because I grew up alone. I want to stop them. As they don't listen to me, I hit them; then they cry and stop fighting.

The fighting with his sisters seems to have increased since the boy's puberty, and the mother is somewhat concerned that the fighting has some sexual meaning. Both parents say they believe the children are aware of the parents' sexual intercourse and that it might have aroused their sexual curiosity. They note that the subject "often sticks his hands underneath the skirts of his sisters or touches their bodies." The mother notes that the second son seems to show an aggressive tendency toward toys and small animals:

> Perhaps he likes to see the insides. Whatever toys we buy for him, he dissects them all. Some toys you can reassemble, but others you can't. He breaks up all the toys we give him, not only the toys but also small fish. When Ichirō catches fish and keeps them in the bowl, Jirō opens up the fish and pulls the insides out. He pulls out the eyes from goldfish and puts them in another goldfish or something of that kind. He catches dragonflies, take their heads off or sticks a match into the tail. He does things of that kind. He seems to enjoy it, although we try to stop him. He does terrible things to small animals, cutting them open and into pieces.

The older boy, Ichirō, shows tremendous ambivalence toward his father and his discipline. Although both parents say that recently the father has hit none of the children, the boy claims that at least once or twice a week he receives a beating from his father. He states, however, that the father very often misses because he is able to avoid him and run away outside. The father chases him, but the boy usually succeeds in hiding himself. He stays outside until late at night and then sneaks into the house and into bed, and usually the father doesn't say anything more about it. He says he was always hit by his father at least once a day as punishment when he was small. When he received severe punishment from his father, the boy often got angry and thought of running away. Especially in the summer, he would sometimes stay away from home the night following a physical attack. He slept a few times in the truck of a lumber company and would go directly to school without returning home. Sometimes his mother came to look for him, and he would whistle to her to let her know where he was hiding. Sometimes one of his elder sisters came to take him home, but when he didn't want to go home he would insist on staying away. Very frequently on these occasions the mother would come to the boy the next morning with a lunch box, and he would eat his breakfast before going to school. Occasionally in winter he would go to a newspaper store for which he was working as a delivery boy, and the proprietor would let him stay overnight. There were several other boys, whose houses were far away from the store, and they used to sleep together.

And yet, withal, Ichirō states that he likes his father, especially recently. He also says that his father makes jokes and talks humorously and makes everybody laugh. He says neither of his parents cares whether he goes to school or not. He likes to read books and magazines about airplanes, jet planes, and battleships. When the interviewer asked him what he wanted to become in the future, he said he didn't know. He likes battleships and he likes war, and he thinks it would be wonderful to be a jet-plane pilot. When the interviewer asked if he did not want to be like his father, he said he didn't, because there was nothing good about his father. Then immediately afterwards he stated that his father was a sergeant after the war and that occasionally he wishes he could enter the Japanese Defense Corps and be promoted to a higher rank than his father's. In contrast to his picture of his father, he sees his mother as "gentle," since she never hits him.

Ichirō describes his delinquency as mainly of a group type, and yet his statements in regard to friends are contradictory. He likes to go to movies and says he sees at least two different movies every week, but he doesn't like to go to movies with his friends. On a holiday he sometimes goes on his bicycle to a scientific museum in Uneo Park, more often alone than with friends. He says he does not like his friends very much, but when he was asked if he had good friends, he said he has three very close friends. When he was in the first and second grades he was often the leader of a group of kids who acted aggressively and broke windows and other things in the school building. He says he was a *gaki-daishō*.[1] When he broke windows at school, the damage was reported to his parents, and the parents had to pay for replacements. He was then beaten by his father. He broke a broomstick at school and was scolded by his teacher, receiving slaps on his cheek. This made him feel angry with his teacher and made him want to quit school. At times he would stay at home, and his teacher had to come to fetch him back to school. When he was in the first year of junior high school, he admits he used to disrupt the class, acting up before his friends for

1. *Gaki* in its original meaning was a starving soul in a Buddhist hell, related to the *pet* of present-day folk belief in Thailand. In Japan the word is still used colloquially without religious connotations. In the Japanese lower class, a complaining child (often a hungry one) came to be called *gaki*. Today the word *gaki* has completely lost its connotations of hunger and has become in colloquial lower-class terms much like the English word "kid." It is not much used by the middle class. *Daishō* is a general of the army. A *gaki-daishō* is a child, usually of mischievous behavior.

fun. The class teacher was a young woman, and Ichirō says, "I enjoyed being scolded by this teacher. I often misbehaved deliberately because I wanted to be scolded."

Ichirō states that since entering junior high school, he has come to like school better. He says that he'd rather be by himself than play with his friends. Nevertheless, he continues to go to recreational centers with those he calls his "best and closest" friends. Two or three times a month he goes roller-skating. He says he knows how to ride a motorbike as well as drive an automobile.

> Although I have not done it very recently, when I was in the second year of junior high school, I picked up a car key and rasped it until it fit into the tiny keyhole of a little pickup owned by a lumber company in the neighborhood. It was very difficult, but I succeeded in starting the motor. I would sneak into the car when nobody was around, would start the engine, throw it into gear, and move the car a little bit forward or backward—not very much, but it was fun.
>
> I knew a man who worked for the lumber company, and one day when he couldn't find his car key, I offered him mine. The man thus discovered who had been playing with the car, so I was severely scolded. Most of the junior high school students around here do the same things. They make their own passkeys for motorbikes owned by somebody they know so they can "borrow" the bicycle when the owner is not around, and they drive it slowly so the engine will not get heated and the "borrowing" be discovered. They drive the bicycle around for a short time and then return it to the place where it is stored.
>
> I did some shoplifting in a candy store when I was a fourth or fifth grader. I never was caught, but one of my classmates was caught while shoplifting and was reported to the teacher. This boy told the teacher that I had also done it, and I was called in by the teacher and also scolded. Although I usually did it alone, we exchanged our information and boasted about our success, so everybody knew what we did. There were about ten boys in my class who were doing this.
>
> Stealing was particularly fashionable when I was in sixth grade at school. It was a group activity; in the evening we would sneak into the school building and into the teacher's room and open the drawer that contained notebooks, papers, and pencils, and we would steal stationery from the school.
>
> In stealing from an ordinary store, we would gather together first and decide to hold a contest to find out who could steal the most without getting caught. We would set a time to get together again and would break up to go to various stores to do a job. We would come back with our loot and eat candies together, but if we stole some larger items, we would return them to the store. It was really fun, but after I learned that it was a bad thing to do, I stopped doing it.

When his sixth-grade teacher found out about Ichirō's shoplifting, he reported it to the boy's parents. The interviewer asked what his parents did to him. "Well, let me see. My mother said it was my business and I could do it if I really wanted to, but that I should stop because it was not good for me or something like that." When asked how he felt, he said:

> I listened to my mother and thought she was right. My father said that what I did had nothing to do with him. He said it was none of his business, but nevertheless he told me not to do so because I was his son. He said it was none of his business, but I should stop stealing because otherwise I would cause trouble to my family. I hated my father at that time because he said I should not do it, but I decided to quit because I thought that, after all, my father was right.

When asked why adults do not do such things, the boy's answer was "Because they are afraid of doing bad things, or even when they are not afraid of doing them they might be afraid of being thought badly of by their neighbors." This latter attitude again reveals that group sanctioning is expected to operate as a very strong motive for good behavior among Japanese.

The boy says that he sometimes lies to his parents. He feels that his parents have little interest in his schooling because neither of them ever attends PTA meetings.

When asked about girl friends, Ichirō admits to having one. (Most of our subjects did not admit to having girl friends.) His girl friend is not in the same class. She is "tall, friendly, kind, and gentle in heart." He says he is not sure if she is attractive or not. He also states that he never actually wants to go any place with her or with any other girl. He says that at school both girls and boys talk about one another and whom they like. Sometimes they even exchange letters in which they write jokingly such words as "love" and "yearning." But he says everybody laughs at this game and nobody takes it seriously.

There is certain evidence that this boy has a rather negative self-image. He says he sometimes wonders if he is not inferior to others, and he refers to himself as having "an empty head." He admits that his bad habits include failure at school. He knows that his teachers do not think much of him because of his tardiness and truancy. Throughout the TAT, he sees people as perplexed or in quandaries, unable to act.

In assessing this case, it seemed obvious to us that the parental discipline and supervision were grossly inadequate. In some part at least, Ichirō's delinquent behavior results from general intrafamilial attitudes that to some degree countenance his casual attitudes about the property of others.

Ambiguous Attitudes toward Authority

An ambiguous attitude toward authority is very clear in the Fuchino case, D-9. Both parents exert inconsistent discipline, and we sense their hostility toward the police for chastising their child. Mr. Fuchino said that when he discovered his child's theft, he hit him and kicked him and gave him relatively severe punishment, although "I didn't like doing it at all," and it seems that the wife also physically punished the child. Yet, in talking to the interviewer, the father reveals a strangely conflicting attitude toward authority and his child's antisocial behavior:

> I told the policeman that we were in the depths of poverty and our child wished to have some money. I asked him not to look at my son too negatively. [The implication was clear that he saw that poverty makes it natural for a child to want to steal.] When a child looks at an egg and feels tempted because he's almost starving, would you punish him? I would not. I would not notice his stealing an egg. By the same token, it would be probably all right, or at least it might have been not so serious, if my son stole things. But stealing cash is something different. It is serious.

The father in case I-7, Mr. Ishisaka, dismisses his son's delinquent behavior as inconsequential:

> After all, even when he does something wrong, it's not as bad as using a deadly weapon. After all, all he can do is do something sneaky. He can't do something really bad but only get involved in trifling things. He's a lazy child, but perhaps this is the disease of the city. This never happens to children in the countryside.

In case D-10 the mother's attitude toward her son's delinquency is very revealing of her own unconscious attitudes. Mrs. Fukitomi stated:

> I heard that it was a necklace my son took. I heard that other children who had gone there first took things like that and therefore my son, who went later, also stole. It so happened that they were watching the store the day he was there, and therefore it was he who was caught. [The implication is that he would not have been caught if others hadn't done it before him, and that it would have been all right to take it if he had not been caught.] It was a department store in Ikebukuro. Yes, he went there and did it, although I don't think he meant it. He had no bad intention. It was simply a mischievous act. He did not really want to have the necklace, but I think, somehow, his hand moved of itself toward it.

Later in another context she states:

> Yes, he also stole doves. Other children stole them first. My son went there afterwards and therefore he took one. A cop happened to come by. Therefore he was caught. I don't think it was worth making such a fuss. There are many other kids who do it more often, who do much worse things.

The word she used for police is a very rude and hostile form—*O-mawari*. The usual form of this word is *O-mawari-san* (Honorable Walk-about). Just saying *O-mawari* expresses a negative, aggressive attitude.

She also stated that when her son's case was sent to the child guidance center, she received a notice asking her to come for an interview. She did not go, "because people ask many bothering questions there and I didn't like the idea." She did not say how often she refused to go before being ordered to do so. In another context, when she was asked what was her principal concern about her son, she first said nothing, but when pressed further she said, "It is his not being studious." She stated then that the son does not like to study and is very negligent of homework. But she quickly went on:

> He does not study, because he does not like it, but you cannot force him to do work, because he has been like that since he was a first-grader. You can't change him so soon. He has never studied since entering school, but I think you can't force him. I don't see any point in forcing a child. It's certainly better if a child studies and likes to study—but after all, a child is a child. You cannot force a child when he does not like it. Accordingly, I'm just hoping that he will learn to live without bothering others too much.

Inconsistencies in Discipline

Those few fathers of delinquent subjects who admitted to some forms of antisocial behavior on their own part also revealed basic inconsistencies in the disciplining of their children. It is possible to see correlations between negative attitudes toward authority, inconsistent discipline of children, and some behavioral irregularities by the fathers in the past, although these correlations cannot be statistically demonstrated, because of the small sample.

Case I-6 demonstrates this pattern quite well. Mr. Ikuta was born in the entertainment district of downtown Tokyo. His father was an illegitimate child reared by an uncle, and his parents were running a prosperous toy shop at the time of the great earthquake and fire of 1923. As he describes it, the quake wiped out their toy business, but his father quickly started a wholesale ice business, which prospered for awhile. An informal union established among ice makers squeezed him out because he insisted on selling below the agreed-upon rate. (This evidence of a cartel among ice dealers is rather surprising, given the usual fiercely competitive attitudes found among most entrepreneurs in Arakawa.) The father again went bankrupt.

Mr. Ikuta, after finishing six years of primary-school education, was apprenticed to a metal manufacturer. As he describes his career, he soon became independent and ran his own little shop, helping support his jobless parents. According to his story, he was continually physically abused by his father for such things as staying out late and visiting prostitutes. (Since he was unmarried, according to traditional thinking he was not really "independent.") The difficulty with his father became so severe that he started to fight back, and eventually left the house, giving up his business. At this point, he says, he joined a gang involved in extortion, intimidation, blackmail, and prostitution, which was a branch of a very large *yakuza*, or outlaw organization. He had frequent contacts with the police and was eventually jailed when a member of a rival group was injured. He agreed to reform by joining the navy and was released. (It was a custom in Japan at that time to accept for conscription men involved in minor crimes, who, if they showed a sufficiently penitent attitude, were allowed to sign up for military service.)

As he describes it, Mr. Ikuta developed a "nihilistic" attitude toward life during his war service. He said he had no religion and did not acquire any. He wondered if anything was worth the effort in life when anything could happen to a man at any time and wipe him out completely. Nevertheless, he felt that the compulsory discipline of navy life had turned him away from his previous delinquent, crime-oriented inclinations. When he returned from the war he no longer had any contact with criminal associates. (In his response to the TAT, Mr. Ikuta relates stories of individuals with secret wrongdoing in the past for which they feel guilty.) Most of his family (a mother and two sisters) had been killed in the air raids on Tokyo, leaving his father alone and destitute. Dealing on the black market, Mr. Ikuta was able to support himself and his father. He went to live with a distant relative and at this time met his wife-to-be.

Mr. Ikuta's memories of his father were continually ambivalent. He remembers that his father was inconsistent in the way he related to his family and would sometimes hit him without warning. Sometimes his father hit him because he was angry with him for fighting with his brothers or sisters. He remembers very vividly his father's throwing a pot of rice at his mother; as he describes it, he tearfully ran around trying to pick up the grains of rice while begging his father to stop. At other times, however, he recounted extremely warm memories of being lifted on his father's shoulders and carried out to watch the shrine festivities. Throughout his description of his father, we see the conflict between feelings of resentment and a need for nurturance, for it is manifest that he wanted to portray his father as destitute and helpless. His father obviously did not help him to assume a stable male identity or to learn to perform well in the parental role. The problem of poor ego control, considered in relation to his life history, can be understood as stemming from inadequate and inconsistent discipline.

This man's Rorschach gives substantiating evidence of a diffuse and immature emotional structure. To the colored Rorschach cards, for example, he gives strong, uncontrolled responses. He also shows poor control in regard to form accuracy, which is lower than one finds in most Japanese. He shows evidence of low tolerance of frustration. There is a great deal also to suggest a schizoid form of withdrawal.

Mr. Ikuta, throughout his projective materials, shows very little concern with achievement. He expresses, instead, a sense of deep personal inadequacy and an undertone of depression. Like many other Japanese fathers in our sample, he uses a kind of pseudointellectualism to cover his deeply felt sense of inadequacy. We see essentially a person in conflict, confused about how to maintain his own independence, while experiencing feelings of deep rebelliousness. In his interviews he manifests considerable ambivalence over accepting responsibility for disciplining his son and forcing him to study. He conforms, on the surface at least, to the expected traditional Japanese cultural values about achievement, although he seems to have very little personal investment in them. He feels deserted and mistreated by maternal figures and suggests that the same thing is happening to his son.

The wife directly attributes to the husband the blame for her son's delinquency. She is not hesitant in describing the inadequacies of her husband and her dissatisfaction with him. In her projective materials, however, she too shows considerable ambivalence about accepting the expected role of wife and mother. On the one hand, she makes up a standard story about maternal self-sacrifice. On the other, she tells a TAT story of a son who catches his mother with another man. We were subsequently told in Mrs. Ikuta's interviews that her husband's father, about ten years earlier, had committed suicide with his second wife by turning on the gas in their house. The older man had gambled away a friend's money, and his new wife, who was chronically ill, decided to die with him. We gain the picture of an unstable, "delinquent" old man, whom his grown son saw with great ambivalence. In this case one can perceive that the delinquency of our subject is definitely related both to the father's ambivalence about authority and to the mother's ambivalence about her role as a woman.

Mrs. Ikuta has seen herself all her life as a "tomboy," who refuses the wifely female role. She is one of several cases in which the wife overtly sees herself as having been masculine and tomboyish in her childhood.[2] She was the fifth child, the third girl in the family. From the time she was small she remembers herself as active and in conflict with her mother, who continually chided her to be more "feminine." She remembers being told once that she should have been born a boy. Most of her remembrance of parental conflict was with her mother, since her father was deeply involved in his business. Part of her memory of her father was his bankruptcy and his abject discouragement, which resulted in his becoming a heavy drinker and putting the family into progressively heavier debt.

As Mrs. Ikuta remembers herself at school, she was excellent in sports and physical education but did poorly in academic subjects. She was forced sometimes to stand up in the middle of the class because she didn't understand what was going on. She felt very self-conscious about the impoverished status of her parents. Her clothes were inferior to those of other students, but she remembers that she refused to ask her mother for better clothes, knowing how poor they were. Her own memory of her mother was that she was a self-sacrificing person who would never scold her husband.

According to her memory, Mrs. Ikuta was never close to her father, who favored an older sister. In spite of her mother's negative attitudes about her tomboy behavior, she describes herself as being most attached to her mother, and she remembers with some regret that she never came home to help her mother or to learn feminine tasks from her. At one point she was sent as a maid to a temple to learn how to become "more feminine." She says she developed a habit of sleepwalking there and had to return home after a year and a half. She attributed her sleepwalking to the fact that she was under some strain because she

2. See the later section on role rejection for other illustrations.

had to leave her mother and was forced to sleep alone instead of in a crowded room with the rest of her family. After her return from the temple, she never again walked in her sleep.

Even today the aging mother is still concerned about her daughter's femininity. Mrs. Ikuta's projective materials reflect a somewhat depressed, hostile, aggressive woman obsessed by the feeling of being threatened by forces larger than herself. The TAT responses reflect a lonely woman with an underlying narcissism of an exhibitionistic type, who feels some positive attitudes toward herself but has not had an opportunity to develop them. Her responses reflect conflict with maternal figures as well as negative attitudes toward male figures generally.

Her son by the time he was in fourth grade had been arrested for stealing books, with several friends. Her husband's disciplinary response at that time was to scold the boy once and say no more. The son's projective test stories, as well as his conscious statements, reveal a far warmer picture of his father than of his mother. He consciously says that he fights a great deal with other members of his family, but he likes his father best.

Although the boy is involved in group delinquency, others tend to see him as an isolate. Yet, as far as he is concerned, he has friends, and his family does things together congenially. This view is not substantiated by either the parents or the teachers. (We classified his case as "isolate delinquent" from the reports of the teachers at school.) The boy somehow felt it necessary to present to us a capacity for getting along with others, which was not borne out by observation.

In the boy's TAT we find most unusual stories of mothers doing negative things. On Card I the mother seems to disapprove of the boy's attempt to achieve. On Card 6BM (a mother-son scene) he leaves home and succeeds, coming back to please the mother. In three of his stories he mentions leaving home and having things turn out better. In others he mentions quarreling. His most unusual and pathological story is given in response to Card 11; the son catches the mother stealing the father's money, scolds her, and talks her into returning the money to his father. The boy mentions money quite often, and somewhere in the explicit emotional understanding of the boy there seems to be some direct relationship between money and love.

In short, all three members of the family show considerable ambivalence about love, and anger about legitimate authority. It would be accurate to classify this case as one in which mechanisms of induction operate, that is to say, where the son manifests in his delinquent behavior unresolved feelings that are still operative in the parents.

"PARENTAL" SUPERVISION ON THE PART OF TEACHERS

Japanese teachers frequently feel responsible for helping out with problem boys. For example, in case D-6, the teacher saw the Funahashis' son as still amenable to change in attitudes but easily led by others, and sought to intervene by getting him a job in a nearby restaurant to break up his contact with other delinquency-prone boys. For awhile this tactic seems to have been successful. The boy worked well in the restaurant and, up to the time of the interview, seemed to be avoiding trouble. The teacher actually does the banking of the boy's salary and keeps a bankbook for him. Nevertheless, the boy's expressed attitude about this activity on the part of the teacher is one of indifference. He states that he doesn't want to work but does so anyway. One surmises that he is incapable of disobeying an authority figure who is taking an interest in him. He still expresses somewhat negative feelings by periodically coming late to school, blaming his lateness on the fact that his sleep is disturbed by the light in the workshop where his parents work late at night. The father of the family expresses concern about the boy's failure to get up in time in the morning, but seems peculiarly powerless to discipline his son about this. One gains the impression that the father is pleased that someone of authority has taken over some of his supervisory responsibility and that he is happy not to assume this role himself.

THE QUESTION OF PEER GROUP INDUCTION

In some sociological literature there is a reluctance to regard family attitudes, either manifest or latent, as prepotent in delinquency formation. Instead, the most frequently cited causes for delinquency are neighborhood conditions and the influence of the peer group. One cannot deny in some cases the influence of delinquency-prone companions as an important stimulus to the start of delinquent activity. It should be emphasized, however, that prior conditions in the family either provide the child with a certain degree of immunity from such potential influences or, conversely, provide certain latent attitudes, predisposing him to seek out conditions or relationships to satisfy delinquent tendencies already present. Emphasis on such delinquent predispositions as being due to family experiences does not in any way devalue the considerable influences of neighborhood or peer group on the probability of actualization of these predispositions.

In fact, our difficulty in locating cases of isolate delinquents attests to the fact that they are a small minority of the reported delinquent cases in Arakawa Ward. Most cases of deliquency involve at least some elements of peer-group induction, which by definition were lacking in our isolate cases. It is clear that children with a potential for delinquency interact with one another to cause mutual induction to illegal activities, and that induction of the inexperienced by older, more experienced boys is a usual pattern.

In Japan, it is not an infrequent occurrence, according to some social workers, for boys who deliver papers to get into some kind of delinquent activity. The strong likelihood of peer-group induction is obvious in such cases. The wife in case D-8, Mrs. Fukuhara, reports her boy's initial delinquency as follows:

Toward the end of last year, my son told us he wanted to work delivering newspapers. You have to wake up at 4:00 A.M. to deliver home newspapers. [Before this] he usually slept until late and didn't have time to eat breakfast, rushing out of the house to school without breakfast. He had a few slices of bread for lunch and ate sufficiently only at supper. We had worried about it. . . . Therefore, we told him that such a late bird couldn't work for a newspaper. But he insisted, and I therefore welcomed the opportunity because I thought our son would eat a good breakfast.

For the first few days I had to wake him up, but he soon learned to wake himself up. When my son wanted our permission to work on the newspaper delivery route I told him yes, and I did not tell it to my husband lest he would be opposed to our son's plan.

He worked hard and was happy. He worked for four months, making a good income, which he spent for his clothes and other things for himself. He started eating a heavy morning breakfast, which made me feel happy. But I was not a little worried about the way he spent his money. He was earning about ¥4,000 a month ($13) and spent it quickly and lavishly on clothes and other things he wanted [an ordinary reaction by a boy to having money].

He was working with a group of his friends. Once he wanted me to allow him to stay overnight with his friends at someone else's house. I let him do so without knowing what would happen. Early the next morning I received a call from a police station. I was asked over the telephone whether my son had left home that very morning. I said yes. The policeman told me I was telling a lie. I said that on the previous evening my son was staying with his friends. This was the first time I had let him do it. The policeman said my son had been involved in stealing and acted as the lookout. I was astounded and couldn't quite believe it. The policeman said the boy was not delivering newspapers but stealing. I was told to come to the police station, so I went. It was still dark and early in the morning. I felt I should not have allowed him to stay overnight with his friends.

He went to someone's house with two of his friends, and while these two boys were stealing pigeons and cutting the wires of the cage, my son was standing guard. The policeman came by, so my son said, "Watch out, the police are coming!" The other two boys climbed up on the roof and they ran quickly, but my son runs slowly and he fell down and was caught by the policeman. The other two boys, wondering why my son didn't join them, returned to the spot and were also caught by the police, and they were all taken to the police station.

The policeman said that my son was the best of the boys. He is not yet accustomed to stealing and was very clumsy at it. The policeman at the station said that all boys delivering newspapers also tend to steal milk from milk boxes that are attached to the gates of the houses to which they deliver newspapers.

According to the mother, her son became indignant and told the policeman that he usually delivers papers before the milkman delivers milk to the houses. Telling this story to the interviewer, the mother voiced her anger and resentment toward the policeman who had treated her son as a thief. The interviewer asked the wife what her husband's reaction was to the son's involvement. The mother answered:

> It seemed that he wanted to scold him and punish him severely in the beginning, but he actually didn't get angry. He reasoned calmly with him for a long time; then he told our son that only children of poor families deliver newspapers to help their families financially and if he wanted to buy something, then his working as a newspaper deliverer would be justified, but it was not right to work just for the fun of spending money. My husband reasoned with my son quite calmly and never got angry. After all, our son was already regretting what he had done and felt hurt. Therefore, we should not touch the wound in his mind.
>
> He didn't want to go to school, and he said he felt too ashamed to go, but I also went to talk to the schoolteacher, who said that, though it was between him and me, stealing pigeons was not that serious. He said there are many other boys who have done worse things. The boys who had actually stolen the pigeons had had their [own] pigeons stolen before.
>
> When our boy was taken to a family court and was interrogated by a family-court investigation officer, the officer asked my son if he ever stole anything else. My son said he had stolen chocolate candies, not because he wanted to eat them but because he wanted to give them to his friends. He stole them because it was thrilling and he enjoyed the sensation of stealing without getting caught. The officer asked my son if he wanted anything, and he answered that he wanted some skates. The officer asked him if he would buy them or steal them. My son said he would work and earn money to save up to buy them; he said that he would never steal anything expensive, and that skates were too expensive to steal.
>
> The officer asked if it was all right for him to steal candy and chocolates, which were not very expensive. My son didn't answer but remained silent. I thought my son was being very honest. Even at such a place as the family court, he didn't lie but remained rather frank. He was telling without reservation what he thought. I thought he was very honest.

The mother thinks the boy was being honest, but in emphasizing the honesty of her son she seems to overlook the fact that her son does not think it very bad to steal inexpensive things. She also makes a point of the fact that the schoolteacher remarked that there were boys who did worse things. One gains the impression that the mother is condoning in one way, at least, the behavior of her son. Previous parental attitudes sensed by the boy may have made peer-group induction more possible for him than it would have been for another.

The son's version of his deviancy was somewhat different from his mother's. He told the interviewer of his fondness for animals, and said that he had delivered newspapers for four months the previous summer because he wanted money to increase the number of pigeons he was keeping at the time. He said he likes all sorts of animals, and that it was fun to keep animals as pets, adding, "It's so interesting and pleasant that once you start doing it you can hardly stop." He quit working after four months, and the interviewer asked him why. He answered, "Well, it was due to certain circumstances." When the interviewer pressed him about these circumstances, he responded, "Well, for some reasons." It was obvious that the boy was trying to avoid telling him about his stealing, which had caused him to stop work. The interviewer, nevertheless, pressed him further for an explanation. The boy then said, "Working early in the morning and in the evening, I couldn't study very well. My parents wanted me to prepare myself for the entrance exam into high school." The interviewer then asked him what had happened to the pigeons. The boy answered that he had had four of them, but three of the homing pigeons had failed to return to their cage when he let them loose at some distant place. The last one had died.

In his attempt to bring the boy back to his experiences with the policeman, the interviewer asked whether he had ever stayed away from home with his friends without telling his parents. "I always tell my parents when I spend the night with my friends, although I have done it only twice." From the tone in his voice, the interviewer felt that at this point the boy was resisting coming any closer to talking about his past experiences with the police. The interviewer resorted to more direct questions: "You have never taken other people's things?" And the boy's answer was: "Yes, I have." The interviewer thereupon asked: "What did you take?" The boy's answer: "I forget what I've taken, but I have taken." The interviewer pursued the subject: "For example?"

> Well, it's hard to recall but, for instance, poker chips or firecrackers that we use for playing poker. I didn't steal them from my friends. I simply borrowed them from my friends and didn't return them. So it's practically the same as taking them. But actually it's borrowing without returning [laughs]. After all, my friends forget and I forget. There was a time when they borrowed from me and both of us forgot, so it's mutual.

The boy showed some resistance in his manner, and so the interviewer tried some more direct questions: "You have taken some things from a store?" "Yes, I did, when I was still in the fifth or sixth grade." "What did you take?"

> Candy, things like that, inexpensive things that you can buy easily. I didn't do it for my own sake. I took it for my friends. There's a thrill in it, you see. It's fun to take things without being discovered. When you steal something and hide it somewhere, then you are told that you are a thief. You say you didn't steal. If the person still insists that you stole it and insists that you return what you stole, then you say: "Let's go to the police station," and you ask the guy what he would do if the policeman searched you and found nothing, proving that you're not a thief. Then it becomes bad publicity for the store, so he wonders if it's really the wise thing to do. He decides not to take you to the police station because he's afraid he might turn out to be wrong. I have never done such a thing [laughs and laughs], but I have heard about it.

The interviewer pursued the point of what happens if you get caught. The boy: "When you get caught, you are immediately forgiven if you return what you have taken. If it's candies and things of that kind, it's not very serious because it's not very serious to steal such inexpensive things." Interviewer: "Therefore you took only small things?" "Yes, small things you can hide, of course."

The boy was attempting in one way to talk about what he had heard rather than his own experiences. The interviewer asked him if it was really fun to shoplift in a candy store. The boy said, "Yes, it is. I have not done it recently, though, because I was taken to the police station once." "What happened?" "Oh, I no longer remember. It was last year." The interviewer asked why he was taken to the police station. The boy, now opening up, said:

> What? Why was it? Was it not pigeons? Yah, I stole pigeons. Well, it's not quite accurate to say I stole them. I simply helped my friends. I didn't do it for my own sake. I was asked, and I couldn't refuse. I couldn't say no. I didn't like it. Well, it's not quite accurate either to say I didn't like it, because it was kind of interesting. It was fun. When I was standing on guard and my heart was beating very fast. It was very thrilling. You can't refuse when you're asked by your friends to help them. If you refuse to help them, you feel very bad afterward. After all, it's a matter of friendship, you know.

He was asked how he felt when he was taken to the police station.

> I felt bad. You see, since childhood I never liked policemen. When I was a child and didn't behave well, people used to say that they would call in the police to punish me, so I never had the idea that policemen were nice people.

The interviewer asked if the boy felt unwilling to meet other people after having been caught by the police. He answered:

> Well, after all, this kind of thing happens to everybody, or at least to those who do trifling things. There are not many people who haven't done something like that. Most people have at least once done something wrong, no matter how small. Everybody has done something wrong, even if it's not seriously wrong.

When asked about his future aspirations, he said he wanted to be an airplane pilot so he could fly freely in the sky. He also wanted to join the Japan Defense Force and to attend the military university. But then he immediately added:

> It may not be very possible for me with the kind of brain I have. . . . Of course, it's very difficult because you've got to have a good brain. Even if I cannot become a pilot, I want to join the Defense Force. I sometimes wish to join the war [laughs]. I am never afraid of death. I never dislike the idea of losing my life. I don't understand why people are afraid of losing their lives.

Rather than citing peer-group inducement to delinquency, a number of the isolate boys complain about mistreatment by classmates and see themselves as rather passive, taking to stealing to satisfy needs and thus compensating for their lack of companionship. For example, in case I-7, the Ishisakas' son was in the fifth year of primary school when he stole money for the first time; he sees his stealing as related to the fact that he wanted some expensive things like a camera or a transistor radio, and he also wanted better clothes. He sees himself as weak, and yet he said he was "insistent" on things he wished to own. He first pressed his father for these things, but the father refused him. When he was arrested for stealing, his father beat him and forced him to leave the house. The boy did not change his ways but truanted more frequently and continued to steal money. He learned to lie without compunction, trying to cover his misdeeds. His mother seemed at times to help him avoid the wrath of his father. Sometimes he would sleep at a neighbor's, but he told his mother, to gain her sympathy, that he had spent the night in a train or in public washrooms.

SEVERE PUNISHMENT AND OTHER INAPPROPRIATE DISCIPLINE AND SUPERVISION

There are many cases of delinquency in which experience of induction through peers or parental attitudes is not clearly perceivable. What is most commonly evident as a source of delinquent attitudes is inconsistent or overpunitive discipline on the part of the father and conflict between parents over discipline. Harsh treatment by a father in such situations is often negated by protectiveness on the part of a mother, which, in effect, emphasizes the arbitrariness of the father's behavior.

In case D-8, which we examined in the previous section, Mrs. Fukuhara describes her husband's harsh disciplinary behavior. Once, although she does not remember the cause, the father punished the boy, who was in the second or third grade, on a snowy day by stripping him of all his clothes and throwing him out of the house. The mother, unable to endure this treatment of her son, persuaded the father to relent and finally brought the boy back into the house.

Mrs. Fukuhara describes the generally uncontrolled behavior of her husband when he is under stress. She states that he is very quick-tempered; when he gets angry he smashes or throws things around, and sometimes he throws good things away. A few years ago when he was suffering from an upset stomach and was worried about his business, he was continually in a very bad mood. She states that he often beat her on the head, "so much that the surface of my head became uneven (*deko-boko*). He would get angry at trifling matters almost worthless to mention." Throughout the interview she interpreted her husband's bad moods as stemming from a tired physical condition caused by his overwork.

In the supervision and discipline of lower-class Japanese children, there is considerable mention of beating on the part of the fathers and of submissive excusing and apologizing to others on the part of the mothers. In case I-11, the boy was beaten by his father, Mr. Ihashi, sometimes so badly that he was unable to go to school afterward. The beatings were related, not to delinquent behavior, but to the fact that the son did not wish to help his father in his tiny factory. One gains the distinct impression that the harsh punishment meted out for the son's defiant behavior was also a means of relieving the father's frustration brought on by financial difficulties. The mother, on the other hand, did not like to scold her children. Mrs. Ihashi has always taken the role of apologizing for her son's wild behavior to others, in a helpless, submissive way. Again, in this case, one notes the general attitude that when children are thirteen or fourteen, the father considers them to be grown up enough "to understand" without being physically punished.

A number of the fathers are self-conscious about their lack of self-control in exercising discipline over their children; they are not reticent in describing themselves as quick-tempered and impulsive. In the case of I-7, the father, Mr. Ishisaka, speaking of himself, says:

> I am very short-tempered and I get angry. When I get angry, I hit my child. Certainly it's not very easy to make me angry. If something happens once, I don't get angry. When it happens again, still I don't get excited. But if it happens three times, I get mad. And my child does the same thing over and over again to make me really angry. . . . I am a man of frank disposition and a strong sense of justice, but if the same thing happens over and over again, I lose my temper. Usually I'm reticent, quiet, and do not commit myself. If somebody insults me once, I let it go, but if it happens twice, three times, I get really angry. I've always been this way since childhood.

The mother's interview substantiates her husband's account. Speaking of his attitude toward the children, Mrs. Ishisaka says:

> I don't know how to say it. He is quick-tempered, and, well, for instance, when our children are watching television quietly, if he doesn't like something, since he himself doesn't enjoy watching television, he suddenly turns off the switch, even when the children are enjoying some program. I would hope he would stop acting that way toward the children. He also wants to talk about his own childhood and criticizes bitterly what our children say. He says things were different when he was a child. I tell him the present world is different from the past, but he is old-fashioned, will not change his mind.

In respect to her son's delinquency, she says:

> My husband didn't take it very seriously in the beginning, but when it happened twice or three times, he became worried. He said that if the child cannot be corrected after doing something wrong, the child is as useless as some wild beast. He says our child should be thrown out of the house. As he reacted this way, it became difficult for me to tell him what our son did later on. My husband would become violent, beat our son, and would tell him to go away. . . . Once the boy was afraid of his father because he thought the father would scold him severely if he found out he had stayed away from school for two days. So he decided to avoid any con-

> tact. He went into an empty house with his own small blanket and transistor radio. He turned a light on and was therefore discovered by the police. A policeman came into the house and found the boy with the transistor radio.

Although the transistor was his own, the police suspected the boy had stolen it, so they took him to the police station and called his parents, who explained to the policeman that the transistor actually belonged to the boy. But the husband found out that the boy had run away from home because he had stayed away from school two days and had been afraid of punishment. When the father found out, he became violent and, in front of the policeman, hit his son on the face. It was a strong blow, and the inside of the boy's mouth was cut. The father said he would take his son to a nearby park and kill himself and his son by drowning in the pond. The policeman got very upset and told the father to quit behaving so violently. The wife states:

> My husband always acts that way when our son does something wrong. He never tries to reason with our son but simply gets angrier and angrier and beats him. He shouts at him without thinking that the neighbors are all hearing him. This is what makes our son feel so ashamed. . . . He told our son to go away but, after all, the child is ours, not someone else's. It's ridiculous to tell one's own child to go away. I told him not to say such things. After all, this is our home. I asked my husband not to say such things, but he always tells our son to go away.

As his wife describes him, Mr. Ishisaka seems to be a total isolate. He never attends recreational meetings of the day laborers with whom he works nor associates with any of them off the job. He doesn't have any friends. He doesn't visit anyone, nor does he invite anyone to his home. Mrs. Ishisaka said that soon after their marriage her husband used to lose his temper when a meal was not cooked well. When he got angry he used to throw things and turn the table upside down. Mrs. Ishisaka says she endured all this.

> I couldn't even argue with him. I was told that I was a selfish, willful creature, and that a woman should agree with him even when he says a crow is white. He told me that as long as a woman remains that way everything goes well within the family, although I know a crow is not white, and [now] if a man says a crow is white I say "Oh, that's right" and remain silent. Only when I notice that my husband is in a good mood would I say that although he said a crow is white, I have never seen a white crow. This is the way I've always been.

In this, as in a number of other cases, the man's behavior is described as changing as he ages: "He has changed. And recently he eats whatever I cook him. He is very serious and hardworking and does not even drink a drop of sake, and he is very reliable."

To the hypothetical question whether she would marry her husband again if she could repeat her life, Mrs. Ishisaka says, "Well, as long as I suffer and endure, there is nothing particularly dissatisfying about life to me. He doesn't drink and become wild. His only defect is his short temper. But I would accept the present situation."

One would think that this behavior of the father would be enough to suggest why the boy has become delinquent. However, as we indicate in describing the mother elsewhere (chapter 9), there is also considerable rejection on her part to compound the picture. What we hypothesized to be an underlying rejection of her son is compensated for by a conscious helplessness over being unable to discipline or supervise the child.

Inadequate Supervision: "Helpless" Mothers and the "Bribing" of Children

One noticeable pattern, not only in the Ishisaka case (I-7) cited above, but in others as well, is compensatory bribery of a willful child who has been rejected for one reason or another.

The wife in case D-17, Mrs. Torihashi, did not seem to accept the subject's birth; she took no responsibility for naming the child, but casually allowed a neighbor to suggest a name when his birth had to be registered, long after the child was brought back from the hospital. She put the baby on a strict bottle-feeding schedule, and she had others feed him most of the time. The child wore a pacifier around his neck and sucked his fingers vigorously. In his preschool years he was what we would describe as a "holy terror." When he was angry and could not do as he pleased, he would attack anyone around—the parents or his playmates. He would threaten to throw things or break them.

The mother never knew what to expect. She felt unable to handle the boy but was reluctant, as she put it, to be "too severe" with him. Because of her feelings about a previous child who had died and about her own strictness with her older children, she let things pass, telling him not to do it again. Both parents would give him large amounts of pocket money to pacify his anger and to serve as a sort of "baby-sitter" while they worked outside the home. The child usually went out and spent the money on cakes and candies, which the parents hoped would make up for "not being able to take care of him all the time."

Mrs. Torihashi describes an accident that happened shortly after their son started elementary school, in which he was shot in the stomach by a cousin with an air rifle. His mother, not realizing that he had been hurt, severely reprimanded him for doubling up in pain and not acting "manly." The boy has committed several delinquent acts involving thefts with other boys. The mother feels "helpless" about coping with her son's behavior.

Maternal Punishment and Inconsistent Discipline

It is not only fathers who show inconsistency about physical punishment of children, although there are relatively few of our cases in which mothers are openly physically abusive. Case I-2 offers an example of basic ambivalence on the part of a mother about discipline. Mrs. Ichitani is afraid she has made her children "too indulgent and carefree" because of her too great affection for them. She sees herself, however, as rather short-tempered. She does things by herself when she can't get others to do them, and accordingly, the children have never worked much for her. She remembers beating her boy severely when he was in the fifth grade because he did not obey her. The boy told her that she should have persuaded him by explaining to him what was wrong with what he was doing. Later she came to consider that she was "always wrong" and decided never again to beat him. She now tries to scold him when no one else is there. She has paid considerable attention to her children, according to her report, but she thinks that she has been much "too nervous" about it.

Her boy has become somewhat detached from her as he grows older, and she feels it is better not to be too close and affectionate with him. He cannot now wash his back in the bathroom. This makes her feel lonely. She does not now ask what he is doing in school because she cannot understand clearly, even though he tells her. She thinks that she is "too ignorant" to understand schooling. The boy does not speak to her now except when he needs money. These latter statements indicate that the mother feels she is being rejected and no longer has any way of expressing closeness, even symbolically; she has no way of providing nurturance in any acceptable form for her child.

Drinking and Parental Authority

Fathers with severe drinking problems have difficulty in maintaining themselves as any kind of consistent authority figure for their children. Case D-16 is an obvious example. Mr. Tsunada, who is an *oden*-cart peddler,[3] is one of the many continual drinkers whom we find in our sample. He and his wife do not own the pushcart they use from late afternoon until after midnight; it is rented, he says, from an *oyakata* (boss), who also sells him his materials. The husband does extra work sometimes in the mornings, preparing *oden* in the *oyakata*'s shop. Husband and wife leave the house late in the afternoon, go to their *oyakata*, load up the pushcart, and take it to places of entertainment where people are apt to buy. Since they have become older and more tired, they try not

3. *Oden* snacks have an ancient origin. O is "honorable"; *den* is an abbreviation of *dengaku*, a form of peasant entertainment, or "music of the rice paddy," a medieval forerunner of Noh drama. *Oden* originated as a boiled yam on a skewer sold from carts during the middle ages to rural folk gathered to watch the dances of a band of itinerant performers. At present *oden* are any assortment of yams, fishcakes, turnips, eggs, or giant radish (*daikon*). These snacks are cooked in a soup broth lightly flavored with salt, sugar, and seasonings. The *oden* cart is a frequent sight late at night in the entertainment areas. It is pulled by hand. A few folding chairs are provided for the customers on one side of the cart, with a curtain extending so that the customer's faces cannot be seen from the outside. The *oden* peddler sits on a stand across from his customers. The *oden* boil constantly in their broth, sending off a steamy vapor, a warming sight during the winter night's chill. Since the prostitution crackdown of 1955–1956, the *oden* cart has been used as a pickup spot by pimps and prostitutes. The customers go to particular carts, where negotiations take place.

to change their location more than once or twice an evening. When they close up for the evening, the husband goes back to the store, takes a nap for a short while, and spends most of the night preparing materials for the next day. He gets an additional ¥10,000 ($33) a month for this. From the peddling itself, the couple make approximately ¥20,000. The husband comes home in the morning and has a heavy meal, drinking about a pint of 80-proof *shōchū*, the cheap potato or rice brandy that is the Japanese equivalent of rotgut whiskey. This almost daily drinking does not interfere with his work, but it seems to have become a necessity for him as a reward, perhaps, to keep him in some kind of balance with a depressing existence.

The son has learned to avoid his generally drunken father. It is not that his father has no ambition for him, although it is apparent from the projective materials as well as the interviews that the son seems very directly headed for a totally delinquent identity. His father says he wants him to "get a good job so that he does not go farther in the wrong direction, but I leave it to him. If he is unwilling, I cannot do anything about it. I only wish that he would get a secure job. I don't care what he does. He can be either a construction worker or an *oden-ya* like myself, as long as he works honestly and does not get into trouble."

He attempts to sound uninterested or helpless about controlling his son, but at the same time he states that he "hits and hits and hits" him (*nagutte, nagutte, nagutte*) when the son does not "obey" him. He states that since he recently has felt a very strong antipathy toward his son, he tries not to hit him too often.

Mr. Tsunada can describe, in vivid terms, the inconsistent discipline he received from his own father; nevertheless, he seems to be incapable of doing anything else in regard to his son. It is apparent that the son's delinquent activity is directly related to the father's drunkenness and inconsistency, as the subject himself seems to recognize. The boy has never liked school and has only rarely done his homework. His parents "never came to PTA meetings," he says. He receives ¥50 a day as an allowance and another ¥50 for buying bread for his lunch, but according to his own story, he spends all his money on *pachinko* (pinball machines) "because I can increase the money so I can buy better food and also cakes and sweets." He says he is good at *pachinko* and it is easy for him to win, so he cannot become interested in other ways of earning money. He says he likes both parents, but immediately afterwards he says, "I like both my parents; even if you like other people, nobody really cares for you or takes care of you (*mendō nanka zenzen mite kurenai*)." He also states that his father, when he's drunk, becomes nagging, but as he soon falls asleep, he doesn't feel much bothered. When the father becomes too difficult, the boy leaves home and doesn't return for a day or two. He says he has a good number of friends (who are all delinquency-oriented) who always put him up. His real best friend is a dog. He says he likes animals very much.

The wife in case D-8, Mrs. Fukuhara, recalls the drunken behavior of her own alcoholic father. Her mother and father were "driven out" of the house by a mother-in-law, so they had to be on their own. As she describes her own father's behavior, he tried very hard to establish some kind of job as a hauler with a wagon. He was a quiet man who could not assert himself with his wife when he was sober, and who seemed to need to drink sake in order to complain and blame his wife. He would sometimes come home completely drunken, go into the toilet, and fall asleep there. Someone would have to carry him out. Sometimes he would vomit, and his wife would have to clean him up. Mrs. Fukuhara remembers once that, when her father came home from a wedding party, he stumbled and fell on the side of the road and lay there in the mud. As she describes her mother's gradual change, she says:

> As this sort of thing was always happening, my mother couldn't afford to cry. She became more and more strong-willed. She became so strong she started scolding her husband rather than being scolded by him. When my father sat down in the toilet and started sleeping, my mother would go in and would carry in a pail of water and would clean him up. She would hit my father, slapping him, saying he was no good. . . . She used to tell me that I should marry someone who didn't drink any sake at all.

Mrs. Fukuhara remembers worrying continually through childhood about her father's drunken behavior. When she went to a village theater to watch the drama, she would come home even before it was over because she was worried that her father would be drunk and bothering her mother. When the father came home drunk at night, she would get out of her *futon* (bedding) and tell her father to calm down and go to bed. She says that her father always obeyed her when she did this and would silently go to bed. One gains the picture that she herself had learned to take an assertive, dominant role toward men. And yet, in her description of her own behavior with her husband (above), she seems to have taken the submissive role in most aspects of their married life.

ADULT RESPONSIBILITY, ROLE REJECTION, AND THE REJECTION OF CHILDREN

A number of women in our sample in the projective-test stories revealed some basic ambivalence about their acceptance of the woman's role (see also chapter 9). As far as we could determine, some of these women's rejection of their role as women was related to what appeared to be feelings of being rejected by their own mothers.

In case D-6, for example, the material is obvious. Mrs. Funahashi said that her own mother never had any time for her, and yet she herself was forced to assume a maternal role with her younger siblings. She was particularly bitter about not being allowed to continue school. She describes herself as "swallowing tears" when she was forced to quit and go to work. Her home situation was one in which her mother was "too busy ever to concern herself with what I felt." Throughout her test materials she reveals hostile and yet dependent, ambivalent attitudes. She expresses the same ambivalence in caring for her own children. After her first interview the interviewer wrote that "although she looks outwardly gay and cheerful, she actually seems defensive and lacking in warmth." The projective materials reveal strong aggressive attitudes in spite of a kind of grudging surface conformity. In the interviews she admitted she should be submissive, but "I don't like to be defeated either." Ambivalence extends into her sense of sexual identity. She is an active person in her work outside her home and seems to be afraid of becoming dependent and passive. She acknowledges quite openly that she really doesn't like to take care of others, and she states in one of her interviews that she dislikes the role of mother and wife. Her continual ambivalence comes out when she describes her husband positively in one respect and then quickly gives a negative counterbalancing description. For example, in one interview she states that her husband is "sympathetic," but then quickly adds that he is "indecisive." It is interesting to note how this wife's active, competitive attitude fits in with the passive, withdrawn stance taken by her husband.

Another example is case D-17, that of Mrs. Torihashi. As a child she felt rejected and uncared for, and as an adult she appears to be somewhat authoritarian, dominating, and independent. Underneath this overt picture, the projectives suggest a person who wants a dependent relationship but is unable to admit it. In her interviews she consciously disapproves of women's dependence on men and states that she envies men's independence. Nevertheless, she contemplates positively the idea that she will be taken care of by her sons in her old age. Attitudes suggesting role rejection come out as she discusses the fact that she was "ashamed" of giving birth and that she was unable to breast-feed her children. One gains a definite impression that her dominating and aggressive exterior hides a deep fear of feminine inferiority. After her marriage, as she describes it, she was uncomfortable around her new family because of their different customs and dialect. Her husband refused to be sympathetic or to support her in the conflicts that arose with her new relatives. Nethertheless, by the time they had their first child, she was able to see to it that her husband complied with her request to change the diapers, a symbolic act of reversing roles. In this case as in others, we see a direct connection between the difficulty that a woman has had with her own mother and her difficulty with the feminine, compliant role in her marriage and as a mother.

One form of role rejection on the part of a wife and mother is a curious one from the standpoint of American social psychology, namely, the decision to give up serving the parents of a dead husband.

Mrs. Iida, in case I-4, was previously married to a man who was killed in the war. She found it impossible to live with her mother-in-law, and as she put it, "I decided to divorce my dead husband." She wanted to take along the son that she had had by this husband, but according to the Japanese law of the time, the child was a child of her husband's lineage and she had no right to him if she left the house. Therefore, in effect, by rejecting her role as a dutiful wife to the dead husband's family, she was forced to give up her own child. This decision cost her heavily. According to her description, she cried for many nights. She had a friend go sometimes to see how the child was being taken care of by the grandmother, and she expressed her wish that she could steal her child and run back to her own parents. She describes one episode in which she found herself no longer able to control herself and went one afternoon to his school when he was in the third grade and asked the teacher to allow her to watch him play in the yard below.

The forced abandonment of her child when she left her first husband's family played no small part in her subsequent rejection of her stepchildren, the children of her second husband. Her own hostility and dissatisfaction with life, which she openly expressed to us, was strongly influenced by her previous marriage. She said she thought, at the time of her second marriage, "It may be my fate not to raise my own child, while I must raise someone else's children for him." She had been told about her present husband by a distant relative, who described him as a widower who was having a hard time raising two children. As she states it, "I entered the marriage without meeting him at all, through a very formal, ordinary wedding." Her rejection of her second marriage extended to the child who was born of it. The husband himself, in the interview, expressed his rejection of the child by saying, "I wanted her to have an abortion, but she said it would cost us as much as the birth and she might as well give birth to the baby. Therefore, the baby was born."

Other cases of role rejection will be discussed in chapter 8, in the context of family cohesiveness and dissatisfaction with marriage, and in chapter 9, dealing with neglect and deprivation.

Role rejection, of course, is not limited to women. A dramatic instance appears in case D-20, that of Mr. Tayama, who, using the contention that he was a second son, refused to inherit his father's business. The father was a wholesale dealer in religious paraphernalia. Since Mr. Tayama's elder brother had already started running a printing shop with fair success, the family did not expect him to take over the father's business, and Mr. Tayama, the second son, was selected to continue the family tradition. When he returned from army training, he was put to work for his father for a period of two years. When he saw that it was a foregone conclusion that he would take over the family business as soon as possible, he fled to Osaka. He states:

> It was not that I did not like being a wholesale dealer, but I thought it was my elder brother's duty to take over the family occupation. Being a younger son, I thought I should not be forced to do so. My brother hated wholesale dealing. I was healthy, stout, and worked very hard for my father. Accordingly, my father wanted me to take over his business. I felt the whole thing wouldn't look right to my relatives if I were to become heir to my father's occupation; therefore, I ran away and went to Osaka. How

> could I become the heir to my father, thus preventing my brother from becoming one? I thought it was against the proper way of doing things, so I went to Osaka.

The resentment of a second son, frequently mentioned herein, was acted out. Mr. Tayama did not do well in Osaka and returned home after several months. Evidently, at this point his father was reconciled to the idea that his second son did not want to be his heir, and allowed him to work with him again without broaching the subject.

Mr. Tayama tried to avoid getting involved in the management of his father's business by way of a marriage agreement prepared for him. The marriage was indirectly proposed by a peddler of bamboo baskets, who was a constant visitor at both the homes. In effect, this rather unlikely *nakōdo* (marriage broker) was used as an intermediary to bring together people who were already distant relatives. Mr. Tayama arranged to become a *muko-yōshi*, an adopted son, since his intended wife was the only child in her family. As he says, "I thought if I were to marry her I would not have to take over my father's business, so I married her." Things did not work out exactly as he had anticipated, for "after my marriage to my wife, my wife's parents and I started wholesale dealing as a branch store of my father's. For about a year my father-in-law and I worked for my father, and my mother-in-law and my wife worked in the branch store." Evidently the branch did not work out and the in-laws went back to their previous occupation of peddling sweets, while Mr. Tayama again found himself working in his father's business as a deliverer, riding on a three-wheeled truck. Some differences of opinion developed between his father and himself in regard to running the business:

> I started criticizing my father's way of handling his business. Arguments ensued. As I learned the business better and became more impatient with the way my father ran it, I complained considerably. Because he wanted me to stay on the job, my father tended to listen to me, especially when we ran out of stock. It was I who had to do all the apologizing and explaining to the customers. I didn't like it. I felt I had had enough of it. [So he had another plan.] I was riding my three-wheeler, and naturally I had to have a driver's license. I thought that if I were to lose the driver's license, I would not be able to ride on the motorbike and I would no longer be able to work with my father, so I decided to destroy it. If I were to burn it completely my father would not believe it, so I burned half of it and, showing him the remaining half, I told him I was no longer able to drive. When I do something, I do it thoroughly. Therefore, probably I am disliked by my relatives. When I wanted to quit I always produced some reasons which necessitated my quitting.

Here we see a man who has resisted taking on the destined task of succession. It is noteworthy that these cases of resistance to the occupational role are prevalent in the delinquent sample.

ROLE DEDICATION IN THE PARENTS OF NONDELINQUENT BOYS

In some remarriages in which the woman acknowledges her dissatisfaction with her husband (see chapter 8), there seems nevertheless to be a complete commitment to the parental role, if not to the marital one, on the part of both parents. Case N-8 is an example of such a marriage, in which the basic cement that keeps the Shiratori couple together is a perseverence in parental role playing. Although the husband overtly states that he is "satisfied" with his wife and admits to being emotionally dependent on her, he has little contact with her. He is dissatisfied with his own occupation, wishes he had better education, and feels that it is impossible for him to move ahead. Yet he continues to work hard and wants to have more income "to live in a better house, so that my son can move further ahead than myself." Repeatedly, throughout his interviews, Mr. Shiratori expresses concern over his well-behaved son's health and education.

Mrs. Shiratori expresses dissatisfaction with her husband; she even admits to periodically wishing for a divorce, but she long ago decided not to get one because "the child needs a father to grow up as a fine man." She voices her lack of interest in sex, but she insists that she is adequately playing her role as a wife by helping her husband in his work and keeping the house as well as possible. But most of all she stresses her role as mother. She says, "The basic principle in raising the child is to teach him to love and trust, and get along well with people."

Her history as a parent was not without problems. After the birth of her child, she had to stay in bed for six months because of heart trouble and asthma, and the baby had to be taken care of by her sister, who came to stay with the family. After this illness, Mrs. Shiratori experienced no further incapacitation.

The dissatisfaction she expresses with her present husband is in direct contrast to her description of her dead husband. She describes her present husband in terms that she also used to describe her own father, "rigid, inflexible, and militaristic," whereas she remembers her first husband only as "kind and affectionate." She considers herself "masculine," and her Rorschach responses also strongly suggest homosexual tendencies. Her TAT stories are about problems that are resolved with an emphasis on harmony between people. One gains a definite impression that she has somehow learned to live vicariously with her own ego residing in her son. She has sublimated her own tendencies toward a masculine identity by dedicating herself to a mother's role.

Mr. Shiratori himself reveals some deeply repressed rebellious wishes and hatreds. He evidences a strong sense of being dominated, which he tries to deny. He uses pseudointellectualism and a sense of self-righteousness as defenses. His wife's description of him as "rigid" perhaps reflects his attempt to suppress basic rebelliousness by a strict adherence to role behavior. His "militaristic" tendency may be a reflection of his need for discipline as an external reinforcement for his superego. What comes to the surface is his strong dedication to his role as father. From what we can determine, his behavior is adequate in acting out this role.

The boy's projective test record, as well as his behavior, clearly suggests that the parents have been successful in inculcating conforming social attitudes in their child. The mother's concern with trust and harmony is reflected in the boy's TAT stories, which show an implicit trust in parental figures. Although he has some concern with potential discord, he emphasizes a capacity for reconciliation and positive relationships among people. His Rorschach responses indicate active strivings, positive feelings, and a high level of intelligence optimally realized. In this family, one finds a positive resolution in areas which in other families result in deviant behavior.

In another nondelinquent case, N-12, Mrs. Sayama is a woman who shows an aggressive competence, whereas Mr. Sayama seems weak and ineffectual. She is equivocal about her satisfaction in marriage. On the one hand, she seems to avoid voicing criticism, but on the other hand, she expresses no positive satisfaction with her mate. As she described her life, it was one of continual hardship and suffering. She would not answer the question whether or not she would marry her husband again were she to repeat her life. She stated simply, "Well, I never gave thought to such a thing. It's too unreal to me." It is clear from the tone of her interviews that she resigned herself to the role of a mother and does enjoy her children. She also tends to give the best interpretation possible to many situations. For example, although her husband never goes to PTA meetings, she emphasizes the fact that "he is not satisfied until I tell him a great deal of what has happened at the meeting and what has been discussed. He is a very concerned and understanding father toward our children." The husband, however, simply states that he leaves everything to his wife.

It seems safe from this and other evidence to assume that what she wishes her husband to be as a father colors both what she wants to present to others and what she emphasizes consciously to herself. She also uses religion to strengthen her role dedication; she is a practicing Tenrikyō member, converted to the sect by her mother-in-law, who had joined previously. Her husband remains totally indifferent to religion. The two daughters in the family are members of the youth group and occasionally join in excursions with other Tenrikyō youth. Mrs. Sayama's interpretation of her religion is that it has kept her "upright" and taught her to be satisfied with what is given to her in life. She believes that it has a positive effect on her children. She also has been a dutiful daughter-in-law ever since she and her husband's mother developed a very strong attachment. She says, "I felt very jealous and angry at first because my husband thought about nobody but his own mother. But he is a son with filial piety. He has taken good care of his mother." Since the mother became paralyzed by a stroke, Mrs. Sayama has taken care of her, sometimes wheeling her in a modified baby-carriage to the public bathhouse. She is known to her neighbors as a dedicated daughter-in-law, as both she and her husband revealed in their interviews. She admits to this with a matter-of-fact attitude, emphasizing that her mother-in-law is "a woman of very strong character, very strict." In this case we see in behavior and attitude what might be described as a paradigm of a woman's acceptance of her social role.

ATTEMPTS AT ROLE RESIGNATION THROUGH RELIGION

In six of our fifty cases, women were affiliated with one of the new religions. In delinquent case D-7, Mrs. Fudasaka had joined a religious sect called Risshō Kōseikai, in which she was active for five or six years prior to a business failure of her husband's. Outwardly the religion was to help her resign herself to the woman's role, but from the way she describes it, she used her affiliation with the sect, in effect, to leave home and stay away. When her husband went to complain about her absence to the leaders, they were able, interestingly enough, to persuade him to become a member himself.

Mr. Fudasaka gave as his reason for membership that the religious organization was a very good guide for living, since they teach people "that a wife should obey her husband and appreciate her ancestors." He also stated that it was good for children, since "they teach one to treat parents nicely and respect ancestors." When he became involved in gambling in an attempt to recoup his business losses, Mrs. Fudusaka was very angry. Her husband indicates that she didn't complain very much, however, because of the religious principles of the group to which they belonged. On the other hand, the husband exploded in anger to his wife, complaining that he failed even though he joined the group. In this case the attempt to use religion constructively did not prevent the appearance of delinquency in a child.

CHAPTER 8

Family Integrity versus Discord, Depreciation, and Dissatisfaction

RECIPROCAL ROLE PERFORMANCE

There are significant differences in the manner in which harmony is maintained and discord avoided among our nineteen normal couples in contrast to those with delinquent children. In respect to general achievement and competence, there is no difference among the fathers of these families. Many fathers in both groups are obviously economic, vocational, and personal failures, but the mothers of nondelinquents maintain respect for the role of the father and allow themselves far less direct criticism or depreciation of the manifest inadequacy or shortcomings of their husbands than do the mothers of delinquents. We were somewhat surprised to find that in the interviews of each mother, more than three-fourths of the mothers of the problem children expressed a direct and unequivocal dissatisfaction with shortcomings of their marriage partner, and many of them described in graphic terms the types of discord and disharmony that characterized their marital life. Although the mothers of nondelinquent children also criticized their husbands, they did so less frequently and less intensely.

In both groups we found many women whose basic personality propensities were not at all in accord with the demands of their sex role. Many of these women felt themselves to be more dominant and aggressive, and even more impulsive, than acceptable role behavior warranted. Yet we felt that the psychologically available techniques of role maintenance, especially the dedication to self-controlled behavior within the role, was the critical difference. It must be noted that on a psychodynamic level, the integrative mechanisms available to mothers of the normal controls were somewhat better than those of the mothers of delinquents; thus the mothers of nondelinquents, whatever their propensities, had better psychological means at their disposal to maintain self-control.

Ideally, the Japanese father was never to be treated in any way that was disrespectful to his role position. Whatever the woman's unrealized need for affection or dependency, she was to treat her husband as the symbol of authority and succession in the family. In our previous work comparing farming and fishing villages (De Vos, 1973, chapter 3), we found in the fantasies elicited by the TAT that, depending on class and role background, the implicit expectations of women could vary considerably from the ideal of the self-sacrificing wife of a warrior. In the farming village, women's fantasy was more clearly in line with traditional normative expectations, and a successful marriage simply for love was never depicted, nor were there any instances depicting a woman's aggressive behavior toward a husband in a situation of discord or dissatisfaction. In the fishing village, however, we elicited a number of stories of women who were physically abusive to a drunken or profligate husband. In the farming village, when a woman was depicted in any violent scene, the source of her violence was her deep sense of responsibility for the careful upbringing of her children. Should her children be profligate, the mother could inflict violent punishment on them.

This emphasis on role maintenance, whatever the personal feeling of the man and wife toward each other, had certain expressive advantages as well as the disadvantage of hindering greater intimacy of communication. There was a sense of security in that the individual knew that, whatever his personal defects, he could maintain himself within the protective armor of his role position. Such a use of role is especially advantageous for individuals with an underlying sense of inadequacy. A person, whatever his sense of personal inadequacy (which, given Japanese standards, is a widespread inner experience), could maintain himself within his formal family pattern without a sense of being threatened. Most vulnerable, of course, is the individual holding the position of family head, since this position carries the expectation of family success and the responsibility for failure. Ideally, the individual was placed *in* the role rather than measured *against* the ideal requirements of the role. For the children being socialized within a family, emphasis on role behavior was ideally suited to foster the continuity in vocational identification useful in a lineage system. Observation of the respect accorded the adult male was a continual psychological inducement to the growing male child to take over the privileges of the same vocational marital position. Identification with the father was fostered at least in respect to the father's role position, whatever the deficiency in the father's capacities as a spontaneous individual.

The traditional Japanese emphasis on role behavior, while de-emphasizing intimacy and companionship between man and wife, also served as a protective buffer against the appearance of discord and disharmony in family life in situations where the expressive and emotional gratification is minimal for both spouses. Therefore, one of the reasons for the relative lack of discord in Japanese family life compared with that in other countries is the degree to which women derive personal satisfaction from being competent in their roles rather than from having a mate who meets their personal needs. In our lower-class Arakawa sample, the woman pictures her role as far less satisfying than one would expect—full of dissatisfaction and perceived disharmony.

In this chapter we shall examine and discuss the subject families by centering on the expressions of marital satisfaction and dissatisfaction. We shall also examine the nature of disruptions and irregularities in the past history of the three generations covered in our case histories; the attitudes the spouses had and still have toward their own parents; and the present attitudes of the young boys about their parents. We shall demonstrate both quantitatively and qualitatively that lack of family cohesiveness is very significantly related to the appearance of delinquent behavior. Before discussing these assessments of family cohesiveness, we shall first present other quantitative features of the circumstances of marriage in our fifty families which had no significance for delinquency but were of some ethnographic value in an understanding of our cases.

CIRCUMSTANCES OF MARRIAGE

We found that the age of the marital partners, or their age relative to each other, and whether a marriage was arranged by others or was the result of mutual initiative on the part of the couple, related neither to marital harmony nor to the appearance of delinquency in a child.

The Time of Marriage

Most of the parents in our sample were married in their early twenties (average age 23). We found that in almost all the families, the husband is older than the wife, as is shown in table 8.1. The assessment of age of couples at the time of marriage produced no significant differences between delinquent and nondelinquent groups. There are expressions in Japanese, *ane-sama-nyōbō* (elder-sister-wife) and *hitotsume masari* (one year older is better), to describe situations in which a wife is older than her husband and further to suggest that when a wife is one year older than her husband the marriage should work out well. There is actually only one such case among our fifty families.

Most husbands are now between ages 40 to 60, averaging approximately 47.5 years of age. The fathers of isolate delinquents show a wider age range, with some under 40 or over 65. The average age of the mothers (41.5) is about 6 years younger than the fathers.

As was expected, there is general correspondence between the end of apprenticeship and time of marriage. In many cases the man's or woman's employer or someone in the employer's family was involved in arranging a marriage as well as in assisting in setting up an independent business. The implicit obligations of the master in an apprentice program often are marital as well as economic. In middle-class families the age at marriage tends to be older than it is in Arakawa families. In middle-class families there is a similar expectation that marriage awaits the end of training, but higher education and advanced degrees at the university take longer than apprenticeship programs, and hence the expected age at marriage of men in the professional segment of the population tends to be in the late twenties.

In Mr. Iida's case (I-4), the pattern of employer responsibility was quite apparent. Also apparent was the employer's familial-like concerns and am-

TABLE 8.1
Age Distribution of Arakawa Couples

AGES OF HUSBAND AND WIFE

	Normals (19)		*Social Delinquents* (20)		*Isolate Delinquents* (11)		*Total Delinquents* (31)		*Grand Totals* (50)	
Age in Years	Hus	Wife	Hus	Wife	Hus	Wife	Hus	Wife	Hus	Wife
35–39	0	7	0	5	2	3	2	8	2	15
40–44	4	5	5	9	3	4	8	13	12	18
45–49	6	2	6	3	2	3	8	6	14	8
50–54	4	3	5	2	2	1	7	3	11	6
55–59	4	2	3	1	1	0	4	1	8	3
60–64	1	0	1	0	0	0	1	0	2	0
65 over	0	0	0	0	1	0	1	0	1	0
Mean age	49.8	44.3	49.25	43.25	47.45	42.9	48.61	43.13	49.10	43.40

AGE DIFFERENCE BETWEEN HUSBAND AND WIFE

	Normals (19)	*Social Delinquents* (20)	*Isolate Delinquents* (11)	*Total Delinquents* (31)
Husband older than wife	19	17	11	28
Husband and wife same age	0	2	0	2
Wife older than husband	0	1	0	1
MARKED AGE DIFFERENCES BETWEEN HUSBAND AND WIFE				
Less than 5 yrs.	10	12	6	18
5 yrs.	2	1	1	2
6–9	4	3	1	4
10–14	3	1	3	4
15–19	0	2	0	2
20+	0	1	0	1
Average difference	5.6	6.6	6.0	6.4

bivalences related to the sex life of young employees. Mr. Iida was sent in his youth to be an apprentice in a small metal shop in Asakusa. He worked closely with the other apprentices and enjoyed their companionship. After several months, however, the owner of the workshop died. The owner's wife gathered the workers together and told them they were free to return home if their parents felt uneasy about having their children work in a masterless shop. No one left, as they all liked the wife, who took over the running of the business and cared for the workers as if they were her own children. To the older workers she would say that it was "natural" for a young man to want a woman. But she would immediately caution that one should not have too many women or spend too much money or he would lose his good health and his equilibrium. According to Mr. Iida, the apprentices felt somewhat in a "double bind." Although their employer was telling them not to spend money on prostitutes, she sounded at the same time as if she were allowing them to do so. The general result was that they were all reluctant to spend any money on women. As Mr. Iida said of himself, he liked drinking better anyway, so he did not go after women.

As he described it, the atmosphere of his apprenticeship was like a large congenial family, the young workers living harmoniously with their motherly employer. At what was considered an appropriate time, his own marriage was arranged by his employer's sister, and he was married to the maid who had come to work for his employer. The familial provision of a wife for him was obviously satisfying to Mr. Iida. He felt that in his apprenticeship he lived in a dependent, family-like atmosphere which fulfilled his basic needs, including that of finding a wife.

Love Marriage versus Arranged Marriage

One of the possible questions specific to the subsequent cohesiveness of a Japanese marriage is whether the marriage was based upon some degree of free choice and mutual liking. Many Japanese marriages are arranged by others, either family, employers, or other mentors, for what is judged to be the benefit of the couple to be married. One might suppose that there would be differences in the rapport or cohesiveness experienced by the spouses, depending on how and why individuals were married to each other. However, according to Blood (1967), who sampled 445 middle-class couples in Tokyo, there was only slight indication of greater cohesiveness in the 296 middle-class love marriages than in 141 arranged marriages. The variations were considerably less than might be expected from a hypothesis that freedom of choice in marriage would lead to greater closeness if not stability in a marital relationship. In our Arakawa sample of 50 couples, 14 were love matches (2 of them are common-law marriages), and 36 were married according to an arrangement made by a relative, a friend, or very often the husband's employer.

We found no significant difference in the number of love marriages reported to us by our control samples (5 of 19) and our delinquent samples (9 of 31). One must conclude accordingly that whether the marriage of the parents was love-based or arranged does not seem to influence delinquency formation in children. In the absence of specific statistics in regard to the type of marriage among the working-class segments of Japanese society in general, we do not know whether or not our Arakawa families differ from the general pattern. We can assume that they are representative of Arakawa Ward generally.

In some of our cases there were discrepancies between the reports of the husband and wife as to whether their marriage was "free" or arranged. In case I-11, for example, the husband, Mr. Ihashi, reports that his marriage was arranged through an acquaintance, whereas his wife claims that she fell in love with Mr. Ihashi and then obtained her parents' consent to the marriage. Our interpretation of such a discrepancy, considering other evidence, is that among the more conservative people of Arakawa Ward, it is still considered more "proper" to have had an arranged marriage rather than a love marriage, and that the husband in this case was somewhat more conforming in his social attitudes than the wife. The wife showed a number of other characteristics of rebelliousness and was evidently more willing to describe having made a love marriage on her own initiative. She previously reported that she completed higher primary school in direct opposition to her father, who thought that education was unnecessary for women. In fact, her father had tried to make her work on the farm during school days, but she refused. She also indicated that she went to Tokyo to work as a maid in defiance of her father's opinion that she should not go to the city.

Even in a "free" marriage, a go-between is sometimes called in to make it more formal and legitimate, and there are instances of an arranged marriage in which the person seeks his parents' opinions and comments on a prospective bride. In case D-8, according to Mr. Fukuhara, the following took place:

> Certainly, as I was still a young man, I was anxious and not very certain. I went back to my home and consulted with my mother. I told her that somebody was introducing me to a prospective bride. I asked if she would meet this woman and tell me if I should marry her. However, my mother told me that she would be *my* wife. My mother said that she would not be able to tell me anything about the girl. She said I should decide, because after all she was going to be my wife, nobody else's. As I was told so by my mother, and as I would not be able to remain unmarried long, and as there was somebody who was kindly arranging the marriage for me, and as I thought it would be better for me to marry, I decided to marry my wife after meeting her once.
>
> Perhaps I do not think in complicated ways about these things. After all, if a man is able and successful in his occupation, he can always get a woman he wants. This was my opinion. Therefore I did not think very deeply about it. I thought that after all I was not yet successful, and I was not qualified to make my own choice. If I would become particular about choosing a woman, the woman would also become choosy, and I thought I could not wait until I became qualified to be choosy about a woman to marry. I thought that if the woman whom I married turned out to be not normal or satisfactory, I could always have a chance to get another wife.

There are a number of culturally interesting passive-dependent attitudes expressed in this statement. First, Mr. Fukuhara indicates that if a person is vocationally successful, he has more opportunity to make his own choice in marriage. Judging himself to be not particularly successful, he must take the candidate suggested by others. A passive role in marital choice, therefore, is seen by him as a necessary alternative for those who have acknowledged themselves not to be successful economically. Another interesting aspect of Mr. Fukuhara's story is the contention that his mother's attitude (as reported to us) was one that encouraged an independence he felt incapable of achieving. She wanted him to determine things for himself rather than calling upon her to make a decision for him. The mother, in effect, was not willing to fulfill the son's dependent expectations.

In some cases a distant or close relative continues to take the responsibility for marriage arrangements even should the first attempt fail. Mr. Sorai in case N-11 was married to his first wife while he was apprenticed to his grandfather in Tokyo. At the time of marriage he was expected to take over on his own, running the family bakery with his new wife. The marriage did not work out, according to him, because of "character incompatibility with a willful wife. She wanted to return to her home when the baby died of illness before its second birthday."

We do not know further details of this marriage. Soon after the divorce, however, he was married to his second wife, who was, according to Mr. Sorai, "a nice, obedient woman." She died of an illness after two years. He was married to his present wife when he was twenty-eight and she was twenty-four. All three marriages were arranged by the same relatives, who evidently considered it their duty to come up with a successful permanent marriage.

OVERALL QUANTITATIVE RATINGS OF FAMILY COHESIVENESS AND DISHARMONY

In attempting to assess cohesiveness in terms of harmony and disharmony, we rated our Arakawa families in four areas: first, *affection for spouse*, in which we rated husbands and wives separately; *mutual discord*, for which we gave a single family rating; *marital satisfaction*, in which we again rated husbands and wives separately; and last, the *boy's attitude toward his parents*, for which we gave separate ratings for the son's attitude toward his father and toward his mother. These four areas influenced the overall rating we gave the families on the Glueck scale for family cohesiveness (see table 8.2). Initially, we attempted a five-category scale running from very positive (++) through positive (+), neutral or indeterminate (0), negative (−), to very negative (−−). Finding we could not differentiate clearly between + and ++, we abandoned the attempt to break down "positive" ratings as to degree of intensity. Neutral, ambivalent, or noncommittal attitudes were rated 0. We maintained two ratings of − and −− to indicate degrees of intensity and dissatisfaction of basically negative attitudes.

The Glueck Ratings of Cohesiveness

In chapter 1 we described the significant differences between the delinquent and nondelinquent samples in our overall ratings using the Glueck scale of family cohesiveness. In the nondelinquent sample, only 7 parental couples out of 19 lacked family cohesiveness to any appreciable degree. This figure was dramatic when compared with 17 of 35 families with delinquents which were rated as having *some problems* of cohesiveness and an additional 11 which were rated

TABLE 8.2
Ratings of Active Discord or the Overt Expression of Like or Dislike of Spouse

	Normals (19)		*Social Delinquents* (20)		*Isolate Delinquents* (11)		*Total Delinquents* (31)	
Discord	Mutual		Mutual		Mutual		Mutual	
Not mentioned	14		8		3		11	
Some	3		9		6		15	
Much	2		3		2		5	
Affection	Fa.	Mo.	Fa.	Mo.	Fa.	Mo.	Fa.	Mo.
Positive affection	9	10	6	1	1	1	7	2
Noncommittal or vague	6	5	10	15	6	8	16	23
Dislike	4	3	2	2	4	0	6	2
Strong dislike	0	1	2	2	0	2	2	4

X^2 (Yates correction)
Discord mentioned vs. not mentioned
N vs. Total Del. $P < .01$
Affection + vs. 0, −, − −
N Fa. vs. Total Del. Fa.: $P < .05$
N Mo. vs. Total Del. Mo.: $P < .01$

0 vs. + or −
N Fa. vs. Total Del. Fa.: $P < .05$
N Mo. vs. Total Del. Mo.: $P < .01$

as *seriously lacking* cohesiveness. Only 3 families in the delinquent sample were judged to demonstrate an adequate degree of family cohesiveness.

The anecdotal material in this chapter, as well as in others, gives striking evidence of how, and in what form, lack of cohesiveness occurs in some Arakawa families whose members never seriously consider actual divorce or separation.

The Ratings of Discord

Histories of interpersonal discord are as apparent in lower-class Japanese families as they are in reports about family life in other cultures. There is no lack of evidence of physical abuse and fighting in a few of our families. In a few other families dissatisfaction appears, although there seems to be relatively little discord; and alternatively, discord may appear without expressed dissatisfaction.

The Ratings of Affectionate Feelings

We attempted to assess expressions of mutual affection or dislike in our samples (see table 8.2), as distinguishable from expressions of satisfaction. Some persons expressed some dissatisfaction with a marital partner, but at the same time made avowals of affection. In the control sample of 19 families, we obtained rather positive avowals of affection from 9 men and 10 women in regard to their marital partners. In the delinquent sample (socialized and isolate) of 31 families, we got definite avowals of affection from only 7 men and 2 women, and most families in these samples could not be rated either positively or negatively. There was no mention of positive affection and there were no expressed attitudes demonstrating lack of affection in 6 men and 5 women in the nondelinquent sample in contrast with 16 noncommittal men and 23 women in the delinquent samples. Generally, we do not feel that our ratings of "affection" or "dislike" are as reliable as the other judgments we attempted, since we did not ask direct questions. Nevertheless, we are presenting the ratings as part of the evidence of our judgment of cohesiveness in the family. Disagreements, arguments, and quarrels were frequently mentioned. Physical abuse (see anecdotes) was often mentioned in the context of drinking on the part of a husband.

Only 5 of the 19 nondelinquent families gave evidence of chronic active discord between the parents, as compared with a total of 20 out of 31 in the delinquent sample. For the social delinquent families, 8 were scored as showing no unusual discord, 9 as somewhat discordant, and 3 as extremely discordant. Among the isolate delinquent families, 3 were showed as showing no unusual discord, 6 as somewhat discordant, and 2 as highly discordant.

There is no necessary correlation between the ratings of marital dissatisfaction (discussed below) and those of discord. In some of the marriages, although no dissatisfaction is expressed, there is evidence of periodic if not chronic discord; 3 of the normal group are in this category. Conversely, in some families in the nondelinquent sample in which there is no expressed discord, one still finds expressions of dissatisfaction with the marriage on the part of some wives. In the delinquent groups, where ratings of discord and dissatisfaction are both more frequent, there tends to be a more general correspondence in the negative ratings. Nevertheless, there are a few cases in which dissatisfaction appears with relatively little discord, or discord appears without expressed dissatisfaction.

MARITAL DISSATISFACTION: ITS RELATION TO A DISRUPTED FAMILY BACKGROUND

Marital Disruption and Irregularities over Two Generations

We have already pointed out briefly in chapter 4 that there is a higher incidence of broken families and remarriage among the families of delinquent boys than in the families of normal children. We certainly do not suggest that divorce and remarriage of parents is the direct causal factor for delinquency formation in children, but the higher incidence of separation may very well be a valid index of a complicated background of disharmony and relative lack of family cohesiveness.

As we indicated in chapter 4, family disruption is not limited to the parental generation but extends to the generation of the grandparents, as reported to us by the parents. A larger number of the grandparents in the delinquent sample experienced remarriage or unlegalized (common-law) cohabitation than in the normal sample. Among delinquent families 18 men and 16 women out of 31 couples grew up in broken households, as did 5 men and 3 women out of the 19 normal couples (less than one-fourth).

The number of nonlegalized unions reported is small for all the groups, but those that were reported were a significant part of the background of the families of delinquents. As we shall now demonstrate, these results on family integrity as related to delinquency are striking when a comparison is made between the expressed dissatisfaction of spouses having suffered a previous marital disruption and a subsequent remarriage and those who have married only once.

Ratings of Marital Dissatisfaction

Being aware of the strong emphasis on role behavior in the traditional Japanese family, we were somewhat surprised by the readiness of the women in our sample to express, rather directly, dissatisfaction with their marriages. Such expressions of dissatisfaction were not limited to the mothers of delinquent subjects, but the degree and strength of their dissatisfaction were much more severe than those expressed by the mothers of normal subjects. We believe that this readiness to express dissatisfaction is partially related to the fact that Arakawa women generally find themselves in a relatively low status within Japanese society, married, in many instances, to husbands who are occupational failures.

In interviewing each of the fifty husbands and wives, we asked them a hypothetical question: "Would you or would you not again marry your present spouse, if you were to live your life over?" Beyond this question we probed into the reasons, either positive or negative, for expressed attitudes about the marital partner. We obtained fairly detailed descriptions of marital life, seeking out illustrative material from our subjects. As a result of these interviews, we finally classified each husband and wife according to the overall estimated degree of marital satisfaction or dissatisfaction, scoring + for very satisfied or satisfied, 0 for ambivalent responses, − for dissatisfied, and − − for strongly dissatisfied.

In general, in all our groups, husbands either were more guarded about giving any response or tended to express mild satisfaction with their spouses, whereas wives tended to be more frankly and openly dissatisfied. The parents of nondelinquents were generally far more positive about each other than were those of delinquents. Of those we could clearly rate as either basically satisfied or dissatisfied, we found 10 satisfied and 7 dissatisfied women in our normal sample of 19, and only 5 satisfied and 23 dissatisfied in the delinquent sample of 31 (see table 8.3).

TABLE 8.3
Marital Satisfaction in First Marriage and Remarriage

	Normals		*Social Delinquents*		*Isolate Delinquents*		*Total Delinquents*	
Degree of Satisfaction	Hus.	Wife	Hus.	Wife	Hus.	Wife	Hus.	Wife
FIRST MARRIAGE	14	14	11	11	5	5	16	16
+ (satisfied)	13	9	6	2	2	2	8	4
o (ambiguous)	1	1	3	2	1	0	4	2
−(dissatisfied)	0	4	2	3	1	1	3	4
− −(very dissatisfied)	0	0	0	4	1	2	1	6
REMARRIAGE *	5	5	9	9	6	6	15	15
+	3	1	0	0	3	1	3	1
o	2	1	5	1	3	0	8	1
−	0	1	4	1	0	2	4	3
− −	0	2	0	7	0	3	0	10
TOTAL †	19	19	20	20	11	11	31	31
+	16	10	6	2	5	3	11	5
o	3	2	8	3	4	0	12	3
−	0	5	6	4	1	3	7	7
− −	0	2	0	11	1	5	1	16

Satisfaction (+) vs. Dissatisfaction (− & − −)
* Remarriage: Husbands + vs. −, − − not significant
$P < .01$
† Total Husbands + vs. −, − − $P < .005$
Wives $P < .01$

We examined the differences between those married only once and those who had remarried. Twenty out of our 50 couples were remarried, 5 among the parents of normals and 15 among the parents of delinquents. In almost all remarriages in our sample, both parties had had previous spouses. Table 8.3 reveals a general tendency for less satisfaction on the part of both spouses in a remarriage, a tendency particularly apparent in the wives. Therefore, one is struck with the fact that although we have selected only officially intact families, the manifest attitudinal evidence directly suggests the relative lack of expressed cohesiveness in the families of delinquent subjects, especially in cases of remarriage.

The pattern of making a second marriage out of a sense of obligation and as a means of economic security is well illustrated in case I-9 (see also chapter 9). Mr. Igayama's first marriage lasted sixteen years and ended with his wife's death at the birth of a fourth child. The present marriage is of approximately nine years' duration. Mrs. Igayama is a deeply dissatisfied second wife and stepmother. She herself had a previous love marriage in which she had both a son and an adopted daughter. Her first husband was killed in the war, but she still clings to the hope that someday he may return, since although he was reported missing, his death was never officially confirmed. Nine years after the loss of her husband, in 1954, she was persuaded by both her brother and her sister-in-law to accept a new, arranged marriage. Since there was some distant relationship between herself and the man (father of the delinquent boy in our sample), her brother argued that she should help her family and help the man take care of his children. He also pointed out that by so doing she would ease the burden on her own immediate family, since she and her children were being taken care of by others. The wife says directly that she made this marriage out of a sense of obligation, and now her dislike of her husband is so intense—and he is so inept at providing money—that she is waiting for an opportunity to leave her husband and go to live with her own married daughter's family. This woman represents an extreme of the pattern of dissatisfaction among the mothers and stepmothers of delinquent subjects.

Dissatisfaction and the Sense of Status Mobility in Marriage

We mentioned in chapter 5 the possibility that some wives would overestimate or exaggerate their fathers' occupational success and social standing in connection with their own dissatisfaction with their husbands' lack of financial success and inadequate, passive personalities. Those women who emphasized that their previous family background was socially better than that of their husbands were found much more often among the mothers of delinquent boys than among those of normal boys (see table 8.4).

When a wife is dissatisfied with her marital life and with her husband's economic inadequacy, does it become important for her that she came from a "better" natal home than her husband or that her father had a higher social standing than her own husband? Or, conversely, if a wife feels she comes from a better family background than her husband and that her father was more successful occupationally, does she feel dissatisfied with her marital life? Both are plausible sequences in the formation of attitudes, although we do not know which is more likely in individual cases. In either sequence, we would expect a correlation between the wife's higher or better family background and her feeling of marrying "down," on the one hand, and her dissatisfaction with the marriage, on the other.

Almost all the women who have remarried, whether in the normal or the delinquent sample, acknowledge little satisfaction in their remarriage. Only 2 out of a total of 20 remarried women express satisfaction. In the normal sample, the 1 satisfactory remarriage was by a woman who perceived her second marriage as an upward move in status from that of her own family, whereas the other 4 saw their remarriages as downward. In the cases of social delinquents, the 1 woman whose remarriage was perceived as upward gave a somewhat neutral rating of satisfaction, whereas 8 rated their remarriages as downward and were very dissatisfied. The result with the mothers of isolate delinquents is inconsistent in that 4

TABLE 8.4
Status Discrepancies in Remarriage and Wife's Marital Satisfaction or Dissatisfaction

	Normals			*Social Delinquents*			*Isolate Delinquents*		
	Rating of Satisfaction			Rating of Satisfaction			Rating of Satisfaction		
Wife's Mobility	+	o, + −	−	+	o, + −	−	+	o, + −	−
FIRST MARRIAGE									
1 or 2 steps up	3	0	0	1	0	1	0	0	1
No mobility	5	0	2	0	1	2	0	0	0
1 or more steps down	1	1	2	1	1	4	2	0	2
Totals	9	1	4	2	2	7	2	0	3
REMARRIAGE									
1 or 2 steps up	1	0	0	0	1	0	1	0	2
No mobility	0	0	0	0	0	0	0	0	1
1 or more steps down	0	1	3	0	0	8	0	0	2
Totals	1	1	3	0	1	8	1	0	5
TOTAL PRESENT MARRIAGE									
1 or 2 steps up	4	0	0	1	1	1	1	0	3
No mobility	5	0	2	0	1	2	0	0	1
1 or more steps down	1	2	5	1	1	12	2	0	4
Totals	10	2	7	2	3	15	3	0	8

Satisfaction related to perceived mobility up or no change vs. perceived mobility down, $P < .01$
Mobility vs. remarriage not significant
Mobility vs. delinquency not significant

out of 6 mothers saw their marriages as either a step upward or as no different from their former status, and only 2 saw their marriages as a step downward; yet 5 out of the 6 rated their marriages as unsatisfactory.

In first marriages in the normal group, 7 out of 14 wives perceived no difference in status in comparing husbands with fathers; 5 out of these 7 rated their marriages satisfactory. An additional 3 of the 14 rated their marriage satisfactory and also saw the marriage as an upward move in status. Thus, 9 out of the 10 women in the normal sample (including 1 remarried woman) who rated their marriages positively perceived their marriages as resulting in either higher status or not lower in status than that of their own families. We repeat that we have no objective evidence of the actual status of people in the grandparents' generation. It may well be that the retrospective description of the social status of the grandparents vis-à-vis the present husband is colored by present attitudes of satisfaction or dissatisfaction. We cannot determine this from our available material. In general, little conscious point is made verbally about status as a source of dissatisfaction, but rather, disharmony is most frequently cited as the direct cause.

Descriptions of Marital Dissatisfaction and Discord

Qualitative assessment of the records has shown that a good number of the wives in the nondelinquent as well as in the delinquent samples directly express marital dissatisfaction without discord. Mrs. Sorai in case N-11, for example, gives the distinct impression that she is not satisfied with her marital life, and yet she does *not* base her dissatisfaction on discord. When asked, she said that she would marry another man if she were to repeat her life, one more quick-witted and clever and more willing to adjust himself to a changing environment and a new age. She says that her present husband is rigid, sticks to old-fashioned ideas, and shows no skill in adapting to a changing society. "I wish he'd learned his lesson when he failed in business." Also, she wishes that he would take more initiative at home in putting things in order, and show some capacity for planning a budget. He is described as completely passive and indifferent to everything since his failure in business. Mrs. Sorai says of her husband, however, that he is basically a "hardworking, honest, and serious-minded man," one who does not smoke, drink, or gamble. She states further that she should feel fortunate in being married to such a man. "Many other men drink and fool around day after day." Therefore, she says that her dissatisfaction is somewhat groundless, although she admits to it freely. As for sexual compatibility, she finds sex "bothersome." She "dislikes it particularly when I am tired." She states that even when she was young she never found sex enjoyable or satisfying. She is now working outside the home and enjoys her work. "It is more fun to be out meeting and talking with other people than staying at home."

Mr. Sorai also expresses marital dissatisfaction. He did not directly answer the hypothetical question of whether he would marry his present wife if he were to repeat his life. He states, however, that he is not sexually satisfied, but he quickly avers that he is "not too interested in it anyway." Mr. Sorai states that his wife talks too much and too fast. We must note that even though their present living circumstances are by objective measures very meager, they both expressed basic satisfaction with their house and with the way their parental roles are carried out, and they find satisfaction in their relationship with their children. Therefore, in this case, although many aspects of mutual dissatisfaction are present, it does not appear to extend to the care or supervision of the children. There were cohesive feelings between parents and children, if not between each other.

The personality picture of the husband is one of an inadequate, defensive pretentiousness verging on grandiosity. One gains the distinct impression that any sustained, stable business venture would severely tax his ego capacities and that he could easily overextend himself in business. The test materials also reveal basically unresolved hatred of both his father and mother and considerable evidence of preoccupation with guilt. Mr. Sorai claimed that his business failure was "due to stuttering." This was the only bit of paranoid-like projection that he seemed to have allowed himself in our conversations with him.

Mrs. Sorai's personality picture is that of a childish but spontaneously open and lively person with perhaps some "boyishness" as a trait. She, too, seems to be somewhat threatened by a potentially dangerous world and easily aroused to anxiety.

The boy in this family, from what we see in his projective material, shows some problems about internalization. He has ambivalent attitudes toward responsibility, which he voices both in the interviews and in the projectives. Nevertheless, he seems to have developed a basically positive, dependent attitude toward authority. At school he seems to be particularly sensitive to the attitudes of teachers and other students, but not much interested in achievement. He is seen as a rather compliant and inoffensive person by his teacher and, according to the teacher, also by his peers. He sees his father as quick and short-tempered and his mother as gentle and understanding. He is very dependent on his older sister, who takes care of him. Authority and the police are presented in a positive light in his TAT stories.

We would judge that in this case the voiced incompatibility of the parents is compensated for by a sense of parental responsibility toward the child, especially on the part of the mother. The presence of the loving and concerned sister in the family seems to make it unlikely that the boy will have problems with authority during his youth and adolescence. His relationship to his father leaves much to be desired, but this shortcoming is not sufficient to cause any overt social problems expressed in deviant behavior.

In case D-7, Mrs. Fudasaka in the beginning interviews did not express her feeling of dissatisfaction with her marriage and her feeling that the marriage was highly discordant from the first. Her husband hedged and did not express so much open dissatisfaction. At the start of her marriage Mrs. Fudasaka lived with her husband's parents and his three younger sisters. She says she felt as if she had entered an upper-status family, much higher than her own, in which there was polite conversation rather than the rude peasant talk to which she was accustomed. She says that her mother-in-law was in complete control of the household, but that she did not place undue pressure on her as a bride. Her father-in-law had retired from work because of his heavy drinking. Her husband, she found out after the marriage, was involved in gambling activities. This discovery was quite upsetting, since she felt that gambling was something that ordinary people would never do. Although she has resigned herself to her marital position, she has never found any satisfaction in her relationship with her husband nor felt any mutuality between them.

Mrs. Fukuhara, the wife of case D-8, is well representative of those women who discussed rather frankly the nature of their continual discord with their husbands as part of their basic dissatisfaction with marriage. We have extracted the following quotes from Mrs. Fukuhara, as she describes her relationship with her husband.

> When I was living in the country, while my husband was in Tokyo, we had a neighbor who was very considerate of his wife. He took great care of her. He would go to the farm, pull out leaves, wash them, and make

them ready to be used in *miso* soup for her. He was commuting to his work from his home, and at home he used to do all kinds of small things for his wife. When he came home from work, he would take over all the little things—household chores—in taking care of his wife. Watching them together, I felt very envious. I thought how happy she must be. So I spoke of this couple to my husband when he came to visit me. I told him that I was envious of this most fortunate wife. My husband said to me, "Would you be happy if I stopped working to help you around the house? Is that what you call happiness?" I couldn't answer and I shut my mouth [laughs].

A few years ago when my husband was very irritable, he would easily lose his temper. He couldn't control himself. When he started nagging me, my children, who were already asleep on the second floor, would awaken and come down, and they would tell him that he shouldn't treat me that way. That made my husband even more angry. He simply couldn't control himself. He would shout that even our children were siding with me. He would yell at them. Therefore, the children had to remain silent. There was nothing to be done. I thought it was his sickness. His sickness was making him behave as he did.

When he was in a good mood he used to tell me that when he lost his temper I should think that his sickness was causing all his anger. I tried not to talk back. I never spoke back to him even when he hit me. If I spoke back to him he would become furious and would hit me more. Therefore I tried to remain silent, even when he hit me and kicked me. Our children were all very sympathetic toward me, and they would tell me not to say a word to my husband. [It might be supposed that Mrs. Fukuhara showed some form of silent resistance and stubbornness when she was letting her husband beat her without saying a word.] Our children were all on my side, and nobody would talk to my husband. That must have made him feel very lonely. It must have made him reflect on his behavior and he started thinking about getting out of his business, which was bothering him. He has been changing over the past few years, and he has become a really wonderful man.

The worst occasion was the time when we had an argument over sending or not sending our second daughter to be adopted by my brother-in-law. He was really furious and angry.

There's another time, but I cannot recall what was the cause. I had to go to our customers to collect money. Before I left home for my errand my husband had already been angry and had beaten me, although I cannot recall what the cause was. I was crying, but I had to go on an errand and I went to Asakusa. I couldn't fight back my tears. When I went into the store of our customer we tried to talk business, but I couldn't help crying. My business client asked me what was wrong, and I told him a long story of my husband's terrible temper. I stayed there a long time. I was treated with supper and received some consoling.

I returned home very late in the evening. My husband was already in bed but awake. I slipped into the bedding. He opened his eyes and started getting angry at me again. I remained silent, covering my head with the quilt. My husband nagged at me. It finally became impossible for me to control myself. I sat on the bedding and told my husband to kill me if he really hated me. I said it would satisfy me if I were to be killed by him. I said I would go out of the house naked so that he could hit me by the lumber pile outside and I could die. I took off my clothes. I pulled at my husband's hand, telling him to kill me outside. This surprised him so much that he stopped being angry. I said I had endured long enough. I finally had made up my mind to be killed. I told him repeatedly that he should kill me if he hated me. He was astounded and remained quiet for awhile afterward.

I went to my sister and told her and her husband our troubles; then they said from the beginning I had spoiled my husband. I should not have been so reticent and lenient, making my husband feel there was nobody really controlling him. I was told that it was my fault. I should not have been so obedient and quiet as I had been.

Really, I allowed him to put all the blame upon me. I shouldn't have done that. My husband used to decide it was always my fault. I was always wrong. My daughters used to say that I was like a blotter or a sponge which absorbs all complaint and blame. There were times when I wanted to run away from my family, leaving all my children behind with my husband. There were times when I didn't care what happened to my life. I wanted to quit. However, more recently my husband has changed and has become really a good man.

According to Mr. Fukuhara, his wife's dissatisfaction with him relates to his tendency to change jobs and to take a gambling attitude toward life.

Mrs. Igayama in case I-9, the stepmother of an isolate delinquent boy, totally rejects her husband and is quite frank in telling why. The relationship, as she sees it, is one of symbiosis. "We live in his house and eat his food. I have to do certain things for him; otherwise the neighbors in the community will criticize me." She told the interviewer quite frankly that she was disgusted with her husband, who "one, has a bad smell in his mouth; two, has defective ways of working; three, provides no satisfaction in sexual relations." Mrs. Igayama has no sentimental feeling for him at all and can think of no good points. She defends herself as not being legally married to him, since she has maintained a common-law marriage. As was indicated earlier, she has never accepted the death of her former husband. "I just let the days pass by. I maintain a strong belief that my own husband will be back someday." She constantly compares her present husband with the husband who was reported missing during the war. Mrs. Igayama expresses equally her open rejection of her stepson (see chapter 9). Her attitudes are illustrated by her description of what he was like when he was eleven years old and did not obey her. "At that time he used bad language and would hide nude pictures." She reports how she found him with a notebook including a detailed story of a man's taking a woman to an island and raping her. She says, "I feel ridiculous sending this boy to high school, since he is not my real son."

It is not entirely out of keeping with Japanese role expectations for husbands to be unfaithful. There is, nevertheless, a hopeful expectation of faithfulness on the part of Japanese wives, who do not always live out the traditional submissive paradigm of tolerating unfaithfulness. Mrs. Tozori, in case D-19, for example, was extremely intolerant of her husband's outside sexual activities, and fought him directly about it. As she describes it, she felt a desperate fear of being deserted by her husband as well as strong dependent needs directed toward him. This fear of desertion by the husband is fairly uncommon in middle-class Japanese women, since the husband, in effect, cannot desert his own lineage and therefore seldom leaves his house to go to another woman.[1] Mrs. Tozori, nevertheless, expressed this as an overt fear, saying that she hated her husband's activities and wanted to punish him by leaving the children to his care. Her anger with her husband disrupted her behavior toward the children, rather than eliciting efforts to protect them from the effects of discord between the parents. One might speculate whether her fear of desertion was not, in effect, a projection of her own desire to leave her children and husband.

Many of the men were noncommittal about satisfaction or discord with their wives. Mr. Fukuhara (case D-8, above), for example, made a statement that expressed male hedging: "There is nothing about her that I particularly dislike. Nor is there anything which I particularly like [laughs]." When asked whether he would choose his present wife if he could repeat his life again, he said, "I don't know whether I could be married to a woman as good as my present wife. My wife is very domestic and I think she is very good-natured. She is very honest and never spends money without my knowing it."

A few of the men are frank in their expression of incompatibility and dissatisfaction with their wives. The husband in D-20, Mr. Tayama, states:

> My wife finished only six years of school. She has never satisfied me. I, myself, do not have much of an education, but I finished two more years than my wife. Also I have had many experiences outside my family and in the army. As a result, my wife's thinking is quite different from mine, but I have resigned myself, saying that after all she is a woman and a woman's thinking is simple.

He states elsewhere that he has rarely argued with his wife because when he gets angry and tells her off, she remains silent and does not talk back to him.

> A woman cannot play her role of wife unless she can obey her husband. There are only a very few husabnds who are ready to admit their mistakes and faults and apologize to their wives. A woman should be able to follow her husband even when the husband is wrong.

When asked whether he would marry his present wife again, he gives no straight answer. He says:

> Well, I think it's the same with both men and women. You might call it fatalism. I tend to respect one's fate. Once you marry a woman and you

1. Overall, on TAT cards, compared with American samples, there is much less expression of fear of desertion among Japanese women.

desert her, you could completely destroy the life of that woman. Many people used to think that way in the past. I think a married couple should stick to each other unless there's some very serious reason for doing otherwise. I do not know how modern women think, but the value standards of the past disapprove easy break-up. Even when you dislike a woman, the negative feeling will eventually disappear. It will not last forever. It is not that I hated my wife thoroughly. Perhaps it is because my wife was a distant relative. We are not like an ordinary couple. [The interviewer repeats his question; Mr. Tayama answers:] You mean if I were to start my life all over again from the beginning? Well, I have never met a proper woman, therefore I cannot answer that question. I presume those who are in the same situation as I would have said the same thing. I do not have any special feeling or particular emotion toward my wife.

In another part of the interview he states he does not feel that his marital life has been a failure, although he admits that his wife is dissatisfied and considers the marriage a failure. He makes this acknowledgment:

> Our marriage is full of defects and shortcomings, both of myself and of my wife. However, there is nothing that can be done about that, and therefore we have stuck to each other. Maybe this is it, even if we were suddenly to become rich by winning a first prize, for example, and if there were good women, I cannot believe I would indulge myself playing around with women. Even if we were to become rich suddenly, my wife would not make up her mind to go to someone else, saying that she could no longer tolerate her husband. If we were to get extra money, she would show me that money and say, "Let's go someplace together for a vacation." I somehow feel that my wife would behave that way. Although I have no prospect of getting such extra money, if it happens I would buy my wife a kimono and reward her many years of hardship.

Attitudes toward Marital Sex and Dissatisfaction

There were no significant correlations, as far as we could determine from the material reported to us, between ratings of sexual satisfaction per se and overall ratings of marital satisfaction. The kind and nature of sexual adjustment reported to us were highly varied and probably highly unreliable. No observable trends appeared to distinguish our samples. There were instances among mothers of both nondelinquents and delinquents of expressed lack of interest in sex.

A wide variety of attitudes toward marital sex are represented in our present sample. These attitudes range from what is reported as a mutually satisfactory, active sex life to patterns of complete dissatisfaction. The frequency of intercourse reported varies widely from couple to couple. There are also differing attitudes toward adultery, some women being tolerant of male sexual activity outside marriage, others very jealous and hostile about it. In general, one might say that our sample is not characterized by a great deal of sexual activity outside marriage, and that in most of the marriages sexual intercourse is not more frequent than once a week. Our figures and interview data are so inexact, however, that we would not dare indicate the rough average of the group. Our findings and discussions must remain impressionistic.

There are little undercurrents of dissatisfaction mixed with statements of relative satisfaction in many of the reports. For example, in case D-9, Mrs. Fuchino reports that she and her husband have sexual intercourse twice or three times a month and she does not feel frustrated. She says that her husband never wanted more frequent sexual intercourse even when they were younger, and she does not voice any discontent. However, there is some indication by the husband that the wife would prefer more frequent sexual activity, and that he feels he does not satisfy her sexual needs completely. The husband says, "In regard to food also, she likes things *shitsukoi*." *Shitsukoi* is a difficult word to give in direct translation; it literally means "insistent and persistently demanding." When a person wants frequent sexual gratification with a partner who is not always responsive, the partner will describe the insistent one as *shitsukoi*. When the word is used regarding food, it suggests food that is rich with much oil, meat, and heavy seasoning. Those who like *shitsukoi* food are also considered to have strong sexual needs. The opposite of *shitsukoi* is *assari-shita*, a word that is also applied both to sexual desire and to food taste.

A number of women, in describing their feelings and attitudes about sexual compatibility, said they were "not interested" in sex prior to marriage. Mrs. Fukuhara, in case D-8, for example, when speaking of her own adolescence, says she didn't have any experience of going out with boys. She was convinced that it was a bad thing to develop a positive emotion toward a man. She never remembers feeling any envy of her girl friends who talked about boys; rather, she felt that those girls were semidelinquents.

> Not that there was no one whom I liked. There were a few men who liked me, but I don't remember going out with any of them even once. Probably I was convinced that it was a very bad thing to go out with a man, or perhaps at the time I was *okute* ["a late crop," meaning a child whose maturation is slow]. One man invited me rather insistently to go out and told me many things. I liked him also, but I couldn't respond to him at all. Probably I didn't show my emotions at all to him.

Mrs. Tayama in case D-20 (see husband's dissatisfaction, above) reported to us how her future husband had attempted to have premarital sex with her. As she tells it, this attempt did not endear him to her, but became part of the basic hostility and rejection she has felt toward him most of their married life. She had been in love with another man but was being pressed by her parents to have an arranged series of meetings with the man (later her husband) whom her relatives had selected for her. She didn't know what to do, since she could not marry the man she loved, and her parents were complaining about her delay in marrying. The families had reached a mutual agreement, and she felt trapped. One day, her prospective husband took her for an outing, promising to meet a mutual friend in Yokohama. They went to a hotel, ostensibly to wait for him. After waiting for some time and realizing it was becoming too late to go home, the wife knew that she had been tricked. Although her escort told her that they could go home if she really wanted to, she became resigned to the fact that she hated it and felt her husband must have felt he could not marry her unless he did something like tricking her into having sex with him.

Mrs. Tayama is very frank in voicing her dissatisfaction with her husband, a dissatisfaction related not only to her sustained resentment about being tricked with sex, but also to his secretive support of his own fmaily and his self-centered attitude. After telling the interviewer that she felt he had partly forced her into the marriage, she said:

> Even after getting married, I felt dissatisfied and angry and resentful toward my husband. Recently, as my mother has become old, I have stopped complaining to her, but when she was in better health I used to tell her frequently how unfortunate I was. My mother told me that they approved the marriage for my sake, not because they hated me. They used to tell me that it was my life and I should accept what was given to me by fate.
>
> My husband says I am not sincere in doing my job at home. He says I work because I must, but I do not commit myself very seriously to do what I do. He doesn't know why, but I know, because basically I'm not happy. My husband often says I do not work sincerely. For instance, when I do laundry, he says the proper way of doing it is to let it dry, examine each item carefully and fix a button when it's missing, fold up things neatly, but I don't do it and simply leave it. My real feeling is that if he wants me to do it as he likes, he should be more warm and considerate toward me. But I could hardly tell him my real feeling because I'm afraid he would get angry and hit me. I never tell him anything, but as that sort of feeling is in my mind, it's bound to be expressed in my behavior and attitude. I feel that basically what I'm doing to my husband is to show my cold feeling toward him.

Although her husband stated that he would buy a kimono for his wife if they were to have money, his wife says, "In my husband's mind there's never an idea of buying anything for me. He himself doesn't care for clothes, not only for himself but for anyone else—me or the children." Mrs. Tayama says she feels sorry for her children, as they are affected by the marital discord. They watch the expression on their father's face and run away whenever they sense he is about to beat them. But recently he seems to have changed and reacts less violently. She adds that a woman living across the street from them said she has been surprised to notice the change that seems to be taking place in her husband with age.

In respect to sex, Mrs. Tayama reports that she never experienced orgasm until quite recently, after her children had grown up and after she was forty. Before that she felt repugnance about sex and felt constrained to participate only because it was the duty of a wife.

Part of the couple's disharmony was over the fact that the husband used to send part of his salary secretly to his own family without telling his wife about it. She would never talk to her husband about anything, because if he got angry he would begin to beat her. She remembers being severely beaten shortly after marriage as a result of an argument, so she learned quickly to remain silent and to limit her displeasure to sulking. When she sulks, her husband becomes huffy, but leaves her alone.

In more recent years, Mrs. Tayama reports, her distance toward her husband seems to have waned and their life is becoming increasingly peaceful. Occasionally, they have even come to joke with each other, saying they made a mistake by marrying. When she complains of suffering by marrying someone she disliked, her husband retorts, saying that that is why she can live as lazily and as carefreely as she does. She feels perhaps he is right.

It is interesting to note that in spite of the husband's dissatisfaction and the wife's obvious continual rejection of him, he has never taken an interest in other women. He constantly rails at her sloppiness and lack of interest in her home, but he seems to feel a basic attraction for her.

In regard to their sexual life, the husband admits to limitations caused by the smallness and crowded quarters of their home. They try to have sexual relations while the children are away, and they frequently have to restrain themselves because of the presence of the children. He says one of the reasons he used to play Mah-Jongg was that he did not like to come home and feel rejected. The wife reports that they have intercourse about every ten days, when the children are asleep. Lately, the children have tended to stay up late, increasing the problem of when the couple can get together. She says they have to be especially careful, since one of their boys often pretends to be asleep and tries to watch them. When the husband comes home drunk, about once a month, he has no sense of restraint, and the wife finds it difficult trying to conceal his sexual desire. All the children know what goes on, and the boy, who is interested in girls, chases after his sisters. He puts his hands on their *futon* (bedding) after they go to sleep or puts his hand up their skirts. Therefore the parents wish to move into another house with an additional room.

This case shows that one cannot assess variables in isolation from one another. The wife's basic rejection of her marriage makes the weaknesses and shortcomings of the husband intolerable. This case could be described in terms of "role rejection" in chapter 7, as well as in terms of "discord" in the present context.

Marital Harmony and Family Solidarity

Our descriptions of marital dissatisfaction and discord should not give the impression that all Arakawa families are filled with dissent, stress, and strain and are on the verge of disintegration. We have already pointed out that even when a husband and wife feel intense dissatisfaction with their life as a married couple, they often manage to be responsible as parents and even to enjoy the satisfactions of their parental lives. Marital dissatisfaction or even discord does not always exert a negative influence upon children. There are a good number of Arakawa families in which husband and wife find themselves in harmonious and satisfactory relationship and in which one sees the cooperative participation of family members.

The Saitamas in case N-9 are a typical example of a couple that express considerable mutual satisfaction and harmony. Mr. Saitama leaves the responsibility of child-rearing completely to his wife. He never goes to PTA meetings or takes on any of the day-to-day problems of his child's education. Nevertheless, Mr. Saitama expresses himself as being seriously concerned with the child's education and future aspirations. He wants his son to become an engineer. He is willing to mention some "weak points" of his wife, such as that she shouts (*donaru*) too much and talks too much. He has no negative attitudes about her doing extra work, does not involve himself with the *naishoku*, and does not know how much money she makes. He does not care so long as she keeps up her housekeeping and spends at least some of her income to supplement their family budget. He does not, in turn, let her know how much his salary is. Similarly, his wife expresses the attitude that she does not care about his secrecy as long as he gives her enough money for food and other necessities for the household. Mrs. Saitama asks him periodically to give her more money, as she needs it for house repairs or for the son's education. Mrs. Saitama describes herself as satisfied, admits that she is rather talkative and frank (*akesuke*), and she sees her husband as introverted (*naikōteki*). She says he keeps very quiet when he is angry; he will remain silent as long as a week. Nevertheless, she thinks they are a good combination. Mrs. Saitama shows a certain degree of dependence on her husband, stating that when important decisions are necessary—such as the purchase of a large item or major repairs on the house—she expects her husband to make the decision. She always remembers to buy a present for him on his birthday, but she admits that "he usually forgets about mine." She says that her husband is very hardworking and a good husband and father. Mr. Saitama describes his wife as a good wife and mother and reliable, although he quickly adds, "I don't think she is very good at managing our family budget. She likes good food too much."

The general impressions gained from the projective test data on this family are typical in showing a kind of fairly prevalent family constellation. Mr. Saitama's Rorschach shows a cautious, noncommittal, well-guarded individual. His TAT shows that he is concerned with possible uncontrolled release of impulses, but counteracts such a tendency by conforming to standards and submitting to authority. One might even describe him as a conformist for whom control of impulses is an end in itself and becomes a major value.

Mrs. Saitama is a fairly active, lively person with somewhat childish hysteroid tendencies, but with healthy, spontaneous aggressiveness. On the TAT, her stories indicate a conforming person, one that submits to authority, and she makes explicit statements that people should conform or submit for the sake of mutual harmony. She controls impulses, not because control is an end in itself, as it is for her husband, but because control is necessary for mutual living together. She is adept at playing the role of wife and mother in the Japanese family.

The son's configuration is not untypical of a future Japanese adult male. His Rorschach record already shows a certain degree of pretentiousness (see Appendix A). He has a good deal of achievement drive, manifested by his desire to produce well-integrated responses. The record in general shows a balance that is well within the normal range. The TAT responses reflect his concern with possible separation. There is some contact hunger and loneliness. The mother is a central figure in his fantasy. Also evident in this boy's TAT is the family concern with maintenance of harmony. He shows feelings of obligation and responsibility in personal relationships.

The Sumi family in case N-13 is another example of a satisfied couple and a harmonious family, although they are financially and psychologically taxed by the presence of their second child, a daughter who is severely mentally retarded. Mr. Sumi was the last of the seven children of a well-to-do man who owned a shipping company. He was raised as a *botchan* (the well-protected son of a wealthy family), but the great earthquake of 1923 wiped out his family's business. At age forty-eight, when he was interviewed, Mr. Sumi was the foreman of a maintenance crew of the Tōbu Railway Company. Soon after World War II, when he was working at the Japan Shipping Company, he became a close friend of his present wife's father, who liked him so much that he married his only daughter to the young man. Although he did not become an official *muko-yōshi*, Mr. and Mrs. Sumi lived with Mrs. Sumi's parents for many years after their marriage. Mrs. Sumi's father and mother liked their son-in-law and used to take his side whenever he and his wife quarreled.

Mr. Sumi, a frank and open person, says he is completely satisfied with his wife and would certainly marry her again if he were to repeat his life. He says she is "*nonki* [carefree] and slow in action, while I am quick-tempered and impatient. I keep nagging at her [*kuchi yakamashiku yū*]." Mr. Sumi is very active at home. He repairs things, sweeps, and cleans their three tiny apartment rooms. He says, "I do practically everything at home except for cooking and laundry. I could do them also if I wanted to, but then I would be doing too much [laughs]."

Mrs. Sumi is a very pleasant, fat woman, talkative and often laughing. As the only child of a strict but loving father and a strong-willed but gentle mother, she looks upon herself as a "well-loved child." At age twenty, at the time of marriage, she was "not willing to marry, as I was still young," but her father liked Mr. Sumi very much and emphasized that he was a really good man who would make a fine husband—serious, honest, and hardworking—so she consented to her father's wish. Mrs. Sumi seems basically dependent upon her husband and says that he makes all the important decisions. She describes him as a very serious-minded (*majime na*) person, and the only complaint she has about him is that he is "gabby" or "nagging" (*kuchi yakamashii*). She says, "I like it when he sweeps and cleans the rooms and puts things in order without complaining and nagging. Then I feel much more grateful to him and appreciate his activities [laughs]."

In the early stage of their marriage, Mrs. Sumi found sexual life "annoying and bothersome," but she soon discovered that "sex was not dirty and obscene, as I used to think before marriage. My husband taught me that." Mrs. Sumi says she is sexually satisfied and has no complaints. Interestingly enough, however, when she was asked when she first experienced "woman's pleasure" (*onna no yorokobi*—a usual euphemism for sexual orgasm in Japanese), Mrs. Sumi apparently misinterpreted the question and told about her pleasure as a mother. She answered, "When I was pregnant for the first time and felt my baby kicking in my womb, I felt for the first time the woman's pleasure."

Mr. and Mrs. Sumi have three children. Their son, the eldest child, received an award for his good school record, which placed him second among the 200 children in eighth grade, and for his good conduct in taking care of his younger, feebleminded sister. The second child, the feebleminded daughter, is a heavy burden for the family, taxing the Sumis both financially and psychologically. The youngest daughter is just five years old. Both Mr. and Mrs. Sumi are proud of their son and say they are grateful to him for not complaining about his parents' devoting most of their money and attention to his feebleminded sister.

In some of the families basic harmony and cohesiveness is maintained in spite of obvious pressure of a characterological nature and of the presence of unresolved forms of sexual pathology.

In a number of marriages the husband has seemed to shift toward a less dominant, even passive, role with age. For instance, in case N-4, the family of Mr. and Mrs. Shimizu, we have a vivid picture of such a man. He described himself as being capable in his young adulthood of taking a great deal of initiative in educational and vocational achievement and more than the usual initiative in establishing and maintaining heterosexual relationships. Mr. Shimizu came from an extremely impoverished family in Kyoto with a totally illiterate father and a mother who could read only the *kana* (syllabary) but no ideographs. He had to quit school after the fifth grade to help out at home, but he ran away from home, got himself a job in a bathhouse in Osaka at age thirteen, and went to grade school at night. He continued in night school through high school and even went as far as taking some correspondence courses from a university. He notes in his history that he fell in love with a woman at age twenty-one, but as she was of higher status, he had to give up the relationship. At age twenty-three he initiated a relationship with a woman who was working in the same factory as he, and married her. Throughout his occupational career he showed a great deal of initiative in starting enterprises and making a success of them, but any possible sustained success was interrupted by the war. After the war he got into black-market activity with his brother-in-law and was caught by the police—a fact he blamed on the brother-in-law.

Something went wrong with the family relationships, including the relationship with his wife. After ten years of childless marriage, he divorced her in

1946. In 1947 he initiated a new marriage with a woman thirteen years younger than he against the wishes of her family. He first formed a common-law liaison with the girl, who, like his original love choice, came from a family whose status was considered higher than his. Their relationship was maintained, and eventually, when the girl's family went downhill, the marriage was recognized and they called on him to help manage the family's affairs. Mr. Shimizu was taken, in effect, as a *muko-yōshi*, an adopted husband, although he denies that this was altogether the case, indicating that both his family name and that of his wife were Shimizu, so that one couldn't really tell whether he was a *muko-yōshi* or not.

The shift toward passivity is overtly expressed in sexual behavior. As it is described to us, Mr. Shimizu initiated his wife into sexual interests, in which he can no longer satisfy her; his wife wishes he were more sexually active. It is obvious that during the course of their marriage Mrs. Shimizu's more aggressive, controlling nature gradually took over. At the present time, Mr. Shimizu has regressed into what is seemingly a dependent relationship, a tendency that must have been an underlying theme in his personality in spite of his past initiative. He has always complained of "stomach trouble," which was most severe from ages twenty-one to twenty-three, during the time he was establishing himself. He had a number of other seemingly psychosomatic complaints at this time as well.

At the present time, in his fantasy at least, Mr. Shimizu is becoming more and more childishly passive. In the Rorschach he gives a graphic symbolic indication of this passivity. On Card II he sees two baby female elephants playing in the water, which is reddish because the sun is reflected on the bubbles. On Card VII, which is usually a feminine card, he sees two weasels licking the buttocks of an elephant. This anal preoccupation is also found in Card IV, where he sees a monkey standing on its head with its buttocks presented. One gets some indication of a masochistic fantasy of himself as some kind of facilitative instrument of the activity of others. On Card VIII he sees two leopards climbing over rocks with the assistance of a chimpanzee, which is helping pull the leopards up. On Card IX he sees a bear climbing up a dead tree.

Such symbolism complements the Rorschach record of his wife, which is full of active and vigorous percepts, some with sadomasochistic features. She sees a lion's face with a mane on Card II, then a bulldog; then she produces a more passive but sadomasochistic response, seeing two bears tied up and hung by their hind legs, still wriggling. She goes back to the same configuration, perceiving it as a vigorously spinning top. On Card III, she sees competition: two men are holding a load together, but one is trying to take it away from the other. She gives a second response to the same figures, seeing them as *kappa* (Japanese mythological water creatures), pushing and fighting. On Card V, she sees two wild boars pushing at each other. On Card IX she sees a coiled dragon with angry, protruding eyes. She again perceives the dragon on Card X, where it rises up to the sky.

The wife's active, aggressive symbolic material is supplemented by exhibitionist symbolism. On Card VII she sees elephants performing. In the inquiry on Card II she sees spontaneously a peacock with its tail spread out. Physically she is quite heavy, and one would suppose she might identify herself more as the elephant of Card VII but would prefer to be the peacock. On Card VII, usually a feminine card, she sees a prickly cactus. The Rorschach responses certainly symbolically indicate underlying tensions about passivity and activity in this married couple—masochism and sadism—but they also express a buoyant acceptance of life.

Their son's identification seems to be in an active rather than a passive direction. In his Rorschach he exhibits responses of potential aggressiveness. He sees rockets shooting out on Card II, a revolver on Card VI, the atomic bomb on Card IX, and insects quarreling on Card X. On Card III, interestingly, he first sees the usual human beings in a rather positive relationship to one another, but follows this up with a dead crab, and then what is usually considered a symbol of maternal destructiveness, a monster spider.

Behaviorally, the boy in the Shimizu family is characteristically described as somewhat "timid." He seems to be recapitulating with his younger sister a situation that his mother, Mrs. Shimizu, describes as having occurred in her own childhood. Her own older brother was rather timid, and Mrs. Shimizu used to fight his battles for him. The boy's younger sister is described as "aggressive and stubborn," and she is also described as helping her brother fight his battles in school.

The mother, perceptively, sees her daughter as recapitulating her own relationship with her mother, who was a dominant personality. One gains a picture, therefore, of female dominance and aggressiveness in three generations of women. Female dominance is now being played out in a family setting of complementary dependent needs on the part of a man.

Withal, everyone in the family describes family relationships as satisfactory. The son sees the parents as happy. Mrs. Shimizu, in spite of her expressed concern with the sexual inadequacy of her husband, nevertheless expresses full contentment with their married life and castigates herself for not being "more wifely" toward her husband. She is preoccupied with two themes: with past poverty and the need for achievement, and with her own aggressive, controlling personality, of which she is very conscious. She made an interesting remark in her interview, saying that when she gave birth to her first child she felt that at last she was a woman.

Sexual Irregularities and Disruptions in Family Life Patterns

Anecdotal material from our case records illustrates the type of sexual irregularities and family disruptions that we have indicated quantitatively to be more characteristic in the family backgrounds of delinquent boys than in those of the nondelinquent group.

The marriage of Mr. and Mrs. Fuchino in case D-9 was initiated by the premarital pregnancy of the wife. The couple met when they were working in a factory together, and they fell in love. Because of the war, Mrs. Fuchino was sent back to her home in the country, where Mr. Fuchino often visited her. She became pregnant, and when the pregnancy became apparent, Mrs. Fuchino's parents agreed to the marriage, which was quickly performed.

Case D-13, that of an itinerant construction worker and his family, is perhaps the most striking example of irregular family life in our sample. These individuals are at the very bottom of the social ladder of nonoutcaste Japanese, being part of a society of traveling groups that work on road-building projects, dams, and other construction jobs, moving from place to place without a permanent home.

In this case, Mr. Tokuda, who was an illegitimate child, has no memory of his father. His mother was eventually married to a widowed Buddhist priest, who had three children of his own. He was taken into this priest's family with his mother while he was still an infant, but soon he was sent out to his mother's parents' house and raised by his maternal grandmother. Mr. Tokuda had a minimum amount of schooling and began working at a very early age as a laborer in constructing dams.

His wife was herself the illegitimate daughter of a construction laborer and of a woman working as a kitchen helper at construction sites. She has no memory of her father, who left without marrying her mother. She was with only her mother during her very early childhood. As Mrs. Tokuda puts it, "It was such a long time ago that I don't remember my mother clearly." She was sent to her maternal grandmother by her traveling mother. We observe in this family a kind of matrifocal continuity in which temporary liaisons with men occur, but there is no lineage pattern whatsoever in the ordinary Japanese sense. Yet, as we shall see, there is hope and aspiration toward "proper" marital behavior.

The vague memory that Mrs. Tokuda had of her own mother was that "she often drank sake and talked with many people at the construction site." One gains the impression that part of the mother's activities was to provide sexual companionship for the construction laborers. Mrs. Tokuda had no formal education; she says, "I am illiterate; I have no education." As she grew up, she also started working as a cook for the *hanba*, or construction-worker coterie. She met her present husband when she was about twenty and he nineteen, both working at the same *hanba*. They began having sexual relations, and she became pregnant and gave birth to her eldest son. Then Mr. Tokuda received notification that he was drafted for war service. The wife's grandmother talked to Mr. Tokuda and made him agree to become a *muko-yōshi*, legalizing his relationship with her granddaughter. They were separated for about three years. Mrs. Tokuda went to Tokyo with her small child, looking for some better chance to survive. Her maternal relatives had died in the meantime and she was homeless. As she puts it, she did all kinds of things to keep herself and her child alive. Finally, Mr. Tokuda returned to Tokyo from the war front, but two years passed before she finally found him. When she did, she discovered that he had been considering "marriage" with a woman whom he had met in Tokyo.

In 1948, Mrs. Tokuda moved into a tiny room with her husband and child. Neither Mr. nor Mrs. Tokuda reported to us what happened between them at the time, but a second child was born in 1949. In 1950 Mr. Tokuda had an operation for a stomach ulcer, and in 1951 a third child, the subject, was born, and quickly thereafter two more. All this time both Mr. and Mrs. Tokuda worked irregularly as day laborers on government relief. Both suffered ill health and claimed welfare subsistence under the *seikatsu hogo hō*, the Life Protection Welfare Law. Both husband and wife joined a new religious sect, Sōka Gakkai, in 1958, and their son also eventually joined the youth group affiliated with it. Mr. Tokuda died during our research contact with the family. The boy has not continued any of the stealing behavior for which he was apprehended at the time we were doing our case study.

In the family of Mr. and Mrs. Ishino, case I-8, we find a history of a broken family and sexual irregularity, coupled with epilepsy and mental subnormality in the wife. As it was told to us, Mrs. Ishino was legally registered as the eldest daughter of a married couple, but she was actually the child of her adopting mother's younger sister; this pattern is not infrequently found in Japan—an irregular birth is disguised by a relative's registering a child as his own. Mrs. Ishino's father was said to be unknown, although Mr. Ishino reported to us that he had once heard from a relative that Mrs. Ishino was the presumed child of her adopting father and her adopting mother's younger sister. However, both state that the truth of this matter remains unknown. Her foster father was the foreman of a construction company and was financially relatively well-off. Mrs. Ishino thinks that possibly her adopting mother had complicated and mixed feelings toward her because of her natural parents' relationships to her, but Mrs. Ishino does not claim to know what her mother's feelings were. She reports that her parents told her that a little before her first birthday she began to have convulsive fits. Whenever she became cold at night she would suddenly lose consciousness; her body would tremble and become rigid. This description suggests epilepsy, but the parents were told by a local doctor that she had a very strong *mushi*, or bug, and that she should be given certain Chinese herbs to help control the "bug." The attacks lasted until she had finished grade school and then for some reason stopped.

From the husband's report, although Mrs. Ishino entered grade school, she was considered mentally retarded and never actually finished. Mr. Ishino did most of the describing of his wife's past to us, telling how she had been recruited to work in a war factory but was returned home, since she could not handle the tasks because of her intellectual inadequacy. While at home, she quarreled often with her parents and began to stay out at night, hanging around a railroad station and associating with a youthful gang of delinquents (*chinpira*). She became known as a prostitute. Her conflict with her foster parents was instrumental in her first meeting with her husband. She had stolen money from her parents, and they punished her severely, forcibly cutting her long hair short as part of the punishment. She had come crying outside a nearby factory, where Mr. Ishino found her when he came off work. He felt sorry for her and told her she could stay overnight at his home. It made his parents very angry; they said they did not want such a "slovenly" girl around. Mr. Ishino himself was staying with foster parents, who had adopted him. Soon he began having sexual intercourse with the girl; she became pregnant, and out of pity he married her. Their subsequent life has been an extremely chaotic one. The Ishinos now have eight children, and Mrs. Ishino has sometimes aided her deliquent son in his stealing activities. The house is in a state of great disorganization. Mr. Ishino's attitudes toward his wife and family can only be considered to be those of a saintly masochist.

The Terayama family (case D-14) also has an example of flagrant antisocial behavior, in this case on the part of a first wife who eventually deserted her home. The couple met as co-workers in clerical jobs, and after going with each other for about seven months they made a love marriage. In talking about the circumstances of his marriage, Mr. Terayama indicated that the wife was the one who had taken the initiative. When asked if it were a love marriage Mr. Terayama responded, "Well, in a way, yes, for my wife."

The wife evidently took the initiative in many matters. Immediately after the marriage she stopped working, and they lived on Mr. Terayama's tiny income. They had a child after three years of marriage. It seems that the wife, during this time and afterward, as Mr. Terayama puts it, "liked socializing [*shakō zuki*]." He says, "She had no idea of economy at all and bought whatever she wanted." He evidently was helpless in dealing with her economic and social profligacy. He said of himself, "I am timid, weak-spirited [*ki ga yowai*], whereas she was strong-spirited [*ki ga tsuyoi*] and also of somewhat fierce temperament [*kishō ga hageshii*]." As he described her, she seemed a rather egocentric, hysterical, and aggressive woman with little control over her impulses. During the time she stayed with Mr. Terayama she gave birth to three sons, toward whom she was somewhat rejecting. He says, "She did not like to breast-feed her babies." Nevertheless, she was strict with her children. She continued to "socialize" even after the birth of three children. It is curious that Mr. Terayama is very vague in describing his wife and yet seems still to be somehow passively drawn to her. Their marriage lasted for about twelve years. Finally, the wife's socializing, which evidently involved flagrantly going out with other men, ended when she got into trouble with the neighborhood wives' association, a mutual financing organization in which the participants pooled money so that each in turn could buy an expensive item. Mrs. Terayama ran away with ¥700,000 and a young factory worker, leaving behind her three sons. Mr. Terayama divorced his wife because he "was encouraged to do so" by his wife's brothers, after they had communicated with the wife, who was living in another part of Tokyo with her new lover. The use of this expression of being "encouraged" reflects Mr. Terayama's basic passivity and his incapacity to act upon anything on his own. It is interesting to note that the wife's brothers felt responsibility to find Mr. Terayama a second wife, a widow, whom he married four years ago and who now helps him take care of his family.

The dead first wife in case D-18 is a tragic example of a woman whose sexual acting out ended in suicide. In this case Mr. Teramoto had an "arranged marriage" with his stepmother's niece, with whom he had had sexual relations when he returned home from war. The girl had become pregnant, and the marriage was brought about as quickly as possible. Their son, the subject, was born less than six months after the marriage. Soon afterwards a fierce battle broke out between Mr. Teramoto's wife and his stepmother. The wife turned out to be an extremely aggressive, impulsive woman, who took out her aggressions on her child as well as on her husband. She fought violently with her mother-in-law, who openly expressed her hatred for her daughter-in-law to her neighbors. Sandwiched between his bitterly complaining stepmother and his explosive, cup-throwing wife, Mr. Teramoto did not know what to do. He became a helpless observer of domestic warfare, and seven years after their marriage, family life became too much for him to bear. To escape from the constant fights, Mr. Teramoto concentrated on hard work, and on getting drunk every night after a hard day's labor. Home became a place for him to return to after midnight, eventually to fall asleep in a leaden stupor. He hardly talked with either his stepmother or his wife, nor did he relate to his increasing brood of children.

For extra income the family rented a room on the second floor to a young boarder, a distant relative, who was a university student—a quiet, studious young man, but also one who had some reputation for playing around with women. The wife quickly became intimate with this student, while Mr. Teramoto remained occupied with work and drink. Sometimes he would return home, as he describes it, "to find his wife and the student intimately talking over a cup of tea." He also heard that when his wife took their children to a nearby theater the student would be seen in their company. Jealous, he drank more and began accusing his wife of preferring the student to him.

One day the wife ran away with the student. The mother-in-law was triumphant, saying she had been right all the time in claiming that her daughter-in-law was "a wicked woman, flirting with many men in the neighborhood." The old woman insisted that the wife should be divorced, but Mr. Teramoto wanted her back. He reported her absence to the missing persons bureau of the police. He went to the student's parental house, expecting to find both the student and his wife there; but she was not. He was told that she had gone back to her own parents. When he followed her there, she looked happy to see him and agreed to return home with him. He hoped that she would change her attitude and that there would be no more trouble.

Three days later he returned home, both late and drunk, to find his wife and the student again sitting close together at the *kotatsu*, talking and laughing. Enraged by drunken jealousy, Mr. Teramoto called his wife a whore and told her he was finished with her. His wife and the student then went upstairs together. He remembers falling asleep. The next morning, concerned with the quiet upstairs, Mr. Teramoto went up. There was no sign of the student, but his wife was lying unconscious. She had taken a heavy dose of sleeping pills in an attempt to kill herself. She was hurried off to the hospital, but complications developed and she died of pneumonia, at age thirty-one. Their eldest son, our delinquent subject, has been told that his mother died of a sudden illness.

Individuals who admit to sexual irregularities sometimes also admit to irregularities with the law. For example, in case I-11, Mr. Ihashi admits rather freely to his postwar black-marketeering activity, which he ran in conjunction with the operation of a small sake and beer bar at the corner of a market. He was concerned, however, that such business irregularities and the poor environment in which he was living were not good for his children. When things got better, he moved to a new location and started up a metal business. During this time Mr. Ihashi maintained an illicit liaison with a woman who was helping him with his black-market dealings. Mrs. Ihashi talks about this liaison rather freely in her interview, saying that her husband fell in love with this woman and that their relationship lasted for about five years. Sometimes he would stay away at night; occasionally he even brought the woman home. This behavior caused serious discord between Mr. and Mrs. Ihashi, and is still remembered by the children. Mrs. Ihashi says that she endured her husband's conduct because he was the father of her children. However, Mr. Ihashi discovered that his mistress was being unfaithful to him and discontinued the relationship. The wife seems not to have displayed much open hostility, but seems to have attempted to take on the submissive, suffering role of the Japanese woman. One gains the impression, even so, that Mrs. Ihashi was not actually fulfilling Mr. Ihashi's dependent needs, and that she was aware somehow of her own inadequacy in marshaling her emotional attitudes to play the submissive wife wholeheartedly. It is interesting to note that on Card 13 in the TAT she constructs a story of a wife who was murdered by a former embittered lover. The husband in the story is seen as being sorry when he finds the dead wife, thinking that no wife could be so good, and he will never be able to get another wife like her. Her stories suggest that her submissive acceptance is related somehow to guilt in regard to her own disavowed fantasies about extramarital relationships.

Mrs. Ihashi's submissiveness is manifest in the handling of her child. She describes how she took on the mother's role of apologizing continually to her neighbors for the wild, aggressive behavior of her son, who often fought the neighborhood children, occasionally injuring them. He uprooted the neighbors' plants, broke glass doors at home, and stole money to buy things. Mrs. Ihashi felt that her son was "most difficult to raise" and that it was she who had to apologize to the neighbors for his misbehavior, as the father "hated to lower his head toward others."

In a few cases, the sexual irregularities of the grandparents produced obvious feelings of neglect or deprivation in the childhood of the husband or wife.

In case I-2, Mrs. Ichitani describes strong negative feelings about the neglect resulting from her mother's irregular sexual life. She is unclear about the sexual history of her mother preceding the marriage during which she herself was born, but her mother had had a child earlier by another man. It was never made clear to her why there had been a separation from this child's father. She remembers that her mother was usually at home during her early childhood but that she expressed no attachment for her children, nor was she at all interested in their education. Mrs. Ichitani remembers being given pocket money only by grandparents, and that among her siblings she was the most strong-minded and stood up best for her rights, although all the others felt the same about the neglect they suffered. In 1935 the family moved to Arakawa, where Mrs. Ichitani entered primary school. Her elder sisters were then adopted out, which came as a terrible shock to her because she had always felt that her whole family should live together. Soon thereafter she too was adopted out to another family. She wanted to go back home when she found that her new parents loved an adopted boy more than they loved her. She eventually was able to go home again, where, according to her report, she was teased by her brothers day and night.

When she was eleven, her mother left home, abandoning her remaining children, the youngest of whom was only six months old. The care of her smaller siblings was left completely in Mrs. Ichitani's hands. She was told by someone that her mother had gone off with a man with whom she had fallen in love. She could understand what that meant, but she hated to hear about it. She lost what remaining respect she had had for her mother, and even though the mother came back home in about a year, the daughter henceforth felt only hostility and antagonism toward her. Eventually, her mother forced her into marriage against her wishes at age seventeen.

Sexual irregularity per se is not mentioned in case histories of the other parents of delinquent children who experienced prior family disruption. What is stressed in almost all instances is the feeling of deprivation and rejection in childhood that colors the remembrances of a disrupted family life.

The story of Mrs. Torihashi in case D-17 is such an example. She remembers her father as a factory worker in Tokyo, where she has lived from birth. Her mother was a cold, competitive woman who showed little affection toward any of her children. Her father was a chronic alcoholic who became abusive to his family whenever he was drunk and who, even when sober, was irresponsible and given to a kind of superficial masculine bravado. The home atmosphere was one of constant dissension, and Mrs. Torihashi remembers envying her happier playmates. When she was six her mother deserted the home and never returned, and her father was left with the responsibility for the four children. He discharged this responsibility by sending Mrs. Torihashi, her next older sister, and her younger brother to relatives, and by selling the oldest daughter into prostitution. From that time on Mrs. Torihashi lost contact with her family with the exception of her next older sister, who used to come and visit her after the family was split. In the following four years, Mrs. Torihashi was passed from relative to relative.

When she was about ten, Mrs. Torihashi was apprenticed to a distant relative who owned a barbershop in the city, a strict, dominating woman who punished her for any mistake. After she finished elementary school she began high school, but she lost interest because her employer scolded her too much for being late to work. During her schooling and apprenticeship she made few close friends, although there were several girls apprenticed with her. Because her employer was also a distant relative, she didn't feel free to complain about the work as the others did. When they would go home to visit their families on days off, Mrs. Torihashi would remain in the shop because she had nowhere to go. The situation became unbearable and she finally left, returning to an aunt with whom she had been living before being apprenticed. This aunt, however, rejected her, reprimanding her and telling her to go back to the shop where she belonged.

There are relatively few reports of sexual irregularity after marriage on the part of a present wife, although such deviancy is reported for the women in the grandparental generation or for former wives. The Torihashi family is unusual in this respect. Mrs. Torihashi reports leaving home and taking a younger lover herself as revenge for her husband's sexual liaison with an older widow who had been working for him in his barbershop. Mrs. Torihashi, whose childhood past we have just described, became disturbed by gossip and "aggravated by my husband's indecisiveness concerning his work activity." She left him and her children and moved away.[2]

About this time, at a public bath, Mrs. Torihashi met a man who was married and out of work and wanted to find a job in the city. She volunteered to help, and they took off together. Her oldest daughter was left with the responsibility for the care of the father and the other children. Mr. Torihashi admits that his children were aware of his involvement with his employee and that they knew this was the reason for the parents' separation.

The delinquent subject in this case was six years old at the time of his mother's departure, and he kept asking when she would return. After seven months, Mrs. Torihashi attempted to send for her children; she wrote a letter saying she had settled in a new job and had found an apartment. Two months later Mr. Torihashi gave up his mistress and came to Tokyo to reunite the family for "the sake of the children's education." When he first arrived, Mrs. Torihashi taunted him about the younger man with whom she had come to the city. Mr. Torihashi became extremely angry; he drank heavily and got into actual physical fights with his wife.

He was doing very poorly and had to change jobs frequently. This situation went on for several months, but finally the family settled into a routine, and from then on there was no reported socially unsanctioned sexual behavior on the part of either parent.

2. When she deserts, a Japanese wife can usually justify leaving her children because technically they belong to the man's family lineage.

Wartime Disruptions

Although it has been mentioned in various contexts, we have not focused on World War II as a generally disruptive event for all Japanese, including the citizens of Arakawa Ward. We should note that a number of the family disruptions reported in both our normal and our delinquent samples were due to wartime conditions and fatalities. For example, in case I-6, Mr. Ikuta returned home from war in 1946 to learn that his wife, mother, younger sister, and twin brother had been killed in bombing raids. Both he and his father were very despondent. He went to live first with his father's family in Ibaragi Prefecture and then with his sister's family in southwest Tokyo. A year and a half later he married his present wife.

In the descriptions given of occupational vicissitudes (see chapter 6) there are a number of cases of temporary disruptions of family life related to occupational necessity during the war period. Some individuals employed in the countryside had to go to Tokyo alone to live with others. They could not take their families with them and had to commute once or twice a month to their families living in the country; these circumstances occurred in cases D-8 and N-11.

In a number of cases relatives sought to bring together families of widows and widowers "for the sake of the children." The fact that there is such general dissatisfaction with these patched-together families is a major finding from our material. Evidently, remarriage is not generally successful for most Japanese; the first marriage seems to be tenaciously held by most women as their primary and lasting commitment.

INTERGENERATIONAL ATTITUDES

Attitudes of Parents toward Their Own Parents

In attempting to gain a three-generational picture, we tried to rate the attitudes held by each spouse toward his and her own parents. In many respects evidence about attitudes was comparatively fragmentary, and some of our ratings are of questionable validity, since they are based on limited data. We present our findings, therefore, with considerable caution.

The attitudes held by the normal couples toward their own parents were generally more positive than those held by the families of delinquents. Ten of the 19 husbands in the normal control families gave generally positive descriptions of their own fathers; 11 of the 19 gave similarly positive descriptions of their mothers; and 3 were generally negative about their parents. The statements of the remaining husbands were either so bland or so ambiguous that one could make no determination. The wives in these 19 families rated their own fathers positively in 10 cases and negatively in 2; they rated their mothers

TABLE 8.5
Overall Ratings of Attitudes Held toward Their Parents by Husbands and Wives

	Normals (38 individuals)			*Social Delinquents (40 individuals)*			*Isolate Delinquents (22 individuals)*		
	Rating of Satisfaction			Rating of Satisfaction			Rating of Satisfaction		
	+	o, + −	−	+	o, + −	−	+	o, + −	−
Husband's attitude toward his father	10	6	3	6	7	7	4	0	7
Husband's attitude toward his mother	11	5	3	7	8	5	6	1	4
Wife's attitude toward her father	10	7	2	5	6	9	1	4	6
Wife's attitude toward her mother	13	1	5	7	2	11	2	3	6
Totals	44	19	13	25	23	32	13	8	23

TOTAL RATINGS IN EACH GROUP

	Normals	*Social Delinquents*	*Isolate Delinquents*
+	44	25	13
o, + −	19	23	8
−	13	32	23
Totals	76	80	44

Significance

Husband's Father	$P < .05$
Husband's Mother	Not significant
Husband's F + M	$P < .05$
Wife's Father	$P < .005$
Wife's Mother	$P < .025$
Wife's F + M	$P < .001$

positively in 13 instances and negatively in 5. Altogether, the ratings were approximately three time as many in a positive direction as in a negative (see table 8.5).

The families of social delinquents present a contrasting picture. In the 20 families, husbands rated their fathers positively in 6 instances and negatively in 5. The wives were even more negative in their ratings of their parents. Only 5 rated their fathers positively, whereas 9 gave them basically negative ratings; only 7 rated their mothers positively, and 11 rated them negatively.

The parents of isolate delinquents were even more extreme in their negative ratings of their own fathers and mothers. In the 11 families, 4 husbands rated their own fathers positively, 7 negatively; 6 rated their mothers positively, 4 negatively. The most extremely negative ratings of all were by the mothers of isolate delinquent children. Only 1 mother rated her own father positively, whereas 6 gave their fathers basically negative ratings. Only 2 rated their mothers positively, and 6 negatively.

Totaling the mothers of delinquent subjects, therefore, only 6 out of 31, or less than a fifth, saw their fathers in a positive light, while 15, or about half, gave their fathers a definitely negative rating (see table 8.5). Only 9, or less than a third, rated their mothers positively; 17, or more than half, gave their mothers a negative rating. These findings of the basic attitudes of parents toward grandparents are very striking. Although some of the findings are fragmentary, they indicate on a group basis the continuance of negative interpersonal attitudes from one generation to the next, which becomes apparent when the parents' attitudes are compared with the attitudes of the boys in our sample.

The Boys' Attitudes toward Their Parents

As part of our general assessment of cohesiveness, we attempted to rate and tabulate the boys' attitudes toward their parents. A number of our subjects were noncommittal, vague, or confused in expressing their feelings toward their parents. Nevertheless, as is shown in table 8.6. a number of boys, in both the normal and the delinquent groups, do express negative feelings toward their parents, particularly toward their fathers. The socialized delinquent boys are characterized by a complete lack of any unequivocable positive feelings toward the father and also by a large number of individuals who were noncommittally "neutral" in their attitudes toward the father. None of the nondelinquent boys was overtly negative toward his mother. Contrary to impressions gained from studies of delinquents in the United States, our sample of delinquents tended to voice more negative complaints against their mothers than against their fathers. A total of 17 out of 31 voiced some complaints (negative or strongly negative) against their mothers, 8 out of 31 against their father. While some further explanation may be possible, we can only interpret this as a cultural difference wherein direct criticism of the father is psychologically more difficult than criticism of the mother. The authority figure of the father in Japan still carries considerable weight even among delinquent subjects. This finding goes counter to our supposition that matrifocality among the Japanese lower class should be corrosive to the image of the father. At least in our interviews, the boys were more willing to be vague than to be critical, somewhat opposite to the findings we derived from the wives in these families.

Following are some examples of the boys' expressed attitudes toward their parents. Despite antagonism, most boys still feel deferential toward their fathers. Their main complaint is physical abuse from the father, but they also express a wish for greater closeness than the father allows.

Describing his feeling toward his father, a delinquent boy in case D-8, Masao Fukuhara, said he was afraid of him. The interviewer asked why he was afraid, because the boy was now big and maybe stronger than his father physically. The boy said:

TABLE 8.6
The Boys' General Attitudes about Their Parents

	Normals (19)		*Social Delinquents (20)*		*Isolate Delinquents (11)*		*Total Delinquents (31)*	
	Toward		Toward		Toward		Toward	
	Father	Mother	Father	Mother	Father	Mother	Father	Mother
Strongly positive +	6	5	0	0	2	0	2	0
"Neutral," or not clear, ambivalent o, + −	8	14	15	10	6	4	21	14
Negative −	4	0	5	7	2	4	7	11
Strongly negative − −	1	0	0	3	1	3	1	6

Father: normal vs. delinquent not significant
Mother: normal vs. delinquent .001

> It is true that I have grown big, and I might fight back with somebody else, even an adult. But I cannot fight with my own father. I don't know why, but after all, he is different. He is my father. He is not a stranger. The father is a father and is different from ordinary adults. I don't feel equal to him. After all, he is the man who raised me, isn't he? Even when I feel I am right and my father is wrong, I do not talk back to him because I somehow feel he would hit me. I am afraid of him, after all.

His main complaint is his father's indifference to him:

> I do not remember any occasion on which my father took me someplace. Last year I went skiiing with my father. This was the first and the last time we went somewhere together. My mother never says she wants to go someplace with me, and I never want to do so either.

The son in case I-11 expressed this attitude toward his father, Mr. Ihashi: "I do not like my father, because he is noisy and capricious and tends to preach when he drinks." Also, "he becomes absolutely fearsome when he is angry." At such times the son hates him. He loves his mother more, as she is continually "tender."

However, the son displays ambivalence toward both parents. This is evidenced by a statement that his mother never gives money or other things with any generosity and that when his father is in a good mood he is a gentle, generous, and loving person, and "much better than my mother." It appears that the son wishes to identify with the positive aspects of his father's personality but that there is no stability in the father's moods nor consistency in his behavior. Therefore, on the whole, he tends to prefer his more gentle mother, and seeks to find security and dependence in his relationship with her. Nevertheless, he feels there is some withholding quality in her that somehow frustrates him. There is no doubt that the boy is aware of his mother's unexpressed hostility toward his father because of a long affair with another woman. But her method of withholding, which is subtle, is somehow there toward the son also, in spite of the outward submission expressed in the behavioral role of a dutiful wife and mother.

Occasionally, the father in this family attempts to hold "a family meeting," as he calls it, so that members of the family can have an "opportunity to express themselves." He is somewhat aware that they do not actually feel free on these occasions, because they fear him. He is vague about what he wants to accomplish in these family meetings. There seems to be a certain degree of self-deception in his assumption of the pose of a modern, "democratic" father to cover up hostile feelings of inadequacy. With all his high-handed, erratic behavior, he is still motivated by a need to be loved by his family and to have them express such feelings toward him. The boy views such family meetings as "nothing but a sham" and "nothing but my drunken father's speeches," indicating how little respect he has for his father.

The family in case I-9 is an example of a negative relationship between a delinquent son and his stepmother. The stepmother, Mrs. Igayama, sees her stepson's shyness and quiet behavior as an indication of "obedience" to her. But the boy sees his stepmother as "nagging, critical, stingy, and gossipy, a woman who does not look after her husband and children." The boy feels that his stepmother is concerned only with her blood child by a previous marriage.

Even in families with nondelinquent children, it is fairly common to hear complaints about well-recognized favoritism toward one child or another. For example, in case N-10, the Sekis, who are basically a harmonious family, there is tension over the husband's favoritism toward his first son by his first marriage. This eldest son, according to the stepmother, is very similar in character to his father, timid, introverted, and unable to speak frankly. He has never opened up with his stepmother or with his stepsiblings. This case is complicated in that there are two other children in the family: the wife's son of her first marriage and a youngest son of the present marriage. The eldest son gets along with neither of the other boys, nor does he get along with his own father. The wife says that she does try to take some special positive attitudes toward the eldest boy because "he is the eldest son and also my husband's son." She kept a wardrobe for hanging clothes in his room so that "his friends visiting him would think that he had his own wardrobe and might even think that he earned enough money to buy one."

A few years ago this eldest son suddenly left home and began living with a woman, making the father angry and causing the other two sons to accuse him "of doing whatever he wants (*kattena koto o suru*)." There has been some reconciliation, since the son is now married legally and has a baby. One sees in the attitude of the mother some attempt to make the best of a favoritism that the father seems unable to disguise. From the brief description we get of this now-married boy, he carried a deep feeling of resentment against his siblings despite his being the favored one. They, in turn, feel resentful of him, and our subject, the youngest son, openly describes the eldest as "having always enjoyed the greatest attention from the parents, and yet he did what he should not have done." Our subject blames the father for being far too lenient with and partial to his eldest boy, the cause of open antagonism between our nondelinquent subject and his father. Therefore he more closely identifies himself with the mother. In effect the subject has at times said that he wishes his father would go away and stay with the eldest son, an obvious desire on the part of our subject to have the mother more to himself. He stated to our interviewer that it is strange he is not delinquent, hating his father so much, but he would never become delinquent because he would not want to worry his mother. He says that because he loves his mother so much he could never think of doing anything to hurt her.

The mother in turn states that "my youngest son does not respect his father," and she adds with vehemence, "absolutely not." She, in effect, sometimes uses her son to have him complain to the father about things she feels but will not express directly to him. She says, "Our son understands how I feel, and sometimes he directly tells it to his father."

Throughout our material the remembered favoritism for another child is a point particularly focused on when parents describe their own childhood in negative terms. When they describe their childhood positively, it is often with some reference to the fact that they themselves were particularly favored by one parent or another.

Some parents still attempt to impart to their sons the sense that as males they have a special position. For example, Mrs. Tayama, in case D-20, says:

> I still differentiate between men and women. I always tell my daughters that men cannot lower their heads even when they realize they are wrong. Therefore, after my daughters marry, unless they learn to respect their husband's position as that of a man they will be unhappy. Although men and women are said to be equal legally, still in Japan women follow men when they are married. Accordingly, after marriage when their husband tells them that white is black, they must listen to their husband. As he always listens to me when I talk like this, my son has developed the idea that he can be more important than his sisters.

According to Mrs. Tayama, her husband equates changes occurring in the attitude of respect accorded the eldest son with his own worries about being taken care of in his old age. The wife says:

> My husband says there is no longer a system in the country which makes the eldest son support the parents. Under the new system all children should take care of their parents equally. My husband tells our son that he is as important as any other child in our family. In the past the eldest son was important, but it is no longer true. All the children are equal.

Nevertheless, the husband still tries to influence the eldest son to see that his special position is related to an expectation of future dependency.

> My husband has long thought that the eldest son is special. Accordingly, our son came to think that he was more important than the other

> children. Actually, we used to tell him that he should be reliable and dependable because he was the eldest son. It seems that he thinks he is important because he is the eldest son and therefore takes care of his parents.

In another context the wife points out that the eldest boy also feels responsible for his sibs, spending on clothes for them the money he earns by delivering milk. The deep sense of responsibility that goes with a privileged sibling position has been discussed elsewhere.

We have included at some length examples of anecdotal material in order to make explicit the nature of the materials we have used to categorize such features as discord, disharmony, and the relative cohesiveness of families in our Arakawa sample. The quantitative summaries by themselves cannot with sufficient cogency indicate the actual differences we found between the experimental and the control segments of our fifty families. To us at least, the evidence is compelling: There are very apparent differences, not only in the attitudes toward responsibility, authority, and discipline (discussed in chapter 7), but also in the quality of interaction and mutual acceptance within these families. Much of the anecdotal material included in this chapter overlaps considerably with the material bearing on considerations of neglect and rejection, love and nurturance, which are the focal points for the discussion in the following chapter. The course of our theoretical position will take on more concrete meaning after the reader has read the detailed interview materials in chapters 10 through 13.

CHAPTER 9

Affiliation and Nurturance

The Experience of Neglect and Deprivation

THE SOCIALIZATION OF DEPENDENCY IN JAPANESE CULTURE

It is essential to examine the characteristics of socialization beginning in early childhood which lead modern Japanese, like those of preceding generations, to emphasize emotional interdependency, whether in the family or in other organizations (Caudill and Scarr, 1962). Caudill, in his intensive research on maternal care and infant behavior in Japan compared with that in the United States (Caudill and Weinstein, 1969), stressed the intensive and continual body contact between the mother and her young children. Compared with Westerners, the Japanese are much more conscious of the satisfaction to be found in body contact and oral sensuality. This consciousness of the pleasures of the body is further encouraged by customs of bathing and massaging, and by the attention to textural details of food, art, and language.[1]

Hovering nurturance, which persists to a far later age in Japanese than in American culture, tends to go counter to the fostering of aggressive independence. The child is disciplined by threats of isolation rather than by the inhibition of free movement.[2] He learns to rely upon ready access to gratifications afforded by his mother. He is not encouraged to distance himself from her or to seek independent means of coping with his environment, as he often is in Western society. In this context of fostered dependency the Japanese also develop a capacity, by passive means, to induce nurturant behavior in others toward themselves. The inductive manipulation of others to secure care of oneself is expressed in the Japanese word *amae* (Doi, 1962).

The child is encouraged to be *sunao*, as *sunao* behavior receives positive evaluative reinforcement. The nearest English equivalent translation, "up-

1. The Japanese language is extremely rich in terms for tactile sensations and other descriptions of texture. Many of the terms used in Japanese depict relative degrees of smoothness, softness, and so on, and have no directly comparable words in English.

2. Takeo Doi (personal communication) points out that when a child is put in a separate room in Japan, he feels he is being isolated from contact with others. An American child in similar circumstances would probably feel that his liberty had been curtailed.

right,"[3] does not convey what is meant by *sunao*. The word has the connotation of being compliant and obedient to the wishes of others. For example, *sunao ni kiku* means to listen without objection or to follow directions compliantly. The opposite of being *sunao* is being *hinekureta* (warped). When a person's need for nurturance and dependency is not satisfied and he feels some acute frustration, he may take to sulking in a characteristic way described by the verb *suneru*, which means to manifest an apparent indifference to dependent needs or, even worse from the Japanese standpoint, to develop a jealous or envious attitude in which one judges that others are favored over oneself. This latter attitude is expressed in the Japanese verb *higamu* (to be "twisted"). When *higamu* becomes a chronic attitude, seen as an integral part of a child's or an adult's personality, he is described as a *hinekureta* person—distrustful, embittered, and cynical.

Compliance and obedience must be maintained so that the child will undertake willingly the increasingly heavy requirements and obligations placed upon him in the school and the home. There is a direct cultural linkage between contentment and compliance; a *sunao* person maintains basic trust in authority and finds it easy and natural to follow the directives of others, with the implicit assumption that he will be taken care of should special needs arise. Only those who are warped in character would suspect, object to, or protest against any legitimate authority.

It is this implicit "psycho-logical" equation stretched through time that makes it possible for young people to endure periods of rigorous training or apprenticeship. It is this equation that is implicit in *oyabun-kobun* paternalistic relationships within the Japanese economy (Bennett and Ishino, 1963), which makes it difficult for the Marxist-oriented labor unions in Japan to develop the cleavages in loyalty necessary to separate workers from management. Even the owners of progressive factories have realized the necessity to maintain worker goodwill by continual central emphasis upon what are termed "fringe" benefits in the United States. For the Japanese worker, these are not fringe benefits but essentials expected from one's boss in an occupational setting. It was this implicit psychological equation that made for the special affectional preference given the eldest son in the traditional culture. Since he was to carry the heaviest burden of responsibility, it was only natural that he be given the most intense care and nurturance.

On a deeper psychodynamic level, being *sunao* sometimes means remaining an extension of the mother's own ego. Many women have strong achievement needs or desires to express potentials for dominance and other instrumental potentials within their personality. Binding their sons permanently to themselves by maintaining nurturant control, the mothers in effect use the sons as a masculine extension of their own egos. This underlying psychodynamic use

3. Derivatively the word *sunao* comes from *nao*, straight, as in the verb *naosu*, to straighten, correct, or cure. The *su* is an emphatic prefix.

of the sons helps explain why many mothers become so fiercely competitive with daughters-in-law, who may seek to intrude and break up the mother's hold.

For the Japanese male who maintains a lifelong dependent attachment to his mother, there is no feeling of internal conflict, no matter how disappointed his wife is in him when he fails to assert himself in conflicts between his mother and herself. Characteristically, the disappointed wife learns, in turn, to manipulate her husband's passive dependence to her own purposes. She also affectively turns to her own children, ensuring the continuation of the pattern into the next generation.

Although Japanese women may be more psychodynamically independent than men in some respects, many of them, through their manipulations, elicit *amae* from a grown son. The role requirements for Japanese women wean them from any expectations they may have had of remaining dependent on their own mothers. Sometimes a young bride transfers her dependent expectations to her exacting mother-in-law, with resultant tension and unhappiness.

The prevalence of alcoholism in Japan (which we saw as severe in Arakawa Ward) receives less attention both from the public and from the psychiatric profession than the same problem does in the United States. Perhaps one reason for this lack of concern is that tensions over dependency, which often underlie alcoholic problems, are considered more "natural" by Japanese than unresolved dependency problems are by Westerners. Only when alcoholism is combined with some form of violent expression does it receive much attention. Individuals who drink more than a quart of cheap sake every day are rarely considered "sick" in any way. We found such drinking habits fairly frequent in lower-class Japanese. In our sample of fifty families the descriptions of a considerable number of fathers and of paternal or maternal grandfathers would classify them as alcoholic in an American clinical setting.

This lack of concern is related to the lack of negative sanctions applied to any form of oral indulgence not leading to the complete disruption of one's required role activities. It is not outside the boundaries of the acceptable male social role to become drunk so long as there is no interference with one's work pattern. In fact, drunkenness is frequently an excuse for social blunders or unseemly behavior.

Our lower-class sample confirms the frequent appearance of stomach complaints among Japanese. Some of these complaints, affecting many more men than women, are apparently of a psychosomatic nature. Cases of so-called hyperacidity (*mune yake*) strongly suggest underlying problems often related to tensions in a job situation. In our sample the complaints seem to disappear when the person quits his job or finds some other form of employment. Some individuals are so severely affected that they remain home "ill," and their wives must seek employment in their place.

The widespread acceptance of insurance policies has contributed heavily in recent times to a de-emphasis of the dependent role of the aged. The attitude that financial provision can be made in advance for one's parents has tended to further the development of nuclear-family thinking in many younger Japanese. Nevertheless, the tendency to avoid responsibility for the care of the aged is nothing like that found in the United States, where beds in hospitals or nursing homes are filled with aging parents who can no longer take care of themselves owing to some form of deterioration. Although there is some increase in the number of old people's homes in Japan, this form of care for the aged is not yet in any way characteristic of the present-day social scene. The aged generally can still depend on their middle-aged children for personal care and assistance.

In spite of this cultural emphasis on nurturance, it is apparent that in Japan, as well as elsewhere, there are relatively deprived children who become delinquents during adolescence, as cases in our sample well attest.

RATING PROCEDURE FOR AFFILIATION, ISOLATION, AND DEPRIVATION

Perhaps one can never hope to "measure" the experience of mutual affection or of being cared for. Our attempts at assessment of the relative presence of affection in a family are admittedly impressionistic. Nevertheless, we felt compelled to attempt some broad dichotomizing of attitudes about affiliation expressed by members of our sample families. Where to draw the line between what seems to be a relatively satisfactory or an unsatisfactory family experience in regard to affiliation and nurturance was not easy in a number of the cases. In most, however, we could find guideposts in our data that gave us some confidence about our judgments.

In general we found it easier to rate evidence for negative features in affectional ties. Data suggesting positive affection and mutual concern for one another was present to some degree in most families. Our clinical task, however, was to look for features of interpersonal relationships associated with the delinquency of the child. We focused, therefore, on the data indicating a relative lack of affection or nurturance directed toward our subjects. It seemed apparent that a few of our subjects were ignored in comparison with other siblings, and thus the fact that a more favored sibling received care and nurturance was of indirect concern to us because of how it might influence the attitudes of our subjects.

We first attempted overall ratings on a five-point scale from ++ to −− of interaction of each parent and subject, but later we abandoned the attempts to differentiate two steps in a positive direction, and ended by rating the evidence of interaction as positive, neutral, "negative" (−), or very negative (−−) in each of the following categories:

Signs of *interpersonal isolation:* Our chief criterion for such ratings was the degree to which the parent seemed to isolate himself from either the spouse or the boy, so that there was little interchange of personal warmth. The evidence used for rating isolation tended to overlap considerably with that used for ratings of mutuality and harmony described in chapter 8.

Signs of *neglect*: Our chief criterion for rating the neglect of a child by either parent relative to expected role behavior was based mostly on evidence that the parent's concern with other activities seemed to result in a lack of sufficient communication with the child or of concern with the well-being of the child, either in the past or at present. Other criteria overlapped considerably with those used in the assessment of supervision discussed in chapter 7. We attempted to maintain a distinction between isolation and neglect, using "isolation" to emphasize emotional withdrawal, and "neglect" to emphasize a preoccupation with other activities and a lack of positive appreciation of a child's good points or sense of personal worth.

Signs of *rejection*: The principal criterion for judging rejection as distinct from neglect was evidence of parental antipathy, suggesting an active rejection or depreciation of the child, not simply a concern with other things that distracted the parent from giving proper attention and appreciation to his child.

Inappropriate forms of *withholding* or "*compensatory giving*": In the area of nurturance, we found evidence of withholding attitudes ranging from the simple withholding of money to more subtle forms, such as withholding of support for educational hopes or the withholding of praise for constructive efforts. We also found forms of what we termed "compensatory giving," a seeming inability of a parent to set limits on demands, which often suggests that he is compensating for a basic withholding of affection or the rejection of a child or the children generally in a family. We attempted to rate these attitudes either as "inappropriate giving" or as "withholding," according to the evidence in the case material.

Subjective experiences of *deprivation*: Our principal criterion for deprivation was subjective descriptions by both parents and subjects of needs unrealized by their parents. In addition to those we shall presently relate, we have already given several relevant anecdotes in the previous chapter that the mothers and fathers in our sample recounted to us as their experiences with their own parents. We also assessed the experiences of deprivation suggested in the accounts of the boys, and took note of indirect indices of deprivation, such as oral symptoms and the history of breast-feeding in the accounts given to us by the mothers and fathers.

One of the better sources of material for these assessments were the inconsistencies and contradictions among the accounts of the three members of each family interviewed. Sometimes inconsistencies appeared between one interview session with an individual and the following one. Contradictory statements very often gave us clues to ambivalent attitudes or desires to distort the past on the part of either a mother or a father or even the boy himself. The boys' interviews themselves were not directly revealing of a sense of deprivation in any direct way. We depended more on the sequence of interviews with the parents, and as a result our ratings of deprivation were perhaps too heavily influenced by evidence of a sense of deprivation in the parents of delinquents in what they related to us about their own childhood experiences, rather than in respect to the children in our sample.

Results of Ratings

The various ratings given in table 9.1 strongly support our overall impression that there is considerable clinical evidence in our case studies that neglect, depreciation, rejection, and a sense of deprivation are key issues in the parent-child relationships of Japanese families in which delinquent behavior appears. Overall, in delinquent families problems of isolation and neglect most characterized father-child relationships, and rejection or a sense of deprivation most characterized mother-child relationships.

Isolation: Our ratings for "isolation" were somewhat surprising in that the fathers of the socialized delinquents were more often rated as isolating themselves than were the fathers of the isolate delinquents. Eleven out of 20 fathers in the social delinquent category showed some form of withdrawal from interaction with the delinquent subject, as against 3 of the 11 isolate delinquent fathers.

Neglect: Because of the lack of independence of the criteria used, our ratings of neglect coincided often, but not always, with those of isolation. It was interesting to note that we gave more negative ratings (8 out of 11) to the fathers of isolate delinquents for signs of neglect than for signs of isolation. Conversely, however, in the mothers of the social deliquents, there were more indications suggesting "neglect" than there were signs of emotional withdrawal or isolation. Generally speaking, few mothers in any of the groups could be regarded as having simply isolated themselves from interaction with their children without some excuse of other pressing activities. Such behavior is far more possible for the Japanese father, who can take a position of distancing or withdrawal without doing violence to cultural expectations.

Rejection: We found the mothers of the social delinquents most extreme according to criteria of active "rejection": 12 out of 20 mothers were rated as rejecting or depreciating a child in some way. Signs of active rejection appeared in 17 out of the 31 mothers in the total delinquent sample. Only 1 such rating was given for the 19 mothers of the nondelinquents.

In critically assessing our own judgments and our ratings of various criteria of affiliation and nurturance, we must point out that these ratings were not made on case material in ignorance of the case category. We cannot discount the possible skewing of our ratings through the halo effect of such prior knowledge. Nevertheless, allowing for such influence, our results are still so striking that we believe the evidence for differential patterns in the delinquent and nondelinquent parents is incontrovertible.

Withholding or compensatory giving: We found relatively little reported evidence of direct "withholding" in either our delinquent or nondelinquent groups. It may be that there is a conscious sensitivity on the part of parents that would lead them to avoid giving us evidence of this sort. At any rate, only 8 out of 62 parents of delinquents and 2 out of 38 parents of nondelinquents gave any evidence at all of "withholding" as distinct from withdrawal or neglect.

TABLE 9.1
Ratings of Isolation and Deprivation

	Normals (19)		Social Delinquents (20)		Isolate Delinquents (11)		Total Delinquents (31)	
	Fa	Mo	Fa	Mo	Fa	Mo	Fa	Mo
ISOLATION								
OK or not reported	15	19	9	17	8	10	17	27
Negative	4	0	8	3	2	1	10	4
Very negative	0	0	3	0	1	0	4	0
NEGLECT								
OK or not reported	18	17	9	9	3	5	12	14
Negative	1	2	9	7	6	4	15	11
Very negative	0	0	2	4	2	2	4	6
REJECTION								
OK or not reported	16	18	15	8	8	6	23	14
Negative	3	1	5	5	2	2	7	7
Very negative	0	0	0	7	1	3	1	10
WITHHOLDING OR COMPENSATORY GIVING								
Ok or not reported	17	17	13	16	8	9	21	24
Withholding	1	1	0	1	2	1	2	2
Very withholding	0	0	2	0	0	1	3	1
Compensatory giving	1	1	5	3	0	0	5	3
DEPRIVATION								
OK or not reported	18	17	16	7	9	3	25	10
Negative	1	2	4	11	2	2	6	13
Very negative	0	0	0	2	0	6	0	8
TOTAL TRAITS PER PARENT								
No negative traits	13	14	4	1	2	1	6	2
One negative trait	4	4	6	5	4	0	10	5
Two or more	2	1	10	14	5	10	15	24

X^2 (Yates Correction):
Nondelinquents vs. Total Del. Fa.
Neg. $P > .001$
Lt. trait $P > .001$
ND vs. Total Del. Mo.
Neg. $P > .001$
Rej. $P > .001$
Depr. $P > .001$
Lt. trait $P > .001$

Total Del. Fa. vs. Total Del. Mo.
Isol. $P > .02$
Rej. $P > .05$
Depr. $P > .001$

However, in respect to "compensatory giving," 8 of the 40 parents of social delinquents and 2 of 38 parents of nondelinquents reported incidents that we interpreted as using money or material objects to placate, bribe, or deflect the demands of a child. Although not significant overall, these results suggest that such "giving" is likely to appear in situations where other means of adequate relationship are not being exercised. Such "giving" appeared most often in parents rated poor in respect to adequate supervision of their children (see chapter 7).

Deprivation: Our ratings on deprivation vary significantly between the mothers of delinquents and those of nondelinquents. No such distinctions appeared in regard to the fathers. Only 10 of the 31 delinquent mothers escaped a negative rating in respect to some signs of deprivation in the mother-child relationships (either in the present or past generation). The mothers of the isolate delinquents were most extreme in this respect; not only were 8 of 11 negatively rated, but 6 of those 8 were rated *very* negatively. (See also the "isolate" cases in the illustrative materials in chapter 8 and the materials in the following sections.)

A caveat is necessary in comparing the very different ratings of mothers and fathers in respect to "deprivation." We included in our overall ratings of signs of "deprivation" reports of bottle-feeding, separation in early infancy, and the like. Evidence of this kind is not pertinent to the ordinary expectations of the father-child role, and therefore there is less on which to rate "deprivation" in the reports concerning father's behavior. The reports made by women were more directly sensitive in discussing feelings of deprivation in respect to their own mothers. We admit that we may have been incapable of finding how feelings of deprivation are indirectly expressed by Japanese men in their life histories. Supporting this possibility is the fact that the men in this sample do not describe dissatisfaction as readily as do the women (see chapter 8). It may well be that for males the overt verbal expression of a sense of deprivation in a mother-son relationship (or even a father-son relationship) is very difficult. Moreover, the men in our cases seldom report any sensitivity to possible deprivation in respect to how their wives treat their own children. Not only may men have difficulty in verbalizing such thoughts, they may not even be conscious of having them.

PATTERNS OF MOTHERING AND DEVELOPMENTAL DISTURBANCES

Although one can make some general assessments and ratings of attitudes of parents toward children or of experiences derived from case history material, few of the features on which our interpretations are based are directly quantifiable. The summary of anecdotal evidence seems to us more convincing than any attempt at presenting a series of tables and ratings. In our study of Arakawa families, we gathered materials from each of the parents in regard to the "problems" they encountered in bringing up their children. We also attempted to have them describe, as well as they could remember, the type of early mothering, including breast- and bottle-feeding, early food habits, and problems with toilet training, as seen retrospectively by both mother and father without direct yes-or-no questioning concerning the appearance of specific symptoms.

From this material two very clear patterns appear, which differentiate sta-

TABLE 9.2

Feeding Patterns and Childhood Symptoms of Nervousness

	Normals (19)				*Social Delinquents (20)*				*Isolate Delinquents (11)*			
Feeding	No Symptoms	Suck, Bite	Enuresis	Total	No Symptoms	Suck, Bite	Enuresis	Total	No Symptoms	Suck, Bite	Enuresis	Total
Breast	16	0	1	17	4	1	3	8	3	2	4(2)*	7
Breast/ Bottle	0	0	0	0	1	1	0	2	1	0	0	1
Bottle	1	0	1	2	3	4	2(2)*	7	0	1	2(1)*	2
Unknown	0	0	0	0	1	0	2	3	1	0	0	1
Totals	17	0	2	19	9	6	7(2)*	20	5	3	6(3)*	11

	Normals (19)	*Total Delinquents (31)*	
Breast-feeding	17	15	
Bottle-feeding	2	9	X^2 $P < .05$
Breast/bottle	0	3	
Unknown	0	4	
No Symptoms	17	14	
Oral symptoms	0	9	X^2 $P < .02$
Enuresis	2	13	
Oral and enuresis	2	17	

*Numbers in parentheses indicate children with both oral symptoms and enuresis.

tistically the delinquent children from the nondelinquent controls (see table 9.2). One pattern, related to feeding activities, shows that 17 out of the 19 normal controls were breast-fed, whereas in the 27 delinquent cases where the material seemed sufficiently reliable, 9 were solely bottle-fed and 3 were fed by a combination of breast and bottle. We tabulated all reports of thumb-sucking and nail-biting and found that no such symptoms were reported by the mothers or fathers of nondelinquents. Parental recollection of such "problems" was limited specifically to children in our deliquent samples. Our material on other feeding problems per se was less clear-cut; relatively few such problems were reported, and they did not seem to be related to delinquent behavior.

A second striking difference between groups in our sample was in enuresis. Only 2 (10 percent) of the 19 normal families reported bed-wetting into school age, as contrasted with 13 out of 31 delinquents, or 42 percent. This finding of some relationship between enuresis and the later appearance of delinquency has been reported previously in the psychiatric literature (see chapter 4).

The fact that in our cases 17 out of 31 delinquent children, or 55 percent, manifested one or more of the specific symptoms of enuresis, nail-biting, or finger-sucking is a startling cross-cultural affirmation of findings in the United States based on psychoanalytically oriented theories in regard to the personality syndromes of predelinquents. Only two out of 19 nondelinquent controls, according to the retrospection of the parents, manifested any such problems. It must be noted that in our nondelinquent group, 1 of the 2 bottle-fed children was enuretic. However, no correspondence between breast- and bottle-feeding and enuresis was found in the delinquent children, 7 enuretics being breast-fed and 4 bottle-fed. Oral symptoms such as nail-biting or finger-sucking were found in 3 breast-fed delinquents and in 6 who were bottle-fed, showing some slight correspondence between bottle-feeding and finger-sucking.

ILLUSTRATIVE MATERIALS ON NURTURANCE

Early Nurturance

Traditionally in Japan, breast-feeding was generally prolonged, extending often into the third year.[4] In present-day Japan, the nursing period appears to have shortened, with removal from the breast sometime between the first and second year. This prevailing pattern seems to be mirrored in our Arakawa cases. In a few of our records, however, we find evidence of the late weaning more characteristic of the past.

In case I-6, the Ikuta family, for example, weaning of the later delinquent took place at about three years of age when a new baby was born. The mother's explanation was that she was so fond of the boy that she could not bear to wean

4. There has been some controversy on breast-feeding reports from Japan. See B. Lanham, (in Haring, ed., 1956).

him, because he would cry. The day his brother was born he was abruptly weaned. That night he slept with his father, and it was reported by the father that he attempted to nurse on the father's nipples. He cried all night long, and the father spent a sleepless and painful night with him. He never again attempted to nurse, according to the parents' reports.

Although we demonstrated some correlation between bottle-feeding and the presence of delinquency, suggesting deprivation, there are instances in our delinquent cases where the early pattern reported between mother and child must be judged to have been quite good, as in the Ikuta case. Nevertheless, the boy developed a later pattern of isolate delinquency. As always, we must concern ourselves with a number of possible determinants rather than locating one or another that holds true in all instances. In the Ikuta case, for example, we found inconsistent fathering. Also apparent in the psychological tests and in the interviews was an obvious role rejection related to sexual ambivalence on the part of the mother.

Only a few of our subjects were separated from their mothers during early childhood. Early traumas caused by separation do not characterize our records, but one possible instance is reported in case I-7, the Ishisaka family. The subject became severely infested with parasites when he was one year old and was hospitalized for several months. The interviewer did not ascertain whether the mother was with the boy in the hospital (a usual Japanese custom) or how long she was with him if she did not stay with him for the entire period. One must take into account that such a period of separation could act as a trauma, possibly creating a negative pattern of interaction between mother and child. In general, however, we do not consider early physical separation in the subjects of our sample a significant variable explaining delinquency.

Isolation and Neglect: Generational Continuities

Continuities in patterns of interpersonal isolation and deprivation are apparent in the case histories of parents. Stepparents in particular are remembered as being nonnurturant and offering little in the way of love. In case D-16, Mr. Tsunada was the third son of five children of an impoverished tenant farmer in a prefecture near Tokyo. His father then married a woman whom he describes as "hardworking, strict, and fearsome [*okkanai*]." "She used to say all the children in the family were good for nothing [*gutara*], like their father." He has no memory of receiving any warmth from his stepmother. She used to complain and criticize her husband, who was a quiet person given to excessive drinking. He had frequent stomach complaints and used to stay in bed instead of working on the farm. The children learned to avoid their stepmother on such occasions because then her tongue was particularly biting and caustic.

Mr. Tsunada's siblings "disappeared" in one way or another. One brother was killed in the war. A sister went to Tokyo and "sort of disappeared." One gains a total impression of Mr. Tsunada's childhood as one of emotional isolation and deprivation. As he describes his present life as a pushcart snack peddler, one sees a continuity of isolation in regard to his own children. His wife works with him sometimes, as they sell *oden* until midnight. He comes home in the early morning and has "supper," consuming about a pint of 80-proof Shochu, a cheap brandy, before he sinks into sleep.

The son feels emotionally isolated from his parents. He describes his father's drunkenness as "annoying," but since the father sinks rather quickly into a stupor, the boy says he is "not much bothered." When his father becomes too *urusai* (nagging), the boy leaves home and does not return for a day or two. He says he has a number of friends who put him up periodically at their homes. The only object of affection for this particular boy is his dog. He says he loves animals very much. On his projective tests he shows rather direct hostile delinquent attitudes, little concern for achievement, and an imperfectly internalized superego. He is afraid of revenge and retribution from others, pessimistic about human relationships, and has a negativistic attitude that pervades his outlook on life. The mother in this family does not reveal much of herself, although one gains glimpses of a stubborn, rebellious, and hostile attitude toward outside authority.

In some of the interviews with the boys, we found a reluctance to admit to their own feelings of isolation in the present, although they were sometimes more willing to discuss difficulties in the past. In case D-8, for example, Masao Fukuhara says, "When I was small, I did not know how to play. When I was a small boy, I played only with girls. It was not fun." In another context, he states rather grandiosely that he has a hundred or a hundred and fifty friends at school, although he has no friends in the neighborhood. However, he adds that he doesn't have particularly close school friends who come to his home to play or talk. Looking back again, he says that while he was in primary school and even now at the junior high school he has had no friends whom he could trust or who were really congenial. He wishes he had a few real friends.

> They should have character compatible with mine. They don't have to be particularly bright. But my parents say that I should choose friends who do really well at school. But as I myself don't do well at school, I wouldn't be able to talk with meaning with somebody who does well. Therefore I need friends who do as poorly as I do [laughs].
>
> True friends visit me, but I never let them into my house because my room is so dark and uncomfortable. Also, I somehow feel that other members of my family are always ready to eavesdrop on us if I talk with my friends in the house.

Although the subject in this case sounds emotionally isolated from all his friends, it is also clear that he attempts to derive emotional satisfaction from what associations he does have and not from his own family members. He says he always has breakfast alone, as his sisters work and leave home early, and he doesn't like to eat with his parents, especially with his father, because then he has to eat with proper table manners. When the interviewer asked to which of his family members he feels emotionally the closest, Masao answered, "There is nobody in my family to whom I feel close. I am afraid of my father. My mother and sisters, after all, are women, and men and women do not understand each other."

He reveals that when he needs a large amount of money, like two or three thousand yen to buy something, he does not borrow the money from his parents, but tries to save his allowance. Sometimes he is able to borrow money from his friends and pay them back later from his monthly allowance. When he was asked by his friends to join in stealing, he couldn't refuse. He says it was not because he was afraid of rejection by them, but that he couldn't refuse their invitation, because "it was a bad thing to do to one's friends."

This boy is also afraid to excel in any way. There is a feeling of fear of competition or, as he puts it, of being "conspicuous" (*medatsu*). Although he is potentially good at sports, he never became any kind of acknowledged athlete. He says,

> I don't like to be one. I hate to be conspicuous in that way. I hate to appear in public. I never wish to show up at public places. . . . When I appear before the public, I become unable to do things which I otherwise can do. I like best to be left alone. When I am selected to be a representative athlete, I decline. Usually I am good enough to be selected. I don't try hard if it's necessary.

He has been given some appointive offices in student activities, but he says he doesn't care for them. "It's not that I ask for them. I was recommended by my classmates and forced into these positions. I was made to do these activities." Evidently he is recommended for such positions because others think of him as considerate. "I like to take care of others, I guess. I think it's because I like to take care of others. I don't like to be conspicuous. I don't want to appear in public. But probably I do like to take care of others without its being known." Among his friends he even avoids fighting in public, saying he prefers secret duels when there is some cause for fighting, although he admits that he doesn't fight very often.

One must not generalize that all delinquents have only negative feelings or are acting out of a sense of potential rejection by their peers. In some of the reports of our socially delinquent children, parents note a warmheartedness as well as aggressive and antisocial behavior. For example, in case D-20, Mrs. Tayama sees her child as very quick-tempered "just like his father," but she also says he "has a tender heart." When the family was in utter poverty after the father's bankruptcy, the boy used to collect empty bottles and sell them for small amounts of money, and he would then buy bread and give it to his siblings to eat when they were hungry. Although he fights aggressively with his sisters, he is at the same time very protective of them. The mother is worried, however, about the direct sexual interests her boy has shown; she has seen him, for example, reaching under the skirts of his sisters.

Descriptions of daily patterns were a source of materials demonstrating the

The artist reflected in his work. (Photographs by Karel G. van Wolferen)

A local shrine. Housewives still evoke the deities of a local Shinto shrine. These *Kami* watch over Arakawa but now share sacred space with commuting trains.

◀ The "Throw-in" temple still serves as a sanctuary for the dead. In Tokugawa times dead prostitutes, no longer of use to the proprietors of the nearby gay quarters, were wrapped in reeds and disposed of, to be cared for by the more compassionate Buddhist monks of the temple.

The tough "manly" spirit of the *Eddoko* of old *shitamachi* is still alive in the attitudes of daily workers, *tobi* (kites) who once also served as voluntary firemen. There is to be found yearly gymnastic competition, in which they fly to the sky on ladders.

Industries of Arakawa

A collector of empty cardboard containers. Arakawa became the "waste basket," or collection center of refuse, for modernizing Tokyo. Nothing that could be recycled was thrown away. The organized waste-dealers even built their own assembly hall in the ward. ▶

Manufacturing slippers inside a house factory. Arakawa was one of the first areas to produce modern clothes. Large mills were established on the banks of the river. Small house-factories became subcontractors in the shoe industry.

To compete in productivity family entrepreneurs work long hours to maximize the possible profits by utilizing their machines. Here a man and wife work late at night producing pencils in their house-factory.

"Company presidents" are ever mindful of their status. Here a small-scale entrepreneur, dressed appropriate to his role, helps one of his four employees box pencils. His "company" is part of a chain of subcontractors, who might go bankrupt with a shift in demand for the particular pencils being produced.

The *oden* cart is being readied for the evening. Nocturnally carts travel neighborhoods or are stationed at convenient spots in the entertainment districts. Arakawa is the home of many of these vendors, who with their entrepreneurial instincts inhabit hovels located in the ward. Here a noodle vendor lives under the tracks of a commuting train. ▶

Work with metal parts now occupies many subcontractors, who keep their noses to the grindstone in the house-factories of the ward.

Entering the alleys. From wider commercial streets one enters into a rabbit warren of narrow lanes, where the invisible networks of subcontracting house-factories are located. Pre-World War II American economists could not envision their considerable contribution to the Japanese war effort. Here the laundry is being raised on a bamboo pole.

Play. People live and play outside as well as inside the tiny shacks that are home to the *Eddoko* of Arakawa. Some fathers love to play with younger children when they are free to do so.

For many housewives child-centered life is a round of community contacts inside and outside the home.

The older "individual" hovels are giving way to several-storied *danchi*—"modern" tiny concrete apartment cells with commercial establishments at the ground level.

The woman often does *naishoku* (hand-piece) work at home in addition to helping out with whatever is produced on subcontract by machine. At night the space is used for family life.

There is a closeness of human contact in the crowded, tiny living areas. In winter there is a feeling of warmth shared by sitting around a *kotatsu*, drinking tea while one's legs are warmed by an electric brazier in a pit under the dining table.

The ever-present laundry does not occupy all the balcony space. Paper carp are displayed high on "boys' day." They represent hope for the next generation. Carp are symbols of manly strength and endurance. They persistently swim upstream, overcoming adversity.

Hope is internalized in the growing child by a "socialization for achievement." The mother's unstinting care inspires children to strive in school.

In a changing city grandmothers can still continue their role in caring for the young while mothers work.

Aging men in Arakawa often live partially in the past. Their function within the family has diminished. They are crowded off into corners by the pace of modern life.

There is stoic continuity written in the faces of all generations.

The heritage of endurance is an essential asset for the subcontract with life in Arakawa.

considerable distance and the lack of interaction among the members of some families.

For example, the usual day for the Torihashi household, case D-17, progresses in the following manner: The wife must go to her job by 7:00 A.M., and she therefore rises earlier than the others. The husband leaves about 8:00 A.M. One daughter works in a local department store, and an elder son works in a steel factory; they both leave early in the morning for their jobs, and each eats breakfast separately. Our subject leaves about 8:15 A.M. for the junior high school. Toward the end of the day the family members return one by one. The son who works in the factory arrives home first, and he prepares dinner for himself and his younger brother. The mother arrives home after 8:00 P.M. By that time there has already been one of the frequent quarrels between the two brothers; the older one has expected respect and help, which is frequently not forthcoming. The younger brother sometimes leaves the house and wanders about in the unpaved alleys nearby, where he may find others with whom to play swordsman until his mother arrives. He sometimes expects her to help him later in the evening with his homework. The father works six days a week until 10:00 P.M., and therefore has little time to spend with his family or talk with his children.

It is obvious from our interviews that the family shares few common interests. As far as our subject is concerned, family activities are limited to one of the adults occasionally taking him to a movie or sometimes accompanying him to the playground. On the day that both parents are home from work, they usually sit at home, drink tea, and wash clothes. In this family each person takes responsibility for his own laundry. One gains the definite impression that each of the family members has learned to shift pretty much for himself in terms of interests, activities, chores, and emotional needs.

Patterns of Rejection and the Experience of Deprivation

A pattern that one can infer from at least one of our records is a family configuration in which a rejected child is the family scapegoat. In case D-6, the Funahashi family, the subject, a fifteen-year-old boy, has gotten into considerable trouble with other youths through participation not only in a number of pranks at school but also in shoplifting and, most recently, in an attempt to steal an autobike, for which he was apprehended by the police. The father of this family, according to his own reported childhood, has been a rather diligent person. However, throughout his interview material, he stresses the fact that his second son is like himself. He seems to equate his own experience of neglect as a child with what his son is now experiencing, but this similarity does not make him feel closer to this son. From the mother's report we learn that the first son is his father's favorite, even to an unfair degree.

The boy's TAT suggests a considerable longing for nurturance and a strong fear of rejection. In the general family attitudes toward the delinquent son compared with his other siblings, one finds rejection glaringly manifest. The wife,

Mrs. Funahashi, is a rotund, seemingly hearty *shitamachi* woman whom we describe in chapter 7 as rejecting of her maternal role. Her son throughout infancy and even in grade school was troubled by bronchial asthma as well as by enuresis. He was seen as a violent and impulsive child in his early grade school days, constantly fighting and sometimes breaking windows. In the boy's projective materials there are indications of self-destructive feelings. His grades have been poor all through school.

The fact that considerable money was spent for treatment of his asthma when he was a child has been held against him by the family. The father in his interview constantly dwelt on the heavy medical expenses that the family incurred as a result of the boy's asthma, seeming to blame the boy for the present financial difficulties of the family. There is obvious distortion of memory; he is blamed for events that happened previous to his birth. The boy was born after the war, in 1948, and yet we are given a story by the father stressing the special care that had to be taken of him during air raids, when it actually may have been the older sibling who needed the care. There are other hints of this kind in the record. We concluded that the boy has become a depreciated scapegoat for the projection of unwanted impulses or difficult feelings that the parents themselves cannot handle. The boy's asthma (itself a psychosomatic symptom often related to an infantile fear of deprivation or abandonment)[5] evidently gave both parents a means of focusing all their internal and objective states of misery on a child who has been symbolically rejected in a number of different ways. The unexpressed aggression in the projective tests of the parents is manifest in the antisocial behavior of the boy.

In the interview materials, there are instances in which a rejecting attitude is directly expressed through feeding practices and in the attitude taken toward a new baby by the mother. To return to case D-17, the wife, Mrs. Torihashi, put her son on a very strict bottle-feeding schedule, from which she did not deviate. Anyone who was around at the time of the feeding was to give the baby his bottle, and since she worked, this was very often a substitute person. In his first years he sucked his fingers voraciously, so a pacifier was hung around his neck, to be available at all times, and he wore it until he was about five years old. His parents reported that when the other children began to tease him about it, he disposed of his pacifier and went back to sucking his fingers. By the time he entered school, he had given up sucking his fingers because of teasing, and now he bites his nails instead. The parents are aware of these oral activities on the part of the child, but they do not link them in any way to the fact that the boy was impersonally bottle-fed or to circumstances that existed at that time or later.

The connection between rejection or depreciation on the part of the mother's mother and her own rejection of her child, which we found in our delinquent sample, is apparent in case I-4. Mrs. Iida describes her own rela-

5. See the discussion of asthma in Fenichel, 1945, pp. 251 and 321–323.

tionship with her mother as basically rejecting. She was the last of eight children, born four years after the seventh child, a daughter, whom the parents had named Sueko, meaning "the last child." Her mother had not wanted any more children, especially since she was forty-eight years old, but she had to accept her, as she put it, as an (unwanted) gift (in Japanese, *sazukariko*). Her mother told her she had not cared whether she were born alive or dead. She was named Tome, meaning "to stop." As a child, she often heard her mother and grandmother say that she was an unwanted burden. She felt that she was given less food and fewer clothes than the older children, and she had to contend not only with her own siblings but also with a nephew her mother took in to care for, a boy one year older than herself. Her mother, as Mrs. Iida remembers it, took very good care of this male child and neglected her. When Mrs. Iida finished her six required years of primary education, she was sent away to become a nursemaid for a family living in Kita-ku in Tokyo. Her employer's family later arranged a marriage for her with an apprentice metalworker.

The deprivation felt by some children as a result of rejection by the parent is well expressed by the subject in this case. According to his parents, when a younger sister was born the boy showed extremely regressive behavior. He no longer wanted to walk and had the parents wheel him in a buggy. He was described by his father as continually touching his mother's breast, and he tried to take the breast away from the new baby. One time his mother caught him putting a *futon* (bedding) over the head of the baby, and he asked his mother to give the baby away "because he did not want her." The mother tried to be gentle with him, feeling "sorry for him." She gave him money, as she puts it, "because I could not take care of him while taking care of the younger baby." The subject, at the age of three years, learned to go out to buy candies with money, an obvious pattern involving compensatory giving.

In the same year his younger sister developed a high fever, and the mother went to stay with her at the hospital, leaving the boy alone during the day. According to the father, he was praised by the neighbors for doing *rusuban* (watching the house) very obediently and quietly. The neighbors said he was *otonashii* (well behaved). The father stated that people said that he was so *otanashii* at times that he was just like a girl. However, during this same period, the child stole a thousand yen from his mother's purse. His mother took back the money and gave him a smaller amount and then hit him. The husband at this time was working overtime in order to increase his income. He left home very early in the morning and came home late, and thus had very little contact with the child.

At the age of five, on the birth of a second son, the boy was put in nursery school. He evidently was somewhat *hinehureta* (twisted or warped). He was punished by being confined in a dark room by his teacher for not obeying his teachers and not conforming to the group activities. He is reportedly still afraid of dark rooms. This isolated boy, when he came home from nursery school, complained of being bullied by others. But according to the mother, after a few months in a nursery school he became "adjusted" to group life.

Mrs. Iida's own impression of her attitude toward her child was that she had "spoiled him" (*amayakashita*) and failed to give him sufficient discipline. He wet his pants frequently at the nursery school and could not take care of himself by putting on and taking off his shoes. As a second-grader he stole toothpaste from a neighborhood store, an incident that was reported to the parents. The mother told of his theft in her interview, but the father never mentioned it, insisting that the son throughout grade school, until the third grade at least, was *sunao* and *otonashii*. After the third grade, according to the father, he became stubborn and *hinekureta*. The father's idea was that the mother had scolded him too severely when he fought with his younger siblings, and as a consequence he had become *higamu* (resentful and envious of others). The mother, in another interview discussing the subject's delinquency, said that after he entered primary school she felt that her love somehow shifted to her daughter, whereas her son became *kimuzukashii* (of difficult spirit) and untrustworthy.

Mr. Iida said that also by the third grade the boy made some bad friends, among them an eighth-grader who seemed to have considerable influence over him. Once he did something to the stove in the classroom during the winter and was told by his angry teacher not to come to class. He did not tell his mother but stayed away from school the next day. The father reports that under the influence of his "bad friend" the boy, in the fourth grade, stole money and a watch at a neighborhood bathhouse. He turned the watch over to his friend and spent his share of the money on cakes and candies. The police picked him up and had his case transferred to a child guidance center, where he received group therapy. The father at this time decided to send him to take writing lessons so as to distract him from contact with his delinquent friend. Soon afterward, however, he stole a classmate's pencil box and wrote his name on it and would not admit that it was not his. His classmates ostracized him, and he had very little contact with others. In the fourth and fifth grades he stole money from other children, and in the fifth grade he would go to an entertainment area to spend it. He stole money subsequently not only from his mother but also from his older stepsister's purse.

The stories in the TAT of the subject in case D-10 (Fukitomi) are examples of a symbolic expression of deprivation in a setting of continual family discord. We find throughout a strong sense of anger about being deprived, and concern with rejection, isolation, and anticipated punishment for wrongdoing.

In interviews the Fukitomi family as a unit gives a feeling of unpleasant gloominess. The son is basically hostile, deprived, angry, and trying to force people to give what they are unwilling to give. The boy's TAT stories convey the familial atmosphere. Card J2, for example: "This is a farm. There is a shortage of water; they're wondering what to do. The woman on the left is thinking of what to do—there is no water—yet they work on the farm." For Card J11 he says:

> This person returned home from school and threw his briefcase into the house and went out to play. He comes back home and this lady [he avoids seeing a "mother," in effect rejecting his mother] is quarreling with his father and therefore this person steps in between them to try to recon-

> cile them. They don't listen to him, but in the end they stop fighting. They'll be all right, and this boy can go out to play again. The father always drinks sake, and the child goes out to play whenever this lady becomes angry. They will quarrel again while he is out.

A traumatic deprivation experience is very evident in case I-9, the Igayama family. In this case the subject's mother was physically weak and described by both father and boy as a gentle, kind woman. She died six months after the birth of a fourth child. At that time the subject was five years old and, by all accounts, very much attached to his mother. He had two older siblings, and after the mother's death the father felt helpless in dealing with all the children. The boy was sent to another city to stay with his father's sister. He did not adjust to the new environment and withdrew into himself, and his aunt found it impossible to draw him out. He developed a habit of bed-wetting every night, and within a year's time he was returned to his father. Many of the traits that had been noted in him before his mother's death were intensified. The symptom of bed-wetting that started again with her death continued for at least six years. His father remarried; the second wife was a distant relative, a widow, who agreed to the marriage out of a sense of family responsibility and obligation. Evidently she was unable, either from her own standpoint or from that of the boy, to develop any kind of positive relationship with him, and in our judgment she seems to have actively rejected her stepson. The boy responded to this unhappy situation with delinquent behavior, stealing money from the home; he had originally been classified as an isolate nondelinquent, and the fact of his stealing came out only in the interviews. He ran away from home several times, and at age twelve he once stayed away for three days.

At the present time (of the interviews) he is overtly hostile to his stepmother and sees her as continually nagging and recriminatory. He now fights back, feeling no compunction to hide his strong hostility. The interview and projective materials bring out the fact that this boy is at present preoccupied with some sexual fantasy. Although he is not known to the police for delinquent behavior, it is obvious that his is a borderline situation and he might well soon come to the attention of outside authority.

According to his stepmother, the boy has been nonexpressive and undemanding of her attention ever since she married into the family. She required him to help a great deal with the housework, and at one time he was also set to work at some handcrafts to supplement the family income. In the details of the boy's experience after his mother's death one sees that he was sent to a family that already had three children, and when his paternal aunt gave birth to a fourth child during his stay with her, the situation of the birth that occurred before his mother's death was re-created.

His relationship with his new stepmother did nothing to alleviate his sense of deprivation. He is well aware that his stepmother regards her marriage as based on economic and obligatory considerations rather than on affection or love. In spite of his isolate tendencies, he has not simply withdrawn but has increased his antisocial behavior. It is psychodynamically important that the time he ran away for three days was at approximately the time a grandchild was born to his stepmother by her eldest daughter.

The picture is not completely bleak as far as relationships are concerned, because the boy does feel some positive attitudes toward his father. Nevertheless, he feels that his father is not supportive of him in his antagonistic relationship with his stepmother. His response to Card 11 of the TAT dramatizes this directly:

> The boy broke something important in the house. He broke a vase and threw away the fragments because he was afraid he would be scolded. When he came back from school his stepmother noticed that the vase was not there, and the boy peered at her from behind a wall. After a time, his father returned from the office, and the boy's stepmother told his father of the event, and his father and stepmother scolded him.

The boy's observation of his stepmother is that she cares only for her own son by a previous marriage and has no regard for him.

Family Disruptions and the Sense of Deprivation in Childhood

In chapter 4 we discussed quantitative research findings relating family disruptions to delinquency. The following excerpts from our cases illustrate the subjective experiences that conduce to delinquent attitudes.

In case D-18, the Teramotos, the stepmother who came in following the death of the first wife describes a pathetic situation of complete neglect, which was obviously related to the chaotic behavior of the parents. The new Mrs. Teramoto describes how shocked she was when she married into a family in which the previous wife had committed suicide following rejection by her young lover. She thought she had been prepared, but the situation was worse than she could have imagined. The family was deeply in debt. The mother had been out every day with her lover. The children were dressed in tatters, and the father returned home only at midnight, drunk. The grandmother who lived with the family did nothing but complain, declaring that she hated the children. The inside of the house was a total wreck. There was nothing in order. This was perhaps our worst case. One wonders why only one child in the family has become delinquent.

In two other cases, the new stepmother also mentioned the neglect of the children owing to the total incapacity of the father to manage the children after his first wife died or left the home. More often, the descriptions of neglect are part of the parents' own childhood memories of separation from parents.

The father in case D-9, Mr. Fuchino, remembers his own feelings of deprivation related to the loss of his father, who died when the boy was three years old. According to his memory, his mother described his father as a man who very much liked to drink. His mother was a driving woman from a fisherfolk family, who had to work hard to raise her two sons. She struggled for about four years alone, but by the time her son was age seven, she found it too difficult and decided to marry again. She married a factory worker who died after only two months of marriage, leaving behind a pregnant widow. After the child was born, she married a third time, this time a fisherman who also had children by an earlier marriage. The mother gave birth to a child by her third husband as well. Mr. Fuchino says, "I hardly have any memory of my mother, but from what I heard, her life was always full of pain and suffering." The reason he has little memory of his mother is that he was sent away from home when he was in the second grade to live with a paternal uncle who was a stone carver. This uncle already had two children of his own and did not welcome the nephew, who meant an additional financial burden. As Mr. Fuchino puts it, he was treated depreciatively as a *jamamono*, a "disruption," and did not receive any warm acceptance from this foster family. He lived there for two years until a paternal aunt, feeling that the boy was unfortunate and lonely, took him in. She took good care of him, and Mr. Fuchino remembers her as a warm, maternal figure. "Whatever other people might say of her, she was a warm and gentle mother for me. I am very grateful to her." He never specifies why others might say something ill about his aunt.

Some of the couples interviewed have poignant memories of a series of separations in childhood. In case I-9, Mrs. Igayama, the rejecting stepmother we have seen above, reports that she was the second of ten children. She was adopted at the age of four by her father's sister, who was childless. She had to travel from Hokkaido, where her parents lived, to Tokyo, and she was never able to visit her own family again. She says she grew up believing that her adopted parents were her real parents, since she had no memory of her previous family. When she was a sixth-grader, she was told about the adoption. She said her adopting parents were always kind and gentle and took good care of her. They had a son, however, when she was seven years old, and then later on, a daughter. When questioned, she seemed somewhat evasive about whether she and these new siblings were treated equally. "It is difficult to expect from humans, after all, that your own children are not different from children of others." She went on to say:

> Well, after all, not everyone has two sets of parents. I have my adopted parents [*sodate no oya*], who reared me, and my real parents [*umi no oya*]. Once my real parents came up to Tokyo with a sightseeing group, and I had an opportunity to get together with them and my real brothers and sisters. Since then I have been corresponding with them and I am no longer in contact with my adopted parents and their children, although they, at this point, still live in Tokyo.

USE OF RELIGION AND MAGIC IN FEELINGS OF DEPENDENCY

We have little material related to religious beliefs as reflecting dependent or nurturant needs. Such beliefs did not seem to be important in most of our records, but here and there we did pick up attitudes about the use of reassuring magical or religious practices in relation to health. In case D-8, for example, Mrs. Fukuhara developed what she called a spinal hernia (*sekitsui-heruniya*) from carrying too heavy things. A cartilage between the spinal bones was crushed and pushed out of place. It was very painful, and she had to be hospitalized for several weeks. She received both massage and acupuncture in 1961, but she still didn't feel well and went for a more thorough examination to the University of Tokyo Hospital, where she was told nothing was wrong.

She then heard of an *o-gamiya-san*, a kind of magical-religious practitioner, to whom she went with her problem. She received a "religious or spiritual investigation," the nature of which she did not state in the interview. She went to a little shrine very close to her house dedicated to "Inari," a vaguely conceptualized deity, the rice god (often confused with the fox messenger who stands at the shrine's entrance). She found that a worker who worked for the Fukuharas used to spit on the dirt that was spread in front of this shrine. The practitioner told her that the deity was very angry and that he was punishing her with the spinal trouble. She was told that she should apologize to Inari by offering *aburage* (fried bean curd), supposedly a favorite food of the Inari fox. Mrs. Fukuhara cleansed the front of the little shrine, apologized to the deity, and went to a bean curd shop to buy *aburage*. On the way to the shop she had to rest three times because she felt very weak and was troubled by her spine. From the moment she bought the *aburage*, she immediately felt better, and after leaving the offering she went home vigorous and healthy. Since then she's been completely well. She was very well pleased and brought the religious practitioner a bottle of sake, one *shō* (about two quarts).

It is to be noted that the father in this family, Mr. Fukuhara, complained of stomach trouble, which he "cured" by giving up working. He is also interested in a new religious movement called the Dōtoku Kagaku Kenkyūjo. Its "moral science research institute," located in Chiba, was initiated by a certain Doctor Hiroyuki. Judging from what Mr. Fukuhara says, people can go to this institute, stay there for a month or two at their own expense, and receive teaching on Socrates, Confucius, Mencius, and Buddha. They are also instructed in the writings of "saints" like Kōbō Daishi, Nichiren, and many other wise men of the past. After receiving such training, they in turn may become "lecturers" and spread the gospel to other people, although Mr. Fukuhara does not seem to have become an active proselyte.

PART III

Family Portraits

The following four chapters illustrate how the techniques of intensive interview, used by social scientists, and of psychological testing, developed by psychologists, have been put to fruitful, complementary use in our attempt to understand community and family life in Arakawa. This intensive case-history approach, with a psychological as well as a social dimension, is as central to our study of family and delinquency as were the quantifications of results presented in the preceding chapters. We would argue that both forms of presentation are necessary. We include here, therefore, the verbatim responses to both the Rorschach inkblot test and the pictures of the Thematic Apperception Test (TAT), and our detailed interpretations. No brief summary of these could do justice to how these interview notes and test materials mutually contribute to an understanding of family processes.

The value of our case approach is not limited to material allowing for psychodynamic interpretations; there is equally valuable material on cultural continuity and social interaction. We learned much from our cases about their detailed experiences in urbanizing. Leaving the countryside in their youth, going into occupation careers, they became gradually transformed into representative *shitamachi* people through a process of "secondary socialization," sharing the attitudes and values of their fellow townsmen. Moreover, we could glimpse in our individual interviews continuities of tradition modified to fit the widespread processes of change going on throughout contemporary urban Japan.

Our cases also reflect how marital and parental role behavior are not only determined but also constrained by social expectations. It is also quite evident how behavior in given family units is expressive of personality variability. The individual—man, woman, or child—inhabits a given occupational, marital, or family role differently, depending on his or her individual psychological variation. Yet withall, each of our four family case histories becomes illustrative of what can still be termed Japanese "national character." We believe the cases selected will well illustrate these contentions.

The family-history materials presented in the following chapters are much condensed from the original verbatim interviews. We have tried to edit, paraphrase, and rearrange material to convey what we observed to be both characteristically "individual" and "Japanese." We have been protective of confidentiality, disguising in some instances by transposing occupations, family size, and similar details. The verbatim psychological test responses, however, are unmodified.

The Rorschach and TAT protocols, highly variant from one individual to another, nevertheless reflect Japanese modalities in perceptual organization, in cognitive and emotional control, as well as in common attitudes held toward self, and in common concerns about interpersonal relationships. Anyone familiar with Thematic Apperception Test stories or Rorschach protocols taken from another culture will recognize how uniquely "Japanese" are some of our materials. These test protocols confirm many of the generalizations reported by us in studies of both rural and urban Japanese samples taken, in some cases, ten to fifteen years earlier and reported extensively elsewhere. There is evidence and awareness of modern change reflected in the TAT responses as well as in the interviews. By and large, however, the thematic material of the 1960s remains continuous with the basic world view and perceptual approach of a previous generation of Japanese.

Our first case is a typical example of rural migration into Tokyo. The husband eventually inherits his wife's family's business and becomes an "entrepreneur" operating one of the house-factories we have described as central to the economic structure of Arakawa Ward in 1963.

CHAPTER 10

Ryūichi Segawa

A Scion of the Samurai Tradition

In commenting on fourteen-year-old Ryūichi Segawa, his teacher says that he is a responsible, healthy, courteous, cheerful, and cooperative student. He is exceptionally popular with his schoolmates, who have recently elected him student vice-president. Although he is only average in his academic grades, he represents in his behavior what the teacher sees as a model student.

The Segawa family (case N-3) lives in one of the better parts of Arakawa in a three-room duplex, which they rent for about $15 a month. They have a nine-by-nine-foot bed-sitting room, in which the parents sleep, and a six-by-nine foot room for the two sons; in a third room adjoining the street they have some furniture-making equipment. The home has a radio, a television set, a sewing machine, and, the pride of the family, a new stereo record player. It is one of the least crowded living arrangements of any of the families in our sample. All four family members spend some time in running their small house-factory, manufacturing small tables and other items of furniture. The father says that out of ¥100,000 gross income a month they net about ¥50,000 ($165 a month). Most of this money goes into household and living expenses plus a little savings each month toward extra purchases.

FATHER'S BACKGROUND

The father, Kenji Segawa, is a tall, thin man who gives the impression of a quiet, serious, and steady strength with an underlying current of nervous tension. He has rather sharp features and strong eyebrows, with relatively deep-set eyes for a Japanese. He was the youngest of two sons and a daughter born to a maker of straw products who lived in a rural farming town in the center of Ishikawa Prefecture in north central Honshu.

He reports that he had a very close relationship with his own father. Although he was a second son and his elder brother was given some of the prerogatives of the first son of the family, he believes he was actually the favorite of his parents. In parts of the interview he describes his father in almost glowing terms, as an ideal man—strong, tough, good at sports. The deep affectional bond between the two was demonstrated when his father climbed a mountain to bring down snow to cool his son's high fever during an illness in early childhood. Mr. Segawa readily expresses his consciousness of a strong emotional dependence that continued into adulthood. "When my father died I felt most lonesome. There were so many things on which I needed to consult with him and get his opinion." From many of his statements we infer that Mr. Segawa saw his father primarily in a teaching role. He pictures his father as a strict man who emphasizes the virtues of endurance, discipline, and self-constraint and who continually stresses the primacy of family obligations over the pursuit of pleasure (i.e., work before sports). Mr. Segawa vividly recalls the severe training he received from his father in proper behavior. He was taught to endure suffering and to be always responsible for his own actions. At school he was to maintain himself well in any conflict with his classmates.

Both parents of Mr. Segawa claim descent from samurai stock, from impoverished branch lineages that were constrained to take on farming occupations for survival. (One not infrequently finds entire rural villages whose origin is similarly traced to a warrier background.)[1] Mr. Segawa's childhood training put emphasis on the samurai virtues of courage, persistence, and an intensely competitive pursuit of ideal standards of excellence. These were summed up for him in a crude local expression, *mara-kuso-konjō* (literally, *mara*, penis; *kuso*, feces; *konjō*, spirit), which somehow added up to "manly spirit."[2] Mr. Segawa viewed his father's discipline as frequently harsh yet always fair. He remembers himself as a somewhat mischievous child—tough, rebellious—who required strong disciplinary measures. He recalls sometimes rebelling in anger against his father, but now he realizes his father was always right. He blames such anger on his own immaturity. He gradually learned to repress such feelings. For instance, he wanted very much to go to middle school, but his father said he couldn't afford it. He says, "That was the end of the story; I gave up the issue and never wished again to go to middle school." He now fully justifies his father's decision, saying, "It was not a right thing for me to be sent on to school. . . . Therefore, now I am very grateful to my father, who kindly trained me from my earliest years in how to run a business." His gratitude to his father is a repetitive theme throughout our interviews; however, as we shall suggest when we analyze his TAT stories, a deep underlying resentment and rebellion remain a submerged current in his psychic life. He is still struggling on one level of his personality with unresolved feelings about the tensions existing in rebellion versus submission, and obedience and conformity versus the exercise of autonomy.

Mr. Segawa gives us a similarly idealized view of his mother. He describes

1. See, for example, the insistence to this effect by the villagers of Niiike, an agricultural hamlet near Okayama city, in Beardsley, Hall, and Ward, 1959, chapter 1.

2. See Nitobe, 1905, and Gibney, 1953. These books illustrate how the military character of the samurai code undergirds the traditional Japanese society. It is a system of social morality based on obligatory commitments to be fulfilled in each prescribed situation to maintain honor and demonstrate loyalty to one's master. It puts strong emphasis on discipline and self-control, which one attains through rigorous training. Although this code was tempered by the incorporation of Western thinking, it is still to be found honored in some rural areas as an ideal of comportment.

her as gentle and consoling to him, and above all obedient and respectful to her husband. This picture is thoroughly congruent with the traditional image that Japanese have of a proper wife and mother, which he relates to her samurai origins.

Mr. Segawa frankly characterized his parents' relationship as one in which the father exercised a somewhat tyrannical role, at times heaping verbal abuse on his wife. As he saw it, his mother's reaction was one of fearful obedience. However, he quickly points out that his father was very dependent on his mother, and he rationalizes the abuse as a necessary outlet for many financial frustrations. The image he paints of his father closely approximates that which his own wife and son paint of him. In another context, Mr. Segawa admits that he thought his father was an unhappy and dissatisfied man, indicating at least some partial conscious discrepancy with his idealized image.

Mr. Segawa has a brother six years older whom he describes as his direct opposite, a quiet, diligent, and serious student. They never had an easy relationship. Even today, Mrs. Segawa suggests that her husband was jealous of his brother's status as a first son; in turn, the elder brother always put a sense of "loyalty of family lineage" before any other consideration in his relationship to his brother. Mrs. Segawa succinctly describes her brother-in-law's concern for the family: "Ishikawa Prefecture is a very feudal place where there is still predominance of man over woman, and the eldest son has a much higher status than the rest of his brothers and sisters, and of course, his 'loyalty to family' is very strong." Consequently, this brother vehemently opposed Mr. Segawa's marriage because of Mrs. Segawa's lower social background. The extent of his animosity was later shown in the minimal help he grudgingly extended to the Segawa family when, after Mr. Segawa's long illness, they were in desperate need of finances and housing.

Mr. Segawa had a close relationship with his paternal grandfather and speaks of him with deep affection. Although his paternal grandmother also cared for him, he expresses no particular memory of her. His perfunctory discussion of the women in his family plus the few stereotyped memories he affords us of his mother may indicate a strong surface repression of any interest in or identity with females. (We shall indicate in both the TAT and the Rorschach test responses that there is a suggestion of latent homosexual tendencies strongly overcompensated for by an emphasis on masculine traits.)

Mr. Segawa completed the eighth grade at age fifteen, after what he reports to have been a fairly successful final two years in school. Earlier, in elementary school, he did quite poorly, but when he entered the higher elementary school (seventh grade) he began to take an interest in academic subjects and studied harder. He also participated actively in school sports and was very proud of his good performances. His spare time was filled with delivering goods for his father's business. After graduation he passed a National Railroad Company test and for a brief period worked near home for this company. Two years later, at seventeen, he passed a second test and was transferred to Manchuria. His father actively supported his leaving home. Mr. Segawa at this point entered into what he describes as "a life of freedom," which he recalls now as the most carefree and the happiest period of his past. "It was like life in paradise, beyond description." It can be speculated that his physical separation from his father relieved him of the oppressive task of fulfilling the father's demands and expectations and allowed him to experience and satisfy his own personal needs. In 1941 he passed the entrance examination for military service and was drafted into the air force. He was in combat for four years and near the end of the war was captured during the Japanese retreat from Singapore. In 1946 he returned home and found employment in a nearby farm-equipment factory, where his future wife's father was acting temporarily as foreman. He fell in love with the foreman's daughter, and in January 1947, at twenty-six years of age, he married.

This marriage created a split within his own family, as his elder brother would not accept his prospective wife, whose family had evacuated from Tokyo during the war without any established ties to the community in which they sought temporary residence; they found no acceptance from anyone. In effect, for Mr. Segawa at least, if not for Mrs. Segawa (see below), they were joined in a "love marrige" initiated by the lovers rather than brought about by formal arrangement of the families concerned. The marriage was strongly approved by the wife's family, who saw to it that the wedding was conducted in what they considered proper fashion.

Mr. Segawa has always seen the love he bears his wife as of a spiritual nature and as a vital part of their relationship of over seventeen years. One finds this a curiously liberal attitude in this otherwise tradition-bound man. He states, also, that although he had "dated and loved" other women, intercourse had been "beyond the limit." He sees it as natural for him only in marriage. He viewed sexual activity as "dirty" prior to marriage and did not participate in any such activities, to avoid a possible feeling of "shame." This puritanical view of sexuality raises the question of how it might be related to unconscious feelings of masculine inadequacy. It is important to note that Mr. Segawa selected a mate who was "totally ignorant regarding sex," and he found satisfaction in taking the initiative "to mold her into the shape I liked." In 1948 their first child, Ryūichi, our subject, was born. One year later Mr. Segawa contracted a serious case of pleurisy and was ill for several months. By this time his father-in-law and other members of the family had moved back to Tokyo to open up a furniture business. During this illness his own brother's "unfeeling attitude" toward his impoverished situation aroused a deep and abiding resentment that has never receded.

In 1950, remembering his previous satisfaction with military life, Mr. Segawa volunteered for the newly constituted Japanese National Defense Force, and again entered military service. He found his time in the National Defense Force thoroughly enjoyable, but a recurrence of his illness forced him to resign in 1951.[3]

3. For some individuals illness is the only way out of an impasse. The body is blamed for a failure to perform. See De Vos, 1973, chapter 5, for a discussion of guilt and its avoidance.

After he resigned from the Self Defense Force, Mr. Segawa and his wife and child moved to Tokyo to live with his father-in-law, whom he assisted in his successful furniture business. At this time the living conditions were very crowded, for Mrs. Segawa's nephew was also living with the family. This was a particularly difficult time for Mr. Segawa, who was struggling to reestablish himself after a debilitating illness and was discouraged over the necessity of leaving what he had hoped would be an army career. He now found himself in the impersonal surroundings of Tokyo, beholden to his wife's relatives both occupationally and domestically. Furthermore, he probably considered Arakawa Ward, where they had settled, a demeaning environment, given his sensitive concern with social background and his own ambitions. This period was in effect a turning point for him, when he had to reconcile himself to what appeared to be his occupational fate—that of a lower-class entrepreneur. His father-in-law eventually left the table-making business entirely to him and with his own son's assistance took over another business elsewhere. The father-in-law and his family thereupon moved out, leaving Mr. and Mrs. Segawa in sole possession of their present establishment. This was considered an act of generosity and kindness on the part of the father-in-law, but it also is not unusual behavior for a father-in-law toward an in-marrying son. Mr. Segawa had been accepted, in effect, as an adopted son of the family, although he never changed his name. Behaviorally, if not in a formal family sense, Mr. Segawa had become a *muko-yōshi*, cut off by his elder brother from his own family but rewarded by his new family by being given a thriving business. Since the Segawa family was of higher status and claimed a samurai background, Mrs. Segawa's family could not realistically hope to have him change his name but were probably pleased to have a family member with such a high-status background. Also it must be noted that Mrs. Segawa's father had a younger son who could carry on his own family name for him.

Mr. Segawa's present life centers around his work and leisure-time relaxation with his family. After their evening meal the entire family remains together, sometimes watching television, sometimes having a congenial game of cards. Each in his own interview expressed pleasure over this shared time. As the father of the family, Mr. Segawa has assumed the traditional role of teacher and mentor in moral virtues. Repeatedly, he stresses how he tells his son he must fight for "the right." He emphasizes the virtues of successful competition, endurance, and self-control. He is pleased because his son has been so obedient to him in this regard, but he nevertheless expresses continual concern over how to be an adequate parent. He recognizes that his own words must be supported by example. He also believes that the influence of his wife on the son is very strong, perhaps greater than his own.

Mr. Segawa's personality is in some respects representative of a number of currents found in the Japanese cultural psychology. A strong authoritarian hierarchical tone colors his perception of social relationships. He seeks personal validation through being continually tempered by training in some discipline. He fully identified with the power and prestige and structure of military life, and found it far more appealing than the less certain organizations of civilian activity. Nevertheless, as a person of lower status, he finds himself in an essentially powerless position outside his family. We will present a further glimpse into the personality of Mr. Segawa after presenting his projective test responses below.

MOTHER'S BACKGROUND

Thirty-four-year-old Mrs. Segawa is a short, stout woman of obvious good health whose clothes seem to be always in slight disarray. She has a positive, cheerful approach to others and a spontaneously affectionate nature. She gives the impression of considerable strength of character, which is expressed in a totally nonaggressive way.

Mrs. Segawa was the firstborn of three children. Her father had been adopted as a *muko-yōshi*. Her parents' marriage was arranged by her grandmother against her mother's will. As reported to us, her father's family also refused to accept the marriage or their son's adoption into another family. The marriage was therefore not officially legalized till her father was over thirty years old, at which time his name was changed and entered into his wife's family registry. In the meantime Mrs. Segawa had been born, and at first she was legally registered as her maternal grandmother's child. As the story is told to us it seems to be an unusual situation, in which the grandmother in effect forced her own daughter into an illegal liaison. The actual circumstances may have been somewhat different from the way they were given to us by Mrs. Segawa.

The marriage of her parents is reported by Mrs. Segawa to have been a continually discordant and unhappy one. She recalls her mother's repeated expression of intense dislike for her husband, and her father's helpless position vis-à-vis both his mother-in-law and his wife. Feeling continually harassed, her father would at times physically attack both women in retaliation. He was continually demeaned by his mother-in-law, who considered him "of little importance." The grandmother maintained tight control as head of the family. The old grandfather scarcely counted; he was described by Mrs. Segawa as a "weak man." She recalls no intimacy of communication ever taking place between her parents, nor any participation in joint activities. Marital discord and personal dissatisfaction led to chronic distancing and isolation among the family members.

Mrs. Segawa remembers her father as a gentle, tender man who was powerless even to exercise any authority over his children. Despite the lack of respect shown him by everyone, she remembers him with strong feelings of affection. In marked contrast, she saw her mother as "socially active" and of "strong character," but distant to her children. She was "incompetent in the woman's task of housekeeping and raising children." Mrs. Segawa was raised by her maternal grandmother, who during her early childhood was her "legal" mother. The grandmother not only cared for her and provided a strong female model but also sustained her through the potentially emotionally damaging marital conflicts she continually witnessed between her parents.

Mrs. Segawa was born and reared in Tokyo in the world of woodworking artisans. She grew up in the lower-class area just south of Arakawa Ward in a maze of tangled, irregular streets. As a small child she was frequently ill and was considered physically weak. She did not like elementary school, although she obtained at least average grades. After school hours she played about very much as a "tomboy." When, close to the end of her elementary schooling, her grandparents moved away, she left her own parents to stay with them. She expresses few positive emotional memories of childhood, and much of what she tells us is given in a matter-of-fact, bland manner. She expressed no jealousy or rivalry toward her two younger siblings, who remained with her parents.

Her adolescence was marked by close relationships with girl friends, with whom she spent a great deal of time. After finishing middle school in 1943, she began working for a department store. Her grandmother afforded her considerable freedom of movement; she could come and go as she pleased. She felt that at this time she was living in a pleasant, permissive atmosphere, supporting herself and feeling independent and self-sufficient. With the heavy air raids on Tokyo, she and her grandparents again joined her parents, and they moved together to Ishikawa Prefecture, where her father had obtained a foreman's job in a local factory. Finding that she intensely disliked country life, Mrs. Segawa returned to Tokyo by herself. However, she found that with the rising cost of living and the disruption that was going on in Tokyo, she could not survive there by herself, and with a deep sense of hardship and failure she returned to her own family. It was at this point that she met and married Mr. Segawa, who had become an employee under her father.

THE PARENTS' MARRIAGE

The marriage had been arranged by Mr. Segawa himself and by her parents. Mrs. Segawa felt totally unprepared. For him it was a love marriage, counter to his family's wishes. For her, however, it was a marriage in accord with the desire of her parents. She was self-conscious about what was considered her inferior social status as the daughter of a poor Tokyo family with no material possessions, but she was aware of her future husband's love for her and readily consented to the marriage. She came to the marriage with no definite ideas or expectations but a willingness to follow her husband's lead and be a dutiful wife.

Prior to her marriage, Mrs. Segawa claims to have made no conscious differentiation between the sexes. She says that she had never experienced any close relationship with a male, including members of her own family. This is somewhat inconsistent with what she told us of her early childhood memories of her father as a soft and tender person. She apparently received no sex education. Throughout elementary school she saw her male peers simply as playmates, and in middle school, as is not unusual in Japan, she had no male friends. Later as a working girl she "dated" on a group basis only. Thus, it is not improbable that she entered marriage without any conscious awareness of the physical aspect of the marriage relationship. She remembers her initial surprise at her husband's request for physical intimacy. She said she was "shaken up" but trusted her husband. A year later her first child, Ryūichi, was born. She recalls no particular feelings regarding the birth of a child or how his presence changed her life.

Mrs. Segawa is actively engaged in running her three-room home and occasionally helping with the factory work, but she devotes most of her time to raising her two sons. Apart from rather uneven housekeeping, she seems to manage these tasks to the satisfaction of other family members. She says that the happiest time of her life is the present.

Mrs. Segawa says that she is not especially fond of children (except her own). She remembers that she did not particularly look forward to being a mother. However, when children came along, she seems to have willingly taken on an active, concerned, mothering role. She feels she has a close relationship with her elder son, Ryūichi, and expresses considerable warmth toward and pride in him. Her positive attitude toward him is obvious both verbally and behaviorally. She states that when he was young she felt she "overprotected him." When he was ill she spent long hours holding him, sometimes throughout the entire night. It is almost as if she feels that for his own good she should not be as expressive as she spontaneously is. It appeared to us that her self-consciously stated "overprotection" was instead an adequate, spontaneous maternal response, which she seemed to devaluate. She consciously expresses a strong belief in a need for psychological independence in her children; it is not usual in our sample to find this so directly expressed. She also says that her babies did not sleep with her but were frequently put to bed alone after their feedings, which is untraditional Japanese behavior.

Mrs. Segawa continues to have a close relationship with her son. She likes to take time out to play with him, and the son shares his concerns and pleasures with her. There is obvious indication on the part of both of frequent and good intercommunication. We received the impression that the mother has lately taken on the role of a "friend" more than that of a hovering parent. She herself maintains a childish or adolescent quality in her interests and behavior, and this may well be the reason for the ready peerlike relationship she maintains with her older boy.

MARITAL INTERACTION

The Segawas' "love" marriage has been exceptionally successful. It is not unusual for such marriages to end in failure.[4] The Segawas do not in any way regret their marriage. Mr. Segawa seems to have achieved a genuine personal autonomy in respect to his feelings about having taken the initiative in a mar-

4. See De Vos, 1973, chapter 5, for a discussion of the difficulty of overcoming the guilt involved in a "free" marriage.

riage choice. Within their marriage they have found a positive affirmation of the traditional expectations of male and female. One might say that whatever failings either of the marital partners manifests, the other is not recriminatory but chooses to selectively perceive what is positive and expected in the behavior of the other. According to Mrs. Segawa, the first years of their marriage were very "happy" and "homey." After this there came problems of illness and financial stress. As she notes, after her husband's illness and the crowded and frustrated living conditions with which they all had to contend in Tokyo, he became increasingly irritable. He was given to outbursts of temper during which he would scold her loudly; at times he would even strike her. Mrs. Segawa seemingly accepted such abuse up to a limit, at which time she set up her own defenses, employing apology, teasing, or even at times a commanding voice to get Mr. Segawa back into a better mood. Thus, Mrs. Segawa saw herself as providing their relationship with the inner control that her husband lacks; however, she also overtly preserves her husband's somewhat authoritarian role by allowing him to project the blame for his outbursts onto her supposed provocations. Their relationship is clearly illustrated in the description of their sex life. Mr. Segawa considers that he initially "trained" Mrs. Segawa in the sex act. Though she at first disliked intercourse, she submitted obediently. Now she says she enjoys it but still waits for his initiative. They always sleep together and have intercourse two or three times a week.

Despite Mr. Segawa's traditional tyrannical rule, he loves and deeply respects his wife and consciously needs her as an object of his basic dependency. "I have a strong love toward my wife. But I cannot express my love but always act high-handedly." His dependence on her is clear in such statements as "She has served me for a very long time very well, and now I feel very grateful." Mrs. Segawa likewise loves her husband, justifying his weaknesses and expressing trust in his continual concern over being a good father and husband.

To summarize succinctly the multilevel interaction between this man and wife, we see on the overt role-playing level the traditional, high-handed, domineering husband and subservient, obedient wife. On the deeper level of personal needs, however, the husband's authoritarianism appears as a defense against his shaky male sexual identity and unresolved feeling of emotional insecurity. The wife's strength undergirds his dependency needs while his weaknesses allow her some sense of control in their relationship. The expected social roles are thus maintained without any serious sacrifice of personal needs. Though both indicate some awareness of this balance of resentment and unrealistic role demands, it is our impression that their interpersonal solution is basically satisfying to them. They seem to be indeed happily mated within the context of traditional Japanese cultural values.

Since they receive satisfaction from their relationship, they are also able to respond emotionally as parents to their children. Their children in turn have generally accepted the expectations of traditional familial roles, although they too must work out ways of meeting personal needs within this family context.

RYŪICHI, THE FIRST CHILD

Ryūichi was the first child, born fourteen months after the Segawa marriage. His father had wanted a son; his mother states that she had no preference. The traditional rule of family descent through the eldest son remained an important consideration for Mr. Segawa. Thus it can be assumed that Ryūichi's position as first son has placed added expectations upon him and that he is being prepared for his eventual role as head of the Segawa family. Now at fourteen he is in the second year of junior high school. He is a healthy boy, short and stout. He is only slightly over five feet tall but weighs 161 pounds, with a look of sturdy strength. In his physical appearance he takes somewhat after his mother. He has a lively, cheerful, expressive personality which has recently made him popular with both peers and adults. With what is perceived as a sincere, responsible approach to people, he usually gains their quick respect. He also has a positive relationship with his younger brother, who is six years his junior.

In his parents' reports, Ryūichi followed a fairly normal developmental pattern. His prenatal development and birth were without complications. For some time, however, he was described as being a "weak" baby with frequent fevers and colds. He was hospitalized for a short period for dysentery when he was about seven months old. Like most Japanese babies, he was breast-fed. Mrs. Segawa feels that she may have been too "mothering" and expresses a conscientious concern about whether she had properly weaned and toilet-trained him. She says that she began quite early but could not force him to comply, since he was a strong-willed baby. He ate well. Mr. Segawa added that while he was crawling he began eating ashes out of the hibachi, or charcoal brazier. Mrs. Segawa had said that he had "thrown charcoal." Evidently, this point of disagreement in their memory of his behavior creates minor dissension in the family. The parents were concerned over this incident and consulted a doctor, who advised them to watch him closely. Subsequently, Mr. Segawa said he broke him of this habit by slapping his hands until he quit. Otherwise he was given considerable freedom in his motor activities.

Ryūichi experienced separation from his father during the time that Mr. Segawa was away with the Self Defense Force, a separation that was extended with the father's hospitalization. The only other time Ryūichi was separated from his family was when he was two-and-a-half and was sent to stay for a month with his grandmother while Mrs. Segawa cared for Mr. Segawa during another illness. At three years of age he was placed in a day nursery while his mother worked briefly outside the home. She remembers, however, that when he returned from the nursery she would play with him.

When Ryūichi was six years old two crucial events occurred: he began elementary school, and his younger brother was born. He himself expresses no very clear memory of either event. His only immediate recollection of his early school experience was that he underwent painful teasing for being fat. He felt at this time some degree of social isolation. His memories of his brother as an infant were expressed positively, and he has no recollection of any pangs of jealousy.

Throughout childhood Ryūichi was considered to be a passive, obedient child because of his generally peaceful and happy disposition. He was positively responsive to the "moral training" of his father. His parents have always considered him a very good child and evidence considerable pride in him. Their attitude is at present obviously mutual, as Ryūichi also expands spontaneously about his close and positive feeling toward both parents.

He says he loves his father best. He finds him a confident and trustworthy teacher and has unreservedly accepted his moral attitudes. He consciously depends on him for guidance and emotional support. For example, before an examination he confided to his father his deep fears of possible failure. He is, however, candidly critical of his father's periodically abusive treatment of his mother, but he says he is not angry with his father, and quickly excuses him on the grounds that he is really "sick," not willfully uncontrolled. One sees here that Ryūichi will not tolerate in himself any conscious feeling of direct anger toward his father.

He views his mother more as a companion or friend, sharing thoughts and feelings. He has more open and direct expression with her than with his father. He thinks that she will buy or do anything for him if he really needs it. He feels that she is a very dependable person.

Ryūichi feels that his communication with both parents is good and free and he may ask them about anything, even such topics as sex. However, we noted that in actual discussion with them he selectively omits subjects that do not altogether fit in with their expectation or perceptions of him. He told us that he had not ever mentioned to his parents that the children used to pick on him in elementary school for being fat.

There is a carry-over of the affectionate, open relationship with his parents into his relationship with his teachers. He views his present teacher as both a consultant and a friend. However, his parents' confidence in and high expectations of him have made Ryūichi somewhat uncomfortable about his grades. He expresses feelings of inadequacy in having to meet their expectations. Although his grades have been low to average, he has recently made some improvement in them. Grades are a matter he does not discuss at present with his parents, because they are not up to his own expectations. We see here, therefore, that although there is a statement of free discussion and he is genuine when he makes it, he guards himself in some areas and is not as openly expressive as he describes himself to be.

Ryūichi is popular with children of all ages, not only his immediate peers. He is looked up to as something of a leader by younger children. He cites instances of acting as an arbitrator in fights and teaching the younger children new games. His two closest friends are boys of his own age; they go out together frequently and have a close and mutually supportive relationship. He also has a wider circle of acquaintances who respect him. For instance, he tells the story of telling a tough *banchō*, or gang leader, in his class to quit smoking in school, and seemingly this boy quit smoking. Whether it is true or not, the pride with which he told us this story reflects the degree to which he has accepted his father's sense of moral responsibility in social situations.

Ryūichi recently has become more aware of girls. He has formed one intermittent friendship with a girl, whom he describes as "active and cheerful." Their relationship is focused on studying together some subjects in which she helps him.

Ryūichi's daily routine begins with a hasty breakfast and departure for school. After school he works about an hour or so at a woodturning machine for his father. He studies, eats dinner with the family, and then watches television. He studies again for a short period before bed. He claims to study about four or five hours a day. He also says he finds time to play and to participate in sports, which are an important part of his life. He belongs to a kendo club where he is learning traditional Japanese fencing, a sport considered to train character as well as skill. He practices judo and is fond of basketball (as was his father). He considers himself a relatively good athlete.

The summer between his first and second years in junior high school was spent in organizing and leading a community project in which some of his peers participated. At his father's suggestion, Ryūichi established a fireguard of boys who policed the neighborhood, inspecting for fire hazards and cleaning up combustible rubbish. Some of the neighbors regarded this behavior as officious, and a controversy arose over the value of having children interfere with other people's property. Nevertheless, Ryūichi continued his activities, and his father argued the case with the neighbors, stressing that the virtue of persistence and dependability learned by the children was more important than whether this type of behavior was necessary for the neighborhood. Ryūichi and his father both accepted the disfavor of a number of their neighbors for being busybodies as the price willingly paid for socially responsible behavior. Later, Ryūichi and his group activities were validated when police, fire department, and school officials all saw to it that Ryūichi received official commendation for safety and fire prevention efforts. Such incidents as this demonstrate how the community supports the inculcation of social responsibility.

Ryūichi now is interested in obtaining further schooling, and he has the hope of eventually taking over his father's place in the furniture-making business. He has no question about his future occupation. At present he has one and a half years of junior high school left, after which he will have to take an entrance examination if he wishes to continue further. His father is encouraging him to attend a senior high school. However, he himself is worried about his capacity to pass the necessary examination. As was noted by Vogel (1965), there is intense competition for these examinations, which are the key focus of the achievement-oriented middle class because later prestige and job opportunities depend on the quality of the high school attended. In the middle-class family the children are incessantly drilled so that they may pass this examination well. The entrance examination is sometimes called by Japanese youth the *shiken jigoku*, or "examination hell." The intensity of the competition, as well as the intensity of the family's expectations focused on this examination, cause many children to develop neurotic symptoms.

Ryūichi says that he would rather go to a technical school, but he has accepted his father's demands and is preparing himself as best he can for an entrance examination to the type of senior high school that would prepare him for the possibility of college. Ryūichi himself is more willing to discuss spontaneously his own fantasies of what he will be doing after he leaves school. He sees himself managing his father's shop, with his father and brother working under him. He is eager to take on family succession, allowing his father to retire officially while he takes on the major responsibility for the success of the business. This pattern of wanting to succeed the father early is the counterpart of the Japanese wish to be able to retire early if a responsible and diligent son shows the capacity to take over as head of the family household. It is therefore a most appropriate wish for a child to become head of his house before he reaches age thirty, even though the father is still vigorous and capable. This is seen not as any form of usurpation of the father's role, but merely as the repayment of the obligation and duty to parents and family. As Ryūichi sees it, he would like to expand the present business to include more elaborate furniture items that all the family could make together. He shows, therefore, in budding form, a continuation of the entrepreneurial spirit of enterprise that we find as a dynamic force underlying the economic activities in Arakawa Ward.

He also expresses other feelings of family obligation. For example, he expressed a spontaneous wish to eventually build his parents a separate house, to "make them happy." He said that such a project would be his first use of surplus money, before any realization of personal desire.

There is little doubt that Ryūichi has closely identified with his father, as Mr. Segawa does with his father before him. Ryūichi is almost exactly repeating in both word and deed the samurai virtues as inculcated in him by his father. Adherence to the principles of diligence, social responsibility, persistence, and endurance, as we have pointed out elsewhere, probably requires a strong underlying motivating force of potential guilt for any deviance in behavior. Guilt arises in many Japanese when there is a failure to meet expectations of family obligations. Under such circumstances there is an acute sense of hurting the parents by one's own failure. Very often, however, this is not stated in explicit terms; rather, concern with shame is the overt conscious expression of underlying guilt. Ryūichi would feel severely shaken by any act of disobedience of his father or any violation of his trust or honor. The fact that such a mechanism of guilt is already present in Ryūichi may be illustrated by his revelation of an isolated incident of stealing. Two years before the interviews he had wanted to buy a model plane, and in order to do so he took money from his mother's purse. In telling of this incident, he added, "I wanted to buy it so badly." He was afraid that if he asked directly he would not get it. However, he felt very guilty and regretful afterwards. "I sure did a bad thing." He resolved this discomfort by telling on himself, and was thereupon severely scolded by his father.

Ryūichi's present sense of high moral standards is indirectly expressed by his statement that "two-thirds of the boys in my class are no good." He has acquired a certain feeling of righteous superiority in his sense of social service that leads him to assume what appears at times to be a "savior" attitude, considering it his duty to straighten others out. His teacher, with some amusement, told how in teaching moral principles to his peers he assumes at times his father's technique—loud and angry shouting.

In identifying with his father's goals and feelings he feels justified in having the same emotional response as his father. In the controversy over his community project his father expressed considerable anger, as did he. His father was not reluctant to gossip about the deficiencies of some of the neighbors, and Ryūichi also is openly critical of them. His father shows considerable distrust of his neighbors, and so does Ryūichi. Ryūichi says that his father was a good athlete, and he is consciously training himself in the same sports his father excelled in. Mr. Segawa notes this identification, saying, for example, "My son's taste in music is the same as mine." On the whole, the boy's identification, on the conscious level at least, involves choosing so far as possible the particular interests and purposes of his father. And yet, we must note that some of the qualities Ryūichi has that account for his popularity are derived not from his father but from his more spontaneously carefree and open mother. In the projective materials below he shows much more spontaneous self-acceptance than is apparent in his tense and nervous father.

PROJECTIVE TEST RESULTS: MR. SEGAWA

The Rorschach Test[5]

In general, the Rorschach protocol of Mr. Segawa is filled with a great deal of symbolism of evil, threat, and such abstractions as "human lust." The overall impression is one of a well-sublimated, benign, paranoid condition marked by a certain aura of defensive pretentiousness that does not reach the level of grandiosity.

Rorschach Protocol[6]

I. (5″)[7] 1. *A bat.* It looked like a bat with its wings spread. This part [points] was especially suggestive of a bat to me. The whole thing resem-

5. See Appendix A for a summary of Rorschach findings with the Arakawa samples.

6. For each of the ten cards that are shown in sequence (indicated by Roman numerals), the spontaneous response is printed first in italics. There follows in contrasting type a summary of the significant responses of each testee to nonleading questions asked to determine form accuracy, location, and the use of other determinants.

7. The time taken in seconds to give the first spontaneous response is noted to provide an impression of the speed and possible unevenness in responses to the cards.

bles a bat. The impression of darkness a bat has, the way of living, like flying during the night. [W FM, FY+ A P (Neut)][8]

2. *Clouds are performing a ballet.* I used to write poems when I was hospitalized in Singapore. This reminds me of the black clouds that covered the white clouds and disturbed the nice enjoyable atmosphere when the sun was just about to go down. After all, this cloud represents the devil; the way it is about to attack this part [points] looks especially evil. [W YF, M- H CL (Prec, Athr)]

II. (5″) 3. *A butterfly and devils are playing.* This is a butterfly [points] and these are devils. This looks like a very frail butterfly. This [points] looks very strong. This is a butterfly's . . . well, I guess this is upside down. I'd say this is very bad, strong, evil. This is shaped like a human. This looks like a head and a face and hands. It looks like he's squatting like this. This is legs and it looks like he's attacking a butterfly. [D M+ (H) A P (Fab Elab) (Arb Comb) (Athr, Dsub)]

III. (40″) 4. *Two human beings in relationships. The representations of human lust, the ugliness in living things.* They are fighting over something. This is heads. This is buttocks and this is legs. This is hands. Looks like they are human but also they look like animals. They are fighting over one thing. Let's see, it is sort of ambiguous; they look like birds, something like crows, I guess. But they do look more like humans. [D M+ (H) P (HH) (Hdpr)]

IV. (55″) 5. *Cohesiveness.* It looks very strong. This part reminds me of a ferocious animal. These are eyes; this is a mouth; this is a head; this represents a human being. This looks like it's pushing down on the ferocious animal no matter what happens. These are hands; these are legs. I guess this is a face. In short, this human is pressing down the fierce animal. It symbolizes fearless masculinity and strong human will. I get the impression that this face looks very strong; it won't lose for anything. Also these hands look extremely strong. [W M, FM+ H/A (Fab, Elab)]

V. (5″) 6. *The whole thing looks like a bat.* This is when a bat has just spread out its wings. I would say these are legs and this is a head. It is facing the other side. I get the impression of darkness. The whole body gave me that feeling, especially this part. [W YF, FM+ A P (Agl)]

VI. (65″) 7. *It is exposing something mysterious.* I can't tell what it is too clearly. It is ambiguous. It seems as though there is something behind this [points]; it looks like a mysterious door, a half opening. I feel like something is hiding behind it. [D YF- Abs (Adif)]

VII. (90″) 8. *Rabbits are dancing.* These are hands and ears. This is a tail; this area looks like ears; this part is around a rabbit's legs. Oh, the way it looks shaggy reminded me of a rabbit. [W FT, FM+ A (Prec)]

8. Abbreviations used in scoring the Rorschach protocols in respect to location; determinants of a response (i.e., form quality, use of color, shading, movement, dimensions of distance); content; symbols of affect; and qualities of thinking are briefly explained in Appendix A, table A.1.

9. *Intimates are meeting. It's hard for them to separate, although they have ill feelings toward each other.* There are two identical people; even when they separate, they feel as if they have left something behind. That face is expressing that feeling. It looks like a human face . . . this expression on the face. They look inseparable. [W M+ H P (Misc)]

VIII. (70″) 10. *The card expresses the desire not to break something pretty. They are protecting it because they will be in trouble if it is broken.* I can't tell too clearly but just pretty . . . the color makes it pretty. This is the head, legs, and the tail. This is the pretty thing [points]. It is hard to tell what shape it is but anyway it is something pretty, and these are protective gods or guardian spirits. [W FC+ Abs Symb (Fab Elab) (Adef)]

11. *Well, it may be a lizard* [*guardian spirit*]. There are two lizards, I guess. And, this one . . . I wonder what it is. They don't want any intruder to come in. [D FM- A (Adef)] [Additional response] It looks like a face, a human face with a twisted personality. I can see a head, hair, and an area from the shoulder to the chest.

IX. (15″) 12. *It looks strong and dignified.* This is an extremely pretty ball, a glass ball. They look like dragons; I think both. They are dragon faces protecting this. Yes, this is a stand supporting this magnificent thing. This harmony of the color makes me think so. The harmony of the dragons' color and the stand color distinguishes the glass ball. Yes, it looks like an ordinary glass ball. The kind of balls you can find at a place like Futamigaura as souvenirs. This ball reminds me of one that contains all sorts of things inside. [W FM, FC+ Abst A (Porn)]

X. (5″) 13 & 14. *The war between good and evil.* They look like evil. [points out 5 areas] Are they spiders? This bright thing with a pretty color made me think of goodness. That is the human mind. [3 areas] Those are all the same human mind. I usually think of bright colors as symbols of goodness in my heart, and dark as the symbol of evil. The shape . . . spiders, the shapes look like symbols of evil to me. [W CSym Abs (HH) D FM+ A P (Athr)]

Card-by-Card Sequential Analysis and Comments

The first response to Card I is a standard bat. Mr. Segawa is sensitive to the overall impression of darkness. Then he sees clouds performing a ballet, an imaginative but somewhat pretentious response. He refers to his hospitalization in Singapore where he saw black clouds covering white clouds, disturbing the enjoyable atmosphere. In the first of his symbolic responses, the black cloud represents "the devil," which attacks the white areas that symbolize some form of goodness. This continual preoccupation with good and evil characterizes the whole record.

On Card II he represents a contrast between frailty and innocence, represented by the butterfly and the devils playing with it. The devils that are squatting and attacking the frail butterfly are what are usually seen as human figures.

Mr. Segawa is almost Dostoevskian in his abstractions and, like Dostoevsky, is plagued by counteractive feelings of the absolute—the polarities of goodness and evil within his own personality. By inference he refuses to give up a concept of innocent frailty as one aspect of himself, an ideal state free of aggression and any need to injure others. These polarities may be sex-linked—an ideal of feminine goodness as opposed to a dangerous potential of masculine aggressiveness that can become destructive.

On Card III the human beings he sees become representations of human lust and the ugliness of aggression. The response shows a schizoid tendency to combine the human and the animal in one form. In Card IV there is a fight between a ferocious animal and a noble, fearless masculinity. In this picture, masculinity is seen as both moral and strong; it is strong because of the strong human will governing behavior, a traditional Japanese value with emphasis on the conquering ability of will power. The ferocious animal is conquered by willful masculinity. This may well represent two levels in Mr. Segawa's perception of his own father. On an unconscious level he may still see authority as dangerous, ferocious, and animal-like; and yet, on a conscious, more human level, he wants to identify with the virtues of strong will and masculine drive.

On Card V he responds with the commonly perceived bat. He emotionalizes his response, emphasizing his impression of darkness. He is an emotionally labile, sensitive man, continually subject to the tempest of feelings that are swirling about deep within him. He sees Card VI as a mysterious half-opened door. Both curiosity and dread of the unknown are represented symbolically here. He has a feeling that there is something hiding behind the door (a very paranoid-like response). Card VII, a "mother" card, is seen as "rabbits dancing," a positive but immature percept; he sees rabbits rather than the usually perceived humans that one might expect from a man of his intelligence. Childhood, with the attentions of a warm mother, was probably for him a period of innocence and dependency. As is suggested by his attention to the textural quality of the inkblots, he enjoys textural contact, by inference a proneness to passive sensuality. On Card VII, when he subsequently perceives human beings, he sees them as antagonistic rather than joyful. It is possible to speculate that the associative progression between these two responses symbolizes for him childhood innocence, whereas growing up, taking on the role of an adult, constrains one to cope with the unacceptable aggression and antagonisms aroused within oneself in the course of human communication. This communication is essentially ambivalent: people are bound together by ties, and yet they grow to hate one another.

Mr. Segawa's response to Card VIII again expresses in a vital, dynamic, symbolic form the basic underlying ambivalent tension between his sadistic aggressive nature and his desire at the same time to preserve and defend a secret, passive, sensual fragility. The card is seen symbolically as a desire not to break something pretty. "They," later identified as two protective guardian gods or spirits in the form of lizards, are protecting a fragile center area with its pastel colors.

The guardians do not want any "intruder" to come in (reminiscent of the quiet Buddha in the recesses of the temple and the fierce guardian figures outside, in Buddhist iconography). In his additional response he sees the human face with a "twisted personality" in the center of the block. In Card IX he sees almost the same symbolism as in Card VIII. A pretty glass ball is protected by two dragons. The ball reminds him of the balls that are used as floats in fishermen's nets that can be bought in some areas of Japan as souvenirs. This fragile ball reminds him of one that "contains all sorts of good things inside." There is a feeling of the fragile part of himself which he still seeks to protect and preserve. He feels he has within him a delicate nature, which he refuses to give up, a precious core of delicacy that is his feminine component. On Card X he projects a cosmic war between good and evil. The colors remind him of goodness, and the darkness, of evil. The spider is the symbol of evil attacking the brighter colors.

This traditional, authoritarian man reflects the dual Japanese soul, the gentle and the rough spirit, or as Ruth Benedict puts it, the "chrysanthemum and the sword." He retreats from reality by use of intellectualizations. He is highly sensitive to threat. He seems to have partially resolved the tensions within him by an overt identification with the masculine authority role, controlled aggression in defense of social values while also a very conscious dedication to a paternal form of nurturance of the young. Why he is more successful behaviorally at this than some of the other men in our sample who show a similar type of Rorschach record cannot be readily answered. We know from his wife's behavioral description that this man periodically gives vent to aggressive feelings, which she quiets by submissive understanding. Perhaps the basic difference is that this wife is somehow capable of sustaining or supporting the fragile ego of her husband. Conversely, when such displays take place in a context of mutual antagonism between husband and wife, besetting problems over the man's sense of dependent passivity or inadequacy which lurk behind his compensatory masculine aggressive behavior are exacerbated, not mollified, when a confrontational approach is taken.

This man is basically suspicious of others, and at the same time doesn't quite trust his own motives or impulses. He finds within himself a potential threat arising out of his own unconscious impulses, which he handles best as a kind of intellectualized projection of aggressive, hostile features onto human society generally. He feels a threat lurking in his social environment. There is also a "latent homosexual" perception of himself as a helpless, frail object that needs a guardian spirit for protection. These "guardian" responses are almost regressive in nature—dragons, lizards. There is no indication that this man resorts to any religious system as a protection; rather, as is true for many traditional Japanese, adherence to inculcated obedience to the family serves as an overarching psychologial protection from the threats of the outside world. The Japanese family system is a quasi-religion that assuages the insecurity of an individual in much the way that, in the more individualistic West, an individual can find solace in his personal relationship with a God.

There are a number of other possible levels of symbolical interpretation. For example, his response to Card VI is strongly sexually suggestive. What is sometimes perceived as male or female genitals is seen as a mysterious half-opened door, behind which something lurks. One gets an impression that he unconsciously fears being overwhelmed by the mysteries of female generativity as well as by the aggressive potential of masculine sexuality.

The TAT

Mr. Segawa produced a rich, complex set of TAT stories. In spite of his interview statements about his identification with his father's wishes, in the TAT he dramatizes his unresolved feelings about coercion and his desire for autonomy. Symbolically, his sense of occupational failure is still related to an inner resistance he has felt despite his following of parental wishes rather than his own inclinations. Not believing sufficiently in himself to resolve his wishes for autonomy, he still feels that he has been rebellious. Hence a lifelong inner tension.

The following are the responses given by Mr. Segawa to TAT pictures. Question marks in parentheses indicate questions raised by the interviewer.

> J1. I got the impression that this person has been raised in a strict environment where he was forced to do things up to this time. He was forced to do the kind of things that don't suit his temperament or his tastes, for instance like learning to play the violin. Since he thinks that he doesn't have the talent for it, he feels insecure about his future. I think he feels uneasy about learning to play the violin itself and will not find any hope in the future. (?) His parents, I think. That's why he can't just quit doing it and rebel against his parents. He really doesn't know what to do. I feel sorry for him. (?) He will have a hard time. I don't think he will get good results. (?) Eventually things won't turn out as his parents wished. Things will not go well either for him or for his parents.

The first story is one of strict parental coercion of a child. The child is caught in the dilemma of knowing that he does not have the taste or talent for what he is expected to do, and yet he doesn't know how to rebel against his parents. One would surmise from the story given for this card, as well as from themes found in the following ones, that in his own mind he has not yet resolved the deep problems of rebellion versus submission, obedience and conformity versus autonomy. Consciously, he has espoused a value system that leads him to identify with a firmly exercised parental role, but unconsciously his positive identification has not been achieved without psychic costs and a continual state of underlying tension. Being "forced" to play is a most unusual story for a Japanese to give. It appears much more frequently in American protocols; the American middle-class ending in such instances is usually one of compliance, whereas the American lower-class ending stresses eventual defiance of the directives to practice.

Another consideration is suggested by this story: Most Japanese cannot readily countenance the idea of having their own personal motivations or feelings go counter to the well-understood pervasive cultural directives to be concerned with achievement. In this instance, Mr. Segawa seems to be free enough to accept some perception of tension over motivation. There is a kind of objectivity that permits him to state overtly that he feels sorry for the boy in this dilemma, indicating some attempts at conscious resolution of this problem in himself. We also might surmise from the story that he may feel himself to be something of a failure in respect to his own aspirations. He has obviously resigned himself to his role in life as a furniture-maker, but his sense of his samurai past gives him a harsh self-standard for measurement, which is indirectly suggested by the pessimistic ending he chooses to give in this first story.

> J2. This is a farm field. This woman has strong motivation to study, but her family is poor. She works hard in the fields, since her family are farmers. Though she's eager to learn, she is not able to go to school. Her mother understands her feelings and wants to send her to school somehow. But considering how her husband feels about it, her mother is fretting very much. But the woman wants to study no matter what happens or who objects. I can tell how strong her feelings are. The mother is worrying, since she loves her daughter, yet she can't disagree with her husband either. In the future I think that the woman will even leave home in order to study.

In his story to this card he draws an understanding mother interacting with a rather rigid father, who takes a negative view of the child's achievement wishes. The mother obviously is caught in the dilemma between her feelings for her child and her dutiful obedience to her husband. The story is resolved by the girl's taking leave of her home autonomously to follow her own interests in studying. We might parallel this story with Mr. Segawa's own history. His father discouraged him from obtaining further education, and, as he stated in his interviews, he was for a time angry and rebellious, but now he sees the wisdom of his father's decision. For purposes of personality integration and the maintenance of his own identity he may not yet be able to countenance a fully negative evaluation of any of his father's decisions. He may still use up a great deal of psychic energy in keeping what seems to be an unresolved conflict from disrupting him. He is freer to show a positive attitude toward personal goals in Card 2, which features a woman as the central figure, than he was in the case of the little boy with the violin on Card 1. There are a number of indications that Mr. Segawa has a rather strong underlying feminine identification. As we will point out subsequently, these feminine features are resolved by a kind of altruistic identification with the maternal role performed properly by someone else. In the Jungian sense, his anima—shadow or female self—is realized vicariously through the expected role performance of his wife and other women. He can identify imaginatively with a woman's plight and problems, and yet he maintains his masculinity by a firm adherence to the male role in his own behavior.

As a boy he probably did not like his father as much as he says he did. He may not have been sufficiently rebellious to hold back from an internalization of his father's values; he feared his father's power but admired his strength. Instead of identifying completely and readily with male attitudes, he may have taken on covertly many features of submerged identification with his mother, who had her own means of placating a dominant male. It is curious that in spite of the suggestion of what his mother was like and the method of relating to him used by his own wife, he perceives women throughout as capable of making autonomous decisions. It is as if in some sense the woman is freer than the man in spite of overt subservience to the male. He readily perceives women as strong-willed in their goal orientations.

> J3. I wonder if this is a boy or a girl—I can't tell whether it's male or female—I wonder which it is. It looks like a girl, doesn't it?—or a boy. I can't tell—it looks like a girl. It doesn't look like a very wealthy family. She seems worried because she was scolded by her parents. Anyway, she was made to separate from her very close friend, her boyfriend. Her parents used their authority to make her do it. I can guess that she's suffering because of that. She looks as if she doesn't know what to do from now on. She is wondering whether she should go to her parents or go along with her boyfriend. Though she might suffer at the time she goes along with her parents, she may gain happiness later if she can suppress her feelings.

In this card Mr. Segawa wonders repeatedly whether the figure is of a man or a woman, again suggesting in this hesitancy some lack of final settlement of his sex role identification. He prefers finally to give a story with a heroine for the card. He sympathizes with the inner state she must be in, since she has been forcibly separated from her boyfriend by her unfeeling parents. Yet he resolves the issue on the side of tradition and the dutiful submission of the child, whereas in the response to the previous card autonomy was the outcome. He presents, therefore, no consistent position but wavers back and forth from one story to the next.

> J6. He looks like a man who was brought up very strictly by his mother. But something happened to make him disagree with his mother. So his mother got mad at him, saying that she didn't mean to raise her son this way. I have a feeling that he is between his wife and his mother. He is trying to make his mother feel better somehow. He's thinking desperately that he has to try hard to make a pleasant home. If he treats his mother kindly it seems that he can maintain peace in his family. I get the impression that he didn't go along with his mother's expectations. (?) The mother intended to make her son think of his parents a lot, but her son always rebels. Because of that, the family members are not getting along so well. It seems to me that he is saying that it isn't so.

To the usual mother-and-son card he gives a plot, frequently found in Japanese TAT protocols, focusing on a conflict between mother and bride. The man who is both son and husband is somehow trying to reconcile them so that he is not caught by the conflicting roles within himself. Again, he depicts a rebellious son who somehow disappoints the expectations of his parents. The first four stories, therefore, have a continuous theme of tensions between opposites. In this story he uses the Japanese expression *itabasami*, the state of being sandwiched between two boards or pressed between opposing forces without a clear-cut identification with either side. Somehow he wishes to reconcile these opposing directions. He uses emphatic language to express the nuances of the state of mind of his protagonists.

> J7. He was forced to do something he didn't feel like doing by his boss. He was forced to do something bad—some kind of bad proposal. He seems to be wondering whether he should accept it or not. Eventually he will accept it, I think. Though it's a bad plan, I guess he will take it. He has a strong character, but on the other hand he looks as if he will be tempted by a bad plan, (?) for instance, something like being an industrial spy—be forced into it.

In this story a young man is being induced by an older person to do something that goes counter to his better judgment, and in a resigned way he complies. This story, certainly on a symbolic level, goes counter to Mr. Segawa's contention that his father's advice was always right. It indicates again a basic ambivalence and an underlying indecisiveness that suggest some obsessive-compulsive traits in this man's personality.

> J8. Delinquents—maybe not. It seems like somebody is being punished among delinquent youths. . . . No, it is not. No, that isn't it. He went to some mountain and got hurt. He will die unless he is rescued soon. He is desperately seeking help. Anyway they [the two people in the light] are so-called death gods in his imagination. He has to be rescued soon. I think he was rescued after all and came home. He is waiting for a doctor to come. Unless the doctor comes soon he will die, so he is waiting for him impatiently. If the doctor should come he will survive, but otherwise he will die. (?) They are friends, I think. (?) I think they are around twenty. Students—just entered college, I think. (?) This is a woman and I think this is a man. But they are just friends, I think.

On Card 8 he quickly gives up on his first spontaneous story, in which one member of a group of delinquents is being punished by the other group members. (The word used by Mr. Segawa was *rinchi o ukeru*, the Japanese adaptation of the English word "lynch," which has a somewhat broader meaning in Japanese.) He selects a passive figure as the "hero," whereas it is more usual to see a figure in the foreground as the protagonist. He then describes a largely passive situation, changing the story to be about someone who was mountain climbing and got hurt, and who will die unless he is rescued soon. He sees the two people in the background as "death-gods," calling on a bit of Japanese mythology that is rare. It harks back to the idea that there were demons or gods in the underworld who would come to take a dead person to the land of the dead, and that if one saw these demons one was about to die. The man is waiting to be rescued, hoping that a doctor will come in time. Mr. Segawa is caught here again in an ambivalent polarity, this time the most basic one of all, the polarity between the forces of death, represented by the death gods, and the forces of life, represented by the doctor. Again the protagonist is passively caught between these two forces. Basically, each conflict that he sees takes place either in the external world or within the person himself; the battles are between antagonistic forces in open conflict even when located within the individual. It is not a battle between levels of personality, the "superego" and the "id" in psychoanalytic terms, but rather between forces that are operating on the same level, either in terms of social directives or in terms of vital urges. He is caught in a conflict of directives, which he has not resolved by a rigid adherence to one or the other. There is much evidence for what could have become distorted paranoid mechanisms in his personality structure, and yet he remains socially adaptive. He cannot directly express some feelings when they are activated. He tends to externalize hostility and to see it as coming from an outside source, but he also tends to direct some feelings inward in a self-destructive way, as a deep sense of inferiority.

> J9. They are husband and wife. They are a couple, and this is the mother. The wife and this girl are sisters—I guess they are. They are his wife and her sister. The husband's mother had such a strong character that his wife and her sister can't live with her. So the man is taking them somewhere else to stay—I have that impression. I think that everybody in the family is going out from the house to leave the mother because she is so strong. They can't just send the girl away, so the couple and the girl are all going out and live separately from the mother. That's why this girl gives me the impression that she doesn't know what to do. The man, too, is having a hard time to decide whether to go along with mother or his wife. Eventually they will leave the house, I think. (?) In short, the mother despises her daughter-in-law. Because of that she also hates her daughter-in-law's sister.

On Card 9 we find a repetition of the story given to Card 6—a man is caught between his mother and his wife. He seems unable to come to an easy final decision on which side to take. However, the final choice is toward leaving the house and the mother. The marital bond is more important than the mother-son relationship. This is a symbolic act of personal integrity—he has not submitted to childhood dependency but chooses adult autonomy.

> J11. This child seemed to be raised in a very gloomy home. I mean that it's the kind of family which has many secrets all the time. This environment caused him to become so curious that he peeks at things like sexual activities. If it were a cheerful, healthy home this wouldn't happen to a child. But there were always some secrets in his family. He reached the point that he peeked at sexual activities, I think. A child like him will commit some sexual crimes as he grows older. It is not a good thing for parents to have secrets from their child, I think. (?) Well,

> I meant some other—this is his mother, but she is having an affair with a man who is not her husband. That kind of secret. That's why the child has such a strong curiosity, I think. (?) No. As a child, he's wondering what they are doing, especially since they don't talk much in front of the child. He's wondering what his mother is doing behind his father's back. I think it's a very bad influence on the child's development.

On this card Mr. Segawa responds directly to the possible sexual implications of the card and gives an unusual story about a mother having a sexual liaison, witnessed by the child, who will go on to commit sexual crimes as he grows older. The story suggests that this man may have a strong unresolved sexual feeling toward his mother in an Oedipal type of configuration and that he has partially resolved this feeling by some reversal of identification, which creates the latent homosexual tendencies we have noted in him. He is oriented here not toward the education of the child, as in many of his other stories, nor to the illness of the mother, but directly toward the mother as a sexual figure. He describes how such occurrences happen only in a "gloomy" family—one in which secrets are kept by husband and wife—and that in a cheerful house that has open communication such a thing could not possibly occur. Constructively, therefore, he puts a great emphasis on communication among the members of his family. On a cultural level, his story indicates the Japanese awareness that parental example determines how a child is socialized—a mother must be dedicated and must not give in to sexual passions if a child is to be properly reared.

> J13. This seems to me he did something he shouldn't—I think that's what it is. He forced the woman—I think he raped her. Later he regrets what he has done, I think. It seems that way. (?) They were just plain friends, I guess. But he forced her, so he's regretful. (?) Well, then—their relationship dragged on, I think. They will probably live "drudgingly." I get that impression.

Again he does not avoid the sexual implications of the card, and directly sees the man as having raped the women. The consequences are that the man feels extremely regretful and is constrained to continue an unsatisfying relationship with the woman. In this card Mr. Segawa gives evidence of an active male sexual identification, which would indicate that some phallic sexuality is ego-syntonic and capable of expression, in spite of the other trends we have been considering in him. His capacity to face harsh reality is related to his capacity to take on a masculine resolution behaviorally. (He is also adequate in his responsible paternal role.)

> J18. I wonder if this is a child. They might be parent and child. Well, I wonder how it goes—to her drunken husband, who has just come home—he is a man who doesn't know or try to think how a woman feels every day in her hard life; then he's doing anything he wants to do. He has just come home. So he's accused by his wife, who is asking what he is trying to do to his household. She is upset because they are going in debt more and more, and besides, her husband is lazy

and no good. I don't think this situation will improve in the future, since he is the man of the house; I don't think their situation will get any better. That's why she's reached a peak of anger.

Mr. Segawa constructs a moralistic story that indicates he looks down on an irresponsible, drunken husband and sympathizes with the wife, who is moved to a "peak of anger" because her husband continues on his course of drinking without regard for his family. In her extreme anger her physical abuse of her husband is justified.

J22. This is—a man and his wife are fighting. I guess that's what it is. They happened to be going out somewhere, and the couple had a disagreement about where to go. Since they decided to go separately, their child doesn't know whether he wants to go with his mother or his father, so he started crying. Usually they get along, I think. Because if they were fighting all the time their children would not cry like this. Since they seldom fight, their child became upset and started crying. I think that they usually get along pretty well. They happened to disagree with each other in town and made their child confused on the street. Eventually they will compromise with each other because of their child's reaction, I think. This is just a temporary thing. (?) They had different opinions about where to go. The woman wanted to go to some fair, while her husband wanted to see a movie. The cause was very simple, I think. The man wants to go somewhere primarily to please the child, but his wife wants to do something with her husband more than with her child. The cause was very simple, like whether they should go to a fair or a movie. I think this is just a temporary conflict.

This story of a quarrel between man and wife is somewhat unusual in that the man is not egocentrically interested only in his own activities; the quarrel is essentially over a difference of opinion about where to take the child. The child is seen as crying, not because he is accustomed to having his parents quarrel, but on the contrary, because this is a rare occurrence and it is upsetting to him. We must note that the card itself directly suggests some conflict because of the way the characters are facing, but Mr. Segawa does not seem ready to countenance this as a chronic condition, and instead views this family as basically a harmonious one with temporary differences. He evidently does not like to envision any kind of chronic conflict between husband and wife. In both Cards 11 and 22 he seems to have less sympathy with the mother and child than with the father. In Card 11 it is the mother who is committing adultery, and on this card it is the father who is more concerned with wanting to please the child, whereas the wife wants to do something with her husband more than with her child. This is somewhat unusual in that the Japanese usually see the mother as dedicated more to the child than to the father, and it is probably unique among Japanese TAT stories to see a wife preferring a husband to a child in a conflict situation.

J27. This is a student, and his friend, a girl whom he admires, seems to be advising him not to do some bad activity like going to a coffee shop, because she likes him. But he's saying that it is all right and is tempting her to come along with him. I get the impression that she's telling him that going to places like coffee shops will be the beginning of bad activities. They are probably classmates. So the result will be that they will separate. I can't think that this student will listen to the girl student. Though they were good friends, this incident will cause them to separate, I think.

On the last card his response, like many of those given to this card in Japan, is to see a coffee shop as a place of temptation, but in this case the young girl is sufficiently autonomous to resist the blandishments of her friends, so they separate instead of the girl's being led astray by her young friend. The woman is depicted here as essentially capable of taking care of herself.

A moralistic-didactic tone runs through the TAT stories of Mr. Segawa, with an emphasis on role responsibility as a dominant feature. It also should be noted that a desire for autonomy is more readily depicted in adult women than in adult male figures. There are instances of achieving autonomy, but there remains a chronic tension—an internal clash between traditional directives to realize oneself and to submit to paternal authority. Behaviorally, all his life Mr. Segawa has opted for role responsibility over private inclinations.

PROJECTIVE TEST RESULTS: MRS. SEGAWA

The Rorschach Test

Mrs. Segawa's overall response to the Rorschach attests to the fact that although there are strong constrictive elements in her personality she is capable of a positive receptivity to others. This receptivity is inhibited by an oversensitivity to threat and a proneness to anxiety. She has a fairly well functioning inner life. She impresses one as being of at least high-average-to-superior intelligence. Authority is symbolized throughout by fierce, angry faces. A depressive moodiness is also suggested by some of the responses. Yet an open, positive responsiveness to bright colors suggests a triumphant optimism in a woman who has retained much of a childlike, dependent attitude in her adult life.

Rorschach Protocol

I. (60″) 1. *This . . . these are eyes. This . . . a cat . . . a really scary face; it looks like it. This is an ear. This is an eye. This is a mouth.* The whole thing looks like it. I don't know why, but it looks like a cat face. It looks as if it is angry. That's why I am frightened of it. It looks as if it is mad. [WS F+ Ad (Fab Elab) (Athr, Aobs)]

2. *It looks like a devil oni. Yes, this looks like a devil. I'm scared of it. All the parts together.* Suppose these are horns, fangs, and eyes. It does look like a devil. It looks as though a child is wearing a devil's mask. Well, a devil's mask . . . when I was a child I was scared of a devil—

maybe that's why. It's frightening. It looks like a picture that a child drew from a real mask. [WS F+ (Hd) (Athr, Aobs)]

3. *I'm not so good at describing a picture. Since I'm not good . . . it looks like a rabbit's angry face; these are ears.* They are ears, a rabbit's ears. This is a rabbit's face. Since the eyes are raised, they give me the impression that they are angry. I don't know how a rabbit looks when it gets angry, but I think it would look like this. [WS F+ Ad (Acnph, Aobs)]

4. *This is the mother . . . and then . . . I get an impression that a person is standing with his arm raised. In the center. That's about all. It is hard.* [laughs] Yes, these are hands. This little thing is a head. These are hips; here are legs—both legs. That is the way I got the impression. The person is standing with his hands up like this, I guess. It is hard to tell whether the person is facing this way or the other. When one dances you know how one makes a pose by putting his hands up from behind like this? [D M+ H (Prec)]

II. (58″) 5. *Is there no relationship between the upper half and the lower? Let's see, I wonder if these people are putting their hands together like this. Sitting. They look to be sitting like this. Let's see . . . other than that . . . It's not a rabbit but . . .* These are hands. These are heads. I guess they would be their arms. These are their knees. [D M+ H P (Neut)]

6. *There seem to be two bears; two cubs. That's about all, I guess. The nose, the legs and the tail* [laughs]. That was the way it looked . . . like that. These are the cubs' noses. These are their ears, tails, and legs. That was the way it looked. These are their forelegs and noses . . . the ones sticking out. [D FM+ A P (Dch)]

III. (90″) 7. *Oh dear! This looks like a ghost (obake). It makes me feel uneasy. This . . . it looks like a ghost, though a ghost is an imaginary thing; it appears like this . . . since the legs are vague.* Altogether there are two ghosts, and this is a soul, since the soul is part of the ghost. It looks like it's detached from the human race for some reason. It looks like sort of floating . . . well, I don't know what to say when I'm asked why it looks like a ghost. It gives me a sort of a funny, scary feeling. [W CF, M+ (H) P (Athr, Agl)]

8. *This is a butterfly . . . this red thing here looks like a butterfly.* Because these are the wings. This part is the center. It is flying. It is completely detached from the rest of the picture. Just the shape reminds me of a butterfly. [D FM+ A (Neut)]

9. *Here seems to be a human face.* Yes, this is a pair of glasses. You know that a person riding on a motor scooter is often wearing a pair of glasses? It looks like that type of big glasses . . . this black area. I assumed this center part is a nose. This white part reminds me of a mask. This center line is the nose; this white area is a mask . . . looks like it's wearing a big mask. [DS F− (Hd) Mask (Misc)]

IV. (54″) 10. *Oh, dear. All odd pictures [laughs] . . . this looks like a jungle*

. . . forest. Dark . . . let's see . . . maybe, I don't have much imagination. Dark, what shall I say? I get the impression that many trees are crowded. Old trees are here. It reminds me of a jungle because some old boughs are sticking out. [W YF Lscp (Agl, Adif)]

11. *It looks like a tree. This is a trunk. This is a tree . . . that's about all.* It looks like a tree standing . . . this dark part. Yes, only the dark part. And this part represents boughs and leaves. Yes, it is a big old tree, something like a cedar. When a tree becomes old it loses all the leaves from the upper part, you know? This is that kind of old tree. [W FT+ Bot (Neut)]

V. (52″) 12. *Oh, this looks like a butterfly . . . that's all. Just a butterfly.* Butterfly feelers. These are wings and legs. The whole shape looks like a butterfly. [W F+ A P (Neut)]

VI. (50″) *I wonder what it is. What is there to remind me of something? I don't know what . . . I can't think of anything.* (Rejection.) [(Arej)]

VII. (20″) 13. *Oh, I wonder if there are two girls here.* Feathers on their hats are standing. These are their noses and mouths; they look like whisperers. [W M+ H P (Misc)]

14. *There are two dogs, too; cute dogs. That's all.* It looks like dogs. You know the kind of dog with a square head like this? I don't know what you call . . . that square-faced dog. There are some stuffed animals like that too. [W FT+ A Toy (Ps, Pch)]

VIII. (49″) 15. *I wonder what it is. . . . It looks like an animal. Maybe a cat.* I looked at it from this side as one whole picture. Then it looks like one animal standing on a rock, since it is putting its legs on something. This side is sky color. It looks like either a tiger or a leopard because of the shape. [W CF, FM+ A P (Neut)]

16. *This is a flower. The lower part is the flower. And a flower vase . . . It's hard . . . that's it.* This red part. I don't know what kind of flower that is, but I don't know much about names of flowers . . . it looks like a soft flower petal. It gives me a soft, tender impression. A flower doesn't always have just one color. Some part is dark and some part is light. Because it is red it reminds me of a flower. [D FT, CF+ Bot P (Pnat, Ps)]

IX. (70″) *Yes, it's hard, this type of picture, since I don't have an interest in it; I don't feel much of anything. The color is pretty, that's all I feel* [laughs]. (Rejection.) [(Arej)]

X. (30″) 17. *This is a flower petal. A pretty flower is blooming. Let's see, it looks like a flower petal, like a happy spring. That's about all. The shade of color is pretty; I don't feel anything other than that.* This is the stem; these are petals, this is a pistil, and this is a stamen. It is a wild flower; it gives me a tender, warm feeling like spring. The flower is just this part. The first impression was this flower, then the color is pretty and a flower;

since the color is warm, it reminds me of spring. [W CF+ Symb Nat Bot (Pnat)]

Card-by-Card Sequential Analysis and Comments

On Card I Mrs. Segawa starts off immediately with a perception of threat. The angry cat face looks out at her. She says, "I am frightened of it," directly, with a kind of volatility sometimes found in hysterical women. The second response is like the first. This time it is the face of a devil, a devil's mask. She admits to preserving the fears of childhood. Then, after seeing a cat and a devil she is not yet content, but again sees another face, this time a rabbit's angry face. The rabbit is usually perceived as an unaggressive animal, but in her response it too is capable of being angry—hence frightening. Then, finally, she gives a more mature response, seeing the human form in the center with arms raised. She does have a capacity for a mature inner life when threat abates. In general in her record, she indicates a sensitivity to inner promptings, which comes out even on the first card. (The perception of human form is only infrequently described for Card I, and when it appears it is usually indicative of a tendency toward introversion.) She has no strong affective association to the human percept; nevertheless, the hands are described as up, in a position that one would find in dancing, which gives it a generally positive feeling rather than one of threat.

On the next card (II) she quickly sees the popular humans. She then sees two bears or cubs in the same area; the fact that they are "cubs," young bears, suggests a certain amount of childish identity in this woman, an impression strengthened by subsequent responses. On Card III, stimulated again by a sense of threat, she handles the usual humans rather poorly. She sees ghosts—also she uses the red side areas of the blot to perceive what many Japanese see on the Rorschach, two *hi no tama*. A *hi no tama* is a floating spirit, a ball of fire, usually found hovering over the graves of the dead. It represents the still-present soul of the dead person. Usually, however, Japanese see ordinary humans here rather than ghosts. Mrs. Segawa's proneness to anxiety causes her to have a feeling of "floating"—a different feeling of helplessness. (The Rorschach record of the young rapist presented in chapter 13 also is permeated with this type of frightened floating feeling that is indicative of his strong anxiety at the time of testing.) Mrs. Segawa remains a somewhat childlike person who has not surmounted basic feelings of threat as she experienced them when she was a little girl. Again, characteristically, she recovers to give another response, this time describing a rather innocuous red butterfly. Turning the card upside down (which she can do with flexibility), she sees a pair of glasses by combining most of the white area with the black into a rather clever mask, which, however, must again be considered indicative of anxiety, symbolized by eyes—although in this instance she has a positive association, referring to the glasses a person would wear when riding a motor scooter, a positive recreational activity.

On Card IV her diffuse anxiety comes out again. She sees a jungle. There is a feeling of darkness that makes it look like a jungle or a forest. She has another depressive association, a large, old tree, a dying cedar. On Card V she sees the ordinary butterfly without any unusual associations. She directly rejects Card VI, which very often carries a sexual connotation. On Card VII she can see two girls with feathers in their hats. She also sees two cute little square-faced dogs, meaning Scotties. She sees, possibly, some stuffed animals. This "mother" card is handled in a feminine, soft way, again emphasizing a kind of childlike, girlish personality.

To Card VIII she give the popular animal responses, seeing a cat or a tiger. She also gives a response popular in Japan on this card, a flower. She indicates on the last three cards a strong positive responsiveness to color, which affects her in a pleasant way. Nevertheless, she is unable to give any content to Card IX. She is overwhelmed by its formal complexity and she is forced to reject the card. On Card X she recovers, seeing pretty blooming flowers and indicating the positive quality in her nature, expressing the feeling of a happy spring. The colors are pretty and their warmth reminds her of spring. The warmth of her personality triumphs over her labile sense of threat.

The TAT

The TAT record of Mrs. Segawa is a rich, open one. No repression of appropriate thematic material is visible, and the stories are well composed and have an emotional and logical consistency. Some show a wish-fulfilling quality, but in general they are mature perceptions of human relationships. The TAT stories suggest that the proneness to threat and the childlike quality indicated by the Rorschach symbolism are not reflected in any general cognitive immaturity or hysterical blocking in her general social relationships.

The following stories are not those of a more masochistic Japanese woman, who romanticizes the self-sacrificial nature of the woman's role. Although Mrs. Segawa sees it necessary to play the woman's role properly in some of the stories, issues are resolved pragmatically rather than in terms of guilt or inner torment.

> J1. This child likes music. Since he was little he has tried hard to be a violinist. But when he reached a certain age he became aware of the limit of his ability and started suffering. He seems worried about whether he should continue to play the violin or not. In the future, well—I wonder what he will be in the future. It is hard to be a musician. I would think that he'd rather put his effort into something else. On the other hand, you will face some kind of hardship in any field, so I wonder if he should keep trying. From the expression on his face I can't picture his being so successful. He will probably play the violin just as a hobby. . . . He looks sort of worried. Really, what is this? I feel that if he were a good player he wouldn't suffer this way. He seems to feel more serious than that. I wonder that I should say—serious? He looks as if he's won-

dering whether he should do it or not. That's all, I guess. (?) I meant that he was wondering whether he should continue or not. He doesn't look as if he'll be successful as a musician. (?) He will play the violin just as a hobby and will do something else as an occupation. I think it's better for him to be successful in some other field. (?) Let's see. What shall I say? It's difficult. Well, let's make it that he will be successful. (?) Let me see. He looks as if he's about a freshman in junior high. I think he is male.

This story is unusual in that Mrs. Segawa depicts the child as becoming aware of the limits of his ability and perhaps of his talent, so that he will not press on with the violin as a career but will turn to something else, in which he will probably be successful. The story is told in empathetic language and may be interpreted as showing either Mrs. Segawa's practical orientation or perhaps her sense of the personal limitations of her own son, so that she does not wish to have someone pressed excessively toward something that he cannot accomplish. There is a delimiting attitude expressed about his being ready to settle for less—possibly a kind of pragmatic, realistic ego-orientation.

J2. Let's see. They are farmers in the country. But this girl doesn't like farming. She became interested in literature and is about to go away from the farm. I think this is her mother. Her mother and father will maintain the same occupation they have had for so long a time. They will continue farming. And they think that they are happy that way. This girl doesn't like farming. So she is planning to go to the city and will try to specialize in literature, I think. It's the kind of living she's longing for as a teenager. Then she will return home. How is it like that? (?) Well, she will marry happily. She will succeed her family on the farm and have a happy married life. I'll make it that she establishes a nice, happy family. (?) She doesn't like it and spends most of her time reading books without helping with the housework. In the future, after she realizes that it was just a pipe dream, she will come back to her parents' home. She marries a man who joins her family by the marriage, for she is the only child in the family. She comes back to make a happy home for parents' sake and everybody's sake. (?) This is her mother and this is her father. (?) Let's see. She's already in the third year of junior high. But she looks older in this picture, maybe about eighteen.

In her story for the second card the achievement theme is again permitted but not actualized. The story is told in a positive way, however. The farmers are seen as happy with their life, but the girl doesn't like farming; she wants to specialize in literature and she goes to the city, but then returns home to a happy marriage. It is most unusual in response to this card for the Japanese to be concerned with the future marriage rather than the achievement of the heroine of the story. Here she can be resigned to farm life because she is happily married and she comes to the realization that what she wanted was a fantasy and that her place is with her family. It is interesting to note that in her story the daughter stays with her family by taking a husband as a *muko-yōshi*. As we indicated, Mr. Segawa virtually became "an adopted husband," although he did not change his family name. The "dreams" of literature are inhibited or foregone in the day-by-day duties of a wife and mother, and yet the tone throughout the story is positive, with no suggestions of tension or conflict. Although there is some indication of what may be a trend toward a creative, positive, self-expressive attitude, Mrs. Segawa has delimited her horizons to find contentment in what life has offered her. One gains an impression that Mrs. Segawa's basic attitude toward her childhood relationships was a positive one, and that she felt some reluctance in leaving a warm, dependent atmosphere.

> J3. She's crying. This is something; something sad happened. She can't tell her father or mother about it. So she came to her room and is crying. Then am I supposed to say why she's crying? Well, what would be a good reason? From the impression she gives, she seems to be heartbroken. A man she fell in love with left her without understanding her. She couldn't express herself—and came home. She's in a state of sorrow and is crying, I guess. . . . Then she will recover from it and spend her youth with ardent hope. That's about all, I guess. How old is she? Let's see. Twenty. It's a woman. I wonder how old she is. About twenty, I guess.

On this card she sees the girl as crying because of a lack of communication. She is heartbroken; her lover did not understand her. It is characteristic of Mrs. Segawa's positive orientation that the girl recovers and regains her basic optimistic attitude toward life. There is some remaining identification with a girlish adolescence characteristic of many Japanese young women who find it hard to communicate their tender, genuine feelings toward the opposite sex. It is an old, commonly expressed Japanese fantasy that the woman is too shy to express her tender feelings and that through these circumstances a love is never realized.

> J6. This is—a mother is angry with her son. He is explaining what happened and apologizing to her. Well, what will be a good story? The mother found a bride-to-be for her son because he reached marriageable age. But this man doesn't want the girl no matter what. He has somebody else in mind. He is telling his mother he doesn't like the girl. So his mother is angry and is asking how he can refuse her offer. Her face doesn't look as if she is angry, though. Her son looks as if he doesn't know what to do. Since he's living in Tokyo, he has to go back. He's saying to his mother that he has to leave now and is telling her goodbye. Then the mother is saying, "Do whatever you want," and is turning away from him. Then he goes back to Tokyo and marries the girl he had in mind. That's all. (?) Well—the mother—no matter what she said—she will feel better about it after a while, though she was angry with him at the moment. She realizes that it's up to her son. (?) The man is twenty-seven or twenty-eight. The mother is about sixty, I guess.

In this story she expresses understanding of an autonomy conflict that arises between mother and son. She sees the mother as angry with her son because he rejects her choice for his marriage and goes to Tokyo and marries someone on his own initiative. The mother nevertheless reconciles herself to her son's autonomy. Although Mr. Segawa may remain ambivalent about traditional and modern values, Mrs. Segawa basically resolves issues in terms of human feelings.

> J7. This is—I wonder what—he doesn't look like the father. This person is worrying about something. I wonder what he is worrying about. Then he came to see a teacher he respected. I can't tell whether it's his teacher or his uncle. Anyway, he came to see this person he respected and confessed to him what he was worrying about. So this elderly person is telling him what to do or not to do. He looks as if he's dreaming—? Maybe not [she whispers]. That's not enough, huh? (?) Let's see. Judging from his age it's probably some conflict in his family. (?) This person, the younger one, is worrying—I guess he has one child. He had some disagreement with his wife. He is thinking of getting divorced. He came to ask him what he thought of it. Then this person is telling him that he'd better settle down and think of his child and various things. He is telling him to reconsider. He advised him to be more critical of himself and to be patient when it's necessary. Then he thought that the older person was right. So he went home and talked with his wife. They said to each other that they would try to get along by correcting each other's faults and consulting with each other. They became good friends. I'll settle it that way. (?) This person is about thirty-four or thirty-five. The other one is sixty-one or sixty-two. (?) I will make him his uncle.

The story on this card raises some questions: first, why is it necessary for the young man to seek advice from a teacher or an uncle? If we look at her description of her father and the relationship between her mother and her father, it becomes apparent that the father was never seen as an individual commanding respect. To gain advice from a man who is deemed knowledgeable, therefore, she would have to go outside her own family. We have no basis for speculating on what experience or impression she may have drawn to create the story of the temporary dissension between husband and wife that could lead to a divorce. We get no impression in her life history materials that she ever felt so inclined toward her own husband. On the surface, at least, she seems to have reconciled herself to her marriage and expresses happy optimism about it. This may be the point of the story, a kind of demonstration that what is needed in human relationships is increased communication and intimacy. We might say that the basic theme that she expresses in several of her stories is how one is to come closer to other human beings. We see from her recounting of her own life history that in her girlhood she did not actually experience a happy family life. Nevertheless, there seems to have been a continual wish-fulfilling dream that she would somehow be able to find such a life in the future.

J8. I wonder what he is holding. This is a knife? It's either a knife or a hypodermic needle or a pen. I wonder what this is. This is a rifle. This person got injured in the mountains, and these three people brought him back. This looks like a rifle. By accident he was shot by a stray bullet. A doctor is not around because it's in the mountains. They tried to take the bullet out and these people are watching—it's like a Western drama. This person is the one who shot him, so he is in a state of shock. He lost his mind wondering what he should do, I suppose. (?) Then they will go to get a doctor, that is, after they take out the bullet. This person will be saved. (?) These three are friends. I guess this person is a stranger. He is a woodcutter or something and went to the mountains. Then he was shot by mistake. (?) They are middle-aged. This person looks young.

Card 8 depicts no theme of willful aggression, rather, a shooting accident in the mountain. It is noticeable that Mrs. Segawa does not identify with the prone victim as much as with the young man in the foreground, who is concerned with the fact that he accidentally shot someone. The person is taking responsibility for his behavior. The story is well integrated and handles all the details of the picture without evidence of any undue inner problem over the expression of hostility or destructive violence.

J9. Let's see. This person is little—the woman looks sad. She went to get—well, this is not a child. She looks like her sister [younger]. Because of her younger sister, she and her husband had a fight. And her husband went back to his family. He had an argument with his wife about his sister-in-law. So he went home. Then his wife and her younger sister came to apologize to him and they are asking him to come back. I think his mother is telling him not to be so stubborn and to go home, since his wife and her sister came to get him. He decided to go home with them since they apologized and came to get him. (?) This man's mother. (?) He was mad at his sister-in-law because she was spoiled. Then his wife told him that he doesn't have to get mad at her like that. Since he was in a bad mood at the time, he told his wife that she had spoiled her sister and they started arguing. Then he left home suddenly. Then this girl [the woman's sister] too came to get him, saying that it was her fault.

The most interesting and unusual feature of this story is the fact that Mrs. Segawa automatically assumes that the man in this picture was a *muko-yōshi*, an adopted husband. She caught herself after she said that he had returned to his own family after a quarrel, and said, "Oh, he must therefore be a *yōshi*." This is interesting because her father was a *muko-yōshi*, and, as we indicated, her husband in effect was adopted into her family without having his name changed. Mrs. Segawa automatically expects that the usually culturally dominant male-female lineage relationship is reversed. The story itself is unique; it is the only one we have found so far that depicts intrafamily tensions of this kind. We also noted in this story that her words for the husband were very respectful throughout. She made the story of a quarrel revolve around a younger sister rather than relating it to something that was directly disharmonious between the marital pair. The woman, as was proper in the traditional style, apologized to the husband for the quarrel. The man is perceived as being quick to get angry, as her own husband is described by both her and the son. The overall story is extremely well integrated and told in a direct way without any hesitancy or noticeable changes in direction. She also described the woman as short—a spontaneous self-identification.

> J11. This is—he is peeking. He peeked at the guest room after he played outside after school, wondering if there was a guest. Then his mother . . . It doesn't look nice—this mother—while her child was out she committed adultery. Her husband was out on a business trip or something—No, I guess this is her husband. He just came home. If he did come home he is sort of funny, isn't he?—Then he [the boy] saw his father's briefcase and hat lying there. He was about to call "Daddy!" when he saw his mother. His mother looked different so he was surprised and kept silent. The child looks about the age for junior high school. What shall I say now? (?) Let me see. Because he's a child he will leave the scene soon—but since he is a child he won't remember the unpleasant scene. If he were an adult he would feel that he saw something awful, you know? I wonder if a child at this age will feel anything like that? It is difficult. What shall I say now? I don't know what I should say now. (?) Seeing his father lying there, the child would say, "Hi, Daddy!" and go back to play. (?) He is about in his first year of junior high school. (?) The mother is about thirty-four or thirty-five. This kind of picture is difficult.

This card is interpreted directly at first as a scene of adultery similar to Mrs. Segawa's husband's story. It suggests that she herself may periodically entertain extramarital sexual fantasies. She does not stay with this story but rejects it. She quickly changes the scene into one in which the husband has come back from a business trip, thus explaining the hat and the briefcase, which probably suggested adultery to her in the beginning. Their child has inadvertently come upon the parents during sexual intercourse. Mrs. Segawa then speculates what effect this has upon a child, whether a child would remember such a scene or not. She finally resolves the question, dismissing it by saying, "Seeing his father lying there, the child would say, 'Hi, Daddy!' and go back to play." She says that this picture was difficult for her. Nevertheless, she does not automatically block or repress but allows her inner life imaginative license. She tends to give things directly as she sees them, although she realizes some social implications of what she is seeing and checks her perception. We would say that she shows some impulsiveness toward a kind of ready spontaneity. She does not ordinarily use repressive mechanisms to keep back her thoughts.

> J13. This is a difficult picture. I wonder why this man looks so sad. I don't enjoy this type of story; I don't know how to make a story about

> it. This woman looks dead. It's hard. I can't think of anything. Do I have to make a story about it? (?) It's not a pleasant thing. I don't want to think about it. (?) Let's see. It doesn't give you a nice feeling. The problem is the thing that made this person start crying. If they were a couple it wouldn't make sense for this person to cry. If they had an affair without being married to each other he wouldn't have to cry either. I wonder if [her boyfriend] left her. If that was the case she shouldn't look this way. Well, she did something she shouldn't have before she married. She did something that her parents were not aware of. She realized all of a sudden what she did. The man probably thought he did something wrong. He looks like that. It's hard to tell about this type of people. (?) Eventually they will get married. They have not much choice but to get married, no matter how much other people object. Because they went this far [brief blank because the tape broke] (?) I think she made up her mind, considering that she went this far. (?) The woman is twenty-four or twenty-five. The man is twenty-five or twenty-six.

Her immediate concern about this picture is with the sadness of the man, which she then tries to shape into some kind of story but has difficulty because for some reason she doesn't like the theme of a woman's being dead. She seems compelled by the direct reality of the card to see a sexual relationship between these figures. The scene bothers her because in most sexual situations there is no need for a man to cry. This observation is almost as if she countenanced casual sexual liaisons. Finally she settles on a theme of a man and a woman who have done "something wrong" premaritally. They have no choice now but to get married, no matter how much other people object. This seems to be a reflection of the fact that there were serious objections on the part of her husband's family toward their own marriage. Her response, compared with other stories given to this card, in effect rejects the masochistic traditional role of women, a theme that is used by many, who give a sad story of a woman who is ill or dying. Mrs. Segawa shows no masochistic trends whatsoever. In essence, she tries to work out the situation as a mutually beneficial one, rather than one in which either the woman or the man is at a disadvantage.

> J18. She seems to be trying to choke her. This is a woman and so is this. This is a woman. This is a second wife and this is the real wife. This second wife came to tell the real wife to separate from her husband. She came in while the husband was out. The second wife insulted her by saying some nasty things. So the real wife became upset and tried to choke her. Then her husband came home and calmed the situation down. The second wife went home. But the real wife seems disgusted with her husband. She became disgusted with him and probably will reach the point that she wants to get divorced. She appears to look like that. She doesn't give me a good impression as a wife. Because of the way she is, her husband might have gone in this direction. Eventually they will get divorced. (?) That's right. (?) Probably he will marry this second wife. The second wife may be a widow. The real wife behaved

poorly. It was probably the wife's fault that her husband had a second wife. It's both of their faults. When a man has a second wife we can't just generalize and say that it's the man's fault or his wife's fault. A man who has a second wife usually has an opinion like that. I personally don't like that sort of thing.

Mrs. Segawa gives an active, complex, evaluative theme of a conflict between two women over a man. A wife is fighting to keep her husband from taking a second woman. Mrs. Segawa first states that after the battle the first woman was disgusted with her husband for being in such a situation and she decided to get a divorce. But then she sympathizes with the second woman, perhaps feeling that a woman who is so openly assertive and aggressive as the first wife may be contributing to the fact that her husband has taken up with another woman. The man then is seen as marrying the second woman. As the story progresses Mrs. Segawa becomes more and more sympathetic with the man and the second woman rather than with the betrayed wife. In the beginning of the story, as she recounted it, it was the second woman who had insulted the first by saying nasty things. But gradually Mrs. Segawa's sympathy with the adulterous husband increases. She ends without deciding, however, saying, "When a man has a second wife we can't just generalize and say that it's the man's fault or his wife's fault." Again, this gives some indication that there may be some positive sexual fantasy in this woman about adultery. It is most unusual for a Japanese woman to give a large number of stories that are focused on sexual themes. In fact, the relatively overt sexual attitudes of both Mr. and Mrs. Segawa are far different from the more restrained attitudes usually expressed.

J22. A father, a mother, and a child went out together and didn't agree with each other for some reason—that is, between the father and mother. They disagreed about which way to go. The child became impatient. The mother hesitated to do anything. Then the father told his wife, "Do whatever you want!" The mother too said, "Do as you want!" So the father is about to ignore them and leave. The child didn't know what to do and started crying. The mother ignored the child and looked in the other direction. The child felt sad because he was expecting to go out with both his parents. (?) Let's see. Since the child is crying on the street, the father is afraid of what other people might think. I wonder if the mother will yield—(?) Yes, the mother—in this case a woman should yield, I guess. Yes, the mother yielded to her husband. So she said, "Let's go together." Then the three of them will go somewhere together cheerfully. (?) While the father wants to go to the zoo, his wife wants to go to a movie or something. So the father said, "O.K., I'll go there by myself." At first the mother insisted on going to a movie, even alone. Then she thought that it would be better for the child to go to the zoo than to a movie where it would be so crowded.

Mrs. Segawa's story on Card 22 is almost the same as that given by her husband. A story given in such parallel fashion by both parents suggests that they have drawn on some actual experience. In both cases the solution is the same: the woman capitulates and reconciles them by cheerfully accepting the husband's decision.

> J27. I wonder if they are classmates. They happened to meet each other in front of a coffee shop. The girl just came out with her girl friend from the coffee shop. Then the boy saw her and asked where she was going. They are standing and talking to each other. And this woman is waiting for her girl friend and is looking at them. She is hoping that her girl friend will come soon. (?) The boy suggested that he will treat both girls to something. So they all went into the coffee shop. (?) This person looks like a college student. They are not in the same class, it seems to me. I wonder if he is her boyfriend. The boy is about twenty-one. The girl is about nineteen.

Mrs. Segawa handles Card 27 in a most natural way. The coffee shop is not seen as a den of iniquity; rather, it is a casual meeting place for two girl friends, who were invited for a cup of coffee by a boy. No sinister implications are given to the coffee shop. Mrs. Segawa is spontaneously positive in her attitude about interpersonal relationships. She definitely believes in autonomy and yet feels satisfied with playing the traditional woman's role as described in our life history material. All in all, Mrs. Segawa's record is one of the most open and straightforward in any of our samples.

PROJECTIVE TEST RESULTS: RYŪICHI SEGAWA

The Rorschach Test

The young Ryūichi Segawa's record is intellectually superior and generally positive. The joys of life triumph over anxieties. One finds a concern with faces throughout the record, which suggests a kind of authority threat that has not been thoroughly sublimated in his personality. This seeing of faces is common in our total sample and suggests that boys from thirteen to fifteen years of age share certain common difficulties with authority.

Rorschach Protocol

I. (5″) 1. *A butterfly, the butterfly family, a moth.* These are wings. This is a mouth. It's not a butterfly. It's a moth. Because the shape of the body and the way the wings are attached to its body resemble more a moth. [W F+ A P (Neut)]

2. *An elephant.* Isn't it called "Dumbo"? Just like that in the movie. The ears are big. It is flying now. These are legs. This is the tail. This is the body. This is the picture as seen from the bottom. The legs are hanging down. The ears are big and it looks sturdy. [W FM+ A O (Pch, Dch)]

II. (13″) 3. *They are dancing.* They bent their legs and are squatting down like this. They are two people. They have masks on. They seem to be happy and gay. If these were their mouths, they look as if they are laughing. They seem to be enjoying themselves. [W M+ H Mask P (Mor)]

4. *They look like dogs' faces. They are opening their mouths.* These are their mouths. And these parts are their faces. There are two dogs—only their faces. It looks like the dogs are barking [form is poor—mouth is center of bulge of white]. [D FM− Ad (Neut)]

III. (14″) 5. *Playing.* This is a ball. Somebody is bouncing it. Two people. [D M+ H P (Prec)]

6. *It looks like a face.* An animal's face. A wild animal. Because its mouth and eyes look fierce. [D F− Ad Face (Athr, Aobs)] [Additional response] It resembles a scene of a bird falling after being shot.

IV. (4″) 7. *A bat.* It resembles a bat because of the black color and the way the wings are spread. [W FC+ A (Neut)]

8. *A robot.* [as seen from the side and below] These are legs. Since we are looking at it from the bottom, the bottom part of the legs are fat and the higher parts look thinner. It looks dignified. Also the shape of the face looks like that of a robot. [W FV + (H) (Misc)]

V. (8″) 9. *This is a butterfly, too.* This is a real perfect butterfly. This is a face. These are wings and the body . . . I wonder what this is called. . . . Do you call it a tail? [laughs] Because the shape of the body resembles a butterfly's. Also the face and tail look like a butterfly. [W F+ A P (Neut)]

10. *Like unusual glasses.* This area is glass. The black parts are lenses. This part is what you put on a nose. This part for ears. The angle of the picture reminds me of glasses. [W FC' − Obj O (Prec)]

VI. (9″) 11. *An animal's skin, that of a lion.* This is the face. This is the body. Legs and hands. This is the whiskers . . . what shall I say . . . like a lion's. The whiskers look like a lion's. The body looks like the animal's shape and texture. [W FT+ Aob P (Ps)]

12. *It belongs to the fish family. It looks like a stingray.* It is a stingray. This shape is. A tail. A face. Actually the eyes are supposed to be on the bottom side—oh, maybe above. The mouth is on the bottom side, isn't it? These small things are supposed to be eyes. Because their eyes are small. I guessed from the flat shape. [Dd F+ A (Athr)]

13. *A fox's face.* This is the mouth. These are ears. This and this are eyes. That's about all. It reminds me of a fox because of the shape of the mouth and the face. Also the way its nose is shaped in a straight line. [D F+ Ad Face (Aobs)]

14. *People have their arms on each other's shoulders. They are dancing.* Two people, a face, hands, legs. This, too, is a leg. They have their

arms on each other's shoulders. Both of them are standing on one leg. They look as if they're running while they are dancing on one leg. I get the impression that they are standing on one leg and putting the other leg behind. [W M(+) H O (Prec)]

VII. (8″) 15. A *donkey.* This part is the face. The whole thing. The part sticking out is ears. This is a mouth. These are eyes. These are hands. I wonder if these are legs—no, I guess they are hands. Then, the body . . . though I can't see the legs. It is turned the other direction but facing this way. The part sticking out on top looks like ears. The area around its mouth looks like a donkey. The way it bends its legs reminds me of a donkey. This is when a donkey has just jumped. [W F M+ A (Neut)]

16. *Antlers.* Antlers of the deer family. This is the head, and the antlers are on the top of it. The antlers are magnificent on the top of its head. [W F+ Aob, Dauth]

17. A *helmet.* These are the ornamental horns. This part is for wearing on a head. A head part to wear. A helmet. It resembles a helmet which samurai wear in a movie. [W F Cg (Porn, Dauth)]

VIII. (10″) 18. A *flower.* This is a flower. This part is the flower petal. The color is gay and the shape looks like a flower so I guessed it as a flower. [W FC+ Bot (Pnat)]

19. A *face. A decorated face.* This part is eyes. This part is the nose. This is a beard. These are some sort of ornaments for hair, I guess. Because they resemble the ornaments at a festival over there. I meant a festival in a foreign country. [W FC—Hd Orn Face (Aobs, Porn)]

IX. (22″) 20. *Unusual . . . this, too, dancing.* These are faces. One by one. Four people. I wonder if they are singing together . . . yes, they are singing . . . four of them together. This is a mike. These are the bodies. This part is legs. These are hands. They put their hands on their hips. I get the impression that they are singing. [W M+ H (Prec)]

21. A *skeleton* [he actually meant a skull]. *Some parts of it are covered with something.* This is the head. Eyes. A mouth. I wonder if this is some cloth, the kind which a magician often uses. The other parts are covered with the cloth. . . . It resembles the cloth which a magician uses. [DdS F − Anat Face (Aob, Bb, Prec)]

X. (14″) 22. *Oh, let's see. A bird.* These are wings. Legs. This is the body. It looks like a condor. Because the wings are big. This is a condor, too. The wings are down and these are legs, two. [D F− A (Neut)]

23. A *rock.* This is a rock. It is bumpy and shows clearly the part which is dark and light in color. [D YF + Nat (Neut)]

24. A *face. An animal's face.* This is an animal's face. These are the horns. This is the nose. This part is eyes. The nose looks like an animal's nose. The shape of the face looks like an animal's too. [D F− Ad Face (Aob)]

25. *A bird.* Shape. [D F+ A (Neut)]

26. A *firecracker.* The way it splits all over reminds me of a firecracker very much. [W CF Fm+ F i (Hh, Prec)]

Card-by-Card Sequential Analysis and Comments

On the first card Ryūichi sees a butterfly, which is a popular response. His second response to this card is rather childish, albeit clever and positive: a flying elephant with large ears, suggested by the Walt Disney film *Dumbo.*

On the second card he sees dancing people with masks, seemingly happy and gay. Throughout, one finds projections of an internal positive state. Then he sees dog faces with open mouths (these are not in the usual areas). The dogs are barking. We would say that there is some covert aggressive as well as passive orality, represented by this and by the considerable attention paid to mouths throughout the record.

On Card III he sees human figures as playing, bouncing a ball, a childish, positive activity appropriate to his age. This is followed again by a fierce animal face "because its mouth and eyes look fierce." He gives an additional response—a bird falling—to the outer red areas of this card. It is an appropriate response, even though it suggests a passive (incurred) aggression. The percept of the falling animal may suggest some tendencies to feel weak and helpless, but such tendencies probably play only a peripheral role in Ryūichi's present behavior.

On Card IV he sees a bat upside-down, citing the black color. Then he turns the card right side up and gives an unusual response, a robot. He uses perspective, seeing the legs as large because one is looking up from below so that there is a foreshortening. As seen from below, the robot looms larger. Ryūichi uses a curious word in describing the robot: he says it looks "dignified." This creates a dilemma, since a robot is not alive but is a subject of external manipulation. A robot is certainly a toned-down type of threatening figure, but rather than countenancing the conscious sense of threat vis-à-vis authority often evoked by this card, Ryūichi gives due respect to it by seeing it as "dignified." Symbolically, however, the figure is seen not as vital but as lifeless and mechanical.

Card V is perceived as the popular butterfly. Then, like his mother (see above), who saw eyeglasses on Card III, he sees a strange pair of glasses that one puts on one's nose. One wonders why two members of this family, given the test independently, would give this unusual response—taking a whole card as glasses covering the eyes. One of the features of sunglasses is, of course, their protective nature; and sometimes, if they are sufficiently dark, one can look out without one's own eyes being seen; but we can only speculate about what such a response might mean symbolically for either Ryūichi or his mother.

Card VI gives him no trouble. He sees it, as it is popularly seen, as skin, and is responsive to the textural quality of the blot. As his second response he sees, upside down, a stingray, a fearful, rather threatening fish. Again, he pays special attention to where the eyes are, debating with himself whether the eyes or the mouth are on the bottom side. The small things (he points to small areas) are supposed to be the eyes because they are small. Then he sees a fox's face, again pointing out the mouth and the eyes. His last response to this card is positive. Seen upside down, the figures remind him of people who have their arms on each other's shoulders, dancing. Each is standing on one leg and has the other leg behind. This shows a positive readiness for close physical contact between humans. There is no sense of antagonism when he sees the human figure; rather, it is evocative of pleasurable contact in activity.

On Card VII he sees a donkey with large ears, adding that it reminds him of a donkey that has just jumped. He does not see ordinary humans. Rather, his percepts are stimulated by the large ears. He is interested in the protrusions on this card. Then he gives another, similar response—antlers, viewing the whole card as a set of antlers, which he sees as "magnificent" on top of a deer. These are seen positively as a male symbol, which comes out more directly in his next response—a samurai helmet, including the ornamental horns mounted on the armored helmet, usually of a chieftain or a noble lord. Ryūichi gives here a response that is scored as an authority symbol. On the Rorschach there is statistically a significantly greater prevalence of such authority symbols in the record of both boys and fathers of the nondelinquent group in our sample than in the records of the delinquent boys and their fathers. We might say that the authority symbols suggest a positive, affirmative attitude toward the authority structure of the culture on a symbolic level. It may also indicate a positive affirmation of Ryūichi's own samurai background and the masculine heritage it entails.

On Card VIII he sees a flower with a good form quality. He also sees the entire card as a "decorated face," an unusual response, in which he sees ornamentation on the hair. The ornamentation of the face is of the type one sees at festivals in a foreign country, a kind of rationalization for this unusual percept. He continues his obsessive concern with faces. On Card IX upside down, he sees four people singing together, physically close, touching, surrounding a microphone and singing together—an original concept that suggests a feeling of interpersonal harmony and accord. Turning the card right side up, he sees something more negative—a skull in the center—but he puts the skull in a positive context, seeing the surrounding as a kind of cloth that a magician uses. Apparently, the skull is seen in the context of a magic performance, giving it again an ultimately positive context in spite of its negative dysphoric associations. The last card, Card X, he breaks up into a number of individual percepts, one of which is again an animal's face. The firecracker in his final response is the only sign of any affective explosion, but again, the context is positive; firecrackers are celebratory and not destructive.

All in all, this is a positive record. One sees throughout the record symbolic indications of a positive social orientation and an anticipation of enjoyment of and cohesiveness in human relationships. Obsessive concern with faces, however, reminds us that there is an unresolved authority threat that remains a strong component of Ryūichi's personality. The percept of "Dumbo" on Card I and the big ears on Card VII, followed by the warrior's helmet, may be symbolically perceived as a struggle away from a negative self-image toward a more positive identification with masculinity. The movie *Dumbo* probably has some personal relevance in this boy's positive use of childish fantasy. Dumbo is a kind of ugly duckling not quite accepted by the other elephants. He learns to put his "big ears" to use and can do something the others cannot do, a rather common positive fantasy that a child might have about being inadequate but, through special efforts, becoming acceptable to others. We recall that Ryūichi did tell us how he was teased because he was fat when he first went to school; in effect, he was a kind of Dumbo who ultimately was able to overcome his difficulty and by now has achieved social recognition from his peers as well as his teachers.

The TAT

Throughout his TAT responses Ryūichi carries a prevailing theme of someone who has taken the side of the law. There are delinquent acts depicted in his stories, but the heroes are on the side of law and order. The boy's strong identification with authority is evident throughout his TAT record, as is his essentially positive orientation toward social relationships.

> J1. It's so hard. I wonder how to play this. It would be lots of fun if I could play it. That's what he is thinking—(?) He was playing it before, but he can't make it sound good. So he is thinking how to do it. Then he became successful after he thought it through.

On Card 1 he takes a healthy attitude toward the task, giving a feeling that to be able to do something would be fun. In other words, there is a pleasure in accomplishment. He expresses the pervasive Japanese doubt about one's own ability, showing that the boy is feeling some inadequacy, and yet the story is resolved successfully without elaboration. It shows a basically optimistic attitude.

> J2. When she was little she used to live in a farm village like this. Now she is a teacher. She's thinking that she will go back to the farm village when she gets older. . . . She used to be in a farm village before. . . . This person . . . this is the mother, huh? . . . Then her child, see . . . is waiting for her child to come home from school.

On this card the success of the figures with the books is assumed; she is already a teacher, and in this scene she wishes to go back to the farm village when she is older. There is no expression of tension or animosity toward farming, but rather a sense of accomplishment. Ryūichi does, however, leave out any mention of the father. There doesn't seem to be any particular tension about this, but the focus of familial relationships is expressed as taking place between mother and daughter. No negative feelings come out in the story, but we may infer a more basic closeness to the mother.

> J3. This is a hospital. A patient fell down because he walked when he was sick and not able to walk. So he looks pained. . . . That's all. (?) Oh, that's right, after that he will be taken care of by a doctor. . . . (?) Details, details, huh? . . . Since he was sick, he fell down because he walked when he couldn't do it. Then he couldn't move any longer. So the doctor came and took him away. . . . That's all.

Ryūichi concentrates on a physical complaint as the gist of the story. The man has hurt his leg by walking too soon in the hospital, not following the advice of authority. The reason for the injury is doing something that one was not supposed to do, a kind of implicit superego punishment here. There is, however, a basic trust in the outer world. The patient will be taken care of by the doctors, and the problem will be solved. On this card Ryūichi suddenly remembers that he didn't follow the instructions for giving the outcome of the stories, and he spontaneously fulfills the task. He is very cooperative and tries to comply with requests.

> J6. She is so old that she can't live alone. So her son is suggesting that she live with him. But she doesn't move. . . . I think they will live together after this. This man is already married. He is suggesting that she come to live with them but she doesn't listen. . . . (?) Gradually they will live together.

For Card 6 the story is the reverse of what is often the theme expressed in response to this card; that is, rather than leaving the mother, the son wants his mother to come live with him. The mother seeks to remain autonomous but finally gives in and is willing to accept dependency on her son. The willing fulfillment of obligations is an interesting assumption. Somehow the mother does not look forward to becoming dependent and living with her son. Here there may be a continual subtle pull on the part of this mother toward her son's independence. The son himself does not accept this completely. Certainly the story does not give any feeling that the mother wishes to keep the son. The opposite seems to be the case.

> J7. Both of them are scholars. They are making a plan. They are thinking how to make it now. Then they will be successful. . . . That's all.

Card 7 is a very simple story of two scholars collaborating on some plan. There is no expression of hierarchy. The story is simply one of cooperative interaction. Notice here that Ryūichi does not give the usual story of the father giving advice to his son.

> J8. This is . . . [he] did some bad things and was shot by that rifle. Then his friend is taking the bullet out of him. These are the dreams he has had. . . . He reflects about his behavior and will correct that from now on. . . . (?) Yes, it is a scene in his dream. So he reflects about himself.

In the story of Card 8 there is a spontaneous reversal. Here the story starts with wrongdoing. He says the boy "did some bad things and was shot by that rifle. Then his friend is taking the bullet out of him." Note that instead of seeing the boy as inadvertently shooting someone with the rifle and thus doing a bad thing, Ryūichi has already created a retribution for wrongdoing by having the boy doing something bad in the past and then being shot by the rifle. A sensitivity to potential guilt is indicated by such a story, seen as a warning dream. The boy reflects about his behavior and corrects it. Here is evidence of a very strong and active superego, which is continually warning him to keep in line.

> J9. A robber broke into this house and somebody in this house was killed. So the son of the family ran to the scene and is looking at it right now. Then he informs the police. (?) I guess the person's father was killed. This man's [in the right foreground] father . . . Oops! May I change that? This is . . . they are living in a different house at a different place. They were informed by the police that a robber broke in and somebody was killed. So they all hurried there. They saw it and are feeling sad. . . . (?) Yes, these people are all living in a different house. The one who was killed is the father. . . . This person [the woman on the left] is apparently married. . . . (?) This old lady is a house-helper, maybe. (?) They will put up a gravestone to let him sleep peacefully.

Card 9 continues the theme of wrongdoing but has it come from an external source. A robber breaks into a house. Somebody in the house is killed. Whatever aggression this boy has he must immediately project it onto outside sources. He himself thoroughly identifies with proper behavior. "The son of the family ran to the scene and is looking at it," he states, and "Then he informs the police." We might say (symbolically) that he himself cannot get away with anything, but that the superego remains well informed about his intentions. For some reason Ryūichi changes the story and for the first time we get what might be some unconscious hostility coming through, as it usually does, symbolically. In the changed story the father is killed, but the destroyed father is placated with a reverential tombstone erected in his honor, allowing the father to sleep peacefully. Ryūichi has a considerable amount of unconscious hostility toward his father. Nevertheless, his strong superego makes him overcompensate in the direction of conformity.

> J11. This woman—this is an inn. And some woman stole something in the inn. This child saw it, found it. . . . The child is about to tell the police about it. (?) The child seems to belong to this house.

Here on Card 11 we get a curious reversal of the usual response in that the guilty person in this story is the woman, who stole something at an inn. The child informs the police—again there is a quick turn to authority. A second question arises out of this story: To what degree does Ryūichi see his mother as doing something wrong? Could this be a reflection of the mother's spontaneously seeing on this card a scene of adultery that a son is witnessing? This is a speculation that we have no way of resolving. A mother, curiously enough, is seen by all three members of this family as potentially committing some reprehensible act. The boy's innocent interpretation is that she has stolen something, whereas both the father and mother see a mother in some adulterous activity.

> J13. It looks a little difficult. . . . This is . . . these two were already married and had lived together in this house. . . . But some . . . because of some reason they started quarreling. . . . Then this man killed her—now he is wiping off his sweat. . . . He is about to run away.

In his story to Card 13, Ryūichi immediately marries off the couple and then sees a quarrel and the man killing the woman. Curiously enough, on this card in contrast to the previous ones, no authority is brought in, and the man is pictured as ready to run away from the scene of violence. One would say that the boy at his age is not ready to cope with the concept of direct sexuality. This is one instance where he can't take the side of the law, and the man has to run away from the situation. He somehow cannot identify with the male figure, therefore the superego reaction found in the other stories does not take place.

> J18. This is a road. Well, this woman got into a car accident and was killed. . . . Her mother hurried here when she was informed by the police. . . . Now she is embracing her. . . . (?) From now on the mother will be forced to live alone. . . . That's all.

Here the violence is accidental, and not an act of any of the principals in the story. A mother is embracing a daughter who was killed in a traffic accident. We would say that this boy in most instances is able to repress any expression of hostility between family members. Nevertheless, he is impelled by some unconscious hostility.

> J22. This is on a Sunday. The child and his parents are about to go out somewhere. For some reason his parents had an argument. The child doesn't like it and is crying. But they become friends again. . . . (?) Because the parents have different interests. Suppose the mother likes Kabuki and the father likes movies. So they argued.

It is most interesting to see that the son's story of Card 22 parallels those of both his mother and his father. We may presume that such an occurrence has been in the experiences of all three members. It also demonstrates that both father and mother do at times assert their own interests and do have conflicts about it. Ryūichi does not, as his father and mother do, resolve the conflict in the direction of a compromise in which the father's opinion predominates. He simply states that they all become friends again. Neither parent is automatically seen in a subservient relationship to the other.

> J27. These two were friends when they were little. They just happened to meet each other. Some other girl student saw this and felt it was distasteful. So she will tell everybody on them [laughs]. This per-

son [the woman] will explain the situation to everybody and make them understand.

We gain here an impression that it is unseemly for students to have a heterosexual relationship. It is considered distasteful by the witness that a young man and woman should meet each other. Ryūichi already shows an internalization of the traditional Japanese attitude that there should be only muted and distant social relationships between the sexes in adolescence if the young people are of a serious nature. In his own behavior he has already learned to moralize and distance himself in relation to women or young girls his own age, representing an ideal, conforming person whose behavior is proper, as seen by authority.

CONCLUDING REMARKS

Ryūichi is not only a nondelinquent; he is also an upholder of law and order. The social recognition he has received for his clean-up campaign for public safety may make him and his father seem to be busybodies to some, but their behavior is deemed responsible and constructive by their society. They have made strong conscious moral commitments on the side of social conformity. Father and son, however, do not escape inner tensions. The father has not resolved his concerns about autonomy, and Ryūichi in the next generation, in turn, carries forward considerable ambivalence about his father. But the balances in the personalities of both father and son are such that they function integratively and responsibly as conforming members of their society. The mother seems to have assumed a constructive, facilitative role, neither controlling nor submissive. She seems to carry the woman's role realistically and positively forward, and in the future the son will probably come to expect the same from his own wife.

CHAPTER 11

Masao Sakai

The Family Hope Does Well in School

The following case history illustrates well the unquenchable optimism and resilience found among many economically deprived Japanese after the war. Despite a history of failure that spans at least two generations, the emotional ambience of the Sakai family is typical of many of the Japanese lower-status families we interviewed. There is a cohesiveness to family life that has sustained them through repeated failure and through perceived personal inadequacy. For many, family relationships are a solace, for they are based on an atmosphere of trust. Rather than deep soundings of inner deprivation, there are evident in the younger generation wellsprings of energy, tapped by an optimistic social and economic ideology inculcated at school as well as at home, namely, that one can succeed if one tries hard enough. There is also in many families, like those in the preceding chapter, the sustaining effect of a family legend passed on, of a time in the rural past when a higher status was held by some members of the family.

In the Sakai family (case N-1), the father has never been successful. He manifests a profound sense of his own inadequacy, which he expresses in a manner characteristic of many Japanese. He uses a culturally condoned excuse of physical illness; only if the body gives out may the individual slip into a dependent role and give up occupationally.

The immediate family now consists of the son Masao, a fourteen-year-old junior high school student in the eighth grade; the father, a forty-eight-year-old janitor in a government building; the mother, a forty-one-year-old housewife; an eleven-year-old girl in the sixth grade; and a five-year-old girl. Masao is characterized by his teacher as a well-behaved, constructively oriented boy who gets along well with his peers and is close to the top of his class academically.

FATHER'S BACKGROUND

Masao's paternal great-grandfather was the head of a small village in Gumma Prefecture, to the northwest of Tokyo. In those days the family had several employees to take care of the housework and the farm. Since Masao's grandfather was the second son among eleven siblings, he could hope for no inheritance. After his graduation from the eighth grade, he went to Tokyo and was first employed in an inn. Then, after working for a grocer for some time, he showed his entrepreneurial spirit by opening his own tiny grocery store. Mr. Takeo Sakai, Masao's father, was the first son, born in Shitaya-Ku, Tokyo, in 1914, to be followed quickly by six other children. At the time of his birth, his parents' grocery store was located near the Asakusa Kannon temple, and visitors to the temple used to drop into the shop to buy fruit and vegetables on their way home.

When Mr. Sakai was four years old, the family moved to Minami-Senju in Arakawa and reestablished their grocery business. Shortly before Mr. Sakai entered primary school, they moved to a yet poorer area in Arakawa. (We are given no explanation of why the family moved so often; our impression is that Mr. Sakai's father, a gentle, warm man, lacked the capacity to remain impersonal and businesslike in money matters.) The parents had one child after another, and their financial condition became more and more difficult. Mr. Sakai at age nine went to work in a neighbor's small toy-shop to help with the family income. His younger brother and sister also went to work in the same shop, the three continuing there for three years, during which the family's financial condition did not improve.

Mr. Sakai was an excellent pupil in primary school and was expected by his sixth-grade teachers to be sent on to middle school, but this never happened. His father had attempted to open another store, which failed, and the family remained financially strained. When Mr. Sakai learned that he had to leave school, he was disappointed, since he had spent considerable time and effort preparing himself to take the entrance examination for higher school.

Mr. Sakai says he used to be known in his neighborhood as a "filial son," obedient to his parents and willing to help them. He describes the warm relationship between him and his parents. For instance, he recalls when his father's business failed:

> It was about two months before I was to go to a middle school. My father told me that his business had failed and unfortunately he could no longer afford to send me to school. He said he was awfully sorry and asked me to go to the two years' advanced elementary school instead of five years' middle school. I was surprised because I had not known about such a possibility, but I felt grateful to my father who had thought of me so much.

Mr. Sakai completed the eighth grade at the advanced elementary school, then worked full time in his parents' shop. He says that since he loved his parents, he wanted to help them without being asked. One can assume from the way he tells his story that he was a sensitive, empathetic boy.

In spite of adversity, Mr. Sakai's father remained healthy and worked hard. He disliked dishonesty or ambiguity in human relationships. He was warm toward people and liked to help them. Loving his children, he used to tell them fairy tales and read books to them at night. Mr. Sakai remembers one episode during the great Kantō earthquake and fire of 1923: When the earthquake began, his father was out selling vegetables, but he was so anxious about the safety of his family that he returned home at full speed, pulling his joggling vegetable cart behind him. When he knew that his family was safe, he sat down and cried in relief.

Mr. Sakai gives a less graphic picture of his mother, seeing her as an *ippanteki* (ordinary) person, not too strict, not too lenient. He says he has no special memory of her, "because she always took very good care of me and was always with me. Rather than buying clothes for herself, she bought all that I needed for going to school." He feels that his parents took exceedingly good care of all their children. His mother took him and his brothers and sisters to visit her relatives whenever possible.

Sometimes, however, Mr. Sakai's "idealizing" tendency sounds a bit excessive. When he was asked, "Whom do you think your parents loved the best?" He answered, "Nothing like that! They loved us all in the same way. Parents do not differentiate among their children. Children are always equally lovable to their parents." He does not remember ever being severely scolded by either parent, let alone receiving any physical punishment.

Mr. Sakai describes how he enjoyed the role of elder brother. His apparent warm nature found expression in being nurturant toward his siblings, especially a brother, who was two years younger. This brother later was adopted by a childless maternal aunt and, after returning from the military, found work in Kanazawa City on the Japan Sea coast. This brother has three children, and Mr. Sakai expresses pride in the fact that the nieces and nephews have become excellent students. He describes with great detail and relish the whereabouts of his other siblings and their offspring, saying that there are frequent get-togethers with those now living in Tokyo. In his large family there were also a number of deaths, some evidently from malnutrition. It was a generally poor family, and some of the siblings faced considerable economic privation.

Mr. Sakai worked in his parents' tiny shop until 1942, when he was about twenty-eight years of age. At that time they were forced to give up their shop because of extreme governmental economic controls that made selling vegetables impossible. The family borrowed one *tan* (approximately a quarter-acre) of farm land and attempted to farm. Soon after, Mr. Sakai was drafted as a military worker, and in 1945 he was transferred to a military research institute, where he worked as a clerk for a short time. The institute closed at the end of the war, and the next year he was hired by a printing company. Wanting to "settle down," he entered a marriage arranged by his future wife's employer.

MOTHER'S BACKGROUND

Mrs. Sakai, Masao's mother, was born in 1921, the second daughter of a fairly poor farmer in a village in Yamagata Prefecture in northeastern Japan. Her mother died of pneumonia during a pregnancy when Mrs. Sakai was seven years old. She says she does not remember how she felt at the time of her mother's death, "since I was too small a child to know."

After the death of her mother, her father married a widow with children.

Mrs. Sakai did not get along well either with her stepmother or with her stepmother's children. Says Mrs. Sakai, "I didn't think she was a very nice person. Even when I talked to her—you know, after all, she was not my real mother. You wouldn't feel natural love. This happens to anybody, I guess."

After a short time, Mrs. Sakai went to live with her father's mother until she finished school, but she did not feel close to the grandmother, either. One gains an impression of general loneliness, for although Mrs. Sakai said she consulted her father whenever she needed help, she felt that with him too she had only a somewhat distant relationship.

Mrs. Sakai finished primary school at age twelve and then worked as a maid for a farmer in a neighboring town for three years, since her family did not have a large enough farm to need her help, and since she did not want to live with her stepmother and her children.

Mrs. Sakai came to Tokyo in 1937 at age sixteen. She was introduced by a cousin into a lawyer's home as a maid, and she lived with the lawyer and his childless wife for three years. She was not kept very busy, and although the wife at times became hysterical, upsetting Mrs. Sakai, she was usually kind and considerate. After a year Mrs. Sakai wanted to leave the home and told her mistress so, but she was, in effect, "refused" permission and was constrained to stay two more years. (Such contracts of tenure for a domestic from a rural area are not written; nevertheless, they are considered binding by tradition in Japan. A work commitment cannot be readily broken off. There are both inner constraints based on obligation and real constraints in that a person who quits a job will not be hired readily by someone else.)

Finally, Mrs. Sakai was able to leave and she went to live with her elder sister, who worked in a wholesale store in Tokyo. She worked there for a year and then decided to leave, as she and her sister quarreled too often. Through an employment agency she found work in a Chinese noodle shop in Shibuya, Tokyo, and lived in the shop. She liked her work there and stayed six years. In 1945 the shop was destroyed by an air raid, and for the remainder of the war she and her sister lived in their home village. Afterward, Mrs. Sakai again came to Tokyo and worked as a maid for a year in the home of a lumber dealer. She was rather old for marriage, and the lumber dealer became paternalistically concerned that she find a husband. A friend of his at the printing company where Mr. Sakai worked was able to arrange for a *miai* (the first meeting for possible betrothal) with Mr. Sakai, who also felt ready for marriage.

THE MARRIAGE OF THE PARENTS

When Mrs. Sakai was introduced to Mr. Sakai in the arranged meeting, she did not find any "bad points" and decided to marry him. She then moved into his house, which had one living room (12′ × 12′) and a workroom (9′ × 9′) and was shared by his parents and a younger sister and brother. Even now it is not unusual for a Japanese woman, after a *miai*, to decide to marry a man not because she actively likes him but for the stated reason that "there is nothing wrong with him" or, at best, that he seems to be "all right" (*yosasō-na hīto*). Soon after Mrs. Sakai moved in, the sister married and left. The newly married couple and the other family members continued to live in a room that was twelve by twelve feet, but even so, they express no feeling of having any emotional or sexual difficulties.

We asked Mr. Sakai if the living arrangement did not interfere with their sexual life. He answered, "No, not at all. Nothing of that kind." ("But you said everybody slept in the same room; and there was no problem at all?") "No, not at all." ("Didn't your wife feel bothered?") "No, I don't think so."

In many of our cases it was difficult to elicit any feeling of constraint about the limitations on sexual privacy of such crowded living arrangements. However, Mr. Sakai is generally more positive about everything than most of our informants. From this conversation, as well as from many other statements, one receives a strong impression that Mr. Sakai is guarded or suppressive about admitting to negative feelings. He tends to paint a picture of his past and his home in which there were no serious problems, nothing extremely good or bad; things tended toward some balance, and everybody was generally content.

Although they had insuffìcent food, clothing, and living space, the new couple got along well from the first. They reported good relations between parents-in-law and the new daughter-in-law. This is not unusual, but it is more usual to have a young wife express some complaint over how she was treated by her mother-in-law. ("How did your wife feel about living together with her in-laws?") "Nothing special. It did not seem to bother her." ("Really?") "Yes. They lived just like parents and child, and there was no problem at all."

Mr. Sakai seems to be a very sensitive person and empathic to the feelings of others and might well have been warm and considerate of both his parents and his wife. This view is supported and confirmed in the wife's interview. Mrs. Sakai considers her father-in-law to be similar in character to her husband. Mrs. Sakai was well accepted and considered to be a frank, pleasant, and honest person in her dealings with her parents-in-law. She came to have a special affection for her father-in-law, almost as if he were her real father, and he, in turn, treated her as if she were his real daughter.

MASAO, THE ONLY SON

Masao was born in 1948, two years after his parents were married. The family (and especially the grandfather) were all very pleased that he was a boy. Delivery was easy. Masao was breast-fed for at least a year and never had any illnesses. From the beginning he was the center of everyone's affection. His grandfather loved to carry him on his back and would take him out on walks. Whenever he asked his grandfather about something, he was given an elaborate and interesting answer. Hence, Masao was reported to continually ask questions from the time he could talk. He never seemed to forget what he learned, and his knowledge expanded rapidly. He enjoyed playing alone, but he also enjoyed playing with the neighbor boys. By the time he was three or four years old he had developed a good sense of humor and often found ways to amuse his friends and the adults as well. By the age of four, he is reported to have learned the Japanese "51 syllabaries" and counting with numbers, although supposedly nobody set out deliberately to teach him. Therefore the neighbors called him a "genius." (However exaggerated these reports by the parents may be, they certainly reflect a genuine attitude of pride in their son.) Masao himself reports pleasant memories of his grandfather's taking him on trips along rivers, through fields, and frequently to a quiet cemetery. The continual warm attention of the grandfather considerably influenced the formation of Masao's positive and loving personality, just as the grandfather's personality had influenced the father. Masao's personality is described by the mother as very similar to that of both his father and his grandfather. It seems that the superior development of Masao's intelligence and his excellent achievement in his studies have been helped by his grandfather and his father, and by an uncle who had an opportunity to go further in school.

In 1954 Masao entered a primary school in Arakawa, where he became the top pupil in his class and was chosen as a member of the class committee. The parents were informed by his teacher that both his studies and his behavior were excellent. They are exceedingly proud of him. His mother happily says:

> I don't mean to boast about my own child, but he has a really good brain. In early childhood he would learn things quickly. He started drawing good pictures before going to school. When he went to school everybody praised him for his very good performance. I don't know if he was as good as the teachers said he was, but anyway, everybody praised him.

His father sought to help him whenever possible, although he says that he respected Masao "and taught him only when he asked for help." When Masao entered the higher grades of primary school, a point beyond the father's competence, his uncle took over helping him with his studies. This uncle was described as being particularly kind and patient with Masao.

The uncle worked at a store making various electrical appliances, and Masao became interested in electronics at an early age. Earlier, according to Masao, when he was in third grade, he made a train out of paper, and since then his grandfather and father have taken him to various traffic exhibits and to a marshaling yard in Tokyo. Recently, he has constructed designs and devices for trains and tramcars. In the fifth grade, he often went to a museum with his classmates.

In 1954, the year Masao's first sister was born and just before Masao entered primary school, his father was fired from his printing job because of what was diagnosed as "increased heart palpitations from overwork." Mr. Sakai rested at home for over a year and a half, receiving unemployment insurance for six months, but after that it seems that the family was forced to live on Mrs. Sakai's small earnings. We do not know how much she was able to earn, but we can assume that the family lived in dire need. In 1956 Mr. Sakai was employed temporarily in a printing company. The salary was low and the position unstable, so in 1958, Mr. Sakai quit his job and found another as a janitor in a government building, in which there was a branch of the Tokyo Public Welfare Bureau. He identifies with the positive purposes of the bureaus he serves and is proud of "being of service." He says his job "gives me many chances to know real social problems and to improve my character." He is satisfied with his position. Mr. Sakai well illustrates a traditional Japanese tendency to pridefully identify with a worthy organization, even by those who hold the most lowly positions. This psychological tendency makes it more congenial to Japanese to think of themselves as part of a hierarchical social organization than to identify directly as a member of a social class.

Since childhood, Mr. Sakai has had an unrealizable desire to become a teacher. In his TAT stories, his wish to improve his "character" comes out clearly. He seems to have had a continuing aspiration to do something for society. This ideal strongly influenced his younger brother, the uncle who is now helping Masao in his studies; although he was graduated from a popular private university and became an engineer, he soon quit his job to become a junior high school teacher. This is most unusual, since engineers have a better future, in companies and governmental agencies, than teachers have. In 1957 the uncle took a teaching job in a suburb near Tokyo and took the grandparents to live with him, and in 1962 he married a kindergarten teacher. Masao often visits their home and stays overnight. The grandparents are pleased by Masao's frequent visits, as Masao is very warm toward them and tries to please them as well as his uncle and his aunt.

Mr. Sakai says his son was never a difficult child to raise. When he did something wrong, Mr. Sakai

> would talk to him rather than scold him. I rarely raised my hand and used no physical punishment. I simply told him that there are things he should not do and told him why he shouldn't do them. He would always listen to me.

Mr. Sakai says his son was always *sunao* (upright, "proper," and compliant),[1] although

> as he grew up, he began to have opinions, and when we [parents] were wrong he would come tell us so. From the time he was a fourth-grader such tendencies appeared. He became a very articulate child. He still is. He says that things should be done in such a way in these days and that I should do it that way, and get rid of my old-fashioned thinking.

When asked what he does when he is criticized by his own son, Mr. Sakai says, "I say, tentatively, that I do not understand his way of thinking, so I will try harder to understand it."

1. For the psychocultural meaning of the term *sunao* in its relationship to the concept of *amae*, see Wagatsuma, 1970.

His son never evokes anger or blame in Mr. Sakai. Occasionally, returning from school, the son fails to hang up his uniform and leaves it untidily on the floor. Mr. Sakai tells his son that he should hang it up. Mr. Sakai feels irritated. "I say if he knows what he should do, he should do it. Knowing what to do and not doing it is no good. I become angry. Sometimes I raise my voice." ("What does your son do then?") "When he is in a bad mood (*mushi no idokoro ga warui*—when his 'bug' is in a wrong place), he sulks." ("Does he walk out of the house?") "No, he would never do such a thing."

Mr. Sakai's achievement expectations of his son are high; he wants to send him to college, yet he wants him to remain *sunao*. He is also concerned with good manners and the ability to act properly in front of others.

Masao has generally been near the top of his class throughout grade school. In his second year in junior high school, he now ranks second in his entire class. "When he was in the first grade his teacher told me that my son had been doing excellently. I had not known it until the teacher told me." ("Did you not pay much attention to your son's school records?") "Well, yes. I used to say that I would be satisfied if my son stayed within the top five."

Mrs. Sakai says her son has never been a problem, that she was not particularly concerned or careful about raising him, nor had she any difficulty. When she is asked what she would want for her son if she were to have any wish, Mrs. Sakai says, after some pause, "Well, when he finishes school I wish him to find a good job which satisfies him, a job in which he will not be mistreated by his superiors." She says she knows that her son wants to go to college. Her own wish seems to be for him to find a job in a governmental office, such as the Tokyo Municipal Office, after he finishes high school. He might consider the possibility of going to college later.

Her basic satisfaction with her son is well reflected in various comments about him.

> He is *sunao* and he understands when I reason with him. Some people complain about their children in junior high school, but we never have any problem with our son. He never talks back to his parents. He is never contemptuous or rebellious. I often hear people complaining about children who don't respect their parents. It never happens with our son. . . . When he finished grade school, his teacher told me that he should go on to become a scholar. The teacher said I had better think of his future as that of a scholar. Well, he is not that good, I guess [laughs].

THE PRESENT FAMILY SITUATION

In 1960, after the uncle and grandparents had moved out, the Sakais' house was expanded with the financial help of Mrs. Sakai's brothers and other relatives, and a part was rented out to others for income. The present house has four rooms: two rooms nine by twelve feet, and two nine by nine feet. Masao's family (the parents, Masao, and two younger sisters) live in one of the nine by twelve rooms. By our criteria of occupation, education, living area, income, and housing, we objectively call this family a "typical lower-class family." Eighth-grade education is average for lower-class men of Mr. Sakai's age. Mr. Sakai as a janitor is earning about $60 a month. We do not know precisely how much income the family receives from room rent or from Mrs. Sakai's work as a seamstress. Even if we estimate on the high side, the total income of the family could not be more than $90 to $100 per month. Until 1957, three generations of the family—five adults and three children—lived in a small two-room house. We do not know anything of the grandparents' resources; they probably had none, since their farmed land had been leased from the government.

In the area in which the Sakais live the small houses are all crowded. Many of the neighboring families live from hand to mouth. In some of these families, both parents are too busy earning a living to supervise their children. One can frequently observe small children buying something to eat and eating it on the street. Their particular area had been known as having one of the highest delinquency rates of Arakawa Ward. One would think that such an environment of hardship and crowded living would promote severe conflicts and clashes among family members, exacerbating any personal deficiencies. It seems, however, that the personality patterns of the Sakai family members allowed them to avoid any such conflict or strain. Each member seems to have adjusted to their group life, not only by adhering to expected role behavior and attitudes but, even more basically, by their spontaneous feelings of satisfaction, cooperation, helpfulness, and affection toward one another.

Mrs. Sakai says her seventeen years of married life have been quiet ones, with little open conflict with her husband.

> In regard to raising children, or any other matters, we have rarely argued with each other. . . . My husband is a quiet person. He would not raise his hand against his children. He does get angry at them occasionally, but he never raises his hand. . . . I occasionally hit the children on the hand, half in joke. But my husband never does such a thing. Of course I don't do it often, only occasionally.

She sounds basically happy with her husband. When we asked her what her husband's good points and bad points are, Mrs. Sakai answered:

> He doesn't have any bad points [laughs]. Well, I am praising my own husband in front of others [laughs]. . . . Well, . . . I never think he is bad or good particularly. . . . I don't know what I like or dislike the most about him. . . . I never thought about anything like that. ("Would you marry him if you were to live your life again?") Well, . . . I suppose, . . . well, if I come to think of it, really . . . you see . . . my husband is really a gentle, kind person, and therefore I occasionally think it would be good if he were a little bit more snappy and decisive [*paki-paki-shita*]. He really has no weak points. He never gets mad, . . . but I may wish something more. . . . I think it would be really better if he would become a little bit *paki-paki-shita*.

Mr. Sakai says he more or less leaves the child-rearing decisions to his wife, although when he was ill and stayed home he often attended PTA meetings "for his son," when he was in grade school. He says that he and his wife have rarely argued over anything since their marriage. "I can say we have almost never argued with each other—maybe once or twice." He could think of nothing he would wish to change in his or his wife's attitudes toward their son, or in his son's attitude toward him. What he likes the best about his wife is that "she has a very clear-cut view of things and is frank. She is not overly meticulous. She is also very cooperative." As for her shortcomings, he says, "If I am to look hard for any weaknesses, maybe it is her tendency to talk loudly when scolding the children. Our children criticize her when she says something unnecessarily loud. This could be her weakness, if it is to be called weakness." He says there is nothing he dislikes about his wife. To the hypothetical question whether or not he would marry her if he were to live life again, Mr. Sakai first refused to answer, saying he had never thought of anything like that. Further pressed, he says, somewhat uncomfortably, "*Are de iinja nai deshō ka*" ("Aren't things as they should be?" or "She is allright just as she is, I guess"). As to sexual compatibility, he reports having sexual intercourse about once every second week.

In this family, cooperative and nurturant values have seemingly been so strongly internalized by each person that none would violate the wishes or feelings of the others. All the male members seem to identify readily with one another. The youthful Masao's values, as reported to us, are identical with those of his father and grandfather, reflecting traditional Japanese morality.

As in many of our families, there is little participation in social or cultural events outside the home. The main leisure activity is watching television. Neither Mr. Sakai nor Mrs. Sakai belongs to any organization in the neighborhood. They both sporadically attend PTA meetings as a matter of responsibility to their children. There is no religious practice nor affiliation with any religious sect. By family tradition they are nominal members of a Rinzai sect Buddhist temple located in the rural farm area where the grandfather originated. This family, like many others in Arakawa at present, does not maintain a set of ancestral tablets.

PROJECTIVE TEST RESULTS: MR. SAKAI

The Rorschach Test

In general, Mr. Sakai's Rorschach responses reveal a well-functioning ego with, however, some sense of inadequacy resulting in compensatory pretentiousness. He gives "whole" responses to practically all the cards. Even when he gives responses to parts of the ink blots, he tries to relate these parts to one another in some manner. This approach is typical of many Japanese protocols. Most of his responses are well perceived, well elaborated, and organized. He has a certain intellectual capacity (one would surmise an above average to superior intelligence). He pushed himself very hard all through the test situation, a push well representative of the high value Japanese place on hard work and effort. His Rorschach protocol also shows many of the characteristic features that differentiate the protocols of the fathers of socialized nondelinquents from those of the delinquents. He gives a number of positively toned aesthetic responses, seeing ornamental objects. He also gives some responses that are indicative of a positive attitude toward authority. His human or animal percepts are quiet or "resting," such responses suggesting a passive, aesthetic orientation to life. He seems nevertheless to accept his own passivity in an egosyntonic way.

Rorschach Protocol

I. (20″) 1. *I feel this looks like a butterfly.* The feeling of spreading its wings. It looks black, a swallowtail from the shape of wings. [W FM, FC+ A P (Neut)]

2. *I feel this is the cross-section of an iris or something.* This is the large part of the flower; this is the calyx. [W F− Bot (Mpret)]

II. (32″) 3. A *chandelier.* The white space in the center is the chandelier shining in the dark. The lower part is the reflection. [WS F+ Hse (Porn)]

4. *Yeah, a lobster is crushed, I guess.* It is being flattened. I see it often in the stores. The feeler looks like that of a lobster. [DW FM− A (Hsm) Z−]

III. (15″) 5. *Two people are talking about something.* They went shopping. They are on their way home with packages. I guess they are women, because they are shopping. [D M+ H P (Pcoop)]

6. *It looks like patterns on a vase, too.* The impression of the outline. Inside are the patterns; the red part is also one of the patterns. [WS FC+ Art (Porn)]

IV. (22″) 7. *Some kind of animal lying down.* I feel it is lying down to avoid the hot weather. The lower part is the front, both sides are the hands. [W FM+ A (Neut)]

8. *It looks like the shape of a bat, too.* When he is hanging down in the daytime, under the eaves. The lower parts are the wings. [W FM+ A P (Dcl)]

V. (27″) 9. *It also looks like a butterfly.* It is spread out, a specimen; the lower projection is the feelers. [W F+ A P (Neut)]

10. *It looks like a map of somewhere.* Somewhere in Europe. [W F− Map (Aev)]

VI. (30″) 11. *It looks like a badge (or insignia) of something.* The upper part is the part by which you hang it; the lower part is the badge. Its shape. [W F+ Orn (Dauth)]

12. *It is something like a flower.* The flower has relatively large petals; the center part looks just like a calyx. It looks like a lily bending toward the front. [W Fm+ Bot (Pnat)]

13. A *sparrow is just about to fly from a leaf.* The upper part is the sparrow, the lower is the leaf. [W FM+ Bot/A (Neut)]

VII. (20″) 14. *It looks like a cactus.* The shape—it resembles one very much. [W F+ Bot (Neut)]

15. *There are Chinese lions before a shrine facing each other.* The lowest parts are stones. [DS F+ Art (Porn, Drel)]

16. *Some kind of ornament.* The lower parts are legs; something to put an incense burner on. [DS F+ Orn (Porn)]

VIII. (16″) 17 & 18. *This looks like a sculpture.* To make a wood print, you put various colors together. The side parts are animals. The lower part is a flower. I can't make out the upper part. It is an imaginary picture or a futuristic picture. There is a feeling of hope. [W FT+ (Symb) A P Mpret (Porn)] [D FC+ Bot P (Arb Comb)]

19. *Well, something like a design of clothes.* Such a pattern is often seen. I think it would make interesting clothes. [W FC+ Orn Cg (Porn)]

20. *Some ornament for burning incense.* A round one. The upper part is the cover being put into such a pattern. I didn't notice the color. [W CF+ Orn (Porn)]

IX. (35″) 21. *Well, I think a warrior doll is standing.* The upper part is the face; both the sides are legs. [W FC+ A (Pnat)]

22. *Yeah, it looks like a firefly shining.* It looks like it is shining in the grass—I mean the dark pink. [W FC+ A (Pnat)]

23. *It looks like flower arrangement arranged.* The upper part is the flower. Artificial flowers are now in fashion. The rest is the shape of a glass vase. [W FC+ Orn (Porn)]

X. (35″) 24. *Animals are gathering together, I think.* [W S FM+ A (Prec)]

25. *I think this is a picture by Picasso.* It is being imagined—the funny unknown land in a dream. The upper center part is a Martian, although the face is not seen. Colorful. [DS FC+ (H) (Aev, Dlo, Mpret) (Arb, Comb, justified by Art)]

26. *It looks like an athletic meeting of animals.* [Subject goes back to his earlier response to 24, above] The white space is a field; animals are gathering together. A wide and open place—a kangaroo and some other animals.

Card-by-Card Sequential Analysis and Comments

On Card 1 Mr. Sakai sees a harmless butterfly and then a cross-section of an iris. Both these responses reveal no feeling of being threatened by the card, the iris response suggesting some intellectualization of affect. The objects seen are soft and innocuous.

On Card II he gives his first "ornamental" response. He immediately seeks out the center white space, turning the card freely. Looking at it upside down, he sees a chandelier. Then comes the only basically unpleasant response of his entire record, a crushed lobster, suggested by the claws. The response is of poor form quality and suggests at the affective symbolic level some underlying passive masochistic feelings. An animal's armored protective shell is crushed—the ego boundaries separating self from world are broken through.

On Card III he sees two women going about the daily occupation of shopping. As in many responses by Japanese to this card in which humans are perceived, they are seen at some work-a-day job, lifting something, working, shopping, or washing clothes. The work orientation pervades the symbolic activities that are perceived by Japanese in the human responses given to the Rorschach. Mr. Sakai's second response, an ornamental vase, is an attempt to construct an integrative whole response. He incorporates the red spots at the sides as coloring in the pattern on the vase.

On Card IV he sees some kind of animal lying down, avoiding the hot weather, in a passive pose. He also sees a bat hanging down in the daytime under the eaves of a house. On Card V he sees a specimen butterfly, again suggestive of his passive orientation. He also reports a vague form, a "map" of part of the earth, "somewhere in Europe," a response that has a pretentious quality, suggesting something "esoteric."

On Card VI Mr. Sakai gives a response that is characteristic of nondelinquent fathers but only rarely found in fathers of delinquents in our samples, a badge, which we score as an "authority symbol." We found a statistically significant, higher usage of religious and authority symbols by the parents and boys in the nondelinquent families than by those of our delinquent samples. For Japanese, these responses symbolize positive attitudes toward social authority, both political and religious. Mr. Sakai follows with another passive response, a flower like a lily bending forward. Then, he reveals again both his need to organize conceptually and the ability to do so; he sees a sparrow about to fly from a leaf, where the upper part of the blot is the sparrow, the lower part the leaf. This type of response requires more than average intelligence.

On Card VII he produces three well-formed responses. First is a cactus of irregular shape, then two sculptured Chinese lions facing each other before a shrine, not only an "ornamental" response but a response at least indirectly related to religion. His third response also has a religious connotation, an ornamental brazier on three legs on which an incense burner can be placed. Hence, on this generally "feminine" or "mother" card, he gives cactus and carved lions, certainly not suggestive of a soft female. In this instance the responses are of excellent quality, but textural hardness rather than feminine softness is elicited.

Card VIII again immediately evokes an aesthetic response. He sees a sculpture or a multicolored woodblock print, a design with animals at the sides and a flower at the bottom. In other words, he sees two of the popular Japanese percepts in this card. They are usually seen separately, but he combines them successfully into a whole configuration. He follows up this percept with one in which the whole of Card VIII is a design for clothes. Still intrigued by this card, he turns it upside down and perceives another ornamental object used for burning incense.

On Card IX he sees a standing warrior doll. The green part is his armor, and the lower part is the pants and skirt worn on formal occasion by samurai. Again, this response is suggestive of an "authority symbol" but subdued and not dangerous—a toy. He then sees a firefly, using the color to delineate the various parts of the body. The last response to this card is a flower arrangement, which is well perceived. Flower arrangement, an art not unknown to men, is today more generally a woman's activity.

On Card X he sees a gathering of animals, and later he elaborates that they have gathered for an athletic meet, with none of the hostility depicted, in such a competitive response where others often see animals fighting with each other. On the intervening response, Mr. Sakai combines the various colors arbitrarily, rationalizing it adequately as a picture by Picasso. He sees in the center the figure of a Martian whose face is not visible.

Mr. Sakai's total of responses is higher than average (twenty-five compared with a Japanese average of seventeen). He gives aesthetic responses to cards held in both the upright and the upside-down position. He has a high percentage (38 percent) of what are scored on my affective scoring system as "positive" responses. He also has a high total of "dependent" responses (16 percent) in the form of both religious and authority symbols. He is very low compared with others in showing "unpleasant" affect, scoring only 8 percent. He receives a high organizational or "Z" score, indicating a need to organize experiences into meaningful, complex patterns—a pattern that is characteristic in Japanese and fits in with what is described in psychology as a "high need achievement." It is significantly higher in the fathers of nondelinquents than in the fathers of delinquents. Mr. Sakai's intellectual drive is used on a fantasy level, since he is attitudinally an observer not a doer. In sum, Mr. Sakai suggests in both the symbolism and the structure of his Rorschach an extratensive person who responds positively but passively to his environment. His passivity is egosyntonic and socially well integrated. His inner life is intellectual and aesthetic rather than introspective. We do not picture him as retiring or withdrawn so much as passive in his relationship with others.

The TAT

Mr. Sakai's TAT record suggests, above all, a paternally hovering, somewhat moralistic approach to meeting Japanese social role expectations.

> J1. He is composing music, but now he is taking a rest for a while. He is thinking of the melody. He has composed music, the melody of

> which he previously had in mind while he was taking a walk. But he finds some parts he does not like. So he thinks of a good melody, sitting over his desk. After awhile he hits upon a good melody and revises some parts of the previous one. He plays it; it goes quite well this time. It is a very beautiful melody. This is a story of a musician's boyhood.

The story given to Card 1 is a constructive one of a boy composing music, but there is a hint of passivity in the promptly forthcoming interpretation that he is "taking a rest" while thinking of the melody. The description is that the boy is working on something that he is enjoying and becomes satisfied with what he can produce in the way of a melody.

> J2. He stops short and is looking at someone. A young man, one of his old friends in boyhood, is coming here. He thinks the young man must be a friend that he played with when they were little kids. Yes, he really is. The young man was very poor in his boyhood. He went to a town and studied hard without any teacher. He had a lot of hardship there. Now he is a nice young man. So this man makes up his mind to make every effort to overcome poverty and to be a nice man like his old friend. (?) I think he is on his way home from the town.

In the second story Mr. Sakai distorts the sex of the figure in order to make his story about two male friends, one of whom has an opportunity to study and succeed (an unusual story, one suggestive of deeply concealed problems with sexual identification); the other man, seeing that his boyhood friend has succeeded, determines to overcome his own poverty.

> J3. He is tired out. His child has gotten lost. So he looks for him to and fro, but he can't find him. He is really tired out. He is walking around here and there to find him, but it is in vain. He asks a policeman to help him find his son, and he finally finds his son. He reflects to himself: from his careless mistake, he made the son miserable, he troubled the policeman, and he himself was tired. So he resolves that he will never repeat such a mistake as this.

Here is an unusual handling of the third card. The slumped figure is a father looking for a lost child. Blaming himself for the child's getting lost and concerned with giving trouble to the policeman, he resolves to take better care in the future. This is obviously a very concerned father and one dedicated to the care of his son.

> J6. An old woman is asking a man for something. It is a story of [mother] getting a job [for her son]. Her son's academic record in his school days is not so good. So, through his mother's connection, accompanied by his mother, he meets a man in a high position of a company and asks him for a job. Coming back home, the son is being admonished by his mother, who says that he should not ask his mother to help in getting a job, that he should do his job hunting by himself, and that he should be aware of all such things, since he has grown up enough to work in a

company. Since then, he has always kept in his mind what his mother told him, and he becomes a kind and good man in the company, though he was a son whom his mother found difficult to manage.

Mr. Sakai's story for Card 6 is interesting because, although he recognizes that a mother will very often try to help a son obtain a job, he moralizes, saying that this is not the way to do it and that the son by his own initiative should seek employment. Throughout these cards, as in some of the previous cases we have cited, we find this moralizing trait in the Japanese stories concerned with the future career of the child. But in this man's responses there is also the avoidance of any direct depiction of disharmony or discord among people. Preoccupation throughout is with the future success of children.

J7. A young man seems to be being admonished by his father. He was a very nice young man, but he troubled his family because of his friend. One of his friends caused some trouble and he was taken care of by the police. As he was asked to help the friend, he made an effort to do so. But this has resulted in his getting himself involved in trouble, which made his family worry about him. Now his father is admonishing his son for his fault in not telling him his experiences. He tells the son that there are several ways to help other persons, and that he is now quite all right, since it is already done, but he should study harder from now on, making use of his experience. Obeying his father's words, the young man makes every possible effort; he becomes a good man and eventually a nice old man.

In Card 7 we see an intrusion of concern with delinquency, but the concern is related to the effects of associating with bad companions. The boy gets himself into temporary difficulty by trying to help a companion. The father's admonitions are successful, and the boy does not get into further trouble. In this and the following story the characters are confronted with something wrong, and they reflect on their own attitudes and possible contributing behavior. They easily feel guilty and make up their minds not to repeat the same mistake and to try to become better. The characters he depicts are never insistent or resistant to their parents or other authority figures, but remain loyal and respectful. The endings of all his stories tend to be positive. In this story, as in others, we see Mr. Sakai's attitudes and ideas readily projected. He wants to contribute to society. He easily feels guilty. One can even see a certain masochistic quality in his readiness to feel guilt, as in the third story. He never expresses any overt aggression. One can assume that he probably cannot readily stand such expressions of aggression in himself, as is shown in the following story.

J8. He seems to be in an operation. This man [on the right side] and his comrade are there. They have been doing almost all things together. They drank and ate some cold food; then his comrade had an attack of appendicitis. He thinks that it is because of him, because he asked his comrade to drink something cold, and that if the cold drink were good enough, his friend would not be sick. After that he appeals to people to keep food and drink clean, and he decides to engage in studying sanitation.

This is almost too much of an avoidance of aggression. It comes out only indirectly in an obsessional way, as moralizing about the need to keep food and drink clean and proper for people so that there will be no illness. Still we find here a Japanese expiatory pattern; that is, if one causes an injury, then he can expiate it by doing something good for society. There seems to be a great refinement of aggressive impulses in this man. The use of reaction formation against deeply buried aggression causes him to be overscrupulous and easily guilty.

J9. It's a farewell scene. I think that he was a high school boy and his scholastic record was excellent, so he took the examination for some university in Tokyo and he passed it. He is going to start now. All his family members are sending him off with encouragement. He has been a nice boy in the village. He will meet a lot of temptation in Tokyo, however. They are encouraging him to overcome these temptations. If he can't overcome them, he will not be allowed to come back home, so he studies hard. Later, he becomes master and head of the family. He becomes a good citizen and is admired by everybody. He becomes a man who is needed for the nation.

We see again in this story themes of aspiration, self-development, and concern with the hero's ability to avoid the temptations of his environment and to maintain innerdirectedness toward his goals.

J11. The child did not obey his mother's words. He seems to be from a rich family . . . probably of the middle class. After he came back from school, he threw his bag aside and he has gone to play without obeying his mother. The mother is at a loss what to do, as her child did not obey her. Her husband must be a director of a company, and he, I suppose, usually comes home late at night. The child must have been brought up by a wet nurse. The fact that his mother did not take care of him has driven him to become the type of boy who does not obey. Therefore, the mother has realized that something should be done about this, and she tells her husband about it. She herself reflects and makes efforts for the child. (?) The child had gone to play, throwing his bag aside, and when he came back from playing in the evening he noticed that his mother was severely scolded by his father. So he is now looking at his discouraged mother with surprise. (?) I think he will be a nice man.

Card 11 is the only negative story Mr. Sakai gives, about a boy who does not obey his mother, and the reason for his disobedience is that not enough care was given to him as a child. The mother employed a nurse and the father was a director of a company and was not home enough. So we get here a moralistic story about a child's disobedience caused by the parents' lack of care. Some of the fathers of delinquents tell these stories repeatedly, but Mr. Sakai tells a negative story in only one instance. In the test of limits at the end, he picked this card as the one he most disliked, because the parents did not show any concern for their child and neglected him.

> J13. He feels sorry that he can't come back home from the company at regular hours every day. As he does not come home at regular hours, his wife is sulking in bed. He is a diligent man. He has a lot of work to do at the company, so he sometimes can't help but come home late at night. But his wife does not understand his situation, so she is being petulant. He is regretful and he feels it necessary to tell her the situation in order to make a good home. And now he is going to talk to her. He has just come back home. His wife was waiting for him, preparing for supper. However, he did not come back early today. As she does not understand her husband's situation, she is angry. As she is sincere with him, it is quite natural for her to be sullen when she feels that way.

On Card 13 we have him responding to this picture, perceived by some Japanese as a woman in a sloppy sleeping posture, with a story of how she somehow behaves improperly or is angry with her husband. As Mr. Sakai tells it, however, the woman is justified. She is sulking in bed, angered by her husband's late arrival. He is conciliatory and understanding, and tries to placate her, saying that since she is sincere it is natural for her to express her negative feelings when they arise. He attempts to reestablish harmony by talking over why it was so necessary for him to come home late. This is somewhat unlike Japanese men's stories in that usually when a man feels justified in his behavior he does not feel it necessary to explain. In results previously obtained from samples, it was more characteristic for the man in the story to castigate the wife for unseemly conduct. Accordingly, this unusual story suggests Mr. Sakai's extremely passive and dependent attitudes toward female figures.

> J18. A mother is telling something to her daughter. I imagine that some of the daughter's friends came back home from Tokyo, where they got jobs and were working. According to their stories, everything in Tokyo seemed to be exciting, so she wanted to work in Tokyo and she went up to Tokyo to work there. However, the facts were quite different from what she had imagined. She was about to fall into temptation, though actually she did not. Therefore she came back home. So her mother is now admonishing her that it would be better for her to work in a city only after she learns much more about the world—to be better prepared if she wants to go up there again. Thereafter she studies, listens to her mother's opinions, and reads many books. She made efforts to be a nice mother. Afterward she will go to a city and get married and be a good mother as well as a good citizen. Here in this scene she thinks that she should have obeyed her mother's advice when she was going up to Tokyo for the first time.

In responding to this card, which is sometimes interpreted as one woman choking another, Mr. Sakai makes sure that aggression is completely removed from the scene. The mother admonishes the daughter, but the story does not give any indication of bad behavior. There is temptation, but the girl listens to the mother, avoids temptation, and, in turn, herself becomes a good mother. Obvious mechanisms of denial are at work.

> J22. A couple is going somewhere with their child. Father wants to go to a park, but Mother wants to go to a department store, as it is a holiday. So the child is crying, not knowing which he should do. Father insisted on taking the child to a park or some other place where they can enjoy the fresh air, taking advantage of this holiday. Mother wants to go shopping at a department store for herself and for the child. They can't agree, so Father turns aside and begins to step away. But they finally come to agree to Father's suggestion that they go first to some fresh-air place near the city and drop into a department store for shopping on their way home in the evening. Mother, as her opinion is accommodated, feels happy and thinks that she will consult with her husband well in advance next time. They will agree with one another in this way next time. (?) As they can't come to any agreement, Father does not know how to deal with his irritation. He begins to step away, but he stops to reflect.

Card 22, depicting a scene which obviously implies disagreement, turns out well. The parents realize that next time they should come to some agreement ahead of time rather than arguing. The focus is obviously on the parental role rather than on the child in this card. The feelings of the child are assumed. Mr. Sakai spends most of the time figuring out how to prevent this type of situation from arising. One gets some feeling that there is almost a maternal identity in this father. In contrast to many responses in which the emphasis is immediately put on the mother's responsibility, we find in his stories a feeling of shared responsibility for the child's upbringing. He picked Card 22 as his "most liked" card because the parents learn to show more deliberate and considerate concern for their children.

> J27. A girl is giving advice or something like that to a boy. Is that the boy's younger sister? He was watched by his sister when he came out of a coffee shop. She is telling him to choose good friends. They are a good brother and sister. He is being given advice by his sister not to go to coffee shops often and to be careful in choosing friends. He is a nice boy, so she worries about him. He is honest, so he probably accepts her advice. She tells him that it is quite all right sometimes to go to such places to understand things in the world. They are really a good brother and sister. They will study hard and be, respectively, a good man and good woman in the future.

In this last card the brother accepts the sage advice of his sister to avoid the temptations offered by bad companions and environments such as coffee shops.

In sum, in this man's record there is no sense of drama. All attention focuses on quickly resolving whatever may come up to deflect a child from growing up well and serving his family and society. Although Mr. Sakai's responses do not make as interesting reading as those of an individual with a sense of conflict, they well illustrate a man extremely dedicated to his role as father. He has in a sense done what many Japanese women do; he has identified altruistically with others when he himself cannot realize his own aspirations. Earlier he had helped his younger siblings realize their goals, and he is now attempting to help his own boy achieve. The projectives indicate with certainty a person with considerable intellectual capacity and a warm and sensitive nature, one who continually seeks out the positive in his experiences and readily uses mechanisms of denial and reaction formation against expressions of aggression. He has had strong aspiration needs as well as needs for self-validation and self-development. He has also deep feelings of passivity, of failure and inadequacy, which are resolved to some extent in his ability to identify with those within his own family who have or will have the opportunity to do what he could not achieve himself. His values throughout are traditionally Japanese. He sees the virtues of obedience, loyalty, respect, and hard work as leading to a happy life of both self-fulfillment and social dedication.

PROJECTIVE TEST RESULTS: MRS. SAKAI

The Rorschach Test

Mrs. Sakai's projective protocols give an overall impression of a simple, pleasant, and likable personality. They would certainly support her husband's statement that she is a frank, openhearted, and optimistic person. The loss of the mother in early childhood and later difficulties with her stepmother have not had a serious negative effect on her personality development. Her Rorschach test responses suggest a basically normal, somewhat introversive record without any indications of pathological disturbance.

Rorschach Protocol

I. (64″) 1. *Though I'm not sure, it looks like a bat, I guess. It is a bat with his wings spread.* His spread wings. There is the body. It has eyes and ears. I thought it was a bat at first impression. The center looks as though it's split. [W FM+ A P (Neut)]

II. (127″) 2. *It is difficult for us dull people. It looks like people drinking a toast.* I can't find the faces . . . oh, here they are. I get the feeling that they have something on their heads, the red parts. In a group, important people, I think. (?) They are men, because they wear hats. [W M, FC+ H (Porn, Dauth)]

3. *The electric lamp, the upper part.* The long electric pole, standing in the evening. The red color looks like the lamp is shining. [DS CF− Obj (Neut)]

4. *The lower part looks like fire.* It is cold, though the stove [hibachi] is not seen here. People are taking warmth, putting their feet on something. The fire is sparkling, the light is reflecting on the bottom of the clothes. [D CF, mF+ Fi (Pnar, Dsec)]

III. (153″) 5. *It looks like an animal . . . I don't know.* From the impression of the pointed mouth I thought it was an animal. It looks like a fox. The legs suggest some other animal, too. [D F− A (Mor)]

6. *Oh, it's not. In the rice field, planting; the rice plant comes across.* It looks like people picking grass. If you don't look at their faces, they look like people. The faces don't look human. [W M+ H P (Misc Adeh)]

IV. (32″) 7. *Two seals are climbing a rock—and the black part is a cliff-like rock.* The shapes of the head and back are like those of seals. From the thick and thin color [refers to shading], I get the impression of a rock. [W FM, FT+ A O (Pst)]

V. (66″) 8. *A person is standing on a leaf and opening his arms. The clothes are spread. (Oh, this is very well drawn.)* The leaf is cut in half. He is extending his arms. I get that feeling. [W M+ H (Misc) (Arb Comb)]

VI. (64″) 9. *It is a straight path. This upper part is, well, a cliff under the mountain. The lower part is a reflection on the lake.* The reflection on the river is like this, just like two put together. The line in the center looks like a path. [W FV+ Lscp (Pnat)]

10. *People in a circus are hanging from a pole or a rope with both hands, though one hand is not seen.* Two people opening their arms and hanging. The center line is the rope or a pole. [W M+ P O (Prec, Abal)]

11. [*Additional*] *A lion opening its arms. The stripes make it look like a lion.* [W FM− A (Neut)]

VII. (109″) 12. *It looks like a dog sitting on the edge of a stone. I don't understand such a picture. It would be surprising if I did!* It looks like a dog on the edge of a stone, looking sideways. Or the dog is about to turn his face aside. [D FM+ A (Neut)]

VIII. (98″) 13. *It is a large lampshade. The lamp is underneath. The lamp is shining above.* You can see such a lamp in a theater. The red line in the lower part looks like a shadow. The light is going up from the part under that part. It looks like it is shining because of the color. [W CF, YF+ Orn (Porn)]

IX. (30″) 14. *Flowers are put in a vase. The upper part is the flower and the green is the leaves. The lower red is the shadow of the leaves.* It looks like an iris. The color is beautiful and I felt it was a flower. [W FC+ Bot (Pnat)]

X. (188″) 15. *It looks like a pattern on a Japanese dress* [*kimono*]. *It is something like sprinkled flowers, and the red is the column of thunder clouds* (nyūdōgumo) *coming up. Summer has come. The green or blue is like leaves.* A pattern of *yukata* [dress] for children. The colors give such a feeling and there are several kinds of things. It's a little too much, though. [W FC+ Orn O (Porn, Pnat)]

Card-by-Card Sequential Analysis and Comments

Here and there in Mrs. Sakai's record one sees evidence of self-effacement about her own abilities. Nevertheless, she rejects no cards and is able to produce well-integrated, whole responses throughout. Her movement responses are all of a positive nature. On Card I she sees an ordinary bat but gives it a sense of movement. On Card II she sees people drinking a toast. She expresses a certain self-effacing attitude toward high social status by saying they must be important men because they wear hats. Next, the red color is seen as a glow from an electric lamp, and then the lower part is seen as fire. For her, fire represents nonaggression or nonviolence; she gives a spontaneous, warm reaction to its hot colors, which for many represent symbolically the dangers of aggression or violence. People are taking warmth, putting their feet on something, and the fire is sparkling, the light reflecting on the bottom of their clothes—a healthy, integrative use of a color.

On Card III she has some difficulty with the pointed face, first thinking it looks like an animal. She recovers from this and decides that they are humans, although she doesn't like the unusual faces. The humans are working, planting rice in the field, bending over—a suggestion of her basic work-orientation toward life. On Card IV she gives a somewhat unusual response, seeing two seals climbing a rock. The movement is of an active, striving nature, and the response is well integrated. On Card V her response is again predominated by a feeling of movement: the person in the center is standing on a leaf, opening his arms to their full span—an arbitrary combination of elements, although well perceived.

On Card VI she gives a well-delineated vista response to objects seen sideways. She manifests a flexible use of all the potential determinants of the Rorschach cards—form, color, movement, shading, and now vista. She can easily turn the cards around, showing none of the submissive, rigid authoritarianism that is sometimes found in the way Japanese handle the cards. (She has a very low total rigidity score.) She sees a straight path with a cliff under a mountain, and the lower part is a reflection in a lake—a beautifully perceived vista. Then she is again stimulated to see humans, and sees circus people hanging from a pole with hands out, followed imaginatively by a lion opening its arms, a not very well perceived response. If we would pick out some underlying theme, the figures with open arms suggest some longing for greater contact on a deeper level of her personality. Card VII is handled nicely, with dogs seen sitting on stones. It is noteworthy that none of her responses show the childish tone found in some women's records. Dogs are dogs, not "puppies," as are often suggested on this card by some less mature women.

In Mrs. Sakai's responses to the last three cards she shows a strong positive reaction to color, commenting on its beauty. She sees an ornamental lamp and shade on Card VIII, and flowers in a vase on Card IX. Then on the last card she sees a kimono design sprinkled with flowers that remind her of the coming of summer. We see no blocking of intellect or incapacity to handle either color or movement. She is able to use freely most of the Rorschach determinants within the fifteen responses she chooses to give to the cards.

The TAT

The TAT responses again show Mrs. Sakai's simple, open nature. She does not completely avoid the possibility of aggression in some of the cards, as did her husband. Nevertheless, most of the stories she gives are of a positive, constructive nature, indicating her basically optimistic attitude about human relationships. She does inject in some of them an issue of conflict, but most of the problems are resolved. The chief picture of the father, however, brings out a certain amount of constrictiveness and withholding; one wonders if this is not to some degree a criticism of her own father's lack of support of her vis-à-vis her stepmother.

> J1. He has a musical instrument and he thinks that he is going to take an exam in music. He is paying all his attention to it. (?) Well, though his family may not be so rich, he will be able to be a musician by studying hard.

On Card 1 the boy is preparing himself for an examination. She brings in a note of poverty, but the poverty is resolved by hard work, so that he will be able to accomplish his goal.

> J2. Well, a girl has some books. This is in a farmer's home. Is she going to school? I think she is going to school because she has some books. She seems to be a high school student. Her parents are here, too. Her parents wanted her to be a farmer, but the daughter wanted to study much more and to be a teacher. Father, standing with his back to them, insists that the girl does not need to have any higher education. Mother, who isn't facing them, seems to be looking aside. (?) No, she does not agree with the daughter but seems to be having an opposite idea. The daughter seems to do her best. Her face shows that she is making up her mind to do her best to accomplish her aim.

The story on Card 2 is one in which a young woman is able to follow a course of autonomy despite the inhibiting attitudes of her parents. She determines to realize her goal for education in spite of the fact that her parents wish her to continue with farming. Mrs. Sakai's statement that "her face shows that she is making up her mind to do her best to accomplish her aim" suggests the strong value she places upon determination to accomplish a goal. She emphasizes the positive intent rather than a negative reaction to parental opposition.

> J3. What is it the man is sitting on? Is it a bed? Oh, no, it looks like a couch. Is he a child? Well, he ran away from his house after being scolded. He seems to be taking a rest; he ran far and was tired. (?) Yes, that's right. He must have been a stubborn boy. He doesn't seem to be afraid at all. If he were, he wouldn't be able to run away from home. (?) It must be a boy, judging from the hands. Girls' hands must be softer than boys'. (?) Probably the father scolded him.

Again we find in this story some concern with tension between a child and the parents; the boy (identified as a boy because of the strength of hand) is *able* to run away after being scolded. She stresses the fact that he is stubborn but also unafraid. We must judge that Mrs. Sakai did have some kind of crisis of autonomy in her youth which she solved successfully. She admires a forceful person, even if he is technically in the wrong in opposing authority.

> J6. He seems to be asking his mother for permission to get married. His mother, judging from her attitude, is not willing for him to get married. (?) That's right. His mother looks angry. She does not seem to be friendly to him. (?) Well, as his mother was told about it without notice well in advance, she must have been surprised. But I think she will gradually understand and accept him. They will mutually understand each other, I believe.

Again in this story there is reluctance on the part of a parent to accede to the wishes of a child. But the story is resolved with gradual acceptance of the child's purpose and ends in mutual understanding. There is no sign of dependency or feeling of having to give up one's own goal submissively for that of the parent. Again, autonomy is emphasized.

> J7. Well, this man is asking that man for some favor. That person is his father, I guess. (?) He may be asking him for some money that is needed to build a new house. (?) Well, judging from his father's severe face, he isn't willing to give him money. He will probably not understand his son.

This again shows a theme in which a father is strict and, failing to understand his son, refuses his legitimate request. Certainly these stories one by one show the theme of surmounting opposition, suggesting her deep feelings that she had to make her own way without the essential support of her father and stepmother. Her attitude toward her father seems to be that he had given her little encouragement for what ambitions she may have had.

> J8. May I add some things that are not exactly in these pictures? They are children. (?) They are actually not such little boys, but . . . their faces look terrible. It's like an injection. Is philopon [a stimulant drug] injected into arms? or stomach? (?) One person is lying on a bed, and two others are beside him. One of those is injecting, and the other is watching him. One of them may have been wounded. The man on this side is anxious about the man injecting. (?) This is a woman, not a man.

She is a wife. She is taking care of him, holding his body so that he does not turn over during the injection. This is hard to explain.

This story shows the fear of philopon (a drug that was widespread in Arakawa in the late 1950s) and of what delinquent children might do. Mrs. Sakai may feel that her children are vulnerable, living in a lower-class environment. However, the story about a possible drug injection is gradually changed to one of illness, and she inserts in this story a helping wife who assists in holding the afflicted man so that he will not turn over during the injecting. One would say from this story that she has a strong identification with her role as a helpmate and that her sexual identity is secure.

J9. She looks like a teacher. She must be a teacher. This person is a mother . . . this woman I mean. The other two are her daughters. They lost their father long ago. One of the daughters works in a company. Well, the other girl is a student of a junior high school. Her class is going to have a picnic, but she can't join it because her family had lost their father and they are poor. So the teacher came to assist her so that she can join in. The teacher says that he will pay for her. I understand it that way. (?) Yes, I have got an impression from their faces that the mother is lonely and her daughters are too.

Her response to Card 9 is an interesting story in that the male figure is seen as a teacher. The problem of the story is poverty; this is, the mother and the two daughters do not have enough money for the student to go to her class picnic. The teacher comes to assist. Mrs. Sakai is cognizant of the feelings and longings that she must have had as a child and is able to express them. One feels that she has overcome in her own personality the difficulties that she experienced in her earlier human relationships. In her view an adequate male is someone *outside* the family (an implied criticism, perhaps, of the inadequacy of her husband).

J11. They are mother and child. He is about to go to school because there is his bag, which is left there. The boy must have been playing some game until time to go to school. He is trying to pull in the bag from the shade of a sliding door (*fusuma*). Mother seems to wait until it is time to say something to the boy. The boy's clothes tell that he was playing baseball.

The boy in this card is treated positively in a situation between mother and child which is a constructive one. There is no tension in the fact that she sees him as playing. It is assumed that play and schoolwork are harmoniously blended rather than in conflict. The story reflects the essential lack of tension and conflict this mother has with her own son.

J13. A woman has gone to bed. Her husband came home drunk. Oh, no, he has been studying until just now. He becomes sleepy, so he is rubbing his eyes with his fingers. (?) Yes, as he has become sleepy, he rubs his eyes, standing up from a chair. (?) Yes, his wife has gone to bed.

She begins a story that would be a typical one of the drunken husband coming home, but spying the books on the table, Mrs. Sakai is able to turn it instead into a constructive one in which he has been studying and, rubbing his eyes with sleepiness, is soon to join his wife in bed. In some cases one would assume that this switch is of a defensive nature, but one can assume that this woman is aware of problems of drunkenness or inadequacy in a husband but does not feel impelled to follow this story line, which would register an implied complaint against men, when she can make up a more positive situation. Again, as in Card 8, she changes a theme from bad behavior to an emphasis on positive role behavior of man and wife.

> J18. This girl is a daughter. She has just come back home from her work. Her mother is gladly holding up the daughter. She says that she is happy to welcome her. They are looking into each other's face. (?) Probably she went up to Tokyo from a rural area for work long ago; and she came back home after a long time.

This card often evokes stories of extreme violence between two women, but Mrs. Sakai is able to see a positive relationship between mother and daughter. In the previous normative sample of eight hundred Japanese TATs this was not an infrequent theme when the individuals were identified as mother and daughter. In our sample from Arakawa there were far fewer positive stories than in the samples we obtained from rural villages. For Mrs. Sakai the card evokes a theme of reunion rather than one of interpersonal tension or violence. The maternal role is perceived as loving and nurturant.

> J22. Father is going to the company. Mother goes on errands with a child. The child is crying, asking her to buy something. But mother does not pay attention to him as she thinks it good for him not to comply. (?) Well, as he grows, I can't tell you exactly about his future, but I think he will be a good man. This tells us that it is bad to bring up a child too indulgently.

The possibility of tension between parents, a frequent theme given to this picture, is not evoked. Rather, both parents are respectively going about their duties. Unlike overly indulgent mothers, the mother emphasizes that it is constructive to deny an unreasonable demand of a child. She says that it is "bad to bring up a child too indulgently." Her attitude toward bringing up her own child is, again, to emphasize autonomy. She does not feel she should be a passive slave to the child, nor do we get the impression that she would reject a child out of a negative motivation. Rather, she is concerned that her child should have the sense of autonomy that she herself possesses.

> J27. They are students. The boy and the girl are both students. The boy is going to step into actual society. She was a classmate of his. I suppose they are saying goodbye. (?) Yes, he is going to step into actual society. They were, I guess, classmates or friends or so.

The story given to Card 27 is an innocuous short story of students who are ready to graduate into adult society. Affiliation is broken up by the assumption of a reasonable role. In one sense this is an achievement story like those sometimes given by successful American executives to Card 6BM, which they see as a son saying good-bye to his mother. Mrs. Sakai throughout emphasizes both autonomy and role responsibility.

Her record in sum indicates a perception of human relationships in which a father figure can be seen as somewhat authoritarian and rigid but the women figures depicted are generally self-motivated and become both autonomous and responsible. There are references to poverty and lack of parental support which are overcome in a positive way. Human beings are expected to be warm and nurturant in fulfilling their roles toward one another, but excessive dependency is not countenanced. This Japanese woman's TAT responses suggest maternal attitudes that would probably lead to an optimal induction of self-motivated achievement in a man.

PROJECTIVE TEST RESULTS: MASAO SAKAI

The Rorschach Test

The boy's record is characterized, like those of many of the thirteen- to fifteen-year-old boys in our sample, by a large number of faces seen coming directly out of the blot. We must consider some form of authority threat operative in a number of these boys. Outside of this material the record as it progresses becomes focused much as his father's record was, on aesthetic, ornamental responses. The Rorschach record does not take on the brilliance that we find in his TAT in language or imaginative constructions. Yet there are some original percepts in his record. The achievement drive suggested is similar to that found in both his parents' records. Their responses too were almost entirely whole responses with a strong organizational drive to combine all the elements of the blot together into a complex configuration.

Rorschach Protocol

I. (4″) 1. *Birds stuck with* tori mochi *[bird-lime]*. Stuck in these parts in the center. The birds are trying to fly away toward both sides, so this center part looks as though it is pulled out. The looks of the wings are like birds. (*Torimochi?*) Not necessarily *torimochi*, but something sticky. It looked to me to be sticky. [W FM, Fm+ A O (Dsub)]

2. *Some kind of bug.* Looks like a beetle, the feeler and the eyes. Because the head and the body look divided. [D F+ A (Neut)]

II. (12″) 3. *Two human beings.* Looks like they're sitting. They have faces, hands, and feet. [W M+ H P (Neut)]

4. *The face of a bear or something.* Eyes, mouth, nose, because the surrounding parts are black . . . a cartoon bear. [WS FC'− Ad Face A (Aobs)]

5. *Also, looks like the face of a clown.* The same place as the bear face. He has makeup because the mouth is red. The clown because it has a black face. [DS FC', FC− Hd (Aobs, Hdpr)]

III. (6″) 6. *Also, two people.* The feet, hands, and heads. If a person throws back his head, the outline of the figure comes out this way. [D M+ H P (Neut)]

7. *Old men or someone are dancing two together.* This looks like bears. So, it becomes an old man, also skinny, holding his leg up. [D M+ H P (Prec)]

IV. (3″) 8. *A bat.* The lower half is the reflection on the water. Then it might be a rock in the shape of a bat. It looks like a bat because the head is like a mouse and wings are projecting in this way. On the reflection, it has also the head and wings, but they are not in the same shape because the waves change the shape. So it is cubic-looking. [W FV+ Lscp O (Misc)]

9. *A bell.* The upper part is the hand; the projection of both sides are ornaments. The center is that which swings and hits. [W F+ Orn (Porn)]

10. *A giant so big that you have to look up.* A fantastic giant. This is the head and hands. He has big feet. The center part is not included. [W F+ (H) (Athr, Afant)]

V. (4″) 11. *A butterfly.* The shape of the feelers and wings. [W F+ A P (Neut)]

12. *A big eagle.* An eagle flying; the wings are put behind. Black, or it might be his shadow. [W FM, FY+ A (Neut)]

13. *It looks a little like a swallow.* The same as the eagle. Inside position, it looks like a swallow. [W FM+ A (Neut)]

VI. (7″) 14. *A fox face.* The upper part is the nose, both sides are whiskers, and the lower projections are ears. [W F− Ad Face (Aobs)]

15. *A little boat.* This is the surface of the water. The mast is in the center with a flag. [W F+ Tr O (Misc)]

16. *A ray.* The body and the tail, swimming vigorously. This is shrinking and about to spread. The shape is very alike. [W FM+ A (Athr)]

VII. (2″) 17. *Two elephants.* Riding on something, though I don't know what. The nose, hands [feet]. [W FM+ A (Prec)]

18. *Two dogs attached to something.* The ears look just like those of

a terrier. Attached to something, also I don't know what. From the shape of the face, body, tail, and legs. [W FM, Fm+ A (Dsub)]

19. *Two girls.* Feet, hands, heads, wearing skirts. The shape of the heads looks still, about to move, though. [W M+ H P (Porn)]

VIII. (5″) 20. *A flower.* [red iris]. [W FC+ Bot (Pnat)]

21. *Some face, though I don't know what.* The face of a cat, the swollen part makes it. . . . There are ears, eyes. [WS F− Ad Face (Aobs)]

IX. (8″) 22. *Some kind of vase.* The upper part is a flower. This is from the shape and color. This part is leaves, because of the color. The center part is the vase; this is the pattern. The large carnation is put in a small vase. [WS FC+ Bot/Orn Z (Pnat, Porn)]

23. *A flower.* From the color of the stem and the look of the flower, especially the look of the joint of the flower and the petals seen as separated one by one. [D FC, FT+ Bot (Pnat)]

24. *Something like a jellyfish.* It has a head; the rest is the legs. Looks just about to move. [W FM− A (Misc)]

X. (9″) 25. *Dead leaves.* Except this and this, all are dead leaves. They have various colors because they are dead. [D FC+ Bot (Pnat, Agl)]

26. *Animals coming together to the flower in bloom.* The color of the petals and stem. The other small ones are the animals and birds coming. This looks just like a bird. [W FM, FC+ A Bot (Pnat)]

27. *Trash swept by a broom.* A broom with a handle. The rest are trash because they are fluttering (*chira-chira*)—nothing to do with color. [WS Fm+ Hh O (Misc)]

Card-by-Card Sequential Analysis and Comments

Masao's first response to Card I is an original concept in which two birds are stuck on bird-lime, or *tori mochi*. They are pulling to get away, but they are stuck. One can speculate about the symbolic meaning of this response. It is probably related to the interpretations to be made of his TAT stories. The boy feels himself wishing to be free and socially mobile, and yet he is held by some of the incapacities of his own family; if he were to break free completely, he would feel considerable guilt. The *mochi* is a ceremonial delicacy served at New Year's, at gatherings that symbolize family togetherness. Masao's second response is much more neutral: it is simply a beetle in the center area of the card. On Card II he immediately perceives human beings sitting; then he gives the first of his direct-on faces, that of a bear with eyes, mouth, and nose, a cartoon bear. He then changes the same basic area to the face of a clown with makeup; it is a clown because it has a black face. The clown is a traditionally disparaged human that may in this instance, given the other materials, be interpreted as a somewhat socially depreciated father. In both the upright and the upside-down position he sees human beings on Card III. This boy has a much more active introspective inner life than his father has.

On Card IV he gives a most interesting interpretation of a figure that is foreshortened. With the card upside down he sees the top part as a bat and the lower part as its foreshortened reflection in water. To make the response more acceptable, he perceives a rock in the shape of a bat that is reflected in the water. The reflection does not have the same shape, because of the turbulence of waves which have distorted it. This is a clever response requiring a superior ideational capacity for its formation. Also on Card IV, he sees an ornamental bell and finally a giant that is foreshortened, so large that one has to look up, making his head appear smaller than his feet. Here we have, perhaps, the opposite of the clown response, an immense, formidable adult figure.

On Card V he uses the same basic area for three responses. (This boy's productivity level is higher than the average. He pushes very hard to give at least two or three responses to every card.) On this card the responses are not widely different, but nevertheless he gives us as alternatives a butterfly, an eagle, and a swallow. The whole of Card VI is seen as a fox's face. Then, very cleverly again, he develops a vista response. Sideways he sees a little boat with its mast on the surface of the water and its reflection on the other half of the card. He sees a vigorously swimming ray on Card VII. He also sees, with good imagination, elephants riding on something, introducing again the circus theme (the clown) seen on Card II. (Note also the circus theme in the mother's perceptions discussed above.) Two attached terriers, again, like the birds, inject a feeling that active animals are unable to become free. Finally, on Card VII, upside down, he sees two female figures, sometimes seen as dancing.

The colors in the last three cards stimulate him very much, as they did his father and mother. He sees a flower. However, a face again intrudes, this time the face of a cat. Card IX is a vase, the upper part flowers, the center part the color of leaves, and the white part a vase—a large carnation in a small vase. Turning it the other way, right side up again, he sees a flower with petals, and finally a jellyfish. On the final card are dead leaves having autumnal colors, a positive response that has some depressive implications. Upside down, he sees a collection of animals coming together toward a flowering bloom. The animals are not fighting, as they are sometimes perceived on other records in our sample. Then, as a curious final response, the whole card is seen to represent residual trash as swept by a broom. The broom and the handle are in the upper part of the blot, and the rest is the fluttering of trash that follows the sweeps of a broom. There is strong movement in this response. The symbolic implications are not easy to speculate about. We might say, however, noting that Masao's father is a janitor, that this may somehow have a symbolic connection with his father's demeaning occupation, just as his first response indiated some inability to get away from the family.

The TAT

This record is a most unusual TAT, for many reasons. First of all is its linguistic style. Masao uses very elegant Japanese, which cannot be conveyed simply by English translation. He has a rich vocabulary, far beyond that usual for a boy his age, and not at all characteristic of his lower-class neighborhood. He has certain stylistic qualities in his adjectives that would indicate a superior educational attainment. Second, the themes given by him are unusual. Some of them are highly original for the TAT, although they are derivative of themes found in Japanese culture. The emotional logic in many of the themes has a peculiarly Japanese quality, which we will point out. In this instance it is much easier to analyze this boy's record culturally than psychodiagnostically, although we will attempt to see how the emotional logic of his themes may in some way pertain to his own personality. For example, the father figure in some of his stories is one of inspiration, despite his own father's humble social position. The father is seen quite positively. What is also present, however, is a possibly unconscious wish to have a better inherited status than has been his lot.

> J1. May I decide the name of persons? Well, I will call this boy A. A's father was a great musician. When A was a little child, his father died, having asked his mother to educate him as a good musician. One day when this boy had grown up, his mother told him about it. He made up his mind to be a musician and began to study hard for it. One day he decided to compose music, playing the violin. On one or another night, he was bothered about it when he was taking a nap. Then he saw his father's face in a dream very clearly. When he awoke, he found there a white sheet of music paper that was blank. Taking up his violin, he resolved again to be a good musician and began to compose music, writing it down on music paper. One day he entered his composition in a music contest sponsored by a music company. His composition was regarded as the best. He was very glad about it. Since then he's confirmed in his determination to be a musician. Some years later, when he had grown up, he was found composing music on music paper with an elegant violin.

Card 1 expresses a traditional Japanese theme of a boy who aspires to be as great as his father. It is the story of a dead father who becomes an inspirational image for his son, aided and abetted by the mother's dedication to his education. His father's face appears to him in a dream, deepening his resolve to be a good musician. He competes successfully and demonstrates his talent in a contest held by a music company. The emphasis is not on the simple act of playing but on the young man's creative capacity. Psychodiagnostically, we may surmise that this boy has some need for an inspirational father figure. He is ready to find some mentor whose paternal interest will inspire him toward upward mobility and accomplishment. The paternal role, positively experienced in childhood, is for many Japanese something to be sought out in later "paternalistic" relationships.

> J2. Is it a field? It's an uncultivated field somewhere in Hokkaido. A girl who was born there began to have a great concern with agriculture and the particular manner of cultivation she was accustomed to seeing since her birth. By careful observation, she found that all the seeds she sowed were frozen by the cold that frequently attacks these areas. She knew that she could not expect any harvest from this type of seed in this area. Since then, she began to attend Hokkaido University and started the study of the improvement of seeds. One day when she saw her father was sowing seeds, she thought all the seeds that her father sowed would be frozen. The following day, she began to experiment with seeds in a laboratory of the school to make them strong enough to withstand cold. Some days after, she found she could find how to improve them so that they could bear cold. She actually sowed a field, but no buds came out. She tried once again and no buds came out; finally, she found what the defect was. She improved the seeds and tried again. Then, two months later, a sprout with two leaves came out. She knew that this type of plant could grow in this area. She decided to wait for the harvest in fall.

The second theme is also one of achievement, but it is again a paradigm of the Japanese achievement concern. The achievement is not simply for one's self here, but in order to improve agriculture. The young woman is motivated to seek through science the improvement of seeds so that the farms of Hokkaido will benefit. There is achievement pressed toward social benefit, a feeling of dedication that emerges from this rather elaborately told story. Psychodiagnostically, there seems to be a full internalization of an achievement drive in this boy. The care given him by his parents has apparently been fruitful in developing a strong Japanese need for achievement expressed in idealistic terms. This boy has no competition from his own father, who has frankly admitted his incapacity to help his boy further with his schoolwork. In effect, Masao has to compete, not with an actual father, but with some idealized concept of a successful, dedicated Japanese.

> J3. One day a lovely boy was born in a family of a town. He kept growing quickly, but when he was two years old something happened to his leg. When his parents noticed, he had already suffered from poliomyelitis. Time passed on. When he was five years old, his leg was completely incapacitated. Since then, he has been spending his life all the time with a heavy heart. He read many books, but it was still dark every day for him. One day when he was reading a book, he found a biography of Abraham Lincoln telling about his emancipation of slaves in a very difficult situation. Since he read this story, he realized that he could overcome his disadvantage by studying hard. He began to study very hard after that.

Masao's story on Card 3 has an idealized theme, very Japanese in nature, showing how a person overcomes inadequacy in an Adlerian sense. The handicap and incapacity of a crippled leg generates a need to compensate by seeking inspiration from books. Interestingly enough here, the inspirational figure is Abraham Lincoln, who came from an impoverished background and became a great man responsible for the emancipation of slaves. From this biography the young boy realizes that he can overcome any personal disadvantage by studying hard. Psychodynamically, we find here some sense of inadequacy in Masao which, through dedicated application, he feels he could overcome. He lives in a fairly tough neighborhood in which physical prowess is highly regarded, and yet he himself is relatively poor at sports. One sees therefore that intellectual activities are some compensation for his inability to hold his own with his peers on a physical level.

> J6. A boy was born in a poor family. The mother deserted the child on a road because of her economic condition. After many years had passed a man called on her one day. She asked what he had come for. The man asked, "Aren't you my mother who deserted me long ago?" She answered, "No, I don't know." While she was listening to him, she was reminded of the day when she deserted her child. She began to feel regret for what she had done. She asked his name, but it was a name she did not know. She tried to recall those days more clearly. She remembered that the boy hadn't had any name yet. She then remembered and told him that the child had had a mole behind his ear. The man found it by using a mirror, and confirmed that she was his real mother. They began to live together happily, spending the money he had earned so far.

Card 6 is another fanciful story with a Japanese theme of a young man who cares for the mother who had deserted him long ago. The mother, because of her poverty, had to desert her child. The child, however, has earned money and henceforth will be able to take care of his deprived and aging mother. This story shows the Japanese feeling that one is committed to the care of one's mother for life. In this account we have no mention of a father, but the relationship between a mother and her son is depicted very strongly. This is generally true for Japanese records. Fantasy of the father in dependent old age is seldom encountered; the emphasis is on the mother. The presumption is that the father has died and the son has replaced the father as the caretaker of the mother. The primacy of the mother-son relationship is not only culturally condoned but culturally sanctioned. Psychodynamically, we gain an impression of this boy's maintaining a strong relationship with his mother. The idea of having the mother desert the child because of economic pressure may symbolize the fact that although his own mother's attention has been taken from him by other activities, he can regain, at some point, the original close relationship with his mother. It is perhaps a regressive underlying wish for the infantile closeness when he had undisturbed primacy in the mother's affection, before his sisters were born. In Japanese stories the mother-child relationship often remains unbroken or is restored.

In the story to Card 7, again the paternal figure is removed, but the price of removal is that one must henceforth work hard and deserve the sacrifice of the distant, idealized authority figure who has stepped out of the picture.

> J7. A boy studied at a primary school. When he was in the sixth grade, he was taught by this teacher. He learned from his lessons that a man shouldn't be selfish and should think of other people's happiness as much as he does of his own. On the following day, his teacher was killed in a car accident. The teacher's figure came to float before the boy's eyes. The teacher's voice, too, echoed in his mind. He realized that what the teacher had taught was really true. He determined to work for people. He worked hard and saved money. When he was going to die, he took out all the money he had saved. There were a lot of paper notes and small coins. He died leaving the message that he'd like to donate all the money to orphanages.

Here again, as in many stories given by Japanese, we have the father figure idealized but killed off somehow. The ideal teacher, killed in a car accident, comes back as an inspiration. Masao is saying in a sense that perhaps it is better to have a dead father whom one can idealize rather than a live one who reminds one of fallibility and inadequacy. The teacher devotes himself to his pupils, and the boy's money is dedicated to others. It is interesting to note the idea of donating money to orphanages. Perhaps this boy feels some deprivation because of the social circumstances of his parents as well as himself. He may already find himself becoming somewhat distant from his parents in occupational ambitions, but his sense of morality about his possible social mobility turns to the succor of those less fortunate.

> J8. When this boy was eight years old, a war began. His father had to go to war. One day his father ran into the home and fell down. When he took his hand away from his stomach, lots of blood streamed down. The boy woke up all the family by shouting. There was a ball in his stomach. All the family members tried to take it out. The father was in great pain. The boy thought that he had to take out the ball; otherwise the father would die. He quickly took his knife from his pocket and removed the ball with it. He put sanitary cotton in it and bound around it. They kept watching him all through the night. When morning came, the birds were singing. The father's heavy breathing could be heard. The boy called his father; then his father opened his eyes little by little. And he sat up in his bed, but he soon lay down on the bed again because of the pain. The father told him, "War is a foolish thing. It is quite foolish that we have to kill others or be killed by others." The boy thought that we should not have any war in this world. Later he started a movement to abolish wars.

On Card 8 we see a feeling of ambivalence toward the father, overcompensated by a retributive attempt to save the father's life, which is spelled out in graphic detail. The story is idealized, intellectualized, and put in the context of larger social issues, as are other stories, such as that in response to Card 2. The possible death of a father is an inspiration to prevent the death of others, a kind of compensation for underlying feelings of guilt. One finds an adolescent pattern in this boy which is found sometimes in European and American adolescents of an idealistic nature who are resolving feelings toward the parents in the larger arena of the outer world. We see here mechanisms of sublimation and intellectualization heavily at work to cover basic ambivalent feelings toward a weak and inadequate father. The language becomes literary and aesthetic, pointing out the arrival of morning with singing birds—an almost poetic dwelling on the last moments of the father's life.

> J9. It was on a winter's night. After a trifling quarrel a man and three others parted. The man had shouted, "All of you get out!" in a loud voice. These three trudged away, suppressing their tears. This man began to reconsider. He began to feel at fault. He ran out after them, following their footprints in the new-fallen snow with a flashlight. Coming to a valley, the footmarks disappeared as if sucked into the depths of the valley. "Ah, they have fallen into the valley!" he said inwardly to himself. Did he feel ashamed of what he had done? Considering his previous act, he said in a loud voice, "I was wrong." He looked down into the deep valley, thinking his mother and the others must still be there. In the darkness his flashlight could not probe to the distant bottom. Again he considered what he had done. "Surely," he concluded, "I was wrong." The idea came to him that unless he killed himself it could not be made right. "I must die." Then he thought rather than thinking of his death he should think of what would happen after his death—its consequences. As he thought further he came to the idea that it was important for him to live rather than to continue to think about the other three. He thought hard, hitting his head with his fist as though to awaken himself. Then again, "After all, I have done wrong!" pressed into his mind. After answering his own questions he leaped into the valley's depths.

This theme becomes even more fanciful. There is again an aesthetic distancing. He evokes a mood with poetic reference to falling snow. He produces one of the most uniquely told stories in our experience with this card in Japanese TAT responses. This is no stereotyped theme but one that reveals an idiosyncratic pattern in this boy. In effect, it is a young man who drives away three unspecified individuals who in the later part of the story become his mother and two others who remain unidentified (note that Masao has two sisters). Reconsidering, the young man finds himself guilty of having destroyed them. He cannot overcome his guilt. He debates with himself, first that his own death would accomplish nothing, but then his Japanese self takes over and he feels he can expiate what he has done only by his own self-annihilation. One can speculate that this boy has had some fantasies about getting rid of his family; he may feel that they are a burden, that he has outgrown them, and that they are perhaps an uncomfortable encumbrance to his future. Yet such thoughts produce nothing but immense guilt, given the love he has been accorded as a favorite child. Masao produces a highly elaborated plot that shows the depths of guilt he would feel should he abandon his family for his own individualistic development. The figure is forced to destroy himself rather than countenance his own future alone.

> J11. A boy went to school. While he was playing with his friends, he noticed that his friends' briefcases were new and shining and their hats, too. He asked his mother to buy a new briefcase and hat like his friends'. His mother answered that she could not buy them because she could not afford to. He gave up his quest that day. On the following day he went to school. His friends again displayed their new briefcases. He told his mother about it. She said that she could not buy such expensive things. He gave up that day, too, and went to bed. There were noises in the next room at night. He got up and went there. He found his mother wrapping her new kimono in a kerchief. He felt it strange for his mother to do such a thing, but he went back to sleep. The following night there was a noise in the next room again. He went there again. There were a new briefcase and a new hat instead of his mother's kimono in the kerchief. He thought about it. He understood that his mother put her new kimono in pawn and bought a new hat and briefcase. He realized from then on that he had to overcome temptation to want whatever his friends displayed to him.

This card shows again that this boy is preoccupied with the guilt of receiving from his parents; that, indeed, they can refuse him nothing, and there is a considerable ambivalence in him about the consequences of his demands on them. The story is very Japanese in showing the depths of sacrifice of the parent for a child, and yet it is curious to have this boy himself give the story. This degree of sacrifice on the part of the parent makes him feel that he must overcome any temptations from his environment, that he is justified in receiving this kind of attention only by a serious application of his talents. The story shows the boy's attempts at self-assurance. He is trying to say to himself here how much his parents have done for him, and that he should not even think of deserting his family. But at the same time this story might also indicate that the boy still wishes his parents to satisfy themselves so that he too can be financially better off, because in his actual situation he needs more money to pursue his interest in machines.

> J13. A man came back from his company. It was dark in the house. He looked around carefully and then he found a woman who was dead. He wondered why she died in his house. He found a letter beside her. He read it. It read that she was a mother whose son had been killed by his car and that since her only son was killed, she would commit suicide to follow her son in death. A cold shiver ran down the man's spine. He felt remorse over the fact that he had not apologized to her at that time.

> He rushed out onto the road and was killed by a large car which was at that moment passing by.

The very Japanese theme on which this story is centered is a mother's use of suicide to express anger and to induce a feeling of guilt in another person who has damaged her life irrevocably. The man himself is killed by another car. Certainly we find in Masao the comprehension that by one's own suffering or death one can induce guilt in another person—an emotional logic, as we have pointed out, that has its origin in the sacrificial behavior of his parents. In a very graphic fashion this boy manifests awareness that he had been indulged to the fullest by sacrificing parents. Consequently, there is a rather open representation of a preoccupation with guilt over any potential hostility. We see a progression through his stories of guilt, beginning with the death of the father in story 8. The theme of guilt becomes much more fanciful in story 9 (the driving away of the other family members) than does his depiction of the sacrificial behavior of a mother on Card 11, which shows awareness of the results of his own selfishness on another person. We notice with Card 13 that this preoccupation with guilt takes the place of any conscious awareness of the sexual implications. In effect, this boy's idealistic concerns on both Card 11 and Card 13 have completely submerged the potential sexual stimulus of these cards.

> J18. One day a woman drove her daughter from the house. It was snowing. Time has passed since then. One day while she was thinking about what she had done on that day, she began to think that she was wrong because she had asked her daughter for her pocket money and acted selfishly. She thought it must be she who was wrong. She rushed out of the house and called her daughter's name many times. Then she heard a voice in the distance. She went there and found her daughter trudging home. She asked her daughter why she came back. The daughter answered that she thought she was wrong and she should have given money to her mother. The mother said that it was her own fault and not the daughter's. While they were repeating the same thing, they realized that both of them were wrong. They went into the house, having promised not to have such quarrels again.

Here we find a mutual feeling of guilt in the two figures as they contend over a question of money. This boy obviously feels some money deprivation, which comes out in some of the stories. He is aware of the limited resources of his family and may be indirectly expressing guilt over the fact that he wants more than a severely limited allowance. Both mother and daughter in this story are concerned with admitting their own fault, so we have here a continuation of the guilt theme aroused by the other cards.

> J22. One day a boy went out shopping with his mother. While he was walking on a street, he found a toy shop and he was looking into it. His mother kept on going, as she did not notice him. After a while the boy looked around him, but he could not find his mother. He thought

how to find her but he could not think of anything. So he cried out. He was crying and looking for his mother among passing people. His mother wasn't there, however. After a short time the mother came back from the opposite direction. She said, "Were you here? I've been looking for you." And they walked away together.

The theme of Card 22 suggests an earlier fear of being deserted by a parent. Perhaps conditions in the family were so poor that this boy felt a potential deprivation that threatened the integrity of the family itself. The story ends reassuringly when the mother returns and they go away happily together. Curiously enough, this story is given in a very spare way, almost as if the peaks of fantasy in the previous stories have drained this boy's capacity for language. The story is bare and direct rather than descriptive, without the well-chosen adjectives in the previous stories.

J27. A student was walking on a street. Then his sister came from the other side, so he tried to escape from her. He failed to do so, however. His sister asked him why he was going to escape from her. He told her that he wasn't trying to avoid her. She said that he must have been looking for 500 yen. After he kept a silence for a while, he told her the truth, that he had been looking for 500 yen that he thought he had lost. He asked her how she knew that. Also he said that she must have stolen his money from his purse. She had found 500 yen on the road and picked it up before she met her brother. She thought someone had lost it. Soon after that she saw her brother coming and she noticed that he had 500 yen. So she asked him whether it was his or not. He thanked her for it and he went away.

A curious relationship between brother and sister is depicted here. (We note again that this boy has two younger sisters.) Problems of money occur in this incoherent story, in which a boy seems to accuse his sister of having taken money from him. This certainly relates to some underlying feeling of economic deprivation; there is nothing in this particular card to stimulate such a story. In the Sakai family underlying feelings of economic deprivation, and perhaps of jealousy, occur where three siblings present the problem of who will receive what little resources are available. The sister in this story is first believed to have taken money away from the young man, but then the sister gives back to him what he thought he had lost. This story is poorly presented in comparison with Masao's earlier eloquence. It is almost as if he has exhausted himself and has little left over for the last two stories.

In sum, we find that this boy expresses to a strong degree an overrefined conscience in his readiness to feel guilt. He is struggling internally with the sense of economic deprivation that he feels in spite of the warmth and care of loving parents. An inner struggle for personal integrity conflicts with a desire for social mobility which may eventually imply the desertion of parents and family.

CONCLUDING REMARKS

The Sakai family in a number of ways epitomizes what we have presented in many contexts as the Japanese practice of parental self-sacrifice through which self-motivated, internalized needs for achievement are passed on to children. Mr. Sakai is a personal as well as an occupational failure, if viewed from the outside, and yet he can identify vicariously with the struggle toward achievement in his child, and by his facilitative attitudes can actually help induce it. Mrs. Sakai plays the traditional role of a Japanese mother not only ritualistically but in a deeply emotional way. She is uncomplaining about her occupationally inadequate husband and dedicated with great intensity to fostering a need for self-actualization through accomplishment in her child.

The transmission of achievement motivation in Japan occurs on every level of society, mediated by parents who themselves often have not achieved but who can induce a need for achievement in their children, just as some parents who themselves have not acted antisocially, in instances already noted, can induce the appearance of delinquency in their children. In both directions, children often act out or actualize behavior that was latent in one or the other parent.

The Sakai family history conveys far better than any abstract statement what we mean by the title of this volume, *The Heritage of Endurance*. For Japanese who have the long view, the eventual triumph that recompenses them for the trials of the present may not occur in their own life, but may become manifest through the internalization of achievement directives by their children. The child knows this deep in his being. He must achieve to justify the painful tribulations of the past generation. The burden of potential guilt is much greater than the cost of work. Should circumstances of limited opportunity not permit actual achievement, the task is passed on to the following generation.

CHAPTER 12

Yokichi Fukuyama

A "Banchō" Reforms

Yokichi Fukuyama was fifteen years old at the time of first contact in our study. In his junior high school he had become the *banchō*, or leader of a gang, an institution that has only recently disappeared from most of the schools in Arakawa. As we discussed briefly in chapter 2, a *banchō* achieved his position by being recognized as the toughest of his class. The more delinquency-oriented boys would elevate such a boy to leadership, which he would use to his advantage in directing covert forms of gang and individual intimidation of the more pliable and timid boys at the intermediate schools.

This case history is of particular interest to us because we were able to reinvestigate Yokichi's activities after a period of four years. We found that this former *banchō* had not continued toward a delinquent career but had redirected his energies toward becoming a youth leader for the Sōka Gakkai religious sect, in which he now can put his aggressive leadership capacities to more socially approved ends. Nevertheless, rebellious ambivalence about authority, or becoming a leader, remains one of the chief characteristics of Yokichi's social attitudes, which are in effect a continuation of attitudes held by his father.

Our impression of the Fukuyama family (case D-2) was that this boy had received, despite some possible early deprivation in infancy, considerable affection and attention from his parents and grandmother, which might mitigate or counteract any resentment that could motivate him toward an antisocial career.

This case also illustrates how peer-group pressures strengthen delinquent tendencies in a given youth. The induction patterns toward delinquency in the peer structure of a lower-class Japanese neighborhood can indeed be compelling, given some propensity or susceptibility prompted by difficulty within the primary family, some latent rebellious attitudes in parents themselves. A youth seeking some form of compensatory reference-group support as an escape from difficulties at home is more apt to become delinquent in a neighborhood or social environment where a high rate of delinquency already exists. There is a mutual introduction into delinquency of boys who experience some of the same difficulties at home. The degree of difficulty varies with those involved. Sometimes leadership is assumed by someone who simply epitomizes for a group its shared delinquent attitude; in other instances, as in Yokichi's case, the leadership qualities recognized by his peers have socially constructive as well as socially disruptive potential.

Yokichi's police record includes joyriding on a motor bicycle owned by the father of one of his friends, without permission and without a driver's license, and twice stealing automobiles. For these offenses he was brought before a family court, but his case was dismissed. Two incidents of violence to a boy whom he attacked with two other friends brought him to court again, but after a careful examination of his background and the opinions of those who knew him, including a sympathetic teacher, the judge decided to suspend judgment. Yokichi is also known to have committed a number of minor offenses, such as truancy, and staying away from home, and numerous manifestations of "incorrigibility."

He lives in a tiny, one-room home in Arakawa with his hardworking parents and four other siblings. He is the second child, having an older sister who is now working to help support the family, and two younger brothers. The background of the parents, the Fukuyamas, gives some indication of the possible sources of antisocial attitudes in the boy, but in the main, this family's history does not supply the compelling clues found in some others, which more readily suggest a destiny of confirmed deliquency or at least some form of socially directed resentment or antagonism.

THE FATHER'S BACKGROUND

Yokichi's father was born Toshio Yamada. He took his wife's name of Fukuyama as a condition of his marriage, being taken into her family as a *muko-yōshi*, or adopted husband. Toshio Yamada's own father, the paternal grandfather of our subject, was an ambitious, spirited man born in a farming village, the eldest in a family of three boys. The land in Niigata Prefecture which was his birthright was so exceedingly poor that he could not see any future in farming. Rather than assuming responsibility for the meager family fortunes as heir, he gave up to his next younger brother his right to inheritance under the then existing laws of primogeniture. He left for Tokyo, where as an apprentice he learned to become a hauler with a horse-drawn cart. He applied himself diligently to his work and after some time returned to his own village, to begin there his own independent career as a hauler of materials for others.

He made no attempt to expand his business by hiring other employees and subordinates. Instead, he organized and instructed several others in his community to equip themselves for hauling service, which had become an increasing necessity, and formed his group into an organization of cooperative but independent haulers. We are told that Yokichi's grandfather applied himself with vigor and energy to his occupation. He expected nothing less in the way of enterprise from his three sons, in whom he sought to instill his own drive and passion for hard work. Two of his sons conformed to his expectations and took on, for a time at least, the father's business. One son chose to rebel and leave home. The rebel was Yokichi's father, Toshio Yamada, now Fukuyama.

From early childhood, Mr. Fukuyama, who was the third son of six siblings, remembers his father as demanding and aggressive, sometimes given to abusive physical punishment of his sons. Mr. Fukuyama states that his father, who felt handicapped by his own lack of education, was strict about his children's education and forced them to study hard and do their homework, but Mr. Fukuyama also remembers his father as very considerate of his children. Although he rebelled against his father, he also came to manifest some of his father's independent spirit. Some of the traits or values of the father are reflected in his own attempts at entrepreneurial success, which have been marked by a number of ups and downs. Mr. Fukuyama describes other "good" traits in his father's character: "He was very reticent, reliable, also good-natured, like myself," thus identifying himself with his father. He remembers his mother as a timid, quiet, kind, and sensitive woman, who would often secretly give in to the children even though his father had said no to their requests.

At a certain point, young Toshio felt he could no longer accept or conform to the demands of his father, and he ran away to Tokyo. Mr. Fukuyama's self-image in his childhood is that he was an uncontrollable boy who was lazy and disobedient, while his elder and younger brothers were studious and conforming to the parental expectations.

Shortly after Toshio ran away to the city, an older brother also came to Tokyo. Though they attended the same school, it is unclear what the relationship between the two brothers was at this time. The older brother completed school, whereas Toshio dropped out. Eventually, the older brother became a high official in the postal department, where he has been able to translate his father's aggressive personality into a rather distinguished career in spite of his rural background.

During the war with China, Toshio was drafted into the army. After receiving a serious bullet wound, he was sent home from combat. He thereupon went to work in the national arsenal, where he gained some proficiency in working with metal, and it was while he was on this job that he met the woman he was to marry.

When World War II ended, Toshio put what he had learned in his work in the arsenal to good effect. He opened a metalworking business by buying some machines that could make metal fittings for furniture. As we infer from his account, he had a repeated tendency to overextend his resources and capacities. Finally, he was forced into bankruptcy and was left with an unresolved debt, principally as a result of the bankruptcy of the principal contractor on whom he depended for his subcontracting jobs to various furniture makers. Mr. Fukuyama's sense of adequacy has been severely challenged by his bankruptcy, from which it has been extremely difficult to recover.

THE MOTHER'S BACKGROUND

Yoshiko Fukuyama was the only daughter of a small Tokyo shopkeeper who made candy. After the birth of Yoshiko, her mother became a chronic invalid and died when her daughter was only two years old. From this one might suspect that Yoshiko had some experience of maternal deprivation. Shortly after her mother's death, her father married a woman who was incapable of conceiving. This stepmother, a very forceful person, was herself the only child of parents who had died when she was quite young. She had been adopted into another family and put out to work at an early age, approximately twelve or thirteen, as a *ko-mori*, a nursemaid for other children.

Mrs. Fukuyama's father had learned his trade as an apprentice in a large and famous confectionery shop in Tokyo. He too, being of independent spirit, wanted to open his own store and was finally able to do so through the assistance of the master confectioner to whom he was apprenticed. This attempt at independence eventually failed, and he and his second wife were forced to become itinerant peddlers of vegetables. As he is described by Mrs. Fukuyama, her father, in spite of all his desire for independence, was far too timid and nonaggressive ever to become a success. Of his character Mrs. Fukuyama says, "He was so quiet that it was not easy to tell if he was around. He was not a good merchant. He was too weak." In contrast, she sees her stepmother as an independent-minded, self-assertive person (*kachiki-na*, meaning "of a winning spirit"). She worked very hard, and Mrs. Fukuyama says, "Mother was the center of our life." It seems likely that Mrs. Fukuyama strongly identified herself with her stepmother, thus becoming herself an independent, self-assertive woman who is the center of the Fukuyama family's life in many ways. Recalling her father and stepmother, Mrs. Fukuyama says, "I think I was like my father when I was a child. I was shy and withdrawn and bashful (*hikkomi-jian*). But recently I feel that I have become more and more like my mother rather than my father." Mrs. Fukuyama's father was not successful in anything he tried, despite the help that his second wife attempted to give him. At one point in the interview Mrs. Fukuyama suggests that the fact that her family are members of the Shingon sect of Buddhism may have something to do with her parents' personalities, since, as she puts it, "In Shingon-shū the women all tend to be dominant and adequate, while the men are simply worthless."

She vividly described how her parents were forced to become itinerant peddlers, with the consequence that she had very little contact with them. Coming home daily from school, she would find waiting for her a dish of candy, set there by her parents before they left on their daily selling activities. She felt that she had an extremely lonely childhood, and this feeling of loneliness is indirectly reflected in some of her projective materials.

It was not until she was nineteen years old that she discovered that her stepmother was not her biological mother. Her response to this discovery, as she describes it, was somewhat emotionally bland, in that she states she evidenced no surprise or consternation at the time. Says Mrs. Fukuyama, "I was *nonki* (easygoing) and did not take it seriously. After all, I was the only child and my mother had always been loving to me."

Yoshiko had relatively little interest in school and soon quit to take a job at the national arsenal, where she worked during the war. Indicative of the stepmother's assumption of family responsibility is her insistence that her daughter should not marry out, ending her family name, but that the husband become a *muko-yōshi*, and take on the name of Fukuyama.

In Japan, to become *muko-yōshi* has been considered as potentially "humiliating" for a man, because it has often meant that he comes under what is sometimes described as "the rule of a willful daughter of the family and a controlling mother," instead of assuming authority as the head of the household. There are a number of proverbs that warn men against becoming a *muko-yōshi*. Accordingly, the interviewer asked Mr. Fukuyama whether he felt hesitant about becoming heir to the Fukuyama family. Mr. Fukuyama's answer was negative:

> As we liked each other, it did not make any difference. I did not feel hesitant or reluctant. You might say, I was not concerned with it at all. I did not pay any attention. However, I must say, my own mother was terribly upset. She cried when I told her that I was going to marry my present wife. She said I could not desert my mother like that. She thought I was deserting her and my family. I did not think I was, so I went ahead with my marriage.

Overriding the objections of his widowed mother, he henceforth came to be known as Fukuyama Toshio. The marriage was probably facilitated by the fact that Toshio's older brother raised no objection.

Mrs. Fukuyama had a negative impression of her new husband's mother. Her description of her is entirely different from that of her husband. She describes her as a rather selfish person, who probably became self-willed "because she had lost her husband early." Mr. Fukuyama had described his own mother as a rather passive, sweet person, and his father as dominant and aggressive.

THE MARRIED LIFE OF THE FUKUYAMAS

The reminiscences of the Fukuyamas are somewhat contradictory. During their initial six months together they shared a tiny room with Mrs. Fukuyama's widowed stepmother. The young couple worked at the same ammunition plant, sometimes having to go to work on foot because of the shortage of transportation. They earned very small wages and were continually pressed for money. The stepmother started to sell dried fish that she boxed, to help with the budget. During this initial period, the relationship was harmonious. Mrs. Fukuyama reports that her stepmother at first was careful in her treatment of her son-in-law. This was also the time when the newlywed Fukuyamas enjoyed their marital life. Mr. Fukuyama recalls that he was drafted again, from six to fifteen months after the marriage, in the final stages of World War II.

Mr. Fukuyama had found his mother-in-law a continual trial. She was exacting, precise, and continually alert for inadequacies, and she eventually exhausted his goodwill. He had wanted nurturant treatment from her, such as he had received from his own mother; he frequently asked her to do things for him and even helped her as a son would do. Instead, he was "nagged" and badgered by her, according to his account.

Before his return from China in 1945, his wife and her stepmother found themselves in extreme financial difficulties. They decided not to evacuate to the countryside but to try to live on in Tokyo despite the daily threats of bombs and the difficulty of finding enough food to keep alive. In February 1945, the Fukuyamas' eldest child, a girl, Keiko, was born. Mr. Fukuyama, fighting in China, had bought a pair of baby shoes and kept them on his person as a reminder of the coming child. The couple's correspondence was all about the baby and their anticipated reunion. Before his return, his wife and mother-in-law had to work as peddlers to maintain themselves. Mrs. Fukuyama states that she resisted any of the opportunities she had to do business on the black market because she did not want to jeopardize "the honorable status of her husband's older brother" and compromise his position as a bureaucrat. With the baby's arrival, she ceased working entirely, and the two women resorted to selling some of their clothes and furniture.

After the war ended, Toshio was sent back to Tokyo, in the autumn of 1945, and he started immediately to work in the black market, acting as a courier for various food items. As soon as he could, however, he went back to his trade of processing metal fixtures. In the meantime, his younger brother came back from the war and needed temporary housing. The elder brother also arrived, since he had lost his home in a fire raid. Thus the Fukuyamas' one-room sleeping arrangements had to provide for the grandmother, the married couple, their infant child, and the two brothers. When the immediate exigencies of the postwar period passed, the brothers found other lodgings. In the meantime, more children were born in the Fukuyamas' household, the subject, Yokichi, being the second child.

By this time Mr. Fukuyama had a job earning about $50 a month. He found he could make extra money at home by doing metalworking on a simple machine that he set up in part of their living space. He became more and more occupied with how to get enough money to set himself up independently with a few machines of his own. In spite of his affection for his children, he had very little time for them, all his energy being directed toward making enough money to buy more machines. He was also able to buy the tiny house owned by his older brother, who had by then become more successful. It was a one-story wooden house with approximately 360 square feet. He remodeled a 6-by-6-foot area into a small metal-processing shop, and the rest of the home was set up as living quarters for the family.

It is interesting to note that whereas Mr. Fukuyama says he bought the house from his brother, according to the wife's account the house was given to him by his brother. Mr. Fukuyama probably did not like to acknowledge his older brother's charity, which would show him at a disadvantage in respect to their relative occupational capacities.

Our impression is that Mr. Fukuyama was too impatient to expand his business. He took on two partners and went into debt for several thousand yen. His partners, both of whom were bachelors, pulled out of the business after a short time, leaving Mr. Fukuyama the sole person responsible for paying back the incurred debts and continuing his business.

In desperation, he had his wife take on part of the processing of the furniture ornaments so that they could keep at least two of his three machines in constant operation. Her husband had her work from about eight o'clock in the morning, right after breakfast, till about nine o'clock at night. The care of the children was given over completely to the grandmother. Mrs. Fukuyama describes how she would interrupt her work briefly in order to breast-feed her child, and then would immediately return him to the grandmother. The home factory had been extended to take over all but a 9-by-9-foot area for living, and the children were bedded in closets at this time. Mr. Fukuyama had established a reputation for diligence and skill in his work and seemed to be doing well, but it seems that at the same time the husband and wife lost something in regard to each other.

YOKICHI'S EARLY YEARS

Yokichi's mother remembers that he was physically weak in the beginning and that she had to go about three times a month with him to a clinic. He had a discharge from his ears that continued intermittently until he started school. He was weaned to make way for his younger brother, who was born about eighteen months after him. The toilet training of the children was left to the grandmother.

There are some discrepancies in parental recall of their children's infancies. The mother said Yokichi wore diapers until he was about two, but the father says he recalls that both infant boys wore diapers at the same time and that Yokichi probably was in diapers until he was about three years of age. The grandmother persistently took the children to the toilet for training, but Yokichi "failed" many times, and on these occasions the grandmother would hit him. However, the parents recall that the grandmother was particularly fond of Yokichi, and the mother says that the grandmother did not "hit him as much" as she did the other children. The father also feels that he himself paid more attention to Yokichi than to the others.

Yokichi started walking at a later age than his siblings. He was seen very early as a sensitive child, and had some anxieties about getting "dirty." He didn't like, for example, to be at a "dirty table." His father thought that these attitudes were instilled in him by his grandmother. Because he was so late in talking there was some speculation that he had something wrong with his tongue that prevented him from uttering words. His younger brother, seemingly, could talk better than he could. Yokichi, however, though starting late, was an able talker by the time he was five years old. The father recollects that Yokichi continually sucked his fingers and bit his nails as a child, which he still does at times. His father keeps reminding him not to do it. In the mother's account she explicitly denies that he has ever sucked his fingers or bitten his nails. She says, however, that he wet his bed until he was about four years old. She also remarks that he had frequent nightmares—all of a sudden at night he would get up, clap his hands, or hit his head against something. This nighttime behavior lasted until he was in the third grade. His mother notes that when he was small he seldom sought any demonstration of affection from her. She believes that he probably thought she was "too busy" to spare the time for him. She recalls that when his brother was born he showed quite a bit of jealousy.

According to his father, when Yokichi was about two years old he would sometimes bite other children of his own age when he didn't like something or when he became angry at what they were doing. This biting behavior lasted until he was about four. His grandmother used to pinch his mouth or spank him for this, but it seems that his parents did little to punish him for behavior of this kind. When the boy was four or five years old the parents took him to *mushikiri* to receive *moxa* treatments for about a year; this is a traditional medical practice believed to calm down an imaginary bug called a *mushi*, which inhabits a child and makes him uncontrollable.

Mrs. Fukuyama in recalling the past says:

> He was such a wild child that we kept receiving complaints from our neighbors about his wild behavior. He would bite people when angry and would pluck out flowers whenever he saw them. He would eat the food prepared by the neighbors for their favorite cat. I didn't know what to do and I even wished I could dispose of him, giving him away to somebody.

One gets the impression that the parents were ambivalent about disciplining their aggressive boy. They relegated his training and discipline entirely to his grandmother, who apparently enjoyed her role of taking care of the grandchildren, through which she could express both her affection and her own aggressive nature.

Mrs. Fukuyama, probably by way of justifying her negligence in playing the role of mother, emphasizes how busy she was, working with her husband when they were struggling hard to make a decent living. She says:

> All my children grew up like bamboo shoots [the implication is that they didn't need care in their growth]; they never even caught cold. After all, well, our business didn't go well, and being at the bottom in poverty we had to work hard. We had to struggle through our poverty and could not pay attention to our children. We had to leave them to my mother.

Mrs. Fukuyama also admits that her stepmother really loved the eldest son, Yokichi, in spite of his aggressive and wild behavior. She also says that her younger sons were all obedient and not like the eldest son. Yokichi's father would not hit him, but instead would try to reason with him. The material about the grandmother's striking as a mode of punishment comes from the mother, not from the father. His own approach was to say such cautionary things as, "When a boy knows he is right, he should go ahead and fight and not lose," or "When you make mistakes, don't hesitate to apologize immediately."

During his preschool years, Yokuchi remained so small that he and his younger brother were often taken for twins. It was only after the third grade that he made a remarkable spurt in growth and began to show interest in sports. Before attending school he had had no playmates among the neighbors' children and played only within his own house with his own brother. It was during his preschool and early grade school period that the parents were extremely busy and seemingly relatively successful. They would take off only two days a month, a traditional practice. They spent these holidays with their children, going out to buy toys for them.

The subject himself revealed little about his early childhood and refused to talk about it. The earliest period for which he offered any recall was the fourth and fifth grades. He recalls that his father never hit him but was somewhat strict. He wasn't afraid of his father in any way, but he never felt any special tenderness toward him either. He first entered elementary school in April 1954; his grandmother was the one who took him to the entrance ceremony.

When he was in the lower grades his mother would sometimes attend PTA meetings. She felt, however, that the time was used by the teachers to "criticize" the parents, and she discontinued going. The father in explaining why he did not attend PTA meetings said:

> I don't have an education. The only people who attended the meetings were the influential people in the area. I wouldn't have a voice in the meeting, anyway. Of course, maybe I'm biased. And also I was too busy. But perhaps that was my mistake. If I had gone to the meetings and had closer contact with teachers in regard to my son's school records, we could have prevented negative consequences.

Scholastically, Yokichi did well up to the time he was in the fourth grade; he was usually in the top half of his class. He was a popular child and was usually seen as a leader of a group that gathered around him. His friends tended to be pleasantly rather than aggressively dominated by Yokichi; he acted as a protector, quickly rising to the defense if anyone in his group was attacked. His mother states that he always has liked to fight for his friends since the time he was in the lower grades, and he still shows the same inclination. In the fourth grade he had a teacher who understood him well and could bring out his positive qualities. Nevertheless, he was a restive and excitable child and easily distracted, and he did create special problems for his teachers. At the suggestion of his teacher, his parents sent him to a special class to learn the abacus better, and they even sent him for a short period to a brush-writing school. His parents would sometimes help him with his homework, a task never assumed by his grandmother. He himself says, contrary to the parents' impression, that he did his homework at school or didn't do it at all, but that his teacher didn't say anything about it, in effect indulging his unwillingness to conform in this respect. The father would moralize about the virtue of hard work, insisting that everyone has equal brainpower and that it all depends on one's own efforts whether he will do better or worse than others. The father insisted that he study for thirty minutes after coming home from school, but nobody directly supervised or specifically encouraged him in his studies. He was left pretty much to himself. Mr. Fukuyama says:

> Up to the fifth grade he did work hard and did homework well. I thought he would become a son who would meet expectations, but things started to change after that. . . . People used to say that he was a very clever boy. When the time came for me to go out of the house to work, he would go to the entrance hall first and take out my shoes and put them before me on the stepping stones. He even cleaned the shoes for me. When relatives and friends came to the house, our son would go to the entrance and put their footgear neatly in order. He was that way until the third and fourth grades, and then he gradually became brash.

Yokichi became interested in sports in about the third grade, and his sports interests brought him in contact with older children. He took to being away from home in sports activities and sometimes would not come home until about seven in the evening. He remembers with pleasure swimming with his friends. He showed an extroversive personality, became a member of a drama group, and was usually chosen as the leading actor in school plays. His popularity made him something of a school hero. Although he was always considered a rather "naughty" child, it was not until after he entered the fifth grade that his antagonistic behavior developed.

AN ECONOMIC CRISIS IN THE FAMILY

At the end of 1957 Yokichi's father was thrown abruptly into bankruptcy. He had definitely overextended his business, having installed a number of new machines and going into debt for close to a million and a half yen ($5,000). Just at this time, one of the furniture manufacturers to whom he was furnishing materials failed, and the checks he had received from the manufacturer were not honored. In a desperate attempt to keep going, the Fukuyamas borrowed money from private moneylenders at a high interest. The debts quickly increased; the gas and electricity were cut off at their home; and they had no cash for food. Mr. Fukuyama said, "We would buy the cheapest vegetables and boil them in a pot and then dissolve the cheapest crackers in it, making a kind of porridge, and we would all eat it as a meal. This sort of thing lasted for almost three months." This abrupt change in his life is still such a tender area that Yokichi refused even to approach the subject when some questions were asked by the interviewer. The family turned down suggestions that they apply for social welfare assistance. The fact that the teachers at school suggested welfare was considered so shameful that the boy continues to feel the shame. Mr. Fukuyama explains why he did not apply for welfare assistance:

> I did not want my kids to feel further misery by being a burden on society. Yokichi's schoolteacher suggested that we receive aid so that we would not have to pay our children's lunch fee at school, but I did not want them to feel ashamed and be at the mercy of the school [*katami-ga-semai*, literally "to feel one's shoulder to be too narrow"]. We said that even if we had to skip our meals we would pay the lunch fee ourselves. I told this to the teacher and also to my children; I said, otherwise we would be as bad as ragpickers.

Here we see the basically entrepreneurial orientation of this man, who does not want to identify himself, even in his failure, with the ragpickers, whom he considers "dishonorable people." (The ragpickers we interviewed in Arakawa professed many of the same attitudes held by Yokichi's father.)

The continual strained relationship with the grandmother came to a head at this time. There were times when the grandmother complained that Mr. Fukuyama provided less food for her at the table than for the rest of the family, and she was especially jealous when Mr. Fukuyama offered his wife something special to eat. Mrs. Fukuyama remarks herself that she was surprised to see the extent to which her mother could feel jealousy toward her own daughter. Mr. Fukuyama, seemingly oblivious to this situation, would attempt to ignore the grandmother's complaints by saying, "Grandmother's nagging again." In an incident that occurred about six months before the bankruptcy, Mr. Fukuyama had been angered to the point of actually striking the grandmother; he had objected to her insistent advice and had told her abruptly, "I'll strike you if you continue nagging me like that," whereupon, in a challenging manner, she had said, "Go ahead." He then struck her, perhaps to his own surprise.

It was part of the grandmother's character and nature that when bankruptcy struck the house and they had no money for food, she insisted upon going out to find work herself in some form of daily labor. She soon caught cold in the cold weather of the early spring and died, perhaps because she had no resistance in the extreme state of malnutrition to which she had been reduced. Both Mr. and Mrs. Fukuyama recall having no money to buy medicine for her. Mrs. Fukuyama's comment about her own stepmother was that "she seems to have been born to the destiny of a hard life, losing her own parents early, living among strangers, marrying an inept husband, and now in her extreme old age faced with the occupational failure of her son-in-law." Mrs. Fukuyama became embittered and openly hostile toward her husband. She recalls that in front of the urn of ashes and the memorial tablet of her mother she outspokenly told her husband that her only happy moments with him were those in which they worked at the factory together right after marriage; ever since his return from the army, she had had nothing but difficulty in her married life. She cried bitterly and told him that she was no longer able to bear it and that she wanted a divorce because their marriage had resulted in a situation in which they could not even buy medicine for her dying mother. Toshio's elder brother intervened and was instrumental in achieving some sort of overt reconciliation at least. Recalling this unhappy moment in his life, Mr. Fukuyama says, "She [his wife] had had her mother to talk to about her difficulty and sufferings. Now with her mother gone, she thought the whole thing was too much for her to take by herself. But that was the only crisis in our marital life. Generally speaking, our relationship has been peaceful and harmonious."

As a result of his business failure, Mr. Fukuyama added religious faith to his guiding principles of "effort and strong will," which had sustained him until that time. Two years earlier he had joined the Sōka Gakkai at the request of a close relative. The membership had little meaning to him at that time, but when hardly any of their near neighbors deigned to attend the funeral of the grandmother, forty members from his local Sōka Gakkai affiliate appeared. He was very touched, and since that time he has become more interested in religious activities. Mrs. Fukuyama joined him, and at the time of our contact, Mr. Fukuyama was chairman of his local organization. Of the thirty families represented in his group, he reports that a large number are widows and their families.

The Fukuyama family was seriously affected by the business failure and the death of the grandmother. Mr. Fukuyama expressed his deep sense of failure by withdrawing into himself, and it was several months before signs of his resilience became visible. Mrs. Fukuyama seemingly became more detached from her husband, although this impression is difficult to document from their personal statements. The most lasting effect of these events was the change of Yokichi from a demanding, aggressive child into a more thoughtful and less expressive person at home. He would often say, when there was little food, "I'm not hungry," and would refuse to eat.

Shortly before his grandmother's death he had seemed to take an interest in clothes and had become self-conscious about his appearance. His father had continually urged him to associate with "good" people, apparently in an attempt to encourage social climbing to parallel his own grandiose schemes for business and social success. All this crumbled about him. At this time also, Yokichi had a strict new teacher, who afforded him no special indulgence in school and insisted that he obey and tone down so as to fit in better with his class. Yokichi's reaction was almost open rebellion. He organized his friends in a little group around him and would refuse to take part in the lesson. The mother's interpretation of this situation was that "he was more easily noticed than the others because of his size, and it was unfair to see him as the organizer of this activity and blame just him." His father's reaction to the teacher's criticism of Yokichi's behavior was to preach that one must be more serious in school; he attempted little else.

The oldest sister, who is not mentioned much in the parents' discussions, at this time withdrew from her school, about which she had always been serious and dedicated, and started to help her father support the family. She transferred from a day high school to a night school so as not to completely cut off her education. Mr. Fukuyama's remark was, "She is doing exactly what my own father told me to do when I was a child—and I couldn't do it." Working in another individual's small factory, father and daughter would start very early in the morning and would not quit until late in the evening. This caused complaints and embarrassment on the part of the other, young employees, because they did not want to come to work so early and would be ready to quit late in the afternoon. Their complaints were conveyed to Mr. Fukuyama, who decided to try to work again on his own. This little episode points up the difference between his basically ambitious and entrepreneurial orientation and the young workers' attitude of willingness to be merely employees.

Yokichi took to staying out at night to play at sports. The father said that he allowed the son to go out, but didn't know exactly when he began to. The impression throughout is that the father could not replace the grandmother as disciplinarian and was at a loss to know what to do with his aggressive and insistent son.

On the subject of the bankruptcy, one might suspect that Mr. Fukuyama suffered some form of depression or mental illness preceding the financial collapse. Mrs. Fukuyama in her interview says she noticed that for about two years before he went bankrupt, he had already lost some of his spirit for work and wasn't doing very well. She actually had to take over at times to manage the business and deal with the contractors. She immediately interpreted his failure as a punishment for her husband's neglect of religion; although he had joined a new religious group, they didn't devote themselves to it, and so "he went bankrupt as punishment."

Immediately after the bankruptcy, Mrs. Fukuyama started making dolls at home. Her husband, too, helped out. Evidently they were very diligent at this and were making a fairly good income, but they had to pay off their large debt and remained poor. Little by little, the Fukuyamas are paying back their debts. They are now living in a house with one room, which they are renting. They lost their old house to creditors at the time of bankruptcy.

Yokichi's behavior at school had become increasingly antagonistic. His father recalls having been called to school by the teacher because Yokichi and some other boys had openly used obscene words. Yokichi had started going to outdoor amusement places, such as roller-skating rinks at the Kōrakuen amusement center, usually with older boys. One of his associates attacked his teacher with a knife. The father feebly attempted to keep Yokichi from playing with this boy and with the gang of which he was a leader.

When Yokichi entered junior high school, no one from his family attended the formal entrance ceremony. On some days Yokichi was forced to stay home from school to help out on the machines, and he was then allowed to go out and stay out until nine at night. His father said he felt guilty about making his children work, and therefore felt they needed some time to go out in the evening.

Mr. Fukuyama gives the impression that during his financial crisis when he had to work very hard he developed a strong emotional dependence on his eldest son, who was physically strong for his age.

According to Mrs. Fukuyama, Yokichi often stayed away from school for as long as five days, helping his parents at work. His mother thinks that his being away from school caused him to dislike schoolwork; she says, "As a result he came to dislike the school and he found playing more enjoyable." It is curious that Mrs. Fukuyama, pointing out what she apparently thinks are the major reasons for her boy's straying away from his schoolwork, does not convey any sense of regret. At this time Yokichi developed a strong friendship with Haruo, two years older than himself, a boy with real leadership abilities, and evidently Yokichi identified strongly with him. Haruo formed a baseball team and planned trips for the boys. Haruo, after some delinquent behavior of his own, seemed to have steadied down and was helping his father at home with his work. Sometimes Yokichi would help them.

Yokichi eventually became the *banchō* of his intermediate school. He used his leadership capacity to organize some of the tougher boys into a volleyball team, and then they squeezed the less aggressive boys out of participation. It was during this period that Yokichi's activities with other boys became delinquent behavior. He began staying away from home, very often staying at Haruo's house overnight; he was never admonished severely for this by his father. He also, both legitimately and illegitimately, used the excuse of volleyball practice to stay out late at night. His parents at this time started to go to religious meetings together in the evening.

In the autumn of 1961 Yokichi was involved in a car-stealing episode. On that day Yokichi had been helping his father, who had had an argument with him. Yokichi decided that living at home was intolerable, and left. With two of his companions he stole a car. They originally were going to drive to a friend's house with the supposed intention of finding some job so that they could maintain themselves. When the friend wasn't home, Yokichi's two companions suggested that they all go to Osaka together, a distance of about 300 miles from Tokyo. Yokichi disagreed with this idea, left the others, and went over to his friend Haruo's house. Haruo, who seems by this time to have reformed his own delinquent tendencies, persuaded Yokichi to go to the police voluntarily and confess the theft. Yokichi followed Haruo's advice and went to the police, stating that he was constrained into the stealing episode by his two older companions. Two days later these two boys were arrested in Osaka in possession of the car. Yokichi's father's reaction to this episode was one of shock and dismay.

> I had never thought that my son would do such an extraordinary thing. I had always thought that he was a basically timid boy [*ki-ga-chiisai*], although superficially he pretends and tries to appear tough. Accordingly, I had never thought he would do such an audacious [*daisoreta*] thing. I felt so disappointed and disillusioned that I could not even shed tears.

He made Yokichi sit for two hours at home while he gave him a stern but heartfelt lecture; there was no physical punishment administered. Says Mr. Fukuyama:

> When a child does something wrong you cannot beat him or kick him for it; it is wrong. I think it is a matter of parents' attitudes toward the child; I mean it is a matter of love, and I have the conviction that I can handle my child in whichever way I like. He listens to me; he obeys me, anyway.

When his son said he would never do anything like that again, the father believed him and did not do anything further about the matter.

Contrary to Yokichi's own subjective impressions, in their interviews the parents do not indicate that there was a great deal of tension with Yokichi at this time. However, he found it impossible to relate to his parents. A physical education teacher at the school took an interest in Yokichi, who was doing very well in his sports activities. The teacher had lost his wife, and he suggested that Yokichi come and live with him. Yokichi stayed at the teacher's home for about a month and then returned home; he had found that he got his way much more in his own home than in that of a stranger.

In January 1962 Yokichi was picked up by the police for threatening one of his school companions and injuring him in a brawl on the street at night. Earlier, the victim's mother had given Yokichi and another companion some money so that they would stop bothering her son. At the time of the interview Yokichi apparently was still hitting and intimidating other boys at school, but the teachers were unable to find out when and how these episodes occurred. Part of this behavior seems to have been related to Yokichi's extreme sensitivity to what he considered a rejection. When another boy who had followed his leadership in the past refused to go along with him, his immediate reaction was to retaliate physically, to intimidate the boy.

In assessing the exercise of discipline and supervision in this family, we concluded that the Fukuyamas provide a good example of parental induction (see chapter 4). The father seems to have lost much of his own externally assertive qualities, outside of those he has focused on hard work, but he takes considerable pleasure in the masculine acting out of his son. The father, as we will suggest from the projectives, has not been able to feel secure with any masculine concept of himself. As a consequence he has pushed his son to become more independent and aggressive. In fact, at one point in the father's interview it was evident that he became angry when Yokichi exhibited any passiveness. He described his son in one such instance in a very disapproving way, as being timid, easily led by others into trouble, and lacking a strong will. The father's ambivalence is expressed in his language. For example, he said in Japanese, "*Yakko-san wa tenko desu-yo*," a difficult remark to put into English, perhaps best translated by a vulgar phrase such as "That bastard always gets what he wants," said with grudging approval, a curious thing for a father to say about a son. The father seems almost to admire his son for being able to push his way through—a quality the father may feel is lacking in himself. While attempting to be "strict," Mr. Fukuyama actually allows his son to get his own way. The father's discipline was rated as "lax or compliant" rather than "strict."

The following statements made by Mr. Fukuyama in various parts of his interview will further testify that he has problems in assuming the role of disciplinarian. Answering the question "What do you do when your son does wrong?" he said, "Well, after all, generally, usually . . . to find out the cause, to see what the cause was . . . I ask him why he did it . . . and tell him to think whether what he did was right or wrong. . . . I tell him to think hard. . . . There is no use of hitting him or anything of that kind. I don't believe that punishment has any effect." In another part of his interview he says, "In our home, as I'm rigid and strict [*kochi kochi*], it is okay that my wife is lenient [*amae*]. It would not be so good if both husband and wife were *kochi kochi* and *gami gami* [nagging]." Describing his delinquent son, he says:

> He is obedient . . . well, what shall I say . . . his will is weak and he is easily provoked. He is timid and basically shy. Although he may look very tough like a member of a gangster group, he is actually very timid and gentle. No need to be particularly fearful about him. I see no problem of raising him. I had no problem in raising him. No matter what he does, he obeys me eventually. [Somewhat contradicting himself, he says] I did not mean to be noninterfering. I wished to treat my son as I was treated by my own father. However, I was said to be old-fashioned [*atama-ga-furui*, meaning "thinking is old"], so after that I thought I might be wrong and I gave my son too much freedom, which I think was a mistake.

There is some discrepancy between the statements of husband and wife about whether they agree or disagree in their opinions on raising children. Mr. Fukuyama clearly indicates that he and his wife frequently disagree in their attitudes toward children. He says, "My wife says I should be more strict, as I am a man." This certainly contradicts Mr. Fukuyama's own previous statement that he is very strict and that his wife is lenient with their children.

> But as far as I'm concerned, times have changed and solving the problem by talking is much better than being simply strict. My wife, however, seems to feel impatient with my attitude. And yet, my wife, being a woman, cannot treat her children roughly. My wife could not possibly handle our kid. I'm not indifferent nor do I let him do what he likes, but I believe in solving problems by talking. My wife seems to feel impatient, but after all, my opinion goes. I am the man of the family [laughs].

Mrs. Fukuyama says there are no discrepancies or conflicts in opinion. She says, "We never differ from each other in anything. We are alike, even in regard to our tastes and hobbies."

The Fukuyama family apparently maintains a certain amount of group cohesiveness, although one feels that Mrs. Fukuyama has long since lost any deep affectional ties to her husband.

SOME PATTERNS IN MARITAL INTERACTION OF THE FUKUYAMAS

An unsatisfactory interaction pattern between husband and wife is evident in the Fukuyama family. Mr. Fukuyama has a basic sense of inadequacy about his masculinity and tries to maintain his feeling that he has authority in his family by distorting his percepts of reality and intellectualizing his ambivalent attitudes. Mrs. Fukuyama is basically self-assertive, strong-willed, and the center of the family, although she may not like to admit it. Commenting on his wife, Mr. Fukuyama says:

> The best points of my wife are her patience and persistence [*nintai-zuyoi*]. She is quite a woman [*erai*]. She stands up against hardship. I tend to feel beaten when things go wrong. But she is different. She is strong. I have many times been encouraged and supported by my wife.

After making this frankly positive comment on his wife and admitting his basic dependence upon her, Mr. Fukuyama cannot answer another question, "What aspects of her personality or character do you like the best?" He simply says, "Well," and no answer comes from him. The interviewer asked, "What are your wife's shortcomings or weak points?" He answered "I don't know. Everything about her is good [laughs]." The interviewer asked further, "What do you dislike about your wife the most?" He answered,

> Well, it is probably because we have too many kids. It may not be her own fault. . . . Well, what shall I say? My wife lacks feminine gentleness [*onna-rashii-yasashisa*]. She does not keep the home neat, although there is certainly not much of a room to keep neat. If I were a woman I would certainly clean up the room and keep it neat, but as I am a man, after all . . . [laughs].

In Japan the ability to keep a home neat, tidy, and clean is often a symbol of femininity, and if a woman fails in this role, the husband often complains that she lacks a womanly gentleness. When asked if he would marry his wife if he were to live his life once again, the answer was positive:

> I would marry my wife again because I need . . . well, I need a strong-willed person to run a business. Basically, I am not the type to run a business. . . . For me, a steady monotonous job like that of a clerk is more suitable. And yet, at the same time, I do not like to be employed by others. Therefore, I need someone who pulls and pushes me in running my own business.

Mrs. Fukuyama says that her husband is a home-loving type (*katei-teki*) and very loving to his children (*ko-bonnō*). She thinks that the children like their father more than they like her. "He tries to do as much as possible whenever he does anything for his children, and they like their father better, I suppose. Well, I certainly take care of them, but at the same time I tend to be nagging when they do something wrong [laughs]." She said that her husband is very serious toward life and work. She also says he is short-tempered. "I shouldn't blame him, because I do not take care of him sufficiently. Probably that's why. But anyway, when he feels frustrated or irritated, he sometimes throws a bottle on the floor and breaks it. I should take care of him better, I know."

Unlike some of the other wives, Mrs. Fukuyama is not always very frank about admitting that she is the center of the family.

> We agree on most things but not like in many other families, where the wife feels that she is one step down. Ours is more natural. Previously I often repeated my own opinion and had it accepted. But recently I think it is wrong, and therefore I no longer do such a thing. There are people who say that it is unfortunate to be born as a woman, but I have never thought that I was unfortunate to have been born a woman. I am basically satisfied with being a woman. The only time when I felt unhappy about my life was when my husband was too good-natured a man, but this no longer happens.
>
> My father used to be very dependent upon my mother, who was a strong woman. I used to think that as my husband was not like my father I would not be forced into the position that was occupied by my mother, but things do not seem to have turned out as I had hoped. As we become older my husband has become increasingly more timid, and after all I have become the center of our household. I have handled a big amount of money like ¥50,000 or ¥10,000 in business transactions; my husband is not self-assertive and strong enough. People take advantage of him, and after all I find myself taking his place in these matters. . . . Generation after generation the woman was always stronger than the man in my family lineage. It is a bad thing basically, though.

Her attitude toward her husband's possible extramarital sexual behavior is a typical traditional attitude.

> Well, occasionally I tell him that I know I do not take care of him as much as I should. Well, I tell him that for the children's sake he should not cause trouble. Therefore, if he wants to play he should play by spending money. As long as he can solve the problem by money, I don't care how much he plays around. But my husband says it is too ridiculous for him to think of it. As long as he plays with commercial women [*shobai-onna*, prostitutes], he can solve the problem by money, not like a mistress but more casual relationships that you pay for. And I say I don't care as long as he limits himself to this kind of relationship. After all he is a man, and I know that I'm not taking care of him as much as I should. It is possibly not my fault [laughs], but after all when my husband was still young he

had to struggle with a failing business and he was preoccupied with his work and never had a chance to play. Maybe this was a good side of our life [laughs].

PROJECTIVE TEST RESULTS: MR. FUKUYAMA

The Rorschach Test

Mr. Fukuyama's Rorschach is characterized by his continual need to defend himself by means of intellectualization. What is suggested overall is an obsessive-compulsive, paranoid-like defensive personality.

Rorschach Protocol

I. Rejection (Arej).

II. (80″) 1. *Looks like the world situation.* The mediocre dirt representing opportunism; it's a reflection of poor social conditions that can't become completely black. The symbolization of neutrality of thought. It looked that way, as there are reddish spots in the black parts. [W CSym (Symb) (Hh) (Fab Symb) Path R]

2. *Looks like clowns.* Two clowns dancing as a joke. [W M+ H P (Prec)]

III. (70″) 3. *Can I see a part of this? The chest area of a human body.* The two kidneys are there. [D F− Anat (Bf)]

IV. (160″) 4. *The walls of a Western-style room.* From the impression of the whole thing, a fuzzy wall. [D TF− Hd (Misc)]

V. (20″) 5. *A butterfly.* The form looks like a butterfly. [He turns the card around and also looks on the back side.] [W F+ A P (Neut)]

VI. (30″) 6. *A fur.* A fur skin of a kangaroo. It must have such a form, and such a touch, fluffy. [W TF+ (Aobs) P (Ps, Mpret)]

VII. Rejection (Arej).

VIII. (60″) 7. *Invasion.* The red parts reveal a fierce animal like leopards. It is about to invade the blue peaceful land. [W FM, CSym+ A P (Fab Elab) (HH) Path R]

IX. (60″) 8. *Volcanic belt in the Earth.* The state of the flame which is erupting through the weak portion of the earth (green part). [W mF, CF− Nat Fi (Hhat)]

9. *The disturbance of peace.* The symbolization of the activity of red evil hitting the weak points of green peaceful land, no matter when or where. [W M CSym (Symb) (Athr HH) (Fab Symb) Path R]

X. (70″) 10. *The customs of the world; union (solidarity).* Because there are various forms and colors. I imagine various countries, their languages, dresses. Because whole things integrated. The customs of the world unite in one. Various shapes and colors are as beautiful as a map. [W CSym (Symb) Path R (Misc)]

Card-by-Card Sequential Analysis and Comments

Mr. Fukuyama totally rejects Card I, an unusual occurrence in Rorschach testing, indicating severe blocking and guardedness. To Card II, after a minute and twenty seconds, he responds, "Looks like the world situation." The red part for him is the "mediocre dirt representing opportunism," and the black symbolizes "poor social conditions." This type of grandiose symbolism is the extreme of the symbolizing tendency found periodically in Japanese records. Intellectually pretentious, it is usually given by individuals who are defending themselves against a feeling of total inadequacy by paranoid grandiosity. Mr. Fukuyama follows this response by finding on the same card two clowns "dancing as a joke." This is the only human-movement response in the entire record. He is not able to see the more commonly seen human figures on Card III, and he totally rejects Card VII, which also usually evokes human percepts. This lack of human movement is related to his poor development of empathic capacities to feel "into" others. (There is significantly less "M," or movement, in the records of fathers of delinquents than in those of fathers of nondelinquents.) As to the content of the human precept, clowns are innocuous, nonaggressive human beings. They can, however, be interpreted as indirectly attacking human seriousness and authority.

On Card III, rather than seeing ordinary humans, Mr. Fukuyama gives an anatomical response, seeing the red areas as kidneys. An anatomical response suggests the turning in of hostility on the self. Card IV evokes a response of poor form quality. He sees a textural quality in the blot, but can make of it only the walls of a Western-style room. This type of response deepens the impression that Mr. Fukuyama is groping with an almost total sense of his own inadequacy. He must feel himself a failure even in his attempts to give pretentious, compensatory responses. His continual intellectualization is in itself not a very satisfying defense. One can infer that he must passively withdraw from all danger of expressing himself aggressively. Such withdrawal would explain why his wife now sees him as totally incapable of the ordinary self-assertion necessary to carry on the business.

On Card V he perceives a simple butterfly, one of the most popular responses to the Rorschach. He sees Card VI as a fur, again a common perception; but again we get the touch of pretentiousness. It is not the fur of a usual animal; rather, he sees it as the fur of a kangaroo. His attention to the textural quality of the response implies that he has a need for receptive passivity. Yet he cannot handle the highly feminine, texturally soft next card, VII. He rejects this card. For Card VIII, in response to the warm colors, Mr. Fukuyama produces a type of symbolism that is characteristic of paranoid conditions: he sees the card as an invasion; the red parts represent fierce animals like leopards, which are about to invade a peaceful, blue land. The color symbolism here is direct, the red representing aggressive attacking qualities and the blue being placid and peaceful in nature.

In Card IX the color symbolism refers to a felt danger of explosions from within. He perceives a volcano with the flame erupting through the weak portions of the earth, the green parts. The color symbolism is in direct "hot" and "cold" colors. In his second response the colors represent a disturbance of the peace, with red as an evil attacking the weak points of the green, peaceful land. He cannot make use of any concrete form in giving his color responses. He resorts to grandiose abstractions with no attention to form. His last response, to Card X, ends on a note of union or solidarity, a hope for the coming together of the customs of the world, languages, and dress, and somehow integrating the world into a happy totality—a fantasy in which hostility disappears under the banner of human solidarity, a cosmic solution to a subjective inner turmoil.

In sum, Mr. Fukuyama's record shows a severe incapacity to maintain himself within normal channels of thought. In a clinical setting, there would be no hesitancy in judging the paranoid nature of his defensive structure. Yet the fact is that he is maintaining himself despite economic failure in some socially acceptable manner in family and society. He can allocate sufficient energy to continue his preoccupation with work; in fact, one can infer that he sorely needs his daily work activities as a stabilizing force. Throughout, he handled the cards very carefully, turning them about, looking for clues to what was expected on his part, but there was evidence that he considered his performance another failure on his part.

Those who work only in clinical practice are sometimes dismayed by the fact that very disturbed records are periodically found in individuals who present no outward clinical symptoms. In our experience this does not invalidate the potential meaning of tests such as the Rorschach, but shows that not all individuals with poorly integrated personality structure manifest evidence of a breakdown. In this instance we do not know whether Mr. Fukuyama has ever displayed overt psychotic symptoms. His wife's report that he seemed to be "disturbed" for two years before the final bankruptcy would indicate that he may not have been able to keep himself going at his usual hardworking pace for reasons of internal disruption.

Another possible source of integration for Mr. Fukuyama is that in sheer pervasiveness of his passive defense he has somehow concerned himself, on a moralizing level, with what one should do positively in human relationships. The benign stance he takes perhaps spares him from the type of paranoid ideation which would see the world full of plots against him. He takes an "above-the-battle" view, from which he can witness the foibles of human beings without feeling that he is too vulnerable or too involved. His escape into intellectual generalizations and moralism is a refuge from immediate demands or pressures of circumstances. His present recourse to religion would act similarly as socially integrative behavior.

This record indicates the need in social psychiatry to differentiate between *social adaptation* and *internal adjustment*. The behavioral materials suggest a continuing attempt at family life on the part of Mr. Fukuyama. He is no social problem. He is *adaptive*, but his personality structure employs the type of psychological defenses that must be considered internally maladjustive when measured in terms of human maturational capacities.

TAT Responses

His TAT material substantiates the strong intellectualizing defenses used by Mr. Fukuyama. There is throughout an overblown and inappropriate quality to his stories. At times, the words he uses, which are difficult to convey in English translation, are inappropriate and pretentious in Japanese. All his stories are in one way or another an ideological statement of values, morality plays in which Japanese ethics are portrayed in action—for example, in success stories about idealized independent achievement. Another theme is the generation gap in modern society. It is not that these stories are unusual for Japanese, but the verbiage in which Mr. Fukuyama's stores are expressed is more grandiose. There is an unsure quality in his use of language. Rather than making declarative statements, he tends to use circumlocutions ending with a question. The test protocol suffers some loss of spontaneity because it was necessary for the interviewer to ask questions in order to keep the flow of the story going. The interviewer seems too intrusive at times, but perhaps the intrusion was necessary to elicit material from this subject. In our judgment, he should have been permitted time to come back to the point of his story spontaneously, if indeed he could. The points of interruption by the tester are marked by parenthetical question marks.

> Are these about elementary school pupils? Perhaps meditating on his "design" and structure of a musical score, well, hoping to be another Beethoven-like genius in the future. (?) His study. (?) He is perhaps thinking of something about a melody. (?) After the surroundings have become quiet . . . supposing he is a sixth-grade pupil, he is already determined to make music his future profession. (?) Since he works with such interest on music until late at night, he must have ability. His efforts will bring him success.

In this first story, there is an overblown idea that the boy is hoping to become a genius like Beethoven or some other musician of that rank. The wording suggests a flippancy that cannot be adequately translated into English. It is as if he belittles Beethoven's attainments, casting doubt on the ability of the child to accomplish anything. Again, Mr. Fukuyama's language indicates a grandiose, distanced approach to problems.

J2. This is a pastoral scene. In the morning. Everybody is on the way to his place of work. (?) They are the mother, the father, and their daughter. Is the girl going out? To work? The mother looks as if she came to see the father and the daughter off, but—he to the farm and she to work. (?) She is about to go out, but her face shows a funny expression, doesn't it? It's not the happy face of someone departing for work. She seems to have some trouble with her mother. (?) She must be a girl who is in a city working. Returning home the night before, she quarreled with her mother. Her father goes out to the farm with her mother, who doesn't seem to feel very happy about her daughter [grins]. (?) Though she is independent, she is not married yet, I think. She returned home in order to talk about that or for something else, but it became a cause of trouble between her and her mother. (?) The father is not concerned about it, but maybe he knows. (?) I imagine there is quite a difference between the girl who once lived in a city and those living in such a small village so far as progress in life is concerned. From their way of using a horse, we can tell they are rather behind the times. Perhaps the difference is the sense of feeling between the young and old. This is quite common in a village even today. From the point of view of the mother, it is ideal to have the girl help in farming work or have her live in the village and marry some man whom the parents will recommend. But the daughter won't like that. In some way the mother and the daughter are against each other.

In his second story Mr. Fukuyama describes difficulty arising between the mother and the daughter, some quarrel about the daughter's attempts at independence. The daughter does not wish to continue to work on the farm, but the mother wishes to have her daughter married off to someone the parents will recommend. This story is told in a very roundabout fashion. Although the plot itself is fairly common, the manner of telling it is not. Also, the story is not resolved in any way. We do not see beyond the immediate situation of dispute and contention between mother and daughter.

There is some ambivalence in Mr. Fukuyama concerning the generation gap that he depicts. He gets a feeling that perhaps intellectually he is on the side of the independent daughter. Nevertheless, the tone and methods of expression show a kind of ambiguity, so that he does not seem to be completely resolved in his own mind. The father is more or less left out of the picture. Mr. Fukuyama is content to indicate the woman's authority as the crucial issue here. The father does not seem to take sides, but is a neutral force in the story. Mr. Fukuyama doesn't specifically eliminate the father by ignoring him, but he specifically denies that there could be any conflict with the father in the story. One gains the impression, therefore, that in his own family situation he would tend to withdraw from situations of conflict.

J3. I don't think this is something Japanese, but . . . (?) This is a woman factory worker, perhaps falling in love with another fellow worker. She lost out and is sad. She had such a happy feeling a moment ago, but

> now things have changed, making a complete about-face. Isn't this the saddest moment for a woman, so to speak? (?) This woman worker should collect herself to try once more in order to build toward her happy future, since she is still young. This moment is the most important for both a girl and a man, though this man [in the story] has already found his mate. Especially in this case it's most important. The people around her must encourage her, for she is on the border between happiness and unhappiness. In a case like this, those around the girl ought to treat her warmly and kindly so as to help rid her of her trouble.

This story is an exhortative one in which the people around are advised to help a girl who has suffered a lost love. Here Mr. Fukuyama shows sympathy for someone else in trouble, and he shows an easy identification with a female figure, disregarding the male as someone who can solve his problems readily, whereas the woman is at a disadvantage. One can speculate as to how much sympathy he expected from others at the time of his own failure. It is all right to help women, but men are expected to take care of themselves—a thought that may have entered into his experience in his own financial bankruptcy.

> J6. This is also the same one as before. A quarrel between an old-fashioned mother with a feudalistic mind and her son of a new era. The old woman is perhaps dividing her property. The son lives in a city and she . . . [changes story]. It must be a marriage problem for the young, as is often true today. (?) There is something about a love affair. In this case he brought home a girl from his city and she is waiting outside the entrance. And the old woman is objecting to it. (?) I think they have lived together by then. He wanted to get the mother's consent for the marriage and came with the girl, but the mother is angry with no will to consent. As he has just stepped in the hall, he is still wearing his raincoat. (?) No matter how stubborn she was, she would realize the change of time into the new life and ideas. So he thought, and he returned with the certainty that she would listen to him explain his plan. Coming to the house, however, he is surprised and annoyed how different her ideas are from theirs. Take, for instance, our way of thinking and that of our children. Since democracy took over the country, even our way of thinking has become old. When my children complain, saying, "Your way of thinking is terribly old," I cannot help worrying once in a while. Am I really old in my thinking? Maybe so.

This story is another description of the conflict between the generations. Mr. Fukuyama portrays the difference in attitude between the younger generation and the older one. Although he castigates the old woman for being rigid and unchanging, he also sees the youth as somewhat hasty and precipitous.

In the course of conversation during the testing he reveals a little more of his grandiosity. He mentions that he "talks easily to people in my own company." He spontaneously characterizes his own very small operation as a "company," which would make him a company head, or *shachō*, a prestigious role in today's Japan. This side conversation preceded his telling the following story about Card 7:

> J7. This is a scene of a successful businessman telling his son how he has striven to build up his success. This son will not be working in the company that his father founded and made successful. The father tells about enduring twenty years and more of hard times. His son is going to work in another company. (?) If he remains near his parents, he will knowingly or unknowingly depend on his father. He has grown to be a man under his father and now will go to another company for further character training. When his personality is well trained and more mature, his father will have him work in his own company. (?) The son will become a man as great as his father, for he is as serious as can be. He will listen to his father and go to another company and take his father's place in twenty years.

This is the story that Mr. Fukuyama selected as his favorite. It is the one with which he identified the most. The story is of a successful businessman who sends his son out to be tempered by the world. The son comes back and takes over, succeeding the father. This is the ideal Japanese father-son relationship and the ideal of occupational success. It is the ideal self-image of Mr. Fukuyama: One struggles and endures and succeeds, and the underlying dependent needs are gratified when an adequate heir takes over and carries on one's work. The hope is that one can retire in time to enjoy life. Whereas the American ideal is to achieve and succeed and get to the top, the Japanese ideal is to get to the top and then have someone else take over so that one can enjoy both success and leisure. The successful man is capable of enjoying the passive dependent relationship in which things are taken care of for him. For those who like to be dominant, retirement is, in a sense, pro forma. One can continue to manipulate from behind the scenes, making sure that one's wishes are carried out.

Another cultural theme that comes out of this story is the realization that if a son works too closely with a father he is likely to become too dependent, or tensions may arise that the son cannot resolve. That is, if the son is to be successful, he has to be independent. This can result in a dilemma. If the succession is direct, the son very often is incapable of standing on his own feet and mustering enough independence in relation to his father, of taking initiative. The story expresses an insightful realization that one must avoid such problems; many Japanese are conscious of the problems of direct succession in a business. It is therefore a tradition in Japan for sons of wealthy merchants to be sent outside their own father's company for a period during their apprenticeship, to learn to be independent of the father, (see chapter 6). Going away from the father's organization also permits the son more contact with the ordinary workers, which would not be possible where an individual is known as the son of the boss. Wealthy merchants often exchange sons, suggesting to each other that they should not be given special treatment but should learn the hard way. This arrangement strikes a familiar chord in American business circles. We can see here, reflected in Mr. Fukuyama's TAT, that he has been striving all his life to become a company president. That is, he has been striving, by buying several machines, to have an enterprise that he can pass on to his children. His hope is to assume the role of the sage who imparts knowledge and wisdom to others. This fantasy covers the underlying deep sense of personal failure with which he has been struggling.

> J8. This is the dream of the boy. The father whom he trusts most is about to be persecuted [*hakugai*] by someone in his dream. So the boy will attack the persecutor with his rifle. The moment his father is to be stabbed, bang! and he is awakened from his sleep. (?) The boy does not know the world of grown-ups. He doesn't know his father nor does he know the relationship of his father to his friends, nor what the circumstances are. Only with the single thought that this is his trusted father, he stands on the side of his father unconsciously, without thinking, and challenges the persecutor. (?) No matter what kind of man his father is, isn't he the only irreplaceable father to this boy? From the fact that such accidents occur, his father is quick-tempered and can possibly be hated by some people. Even though such a serious affair never occurs, he might have quarreled once before this boy; now he sees such a dream. Such a trifling quarrel of his father stayed in his mind and comes out in his dreams. When he wakes up to the sound of the gun, he finds his father beside him and is very glad.

Mr. Fukuyama tells an exceptional story for Card 8. Whereas it is not uncommon for subjects to describe an accidental shooting of a father by his son, most uncommon is a fantasy in which the boy shoots the persecutor of his father. His use of the word "persecutor" has a somewhat paranoid quality to it; however, as the story progresses, the persecution is seen to be perhaps justified by the father's behavior in the adult world, of which the son is unaware. This story is a different version of the preceding story of a father's retirement and the son's taking over the business. In this story the father shows dependence on the son's love as a source of protection. Mr. Fukuyama is dependent on his son's aggressive qualities. This attitude comes out during the interview material as well. There is some ambivalence in Mr. Fukuyama concerning his son's delinquency. On some levels he enjoys his son's capacity for aggressive behavior. In a curious way, he wants to find himself in a passive relationship to his own son. He idealizes such a relationship as showing that the son loves the father and wants to be close to him. The son thus becomes the protector of a father who sees himself as persecuted and wronged by society, a most peculiar relationship between father and son, with latent homosexuality deeply buried.

> J9. This is a common case in the city. This older brother used to feel loving toward his sisters, but following the trend of the times, he joined some "in" group like the *gurentai* or hooligans. He thinks much of his sisters on the one hand, and on the other he is rebelling against something. Those are his sisters and this is his mother. Though he used

> to be their good brother, he committed some crime and a summons has been sent to him from the police. After he committed a crime and returned home, he still acts like a good brother. When a policeman shows him a summons, he knows what it is for and goes out without argument. His sisters say, "Brother, please be sure to redeem yourself from sin and return straight home"; they have tragic faces as they see him off, as you see. This is a scene in *shitamachi* Tokyo, I think. (?) His father doesn't seem to be living. (Then are there four of them in the family?) Yes, as there is no living father in this family, this boy thinks much of his family. So he expiates the crime he committed by chance, and his family will become happy enough to be laughing merrily again in some months. (?) It must be one of those things. A person of his age can be affected by the fact that his father is dead; having his own way at home, he probably comes to have a dual personality, because there is no nagging father at home. A son among women cannot help being the one man or boss. Yet this man thinks much of his sisters and parent. He doesn't have a bad nature, but acted badly accidentally.

From the response to this card one can see that Mr. Fukuyama is describing the personality of his own boy as he sees him. He views his delinquent behavior as neither serious nor indicative of a "bad" personality, but as due to circumstances. He seems to excuse his son's behavior as inadvertent rather than internally motivated. There are other peculiar features to this story. He states that since there is no father in the family, this boy can't help being boss. By identifying with his son, Mr. Fukuyama may be expressing his feelings about his own dead father and a wish that he could have been the boss of his own family at home without competition. The paternalistic role still played by his elder brother is given no expression in these stories. The Japanese concept of expiation and reform carries the story to a happy end.

> J11. A high school boy, this boy is. [Long silence] It is hard to understand how . . . [long silence] I don't understand what the situation is. The woman is not dressed for going out, I suppose. (?) A mother and her son. The mother is wearing long undergarments. This home seems also a fatherless home. They don't seem to be in trouble financially, though. Someone connected with the dead father . . . must be his immediate boss at his company. She is forced to do something by this boss, and that boy peeps. How shall I explain? What is called "power" must come as a fairly big spiritual blow to this boy's feelings. (?) The man is the immediate boss of the dead father. He used to be the best friend of the boy's dead father and visited the father's house as intimately as if it were his own. And now he gets into a shameful relation with the boy's mother and the boy witnesses it. (?) She is not the kind to take such initiative by herself, but in fact some financial aid was given by the company when the father died, and she is under an obligation to this person.
>
> I wonder how she feels in such a situation. Naturally, she shouldn't take any initiative in this deed, but she seems to be obeying the man's lead, though in low spirits. It seems to be in the evening when the boy

> returned from playing baseball or something. As she did not think he would return yet, she has left the sliding doors open, which are usually kept closed. She felt at ease, believing that the boy would not come home yet. (?) He will put up resistance against this "power" first of all. The boy is in the first or second grade of junior high school. (?) So before long he will blame his mother for what she does. So she realizes that she has submitted to "power" and moves away from here to live in a smaller house, more humbly, where she can rest mentally, and where it is good for the child's study. She will live in the world for themselves only, free from vexation, with positive expectations about the boy's future, dedicating herself to him.

It is difficult to indicate in the translation the type of hesitant failure of words that occurs in this story. Some long pauses occur in the beginning. Mr. Fukuyama is struck by the sexual implications of the scene. He finally pulls together an interesting story of a mother's sexual activities with her husband's former superior. Throughout the story he uses the word *kenryoku*, meaning "power" or "authority," authoritative power, in a rather peculiar way: the boy is seen to experience "power" as an improper use of force on a financially defenseless woman. The mother, however, is able to pull herself free and, by living more humbly, to devote herself to her son's future. There may be an undercurrent of identification with the woman who must submit herself to outside power, suggestive of an unconscious homosexual orientation in this man. The vision in this story of a passive sexual subjection may be in line with an undercurrent of a passive homosexual concept of taking in power or being dependent on masculine power. Mr. Fukuyama's Rorschach is much more definite in this respect, where his symbolic responses describe the invasion of evil forces.

In his TAT he is much more consciously in control, so the stories he creates never lose coherence or plausibility. In his interview material he periodically expressed concern with the evil, attacking nature of the Socialist party. He views Sōka Gakkai as a counterforce to prevent the socialists from taking over. In his concern with political power, he expresses a personalized, symbolic fear of attack. One feels that this man has had grave difficulty in identifying with masculine power directly and sees himself constantly at a disadvantage, facing attack from others. In defending himself in terms of his masculine self-image, he must be on guard to protect himself from the penetration of evil forces that are encroaching on him.

> J13. A sister and a brother [silence]. It must be that the older sister is engaged in some "gay trade," such as work at a cabaret, and the brother works during the day and goes to the university in the evening. When he returns from school, for some reason . . . his sister . . . The sister works and gives him money for his tuition to send him to school. . . . Living together in an apartment is not easy for them, and the sister has sold herself to some man in secret so as to be helped financially by the man. She had finished with one "patron" for some reason and has

> gotten herself another patron, which leads to a triangle love affair. As a result she has been killed here. The brother, who did not know the facts till now, returned home just then and realized that his sister has sent him to school by sacrificing her own person; for the first time now he laments, crying. He only knew she worked as a hostess at a cabaret. People say those hostesses usually earn fifty or sixty thousand yen a month, but actually they cannot earn that much, but about thirty thousand at best. So this family could not live on thirty thousand yen, and the sister sacrificed herself for her desire to make her brother a respectable man in society. (?) Perhaps coming from the country this boy had a strong hope to succeed. The brother will probably study hard in order to be a great man so as to follow his dead sister's will.

We have here another fantasy of a woman who submits herself sexually for the benefit, in this case, of a brother. It is rare to have a brother-sister story given for this card, here with a directly sexualized sister who is sacrificing her own person for the benefit of her brother's education. The theme of self-sacrifice is not unusual, and it is not uncommon for a young girl to prostitute herself, especially in the northeastern regions of Japan. So it is not the story itself that is unusual in the Japanese context, but Mr. Fukuyama's perseverance in this theme, having already given a plot of sexual submission to Card 11. Such plots sometimes appear in Japanese films, the result usually being the downfall of the unsuspecting brother, who goes bad after he finds out what his sister has done. There is an unusual interjection in this story of a triangular love affair, in which the sister is killed by one of her lovers. The male figure of this story and of the previous one is an innocent bystander, a voyeuristic witness of the sexuality of a mother in the one case and of an elder sister in the other.

> J18. This is a gloomy home. The mother has placed all her hope in her only daughter and tried hard until her old age. Nevertheless, the daughter becomes depraved. This will result in a parent and child suicide. She used to be very good before reaching this age. Once she had attained adolescence, however, she went wrong against her mother's wishes and was cast off by her lover. And now she has returned to her parent, on whom she has to depend in the end. I'm afraid too much fondness can cause a child to go wrong. (?) For her it is the end of all expectation. Her daughter who has been her only hope is degrading herself, and she will perhaps kill her daughter and herself.

This card also evokes a situation of sexual depravity, and it ends in a double suicide. The mother has been disappointed in her daughter, who has had a sexual affair that has ended badly. The story of a double suicide from this card is significantly frequent in our deliquent records, in contrast to the nondelinquent records. Stories reflecting the feeling of responsibility of the mother for the daughter's proper behavior are not uncommon in Japanese material.

> J22. On Sunday the three members of the family are going out for amusement, but the father and mother become antagonistic toward each

> other and the poor child becomes involved. The result is that the father goes on to have some fun by himself, and the bewildered mother finds some amusement with her child to calm herself down and then returns home. (?) Well, their feelings are . . . The father works outside and sees and hears a lot, but the mother stays home. So the direction the wife wants to go and the direction the husband wants to go are different, though the child is agreeable to going any place. So I imagine this occurs because of the difference of the parents' opinions as to where to go. Later on, when they all return home, there will be another quarrel. Not so good. Anyway, such a situation happens easily in most families, doesn't it?

In this card he paints a picture of a basic disharmony between parents which results in an outright quarrel. He does not resolve the issue by seeing any establishment of understanding between the parents, but pictures chronic tension between the husband and wife. The identification, again, is more with the woman in the story than with the man. The child is a passive bystander.

> J27. A senior high school student. This boy doesn't make good grades at school, and a girl student in his class hopes to help him get grades at least as good as the middle place in the class of students. So she caught him when he had just come out of a coffee shop today, and she persuades him to study and do well. They are in the same class. Just a friendship. (?) Well, the one talking may be taking a leadership position among girls, and seems to be well trusted by her classmates. While she speaks, perhaps the others refrain from making a fuss. She is in the same group, I think. (?) More here, I suppose. (?) She is, after all, a leader-like person and makes good grades. So he listens. To a boy he would say, "Shut up. What are you talking about? Let's go in here!" With a girl, however, he seems to become serious. Without waiting for the time to come, this boy will be inspired to do well at school. He is timid by nature, I suppose.

In this story, Mr. Fukuyama has the man deferring to the leadership of the woman and changing his behavior to conform to her wishes. The woman is seen as a capable protagonist here, and again the male figure in the story is depicted as passive in relating to a woman.

In sum, Mr. Fukuyama sees many of the stories from the standpoint of a passive witness. One has the impression of a willingness to be dependent on other figures, be they an assertive woman or a successful son. He also has some passive sexual fantasies in which the source of sexual aggression is outside, from some figure who is not depicted in the story. The figures in the stories themselves remain passive witnesses to the encroachment of outsiders. In the one story, to Card 11, he symbolically names this outside source of sexuality as a "power." We have a picture of a man who has stabilized himself in a passive, detached role as a witness to life. Nevertheless, we also note paranoid structuring with latent homosexual implications appearing on the periphery of his stories.

PROJECTIVE TEST RESULTS: MRS. FUKUYAMA

The Rorschach Test

Mrs. Fukuyama's Rorschach record shows her to be a person of high average to superior intelligence, with an intact ego, generally functioning adequately from a psychological standpoint. She reacts with egocentric affective spontaneity in her social relationships. She has some underlying masochistic hysteroid personality propensities and is given to the use of counterphobic defenses to protect herself from easily arousable feelings of threat. She may at times manifest depressive moods.

Rorschach Protocol

I. (15″) 1. *This is an animal's face?* It looked to me like an animal's face, with these openings for eyes and these for ears. At my first glance it looked like a cat's face. It looked a little like an angry cat face. [WS F+ Ad A (Athr)]

II. (15″) 2. *In a way it looks as if people are facing each other. But I don't know. I have no idea.* Watching it carefully, I see the two are the same, though I thought they were folding their palms, each facing the other. (?) The red parts are faces, and they fold their palms. The lower parts are knees and look wounded now. This is a sitting form. (?) This is red here. (?) I did not feel so there. [W M, CF+ H, Bl P (Hh Hsm)]

3. *These open areas look like electric light bulbs.* The red lower part is the bulb and the white part is a shade, but that is rather funny. It is only a shade. [DS FC+ Obj. Porn]

III. (10″) 4. *Looks like persons are doing something.* It seems someone is lifting something. (?) The whole of it made me think of a man bent at his hips to pull something up with his hands. [D M+ H P (Adeh)]

5. *I find something gloomy in it.* (?) The red part seems like a human fire spirit (spirit-fire symbolism—a ghost), and the person himself is not alive. (?) I imagined it to be in connection with a human spirit. I'm afraid it's not a man in our world but a skeleton. (?) The red part is almost swaying. [D Fm, CF+ Spirit Athr]

IV. (10″) 6. *It looks like a beast's hide.* Here is the neck and the skin is opened flat, I suppose. Here are eyes, paws, and hind legs. Not so big, but a tiger or a leopard. At first this [the neck] seemed to be an animal and the back pattern a fur. Looks like a rug. [W FT+ Aob P (Ps)]

7. *Looks like a bat opened flat, with wings here.* Legs are small. It was opened to be used for a science class. This is the head. [W F− Aanat (Hsm)]

V. (11″) 8. *This . . . like a bat with its wings spread flying.* It is too stout for an insect. It looks like a bat. These are the head and wings. [DS FM+ A P (Neut)]

9. *A bird which is close to a beast.* It is not so lovable a bird. (?) It has horns and the wings are not of a good shape. [W F+ A (Hhad)]

VI. (27″) 10. *Something like a beast? A goat?* An animal which is not so fierce. The lower part of the body looks like that of a goat. Also . . . looks like a sheep too. It is fat somehow. (?) The body length is short and fat. Also the body line seems smooth and soft. These are paws and hind legs with a goat-like bearing. This part seems to be fur of a sheep. (?) Looks blurred. [W FT− A (Neut)]

VII. (23″) 11. *Looks like a camel put together arbitrarily. Looks like some animal.* This is the hump, these are the hind legs and paws. With this attached here it would be the head. They are drawn as they are . . . by a little child. (?) I don't see eyes and mouth here . . . , as it is a child's drawing. [W F− A (Hhad Dch)]

VIII. (9″) 12. *A beast.* It looked something like a bear. These are the two hind legs, and it looks as if it was walking with two paws. As for this, it imagines a mountain where it is walking. (?) No, just imagining. [D FM+ A P (Neut)]

13. *A butterfly.* A butterfly shape. (?) It has the wings spread. It is not alive. It's a butterfly used as a specimen. [D F+ A (Neut)]

14. *Looks like a flower with four petals, and this is the center.* (?) The color and the shape. The color is pretty. [D FC+ Bot P Pnat]

15. *In the mountain where snow is about to melt there is a bear, and also an alpine flower is blooming.* (?) The color is soft and gives a bright impression. [W FC+ A, Bot Pnat]

IX. (30″) 16. *I don't understand this. This, I suppose, is a flower, but . . .* Looks like a flower, like a peony upside down. This is the center of it. (?) It's red, though the shape doesn't look like so. It's not a peony but some flower. [D CF+ Bot (Pnat)]

17. *Looks like a picturesque sight seen from above.* This is a lake perhaps, and there are some mountains around it. The blue parts are the higher areas in mountains. . . . The color of trees and the brown parts are the lower area. (?) I didn't notice it. [DS FV, CF+ Lscp A (Pnat)]

X. (10″) 18. *Looks like various leaves, dead trees, leaves all turning to red and also naked trees.* This is the tree, dead without its leaves. They are the roots that have died. (?) It's a dead color and it has no leaves. This is the prettiest black tea color we see in the last pouring from the pot. This has faded out though. . . . (?) All others are connected with red leaves in fall. As a whole I get the feeling of fall with reddening leaves. [W CF+ Nat (Agl Pnat)]

Card-by-Card Sequential Analysis

On the first card Mrs. Fukuyama sees the animal face directly looking out. This is a not uncommon response (especially in the boys) in our present set of protocols from Arakawa. She enlivens the face as potentially threatening, that of an *angry* cat, projecting an emotional tone into the percept. This suggestion of affective lability is deepened by her response to Card II. There, while she perceives the humans very well, the red color in the lower part of the blot is interpreted as wounded knees. Her use of the red color as blood indicates a hysteriod type of affective reactivity.

On Card III she again readily picks out the human percept. Again she shows some affective lability, sensing that the card is permeated with a feeling of gloom. She then refers to the "fire spirits" frequently perceived by the Japanese in the lateral colored blots; the spirits of the dead are often conceived as hovering over graves in the form of a red light or a fireball. She turns the human figures into skeletons. Thus, she organizes this card into a fearful, gloomy subject.

On Card IV she again gives the most frequent or popular response to the card and sees a beast's hide. She is sensitive to the fur and is concerned with the size of the animal; though she perceives it first as a tiger or a leopard, she says it is not large. She counterphobically decreases the size, making it a smaller tiger, and tones down the potential fearful quality of her percept. She is basically conformist in her thinking. She does not go far out in terms of her social perceptions, yet she enlivens her response with affective qualities suggestive of a reactive extratensive personality. In contrast to many of the mothers of socialized delinquents, Mrs. Fukuyama's record is a fairly open one and shows less rigidity and constriction than the average. In an additional response to this card, "a bat opened flat" for a science class, one notes a sadomasochistic tendency but one that is well encompassed by the usual stimulus value of this card. Nowhere does she reach far to give poor percepts to express her affective tensions.

Her response to Card V again is a popular one, but she sees it as a rather oppressive bird that has a frightening quality to it. On Card VI she perceives a goat, which is of fairly poor form quality. She states that it is an animal that is "not so fierce," another indication of her counterphobic quality. On Card VII, she does poorly. She perceives a particular area as the hump of a camel, then sees the whole thing as a camel that is drawn "arbitrarily" by a child. We see here a clever use of forced logic. That is, her initial percept is bad, and yet she gives an inclusive naturalistic percept that it looks bad because it is drawn by a little child.

For Card VIII she shows a positive responsiveness to color. Animals are frequently perceived here, and she sees them as bears walking on a mountainside. She then sees a butterfly and describes the colors in positive terms; she sees the white space as snow that is melting, and the flower gives her the feeling of alpine flowers in bloom. Again there is an arbitrary juxtaposition. Her affective responsiveness is of a positive spontaneous nature, indicating the capacity to react in an affirmative way to her environment. On Card IX she again sees a flower and then again gives a vista response, looking at a picturesque view from above, a lake with mountains surrounding it, the blue-green parts being the higher areas in the mountains. The color of trees is brown in the lower areas. This is a nicely handled percept, indicative of the love of nature. Such responses are characteristic of Japanese percepts, where subjects are able to employ different colors on this difficult card to give some integrative impression, even though there is no definite form.

To Card X she continues the theme of colors of nature—dead leaves that have faded. For her the card has the feeling of autumn, covered with reddening leaves.

These latter responses tend to overcome the negative features of the initial phobic and fearful responses given to the first cards, suggesting positive affective strengths as a balance in this woman.

The TAT

> J1. Is this person someone studying composition? Studying about many things—how he should compose music. . . . Looks like he's at his wit's end. I think he will compose a kind of soft, solitary music, not cheerful in tone. (?) Perhaps he is lonesome in actual life. For some reason . . . (?) Being lonesome . . . thinking of sad, quiet music. Reflecting his own loneliness, . . . for he is lonely at home. Either his father or his mother is absent, and so he is not well-off. Wanting affection and warmth in the family, he is devoting himself to music, I think. . . . (?) A boy. Seems like he is in the music room at school by himself. The whole picture gives a somewhat gloomy impression. It seems that he is meditating without being aware of darkness descending. (?) I think he will find some support in his music.

In the first story Mrs. Fukuyama sets a tone of loneliness and isolation. She responds to the card much as she did to some of the Rorschach blots, and finds it gloomy. She does not express an achievement theme or a concern with inadequacy; instead, the whole tone of her story is the loneliness of the child and the fact that he seeks solace in his music. We get an impression, therefore, that she has feelings of isolation which may stem from an early feeling of deprivation. This emphasis on loneliness reflects her lonely childhood; both her natural mother and her father died when she was young.

> J2. Is this a scene in a farming village? Living in the farming village, she is trying to study hard at school to ensure a good future, I think. She is young and hopes to have a big future. These are people from the same village, a working man and wife together . . . but they don't look like they are talking face to face. The lady in the back is just resting, forgetting everything. In a village like this, very few would

> consent to a daughter studying. But the young these days like to study, whether or not they will do well or become famous. It will not help the family's living, but her parents decide to strain themselves to send her to school in the end . . . perhaps. The girl looks like she is going somewhere for study. (?) She does not like to lead a farmer's life but hopes to establish herself as a scholar.

To the second card she tells an achievement story in which the young girl, disliking the farm life, decides to work hard at school and make a scholar of herself. She pictures the parents in the background as unusually supportive, considering the poverty of village life. The parents sacrifice themselves financially so that the daughter can become successful. Mrs. Fukuyama then moralizes and says that there are young people today who like to study, whether or not they make anything of themselves as scholars. She is critical of the fact that education has been made easy and available to those who do not work toward a career. There is an ambivalent attitude here toward education. On the one hand, she recognizes that education demands hard work if eminence is to be achieved, and on the other hand, she feels that perhaps it should not be made available to those who do not apply themselves to their studies. She nevertheless sees the parental role ideally as helpful. Although she is concerned with loneliness, as is indicated by her story to Card 1, she also has the standard Japanese concern for achievement and expresses it in a traditional Japanese way. She does not end the story with an emphatic statement of success, but leaves it as a hope for the future. The goal for which the girl is aiming, that of becoming a scholar, is somewhat unrealistic for a peasant girl. We must note that thematically the successful achievement of women is given almost as readily as that of men in TAT stories in Japan. The Japanese do not apply a sex role differentiation to their concept of achievement. It is seen as a virtue for both men and women.

> J3. Perhaps this person gets drunk and falls down this way. This is a man, I think. Maybe he gets drunk and has fallen down some place, such as a waiting room in a station. (?) On the way back from his office he was taken to drink by his fellow workers and is drunk. Looks young, so cannot drink much. An elderly man wouldn't drink in this manner. The young don't know their capacity to drink. He will wake up after a while and be ashamed of what he has done. He doesn't know himself, after all. Those who cannot drink much are likely to get drunk this way. (?) Some time later he will get back to himself and feel ashamed of himself. And he will go home. (?) A man like him is likely to be living alone, staying in an apartment. (?) At a party following a regular company party or some party of that sort, he was forced to drink heavily despite his being unable to drink.

Mrs. Fukuyama makes of Card 3 a story of a drunken young man who can't hold his liquor. This is an unusual theme for this card. She seems to be critical of a young person's not being able to hold liquor properly, as older people can. This is the second time in three stories that she has made a statement about the inadequate capacities of youth. In the preceding picture, the young are seen as willing to study, but perhaps they are not able to push on to an ultimate goal of being a scholar. In this story they drink without knowing how to handle themselves. She is evidencing her side of the generation gap, which she feels is present in Japan.

> J6. A parent and a child. A son and his mother had some trouble, and he hurt her feelings and doesn't know how to excuse himself. (?) Coming home late. A young couple had some trouble with the mother-in-law of the bride, cannot find a good opening to explain. She seems that angry. (?) I imagine that the young couple had a good time until late at night outside the house, and the mother was angry with them. If her son was unmarried there would be no conflict. Once there is someone from outside the family, things get complicated. The son is anxious to please his mother, it seems. (?) He does not defend themselves so much, but apologizes, saying that they were wrong, only in order to reconcile themselves outwardly at least. The mother feels lonesome and "left out" by the young couple. She looks rather cold on the whole.

In her response to Card 6 Mrs. Fukuyama again demonstrates a feeling of difference between the generations, and in her story the problem is not between the mother and son but between the mother and the daughter-in-law, with the suggestion that a modern woman goes out late at night and so tension develops between the traditional mother and the nontraditional daughter-in-law. The son dutifully apologizes for their behavior so as to reconcile himself and his wife with his mother, but the statement is then that the mother feels lonesome and has a feeling of *higami* (verb, *higamu*).

(This word is not directly translatable into English. *Higami* is a kind of anger aroused by frustrated desire to be loved, and partially directed toward oneself as well as toward the source of frustration. It is a complex psychological term showing a Japanese awareness of the fact that the desire to be loved when frustrated results in an anger very difficult to handle. Partly what happens to the person who is *higamu* is a feeling of deep anger with oneself for being in the position of dependent helplessness in not having one's desire to be loved fulfilled. There is the supposition in the person with *higami* that he deserves to be taken care of, and therefore an unconcerned frustrator, regardless of the appropriateness of his behavior, evokes resentment and anger. There is also the feeling in the self that one has been diminished by being ignored, while other people enjoy acceptance and care, so that in retribution the injured one acts in a retaliatory way, attempting to induce guilt in the other. Hence, self-destructive behavior is played out in order to "punish" the frustrator. This type of psychological "game" is related to what has been described elsewhere in relation to suicide. [De Vos, 1973, chapter 17]. The extreme *higami* reaction resulting in suicide is a means of hurting the frustrator as well as hurting one's self for being susceptible to one's helpless involvement. One also finds evidence of *higami* in a Japanese form of excessive drinking called *yake zake* (drinking out of desperation). The

Japanese *consciously* recognize a type of emotional response that is most often discussed in the psychoanalytic literature of the West as an unconscious motivation. There is no comparably explicit term for conscious *higami* in the Western vocabulary; one must discuss it by a circumlocution. *Higami* is related to the term *amae* discussed in chapter 2. As Doi [1971] describes it, the wish to be passively loved and attended to is more conscious and egosyntonic in the Japanese mind than it is in the West.)

> J7. This is not at home, but at some gathering outside. Teachers at school or executives at a company, for instance. Not pleasant conversation, but rather about a difficult problem. (?) If at a company, a problem concerning the running of the business; if at a school a problem concerning children. They are discussing some problem that they have faced recently. (?) A principal and a teacher talk over a shameful affair that occurred at the school or some accident that took place. (?) The principal says something and the teacher gives his thoughts. (?) They are engrossed in some serious affair. I'm not certain. (?)

To this card, Mrs. Fukuyama avoids giving the father-son theme that is most often given and sees it rather as a discussion between two authority figures concerning some serious happening. There is no depiction of conflict with authority. We may infer some avoidance of seeing a father and a son in a discussion, either in a positive or a negative sense. One sees Mrs. Fukuyama's basic concept of her world as a negative one in which people have to contend with problems continually. There is little indication of any spontaneous optimism in her.

> J8. Some crime is going to be committed. Is this person going to commit homicide? Looks like a student. This is maybe illustrating young people's spite or holding a grudge or something. The two are going to commit homicide and . . . (?) Well, what is this at the bottom? As the picture is not clear, I suppose this is his imagination. He is afraid of such a terrible thing happening suddenly and he will go away to some safe place, I think. (?) There has been something between them. Either a disagreement, conflict of opinions, or hatred among the students, and he imagined such an awful scene and is going away to tell someone about it. He is afraid not of himself but of his friend being killed. Their enemy is a kind of delinquent. So he fears the worst situation and goes to tell it to his teacher or a person of higher status. (?) I imagine he will ask them to help prevent the worst from happening.

This story represents a not uncommon fear of retribution in many Japanese. If one injures the feelings of others inadvertently or otherwise, one may be subject to retaliation or vengeance. These stories appear frequently from both delinquent and nondelinquent subjects. In this instance the person imagining the happening is frightened and goes to seek the protection and counsel of a teacher or, as she puts it, "a person of higher status" who can help prevent such an occurrence. Mrs. Fukuyama would like to have some protection, some powerful individual on whom she could be dependent. There is an underlying tone in her responses of wanting such protection from a higher authority, and we presume that this is a rejection of the powerless and impotent occupational role of her husband, as well as implicit criticism of him as too ineffectual to take any strong role in emergency situations within the family.

> J9. A fight within the family? No, perhaps some mournful event has happened. Someone—maybe this young lady's father—died, and her brother and sister have gathered here. Their father died in some accident such as a traffic accident. (?) The older brother, the younger sister, and her older sister. This person must be a servant. The mother is not here. I wonder if she is dead. If the father died in the house, they would throw themselves over the body, crying bitterly. But this is like the Mikawashima National Railway accident, so . . . the older brother and sister are mature enough and all of them are more grown up than the time when their mother died, so it isn't so bad. (?) The brother and sister will work, as they have been working.

Mrs. Fukuyama rejected her initial spontaneous reaction of seeing the scene as representing a fight within the family. For some reason she has to deny this and change her story to one in which the family members are gathered around, mourning the death of the father. Interestingly, she sees the maternal-looking older figure in this picture as a servant. She sees the mother as having died earlier so that the children are able to react to the second death with more maturity. In removing the mother from this scene she may be rejecting the responsibility tied to the role of mother. She may not want to have to take charge of difficult situations, and thus avoids having to consider it.

> J11. Are they mother and son? The mother is changing her clothes? The child did not know this and perhaps peeps in, thinking of entering her room. As he is old enough, perhaps he has felt something, wondering whether he should not see his mother doing something. (?) In the second or third grade in a junior high school. A child at that age regards his parents as individual. (?) She looks like dressing, fitting her clothes here and there better to her person. She is perhaps engaging herself in this kind of feminine action. He may have found something of the other sex in her, his own mother. He was at that moment shocked, realizing that he should not go in. Though he doesn't take it seriously, he will not enter, but goes out to play, I suppose. She doesn't know he is there. I am not certain whether she has returned from outside or just is changing her clothes. (?) The father is perhaps not in, working at his company.

This is an unusual story in which the boy is depicted as suddenly becoming sexually aware of his mother, who is either changing her clothes or primping herself in a feminine way, with some sexual connotation. The boy does not enter the room, and the mother is described as unaware of the boy's presence. The story certainly indicates Mrs. Fukuyama's own awareness of her son's sexual interest. It is a peculiar story to give spontaneously. It would indicate that she has some narcissistic preoccupations, which are more prepotent, in her case, than concerns expressed in such story themes as those about the boy's schooling or the visit of a teacher or a boy playing baseball rather than studying, which are often given to this card. Mrs. Fukuyama avoids giving any indication that there may be another man present (as represented by the hat and the briefcase). Rather, the father is depicted as being away, and the woman is by herself, changing her clothes. We found both in the father's stories and in those of the mother direct and unusual sexual content, which would suggest some undercurrent of unexplored sexual fantasy in both parents.

> J13. Maybe a woman—I get the impression that she is dead. These two people found it difficult to continue and killed themselves. The woman dies first, perhaps with a drug, and the man, failing to die, is now suffering. They wanted to end their problems by death. (?) Maybe they were not able to marry. The woman is out of some gay quarters and the man grew up in a status-concerned family that will never allow them to get married. (?) He failed to kill himself at the same time. He suddenly became confused. He hesitated. (?) Just as we change our mind easily at a slight interference, he came to feel there is not much reason for him to die. So he is suffering in regret. I suppose he will surrender himself to the police as justice guides him and submit to a sentence until his agony of conscience goes away.

The story in effect depicts a man who cannot follow through in an act of double suicide with a prostitute. A status-conscious family is depicted as preventing marriage between the man and the woman working in a cabaret. The man is depicted as too weak to follow through with their plan. He changes his mind readily, suffering regret for his action, and will probably surrender himself to the police. As in so many Japanese stories, the police and justice are used here to help salve one's own conscience. One does not attempt to escape the consequences of bad behavior, but seeks to gain absolution through submission to some form of official justice for expiation. In the Japanese lower class there is an attitude toward police, which comes out in these stories, that is far different from that found in American lower-class individuals. The conflict between the generations and between tradition and free expression appears again in a different form in this story. This time, Mrs. Fukuyama sides in the traditional sentimental Japanese way with the plight of lovers who can find no solution to their problem.

> J18. This young girl did something wrong and killed herself. Her mother is holding her daughter, crying with deep regret. (?) Perhaps a man and woman problem. She looks to be a strict mother and restrained her daughter too much. So maybe she committed suicide in rebellion against her mother. Mothers are apt to restrain their children's freedom only because they love them, but this mother's restraint of her daughter led to the happening the mother is regretting now. (?) I feel there is no

> father in the family. Even if there is, he is stubborn, and there are the grandfather and grandmother, too. And the mother is among them, it seems. There are two children, but the older brother of the girl seems to have been away from the home, since this house is too strict on the children. Anyway, he cannot get along with his family as it is. So the girl put up resistance to the family by killing herself, and her death made her mother realize for the first time how wrong she was. The old family system is the cause for this tragedy.

In response to Card 18 Mrs. Fukuyama gives a story of tragedy resulting from the effect of the old family system on youth. But the first sentence of her story is that the girl did something wrong and then killed herself. This quick evaluation of the girl is quickly rejected by castigating the rigidity of the mother and the lack of freedom given children. Here is a curious underlying ambivalence. There was, first, an implicit assumption that the girl's behavior was improper and probably of a sexual nature, and yet the mother is specifically blamed for putting the girl in a situation in which she resorts to suicide. Mrs. Fukuyama's symbolic generalization in her stories is more characteristic of the men's records. Most Japanese women do not create generalizations in the course of their stories; this is not to say that there are no morals to be drawn from women's stories; it is rather that they are more implicit. Mrs. Fukuyama, however, gives several stories in which she has explicit endings demonstrating that the old family system is the cause of tragedy. Again, her story to Card 18 depicts a conflict between the generations.

> J22. The mother and the child are going some place and waiting for something. Her older child has gone back to get something he forgot to bring. The man is passing by. (?) The child may be crying for something, and the older boy has gone to buy it. And the mother is looking at her older child buying something, as there is a store in the vicinity. The younger boy is preschool. He wanted something to eat, I imagine. Not a toy. He wanted something to eat when he saw it while walking. So his mother sent the older son to get it. (?) Yes, when the mother gives it to his boy, he stops crying and they go.

This picture usually evokes some theme of conflict between husband and wife, since two figures are facing in opposite directions, and the small boy in the center is usually seen as crying, wanting something. Mrs. Fukuyama immediately saw the mother and child as going someplace and waiting for something. Then she introduces an unusual character, an older child who has gone back to get something he forgot to bring. Here we may have a spontaneous rejection of the father in the picture—either because the possibility of a conflict is rejected or, on a deeper level, because of a desire to go out with a child as a male substitute for the father. This would fit in with the peculiar handling of Card 11, where the boy becomes sexually aware of the mother, who is by herself without a husband. In this story, after the older child has gone back to get something, Mrs. Fukuyama identifies the other figure as a man passing by. From this point on she makes a plausible, coherent story. We have already noted in her Rorschach protocol that she has a type of intellectual facility that allows her to recover from her potentially dangerous spontaneous emotional reactions. In her TAT stories she again displays an ability to get around her first reactions by creating an alternative story that takes the situation far away from what she initially perceived spontaneously. She did this in several instances, first giving a sentence and then recovering from it, taking a new tack and going on.

In this story, the mother is looking away, from both the other adult figure and the young child. The introduction of the older child into the story may have been prompted initially by the adult male figure moving away. The figure was perhaps then perceived as too mature for that of an older, adolescent son and was changed quickly into a passerby. The older child is not present in the picture but absent on his mission to obtain something for the younger boy. One must consider a dynamic need to eliminate a father from the story, one way or another.

The story also describes a mother who seeks to quiet a demanding child by satisfying his wishes, a fairly common story for Japanese mothers. One would presume that Mrs. Fukuyama handles her children somewhat in the manner depicted in the cards, acceding to them when they are demanding.

> J27. They are students, still in the third grade of junior high school, or they may go to senior high school already. They look like they are playing around during the daytime. I wonder if they are good students, both girls and a boy. They look like they are fond of loafing and now gather for no special purpose but to chat. With nothing to do but play around during the day, maybe they are cutting their classes. They don't seem to be on the way back from school. (?) Yes. I think they are going astray, killing time here and there, meeting for no purpose but for silly merrymaking with no concern for study.

On this last card the coffee shop scene is used to portray a lack of serious purpose in students. Mrs. Fukuyama specifies that they are in the third grade of junior high school, which is the grade her son was in at the time of the testing. The card is used in a negative way to indicate the self-indulgence and purposeless behavior of misguided youth. She does not, however, refer back to family responsibility, as men often do in their moralizing stories.

In sum, Mrs. Fukuyama reveals in the TAT stories some underlying need to reject a husband or a father figure. She seems to be playing a complementary role to her husband in his desire to have his older boy, the delinquent subject, Yokichi, express masculine-aggressive functions the father finds incapable of realizing in himself. The mother's substitution of the older boy for the father has unconscious sexual implications of which she is at least partially aware.

Mrs. Fukuyama is ambivalent about traditional authority and about the possible responsibilities of the maternal role in resolving difficult family situations. She is at the same time moralistic about improper behavior on the part of youth. Finally, there is present some maternal warmth and giving. One might say that she is not rejecting of her children, but is confused about what role she is to play, and what role her older boy is to play in the family.

PROJECTIVE TEST RESULTS: YOKICHI FUKUYAMA

The Rorschach Test

Yokichi's Rorschach record confirms our general impression of a boy with a high average to superior mental capacity. It reveals, however, an arbitrary "forcing" of conceptual integration in his organizational drive. He gives a number of responses that are arbitrary combinations of elements that do not belong together logically. Such responses can be interpreted as suggestions of both psychopathic and paranoid trends. His record also reveals some features suggesting the presence of neurotic mechanisms (and sadomasochistic concerns) that interfere with the spontaneous expression of affect. Yet, as the record continues, there is progressive recovery from initial difficulties. On a symbolic level, the responses become more positive in nature, indicating a capacity to react to his environment in an enlivened, positive way. What is lacking is some indication of present maturation occurring in his inner life. He is much more capable of envisaging animals in his responses than of perceiving humans (a sign of immaturity). He sees only one clear "standing" human percept, whereas the animals he perceives are engaged in various activities. He also characteristically perceives childish games and toys—all in all, an immature individual who feels himself driven beyond his means. He is capable of an interpersonal heartiness that may at times hide shallow fabrication, and he has an immature perception of human relationships.

Rorschach Protocol

I. (32″) 1. A *bat.* Because it has a nose and the wings; his wings spread, perched. The form looks like a bat. [W FM+ A P (Neut)]

2. A *beetle*. The beetle has his wings spread; they are broken. [W F+ A (Hhad)]

3. A *mask of a devil* (oni). Nose, eyes, and horns are there. [W S F+ (Hd) Mask (Athr)]

II. Rejection (Arej).

III. (30″) 4. A *fly.* There are eyes and claws. First I say black eyes and the form of the whole thing and also black color. [D FC′+ A (Neut)]

5. An *insect.* This black part is . . . it looks like it is watching—or aiming at something. Here are claws. The color of the eyes is dark and sharp-looking. [D FC′+ A (Athr)]

6. A *roach . . . its claws.* The same as before [above]. [D F− A (Adis)]

IV. (32″) 7. A *bearskin.* Because it's black. Also from the shape of the head and legs. Something like a rug. [DS FC′+ Aob P (Neut)]

8. *An opened-up slug.* From the impression of eyes and mouth. It's slimy, and the outline of its body is uneven. [D FT− A (Hsm Adis)]

V. (30″) 9. A *bat.* With his back this side because I don't see any eyes. He is flying with spread wings. [W FM+ A P (Neut)]

10. A *kite.* Toy kite. The sides are too long and projecting. This is the head and the tail. [DS F+ Toy (Dch, Prec)]

VI. (25″) 11. A *dragonfly is on a bearskin.* There are eyes and wings, so it looks like a dragonfly. The lower part is a bear rug, with the head and paws and legs. From the shape and color it is not real black. [W FM, FC′+ A P Z− (Arb Comb, Ps)]

VII. (25″) 12. A *human being standing on both his feet.* The upper half of the human body. The face looks like a human. Well-carved face profiles. Two are facing and looking at each other. [D M+ HP (Neut)]

13. *Dogs.* They have tails and the noses are projecting, playing *niramekko* [outstaring each other]. [D FM+ A (Pch Hcmpt)]

VIII. (44″) 14. A *flower.* From the color and the shape. [D CF+ Bot P (Pnat)]

15. *Red bears on a cicada.* The cicada is pulled from both sides. The shape of the head is like a cicada. It has eyes. The red bears come from the shape and the color. The legs of the cicada are under the body because it is seen from above. [W FM+ A P Z− (Arb Comb, Pch)]

16. *Weasels are on a flower.* Weasels are playing. [D FM, FC+ Z− (Arb Comb, Pch)]

IX. (21″) 17. *The rising sun.* There is light. The surrounding red parts are like dawn. [D CF+ Nat (Pnat)]

18. A *flower upside down.* There is a color; it looks like a twig; the flower looks like a chrysanthemum. [D FC+ Bot (Pnat)]

19. *Crabs are hiding from the sun.* In the twilight when the sun is setting, crabs are showing only their claws; the bodies are not seen and are behind this. The color is like twilight. [D CF, FM+ A (Adef)]

X. (13″) 20. *Flowers.* Flowers gathered together—small flowers gathered together. This is the cluster of the flowers; this is the dead twig with a dark feeling—no leaves. Brown color . . . you can see in the field these various shapes. The impression of the whole color. [W CF+ Bot (Pnat, Agl)]

Card-by-Card Sequential Analysis

The first response to Card I is the standard, popular bat. Yokichi then sees a beetle, revealing somewhat sadomasochistic concern—the wings are broken.

He then produces a response found in the records of a large number of Arakawa youth, a head-on picture of a mask or face, in this instance the mask of a devil. The second card is totally rejected, a most unusual occurrence for Card II, and certainly indicative of what is often called "color shock." (There is some indication statistically that delinquents as a group handle color more poorly than do nondelinquent subjects. We found a significant difference in the direction of better form of dominant color responses in the nondelinquent than in the delinquent subjects, signifying better control over their emotional reactivity.) Eventually, Yokichi is able to use color in the last three cards, but the first appearance of color is apparently very upsetting.

The content of Yokichi's response to Card III is poor. He does not see human figures. He sees a "fly," not a pleasant object, with emphasis on its black eyes. Then he perceives another insect in a right-side-up position, an insect that is watching or aiming at something, and finally what he says is a roach, a "disgusting" animal. Symbolically, he may have some very negative perceptions of what a human being is like, despising himself as well as others. From Card IV on, he seems to have recovered some equilibrium and begins to do better. He is able to see a black bearskin rug. But then he immediately gives an opened-up slug, "slimy" in its outline. There is also a sadomasochistic element here, another "repulsive" response like the roach.

On Card V he sees a bat, a response of neutral import. Then he sees a toy kite, his first really positive response to the cards, a toy being a pleasant albeit childish object. On Card VI he gives an "arbitrary combination," seeing a dragonfly on a bearskin. Both parts are individually well perceived, but they are not compatible when one considers the relative size of the two objects. On Card VII he sees two humans simply looking at each other. Then he sees within the same area dogs with tails and noses projecting, playing a childish game, attempting to outstare each other till one or the other laughs.

He perceives a flower on Card VIII, a popular Japanese response. Then he gives another arbitrary combination of red bears on top of a cicada. "Red bears" is an artificial blend of color and forms even more arbitrary when bears are related to an insect without attention to the disparity in size. Yokichi follows up this response with a second arbitrary combination of two weasels playing on a flower. On Card IX he sees the rising sun in the upper area of the card, which is not badly perceived, a rather original response. Then he sees a flower upside down, again fairly well perceived. Then he gives a clever response, which borders on being another arbitrary combination, in which part of the blot covers the main parts of two crabs that are hiding from the sun in the twilight. On Card X he again sees flowers, but then he concentrates on the dead twig in the middle, and it leaves him with a "dark feeling," since there are no leaves. A depressive mood intrudes itself in spite of the bright colors.

To summarize, there is intellectual drive in this boy, but judgment and logic are lacking, as a number of his responses show. There is severe difficulty with spontaneity and reactivity. However, we see some recovery of his capacity to take a more positive, optimistic attitude toward his environment. The nature of the arbitrary combinations in his responses suggest that he characteristically uses spurious logic to force circumstances to be seen by himself and others in the way that he would like them to be seen. Inferentially, he has conceptual traits that could be used in a psychopathic way, if turned outward to convince others. The fact that given his potential intelligence he is able to produce only one human movement response (to Card VII) suggests that he does not have sufficient inner resources to absorb the reactive, impulsive tendencies that lead him to act out when under stress.

The TAT

Yokichi's TAT record reflects some interesting stylistic mannerisms in expression. He uses a number of free and spontaneous words, but at the same time he often speaks in convoluted sentences reminiscent of his father's style, where phrase is piled upon phrase before he reaches the end of his sentence. The language is sometimes colorful and expressive. Yokichi picks words that are graphic, showing a considerable intelligence. His stories are filled with scenes of violence and aggression, some of which he tones down as he goes along. There is no question that his immediate response to interpersonal relationships is one of antagonism. In several instances he avoids the use of close relationships in his stories. He gives a considerable number of stories of death and crime.

> J1. A boy musician comes to a painful dead end in regard to his art. He does not know how to proceed. It is all right with this kind of explanation? Coming to a dead end is quite common, as you know. When you come to a certain point you cannot go beyond. He comes to a dead end and is thinking about it. (?) He wishes to be able to do well. It's dark, isn't it? [expressively] Is it not his own room? He is twelve or thirteen. (?) He may solve it by studying music only. If he devotes himself only to his music his problem solves itself. Judging from this, his parents don't seem to be alive. He is all alone . . . raised by a church. He is in a room there. I cannot tell the rest. Most orphans live in such places, don't they? (?) Yes, this child is an orphan. (?) He . . . I don't know. . . . (?) He is solitary, lonesome. He consoles himself by playing music.

This first story starts with the boy musician at an impasse. He cannot seem to resolve some problems with his music. Perhaps Yokichi at the time of the testing felt that he wasn't going anywhere and felt isolated and misunderstood by his family. These themes continue throughout his stories. In his story to Card I he rejects the idea of parents, seeing the boy as an orphan who is brought up by a religious group. Yokichi shifts from the boy's concern over an impasse in his music toward a statement of the boy's feeling of deprivation and isolation. The musical activities of the boy in the story are seen as a means of consoling himself for his isolation from others. A shift appears also in the language in which Yokichi tells the story. His opening phrases are much like those used by his father, rather grandiose, in a convoluted style hard to translate from the Japanese. Then, when he talks about isolation his style becomes more direct and personal, and there are momentary blockings in his expression as if he is groping for a means of communicating deeper feelings.

The first part of the story ends with a typical Japanese value: if one pours into one's tasks a sufficient intensity of concentration, effort, and sense of purpose, one can conquer any situation. Then suddenly Yokichi shifts into a theme of deprivation, which is to reappear in some of his other stories. In actual life Yokichi seems to be an outgoing person who has many friends and acquaintances. Overtly he is of a boastful and aggressive nature, but underlying such behavior we get a glimpse into another stratum of his unsatisfied needs, which, interestingly enough, he is free to express. This direct symbolic expression of isolation is a positive sign in this boy.

> J2. A farmer's family. They are working on the farm, except for the daughter, who only studies, for some reason. We can tell it from the dark, unhappy expression of the mother. The daughter studies hard, saying one has to have education for the future. So she goes to school and catches up on the knowledge she has failed to receive. (?) As the family is not well-off, the mother does not fully agree. (?) Her father is indifferent. (?) He seems to be against it in the picture, though he doesn't show this openly, but just from the way he looks. (?) She feels that they must work on the farm, as they have no education, but she doesn't like it. "I will be a respectable person. I don't like to remain as a country person doing farming," she says.

Yokichi is rather sensitive to human posture and demeanor. He "reads" others for signs of approval or rejection. This characteristic is brought out in this story. He projects into the picture of a farm scene a feeling of tacit disapproval on the part of the parental figures. The brooding face of the woman and the posture of the father facing away indicate that the parents do not approve of the young woman's plan to obtain an education. Yokichi interprets these figures as representing unfeeling and somewhat inhibiting parents. He uses an interesting phrase, "catches up on the knowledge she has failed to receive." This is almost a conscious indictment of his parental home. Yokichi feels that his home has failed to provide him with the proper training for success in the external world.

The daughter in his story gives no indication of being swayed by parental opinion. She regards the parents' hard farm labor as due to necessity because of their lack of education, and she does not want to be caught permanently in such a life. Knowing his home circumstances, we find a direct reflection of Yokichi's own present attitudes. He wants to reject the poverty and stalemate faced by his own family. But as he reveals them in this story, his strongest motives are to get away from, rather than to go toward, some well-conceptualized achievement plan.

> J3. In a prison or some place, a woman is crying, as she fought and got beaten up. I'm not sure, but she did something wrong for the sake of her child. She did something wrong for the child and was put into prison, where she was beaten up. So she is crying now because she did not obey or was brash [*namaiki*—raw-spirited] concerning something. (?) She thinks she did it for the child, so you can't blame her. (?) She stole something for the sake of her child and was put into prison. The child is in an orphanage. She will be in for three to four months. (?) She wants to work earnestly, but cannot find a job. So I am not sure if she can be a normal person despite such a situation. I do not know if she can. If she can, I think she is great.

This story expresses a type of thinking that is often found in delinquents, that is, that the delinquent's behavior is justified by circumstances. Authority is rigid and incapable of understanding, and one's behavior is judged wrong by an unfeeling society. In his story Yokichi gives a defensive affirmation of a woman who has fought, but has been beaten up and is crying. Now imprisoned, this woman has stolen for the sake of her child. Yokichi's immediate reaction, as in a number of his other stories, is to see the card in the context of violence and aggression. The heroine is depicted as a victim of circumstances. She would really like to work but she can't. She steals and is imprisoned. He is not sure if she can avoid being deviant, given her circumstances. The whole story is given in an expressive, spontaneous, childish, colloquial tone, hard to convey in translation—quite different from the way he began in response to the first picture. Again, we note some direct feeling of childhood deprivation, expressed by his stating that the woman's child is now in an orphanage. In his delinquent protest, an inner sense of deprivation is transmuted into a feeling of social inequity.

Another aspect of this story worthy of note is the fact that the woman first actually fought and "got herself beaten up." The reason she was beaten up was that she was *namaiki*, or brash, a difficult word to translate. This word has a provocative, insolent meaning in Japanese (Yokichi uses it again in the following story). A person who is *namaiki* is presumptuous, behaving in a way unbecoming to his social status, such as a child toward the parents, or a pupil to a teacher. For example, a woman who smokes cigarettes is considered immodest and therefore *namaiki*. Teachers often consider a *banchō* to be *namaiki*, and he, in turn, in maintaining discipline in his gang, will call a boy who does not show him the proper deference and fear *namaiki*. It is a word much used among delinquent boys, and is often used to explain why somebody should be beaten up. The word was used by Yokichi in this fashion in this story.

> J6. In a family an old lady and her son are quarreling . . . speaking harshly. The son is beseeching her, but she doesn't pay any attention. (?) They are quarreling over a money matter. (?) He has given all his salary to his mother and is short of pocket money. He asks the mother to raise the amount of his allowance. She says he is brash [*namaiki*], but the

son insists on getting more. The son leaves home to rent an apartment where he will live, not giving a damn about the situation. (?) The mother lives alone.

Again we have an immediate scene of quarreling. The young man wants his mother to return part of his earnings and is refused. He is not at all polite and leaves the house. Yokichi uses a colloquial Japanese expression, which we have translated as "not giving a damn," to explain the feeling of the young man when he is leaving the house. Again Yokichi describes the young man as being *namaiki*, and we get the impression that he identifies very much with a person who is capable of assuming this attitude toward others. He states that the mother henceforth lives alone, suggesting that the mother is punished for her refusal of her son's demands. In his story we get the direct impression that Yokichi will not bend to others but expects that others will eventually bend to his will. This attitude recalls the ambivalent, negative, but covertly admiring expression of his father, *Yakkōsan wa tenka desu-yo* ("That bastard always gets what he wants").

J7. I don't understand. . . . [long silence] (?) The two are talking over something. (?) Judging from the expression of their faces, they are talking about something wrong. (?) A father and son. The old man started to discuss something bad to be worked out by the two of them. (?) [long silence] (?) Burglary or something. (?) They break into some store, the son watches outside and the father goes inside, knocks down a guard there, and comes out with money from the store. So they run away toward the mountains, and in the end they are caught by the police. A parent and his son are the best unit to escape from police search. The son cannot possibly betray his parent. So a parent and son combination is better than other kinds of combinations.

Yokichi here creates a very provocative story. Rather than seeing the father as a source of inspiration and respect, Yokichi has a father and son joining together to commit a burglary instigated by the father. Courage expressed by violence again appears; the father is seen knocking down a guard and coming away with money. Yokichi ends the story, however, with both of them eventually caught by the police. On Card 3 he has a mother committing a crime, and now in response to Card 7 he sees a father committing a crime, involving his son in his own antisocial activities. We see here too that Yokichi is somewhat egocentric. On one level he is saying symbolically, "It isn't enough that I am delinquent, but I'll have it that ultimately my parents will join me in my delinquency," an egocentric, provocative attitude toward authority generally, and expressing a dominating feeling over his parents. Instead of a story with a moralistic father who advises his son in the proper way, he gives one in which the father teaches the boy how to commit a crime. Can this not be interpreted on one level as a disparagement of the parent? He states that a parent can be sure of his son, who cannot possibly betray his father. The language used is brash. The father is called an "old man" in a rough and disrespectful way. Yokichi can, of course, also be indicating an unmet desire for more informal closeness with an older figure. He wants to be dependent on an aggressive, competent male, even if this competence must be expressed antisocially. Throughout, Yokichi expresses a pervasive cynicism toward humans generally—a "wise guy" attitude.

> J8. Among the group of gangsters a woman got hurt. A bad quack doctor in the town and a drunkard are going to operate on her. (?) The one on the right is the quack, and the one on the left is the drunkard. The doctor has been bribed by the boss of the group to operate secretly on the woman, who is a member of the gang. A boy runs to report this to police headquarters, and they are captured at the end, the quack and the gangster. (?) Looks like an urchin-gangster and not the kind to commit a wrong willingly—a messenger boy. (?) She had some business in smuggling goods and got shot with a gun. (?) Somebody of the other side. (?) Somebody on the side that she had business with. Here is the gun.

This story brings a provocative attention to underworld figures. It depicts a wild happening in the world of the *yakuza*, or gangsters. Again there is disparagement directed toward adult figures in that the two who are conducting a secret operation on a woman (perhaps suggesting negative feelings toward his mother) are a "quack doctor" and a "drunkard." Yokichi disparages the whole gang and sees the young boy in the foreground going to the police station so that they are all captured. The boy is seen as someone who still has a conscience and will not willingly commit something wrong. There is a direct suggestion here of Yokichi's ambivalence at this time about his delinquent identity. There is here a kind of flaunting of a delinquent concern with crime. Yet, in this story and the preceding one the police are not outwitted; ultimately those doing wrong come into their hands. The police authority may be unconsciously seen as an inescapable force, a superego retribution from which one cannot flee. One must pay for one's wrongdoing. This attitude toward the police is common in the records of Japanese delinquents, in contrast to the more defiant attitude prevalent among those in the United States.

> J9. This is a scene in which a father leaves home on business for somewhere far on a cold winter day. His child, wife, and mother see him off together. He will die from some accident in the place where he went for business because there is a dark atmosphere hanging over these people. The story ends here. You see, it happens quite often. He goes over there and meets an unexpected accident, an automobile accident or something, and is killed. Consequently, without the father the family has no one to earn money and becomes unhappy. He is seeing his father off and feels somewhat uneasy. (?) She feels the same way to a certain extent, but the child is more sensitive and feels an ominous premonition. Am I supposed to say more? Is this all right?

Yokichi makes up an unusual story for Card 9 also, suggesting his present ambivalence about his father. He gives a story in which a father is killed by an accident, a story that carries a tone of concern over the possible loss of a needed figure. The father dies after he leaves home on a trip, and the sensitive child has had a premonition that something bad will occur. It is as if Yokichi cannot see a family scene without anticipating some disaster. There is direct expression here not only of a hostile wish but also of a tender feeling of wanting more closeness with his father and worrying about his possible loss. It is interesting to note that the more violent delinquent Japanese boys are apt to give a story of the accidental death of a father, whereas Japanese generally are more apt to give stories of illness to account for the loss of a parent.

> J11. This is a story of a mother who remarried and her child by her former marriage, who had come with the mother to his stepfather's house. The child would not become close to the stepfather, and the mother is worried, standing in between. For the child to call him "father" is impossible, and he ignores his stepfather. But the mother is anxious to please the father. Later this problem is solved, and the three get along well. (?) The mother is seeing the father off to work. The child is worried, curious to see how it is, what the situation is . . . how they are when the father goes out. It is not yet a full year. It is not long yet, and he is already thirteen or fourteen. So he cannot be friendly with the stepfather so easily. His mother is worried, standing between the son and the stepfather. As days go on and the father gradually gets more gentle toward him, they will get along well. (?) As the child is brought by the mother, the father hopes to love him, but has left him alone, since he was twisted and obstinate. As days pass they become good friends.

The search for some kind of closeness is again depicted in this story of the initial antagonism between a stepchild and his father. The "twisted and obstinate" child gradually learns to give up his defenses and becomes good friends with the father. The emphasis here is on the father-son relationship rather than on the mother-son relationship, as it is in many stories for this card. There is a covert note of sexual curiosity in the middle of Yokichi's story; the mother is seeing the father off to work and the child peeks in through the door, but what is given expresses not so much sexual curiosity as a curiosity about how people get along—how they relate positively. This is what Yokichi wants to witness, some kind of positive, close relationship between parental figures.

> J12. A man got married and goes on a honeymoon with his bride. This is at a Japanese-style inn, on the honeymoon. The bride is dead of some cause, and the man is lamenting. (?) Poisoned from eating or something like that. She died as if in the state of unnatural death. (?) By something like a poison. She died and the cause was not clear, and the man is sad and crying. . . . Later on he gets another bride. (?) The police come to investigate many things and find the reason. So he goes to a crematorium, has her body burned, returns with her ashes, goes to a Buddhist temple with it. After her anniversary he will marry again.

This is an unusual story. Yokichi still represses any direct concern with sexuality. He sees the scene as a honeymoon; however, the wife is poisoned and dies. The man is blameless here of any act but is sad and crying. It is interesting to note that somehow the dead bride must be promptly replaced in Yokichi's fantasy associations. Yokichi brings the police into his story to investigate the reason for her death; he also graphically describes what happens to the dead, in unusual, explicit detail that is rarely given to this card. Although there is violence in Yokichi's response to other cards, in this situation, which often elicits stories of violence, a man is not violent to a woman—the cause of her death is something external. One could guess from this that Yokichi is considerably inhibited in respect to sexual relationships with women, that his bravado and aggressive activity may be strongly inhibited when it comes to the opposite sex.

> J18. They are a mother and her daughter. The mother becomes gradually insane and at last tries to strangle her daughter to death. This happened several times every evening, and finally the daughter is killed. And the mother dies mad. . . . (?) When the father died, she perhaps got a shock strong enough to drive her out of her mind. The family is the two of them, the father having been dead for about a year. By the way, he was a captain of a ship that sank and he died in it. Then the mother becomes mad.

Violence occurs again. The daughter is not seen as doing anything bad to provoke the mother, but rather it is the father's death that acts as such a shock to the mother that she gradually becomes insane. The father is given a heroic death in being the captain of a ship that sank. Yokichi seems to have exhausted his concern with delinquency and is now giving more ordinary stories in which delinquent activity plays no role.

> J22. A couple, the father and the mother, and a child are going some place. Then the mother opposes the father and they quarrel. So the child is crying in between. As the child started to cry, they come to compromise and go to the Ueno Zoo or somewhere. The father believes the zoo is better for the child and insists on going there. The mother wants to go to a botanical garden. Thus they disagree with each other, saying, "Have it your way. I don't want to bother with it anymore." And the child begins to cry. So they are sorry for him and begin to compromise. . . . He is five or six years old. (?) As the father is not usually at home as his mother is, he does not like to see the father being hard on the mother. He hates him. So it seems. (?) It is not that he loves his mother better than his father but that he hates someone who is hard on her. Just quarreling in words, when they disagree with each other. (?) Someone says, "Let's compromise and go to the zoo." So they go to the zoo.

The story for Card 22 is a simple, direct story of parental disharmony. The child of five or six years old is caught in between, and Yokichi directly states that the child hates the father because the father is hard on the mother, then quickly states that he does not love his mother more than his father. This story has a certain amount of wish fulfillment, in that the parents resolve their conflict and go to the zoo. The small child can be made happy. Yokichi may still have a considerable hope that harmony can occur between parents. He permits himself to have feelings of sensitivity underneath his bravado, as we noted in the first story.

> J27. A university student is inviting a girl friend to enter a coffee shop with him. The girl says that she doesn't like such a place and suggests going to some other place. So the man says, "Well, then, let's go to another place like a restaurant." (?) They belong to the same club at a university. (?) She [third figure] knows them a little and watches them—what they are doing. She never spoke with them, but is on the same campus and knows their faces. So she watches them. (?) She wonders why they are doing this and that in the middle of the street. (?) Perhaps they realize it a little, but are too occupied in their talk to mind it.

As in other records, the coffee shop is a place that a girl who wants to date decently will not enter. They are observed by a spectator who knows them. Yokichi is saying that people do observe your behavior; they know who you are. Japanese generally are aware that it is difficult to hide one's behavior. Yokichi is expressing awareness of the sanctioning processes of his society.

Throughout the TAT protocol Yokichi appears to be much more preoccupied with resolving the relationship with the father than with the mother. There is even some rejection of the mother—for example, in his response to Card 6. Card 11 depicts a situation that could suggest a sexual liaison between a mother and another, but in Yokichi's story the briefcase suggesting the other man is quickly used to indicate a new marriage. From then on the whole story becomes a preoccupation with the possible relationship with a new father, another search for a father, with some hope expressed that the relationship may be straightened out. One sees in Yokichi, therefore, some basic latent homosexual structuring, which on a level closer to consciousness comes out as a defensive and provocative, delinquently oriented masculinity with a feeling of distance from women. One would suppose that there is a great deal of sexual repression in this aggressive boy, who was sanctioned in school for shouting out the word for female genitals in the classroom. In such behavior he is showing bravado, an approved delinquent masculine activity. But underneath, not only has he not resolved his own relationships with his parents but he is not secure in taking on the masculine psychosexual role. One can look at his aggressive behavior in yet another way. He is still, at age fifteen, expressing this behavior, as do many preadolescent boys, as a substitute for repressed sexual interest. Yokichi wants a warm, conflict-free dependent relationship on a strong man. At the time of testing he was not yet ready to identify fully with strength in himself, in spite of the external show of defiant bravado.

A FOLLOW-UP

After a period of four and a half years we interviewed Yokichi again. We found that, although he for some time had continued with his delinquent gang leader's role behavior, he had stopped short of a fully delinquent career. He now talks about his previous delinquent behavior as "immature episodes." He is fully committed to a job, and in the evenings he directs a Sōka Gakkai youth group in his neighborhood. He talks about automobiles as an abiding interest. It is difficult to obtain from his conversation a full picture of his experiences with young women. One suspects no satisfactory resolution about heterosexual behavior. His confident bravado does not hold up well in this area. He did talk at length about the sexual practices of some other boys in his group who pooled resources to rent a room that would be used by several couples for sexual purposes. In his view, such practices were widespread in the Arakawa neighborhood. Some of these liaisons would become more permanent and drift into common-law arrangements.

Yokichi mentioned that his father is doing better. His entire family is occupied again in maintaining a small metalworking factory. His own religious convictions seem to be quite sincere. He still seems to justify much of his behavior in the past as a response to the unfeeling attitude of adults. For example, as we noted earlier, he joked about the fact that one teacher got what he deserved when one of his pupils struck him because the teacher tried to discipline him. Our impression was that enough teachers took an interest in Yokichi in school, recognizing his undoubted talents for leadership and his physical competence in sports, and the hidden tenderness which he usually disguises behind a "tough guy" facade. From interested older men he could respect he did receive sufficient emotional support to prevent him from casting his lot completely with a delinquent gang.

The institution of *banchō* has disappeared from his former school, and Yokichi's attitude is that this is probably a good thing. He feels that the reason for the disappearance of this institution is the greater rapport between students and teachers. Several teachers take a direct interest in their students, a number of them showing unusual understanding of youthful problems. Organized adolescent gang behavior, to Yokichi's knowledge, has diminished in his particular area.

Yokichi still considers himself to be a fighter. He has found a legitimate cause now in the teachings of Sōka Gakkai, for he can marshall his aggressive feelings without feeling guilty. He can obtain the response and interest of others, which he needs to dispel his feelings of potential deprivation, by becoming a nurturant leader of other youth and finding a continual appreciative response in their company. Since his present activities are legitimate and sanctioned, he no longer needs to feel any guilt over his continuing sense of protest against unfeeling authority or an ungiving society. Within Sōka Gakkai others with the same feelings now channel them into a criticism of corruption in government and a puritanical concern with the lack of purpose and direction found in ordinary life. He has found in Sōka Gakkai, therefore, an ideal outlet and the means of expressing both his aggressive feelings and his needs for affiliative contact and social recognition. Earlier, while he functioned as a *banchō*, his leadership gave him recognition, but he could not fully reconcile his protest by means of a completely delinquent identity. It is not that he ever admitted to himself any sense of guilt for his violence or stealing, but rather, as we see in his stories, that he tended to justify this behavior and even to take a certain defiant pride in being considered *namaiki* by others. He recalls that he could not realize dependent needs through his ineffectual parents, for which he still blames them openly.

During his delinquent career Yokichi was living out his father's own vicarious fantasies in their socially constructive, as well as potentially antisocial, directions. Yokichi was, in spite of his antisocial attitude, success-oriented, leadership-oriented, and he attempted to have the "guts" to demand what he wanted from life (all unrealized wishes of his father). Yokichi was in effect partially rejecting his parents in the name of values that they themselves espoused but could not actualize. Today he seems much more accepting of them, to have become reconciled to their inadequacies and to be attempting to maintain his self-confidence in what he himself is doing. We can look back at his series of violent, aggressive acts and his stealing of automobiles as a symbolic expression of an aggressive mode of achieving recognition, and a symbolic taking of what he was not given in an attempt to assuage an inner sense of deprivation. Such interpretations of etiology of delinquent behavior are frequently made in clinical assessments of American cases. In this instance, they apply equally well to a Japanese.

There are some differences, however. In Yokichi we found even in his delinquent period a more basic acceptance of authority, which seems to be true for many of the Japanese delinquents in our sample, compared with more pervasively defiant American youth. In Japan the cultural tradition continues to give a legitimacy to authority which is far more deeply ingrained than in the American culture, where authority is always questioned and not automatically assumed to be correct.

Yokichi, when we last met, continued to express throughout our interview feelings of energy and activity. He continually views people as taking an active stance, sometimes defiantly but always actively. He does not talk about people in a passive sense. They are always the initiators of activity.

CONCLUDING REMARKS

In the Fukuyama family, as in our other families, we can see the son's personality structure, particularly his delinquent behavior, as a product and an integral part of intrafamilial dynamics involving the conscious and unconscious processes of his parents. Mr. Fukuyama, for all his dauntless determination to achieve and his tireless hardworking tendencies, is basically a passive, dependent person, probably with some unconscious undercurrents of a passive, homosexual nature. All his life he has been using intellectualization and a somewhat grandiose, distant approach to reality as his major defenses against his deep sense of inadequacy; these same defenses might very well have been conducive to his social failure in spite of his continuous endeavor to realize his desires for achievement. Because of his underlying sense of inadequacy and passivity and also his unresolved emotions toward his own father, Mr. Fukuyama has difficulty in identifying with a masculine power and authority role within his family.

Mrs. Fukuyama, on the other hand, is self-assertive, occasionally even aggressive, with a well-functioning, realistic ego, although her assertiveness might very well be her defense against an underlying masochistic, hysteroid tendency and a deep sense of loneliness and isolation. Her identification is clearly with the stepmother who reared her and who was the center of the family's life. Although Mrs. Fukuyama once wished for a husband whom she could "depend upon," it turned out that she, like her mother, is the center of the Fukuyama family. Aggressive and assertive, Mrs. Fukuyama shows some avoidance of taking the role of tender, gentle mother. Both parents, because of their own inner problems, relegated the care of their children to the grandmother; a financial crisis and the need for hard work provided them with an excuse to do so. This, seemingly, created in their son, Yokichi, a deep sense of deprivation and a need for dependency and closeness, and these tendencies became acute with the death of his grandmother, who was for him a mother surrogate. Simply stated, this was the pattern of family interaction in which Yokichi grew up. His father failed to offer him a firm masculine model. And yet the father, with his intellectualized moralizing and ineffective attitudes toward the son, also encouraged Yokichi's aggressive masculine tendencies. It is as if the father obtained vicarious satisfaction from his son's overtly aggressive, antisocial behavior. Furthermore, when his business failed, the father showed overt dependence upon his son. Disappointed in her husband's basic weakness and with a deep need for dependency on a more masculine man, Mrs. Fukuyama turned toward her son for the satisfaction of her needs. There is evidence that she even had some narcissistic fantasy, seeing herself as a sexual object vis-à-vis her own son.

Yokichi, in turn, had little opportunity to satisfy his unfulfilled need for dependency and closeness. His delinquent gang behavior was, in some sense at least, meeting parental expectancy, but it also served to create relations with others which partially satisfied his search for closeness. It also may have served as the expression of his anger toward his own parents and against a society, which Yokichi, as a young boy, felt was not treating him fairly, which did not give him what he wanted, and which pushed his family into financial disaster.

CHAPTER 13

Takeshi Ikawa

A Fifteen-Year-Old Rapist

By age fifteen, Takeshi Ikawa had raped several girls and had participated in a number of thefts. He was apprehended by the police and was subsequently sent to a juvenile detention home. Takeshi is the only child of his father's second marriage, the youngest in a family of four boys. The Ikawa family (case I-5) lives in the back of a small candy and tobacco shop in Arakawa. The father, Hideo Ikawa, age forty-nine, is employed as a bookkeeper in a clothing store. The mother, Takeko, age forty-four, manages the tobacco shop while the father is at work elsewhere. Takeshi lives with his parents, three half-brothers, and paternal grandmother in two tiny rooms.

THE FATHER'S BACKGROUND

Mr. Ikawa was born on Oshima, an island in the Pacific directly south of Tokyo Bay which is now under the administration of Tokyo. He was one of two sons of a widowed mother. As Mr. Ikawa tells the story, his mother had the sacrificial virtues expected of a dedicated woman. She supported her two boys and even went without food at times so that they would have something extra. The mother was considered to be very strict. She continually emphasized that they should in no way be dependent on others outside the family and that they should never under any condition enter into debt to anyone else. Strong-willed in raising her sons, she has continued her dominance over Mr. Ikawa even since his marriage. In the interviews, Mr. Ikawa gives the impression that he maintains a strong respect for and an emotional attachment mixed with affectionate gratitude to his aging mother.

He describes his father's family as relatively wealthy landowners in the village where they lived on Oshima. His father's elder brother was the household head of a joint family whose son became the school principal, then village head, and finally mayor of the community. The paternal grandfather was described as having been a bright scholar who received prizes in school. However, Mr. Ikawa's father left home when his elder brother married, and he eventually established himself as an assistant manager for a small shipping company making its money from tourists who visited the island on weekend excursions from Tokyo.

Oshima, with its active volcano, was at this time attracting more and more visitors from Tokyo and elsewhere on Japan's main island, Honshū. It had been used as a place of exile for criminals during the Tokugawa period, and it kept its reputation as an "isolated" island even after it was put under the administration of the Tokyo municipal government in more modern times. People saw it as an exotic place, with its famed camellias, whose seeds produced an oil for women's hair, and its dark-blue-and-white gridded cloth (*Oshima-gasuri*), used for kimonos. The girls of this island were said to have hearts in which "passion flowed like the volcano's fire." Seeking a romantic atmosphere, many novelists, poets, and students paid visits to the island. To do so they had to suffer a rough voyage across Japan's turbulent Black Current, which flows south of Honshū. There was a time when the island was known as an ideal place for suicide, committed by leaping down into the volcano's crater. Much commercialized in the post–World War II development of the tourist industry, Oshima with its elegant mountain profile seen in the distance from Japan's Pacific coast evokes in many people a romantic yearning for life "remote" from it all. Aside from its specially cultivated flowers, the land is too arid and barren for agriculture. The farmers living there have been able to eke out only a bare subsistence from the poor soil.

Members of the Ikawa family gradually left Oshima for the city. A number of Mr. Ikawa's cousins and other family members who one by one migrated to Tokyo are doing well financially. His younger brother is now working for a bank. Talking about his own occupation as bookkeeper in a clothing store, he considers himself to be the only "failure," living in a poor area of Tokyo and remaining in a relative state of poverty compared with others in his family.

In describing what he remembers of the character of his own father before his death, Mr. Ikawa recalls that his father was not very strict with the children. He has no memory of ever having been scolded by him, for example. It is his impression that all disciplining was done by his mother, who sometimes nagged or scolded him when he didn't behave. His father was a quick-tempered person, but he never got angry with his own children. The father was meticulous in his personal behavior and was concerned that things should remain neat about him. When his room was not cleaned to his satisfaction or his children's clothes were not neat, he would point out these failings disapprovingly to his wife.

When Mr. Ikawa was about ten years old his family moved to Tokyo, where his father had been offered a job in the Tokyo office of the small Tokyo-Oshima Steamship Company. Following his primary education, Mr. Ikawa was sent to a commercial school in Tokyo, where he was followed shortly by his younger brother. During this period his father died, and his mother took on full-time care of her boys. He remembers with some emotion that his mother would starve herself when one of her boys was ill to buy some fancy, healthful fruit in a downtown store in Tokyo. He emphasizes his mother's virtuous dedication and strictness in bringing up her sons. For example, she stressed the need to remain financially independent:

> It was all right to give others money but one should never become a financial burden to anyone else. A person who respects himself does not become a burden on others no matter how shabbily he must dress or what

> poor meals he has to eat as a consequence. For, be he well dressed and well fed, he is nevertheless worthless as a human being if he causes others trouble and invites blame and criticism as a consequence.

Mr. Ikawa showed some ambivalence toward his mother's rigid moral teachings. He says, "Of course, in a society like the present one, one would probably have no chance to become successful if one were to remain so rigidly virtuous." He recalled a case of a well-known public prosecutor who refused to buy rice on the black market; rice was severely rationed after the war, and it was supposed that he actually died from undernourishment as a consequence. Mr. Ikawa points out that he may have been very moral but not very wise. He says, "Therefore I always try to tell my own children not to be too rigid. Times have changed." He disagrees with his mother's idea that a salaried man should come home immediately from work. He says:

> We do not live alone on a mountain. We have friendships to keep; we have acquaintances with whom to associate. It is human to enjoy movies occasionally—that is what I tell my children. My younger brother also tells my mother that the children are living in a different world from the past. In my mother's day it was a luxury to have a radio. It was even a luxury to take a streetcar, and people would walk to save money. You cannot tell the children today to do the same thing. I tell my mother not to impose her standards upon her grandchildren. She is now eighty and therefore can no longer talk much to them. She nevertheless recalls all the difficulties she has gone through herself, and it is understandable that she thinks the way she does.

As he recalls how his mother and father resolved conflicts, he remembers it was the father who gave in. He sees the reflection of this in his own behavior:

> When I have any conflict with my wife it is usually I who, for harmony's sake, gives in. I tell others that the secret of happiness and harmony in the family is for a man to be *kyō-sai-ka* [literally, a person who is afraid of his wife—a henpecked husband]. Perhaps the *kyō-sai-ka* may be too strong a word—what I mean is that if you have an idea that your wife is simply an "instrument" you cannot have a very harmonious home. A wife is dependent on her husband, and a husband depends on his wife. There must be cooperation.

From the traditional standpoint such a husband would be called "henpecked" because in the past the wife was considered much inferior to her husband.

> My wife does not see it my way, though. She says, to the contrary, that I'm not a henpecked husband but a real tyrant. But actually when any argument arises between me and my wife, I avoid the situation and remain silent.

He sees his mother's effect on his personality as making him somewhat passive:

> I'm afraid I lack resolution and tend to be indecisive. I tend to be too careful, being concerned about whether I might be laughed at by others or

> that I may cause some trouble to others by doing something. Sometimes I am so concerned with such things that I lose my chance to act. I tend to remain reticent because I think of what others will say if I state my mind. I am very much concerned about others' responses to what I say and what I do. Therefore, I am afraid I am not very well equipped for a society where a fight for survival is fierce in nature. As Buddha himself said, "A lie is sometimes expedient."

In another context, however, he paints a somewhat different picture of his own character. He says, for example:

> I tend to lose self-control and get excited and quarrel, even with my superior, and I have been forced on occasion to quit my job. I never start quarrels for my own sake but always out of concern with those working under me. When I see somebody in financial difficulties, I cannot help but try to do something for him. I somehow cannot remain indifferent or uninvolved. Suppose a man who has a wife and three children receives only ¥15,000 a month. When I see such a man working in my place I cannot remain indifferent. I go to my boss and tell him that this man needs to be paid more, otherwise he and his family cannot reasonably live. If he has to find a side job to supplement his income, he cannot devote himself to his work for our company. He may even be tempted to become involved with some kind of embezzlement. I would not complain if the whole company itself were not thriving. But the top people are living luxurious lives and ignore the financial difficulties of their employees. This is not right. I tell my boss this. I always speak for other people. I have never complained about my own income, never.
>
> I have always been this way, even in childhood. When I found some friends of poor families wearing torn clothes or something shabby, I used to take them home and ask my parents to give them my old clothes. My mother often tells me that when I was a child I was always thinking of others. My parents even wondered if something was not wrong with me, being so concerned with other children's problems. . . . I can't seem to control myself when I want to help others. I know I should not be this way. I tell myself I'm not living alone in this world; as long as I am a member of society I should behave like others, according to certain rules. I know it and yet I feel involved—I simply forget it. I get into quarrels with my superiors; however, I never act violently. I only argue. I hate violence. When I was in the second or third year of commercial school, I once hit a friend. I apologized to him immediately. I suffered from a bad conscience for a long time and I decided never again to act aggressively toward others.

He considers himself a good-natured man. "If someone acts toward me aggressively I may feel challenged or provoked. However, when the same person acts friendly to me afterward, I can readily accept him as a friend—my mother says that nobody among my relatives ever speaks ill of me."

Mr. Ikawa has been married twice. His marriages graphically represent how the relationship between a mother and her eldest son can intrude upon a married couple. His first marriage took place at a fairly early age and ended in divorce, even after the birth of three boys. He explains:

> I had a very close friend at commercial school. He had a younger sister. He wanted me to marry his sister, although I had never met her. I thought she must be a very nice woman, as she was the sister of my best and closest friend. After I left the commercial school I found a job in a perfume company. I was hired because the president of the company was an alumnus of our own commercial school. When I went for an interview and he found that I was from his school, I was hired. I felt ready to marry then. I talked with my mother. My good friend talked to his parents and his sister. Fortunately, the status of our families did not differ much. My friend's parents were impressed with my mother's character and how she had raised her children alone and had been able to send both of her sons to the commercial school. They were agreeable to marrying their daughter to the son of such a woman.

And yet the marriage did not work out. Asked about the reason for his divorce, Mr. Ikawa replied, "Character incompatibility between my mother and my wife. They could never get along well at all." As it came out in the interview, what he meant was that his mother had never approved of nor accepted his wife.

> My wife was very, very sloppy and had a character really different from that of my mother. My mother is an old-fashioned woman who cannot tolerate things being done improperly. My wife simply could not do things right. Everything she did was incomplete or inadequate. For instance, when she sewed *tabi* [Japanese socks] the size of the two *tabi* would differ and no one would wear them. When she sewed a shirt for her child the neck would be too small and the child's head would not fit through it. This did not just happen occasionally but always. Something must have been wrong with her character—a character defect. If what one makes is always defective it's better not to do anything, and yet she could never admit her failures. She never said she was sorry. She never tried to improve herself. My mother would point out her failures to her, and she would actually talk back without admitting her own fault.
>
> I wanted at first to do something myself to effect some reconciliation between my mother and wife, but I was not very successful. The conflicts between them became more serious when I meddled. Therefore I just stayed out of it. When my mother and my wife started quarreling, I would leave the house. During the war we lived in the country, where my relatives lived close by. All my relatives thought my wife was a terrible woman, sloppy in her work and impudent to her mother-in-law. As all of them were of the same opinion, I decided to divorce her.

He never speaks about the fact that she was the mother of his three children, nor anything about his own affection for her. These attitudes are typical of men who maintain strong attachments to their own mothers.

His second marriage was to a widow who had been married to one of his cousins. Soon after marriage her first husband was killed in the war. "Our children were still young and my mother was looking for a good wife for me, one who would take care of the children and household chores. As my mother knew about this woman and her family background, my mother thought she would make a good wife for me. So it was decided."

THE MOTHER'S BACKGROUND

Mrs. Ikawa is a reticent talker, who reveals little about herself or her attitudes. She is an anxious and self-effacing person, and seems to feel easily threatened. Her characteristic defense is to retire and comply. She gives the impression of being a dutiful, simple-minded housewife, who may be somewhat self-preoccupied and distracted by inner problems that find little direct external expression.

Mrs. Takeko Ikawa was born in 1919, in a farming village in Chiba Prefecture to the east of Tokyo. She describes her own father as being of a submissive nature and her mother as very domineering. She herself was sent to Tokyo at age sixteen and received two years' training for nursing. She had just established herself as a nurse when her marriage to her first husband was arranged in Tokyo. The couple were married only one month when he was shipped to the war front, where he was killed.

Mrs. Ikawa's father had been a cavalryman in the Imperial Guard when he was young, and after his marriage he had farmed the family land. He was regarded by everyone as a quiet, reticent man. Mrs. Ikawa's paternal grandfather was once a fairly large landowner who had served as village head. He became embroiled in some political activity that forced him to be away from home, and as a consequence he lost much of his property.

Mrs. Ikawa describes her grandfather as a person who did not extend himself much to children. She said, "Although other children's grandfathers usually took their grandchildren places, my grandfather never took us." She never remembers any quarrels between her parents. She was never scolded by her father, and yet she felt afraid of him and could not talk to him freely. She believes that since her father grew up without experiencing any great financial difficulty, "he lacked considerate feeling for others." Her mother used to say that a person needs to experience hardship and tribulation; otherwise he never develops a feeling of sympathy for the difficulties of others. Her happiest experience in childhood was being taken to her mother's home, where her maternal grandmother was especially fond of her.

Mrs. Ikawa is explicit about her present husband's mother, with whom she has had to live for most of her adult life.

> She is an old-fashioned woman. She is now blind, which makes her more difficult. Although I myself think that I am doing things right, she does not think so. She says that I do things in a very careless, sloppy way. She says that since she is now blind and cannot see, I do things poorly and make a monkey out of her. It is not true at all. I think I have had a very hard time.

Because of continual difficulties with her mother-in-law she returned home on several occasions, wishing to break off the marriage. Each time she was told by her own parents to endure it, at least until her own child was older.

> When I took my mother-in-law to a public bath, holding her hand and carrying my baby on my back, I had to wash my baby and then my mother-in-law and would as a consequence have no time to wash myself. On such occasions my mother-in-law would still complain and blame me for what I did or did not do. It was just too much for me to bear. . . . I think my husband thought it would make the situation worse if he spoke and therefore he decided to stay out of it. I wished sometimes he would try to help out.

In Japan children stay with the father, for they belong to the father's lineage, and so upon Mr. Ikawa's divorce from his first wife all three children remained with him and became the responsibility of the new wife. Takeko says that from the beginning she could always get along well with her stepsons. The father seems to have had more time to demonstrate responsibility with his older sons than with her own child, who came later.

THE PARENTS' VIEW OF TAKESHI AND THEIR OTHER SONS

Concerning his children by his first wife, Mr. Ikawa says:

> I have always considered my children just ordinary. I never wanted them to be extraordinarily successful—for instance, to become a millionaire or government official. I told them that society evaluates college graduates higher than those who only finish high school, but I also told them to decide what they wanted to do for themselves. I suggested that they would become better balanced if they engaged in both studies and sports.

The eldest boy did not want to go to college, and went to a commercial high school. The father notes that this son did not want his father to use any personal connection as a means toward getting him a job. Instead, he decided to take a competitive examination for which he was recommended by his school. He applied to Mitsubishi Electric and, having passed the examination, is now working for them. The father states, "As a parent I have very complicated feelings. He is growing up fast. As far as my feelings are concerned, he is still a small child, and yet he is living his own life now."

His second son was an average student while in the elementary school, but began doing exceptionally good work in his first year of middle school. He was considered the top student in over three hundred students. In the third-year class, however, he started suffering migraine headaches.

> A doctor in our neighborhood could not cure it. We took him to a large hospital, and the doctor said it was a nervous disease and that it was

> hard to cure. He said that he could do an operation but that he could not guarantee its effectiveness. We did not want our son to suffer from a painful operation without the prospect of being cured, so he did not have the operation, but as he continued having headaches it was necessary for him to stop studying. He said he did not want to go to college, and he went to a commercial school instead. While in the second year at the commercial school he had an operation that seems to have made his condition better. He became interested again in the idea of going to college and started studying hard. He passed the examination for Chūō University, and is now studying law.

Mr. Ikawa thinks his third child, in junior high, is "fairly average" and has no particular problems.

At the time his first three children were going through grade school, Mr. Ikawa reports, he was very active in the PTA. He mentioned that there was a time at the PTA when the "communists" were coming to the general meetings and attacking the chairman and the executive committee about their budget. People became so afraid that no one volunteered for the chairmanship. At this point, Mr. Ikawa said he was not afraid and took over the chairmanship. During the time he was chairman, he said, "I think some people in the PTA did not like me and my way of doing things. However, if you wanted to be liked by everybody you would never accomplish anything." From the mother's interview we gather that most recently the father has not been active in the PTA. In fact, he has had very little recent contact with the school. According to the mother, "Having my old mother-in-law at home, I could not attend PTA meetings very often." One gains a distinct impression, therefore, that the father was much more involved with the schooling of his older boys than with his youngest son. The mother shows less active involvement than is usual.

TAKESHI'S DEVELOPMENTAL HISTORY

The Ikawa's youngest son, Takeshi, the second Mrs. Ikawa's only child, was born not long after the marriage. Mrs. Ikawa says, "I wanted to have my own children and was very happy when my son was born." She quickly adds, "Although when he does wrong I wish he had not been born."

As a young child he seemed to give them no special problems. While still quite small, he went to bed alone without any fuss. Mr. Ikawa remembers discussing with his wife that their boy was "easy to raise." Bed-wetting was occasional, however, until he was in the fifth grade. Generally, Takeshi seemed to his parents no different from the other children except that "he eats meals somewhat more slowly than others, and he dislikes meat."

The first indication of the boy's delinquency was thieving, which his father first noticed when Takeshi was in about the fourth grade. At that time he took ¥3,000 out of the drawer in his parents' store and treated a friend of his with the money. The parents knew nothing of this until the friend's mother came to them with a box of strawberries as a gift to express her gratitude for their son's having been so nice to her boy. They then pressed their son, and he confessed what he had done. They told him next time to ask for money instead of taking if from the drawer. Mr. Ikawa says, "I had heard of this sort of thing happening not infrequently in a store-owning family, and since it's not so unusual for children to take money from the parents without meaning to steal, I did not think it was too serious." As far as the parents know, the boy has not stolen from them since. The father's bland remarks about stealing did not conform to the facts known by the school; other acts of stealing by the boy have been reported. The boy himself in his own interviews admits to more stealing than is mentioned by his father.

Takeshi's deliquency was not limited to repeated stealing. At the age of fourteen he had his first experience of what is described as rape—the degree of compliance by the girl is not clear. He witnessed a friend of his raping a girl, after which he himself also forcefully attacked her.

> First I felt quite disgusted, but then I somehow impulsively wanted to do it very much myself. Then I wanted to repeat it. This first experience left the strongest impression on me, and it still remains in my mind as if it's printed there. I also thought I would not be caught, as my friend had gotten away. When I did it later myself, I would tell myself that I would not be found out. But afterwards, each time I was constantly afraid of being caught. When my teacher would call me to his office I always felt a kind of shock, thinking that they had found me out at last.

Takeshi had been apprehended by the police shortly before our contacts with him, and was subsequently to be sent to a detention home. In the boy's interview materials at this time, there is very little expression of what might be considered guilt about his delinquent acts. He seems to have been most concerned with having been caught. When he was asked how he felt when he was caught he said, "I wondered why they had found out and how come I had been caught—I still can't answer that. The harder I think and the more I wonder, the more I feel confused. I still don't know why I was found out."

He says about his stealing that it was not because he liked the feeling of excitement in stealing but because he needed more money. He said he had been given some allowance but he "needed more." He liked spending money on children at the playground, going to movies, and treating his acquaintances to snacks. He liked to show much money to them and make them feel envious of him. One gains the impression that this boy was desperately trying to buy contact with others and that his stealing was a means of having enough money so that other boys would show an interest in him. He says, "Recently I have felt more satisfied and do not want more money."

We were unable to obtain any detailed and relevant information about the patterns of family interaction and of child-rearing, and therefore we cannot reconstruct the process of the boy's personality formation. The following remarks made by the boy may suggest the feelings he now has toward his family members.

Concerning his grandmother, who used to discipline him, he said:

> When I was a small child I felt annoyed at my grandmother for telling me uncomfortable things. Recently stranger thoughts come to my mind. When my grandmother bothers me too much I frankly feel I wish to kill her, or something like that.

About his parents' discipline he says:

> When my mother tells me to be careful about my words, to talk more politely, or something like that, I feel rebellious. It is okay if she is not too persistent, but when she talks too much I feel I should talk back. I don't like to let her talk. . . .
>
> My father's not so nagging. When he is angry he is angry. But when he is friendly he is friendly. But I don't think I can say that I like my father. I think I like my mother better, even when I quarrel with her. . . . I feel somehow as if my father were a stranger. . . . Especially recently I feel a chill in my back when I see my father's face. I feel as if I were with a policeman. . . . My father does not tell me to study hard as my mother does. In this regard I think I like my father better than my mother.
>
> When I quarrel with my mother I tell her I want to become a real delinquent. She says, "Go ahead and try," and then I can no longer be angry with her. My mother has known my character well since my childhood. Because she knows my character well, she knows that I am too cowardly to be a delinquent even if I tell her I will be.

He says that he gets along with his second and third brothers but not with his oldest. He finds that he can talk much more easily with his mother than with his father. He frankly says that he does not like his grandmother very much.

> I know my grandmother means well and wants to make me grow up well, but she keeps bringing up what happened in the past [meaning his delinquent behavior] and I get angry. Grandmother and mother quarrel frequently—whenever they have time for it. My grandmother blames my mother, saying that as my mother did not raise me right I have become a bad boy. I get angry at my grandmother, and I have quarreled with her. My father tells me to stop and I stop.

Of the possible sources of this boy's sexual delinquency, the father says, "In short, he [the boy] slept with my wife until he was in the fifth or sixth grade. I wonder if this had any effect on him?" It must be noted that this is most unusual even in Japan, where a child, especially the youngest, is allowed to remain close to its mother for a much longer time than is true in the United States. It is safe to assume that the boy was sexually stimulated by sleeping in his mother's bed until he was twelve years old. He is known by the police to have stolen women's underwear on one occasion. In this case we see that the psychological, intrafamilial factors are much more prepotent than the outside, social-environment factors.

The father seems to be quite aware of the unusual sexualizing of the child by his mother. When asked why his son slept so long with his mother, the father replied, "Well, it was from force of habit. When he was a small child he slept with my wife, and it continued without our thinking about it very seriously." When asked if he felt that sleeping with the mother was a cause of his son's delinquency, the father replied, "Well, he slept with my wife, and if he was a precocious child, touching his mother's body and things of that kind caused him to become interested in a woman's body . . . I think that way."

One wonders, when the father is so aware of psychological motivation now, ex post facto, why there were no precautions taken earlier. Since this particular father had a strong and continuing attraction to his widowed mother, one can speculate about his unconscious induction of a similar relationship between his wife and his youngest child, aided and abetted perhaps by the fact that the parental sexual relationship was at best a muted and infrequent one. Mr. Ikawa's mother had remained his primary attachment throughout his two marriages. We should consider the identification patterns in this family that led to the incestuous sexual stimulation of the boy: the father, with his strong unconscious attachment to his own mother, identifies himself with his son, and his wife with his mother, thus creating the image of his desired closeness between his mother and himself. By implicitly encouraging the close tie between his wife and son, the father experiences vicarious satisfaction of his own incestuous wish for his own mother.

There are numerous cases found in clinical settings of impotence or at least a tendency toward impotence or sexual inhibition between husband and wife in family situations where the mother fastens tenaciously onto her son, usually the eldest. This mother-son relationship is in effect sanctioned by the concern for lineage in the Japanese system. It is positvely sanctioned for the eldest son to take permanent care of his mother and to put the interests of the mother over those of the wife when quarrels arise. The relationship usually remains well sublimated, and only rarely, as in this case, does the pattern result in the sexual pathology of a child. Here there may have been seductive interplay between mother and child (see the projective results of Mrs. Ikawa), the husband offering no counter to it but in effect condoning and abetting the situation.

The boy says that he daydreams a lot.

> I thought of becoming a wealthy person and spending all my life just playing. . . . I would live alone so that nobody bothers me telling me what to do . . . I don't like to be told what to do. I would go many places by car—I would be really wealthy. . . . I also daydream about a monster attacking my neighborhood. Houses and everything get smashed under the monstrous huge feet. Everybody is crushed and only I escape. The earth comes to its end and only I am left alone. . . . Things like that.

The boy's frequent "daydreaming" appears to be an outer sign of the severity of his internal psychic disturbances (see projective analysis).

PROJECTIVE TEST RESULTS: MR. IKAWA

The Rorschach Test

Mr. Ikawa's own basically suspicious and guarded attitudes were reinforced by the fact that he felt defensively provoked during his visits to a counseling center with his child, where he went at the firm insistence of the boy's teacher. He claimed to the tester that someone had said he was "reluctant to reflect on his own involvement in the delinquent behavior of his child." He had developed a defensive attitude toward the clinic, stating that the staff members were accusatory toward him rather than helpful to his child. His attitude toward the testing situation, therefore, is greatly influenced by his general negative perception of all professional personnel administering tests and conducting interviews.

Mr. Ikawa's Rorschach is not exceptional to any great degree, but it is a fairly normative record. There are some features of the record, however, that are worthy of consideration because they reflect idiosyncratic aspects of his personality.

Rorschach Protocol

I. (7″) 1. *It is a bat.* It looks like a bat, judging from the color and the shape; besides there is its face in the center. (?) Although I have never held a bat in my hand, I think the wing is somehow different from this. I think a bat has only one pair of wings and is somehow different. It should project in this way. [He is pointing to part of the location chart.] There are holes here, but I think a bat should have a pair of wings. This part looks different. If it does not have these parts, then it is a wing of a bat. Since this has these holes, it looks strange; but a bat is most likely. [W FC′+ A P Neut (Correctness Rigidity)]

II. (60″) 2. *Looks like dancing.* Two persons are dancing, clapping their hands. They've just opened their hands. This part is a foot, jumping. They are not clapping the hands of the other; they are clapping their own hands. Each of them is holding his hands high. This is a back figure. This is a neck. The faces are not shown, though. [W M+ H P (Prec)]

III. (35″) 3. *Looks like two women are washing.* This looks just like a woman. I think so, judging from the swelled-out breasts. The white part is an apron. Seems they are cooking, holding something in their hands. (?) Some utensil in a kitchen. [D M+ H P (Neut)]

IV. (37″) 4. *Looks like an ox is dashing toward this direction. I can't imagine anything else.* This is the head of an ox, and this is the front leg. Since it is dashing toward me, it looks fearful and looks like an ox. That's all that I thought. [W FM+ A P (Athr)] [Additional response]: Looks like the hide of a cow. [When he was about to change the card]: Let me see, it looks like the hide of a cow. How do you call it? A stuffed animal? It is unfolded. First time, I thought it's a rushing cow; but if it is so, it is strange because the anus is seen; so it must be a stuffed cow. I think so, judging from the anus.

V. (28″) 5. *Looks like a bat is flying.* It looks like a bat flying; but I don't know actually. I have seen the shape of a bat in some book and know how it flies. It just lowered the wings after having flown. How do you say? It looks like when a bird lowers its wings after flapping them. When it is flying, I think it opens its legs like this. That's all. [W FM+ A P (Neut)]

VI. (80″) 6. *Looks like a dragonfly about to fly off.* It looks strange for a dragonfly; but I can't imagine anything else. I judged this as a leaf, a big leaf of a fig tree. Although it is not satisfactory, I thought it is a dragonfly. [W FM+ A (Neut)]

VII. (24″) 7. *A Shinto priest is reciting a prayer.* Two Shinto priests wearing long hats [*e boshi*] are facing each other. They are folding their hands. Putting their arms under the sleeves, they are reciting a prayer. This looks like a figure of a court noble, which I have seen in some movie, but this kind of costume cannot be seen in the present society, so I changed the figure of a noble into that of a priest in a modern sense. [W M+ H P (Drel)]

VIII. (91″) 8. *A bear which is hunting around food is reflected on the surface of the water. I can look at this card in any way, can't I? This way, or this way . . . nothing else.* If I look at it vertically, I can't imagine anything; so I looked at it this way: it had four legs, so looks like an animal. It looks like a bear. It's impossible for an animal to walk vertically; so I looked at the card horizontally. The shape looks like a bear. Tensing up the legs, lifting up a foot, a bear walks from a rock to a rock in search of food. This half of the picture is the same; so I thought it is the reflection of the half on the surface of the water. It's impossible to think it is a mirror. [W FM+ A P (Neut)]

IX. (166″) 9. *Well, I don't know. I can't imagine anything.* (?) *I can't see anything at all. Is that all right?* I can't understand. I can't imagine anything. [(Arej)]

X. (101″) 10. *If I dare say so, it looks like a poster of an Olympic Game. It looks like a flag of five colors; among them I think I can see the Japanese flag, which has a red sun in the white cloth. It also looks like two athletes shaking hands.* This is difficult to imagine; so I simply judged from the color. There are five colors, one, two, three, four, and five. So it reminds me of the five basic colors for the Olympic Games, and these men make me imagine that they are shaking hands. And I thought of this as the Japanese flag; that is why I think that this is a poster of the Olympic Games. [WF CF, M+ H/Art (Porn)]

Card-by-Card Sequential Analysis and Comments

On Card I, Mr. Ikawa sees the usual popular bat, but quarrels considerably with the form accuracy of the blot. It is not that his perception of the bat is wrong, but that the blot area is inadequate. There are holes where there should be a solid mass, and the wings are not quite proper for a bat. One infers a kind of querulous, indirect form of hostility expressed through criticizing an ordinary form percept. There is a suggestion of some rigidity in his personality. On Card II he immediately perceives what is a usual percept—dancing figures. But, for some reason, he needs to change it. He has to point out carefully that they are clapping their own hands rather than clapping hands with one another. There is some symbolic indication of withdrawal from too spontaneous, active interaction with others; nevertheless, he is able to see a constructive, positive theme. In this card and the next one he reveals his basic introversive orientation, ignoring the color and paying attention to human movement.

On Card III he again gives a normative popular response in which he constructively integrates the two figures seen as women who are washing, the white part being aprons, or they may be cooking something. What he sees is the prosaic work activities of women. The next, Card IV, he enlivens with some feeling of threat, seeing a rushing bull or ox coming in his direction, a rather fierce animal. He perceives the head area very well, and the rest, although of poor shape, is pulled in to give this enlivened percept. Later he gives an additional response to this card, the hide of a cow. A hide is a popular percept, although it is unusual here in that he explicitly includes the anal region or buttocks.

On Card V he gives again an ordinary popular response, which he describes at some length, enlivening it with flying and lowering of the wings. In each of his responses so far his main perceptual point of origin is his sensitivity to human and animal movement, a strongly introversive orientation. Card VI he sees as a dragonfly about to fly off. He says it looks strange for a dragonfly but he can't imagine anything else. He judges the remainder to be a leaf. An achievement push is suggested by his need to produce an integrated whole response to the entire area of each card. The response to Card VII is a well-perceived and fairly original one of two Shinto priests facing each other and reciting a prayer. Again, he demonstrates possibly superior intelligence in his ability to perceive complex organization. Equally demonstrable of this ability is his response to Card VIII: he sees a bear hunting around for food. Looking at the card sideways, he sees the other half of the card as a reflection of this scene on the surface of water.

Card IX, however, is too much for him, and he finds it necessary to reject it (not unusual among Japanese). The last card he organizes in a daring way, seeing it as poster for the Olympic Games, with flags of five colors. This is his first use of color, which he handles well. In the center he sees two athletes shaking hands, another human-movement response.

Overall, therefore, we see a man who is certainly of high intelligence and capable of complex conceptualization. He likes to think analytically and deductively. He is capable of creative or original thinking. He manifests no unusual content that would have to be considered suggestive of any particular pathological preoccupation. One would say from his Rorschach that he is attentive to his social world, but more introversively oriented than responsive to his outer environment.

The TAT

Mr. Ikawa gives a guarded, emotionally detached, and careful protocol. Nevertheless, he cannot fully guard against revealing some initial reactions. In several instances he quickly changes stories he believes are too revealing. His use of Japanese is cautious and somewhat ambiguous. He does not carefully delineate any statements, almost as if he does not want to state anything so directly that it can be assumed to be an attitude of his. The relationships within the stories are also handled in a very guarded way. There is little warmth depicted.

> J1. Is this a violin? A violin and a music book. It seems to me that he has been practicing the violin according to this music book, but there are some parts he can't understand. What shall I say? Anyway, there is something that he can't understand. Since he cannot play well, he is thinking. (?) It is, I mean, that he can't play well. So he is thinking deeply. (?) That's all that I can say. (?) I do not think this is a lesson at school, but he is playing the violin as his hobby. Suppose he is having a lesson at school; he looks like a junior high school student. In junior high schools I do not think they give lessons in the violin; they just have a music class. It's impossible to think that this junior high school has a class for the violin, so I think he is practicing the violin at home as a hobby. If I say, "He came to a deadlock," it sounds too serious for him, since he is not desiring to be a music expert, just that he is thinking that he can't play as well as he wants. He will try once more. Well, I should say several times rather than once. At the first moment I saw this picture, I thought he was tired of playing the violin, but now it seems he is thinking.

This is not the usual positive achievement story. There is frequent repetition of a feeling of inadequacy. The boy seems unable to continue. Mr. Ikawa almost explicitly denies any future time orientation. The boy is simply studying the violin as a "hobby" but can't play it as well as he would like. Mr. Ikawa indulges in some lengthy verbalization without giving much in the way of actual dramatic content.

> J2. I don't know what this is. Isn't this Japanese scenery? Somehow it's dark, so I don't know. (?) The picture is dark. It's dark—subtle or crafty. This is a mother and a father and a daughter. I can't see this very well, but it looks like a rock. It's hard to tell. Since it is dark, I don't know what he is doing. I think he has something in his hands but I don't

> know what it is. And I can't tell whether this is a rock or a rice paddy or a farm. . . . So, I have to imagine, right? Well, I think this father has a horse. He is engaged in agricultural work. Well, I think this is a farm. His wife has brought lunch or something like that. (?) The daughter came here to talk to her father about something, but her father gave her a curt answer, so she is sulking. She is not facing toward either the father or the mother. And it seems that she is sulking and that somehow she gets angry and is showing her feeling on her face. (?) Perhaps the mother doesn't know. Perhaps, as soon as the mother has finished her errand with the father, she will go home with the daughter and will listen to her. I mean the daughter will talk with the father and she will get an answer. (?) I get the feeling she is an ill-natured person, I mean in the picture. I wish you could test me with a brighter picture, not with this sinister one. (?) The trouble is I can't imagine what kinds of things the daughter wanted to talk over with her father. Just this or that, I think. If I know it I may be able to give you a conclusion, but I just don't know.

His response to Card 2 again exemplifies a cautious, suspicious approach and a tendency to project a great deal of his own covert antagonistic feelings into the testing situation. He criticized the picture as too dark to be seen clearly and uses an unusual word, meaning subtle or crafty. This usage recalls his own verbalization during the interview, "As Buddha said himself, 'A lie is sometimes expedient.'" He would like to present himself as a nonhostile person, but admits in the interview that his wife sees him as hostile and tyrannical at times. This remark seems to be some indirect reflection of his attitude toward the test situation as a devious and crafty device used against him. Toward the end of the story he complains that he wishes to be tested with "brighter" pictures, perhaps to give a better picture of himself. He identifies the three figures in the farm scene as father, mother, and daughter, but then deflects his attention to a "rock" and defensively says that he doesn't know what the male figure is doing; he has something in his hands but he doesn't know what it is. Subsequently, he sees a workaday scene. The father with his horse is doing his farm work; the mother has brought lunch, and the daughter has come to talk to her father. He perceives this as a negative, conflictual relationship. The father rejects the daughter's wishes, so she is seen as "sulking." He identifies only with the male figure. It is unusual for this picture to be a rejection of a daughter by a father. One would surmise from this story, in which Mr. Ikawa focuses on the man as a protagonist in a picture with a woman's figure in the foreground, that he is usually egocentrically concerned with himself and his own internal states. He may at times find himself in an antagonistic relationship with another, not having anticipated the other's reactions to him.

> J3. Since this woman wears shoes, I think this is outside. [long silence] I can't think any more. [Mr. Ikawa thereupon asked the purpose of this test and he expressed his indignation at having heard from somebody that Mr. such-and-such at the counseling center had talked about him and remarked that he had no ability to reflect on himself. The ex-

> aminer talked with him for about thirty minutes and after that he said he understood the purpose of the test and continued with it.] I think this is outside, since she wears shoes. (?) But if I don't think that way I can't reason so I want to think that way. But I am stuck and can't think any more. (?) Yes, I think so, since she wears shoes. But somehow it looks like a sofa; then it should be inside the house. If this is a sofa, then this is not outside but a corridor somewhere. (?) The corridor at some theater. If it is a corridor, no wonder she wears shoes. I think this is a young girl. Well, I will decide she is outside. She is weeping, abandoned by her lover. The lover has already gone somewhere. This would be enough. (?) Well, I think she has been waiting. (?) No, he came, but they had a quarrel and he left and she is weeping here.

In this story the guarded negative attitude noticeable on Card 2 explodes into an overt discussion of his suspicions about the purpose behind his being tested. He says to the examiner that the testing seems to be aimed at accusing him for his son's behavior. He is somewhat mollified by the reassurance that the tests are part of a university research project, assuring him of anonymity. However, we note that even a half-hour discussion, with an affirmation on his part that he now understands the purpose of the testing and will continue, does not alter his guarded attitude in telling his stories. In this card he focuses on whether the figure is inside or outside the house. He worries over the propriety of wearing shoes within the house. He finally gives a quick, standard reason for the "crying," a lover's rejection of the young girl.

> J6. This is a mother and her son. The son has come asking his mother if he can borrow some money. Then the mother said coldly, "I have no money to lend you." The son is not an heir and he doesn't live in his mother's house, so he doesn't know what to do. (?) Yes, he is married. (?) Because his wife is going to have a baby. (?) Rather I would say that this son and his wife have no idea of how to save money and have no money at all now. So the mother thought it was good to discipline them by refusing to lend them money. (?) He will plead with his mother, and finally she will compromise and lend him the money.

This is his third successive story of rejection, an unusual sequential occurrence. On this card we have another form of rejection: a mother rejects her son's request for money. First the mother is depicted as acting coldly, but then Mr. Ikawa reasons that she may have been right, since the son and his wife do not know how to save money properly, and the mother thinks it is "good to discipline them" by refusing to lend them money, and this is strongly reminiscent of his actual marital life.

> J7. They are a professor and his assistant. He is not a student any more, but after he graduates he stays at school and keeps up the relationship with the professor. They are making arrangements for their research. Well, not making arrangements, but rather the assistant is re-

> porting his research and the professor is making comments on it, I think. (?) It seems that he trusts the professor wholly. (?) He also loves his assistant and gives him considerate advice.

The story here contains positive nonconflictual themes in a discussion between a younger and an older man depicted as professor and assistant, who are doing their research together. Mr. Ikawa explicitly needs to state that the younger man trusts the professor wholly and that the other man loves his assistant and gives him considerate advice. Following the three pictures of refusal, this is a change of pace wherein a father-son relationship is idealized. It is almost as if he were self-conscious on this card, thinking that some statement of a father-son relationship was required of him. Seen by itself, this is a positive story, but seen after three stories of rejection, it may be indicative of a kind of compensatory response to what he did on the three previous cards. Note also that in the explanation given to Mr. Ikawa about the purposes of our research, he was told that it was being done under university auspices, so his picking out a "professor and his assistant" in giving a positive story indicates that he is being cooperative and in effect trusts academic people and their purposes.

> J8. He has a dream while sleeping. This child . . . this child, yes, it is this child—he has the same face. (?) Yes, it is a boy. This is in a dream—I don't know. . . . In a dream he broke into the other's house with his friend. A dream is a dream. [Shift of story]: The child has a desire to become a doctor. He has a dream that he has become a doctor and now is assisting the other doctor in performing an autopsy. I think they are opening up this dead man because he died a strange death. He is a budding physician. This is his teacher and he is his assistant. The teacher is opening the body with a surgical knife. (?) There is no relationship between them. If I emphasize that there is no relationship between them, then it is possible to think that he is a police physician.

In this card Mr. Ikawa catches himself. He starts out giving a story of a delinquent boy dreaming of breaking into a house with a friend. He emphasizes all the while that it is a dream, but then he thinks better of it and starts on a more constructive theme in which the boy, who desires to be a doctor, has a dream about assisting another doctor in performing an autopsy to ascertain the nature of a "strange" death. Things are not what they seem on the surface; something has to be examined and analyzed. We get the impression that this man uses, unsuccessfully, a reaction formation when he catches himself expressing an attitude or a perception that he does not wish to become overt. The second story, with an achievement theme, is another example of what he did on Card 6, describing a more positive situation than the one he spontaneously perceived. Some form of intellectualization or reaction formation is called upon by this man for defensive maneuvers in coping with his environment and social relationships. He is intelligent and sometimes is able to rationalize himself out of a difficulty.

J9. Is about to go out. This is a son and a daughter and a mother. (?) Yes, this is a daughter too. They are sisters, and this man is the husband of this girl, and the son-in-law [*muko*] and the mother are not getting along well. They had trouble and the son-in-law left the mother's house. And the daughter tried to go out with him. The sister also wants to go. (?) Since the daughter is extending her hands, she is trying to go with the husband. What should I say about going out of the house? They do not mean to leave the house forever. . . . Since he feels fretful, he must have thought it was a good idea to go out for a walk and then come back. (?) Well, I think she admits it was her own fault and forgives them, allowing them to go away.

In this story Mr. Ikawa starts out suggesting a disharmonious family situation. By the end of the story he has toned it down to a less serious situation, one that can be resolved. The story features the problems of an adopted husband, a *muko-yōshi*, who cannot get along with his adopted mother (or mother-in-law). This story is in fact the very opposite of what occurred in his own two marriages. His first wife was finally sent home because she could not get along with her mother-in-law. When we consider his previous stories of rejection we wonder how much this man actually wanted his first wife to leave and how much he simply acceded to the mother's wishes. One gains the impression that his own emotional ties to his mother were such that he felt no compunction about having his wife sent away. In this story to the TAT he reverses the sex of the figures and creates a similar situation, though one with a much happier ending than occurred in real life between his first wife and his mother.

The manner he uses in shifting and toning down the negative features of his story as it progresses is similar to his more abrupt change of story on the preceding card. One must assume that his defensive use of reaction formation at times occurs after the fact, only after a situation has already been resolved. In other words, his ego censorship does not spontaneously cause him to avoid negative perceptions. He seems only to become aware of the implications of some of his reactions or impulses after they have already been expressed. He has a kind of guarded awareness and alertness by which he hopes to prevent any compromising revelation.

J11. The son had pleaded with his mother to buy something he wanted. He went out shopping. When he came back his father was already home. The son is afraid he may be scolded by the father for what he bought and he wonders what his mother's reaction is. (?) She also does not know what to do, since she allowed her son to buy something without the father's consent. (?) Well, I think he will go into the house soon. (?) I can't see it here but I think he has it beside him. It might have been a small matter if they had bought after consulting the father, but they have failed to do that, and that's why they feel so awkward. The mother is thinking very hard about how to talk about this. After she finishes talking with the father, the son will go into the house with ease.

This story embodies an interesting perception of a kind of conspiratorial attitude uniting son and mother in opposition to a dominant father. The story begins with the statement that the son had pleaded for something from the mother. The mother gives in to the son, but they then both become concerned with what effect this will have upon the sterner father, who has not been informed. The father is made to seem a tyrannical figure. Mr. Ikawa states that the woman gave the son the money without telling *danna*; this usage in Japanese is often a pejorative way to refer to a husband, because, although *danna* is an honorific (master), it can express a negative attitude when it is used without the usual final honorific *san* (or *sama*). Here, therefore, Mr. Ikawa conveys an ambiguous attitude toward the position of the father as an authority figure; although in this story he depicts a dominant, powerful father, we get the impression that he does not identify with such a father or with such a role. His perception is that such a father is a kind of tyrant around whom the mother and son must walk with care, and yet he sees the role as a legitimate one, which must be recognized. The mother takes on a traditional role of intercessor between the son and father and straightens out the situation so that the son can reenter the house "with ease."

> J13. This is, of course, a husband, isn't he? And then . . . the wife . . . let me see . . . she consults a doctor. She is sick and the husband has been told by the doctor that his wife has an incurable illness and so he is weeping and turning away from his wife. She does not know about this yet. But she is seriously ill. That's what I imagine. (?) Yes, she has been sick for a long time. Although it seems strange that if she is sick she is not covered. She is still alive but she is dangerously ill. Being informed of this by the doctor, the husband is weeping and turning his back toward his wife. (?) Of course, after the doctor is gone he is weeping. (?) No, I don't think they have children.

Card 13 starts out as a common story of the illness of a wife and the husband's concern over her condition. In the middle of the story, however, he notes that the woman's breasts are uncovered and says that her body is uncovered in a manner that would be strange if she were sick. However, this impulsive breakthrough toward a more sexual plot is stifled and he goes back to his original story. This abrupt shift again shows an unsuccessful repressive mechanism in his conflictual thoughts. He may be given to impulses that he has to quickly put down to maintain what he thinks is a socially conforming facade. Again he uses a derogatory term for a husband, *teishu*, which is most frequently used rudely by one woman talking with another about her husband when she wants to derogate the husband's status. Used politely, the word would have an honorific in front of it. The word *teishu* is sometimes used by men in a derogatory sense toward another husband, in taking a positive or sympathetic attitude toward the wife; it is a way of indicating a preference for the wife in a relationship while expressing some hostility toward the husband. This usage again seems to indicate in Mr. Ikawa a basic lack of acceptance of the dignity of the husband or the father role in a marital relationship. In two successive cards he derogates the husband by a subtle use of terminology. He also uses the word *danna* again, with its derogatory implications, in the context of this story, as in the preceding one.

> J18. A mother and her son . . . a son . . . a mother and a son. The son has done something wrong, has made a mistake, and the mother is scolding him. The son is a youth, of age twenty or so, I think. (?) Well, rather than scolding, the mother is lamenting, not scolding but lamenting. She is almost embracing her son and lamenting, "Why have you done such a bad thing?" (?) The son naturally feels sorry and apologetic toward his mother and he listens to what his mother says. (?) He has no antipathy toward his mother. He knows that he has done wrong, that what his mother says is right. He is repenting.

We find on Card 18 an immediate toning down in Mr. Ikawa's language. He first says the son did "something wrong," in a phrase that usually has serious import. Then he quickly states that the son had made a "mistake," which has a much lighter, less serious sound in Japanese. Again, we see in his reaction to the stimulus value of the picture a need to inhibit or understate the seriousness of the matter around which he is constructing his story. The mother's scolding is toned down into a lament, in which "she is almost embracing her son." If we take into account the nature of the picture itself, we see he has avoided recognizing a posture that is frequently seen as a man choking a woman and has toned down any implications of aggression in the picture. The result is a guarded story in which he goes out of his way to say explicitly that the son has no antipathy toward his mother but admits that what she says is right and repents his misbehavior.

> J22. They are parents and child. They are going somewhere. But the father and mother have different opinions as to where to go. The husband wants to go this way, but the wife wants to go that way. They had a quarrel and the child was torn between them. But after all I think the wife will follow her master's will. (?) She wanted to do some shopping. (?) Since the father has already started walking and the mother is standing there, I think the mother will be forced to follow the father.

In this story his pejorative use of words to describe the head of the family swings to the other extreme, and he uses an exceedingly polite phrase, *goshujin*, to describe a willful husband. A quarrel will be resolved when a dutiful wife follows her *goshujin*'s will. The story is an assertion on the part of Mr. Ikawa of his right to make decisions that must be followed obediently by his wife, in spite of differences of opinion. One gains again a distinct sense of his considerable ambivalence toward his own position as father and husband. Perhaps it is a role that he likes to take, but feels some reluctance about assuming. It may well be that he could not attempt to assume this role with his present wife without meeting considerable opposition, which must be seen as coming both from within himself and from without.

> J27. These three are all high school classmates. These two are going to drop into a coffee shop. But his first girl friend is watching for him, and so he is hesitating to go into the coffee shop with this other girl. His first girl feels jealous and has an argument. The other girl will not drop into the coffee shop but will go away. The boy and the first girl will go into the coffee shop. (?) Yes, the girls know each other. (?) The other girl did. The other girl asked him to go but on the way he met his real girl friend, so he hesitated to go in with this other girl. Then this other girl got mad and went away. (?) It seems that she has no particular feeling toward him. But this other girl seems to be serious about him.

Card 27 is seen as a triangular situation in which there is competition between two girls for a boy. Again, as in the second card, the focus is egocentrically turned toward the male figure. Mr. Ikawa is self-centered and expects things to revolve around him. His social attitude toward the coffee shop setting is not disapproving, as it is for some Japanese, and he accepts it as a place to meet, and concentrates in the story on the jealousy of one girl for the boy. In general he does not moralize as do some of the other fathers in the sample. Instead of describing the evil effects of bad benavior, he tries to organize his stories so that they will reveal only normal problems reconciled in one way or another by proper adherence to expected social roles.

PROJECTIVE TEST RESULTS: MRS. IKAWA

The Rorschach Test

Mrs. Ikawa's record is fairly normal. There is no unusual symbolism, and the response form level is adequate. She is able to give satisfactory responses to each of the cards, with perhaps the exception of Card IX.

Rorschach Protocol

I. (8″) 1. *A bat. I can't imagine anything else.* Wings? This spreading part looks like a wing. (?) Since the shape looks as if it were about to fly. [W F+ A P (Neut)]

II. (38″) 2. *I get the feeling that it is a lake. Nothing else.* The inside looks like a lake, and the surrounding is a mountain; it seems like a high mountain. (?) I feel that way; I don't know why. It is a lake on a cloudy day. [WS FV, FY+ Lscp (Pnat)]

III. (44″) 3. *I get the feeling that men are pulling something toward each other.* Pulling something . . . (?) It looks like a heavy thing. . . . (?) Well, they are men; seems they are doing some physical exercise—sports or something like that. I feel that way. [D M+ H P (Prec)]

IV. (20″) 4. *I get the feeling that an animal's hide is being pinned down.* It is a wild beast, but I get the feeling that it is only a hide. (?) Since it has the feeling of thinness, I feel it is the hide. If it were a living being it would have the feeling of thickness. I get the feeling it is thin; it is only the hide. [W Fm, FT+ Aob P (Neut)]

V. (24″) 5. *It is a butterfly.* It has wings and the shape reminds me of it. [W F+ A P (Neut)]

6. *Two horses are collapsed.* Judging from the shape of an ear, I thought it was a horse. [D W FM− A (Agl)]

VI. (14″) 7. *It is a musical instrument. It looks like a violin.* (?) The upper part looks like the upper part of a violin. [W F+ Mus (Prec)]

VII. (14″) 8. *It is a mountain, a high mountain; the mountainous area.* A high mountain; the mountainous area. I get the feeling that the rocks are projecting. [W FV + Lscp (Pnat)]

VIII. (17″) 9. *Two animals are climbing a hill.* This part looks like a bear or something like that. I feel so judging from the shape. [D FM+ A P (Pstr)]

IX. (42″) 10. *It looks like a fight among animals.* It looks like an animal. (?) Looks like wild beasts. They are beasts, aren't they? There are four. I feel that way from the hair and the rough impression. [D FM- A (HH)]

X. (14″) 11. *I get the feeling that it is the bottom of the sea.* Living things are the bottom of the sea . . . the root of a tree . . . and seaweed. [W FC+ Bot (Neut)]

12. *Fishes.* And small fishes. The color as well as the shape of seaweed looks like this. [D FM+ A (Neut)]

Card-by-Card Sequential Analysis and Comments

On Card I Mrs. Ikawa sees a bat about to fly, an ordinary percept. Card II symbolically suggests retreat and distancing. She starts with the center area of the blot, sees a lake, and then gives a vista response: surrounding the lake is a mountain, a high mountain. Then she says that the total impression is of a cloudy day. We get a suggestion of a capacity to withdraw or to distance herself, as well as an impression of diffuse anxiety. The color of this card is avoided in describing the landscape. On Card III she shows a normal capacity to see the usual human percepts. The humans are activated in a fairly strenuous way, doing physical exercise or sports. She gives the feeling of an active, assertive, inner, kinesthetic experience.

In Card IV one gains an impression of her tactual sensitivity and sense of threat. She sees the hide of a wild beast but then tones it down, taking out the threat: "It is only the hide." On the first four cards she has given three popular responses, showing a firm capacity to think in the standard channels of her culture. Card V is another popular response, the usual butterfly. Then she gives her first idiosyncratic response, seeing two horses collapsed against each other. Sometimes the two sides of this blot are seen as animals aggressively charging into one another. Her response gives almost the opposite feeling, suggesting some form of inner withdrawal of vitality, a resort to passivity.

Mrs. Ikawa handles Card VI in an adequate way. A "musical instrument" with good form quality is seen, and she exhibits a perception of positive content. On Card VII she again evidences a kind of distancing, seeing a mountain area with projecting rocks, on a card that is often evocative of a tactile or feminine mood. We might speculate in terms of psychodynamics that the distancing she evinces represents some feeling about maternal warmth and even possibly about her own feminine sexuality. The next response, to Card VIII, is another assertive movement response—she sees animals climbing a hill. She pays no attention to the color. So far she has demonstrated an extremely introversive record, giving no sign of warm or "hot" affective reactivity to her environment, which is usually indicated by responsiveness to the colors on five of the Rorschach cards. Only on the last color card, Card X, does she perceive color in an integrated percept.

On Card IX she gives her only directly aggressive response. She perceives the card, with a moderate use of form, as a fight among animals, four beasts. Instead of using the bold colors of this card, she gives texture as a determinant, saying that they look like wild animals because they are hairy and that the card gives a "rough" impression. On Card X she demonstrates a constructive integrative mental capacity. She integrates color in a general overall scene, which is very common in Japanese records. She sees various objects of the bottom of the sea, selecting the root of a tree, seaweed, and small fishes. This last response is fairly well integrated and indicates her capacity for conceptual organization; although she displays this without the superiority exhibited by her husband, one must judge her to be of at least high average intelligence.

Her overall record is heavily weighted in the direction of movement and vista responses, both indicative of an introversive orientation. She also distances herself and shows signs of anxious withdrawal, although she is also capable of active attitudes of an aggressive nature.

The TAT

In general this is a sparse and reluctant TAT record. Mrs. Ikawa employs a vague, nonforceful kind of woman's Japanese, continually asking for reassurance and making statements in the form of questions. She often uses the word *are* (that) instead of being specific about what she means. There are long pauses where she seems to be ruminating on what to say. The stories are given in a choppy, distracted way. She does give a number of stories emphasizing common

Japanese interpersonal concerns. In the end, however, we gain an impression about inner tensions, while she presents an overall picture of a withdrawn, nonassertive person. There are suggestions of sexual seductiveness toward a son.

> J1. [Long silence] About music [silence] . . . (?) Oh, I see. (?) Better . . . better . . . I think he is trying to make better music. (?) Well, about fourteen or fifteen years old. (?) In the room. At night in a very quiet room. And he is trying to make music (?) because he likes music. (?) He will be a great musician and establish himself in society.

The first story is a simple one in which there is little elaboration. A boy in a quiet room is trying to make music. Her emphasis is on the boy in his quiet room, and she seems to be content with an isolated quiet situation. There is little elaboration of a success theme or concern with future time. The ending is perfunctory and does not give any impression of a strong achievement motive or concern with the hard work that goes into striving for achievement. We gain a glimpse of a withdrawn person.

> J2. Do I need to talk about all these people in the picture, or may I just talk about one or two? One evening [long silence] (?) The man [long silence] (?) This . . . is this . . . This man is plowing, and the woman seems to look at something. (?) They may be husband and wife. (?) He is asked something by this person. (?) If she is a schoolteacher, she is asking about their child. (?) Yes. (?) Yes, on the way back from school. (?) Well, about the grades of their child, something like that. (?) No, I don't think so; she is just talking on her way by.

In Card 2 she makes a self-effacing statement as if the picture is too complicated for her to handle with "all these people," in spite of the fact that there are only three people in the card. It is as if she feels very uncomfortable in coping with complicated human relationships and cannot relate easily to others. Withdrawal seems to be her principal mode of defense. The tempo of her presentation is long and drawn out. There is no elaboration or enlivenment of plot. The young woman is seen as an authority figure, not as a child, who comes by, inquiring about a schoolchild and his grades. One gets the feeling that Mrs. Ikawa is readily intimidated by outside authority and feels herself threatened and uncomfortable in the presence of others. She seems to be afraid of being interrogated by someone on the outside. She would not defend herself by any kind of intellectualization. Instead, she is probably often paralyzed by a feeling of threat coming from individuals of status.

> J3. It seems this is the same. (?) The boy is tired after play and he is sleeping, leaning over the bench. (?) Some place where there are benches. (?) This is in a house. (?) A bench—what do you say?—looks like a bed. It looks something like a bed. This is the inside of a house, although he has shoes. (?) About twelve or thirteen years old. (?) And what will happen? [long silence] Yes, I know. (?) Because he is tired after playing. (?) May I change what I said? I think he had a quarrel with his

friend, and he came home and was crying. Yes. (?) Well, I think he had a difference of opinion with his friend. (?) For example, about the baseball game. (?) Let me see, I think he will tell somebody. (?) His mother. (?) In this case? Let me see, I think he will listen to the parents' opinion. (?) I think he hasn't talked to the parents yet. While he was crying, he has fallen asleep, leaning over the bed. It also seems to me that this is a girl. (?) [long silence]

In the third card Mrs. Ikawa sees a tired boy who is sleeping. The story is quite innocuous. Any suggestion of tension in the story as far as the boy is concerned comes from peers rather than from parents. Instead of sensing a disciplinary problem here, she sees the child as having quarreled with a friend and now is crying. She needed constant prodding to give any form of story.

J6. They are a mother and a son. They have visited somebody's house. (?) Well, the mother and the son . . . It seems to me that they plead with somebody for something, for example, asking a favor for getting a job. (?) Well, a boss of a company or somebody like that. (?) A boss of some acquaintance or somebody like that. Let me see, it's the son. (?) He feels uneasy. He is wondering whether it is possible or not. (?) About twenty-three or twenty-four years old. (?) His character was not adaptable to that job.

In Card 6 a mother goes with her son to plead for a job, assuming a traditional role. Again one can see here deference to people of high status. There is no tension depicted between mother and child. The son is shown as being anxious over whether it will be possible to obtain a job. (Mrs. Ikawa expects the interviewer to encourage her before continuing her story.)

J7. They are a father and a son. They are opposing each other in their opinions. (?) [long silence] Well, I think it is something about their company. (?) Well, the father and the son belong to different generations. The son insists on something and the father has a traditional opinion, and they are in conflict. The son insists that he is right, and the father insists on his way. (?) They don't compromise. (?) After a good deal of discussion, I think they will understand each other. And they will solve the problem satisfactorily. . . . I'm sorry I can't speak as I want to.

On this card she gives a basic theme of father and son who belong to different generations and have different opinions. She sees that they are both of strong opinions, but she tones down the conflict by saying that this is merely a difference of opinion and she sees the possibility of ultimate reconciliation.

J8. Inside of a room? [long silence] Has there been a fight, here? . . . (?) Aren't they gangsters, or something like that? (?) All of them, four of them. (?) This one has something like a knife and is about to stick it into this one's belly, it seems. . . . This person is not a part of it. (?) He is afraid of looking. He has turned his back, hasn't he? These two are companions, aren't they? (?) Some trouble concerning money, I guess. Something of that kind. (?) Or, perhaps this person is a woman, twenty-seven or twenty-eight years of age, and she is the wife of this person. Something like that, perhaps. (?) This is inside of a house, the house of this person. (?) This person is thinking of stabbing the belly of this person. (?) He has not yet stabbed . . . he is just thinking of it. (?) [long silence] Well, if the person actually stabbed this one, that would be a serious problem. (?) He might actually stab the person, depending upon circumstances. . . . (?) Or he is just threatening. [long silence] Perhaps this person is unconscious, I wonder. . . . (?) He was anesthetized and has been carried to this place, while unconscious. . . . (?) They will be charged with a crime, won't they? (?) I think they will be caught before stabbing. (?) Or, perhaps this woman may report the crime to the police.

In this card a theme is evoked of gangsters fighting, but by the time the story ends Mrs. Ikawa has not allowed the person to be stabbed in the belly. She takes the younger figure in the foreground, sees him as frightened, an emotion she can probably readily identify with, and then, in a sense making the identity closer, changes it into the wife of the other figure who is frightened, and finally goes to the police so that she can save her husband. The whole story is expressed in a vague and indecisive manner, in very imprecise language. Seemingly threatened by the aggressive stimulus of the card, she finally stretches the story, suggesting that the woman can save the victim and that the knifing itself will not take place. Again we see Mrs. Ikawa as a woman who is more consciously threatened than concerned with her own aggression.

J9. The husband is going out somewhere. And the wife and the mother are seeing him off. (?) That one is the wife. (?) This one is their child. (?) Looks anxious, so I think he is going to see a doctor at a hospital, since he feels sick. Somehow they all look anxious. (?) The wife, the mother, and the daughter. (?) He is going to a hospital, I think. (?) Yes, by himself. (?) Well, I think he will enter the hospital. (?) He has heart trouble. (?) No, he has suffered a little bit. Somehow they look anxious and worrying.

Her responses to Cards 9 and 11 suggest an internalization of a preoccupation with illness as a defense against unacceptable feelings. The focus of the story for Card 9 is the illness of the husband; the wife is anxious and concerned.

J11. The mother is sick. The child is about the age of a student in first year in junior high school. Before he goes to school he wants to see his mother because he is anxious. (?) She is thinking. (?) She is thinking about her sickness and about her child. (?) I think she has always been weak in her health. For one year she has been a sickly person. (?) He will go to school.

In Mrs. Ikawa's response to Card 11 it is the mother who is ill and the boy who is anxious about the mother's illness. The focus of interaction here becomes anxiety over illness. In this story there is an avoidance of the sexual theme that is picked up in some of the Japanese records.

> J13. A boy, isn't he? No, he is a man. He is boarding somewhere. While he is out, she is doing something; perhaps she is his mother. (?) Somehow, let me see, she is tired and is sleeping in a "slovenly" way. And then her son has come back. He is weeping and feeling miserable. The mother is exhausted from her effort to earn a living. I think she is working somewhere. (?) Well, I think she is doing some entertaining job. Looking at the mother's sleeping, the son feels miserable.

Card 13, with its suggestive sexuality, is rarely seen as a mother-son card; Mrs. Ikawa sees first a boy, but then she changes it to "No, he is a man." Only then is the woman seen as sleeping in "a 'slovenly' way." Her son witnesses this and is weeping. One senses here a kind of suppressed sexual exhibitionism on the part of the mother in the story, which is witnessed by the young boy. This story takes on considerable meaning when we realize that according to her husband Mrs. Ikawa slept with her son until he was about twelve years of age. There seems to be a hysterical problem in this woman in respect to repressed sexuality felt toward her own child. We would surmise that in some situations the repression is aided by withdrawal into concerns with illness or by retiring into isolation. But what she is retiring from, perhaps, as is suggested by this story and other evidence from the interviews, is a sexualization of the maternal relationship with her child.

> J18. Is this not a daughter? I wonder if the mother is at her wits' end and is strangling her daughter? Perhaps the daughter is feebleminded or something like that. At the beginning, I think she tried to cure her child, . . . but thinking of the child's future (?) . . . I think she will kill her child.

In Mrs. Ikawa's response to Card 18 the mother is seen as strangling her feebleminded daughter in a type of mercy killing, resulting from the mother's contemplating the sad future of the daughter. To Mrs. Ikawa this is not a scene of anger at a child who does wrong, but rather the killing of an innocent, helpless child, so that the scene is one without malice or aggression, even though it involves the killing of a child. Throughout her TAT Mrs. Ikawa avoids any delinquency theme. It is as if she is not concerned with a deliquent child. The children perceived on the cards are helpless or proper children who themselves are nonaggressive.

> J22. The parents and their child go out somewhere. The parents had a quarrel over their child. Perhaps it was about a toy for the child. The mother wanted to buy a toy the child wanted, but the father said no. And the child is crying. So they decided to go back home. Since it seems that the father also loves his child, he will calm the child and will take him home. (?) He already gave up this time and is hoping the parents will buy it next time. So he will go back home. (?) Generally, they

are in agreement. But at this time, they had a different opinion. It is a temporary conflict between them, I think.

On this card, Mrs. Ikawa perceives a fairly common theme, given the nature of the card. It is the father who is seen as denying the child, but this situation is quickly rectified, and she adds that the father loves his child and will take him home. The child has given up his request this time but hopes that the parents will comply the next time. Mrs. Ikawa says that this is only a "temporary conflict," that they are usually in agreement. She avoids any implications of basic disharmony.

> J27. They are high school students. A high school classmate is asking to drop into a coffee shop or something like that. This person is watching these two students. (?) Just passed by . . . there are no relations between them. (?) On the way back the boy was asked to stop. (?) I think they are not "serious." While they are walking . . . they are in the same class. (?) He says, "Let's go next time." [laughs] He has something to do. (?) I think they will say good-bye.

We get a completely innocuous handling of this card. There is no concern with any possible delinquency or improper behavior on the part of the students in front of the coffee shop. It is simply a passing occasion in a student's life.

In general, therefore, when we look at Mrs. Ikawa's TAT the only reference to any kind of improper behavior within the whole record is that of a mother (J13) whose body is exposed to her son. Mrs. Ikawa employs hysterical repressive mechanisms to avoid awareness of her seductive influence on her son. Her attitude toward outside authority seems to have a defensive quality. The TAT suggests the possible presence of an inductive family pattern in which there is implicit sexual collusion among the family members, which has resulted in the boy's sexual behavior.

PROJECTIVE TEST RESULTS: TAKESHI IKAWA

The Rorschach Test

Takeshi Ikawa's record is one of the most severely disturbed in our present sample; it is highly suggestive of incipient schizophrenic thought disturbance. He shows an incapacity to delineate concepts clearly; they encroach on one another, and he is not capable of keeping them separate. He uses certain queer verbalizations that deepen the impression of "dynamic" feeling throughout, either of fear or of floating.

Rorschach Protocol

I. (7″) 1. *I get the feeling that this is a fearful impression. It looks as if it is coming this way.* Because there is something like a wing. Looks like a butterfly as well. The impression that some things are combined. The top gives this feeling. The side is like a butterfly because the parts are not combined but separated. Because it has protrusions. I feel that it is open and coming this way. [W FM+ A P (Athr)]

2. *Weird or . . . The impression that various animals are "combined."* The wings and others look like a butterfly's, but the top looks like a snail. [W F− A Z− (Fab Comb) (Afant)]

II. (13″) 3. *I feel that this is also like a combination of animals.* Sometimes like a snail. As a whole, it is weird, I feel. Seen individually, it forms something. Bears [pointing to hands and legs] and snails . . . Looks like a snail because of the slender shape. [W F− A Z− (Fab Comb) (Afant)]

4. *I get the feeling that it is a fur.* I get the feeling that something was stretched and pinned down [*hatte aru*]. I feel so because of the shape of the bear. [W Fm− Aob (Contam) (Neut)]

5. *I feel two of something doing something together.* Something like a snail or . . . not a person, not a human being. Two things are talking about something to each other, I feel. Because it looks as if the hands and legs are being moved by them. [W M− (H) (Fab Comb) (Afant)]

III. (15″) 6. *Lonesome feelings.* I get the feeling that it is a spirit fire. I have a weird and lonesome feeling because of it. Something slender is floating in the air. [D CF, mF+ Rel (Athr)]

7. *Also a combination of human beings or animals. "Something is being done."* The faces and others give the impression of an animal. The figure is like that of a man. I feel that they are disputing over something. Doing something, looking at faces and others. [D M+ (H) P (HH)]

IV. (11″) 8. *Fearful feeling. It looks as if it were ready to charge me.* This looks like a leg. It gives the feeling of bigness. Because the leg is like it is moving. Neither man nor animal but something. [D M− (H) (Athr)]

9. *Like a fur.* I feel that something is put on and is spread. This may be because it is black. As the fur is spread and put on. [W FT+ Aob P (Neut)]

10. *Looks like a snail.* Protruding tentacle and other parts a little bit. Because it is of slender shape. [D, F+ A (Adis)]

11. *Looks like a combination of something.* Like a snail, like a monster, like a combination of furs. [W F+ A/H (Z− Fab Comb) (Athr, Afant)]

V. (12″) 12. *I feel it is a butterfly. The feeling that something is flying, a weird feeling.* The impression of wings and others. From the leg part. Spreading the wings and looking this way, so it looks like . . . No, it's facing that way because it has wings. Because the wings are not regular but protruding. It would be good if there were no protrusions. [W F+ A P (Weird verbalization) (Neut)]

VI. (9″) 13. *Looks like a tiger's fur.* Because the protruding parts are like legs and the top is like a face. The feeling that something is sticking to it. Because it spreads out and I see two. The legs and others. Only one should be seen if it's not a fur. I feel some pity. As it is being spread and stuck [pinned], it gives me the feeling that it is dead. [W Fm+ Aob P (Hsm)]

VII. (13″) 14. *I get the feeling that it is a combination of a cow, a horse, and a man or something like that.* The face and the mouth are like those of an animal, but the leg and the body look like a human. Like dancing, because it is spreading its arms. A little bit weird. Weird when seen as a whole. [W M− (H) (P) (Fab Comb) (Afant)]

VIII. (16″) 15. *I get the feeling that it is a mixture*

16. *of animals and*

17. *plants.* The sides look like tigers as there are four legs, and this as a whole is like a flower. As it is spreading and the shape is like a wing. [W mF− Abs Fab Comb (Afant)] [D FC+ Bot (Pnat)] [D FM+ A P (Neut)]

18. *I get the feeling that it is bones.* As it is not neatly organized and has notches. Slender bones and thick bones are mixed together. Looks like bones, as there is a center and they spread as a whole. Beautiful. Because pink and orange colors are used. All are sticking to one another and doing something, as if animals, plants, and bones are stuck together. [D mF− Anat (Bb)]

IX. (10″) 19. *This represents the feeling of this being a human bone.* There is a center and it looks like a bone. [D F− (Anat) (Bb)]

20. *It represents something like a map.* A foreign map or . . . Protruding and like a map. As the vacant part is like a lake. The colors are like those of a map. The colors are beautiful. Many colors such as pink are used. [WS C/F− Map (Aev)]

X. (10″) 21. *There are things like seaweed*

22. *and things like birds.* A thing like seaweed looks like a tangle. It's slender. A thing like a bird is like a hen, as it is small. It gives a weird feeling as there is no bird in the sea. [DW F− Bot (Fab Comb) (Arb Comb)] [D F+ B A (Neut)]

23. *It gives me the feeling that something is floating in the sky.* Have the impression that each one is floating. Like a will-o'-the-wisp. Red and yellow and others are beautiful if seen individually. [WS m,CF sky (contam) (Pnat)]

Card-by-Card Sequential Analysis and Comments

To Card I Takeshi states immediately that it gives him a fearful feeling that something is coming his way. "It" is not clearly defined in the beginning; it turns out to be a butterfly. He is concerned in this card, as in some of the others, with the irregular protrusions at the sides of the card. He sees some weird combinations of animals. The little protrusions remind him somewhat of a snail. He is to see several snails in the subsequent cards. The snail symbolically is a rather disgusting type of small animal and one that is weak and boneless, protected by its own circular house into which it can withdraw. In his response to Card II the boy again shows some loss of a sense of reality, an incapacity to keep objects separate. We infer that he also has some difficulty in differentiating between what is inside himself and what is outside, in the external environment, a basic deficiency in schizophrenic thinking. He sees again a weird combination of animals, bears and snails, and produces a rather incoherent response. He has an autistic feeling of movement going on. He cannot define the humans, even though he finally sees them, and he puts it in rather confused Japanese: "It looks as if the hands and legs are being moved by them."

On Card III he repeats explicitly the feeling of lonesomeness that permeates his TAT responses. He sees a floating "spirit fire," which gives him "a weird and lonesome feeling." Then he sees a human form, but it occurs in a "confabulized combination" (Rorschach terminology) of human and animal. His verbalization is in an extremely unsteady, queer Japanese. In response to Card IV, he has fearful feelings of something charging directly at him. He sees the motion in the legs but can identify the something neither as animal nor as human. He sees the popular "fur" percept, then produces another snail response. He sees "a protruding tentacle" and other parts, which he does not define. Finally, he sees a confused combination of something, like a snail, like a monster, like a combination of furs.

He perceives on Card V the popular butterfly, but with a peculiar verbalization. He says, "I feel it is a butterfly. The feeling that something is flying—a weird feeling." Although he tends to perceive the ordinary, usually perceived areas on this card, as well as on others, it is with a peculiar intrusive, unreal feeling of being moved that cannot be integrated with his percepts, giving his responses a schizophrenic tone. In Card VI he sees a tiger's fur, which is often perceived, but again he expresses a subjective emotional uneasiness. He feels a sense of "pity" at its being spread and stuck by pins. It gives him the impression that it is dead. He shows himself here to be a very sensitive boy, quite unlike what we might think a callous rapist would be like. Nor does this boy offer any sexual content on his Rorschach. Instead, we get the feeling of an overwhelmed ego that can no longer function adequately.

On Card VII he sees a peculiar combination of horse, cow, and man. He perceives dancing by something that is made up of the body parts of various animal forms. Overall, as in both his parents, we get a picture of a highly introversive boy, but his ego is too disorganized to give valid, socially accepted percepts. In Card VIII he again picks out what would be usually perceived areas of the card. He sees the Japanese "popular" response, a flower, and the popular animals as tigers. His least appropriate response to this card was "the feeling that it is bones," which he cannot integrate—slender bones and thick bones are mixed together. He ends by expressing a confused feeling that they are sticking together and doing something, as if animals, plants, and bones are stuck together, in a confused configuration whose elements he cannot keep separate.

Again to Card IX the feeling of bones comes out. Then he responds to the space area as depicting a lake on a map. He responds positively to the color, saying that the colors are beautiful, but he cannot integrate them into any percept, and produces a vaguely perceived "map." In responding to Card X he struggles with the fact that he sees a marine view but there are birds present, and he argues with himself, saying that it is a weird feeling because there are no birds in the sea. Again, as on Card III, he sees some spirit fire or "will-o'-the-wisp" floating in the sky.

The prognosis for Takeshi must be considered poor. What is regarded as poor schoolwork or laziness by his parents and teachers is, according to Rorschach evidence, probably symptomatic of an internal autistic withdrawal, which leaves no psychic energy for such constructive tasks as a systematic application to school assignments. When we look at the amount of raw affect poured into his TAT stories, in combination with this psychotic Rorschach, we feel safe in making a diagnostic evaluation of this boy as schizophrenic.

The TAT

Takeshi's TAT stories are in effect a continual series of statements about inner feelings of loneliness and depression. The faces of all the figures on the cards either express to him inner states of loneliness or have some strange or eerie quality. Schizoid withdrawal is apparent throughout. The time taken before commencing his stories was somewhat protracted. It took him over a minute before he responded to the first picture, to the second one nearly a minute, to the third almost two minutes. He gradually warmed up to the task, however, and by the end was responding rather rapidly to each of the cards.

> J1. This child has a face suggesting he doesn't like to play the violin. His face seems to be somehow unhappy. He gives me the feeling of being lonely. That's all.

In this card, as in many of the following, Takeshi pays attention first to the facial expression, which he seeks to read. The boy's expression suggests to him a lack of interest in playing and that he is unhappy. There is nothing more given in the story except an inner feeling of loneliness. Throughout the following stories he either notes the facial expression or refers to the feeling given to him by the card—almost invariably that of loneliness and isolation. There is considerable hesitancy and blocking.

> J2. Gives the impression that each is doing his own thing for some reason. Mother is thinking about something and the woman seems to be looking at some book. The man is doing something to the horse. Gives the impression of poverty. That's all.

In Card 2 the boy sees that each person is doing something. There is no interaction, but each person is active. And he stated in the test of limits afterwards that he liked the card because everyone is "doing something." One gets the feeling that he perceives the world as full of self-preoccupied people, none of them attached to him in any way. He feels a sense of poverty and deprivation within himself, which is projected continually into the environment.

> J3. Seems to be crying. Seems that there is some trouble with the leg. That's all. (?) Crying, clinging to the chair, and pressing the face against the board. The impression is that the leg is injured.

This picture evokes a story about an injury. A person, whose sex is not defined, is seen as crying over an injured leg, clinging to a chair, and pressing his face against a board—a desolate picture of abject helplessness, loneliness.

> J6. Gives the impression that this man is unable to say what he wished to say. This woman expresses an unwillingness to listen. I get a feeling of loneliness. Both have faces that look tender. That's all.

In responding to the mother-son card all he can say is that the man is unable to communicate and that the woman's expression indicates an unwillingness to listen. Therefore he has a feeling of loneliness. However, he feels, looking at the faces, that they are both tender. Throughout this record one finds no expression of any active attitude toward aggression, although various stories include either injury or killing being done by someone. His identification always seems to be with the passive victim of this aggression.

Card 7 was not given to this subject; it was inadvertently skipped by the tester.

> J8. Two persons are trying to kill something at the place of one of them. Fearful atmosphere. The other one is going to the police station to tell it, so it seems. . . . That's all.

On Card 8 Takeshi sees the two people as killing another person. He comments on the fearful atmosphere and says that the remaining person in the foreground is going to go to the police station and report what is going on. There is an appeal here to outside authority, the police, in a situation of violence.

> J9. Four persons seem to be in conflict. The woman and the child seem to be leaving home. The man keeps silent. Seems to be leaving and taking the clothes and therefore the child seems to be lonely. Also the old woman seems to be lonely too. That's all.

Card 9 elicits from Takeshi a theme of family conflict. Usually when this card is so used it is the male figure who is seen as leaving, but in this instance the women seem to be leaving the home. Takeshi identifies mostly with the child who feels lonely in this situation, but he also sees the old woman as responding with a feeling of loneliness to the impending separation.

> J11. The child seems to be watching what his mother is doing. The child seems to be surprised. He keeps looking at what his mother is do-

ing. The mother looks somehow lonely and is thinking about something. That's all.

This card often stimulates some impression of sexual curiosity, but Takeshi is so vague about what is going on that we do not know what sort of perception he had. The only thing he expresses is the child's feeling of surprise, watching what the mother is doing. Again, the figure of the mother herself expresses loneliness to Takeshi. We get a feeling that for him this pervasive feeling blocks out and takes over so that any other affect becomes secondary or muted.

> J13. Seems that the woman has been killed. The man seems to be crying after seeing that the woman has been killed. As it is dark, it gives the impression of loneliness and fearfulness. That's all.

On Card 13 he sees a woman who has been killed by some unspecified person. The man is crying. There is no elaboration on what the relationships are in the story, but the fearful affect of loneliness and fright are conveyed.

> J18. This old woman is somehow going to kill this other woman. This old woman gives me an eerie feeling. It is dark, and the woman who is attacked seems to be trying to avert it.

In Takeshi's story to Card 18 we find the figure of an old woman, who is seen as eerie, inflicting violence on the younger one, who is attempting to protect herself. Again the identification is with the passive victim. After the test was over, Takeshi said that he disliked this picture.

> J22. The child seems to be crying. Well, well—he seems to be lost. The passersby are passing without paying any attention to the child. Usually someone would take him to the police station, but they seem to be passing him by.

On Card 22 Takeshi sees no one paying attention to a crying child. Not only has he been abandoned but also the passersby pay him no heed, so there is no one even to take him to the police station. He is completely helpless and rejected.

> J27. Two seem to be in dispute. The woman who is watching gives me a strange feeling. That's all.

The last card is again seen by Takeshi as a dispute. There is no card that he sees as a happy relationship. He sees the two people standing in front of the coffee shop as arguing, and he says the woman who is watching gives him a strange feeling. There is a sense of unreality running through his whole TAT which deepens our feeling of his schizophrenic withdrawal. We must also see this record in respect to the situational crisis confronting Takeshi. Shortly after he was given this test he was sent to a detention home. His feelings of loneliness and rejection must certainly have been aroused to their fullest degree by his impending institutionalization.

CONCLUDING REMARKS

After examining both interview and projective test materials obtained from the Ikawa family, we find that Takeshi is a severely disturbed boy showing schizophrenic features, who seems to have been driven to his rape activities by a strong, perhaps semiconscious, incestuous attachment to his own mother. Self-consciously, he is a compliant, passive figure in his own eyes; he says, "When I quarrel with my mother, she says, 'Go ahead and try to become a delinquent.' Because she knows my character well, she knows that I am too cowardly to be a delinquent."

It is difficult to determine the degree of sexualization of his relationship with his mother without much fuller revelation from the parents. From the mother's own story told for TAT Card 13, though it is the only clue available, one might speculate that there was some active but indirect unconscious seduction of Takeshi by his mother during the time he was sleeping with her, which ended when he was twelve years old. We have also seen some indications of unconscious induction on the part of the father, who might have obtained some vicarious satisfaction of his own incestuous attachment to his mother by observing his wife and son sharing a bed.

Seen superficially, Mr. Ikawa, with high average intelligence and basically introversive orientation, has lived much in accordance with the traditional Japanese values in regard to his role as a son to his mother; he has maintained feelings for his mother that have been even stronger than those for his wives. When his first wife was rejected by his mother, he remained passive, siding with his mother. His basic attitude has continued to be the same in his second marriage. In most cases in Japan, however, the attachment between mother and son is well sublimated, so that the undercurrent of sexuality remains well hidden and does not disrupt the ego functioning of the family members. In the Ikawa family it does not remain thus hidden. Only in this regard does this family differ from most Japanese families in which the husband often keeps a stronger tie to his mother than to his wife.

We can speak in a similar fashion of Mrs. Ikawa; it is prevalent and culturally sanctioned, especially according to the traditional values of Japan, that a mother, rather than being the sexual mate of her husband, assumes a role of desexualized dedicated caretaker of her parents-in-law, her husband, and particularly her son. Having a husband who is more strongly attached to his own mother than to his wife, the wife, in turn, develops a stronger tie to her son than to her husband. In most instances, however, such an attachment is well sublimated, so that the undercurrent of sexuality remains hidden. In the Ikawa family as we have said, it was not sublimated, and Mrs. Ikawa's relationship with Takeshi was sexualized, leading to serious disturbance of his ego development.

Mrs. Ikawa in her projective material suggests an introversive person capable of responding to threat by affective withdrawal as an ego-defense. Withdrawal behavior in the mother occurs within a generally intact ego, but the experience of such withdrawal by her infant could have had severely damaging effects. We may speculate that although the mother herself shows no signs of schizophrenia, the son's ego development may have been deeply impaired by an experience of insufficient closeness to his mother during infancy and early childhood. Takeshi's apparent withdrawal in the direction of schizophrenia may be explainable in these terms, hastened by the threatened breakthrough of direct sexual feelings about his mother. The boy's active stealing from his parents no doubt reflects his feelings of deprivation and his desire for warmth, which he sought by taking money and buying friendship with his peers.

The nature of Takeshi's difficulties is at best highly speculative on the basis of the incomplete knowledge provided by our interview data and projective test protocols. More extensive contact over an extended period would have been necessary for us to gain a more complete understanding. However, it should be noted that there were definite introversive trends in both the Rorschachs and the TATs of the mothers of other isolates in our samples. In effect, an introversive trend was the major difference distinguishing the mothers of isolate children, delinquent or nondelinquent, from the mothers of more social delinquents.

PART IV

Conclusions

The discussions and the results reported in the foregoing chapters are too complex and varied for us to attempt here more than a brief recapitulation of the general conclusions we derived from our several years' work on family and community processes in Arakawa Ward. These conclusions, extending beyond our empirical data, are related to the general processes of continuity and change in this area of Tokyo as part of changing Japan.

In assessing the purpose and organization of this volume we should note that our intention in including detailed anecdotal material was not simply to document the differences in the relationships of family members in our experimental and our control samples. It was even more our purpose to document the inner experience of Japanese family life and its heritage of endurance through three generations from the rural premodern past to the present day. We sought to present a narrative documentary in addition to a well-demonstrated social science treatise. We hoped to give the reader a feeling for the way humanity is shaped and expressed through the specific cultural mediation of Japanese traditions. We have sought to do this by making the social context of culturally patterned behavior understandable. The reader, whatever his cultural or ethnic background, should be able to recognize, in the people presented in this book, basic similarities to people he or she knows in other societies, even though role expectations are in some respects uniquely "Japanese."

CHAPTER 14

Genesis of Delinquency in Family Processes

Granting that overall indices of crime and delinquency are related to patterns of social and community cohesion, it is nevertheless true that even in those areas of the United States with the highest delinquency one finds only a minority of youth deeply involved in deviant behavior. Hence, although the sociological approach gives some indication of the social patterns leading to relatively high indices of deviancy, one must turn to more intensive psychocultural studies to find out why given individuals in a community are selectively vulnerable. We believe that in the present volume, reporting our own research, we have been able to adduce considerable evidence that certain attitudes and practices of parents are selectively related to the appearance of deviant behavior in one or more of their children and that these patterns are relevant cross-culturally. Despite the limitations of the size of our sample of Arakawa families, we have documented a number of significant differences in family atmospheric conditions that distinguish those families with a child manifesting some form of deviant behavior related to property or person. We have gone into considerable detail in presenting the actual life-history materials of our cases, since we consider the materials themselves as better demonstrations of our findings than our attempts to quantify particular characteristics of family interaction. It is our general conclusion that, despite some differences in family role expectations in the United States and Japan, many of the generalizations concerning parental behavior that are advanced in the American or European psychological literature on delinquency hold up equally well in Japan.

Our study perhaps has an advantage over many earlier studies in presenting a detailed examination of parents and retrospective accounts of grandparents. Previous publications in this field have generally been based only on work with the subjects themselves in an attempt to reconstruct what family life patterns were like, and to our knowledge none offers results of psychological testing of parents. Our findings concerning the differences in family cohesion and interpersonal attitudes of parents toward each other in delinquent and in nondelinquent families seem to us incontrovertible. Our individual ratings of traits, while admittedly highly interdependent, are an attempt to be as objective as possible with clinical interview data.

PERSONALITY VARIABLES

We have presented separately our quantitative results with the Rorschach records (see Appendix A). Orin Borders helped develop a computer program that tested significant quantitative differences in the Rorschach records which distinguished our delinquent and control samples by nonparametric means. We made a direct comparison of the various Rorschach scores related to intellectual approach, to emotional responsiveness, and to introceptiveness. Additionally, we applied overall quantified assessments of rigidity and maladjustment, using scoring systems initially developed by Seymour Fisher (Fisher, 1950). We also compared our Arakawa records with the system for quantifying affective symbolism developed by De Vos in his previous comparison of Japanese-Americans with American control samples (De Vos, 1955).

We have concluded that it would be extremely hazardous to attempt any use of the Rorschach to diagnose "delinquency" in individuals. As we have indicated, delinquency behavior is not related to any specific personality syndrome. Nevertheless, our results indicate that there are systematic differences to be noted even in our relatively small samples of delinquent subjects and their fathers and mothers (see Appendix A).

For example, in comparing the records in regard to affective symbolism, we note that the members of families with delinquents produced a significantly higher percentage of "neutral" or "evasive" percepts, unenriched by emotional elements. In contrast, the members of the control sample, especially the sons, gave a significantly greater number of "dependent" responses. Most notable were the responses reflecting a positive perception of symbols of authority and the responses that suggest a positive attitude toward childlike dependency. Members of nondelinquent families also showed a significant number of other responses indicative of positive attitudes. There were significantly more responses of a positive sensual or narcissistic nature. There were responses suggesting personal competence and assertive striving as well as the perception of objects deemed ornamental or recreational.

In general, the nondelinquent family members gave more open records, with greater affective responses, greater capacity for introception and intellectual organization, and a freer emotionality, both symbolically, in imaginative perceptions, and structurally, in a more balanced type of personality. In contrast, among the delinquent families there was more evasiveness, guardedness, and rigidity, resulting in both intellectual and emotional constriction. The records of the parents of isolate delinquents in some instances revealed more maladjustment, but the smallness of the sample did not allow these tendencies to approach significance. In general, we found that our Rorschach evidence corroborated the findings of our intensive interviews.

However, if overall configurational studies of personality pictures were used instead of statistics on particular Rorschach or TAT items, we would hesitate to suggest that it is structural "personality" differences per se that make for the difference between the delinquent and nondelinquent groups. Rather, we find some intensification of given traits that are perhaps less balanced by other personality features in some of the parents of delinquents than in normal subjects. But these indices could not be used predictively with any great success; one could not, simply by using the Rorschach test, determine differences between delinquent parents and nondelinquent parents which would be so diagnostic that they could be applied without significant error to a new sample. It is our contention, rather, that the important differences between the two groups are to be found in our ratings of family interaction and of expressed attitudes, either overt or indirect, or in fantasy material on the TAT, related to behavioral deviations from expected social roles. The case history materials as they reflect the cohesion of the family and the expressed love of parents for each other or for their children reveal more critical differences between the parents of nondelinquents and delinquents than do attempts at assessing structural personality characteristics. Basically, then, whatever the origins in personality, one must see that attitudes toward authority and propensities for deviant behavior ultimately are more readily linked with given role behavior within the family and with expressed family attitudes than with personality structure per se.

Some of our nondelinquent boys showed negative personality traits in no way dissimilar to those in boys who had records of stealing and who showed other symptoms of negative attitudes toward social norms, including those directed toward authority. It is in the ways in which these boys relate themselves attitudinally to what they are doing that one finds differences. Attitudes on the part of children which cause them to become delinquent, from our evidence, are causally related to prior attitudes on the part of parents toward each other and toward the subject who becomes deviant.

It is perhaps surprising, given the small sample size, to find that such symptoms as enuresis on the part of the child and bottle-feeding on the part of the mother do indeed show up significantly more often in the records of delinquent subjects than in those of nondelinquent ones. Again we relate these behavioral indices to covertly negative interpersonal attitudes on the part of child and mother, respectively. Our ratings of inconsistency and laxity in discipline or supervision exercised by the father or mother, as indicated in interview data, certainly are related to traits of character, but such behavior is even more directly related to basic attitudes about the importance of doing a good job in the role of parent. The parents of nondelinquents, whatever their personality difficulties, seem to be more capable of mobilizing their efforts in such a way as to fulfill the needs of discipline and consistency in sanctioning, on the one hand, and of the expression of love and appreciation as well as nurturance, on the other. They seek to fulfill as well as they can the emotional needs of the growing child.

Measured in terms either of status-appropriate behavior or of interpersonal behavior with the child, the parents of delinquents show greater internal inconsistencies. On the indices of status characteristics we used to estimate social class position, the parents of nondelinquents showed a greater consistency in the levels of eduation, occupation, and living circumstances than did the parents of delinquents. The question arises whether "status-displastic" elements in the families of delinquents, such as being more highly educated than one's occupation requires or living in poorer circumstances than one's occupation warrants, are simply secondary to other inconsistencies in behavior or whether they can have a determinative role in creating further inconsistencies. Our opinion would tend toward the former conclusion rather than the latter. We believe that the parents of delinquents are less apt to react positively, despite economic or social difficulties.

With respect to social role behavior, the parents of a potential delinquent have greater difficulty than do those of a nondelinquent in accepting the requisites of the role of a parent or of a spouse. They also have greater difficulty in accepting the limitations of others and are more ready to express dissatisfaction or frustration in regard to deficiencies of others in expected behavior.

The parents of potential delinquents are also more apt to be inconsistent in discipline, to show favoritism in their treatment in children, and to employ more physical means of expressing themselves, using less constraint in this respect than the Japanese norm. We found among the delinquent mothers that almost half resorted to striking the subjects in our sample, whereas only a little over 10 percent of the mothers of nondelinquents resorted to such practices. However, the incidence of physical punishment by fathers seemed to suggest no significant difference between the two groups. Use of physical punishment on the part of the mother, which goes against cultural norms, attests to her incapacity to use other means of asserting authority effectively. Although it might be taken as a lack of a mother's capacity for self-control over hostile propensities, it may more simply indicate that she is helpless and ineffectual rather than sadistic. Many children in the delinquent sample expressed complaints or dissatisfactions about parental favoritism for other sibs, whereas such feelings appeared in only a few reports among nondelinquents. This form of resentment, coloring the negative attitude of a child toward his parents, may or may not be based on actual conditions; it does point out that the delinquent child perceives himself to be in a relatively unfavored position within the family.

It might be argued, to explain the differences between our positive and negative ratings, that people are simply telling us what they want to tell and hence that individuals in families without the problem of a delinquent child are apt to suppress any negative attitudes, since to express them would be out of keeping with their usual understanding of their lives. We would argue that the relative readiness of the families of delinquents to express negative attitudes about other family members attests to a lack of cohesion in such families and to a lack of willingness to overlook the limitations of other family members or of their physical or social environment. Even on such vague complaints as "nagging" or unfair treatment (whatever is meant by these), we find that the delinquent boys see themselves more beset by their parents than do the nondelinquent ones. More than half the delinquent boys see their mothers as somehow "harassing" them, compared with only one-sixth of the nondelinquent sample. The complaints of the delinquent sons about their parents are diffuse and imprecise, but they do reflect dissatisfaction with the adequacy and appropriateness of parental attention or discipline.

In our study we found family size and sib positions to be relevant to delinquency. These factors can be sources of relative neglect experienced as such by some children in growing up. In Japan it is a common observation that the eldest son has been treated differently than other children in the family. It has often been said that in the patterns of urban in-migration, it is more often the second sons of rural families who go into the city. We therefore explored sibling position of both the parents and the children in our sample. We found some differences that were significant even for our small sample. In the present generation, we found a lower average number of children (2.95) for our normal controls than for either the isolate (3.45) or social (3.75) delinquent groups. In the sib position of normal and delinquent controls, we found a position of middle or second son overrepresented.

Going back one generation to examine the sib positions of the parents, we found that it was less important to examine sib position of a child regardless of sex, but highly relevant to examine the sib position of the parent with sibs of the same sex. Three out of 19 fathers of normals, or 16 percent, were second sons, compared with 18 out of 31 fathers of delinquents, or 58 percent. This would appear to be a highly significant difference. Over 35 percent of the mothers or stepmothers of delinquents were later-born daughters, compared with 2, or about 10 percent, of the mothers of the nondelinquent sample. These figures suggest a position of relative neglect found in the parents of delinquent subjects which may contribute to the relative neglect of one or more of their own children—in a sense a passing on of a pattern of experience which contributes to deliquency, in some degree at least, given other convergences of experience. Such a finding is in line with what has been often commented on in other societies in comparing the favored treatment of oldest sons with the treatment of other children. The relative neglect of younger daughters in large families is less often commented upon.

The conservative acceptance of authority is highly counterindicative to the appearance of delinquency in a child. In the Arakawa sample, at least one-third of the fathers of delinquent subjects showed some form of rebellious attitude toward authority, compared with only 1 father in 19 in the nondelinquent group. Almost one-third of the mothers of the delinquents showed rebellious attitudes in one way or another, whereas only 2 mothers of nondelinquents did so. Admittedly, this is a vague area in which to attempt objectified scoring. We did find, however, that when we added up signs of willingness to countenance culturally disapproved behavior, there were significant variations related to the appearance of delinquency in children. In sum, the parents of delinquents manifest difficulties in assuming and carrying out authority in a socially acceptable way, and a significant number of such parents evidence difficulty, dating from their own childhood, in accepting some forms of social authority and in willingness to exercise restraint.

THE GLUECK RATINGS

Our own intensive study of fifty Japanese families produced very apparent differences between delinquent and nondelinquent samples when we rated our cases in accord with the Glueck criteria (see chapter 3). In respect to fathers' discipline, we concluded that 58 percent of the fathers in our nondelinquent sample showed adequate, consistent discipline, and none of the fathers of delinquents. Conversely, in the same percentage, 18 out of 31 fathers of delinquents evidenced withdrawal or laxity in their discipline. Only 1 father of nondelinquents was so categorized.

In respect to the mothers' supervision, only 2 mothers of delinquents obtained an optimal rating; half, or 15, showed unsuitable maternal supervision. Of the mothers of nondelinquents, 18 out of 19 were rated as good in this respect.

On the ratings of affection or love only 2 of the nondelinquent fathers were rated unsatisfactory compared with 16 (over half) of the delinquent fathers. No mothers of nondelinquents were rated unsatisfactory in this regard, whereas 19, or 63 percent, of the mothers of delinquents were considered by us to show insufficient maternal affection in one way or another.

In respect to family cohesion, no nondelinquent families were rated as unintegrated or totally lacking in cohesion, whereas we rated 11, or 35 percent, of the families of delinquents as totally unsatisfactory. Twelve families of nondelinquents, or 63 percent, were considered to show sufficient evidence of cohesiveness, compared with only 1 such family among those of delinquent children.

There is no question in our minds that in spite of the obvious rigidities entailed in rating families in either a trichotomous or dichotomous classification in respect to these criteria, these ratings do strongly point up significant differences between the families of our delinquent and nondelinquent subjects.

FAMILY DISCORD AND DISSATISFACTION

Only 5 of the 19 nondelinquent families gave evidence of chronic active discord between the parents, compared with 20 out of the 31 delinquent samples. One must note that nondelinquent families are not without discord, but, as such overall measurements as the Glueck scales signify, it is the compounding of a number of negative features in family life that ultimately makes for a delinquency problem in children. Family discord, given sufficient love on the part of parents for the children and other positive sustaining features, will not of itself lead to delinquency.

In attempting to score our records from a number of interlocking traits we found that there is no necessary correlation between ratings of marital dissatisfaction and those of overt discord. Some parents mentioned frequent quarrels and interpersonal difficulty, yet did not consider themselves to be dissatisfied with their spouses, whereas others expressed deep dissatisfaction without any mention of overt discordant behavior.

In our small sample, spanning three generations, discord and dissatisfaction were reported for the grandparents as well as the parents in the families of delinquents, whereas both parents and grandparents of boys in our normal control sample have a general history of intact marriages. Nonlegalized unions and separations of various sorts were more frequently reported in the histories of the delinquent sample.

Given many of our presumptions about the noncomplaining Japanese attitude toward marital life, we were rather surprised by the overt expression of dissatisfaction in our interviews. Twenty-three of the 31 wives in the delinquent sample, or 74 percent, expressed dissatisfaction with their marriage, compared with 7 out of 19 in the normal sample, or 37 percent. One contributing factor, of course, is the fact that Arakawa women generally consider themselves to be of relatively low status within Japanese society and see themselves as married to husbands who have become obvious occupational failures. Again, we must note that the expression of marital dissatisfaction is not sufficient by itself to cause the appearance of delinquency; such dissatisfaction must be coupled with other factors for a cumulative effect. In our attempts to relate marital dissatisfaction to perceptions of status mobility, we found that, in general, women who are remarried are much more apt to express dissatisfaction with the second marriage than with the first, and that they are more apt to see their second marriage as downwardly mobile. The greater number of disruptions of first marriages in the delinquent sample is therefore compounded by the larger number of remarriages to produce the greater expressions of dissatisfaction among the mothers of delinquents.

In general, then, we added nothing to what has been previously described psychologically in understanding the genesis of deviant and disturbed behavior in children. Our study, however, by being comparative and examining in detail the same problems in Japan as those reported in the United States, deepens the conviction that particular forms of interpersonal relationships and difficulties cause later disturbances between the individual and his society. Finally, it must be noted that what the children did that was defined as delinquent was in most instances to violate laws with regard to stealing or to assault another person. Deviancy in thirteen-to-fifteen-year-olds is not of a political nature; it is not a social critique nor a blow to the structure of society; it often points mutely but directly toward their parents or peers or immediate authorities. It is therefore truly symptomatic of an insufficiency in interpersonal relationships. Most negative or antisocial attitudes have their genesis in early experiences within the family.

CHAPTER 15

Belonging and Alienation in Comparative Perspective

In Part One we briefly reported how our work in Arakawa gave us some direct impressions of why both general economic conditions and community processes seem to have contributed to a decline in delinquency within the ward. What goes on in community behavior within Arakawa differs greatly from what is described as occurring in lower-class neighborhoods in the United States. There are manifest social problems to be observed in high-delinquency urban residential areas in America that contrast markedly with what we observed in Arakawa.

From our general observations we obtained some indirect evidence of the effect of economic conditions on the rate of crime and delinquency in industrialized Japan. From the close-up perspective we gained by studying an individual ward, we saw that increasing prosperity may have an indirect effect of increasing voluntary activities related to neighborhood betterment and social involvement. A diminishing incidence of delinquency results to some degree from increased voluntary community involvement and does not simply reflect the effect of increased economic gain within families. One must look at the effect of economic conditions as they influence the day-to-day behavior of individuals not only within the families being studied but also in formal or voluntary organizations within a community. What individuals choose to do under conditions of increasing prosperity is related to culture patterns. When Japanese small entrepreneurs over fifty years of age have some leisure time they are very apt to devote it to some form of voluntary community activity. This does not occur in American neighborhoods to the same degree; many more Americans find their leisure-time pursuits outside their own neighborhood.

A second form of economic influence on community in Japan is derived from the manner in which residential property can or cannot be bought or sold. Japanese cannot emulate the extremely high rate of residential turnover we have witnessed in major American cities since World War II. The problems inherent in buying and selling property or changing residence are quite different in Japan. The economics of residential change determine whether people remain in or change neighborhoods. Japanese neighborhoods retain an economic and occupational heterogeneity, not only because Japanese are loath to change their residence, but also because economic forces make rapid turnover and self-selecting segregation solely in terms of occupational or economic status less thorough than in the United States.

There are also cultural patterns that determine how people migrate into the cities and where they find residence. In brief, Japanese economic and social patterns combine to make the Japanese neighborhood community heterogeneous in social class and community commitment. Communities there remain more "face-to-face" in daily contacts; there is less anonymity even in prevailingly lower-class districts with some residential turnover. The cultural homogeneity of Japanese society in Tokyo creates residential patterns in which ethnic divergence or minority status is relatively absent.

We demonstrated elsewhere (De Vos and Wagatsuma, 1966; Lee and De Vos, 1981) that this absence of minority issues is not entirely true for other cities. There are cities such as Kyoto, Osaka, and Kobe which have populations with a large percentage of minority ex-outcastes and Koreans. There, in specific areas, we did find delinquency patterns and rates that parallel those found in American ethnic ghettos. We reported, for example, that in the city of Kobe, where the outcaste or former Eta population comprises nearly 7 percent of city residents, youth from this minority group have significantly higher rates of delinquency. They have an average, per capita, of four times as many arrests for delinquency as youth from the majority population. Also, the Korean minority showed seven times the majority delinquency rate. However, the low delinquency rate in Japan generally reflects the basic homogeneity of the Japanese population. Minority youth who live in urban ghettos are a relatively small percentage of the population and do not significantly raise the overall statistics.

JAPANESE INDUSTRIAL URBANIZATION AS SOCIALLY AND PERSONALLY NONTRAUMATIC

The social patterns we described briefly for Arakawa Ward in Part One are patterns that are found in the heterogeneous neighborhoods in which the majority population lives in a Japanese city, whatever the relative degree of economic hardship of an individual family. There are culturally persistent social patterns that tend to integrate city dwellers rather than alienate them from one another. Patterns of urban movement, geographic and social, do not show the centrifugal features found in American migration patterns. Rural-urban movement in Japan takes place, generally speaking, within a shared set of cultural expectations. In contrast, traditions of urbanization within the American city involving immigrant ethnic groups as well as racial minorities have in our judgment been more personally and socially stressful and more conducive to social dislocation. Hence, one finds in American cities not only higher rates of delinquency but higher rates of mental breakdown and other symptoms of social dislocation in a migrant in-moving population.

The general lack of increase in juvenile problems in Japan, despite the possibilities for impersonality and anonymity that exist in any large city, can be attributed to the relative degrees of formal and informal social control which continue on a neighborhood face-to-face level in respect to youth.

We were impressed with the number of voluntary associations joined by our informants in Arakawa. Such joining behavior is characteristic of Japanese petty entrepreneurs and merchants. Voluntary organizations devoted to economic purposes intertwine with other voluntary organizations related to the political life of the community and to informal social life. We reported in chapter 2 our detailed investigation of who becomes a voluntary probation officer. These are community leaders selected to supervise up to three juveniles put in their direct charge. Several volunteers are in turn supervised by a paid professional. Voluntary "big brothers" and "big sisters" exist in the United States, but there is nothing resembling the systematic use in Japan of voluntary supervisors drawn from the delinquents' own neighborhood. Outsiders are not used. Then too, many of the police live in the area they patrol, hence they personally know many people living within the neighborhood for which they are responsible. They are not perceived as outsiders, although they are under the jurisdiction of a centralized urban authority. Teachers also tend to live in the communities they serve. Parents, teachers, and police can have, therefore, off-duty communication as well as professional functions. Also, Japanese parents do not resent the surveillance of their children, both formally and informally, by auxiliary personnel who report to the police suspicious behavior on the part of juveniles.

We described briefly in chapter 2 some of the voluntary community activities in Arakawa. Such activities lead sometimes to success and sometimes to failure, but in either case they demonstrate that the community is alert and readily aroused to action. We observed, for example, that concerted action by teachers and police broke up a network of juvenile gangs with their aggressive leaders or *banchō* which had intimidated other junior high school students for years. We described a campaign to "brighten the life of the community." We also noted that one entrepreneur, seeking to open a striptease theatre in the area, successfully outmaneuvered attempts by neighborhood groups to prevent his "business activities" in the vicinity of a school. In each instance, however, we were impressed with how individuals in the neighborhood were concerned, involved, and above all, organized in typically Japanese patterns of interaction.

We felt that Arakawa Ward was in essence a microcosm of what we would find in other Japanese neighborhoods. The differences in Japanese urban neighborhoods (as observed) and in American lower-class neighborhoods (as described), are, therefore, in our judgment, "cultural" as well as social. That is to say, Japan today is an industrial society with crowded, noisome cities. One might, therefore, expect the conditions of urban life in Japan to show social conditions comparable to those found in the United States. People in poor housing in Japan, however, behave differently. Arakawa residents do not evidence what Oscar Lewis described as the "culture of poverty." It is obvious that other cultural traditions intervene. The "paternalism" found in Japanese industry is found as well in local urban wards. Older men will take direct responsibility for young boys in their own neighborhoods who have become delinquent. Such active, personal intervention does much to cut down recidivism. Some of these men even find it possible to hire former delinquents or criminals in their small businesses. Direct relationships counter the types of impersonal prejudice encountered by members of the proportionately larger American ethnic minorities. In short, the Japanese system may be hierarchical and organized in terms of differences in vertical status, but it is also more personal and more enveloping for the majority of Japanese.

The social networks existing within a Japanese community are part of the cultural tradition. It would indeed be difficult in the United States—given not only the economic circumstances of multi-ethnic American city life but the continuing problems of ghetto segregation and residential selectivity according to income occurring in American patterns of urban mobility—to produce the type of informal voluntary organizations that so characterize the wards of Japanese cities.

The people of Arakawa Ward are not losing a strong sense of family and community in their day-to-day living, whatever the forces of change going on. In our anecdotal material we have sketched out a view of the life-style, the work and leisure activities, of people in this ward. As our case history material in the later chapters reveals in detail, many of the people of this ward in the course of three generations have experienced a general movement from the rural countryside into an urban, industrialized society. They have been socialized into this new way of life by means of a townsman culture that was in existence among merchants and artisans from premodern times. To generalize: In the present, as in the past, urbanizing processes have not been personally or socially disruptive for Japanese. There is no appearance of general alienation or of anomic disorganization. Rather, as we witness in this area of Tokyo, settled heavily only since the 1920s, community forces continue to integrate the individual and his family into more or less encompassing if not entirely satisfying larger units of social organization. The so-called *shitamachi* traditional townsman culture of northwest Tokyo has moved north into this new territory, and maintains enough organizing force to counter the general processes more recently generated by heavier industrialization which are suburbanizing Tokyo to the west and southwest.

The evidence presented in Parts One and Two attests to the operation of processes that preserve or augment social integration rather than those that cause dissolution. It attests to the creation, concomitant with population growth, of a functional neighborhood rather than a disorganized slum, even in an area we chose specifically because of its reputation as the "wastebasket" of Tokyo. It attests to the working of a culture characterized by flexibility in the face of change rather than by incapacitating rigidity.

Our first conclusion, then, is that Japanese urbanization in the modern period is not producing severe problems of personal or social disorganization. Indeed, the contrary is true: Urbanization, as far as the urban in-migrants are concerned, is relatively nontraumatic. This conclusion is similar to those recently advanced by other anthropologists studying urbanization in a number of different cultural settings. For example, Edward Bruner, working in Sumatra (1976), found urbanization a positive rather than a stressful experience for those moving to the city for work. Alex Inkeles, in a well-controlled comparative survey of six highly different cultures in respect to indices of mental health, came to the same conclusion (Inkeles, 1976). Indeed, the effect of urbanization in Japan today may now be more deleterious to the remaining rural population than to those coming to the city (Sofue, 1976).

ACHIEVEMENT MOTIVATION IN JAPANESE LOWER-CLASS SOCIAL SEGMENTS

The second of our major conclusions supported by this study is related to the socialization of achievement motives in Japan. This present work deepened our convictions about the general pervasiveness of a self-initiated achievement drive in Japanese. Although we picked an area of Tokyo that included the lowest occupational strata to be found, we observed that the same value attitudes related to achievement strivings were generally operative in them as had already been so well reported for middle-class Japanese and for rural villagers by a variety of authors. We found this to be true despite the fact that many of our informants were occupational failures who had participated to their disadvantage in a very competitive society. They were the failures who, according to Adam Smith, were destined to suffer the consequences of relative inefficiency in the economic marketplace. From the outside the dwellers of Arakawa might be perceived as victims of social or economic processes, but this view was far from that subjectively experienced by the participants. By and large, people in Arakawa were still positively oriented toward some attempted realization of competitive success as family units. Though many parents failed, they held hope for the relative success of their children. Arakawa dwellers subscribed to the economically productive virtues of long-range persistence, continuous striving, hard work, and frugality. Their individual lack of success, whatever the stipulated causes, was seldom attributed to the fact that failure for some, as well as success for some, was inevitable in a capitalistic economic system. They were thoroughly socialized to become active participants in the system within which they found themselves.

Only at the very bottom of the occupational range represented in Arakawa, among flophouse-dwellers, does one find the true "drop-outs," mutely critical of their society. Their number, considering the total population of Tokyo, or of Japan as a whole, is extremely small. As we have indicated, from an economic standpoint, Arakawa is a positive, productive part of Japan, not a socially unorganized area of unemployed, apathetic, or hostile slum-dwellers on welfare. Nor is it a community of political militants with a deep sense of their own economic exploitation, such as one finds on the peripheries of Paris, in the so-called Red Banlieues of workers supporting the Communist party. Arakawa not only pays for itself economically, it is also an essential functioning part of the economic structure operative in Japan.

SOCIAL COHESION: THE EXPRESSIVE FUNCTIONS OF PATERNALISM

A third related conclusion is that Arakawa does not manifest either the social alienation or the class consciousness one would predict from a direct a priori application of Marxian theory to Japan. The reasons are to be found in the cultural, historical continuities of social organization and the way individuals within families are socialized into a pervasive social network, usually hierarchically structured. The reasons are also to be found in the expressive satisfactions found in Japanese paternalism, a still operative form of secondary socialization following upon that occurring within the primary family. The network of supposedly independent entrepreneurs in Arakawa is in actuality socially as interdependent and as complementary in nature as the more characteristic formally organized hierarchical structures discussed by Chie Nakane in her volume *Japanese Society* (1970). Nakane distinguishes between two types of "belonging." There is that type of belonging found in groups she terms "attribute" groups, whether entered by birth or by achievement, which may take the form of clans or kinship lineages, or be designated by class positions or by occupational definitions such as plumber, carpenter, or professor. She contrasts all such groups with a second type of group identity, produced by a "frame." For Nakane a frame is a situational-historical definition of belonging—such as belonging to the Ford Motor Company, the *New York Times*, and so on. The strongest sense of commitment or loyalty found in Japan is to such a group. One joins a frame group for life. In joining frame groups of one kind or another, Japanese have the experience of working together on common objectives. Since these groups are by definition overtly cooperative, they permit only covert competition among members. Nakane cogently analyzes the way cooperation is emphasized in "team" efforts shared by all members of a hierarchically defined frame cluster, such as a manufacturing company or even a university, which tend to function in direct competition with other similarly constituted social units.

The material from Arakawa Ward on supposedly "independent" small-scale entrepreneurs is in agreement with Nakane's contentions. Competition in Arakawa, however, is usually among actual small family units rather than among larger, quasi-familial company organizations. The network of social relationships as subjectively experienced in Arakawa impels many individuals to define themselves as leaders of "independent," small, occupational units in direct competition with those performing similar operations. At the same time interdependent cooperation occurs among those in complementary relationships, comprising "sets" of subcontracted companies working on the same general order, as we found well illustrated among the small-scale manufacturers of Arakawa.

Seen psychoculturally from our theoretical perspective, this propensity to join supportive organizations is an integral part of Japanese socialization experiences, which also emphasize interdependency in a hierarchical sense of precedence in time by seniority. Many Japanese are still part of a "heritage of endurance," still part of a "Japanese" culture that organizes its people both individually and collectively toward the realization of ends that are often collectively perceived, whatever the individual goals of relative success are vis-à-vis others. Such organization is accomplished with surprisingly high morale on the part of its participants, surprisingly little dissension, and surprisingly high success in comparative world economic terms. The traditional Japanese social system and its dual economy of large and small industries has enabled Japan to actualize a gross national product that rivals that of the industrial giants, the U.S.S.R. and the U.S.A. (De Vos, 1973, chapter 7).

Our particular study in Arakawa has been oriented around the individual and his motivations in the context of family life, rather than being a detailed study of the economic, social, and political forces now operative in Japan. Nevertheless, our study offers evidence that the *shitamachi* culture of the premodern Japanese townsmen is still a force determining the direction and speed of change in Japan. The sociological forces of modern industrialization may swamp this residual thrust of the "heritage of endurance"; but from a social science standpoint, to understand Japan as it joins a thoroughly interrelated world society one must give heed to such cultural-historical forces, as well as to those cogently but imperfectly spelled out in Marxian theory for Western cultures. There is much to be said for giving theoretical attention to the stubborn persistence of "irrational, expressive" psychocultural patterns of socialization that resist the supposedly irresistible, instrumentally directed forces of economic determinism in Japan as elsewhere (De Vos, 1973). An analysis of vertical structures in Japanese social organization (see Hsu, 1975) helps to spell out why there is so little evidence of class alienation in Japan as compared with Western and even Soviet industrial societies. It is our further contention that this cohesiveness is to be explained by special features of Japanese "paternalism" as it is experienced emotionally by Japanese.

The purpose of this volume was not to produce a sustained theoretical critique of what we believe to be the relative inapplicability of certain aspects of Marxian economic theory directly to Japan. Our objectives have been more modest, namely, to examine in microcosm one symptom of social disorganization or alienation—delinquency—as it is generated in particular urban families during a period of rapid social change. From this vantage point, however, we find that we do raise some issues that must be considered in detail by others in order to produce a satisfactory comparative economic or political theory applicable to Japan as well as to Western states.

NURTURANCE: ACTUALITY AND ILLUSION

Central to a psychocultural analysis is a thorough consideration of the nature of the subjective experience of exploitation from an expressive as well as an instrumental standpoint. One has to examine, for example, how particular emotionally satisfying or expressive features of a nurturant, superordinate role can conflict in the inner experience of the Japanese employer with the instrumental advantages to be gained by the uninhibited economic exploitation of his subordinates. Conversely, one has to examine how the exercise of culturally patterned, dependent expectations on the part of subordinates can in certain instances distort the perception of the actual situation so that the subordinates hide from themselves the degree to which they may have been victimized by exploitation on the part of their superiors. One can make the extreme contention, for example, that instrumental or economic exploitation as a social problem does not exist until it is consciously perceived and well defined as such by the individual subject to it. This lack of readiness by the Japanese worker or marginal petty entrepreneur to perceive himself as "exploited" is a point of considerable frustration to the leftist political parties in Japan. One may generalize that most Japanese workers choose to continue to think in positive personal terms about their superiors rather than perceiving themselves as "used" impersonally by them simply as a means toward economic gain.

Countering a Western type of alienating class-consciousness in Japanese is a type of economic and social paternalism which is still felt to be mutually satisfying by those in subordinate as well as those in superordinate positions. Such an expressively satisfying paternalism can offset the alienating processes involved in more impersonal instrumental situations of class exploitation. From a psychological-motivational point of view, paternalism in Japan works because there is reciprocal personal identification between superordinate and subordinate individuals. Status differences do not cause impersonal distancing and lack of emotional concern between those on different levels of Japanese status hierarchy; therefore there is emotional interchange of a type that is rarely experienced between present-day superiors and subordinates in a Western contract-oriented economic setting.

Paternalism and Dependent Gratification

Paternalism in Japan has been real; those in the *oyabun* or parent role position do indeed relate to their subordinates as if the subordinates were their charges, not simply faceless individuals from whom one obtains maximum productive output. The subordinate is not depersonalized or treated as a machine. (Even in Western capitalism there is now some awareness of the fact that one has to treat one's workers at least as well as one's machines to maintain proper functioning without disruption or the need for costly replacement.) As we have illustrated in our discussions of apprenticeship in Arakawa, seen from the outside the *iemoto*, the occupational mentor—if not the actual parent—might be observed to exploit the young economically for their labor. But seen through the internal perceptions of the Japanese themselves, this apprenticeship is conceived as a reciprocal payment of present labor for future-oriented training in a skill. Apprentices are paid poorly if at all, but the apprentice is learning a trade by which he is later to earn his own living. And, indeed, the apprentice sometimes inherits the master's job. This is not to gainsay that in many occupational situations in Japan there is indeed a lifelong perpetuation of *kobun* status, in which individuals remain subadult throughout life, continuing their emotional and financial dependency on an *oyakata*, or parent figure, who periodically rewards his followers with symbols of appreciation or nurturance. Such ties remain highly emotional, internally reinforced by feelings of potential guilt if the subordinates do not repay their benefactors, and—what is often missed by the Westerner—guilt on the part of the benefactor if he fails to give proper care to his subordinates.

Some Western observers might concede that an apprenticeship situation is tolerable when one can identify with future privileges to be reached by seniority. This is perhaps more quickly understandable than are situations of lifelong dependency. Those espousing the modern Western concept that all normal individuals in a society should reach the status of independent adulthood are disturbed by the readiness of some cultures to value the permanently dependent role as a positive feature of a society. Western theorists do not like to accept the fact that Japanese paternalism gratifies expressive needs for dependency; such gratification, they think, is irrational in both personal and economic terms.

This seeking to continue dependent gratification is related emotionally to the way that many Japanese are socialized in their early family experiences. A primary feature of Japanese socialization is the manner in which strong dependency needs are developed and sustained by the culturally typical pattern of maternal nuturance directed toward the young. This early childhood pattern is reinforced in later secondary occupational socialization by the manner in which passive compliance is periodically rewarded. The individual learns to seek continuing gratification in this manner. He not only learns to expect it but learns to some degree to distort his perception so that he will achieve fancied gratification from those in superior positions.

This latter observation of characteristic Japanese distortion toward the experience of fancied care and gratification from others is well brought out in descriptions of Naikan therapy often practiced with delinquent youth (Reynolds, 1980). The individual sits and contemplates or meditates on how he has been ungrateful in the face of the supposed benefices given by his or her parents, stepmother, or other parental authority figures who are culturally expected to gratify the individual's need for nurturance.

The distortion process is a highly complex matter to be further explored psychologically and culturally. In like situations in the West, the individual more candidly observes an unnurturant family environment and turns outside the family to religious beliefs. He is taught not to expect nurturance from those who cannot give it, but to overcome resentment by turning to a universal source. In fact, the seeking after dependent nurturance only within the family is culturally discouraged. Individuals are supposed to learn to be less emotionally dependent. We cannot overemphasize this cultural historical difference in ways of achieving emotional security. One central function of Christian beliefs is to give the individual the assurance that there is someone who cares for him, who will take care of him, recognize his deepest needs, someone who understands and accepts. This person is not a physical being in the actual social environment, but is either the Virgin Mary or Jesus Christ. God the Father is for many too aloof an authority figure to concern himself with individuals, but his compassionate Son or the mother of his Son are considered approachable figures from whom to receive a sense of care and concern. In turn, one "gives" oneself over to Jesus. One finds a release from the petty resentments of life and can then experience a flow of love. The Japanese generally have no such religious recourse, although some have found reliance on figures such as Kannon, an Oriental goddess of mercy, to be emotionally satisfying. In most instances, however, Japanese are constrained to find the illusion if not the reality of "giving" within the primary family or in some occupational transmutation of the primary family relationship so that individuals in parent-like roles tend to be imbued with capacities to give, and a desire to give, which indeed they may not possess. Japanese are wont therefore to feel gratitude toward prominent individuals who have done very little to deserve such feelings. It is often curious to visiting Westerners to find Japanese expressing a feeling of gratitude for behavior to which they themselves gave little thought. They do not well understand the need for a Japanese to feel in some circumstances that someone has cared, has given special attention—has indeed inspired him, has released his energies productively, and has freed him from the necessity to feel resentful toward an impersonal, ungiving world.

Endurance

A second feature of Japanese socialization is a capacity to sustain oneself through present adversity toward the realization of a goal. Endurance, the theme of this volume, is a continual test of a virtuous capacity to win out in the end, to "succeed" in both senses of the word: to accomplish, and to inherit at some time in the future from those to whom one has played the inferior role. There is nothing demeaning about being a pupil. Nineteenth-century Japan was open to learning from the West because there was no sense of one's pride being wounded by absorbing knowledge when one knew it was for the purpose of future mastery and independence.

Vicarious Identification

As a third feature of Japanese socialization, the development of empathetic capacities for vicarious identification is crucial to responsible paternalism. We have already noted the psychological identification of a mother with the success of her male child. The same capacity is to be noted in an inferior's vicarious identification with a superior role. It is less frequently noted but also true, however, that an individual in the superior role in Japanese culture identifies in some way, covertly if not overtly, with the person in the inferior role. What is rarely considered is the fact that there is a similar potential for guilt on the part of males toward their mothers, and of superiors toward their inferiors, which is a deeply internalized part of a Japanese sense of status responsibility. Without taking into consideration the way in which such features are emphasized in Japanese socialization, one cannot explain why Japanese society is so well knit together in vertical structures by expressive, affectional ties instead of by the instrumental contractual bonds required in the West.

In Japanese society the capacity to endure in order to succeed reaches its apotheosis in the role of married women. Women identify readily with males who are carrying out their expected role behavior, an identification that is an essential part of the capacity to feel a deep sense of accomplishment as a mother. This capacity for endurance on the part of the Japanese woman permits her to go through what seem to be almost incredible acts of metamorphosis in later stages of her life cycle.

As we have suggested in some of the anecdotal materials given above, the housemaid can be construed as being at the larval stage of the gracious hostess in her own home, and the meek bride as being at the pupal stage of a later horrendous mother-in-law. Similarly, the eager male apprentice, for good or ill, is potentially the larval stage of a future dominant master, although many males continue to carry on a larval existence throughout their working lives, as more or less well cared for drones hoping for better success for their children. The fact that the final stages of metamorphosis do not occur for all in the same way does not negate a Japanese cultural climate of relatively high worker morale. Psychologically at least, if not actually, it is as if Japanese are in various stages of "becoming" during a life cycle projected into the future. This gives them a sense of forward thrust into an optimistically conceived future; looking forward for one's progeny if not for oneself, one remains at the same time in a dependent position within hierarchical relationships.

The Western image of "paternalism" connotes an instrumental-exploitative use of a contract-bound labor force toward whom a boss feels little or no sense of personal involvement, let alone belonging. The Japanese, in contrast, tend to believe the political and social myths about their nation, about their company or their occupational groups, or about their family collectivity. The *oyakata* is supposed to have "parent-like feelings"; the good parent is assumed to provide for his dependent children—whatever the reality. There are positive fantasies of protective consideration directed to such superiors as bosses or "company presidents" which reinforce an internalized sense of responsibility on their part. Employers are not psychologically free to dehumanize their employees into numbers on statistical tables which give abstract projections of maximal efficiency. Many Japanese industrial leaders, as well as the small-scale entrepreneurs we have described, are caught in an inner necessity to play out the benevolent aspects of an idealized wise "company president," spontaneously concerned with the welfare of his workers.

For individuals who can hark back to their own previous status as young apprentices, there is a personal capacity to identify with an eager youngster who is dependent on an older leader. On a deep psychodynamic level in Japanese hierarchies one finds an age-status network of affection binding Japanese of sharply different statuses to one another. This sense of expressive rapport transcends status differences that more characteristically alienate individualistic Westerners from one another.

Since the subordinates have no instrumental power in the Japanese status hierarchy, they can only hope to induce kindness in their superiors by invoking feelings of nurturance and appreciation from them. If fate puts them in the hands of a harsh authority, they have no recourse but to endure and hope for change in the future. Japanese must find their rewards in positive expressive aspects of their dominant-subordinate relationships, since they have only recently begun to create in their social institutions instrumental guarantees to ensure or secure what Westerners consider the "rights" of justice extended to the weak. What is sometimes difficult for Western observers to apprehend is the combination of nurturance and control going both ways; in Japan not only is nurturance used to control, but control sometimes is also a means of bestowing some expression of nurturance. Having had early gratification of his own dependent needs, many a Japanese boss is constrained to find social means to bestow on others what to a Westerner would seem to be an almost maternal need to nurture. This need constitutes a profoundly significant part of Japanese social consciousness and sense of responsibility.

It must be noted that a system of reciprocity of expectations between superiors and subordinates works only when the subordinates believe that they will be rewarded if they perform properly in their subordinate position. (The system, therefore, implies a necessary sensitivity to the expressive needs of subordinates on the part of superiors, rather than simple exploitation of the weak.) In many of the processes of socialization found in Japan there is indeed a particular kind of internalization socialized into those who are to assume status-authority positions. This process starts with the strong dedication of the mother to her role as responsible socializer, a dedication to role that requires considerable desexualization and the general giving up of the gratification of immediate pleasures on the part of the mother.

The role of the samurai bureaucrat in the premodern culture required him to be as truly dedicated to his job as a mother to her children. Westerners may hear much more about samurai as swordsmen than about samurai as dedicated administrators who were relatively uncorrupt and who attempted to govern with an exceptional degree of equity and fairness. Many samurai had strongly internalized values regarding public service, so that they performed optimally in their role as governors and administrators.[1] Authority may have been feared in Tokugawa Japan, but there was a general respect for it. This is not to gainsay the periodic rebellions of the peasants against improper treatment; these were indeed symptomatic of misrule and corruption in local instances. Generally, however, the system worked; there was enough honesty to keep it going. Therefore, individuals who held positions of authority were invested with a certain moral ascendancy by their subordinates. There was not apparent in Japan the obvious split appearing in the West between idealized spiritual authority, on the one hand, and rebellious, self-righteous hatred of the corrupt power of the state, on the other. In the West, individuals in the religious hierarchy were supposed to be more dedicated than those in the secular hierarchy, whereas in Japan if there was any counterpart of Western religious authority it was to be found in dedicated civil bureaucracy.

This is a most complex topic, which cannot be discussed further here. Suffice it to say that present-day Japanese governmental administrators and even local police generally inherit considerable public respect. As we have indicated in the case histories from Arakawa Ward, whatever negative feelings about authority appear, authority is generally respected and is seldom perceived as being so venal as to be thoroughly distrusted. Authority figures—political, administrative, and familial—are, for the most part, granted a degree of respect rare in the United States. It is emotionally feasible, therefore, for Japanese to expect dependent gratifications to be awarded for performing morally prescribed compliant behavior. The belief found in Western religion that moral obedience gains God's reward of nurturance is similar to that directed by many Japanese toward civil authority.

Japanese Interdependency: A Contrast to the Western Experience

The existence of such a pattern of emotional interaction in a hierarchical social structure is highly repellent to Western theoreticians, and to modern Japanese Marxist theorists as well. They choose to ignore its operational force in Japanese society, and elect the Western model of society as the basis for social analyses. Those Japanese social historians who are influenced by Marx emphasize rational instrumentality and ignore the continuing force of expressive needs that permeates occupational as well as familial hierarchical structures in Japan.

Any appraisal of Western cultural history since industrialization constrains one to perceive that the class system in many Western nations has tended to be

1. See, for example, the descriptions of samurai bureaucrats in a number of chapters of Craig and Shively, eds., 1970.

an alienating one, causing a weakening of emotional ties and mutual antagonism between different occupational strata of the society. Western societies are not knit together, as is Japanese society, with a mythology of quasi-parentage or extended quasi-familial vertical networks of obligations that act as constraints on raw exploitation. The social cleavages resulting from differential status in American and European societies are not tied together by the particularistic familial morality that permeates the Japanese social system. This "particularistic" quality in traditional Japanese society, with its Confucian ideals, is often criticized by both Western and Japanese theorists in contrast to the supposed "universalism" guiding Western societies of Christian origin. On close examination one observes that the supposed Western universalist orientation has certain innate inconsistencies impeding realization. There is no doubt that the moral system considered by most Western thinkers to approximate the human political, economic, and social ideal has emphasized the principles of a broad human brotherhood transcending particularistic tribal or "national" loyalties. In this moral system there is also emphasis on the maximization of individualism and on autonomy as an ideal. However, the history of Europe is one of chauvinistic loyalty and the particularisms of individual national states. Moreover, Western cultures have been prone to collective dictatorships of the right as well as of the left in political organization, and prone to severe alienating class cleavages in economic organization.

Western societies can be perceived to bind potentially antagonistic individuals and groups together by instrumental contractual bonds sometimes enforced by raw power, as Hobbes analyzed it. In such a system one cannot depend on positive expressive needs to maintain patterns of acceptable reciprocity. In this sense Western societies have, indeed, gone far from the particularistic social reciprocities of European feudalism toward a more impersonal sense of formalized contract relationships depending upon a mutual assertion of "rights." Emotional feelings, whether positive or negative, are a hindrance to the development of a system of law based on an abstract universalized sense of justice. It has been, and continues to be, very difficult for Western societies to overcome the particularism of individual states and to achieve recognition of contracts binding beyond the national boundaries. This ideal comes into serious conflict even today with the basically particularistic concept of national sovereignty.

Moreover, the states of western Europe and the "new world" of North and South America, although supposedly similarly oriented toward universalistic Christian ideals, are highly divergent from one another in degree of adherence to universalist precepts in law. Similarly, the supposedly more particularistic societies of Asia influenced by Confucianism—China, Korea, and Japan—are far from resembling each other historically in actual social organization. A comparison of ideological traditions alone gives us no direct picture of differences or similarities in social organization, nor of the expressive forces binding individuals together socially. Confucianist China developed far differently from supposedly Confucianist-oriented Tokugawa Japan. Seen psychoculturally, China did not develop internalized patterns of commitment and loyalty toward vertically organized extrafamilial groups such as occurred in Japan. Hence, simply contrasting "particularism" in Japan with "universalism" in the West may be a most misleading way to attempt to conceptualize differences in psychological motivation or social structure, either between any given Western nation and a nation of Asia or among the states of either region.[2]

Nevertheless, there are some historical parallels to be observed in a broad comparison between the premodern patterns of Japan and of western Europe. Medieval Europe had vertically structured social organizational patterns based on manorial units with vast status disparities between the nobility and the serfs. There were also status differentials by age and seniority within the merchant and artisan guilds that developed around commercial activities in the towns and cities. These particularistic systems in European feudalism were eventually supplanted by an impersonal colonial mercantilism that "rationalized" human relationships as well as machines within the state and, in addition, dealt with foreigners according to systems of impersonally reckoning gain and loss. "Cost accounting" was not lacking in the reckoning of Japanese merchants in considering the work of direct subordinates; they were indeed maneuvering for gain, but they continue to be caught in a system of expressive as well as instrumentally determined social relationships in which systems of reciprocity have been maintained as central to social structure. Curiously, vertical organizations in Japan have increased rather than diminished with the development of modern industry.

Marx, in his vision of the history of Western culture, saw in nineteenth-century society a social system that had been governed by a corrupt and decaying feudal nobility which was supplanted by a system leading to the bourgeois' more impersonal exploitation of workers. In his view the national states would eventually be overthrown by the forces being engendered in them—principally by the general social alienation separating social classes one from another, and then by alienation of the worker from a personal identification with his occupation. His is a European vision that is disturbingly realistic to modern Westerners. Important in this vision, and central to it, is the dilemma of individualism as re-

2. Japanese paternalism with its potentials for a particularistic totalitarian social outlook can be considered potentially more congenial in some respects to a fascist type of national socialism than are societies or nations supposedly oriented toward a universalistic socialist ideology. Yet, as has been demonstrated in various Western governments of the left, it is difficult to plan universalist programs that are not to the economic advantage of particular internal classes or ethnic social segments. In the Soviet Union, supposedly committed to international socialism and a respect for the integrity of its various ethnic social segments, there is an impasse in Communist attempts at "international" thinking. The dominant Russian ethnic group in control of the state tends to "russify" or integrate its subordinate minorities, sometimes with considerable covert social tension. Universalist international ideologies are very difficult to reconcile rationally with conflicting ethnic groupings, as well as with historically arbitrary political boundaries.

Japanese particularism seems to be coterminous with ethnic identity. Hence, internal political dissension derived from ethnic pluralism is minimal, allowing for easier distancing from those who do not belong or are not "Japanese." In this respect, Japanese tend to be "racists." See further discussion in De Vos and Wagatsuma, 1966, and Lee and De Vos, 1981.

lated to personal gain and the consequent instrumental exploitative use of man in a social structure determined by impersonal economic forces. Man conceived as a rational animal, in Marxist terms, when he comes to live in a class society finds it profitable, and hence satisfying economically, to exploit those beneath him in power and status. He does not maintain personal identification with them. What Marx therefore deemed necessary, rather than any system of personalized, particularized reciprocity as in Japan, was a spiritual breakthrough toward a universal regard for one's fellowmen that went beyond regional, ethnic, and national identities as well as beyond class affiliation. The universalistic-individualistic polarities in the Marxian vision of man are seen as antagonistic to one another; on the one hand is the social need of a universal brotherhood to be achieved only by a proletarian revolution and, on the other hand, the manifest bourgeois propensity to actualize a greedy self-oriented individualism that seeks out maximization of good for one's self by instrumental means, including political-economic class alliances.

This image of man in society is far different from that underlying the indigenous Japanese particularistic attempts to conceive of themselves collectively as a society based on an extended familial network. Japanese society places everyone somewhere within a hierarchical status system that is consensually dedicated to the realization of totalitarian collective goals. The Marxian image of man, caught between seeking individual gain as a merchant and pursuing a moral imperative for universal commitment to brotherhood as a worker, is therefore vastly different from the image presented in some of the Japanese chauvinist theories about the nature of Japanese society. Whatever the acceptance or rejection, emotional or rational, of Marxist theory, it is part of the Western intellectual tradition. Ethnocentrically, Western theorists are apt to apply it too quickly to Japan, without examining the "irrational" or expressive patterns related to social structure, which are very different in class-oriented Western society from the vertical reciprocal hierarchies still sufficiently operative to help bind together the Japanese. Western theorists are apt to dismiss too quickly previous Japanese perceptions of their own society as "mythological" rather than "objective" or "rational" without examining the emotional validity of these perceptions as symbolic representations of collective forces that are demonstrably operative within their society. One must acknowledge that irrational, antieconomic motivations play as great a role in history as those directed toward economic maximization. Without crediting the meaning of such perceptions one cannot understand the collective forces in Japanese society or, for that matter, the sources of totalitarian strength periodically manifest in European society as well, whatever the vast differences in traditions of particularism or universalism. The feeling of moral outrage aroused in a universalist conscience does not of itself lead to an understanding of some sources of collective behavior in society.

Today it is the Japanese espousing a Western capitalist ideology who seem to be capable of motivating the type of worker morale that socialist theorists suggest should occur only in a well-managed socialist economic system. What the theorists curse as the hampering effect of traditional cultural attitudes that prevent the realization of workers' gains are seemingly, to some extent at least, now being utilized in Japan for collective national economic efforts. The Japanese are economically successful partly because they are able to carry forward expressive and hence irrational attitudes inherited from a feudalistic premodern past.

We have concluded that the horrendous living conditions of workers and petty entrepreneurs in Arakawa Ward have not turned the inhabitants into bitter critics of their society, nor have they caused social disorganization among them. This situation may change; however, in the time span of our studies, the Arakawa dwellers were still committed to getting ahead through education and hard work as relatively well integrated members of their society, whatever the objective reality of their economic life.

Our major conclusions, with their further implications, derive from our empirical investigation of occupational socialization at a time when the apprenticeship system was still operative throughout Japanese society in the 1960s. Our illustrative material in the historical present of this period attest to how the individual at the time of puberty is introduced into this system, and eventually acquires skills. The individual is trained to develop a future time orientation; he maintains a sufficient degree of social trust that he is willing not only to forego immediate full payment, but even to undergo what seems to be harsh exploitative treatment in return for the promise of future paternalistic support. There are also the gains related to increasing competence and to appreciation, not easily obtained, for meeting established standards of excellence. In sum, there is a realization of inner satisfaction through meeting the internalized standards that are part of apprenticeship training. From this standpoint then, apprenticeship in Arakawa for both men and women is a form of secondary socialization following upon the normative patterns of early primary family socialization. The Japanese are socialized to gain certain reciprocal expressive satisfactions on all levels in an interdependent social system. Such gratifications counter the potentials for alienation in a potentially impersonal industrial society.

One index of alienation is delinquency in youth. It must be noted that in Japan, after a postwar surge, indices of youthful delinquency among lower-class youth are going down rather than up (De Vos and Mizushima, 1973; De Vos and Wagatsuma, 1973). Today throughout Japan it is the youth from relatively higher status backgrounds, when they become students, who show more restiveness and feelings of social alienation. There is a growing malaise about the increasingly impersonal, albeit vastly expanded, system of advanced formal education in the universities. College students are showing more signs of personal and social stress than are the youth entering work in either large-scale or small-scale industries. What is often lacking for students is any sense of personal interaction with their mentors. The teacher's role has become not only distant but also more impersonal. In contrast, industrial workers or youth entering business firms become part of organizations favoring a sense of belonging.

For noncollege youth, Japanese hierarchical society, compared with American society with its more stringent forms of age segmentation, still, to some degree, bridges the generation gap induced by rapid social change. It is the Japanese upper- to middle-class youth who, as students, more prevailingly go through a crisis of commitment respecting occupational choice. The period of worker apprenticeship, whatever its hardships and strain for the individual, is not for most a period of protest or alienation. In brief, the apprenticeship system, where it remains, is a force for maintaining social cohesion in modern Japanese society.

PATTERNS OF COMMUNICATION WITHIN THE URBAN COMMUNITY

Finally, in comparing Japan with the United States, we have arrived at a set of further contentions concerning community cohesiveness that would benefit by further detailed investigation. These contentions are related to our understanding of the meaning of poverty (Lewis, 1959, 1966). Poverty has to be understood as a state of mind. Although economic dislocation, social degradation, exploitation, and deprivation of meaningful work are part of lower-class life in many industrial societies, one can also find contravening traditions that sustain given social groups, preventing the full appearance of a subculture of poverty. We have tried to present in this volume a picture of what seems to be a slum area that, when closely examined, shows relatively few of the personally and socially disruptive features we have come to associate with life in an American slum. Arakawa does not show patterns of hostility or animosity toward the general society, but on the contrary is demonstrably very much an economically productive part of present-day Japan. We have discussed the way in which individuals are socialized into this community. There are some other sociological forces related to community life that must be further examined to stress the differences between Arakawa and the type of communities in an American city. One can find some evidence of the culture of poverty in Japan among minority Koreans or among the former outcastes, a still socially alienated segment of Japanese society living in ghettos in Kyoto, Nara, Kobe, and Osaka; but this was not the situation in Arakawa Ward (De Vos and Wagatsuma, 1966; Lee and De Vos, 1981).

One of the principal features of Arakawa was its heterogeneity. An urban community such as Arakawa remains socially viable because it is not composed of people all on the same social level or all suffering from the same problems. Heterogeneity has been maintained because patterns of geographic and social mobility in Japanese cities such as Tokyo have been considerably different from those in cities in the United States. People do not move rapidly in and out of the Arakawa Ward; most come to stay. As we reported in our statistics, there is both in-mobility and out-mobility, but it is far less than that generally reported in cities in the United States. Moreover, the mobility toward the peripheries of this area is not that of people moving out as they improve themselves economically; on the contrary, those who have failed have a tendency to move into the less settled, peripheral, semirural areas not yet as organized socially as Arakawa.

Arakawa is peopled not only by the merchants who have stores there and by the artisans with their tiny house-factories, but also by individuals of professional status who serve the community. Many of the teachers and policemen serving the area live in the community. They identify personally as well as professionally with their community, and are part of its social life and its voluntary community organizations. They do not seek to move out. If their economic circumstances permit better housing, they stay and improve the structures they live in. They enter and stay in the voluntary associations that make up the networks of communication we have described. In brief, a heterogeneous group made up of individuals of varying status levels is committed to the community in which they live.

There is little sense of alienation related to authority in Arakawa Ward. Authority figures are conceived of as part of the community, not separate from it. The police in Arakawa are not seen as an occupation force; they have personal relationships with the individuals and families living there. They communicate directly with the teachers and the parents. They do not show the impersonality or the interpersonal hostility that occurs in the United States between the police and minority individuals in lower-class neighborhoods. We discussed the activities of concerned Arakawa citizens directed toward the delinquent behavior of youth. We raised the question of whether community campaigns have any direct effect on delinquency. We suggested that what is termed by psychologists "the Hawthorne phenomenon" is at work; this phenomenon was described in a social-psychological study of worker morale in an American factory in which it became evident that morale was affected not by what color walls were painted but by the fact that someone cared enough to paint the walls. So too, perhaps, in the life of a community what matters is not that volunteers pass out balloons and have meetings, but that individuals within that community are committed to its collective betterment. Such concern to be effective must arise out of the community itself. Professional workers can only assist successfully when they work *as part of a community* rather than as part of an outside professional authority, however benevolent its objectives.

In short, the forces of change as they influence Arakawa did not yet show a disintegrative effect at the time of our study. The social traditions into which the dwellers of Arakawa were integrated were sustaining even during such vicissitudes as those experienced by individual families, which we have amply documented in this book. The social deviancy present in Arakawa, as elsewhere in Japan, shows no indication of serious increase. We cannot of course predict what will happen at some future time should radical economic change cause serious disruption within the occupations represented in Arakawa. In general, one must conclude that the centripetal and centrifugal community forces remain in balance at present. If anything, Arakawa Ward is moving in the direction of further social integration. The decrease in the incidence of juvenile delinquency is one significant index of the relative social integration of Arakawa Ward.

We again affirm, as we have in previous work, the necessity in social science to use a multilevel framework in understanding behavior, one that takes full cognizance of societal forces, the nature of social structure, and social organization, on the one hand, and is, on the other hand, directly concerned with psychocultural motivational factors. It is safe to assume that Arakawa Ward in the 1960s, given many of the difficulties of living—the substandard housing, the crowding—would have produced a much higher delinquency rate if it had not been for the fact that within these inadequate housing units we found a large majority of intact, functioning families giving their children sufficient love and emotional gratification to sustain them through an adolescence that would have been intolerable for individuals less nourished by a heritage of endurance. How will this heritage be passed on to following generations? Time will tell.

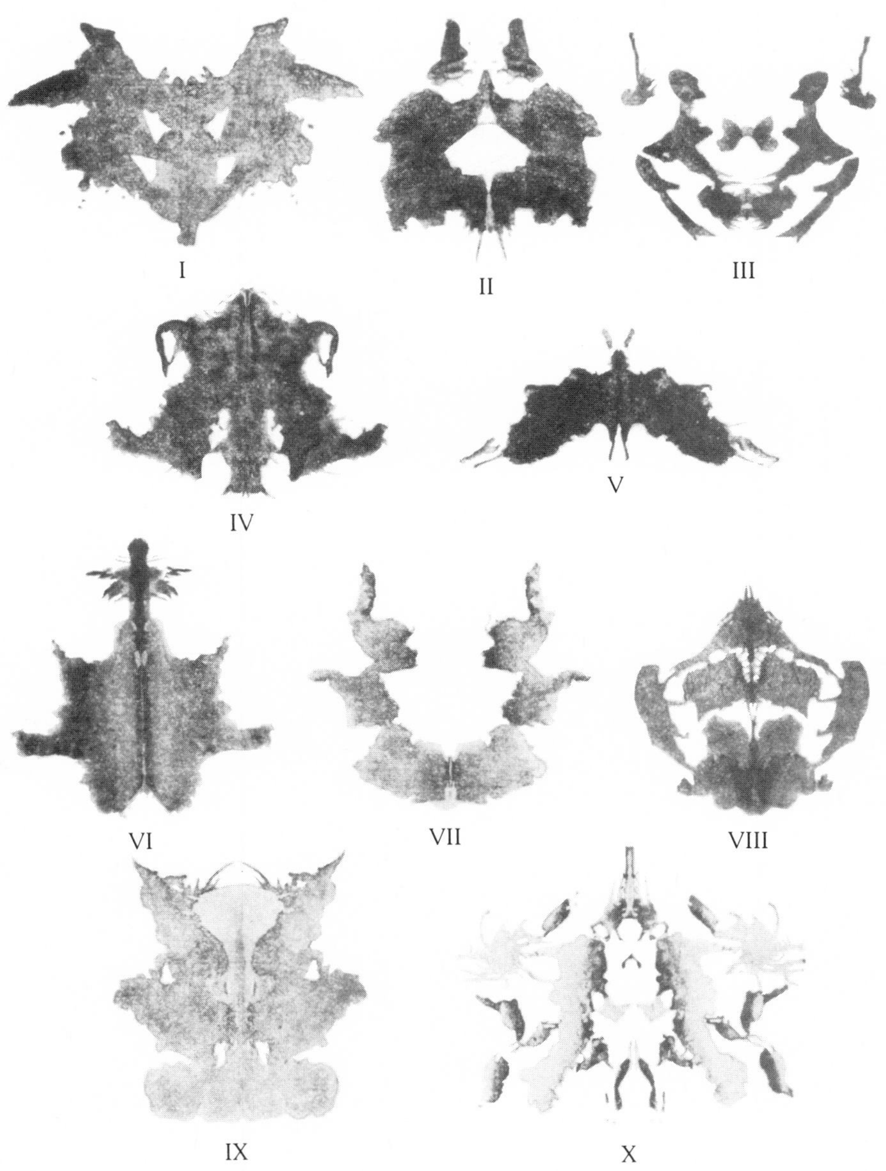

Illustrations of the standard Rorschach blots.

APPENDIX A

Comparison of Rorschach Test Results

The Rorschach test, a standardized series of ten inkblots—five black and white, five partly in color—has been widely used by clinical psychologists and others to differentiate between neurotic, schizophrenic, and normal subjects. It has also been used, periodically, in nonclinical research concerned with differences between groups in respect to personality variables.

De Vos (1952, 1954, 1955) initially used the Rorschach in Chicago from 1948 to 1950 in a study of personality differences between immigrant Japanese and their American-born children. The results were highly differentiating; they indicated a change in the American-born Nisei generation toward American normative patterns of perception. Subsequently, De Vos collaborated with scholars at Nagoya University from 1953 to 1955 in a large-scale sampling of 800 Japanese from three villages and two cities, using the TAT and Rorschach as well as other personality tests.

The Rorschach results in Japan were reported by Murakami (1959, 1962), using a scoring system that included standard symbols as well as the De Vos system for scoring affective inferences (De Vos, 1952). (See table A.1.) Scoring revealed an overall pattern similar to that obtained from records of American Issei immigrants by De Vos in his initial study. For example, whereas the overall level of personality rigidity is considerably higher than for American subjects, the sense of social reality is strong. The Japanese reveal on the Rorschach a higher regard for good form in the percepts than do American subjects. There is considerable overlap between the two populations in which are termed "popular" or frequently seen percepts indicated by the symbol P in table A.1. The Japanese however, are less apt to utilize some particular small details that are popular for Americans. In contrast, they produce a popular response in the form of a flower given to the center of Card VIII, which does not appear often in American reports.

Characteristically, the Japanese give far fewer responses than do American subjects. The average total number of responses for Japanese is approximately seventeen, with twenty-eight to thirty-two responses reported for American populations. The Japanese, by and large, strive to give single, well-integrated responses to each card, showing a strong intellectually organized drive. Americans are more apt to give a simple response to some detail of the card when they

Table A.1
Rorschach Scoring Symbols

TIME

00″ (Time of first response)

LOCATION

W	(Whole Response)
D	(Usual Detail)
Dd	(Rare Detail)
S	(White Space)
Rej	(Card Rejection)
P	(Popular Response)
R	(Response Total)

DETERMINANTS

F	(Form)
F+	(Good Form)
M	(Human Movement)
FM	(Animal Movement)
m	(Inanimate Movement)
Fv	(Vista)
Y	(Shading)
C	(Color)
T	(Texture)
C′	(Achromatic Color)

CONTENT

A	(Animal)
A/	(Strange A)
Ad	(Detail)
Aob	(Object)
H	(Human)
H/	(Strange Human)
(H)	(Human-like)
Hd	(Detail)
Bl	(Blood)
X-ray	
Atb	(Bone Anat.)
Atf	(Flesh Anat.)
Dis	(Disease)
Sex	
Anal	
Death	
Exp	(Explosion)
Fi	(Fire)
Cl	(Cloud)
Fd	(Food)
Cg	(Clothing)
Emb	(Emblem)
Orn	(Ornament)
Stat	(Statue)
Art	
Mu	(Music)
Rec	(Recreation)
Toy	
Imp	(Implement)
Hh	(Household)
Sc	(Science)
Mech	(Mechanical)
Rel	(Religion)
Anth	(Anthropology)
Bot	(Botany)
Geo	(Geography)
Lsc	(Landscape)
Nat	(Nature)
Cave	
Arch	(Architecture)

AFFECTIVE SYMBOLISM

Hostility

Hor	(oral)
Hdpr	(depreciative)
HH	(direct)
Hcmpt	(competitive)
Hh	(indirect hostility)
Hha	(ind. host.-anxious)
Hhat	(tense)
Hhad	(distorted)
Hsm	(sado-masch.)
Hden	(denial of host.)

Anxiety

Arej	(rejecting)
Acnph	(counterphobic)
Aobs	(obsessive)
Adef	(defensive)
Aev	(evasive)
Adif	(diffuse)
Agl	(depressive)
Adis	(disgust)
Abal	(unbalanced)
Acon	(confused)
Asex	(sex confusion)
Adeh	(dehumanized)
Athr	(threatening)
Afant	(fantastic, strange)

Bodily Preoccupation

Bb	(bone)
Bf	(flesh)
Bn	(neural)
Bs	(sexual anat.)
Bso	(sexual organ)
Ban	(anal)
Bdi	(disease)
Bch	(childbirth)

Dependency

Df	(fetal)
Dor	(oral)
Dcl	(clinging)
Dsec	(security)
Dch	(childish)
Dlo	(longing)
Drel	(religion)
Daut	(authority)
Dsub	(submissive)

Positive Feeling

Por	(oral)
Ps	(sensual)
Pch	(childish)
Prec	(recreation)
Pnat	(nature)
Porn	(ornament)
Pst	(striving)
Pnar	(narcissistic)
Pcopt	(cooperative)
Pden	(denial of pos.)

Miscellaneous

Mor	(oral)
Man	(anal)
Msex	(sex)
Mpret	(pretentious)
Mgrand	(grandiose)
Mi	(indefinite)

Neutral

N	(neutral)

do not perceive a total, complex, integrated percept. The Japanese are more apt to reject a card when they are unable to give what they believe to be a satisfactory response.

The Rorschach test has been adopted by a number of clinical psychologists in Japan for diagnostic usage in determining psychopathology, using the same criteria applied in the United States. It differentiates well among individual Japanese in respect to the personality variables used in clinical diagnosis. Therefore, it follows that the test can be used to distinguish normative patterns in subgroups of Japanese, as in this study.

We used the Rorschach in assessing the individual family members in our sample and as an aid to understanding the personality dynamics underlying expressed attitudes and observed behavior during interviews. We were also interested in whether there were any diagnostic features that would be indicative of personality differences that could distinguish between delinquent and nondelinquent subjects and their parents.

Whereas we can report that we did find significant statistical differences between experimental and control groups, none of these differences permit an individual diagnosis related specifically to social deviancy. That is to say, the differences we can report remain statistical rather than clinically diagnostic as individual traits separating delinquent from nondelinquent. Nevertheless, our overall results are worth reporting because they are directly supportive of various assumptions about how and why particular personality patterns may contribute to the appearance of delinquent or criminal behavior in particular individuals.

PERSONALITY RIGIDITY AND MALADJUSTMENT

Throughout De Vos's work with the Rorschach test, he has used two complex scoring devices for assessing Rorschach variables that produce overall quantifiable ratings of comparative rigidity and maladjustment. These measurements developed by Seymour Fisher (1950) have been found to be valid measurements differentiating Americans (De Vos, 1952) and Japanese (De Vos, 1955) and Algerian Arab samples (De Vos and Miner, 1959; De Vos, 1961). (It is not possible here to explain these measures in a brief way. The interested reader must refer to more technical discussions in the papers by Fisher (1950) and De Vos (1952).

The overall totals in this study collectively show significantly more rigidity in members of families with a delinquent son (see table A.2). Higher rates of rigidity in the mothers contribute most to this statistical difference. The scores of the fathers, though generally higher, are significant only at the 10 percent level. A larger sample would of course probably show statistical significance. The sons show the same trends but to a less significant degree than their parents.

Of the twelve criteria in the overall rigidity scale, the most characteristic difference is found in the tendency for members of the delinquent samples to give simple form responses unenriched by other determinants, such as shading,

TABLE A.2
Differences in Total Fisher's Rigidity and Maladjustment Scores and Various Specific Subscores

	Normals				*Delinquents*			
	Fa	Mo	Sons	Tot	Fa	Mo	Sons	Tot
Total rigidity score	37.17	29.78	32.83	33.26	46.17*	44.17‡	39.20	43.18‡
F% (percentage pure form)	53.89	51.89	56.22	54.00	63.70*	66.07†	64.93	64.90‡
F(v) (indefinite form)	.50	.78	.94	.74	.27	.73	.70	.57
Z (organizational responses)	5.61‡	7.00‡	6.83‡	6.48‡	3.20	3.57	4.40	3.72
No card turning	.50	.67	.50	.56*	.30	.47	.43	.40
Total maladjustment score	42.00	34.94	38.11	38.35	48.33	47.87†	44.03	46.74†
Total popular responses (P)	5.22	5.11	4.67	5.00*	4.70	4.70	4.23	4.54
No popular on Card V	.67	.83	.67	.72	.87	.86	.93†	.89†
No popular on Card VIII	.56	.67	.61	.61	.83†	.80	.63	.76*
Animal percentage	55.28	46.17*	55.78	52.41	56.83	55.03	57.63	56.50
Humans (H)	2.17†	2.50‡	2.61†	2.43‡	1.00	1.30	1.50	1.27
Human detail (Hd)	.28	.41	.72	.47†	.13	.20	.37	.23
"Humanoid" responses	.39	1.00*	1.11	.83	.60	.46	1.17	.74
Esthetic Responses	1.17†	.78	.67	.87†	.23	.77	.23	.41
Anatomy	.72	.94	.17	.61	.86	.67	1.07†	.87
Sex, anality	.28	.22*	.00	.17*	.13	.03	.00	.06

*($P < .10$)
†($P < .05$)
‡($P < .01$)

color, or movement. By contrast, the nondelinquent controls are more apt to enrich and complicate their responses. They also show more attempts to organize their percepts into more complex integrated patterns.

One sign of rigidity to be found generally in Japanese is the accepting of the Rorschach cards without attempting to turn them around to look for other possible responses. In this study it was the nondelinquent who demonstrated this general tendency toward less card-turning, showing thereby a more passive, submissive attitude toward authority than evidenced by the delinquents. (The card is presented in only one direction by the tester, and this is presumed by many Japanese to be the expected and only "correct" way to hold the card.)

Mean scores on Fisher's maladjustment scale were significantly higher at the 5 percent level for the members of our delinquent sample. The main contribution to this difference was made by the mothers of delinquents, whose mean score by itself was significantly higher than that of mothers of the control group.

The maladjustment scale of Fisher is highly complex, composed of many variables (Fisher, 1950; De Vos, 1955). In general, they first include what are termed perceptual "approach" variables (the ratio of responses to the whole of the card, or to large details, or to rarely seen details). They also include the adequacy of form, the perception of movement, color, and shading, and the content of the responses. The scale also includes the possible appearance of peculiar thought processes. The subjects showed no difference in approach variables with the exception of the greater complexity of organization found in the percepts of the controls. Differences in the content of the responses showed some slight trends. Members of the delinquent group all give significantly fewer responses involving humans. The delinquent sons tended to give more anatomical responses. The lack of enrichment in the delinquent records suggested that constriction and rigidity contributed more to maladjustment than did signs of looseness or poor reality contact. The records as a whole in both groups gave us little indication of autistic or pathological thinking or inadequate sense of social reality.

MEASURES OF INNER AND OUTER CONTROL

The most notable differences between groups was in what is regarded in Rorschach assessment as the areas of "inner control" and "outer control." The use of kinesthetic or movement responses (M) is assumed to reveal a capacity for an "inner life," hence "inner control"—the ability to problem-solve in thought instead of resorting to externally observable behavioral responses to resolve inner impulses or promptings.

The color responses (FC, CF, C) measure "outer control"—the ability to modulate in a controlled way one's reactivity to outer stimuli. The results obtained with the delinquent samples suggest an excessive utilization of ego constriction. Such overall constriction prevents either more modulated responses to one's own inner impulses or ego-modulated reactions to emotional arousal by outside stimuli or both. Hence, one assumes there might be the periodic appearance of uncontrolled behavior, which could make some social difficulty for the individual.

Deviant behavior in many instances is consequent to a lack of inner control, outer control, or some combination thereof. For example, it can result from strong impulses to express hostility or resentment. Some delinquents "need" to flout authority. Other deviant behavior results from immoderate or uncontrolled reactions to outer provocations. In contrast, a nondelinquent person can "keep his cool" despite provocation, exercising a wariness about inducing social disapproval. Some individuals can be termed "hostile" or be given to aggressive behavior arising from within; others are uncontrolled in their reactions and thereby become alienated and are treated as immature or deviant. Of course, the behavior of most deviant individuals is some composite of inner promptings and what are to them excuses provided by the periodic provocation of their social environment. In brief, a typical delinquent has resentful attitudes, which he can act out and thus justify, pointing out that he is rejected or treated badly by authorities or adults generally.

Measures of "Inner Control"—Human Movement Percepts

The most highly significant differentiation appears between our samples in the use of human movement (see table A.3). The capacity for kinesthetic interpretation of the Rorschach blots, whether it be in the form of human, animal, or inanimate motion, was more freely given by the nondelinquent than by members of the delinquent group. The suggestion is, therefore, that there is greater constriction of inner life in the delinquent sample and, therefore, a lack of maturation of a self-conscious concern with human motivation.

Our finding is consonant with one of the major assumptions of Rorschach diagnosis concerning ego constriction versus ideational freedom. It is therefore a significant substantiation of the meaning of this variable in Rorschach interpretations. There are numerous reports that agree with one another that individuals institutionalized for delinquent behavior in general tend to be more "motor"-oriented in coping with their environment; that is, they are less apt to fall back on resolving problems in their minds before acting them out. They are less apt to use ideational methods of coping with their environment and more apt to use more direct, physical means. Another way of looking at "inner control" comparatively in personality patterning is that some individuals are better able to interpose forms of ideational control which can modulate the direct expression of attitudes or impulses. In a stress situation such a person can experience emotional arousal internally without making a visible outer response. According to clinical inference, the capacity to see human movement on the Rorschach is related to forms of self-control over behavior which in their broadest sense can prevent an individual from getting into social difficulty. He or she can consciously inhibit the commission of any act that would be socially disapproved.

Some of the fathers in the nondelinquent sample occasionally produce a movement response of "poor form" quality. That is to say, the percept given does not correspond well to the shape of the blot area. Such responses are a minor indication that some of these men show certain marginal psychological qualities that may relate to their occupational failure. These men show some indications in their human-movement perceptions of a form of maladjustment that can be socially maladaptive. From a psychological vantage point, while they see more human movement than the fathers of delinquents, by this fact they also reveal, more openly perhaps, some proneness toward "looseness" rather than rigidity in

TABLE A.3
Significant Differences in Movement Responses

	Normals				*Delinquents*			
	Fa.	Mo.	Sons	Total	Fa.	Mo.	Sons	Total
Total human movement (M)	2.33 †	2.78‡	3.78†	2.96‡	1.27	1.47	1.87	1.53
M with minus form	.28‡	.06	.72	.35*	.00	.10	.17	.09
M on Card III	.78	1.00	.83	.87	.70	.53‡	.57*	.60‡
Active M	1.17†	1.22	2.17‡	1.52‡	.53	.80	.80	.71
Passive M	.72	1.22†	1.06	1.00†	.57	.50	.73	.60
Animal movement (FM)	3.83*	4.78*	3.83	4.15‡	2.57	3.03	3.40	3.00
Active animal movement	2.06*	2.61*	2.78	2.48	1.17	1.47	2.10	1.57
Total inanimate movement (m)	.67	1.78‡	1.17	1.20†	.53	.80	.83	.72
Total active movement (M+FM+m)	3.33†	4.67†	5.00*	4.33‡	1.93	2.60	3.47	2.67
Total passive movement	2.39†	3.00†	2.39	2.59‡	1.40	1.50	1.67	1.52

* ($P < .10$)
† ($P < .05$)
‡ ($P < .01$)

their thought processes. Nevertheless, statistically the nondelinquent fathers do not, as a group, differ in overall maladjustment scores.

A Rorschach sign of interpersonal difficulty that characterizes the parents of subjects in the delinquent samples is their relative inability to see human movement in Card III. The shape of this blot makes it fairly easy to perceive human figures. In cross-cultural findings this card most frequently elicits the human form. Seventeen out of 18 of the mothers in our nondelinquent control do see human movement in this card, whereas only 16 out of 30 of the mothers of delinquents do. This is a highly significant difference. The difference is also significant in their sons. Among the nondelinquent controls, 16 out of 19 gave a human-movement response to Card III, in contrast to only 17 out of 30 among the delinquents. Obviously, according to Rorschach assumptions, the failure to see the most commonly perceived human form indicates some problems in experiencing positive social attitudes. The fact that this response, by comparison, is so obviously lacking in many of the delinquent subjects and their mothers goes along with expectations that they will have difficulty in the expression of ordinary social attitudes. (Our samples of fathers were little different on this variable.)

One can differentiate among the human-movement responses by classifying them into those responses that indicate an active "extratensive" or active quality and those that are passive or stationary in nature. The normative controls tend to give many more active or expanding-movement responses than do the delinquent subjects. While the delinquents also give fewer passive-movement responses, it is the actual difference in the number of active-movement responses that most strikingly distinguishes the two samples. This finding suggests that the nondelinquent controls are more apt to take an active, constructive, and outgoing stance in interpersonal relations.

This use of active movement appears in the fathers of nondelinquents more in their animal responses. The fathers of nondelinquents are significantly more apt to give animal-movement responses than are the fathers of delinquent subjects. The animal-movement response (FM) is usually assumed to indicate underlying attitudes that are of less direct relationship to conscious control. They arise out of the more primitive, less consciously controlled levels of personality. They are less apt to be expressed with mature modulation. Also, all the nondelinquents produced more inanimate-movement responses (m) such as rocket ships or blowing wind than did the delinquent subjects. These responses are sometimes indicative of underlying tensions in more highly differentiated, complex types of personality. The fact that these responses appeared in the nondelinquent sample, especially in the mothers, attests to their generally more open personality patterns compared with the more constrictive ones found among the delinquents.

When we combine all forms of movement—human, animal, and inanimate, active and passive—we find a significant difference beyond the 1 percent level between the total normal and the total delinquent sample. The greatest difference, however, is in the total active movement in all nondelinquents—parents and sons alike.

Perception of Color and Shading in Rorschach Percepts—"Outer Control," or Control of Affectivity and Responsiveness to Stimuli

We find a greater constriction among the delinquent samples in the use of color (beyond the 1 percent level of significance). The sons themselves, however, do not show as significant a difference in the total use of color as do their parents (see table A.4).

Not only do we compare in the Rorschach the overall use of color (Sigma C), but we differentiate among color responses that appear in percepts in which the form is dominant over the color (FC), in percepts where the color dominates the form (CF), or in responses in which the color is perceived with little concern with the form (C). Form-dominant, or FC+ color responses, according to Rorschach assumption, represent a well-modulated, mature control over one's emotion; we find significantly higher FC in the fathers of nondelinquents than in those of delinquents. Interestingly enough, some of the nondelinquent sons produce some poor-quality form-dominant responses. One can say, therefore,

TABLE A.4
Significant Differences in Color and Shading Reactions

	Normals				*Delinquents*			
	Fa.	Mo.	Sons	Total	Fa.	Mo.	Sons	Total
Good form, dominant color (FC +)	1.67*	1.94	1.78*	1.80‡	.93	1.20	1.03	1.06
Poor form, dominant color (FC −)	.17	.06	.44*	.22	.10	.13	.17	.13
Pure color (C)	.06	.11	.39†	.19*	.10	.13	.03	.09
Color symbolism	.17	.11*	.11*	.13	.13	.00	.00	.04
Total color responses	3.28*	3.67†	3.33	3.43‡	2.20	2.37	2.47	2.34
Total shading (Y)	3.17*	3.22	2.28	2.89*	1.96	2.30	2.37	2.21
Texture (FT)	1.44	1.56*	1.17	1.39†	.93	.80	1.07	.93

* ($P < .10$)
† ($P < .05$)
‡ ($P < .01$)

that some of their affect may at times have a forced quality to it; that is, the expression of affect may be somewhat artificially controlled in some of the nondelinquent sons.

The perception of shading and texture is related to a passive sensitivity, according to Rorschach assumptions. Perceptions of diffuse shading can indicate anxiety, whereas attention to the textural details and qualities of the percepts suggests a kind of passive, tactual sensitivity to the outside world, when such responses appear to any significant degree in a record. Consonant with the overall greater openness in the nondelinquent group as contrasted with the constriction of the delinquent group, the total score for *texture* (FT) is higher for the nondelinquent sample. The greatest difference between the two groups is found in the mothers. The overall difference in the *shading* (FY, YF) or *vista* (FV) responses show trends but do not reach significance. The sample as a whole in respect to such variables conforms well to the previous normative samples obtained in 1954 and reported by Murakami (1959, 1962).

AFFECTIVE SYMBOLISM

De Vos has developed a system of objectifying symbolic interpretation of Rorschach responses. His scoring system has a high reliability when utilized by experienced examiners (De Vos, 1952). The affective implications of the responses are scored in five major categories—hostility, anxiety, bodily preoccupa-

TABLE A.5
Mean Differences in Affective Symbolism in Respect to Total Summary Categories and to Specific Subcategory Responses

	Normals				Delinquents			
	Fa.	Mo.	Sons	Total	Fa.	Mo.	Sons	Total
TOTAL PERCENTAGE OF HOSTILE RESPONSES	13.33	8.89	15.33*	12.52	9.83	10.87	10.10	10.27
Hor (oral hostility)	.56*	.39	.50	.48	.17	.20	.30	.22
Hcmpt (competitiveness)	.11	.17†	.39*	.22†	.13	.00	.10	.08
Hh (indirect hostility)	.39	.72	.89*	.67*	.17	.67	.30	.38
Hsm (sadomasochism)	1.00*	.56	.83	.80*	.43	.60	.38	.47
TOTAL PERCENTAGE OF ANXIOUS RESPONSES	16.89	17.50	22.06	18.81	21.90	21.90	24.60	22.80*
Athr (threatening percepts)	1.06	1.78†	2.50	1.78*	.67	.87	2.13	1.22
Aev (evasive percepts)	.28	.11	.11	.17	.57	.43*	.30	.43†
Abal (loss of balance)	.06	.06	.39*	.17	.13	.10	.03	.09
Acnph (counterphobic percepts)	.17	.44*	.06	.22	.20	.13	.23	.19
Agl (dysphoric-depressive percepts)	.56†	.33	.28	.39	.17	.47	.43	.36
TOTAL PERCENTAGE OF BODILY PREOCCUPATION	2.78	3.11	.50	2.12	5.43	2.00	3.60*	3.68
Bb (bone anatomy)	.06	.11	.00	.06	.37†	.23	.53†	.38†
Bdi (disease or decay)	.00	.00	.00	.00	.17	.13	.07	.12
Bs (sexual anatomy)	.00	.12*	.00	.04*	.00	.00	.00	.00

* ($P < .10$)
† ($P < .05$)
‡ ($P < .01$)

tion, dependency, and positive responses—plus a category of "neutral" percepts in which affective material is not sufficiently notable (see table A.1). In contrasting the groups we noted that the delinquent group produced significantly more neutral responses lacking any affective meaning. This neutral tone to the responses is related to the general constriction reflected in the rigidity scores already mentioned and in the results with the major determinants.

TABLE A.5 (*continued*)

	Normals				*Delinquents*			
	Fa.	Mo.	Sons	Total	Fa.	Mo.	Sons	Total
TOTAL PERCENTAGE OF DEPENDENCY PERCEPTS	7.83*	10.00†	8.83‡	8.89‡	4.73	5.57	3.37	4.56
Dcl (clinging or hanging percepts)	.33	.44	.39*	.39*	.20	.23	.13	.19
Dch (childishly toned percepts)	.61†	1.22†	.94†	.93‡	.23	.53	.33	.37
Drel (religious percepts)	.11	.39	.06*	.20	.20	.33	.00	.18
Daut (authority percepts)	.56†	.56	.56‡	.56‡	.10	.37	.10	.19
Dsub (submissive percepts)	.28	.33	.17*	.26	.20	.20	.00	.13
TOTAL PERCENTAGE OF POSITIVE AFFECT	23.67†	25.44‡	20.61†	23.24‡	14.83	15.50	12.77	14.37
Ps (sensual-body percepts)	.56	.56	.67	.59†	.37	.33	.37	.36
Pch (child play)	.44	1.17†	.17	.59†	.30	.30	.20	.27
Prec (recreation activity)	1.17	.94	1.67†	1.26†	.67	.67	.70	.68
Porn (ornamental percepts)	1.61†	1.33	.56†	1.17‡	.40	.73	.20	.44
Pst (striving percepts)	.39	.89*	.83‡	.70‡	.30	.33	.20	.28
Pnar (body narcissism)	.11	.28	.22	.20*	.10	.10	.07	.09
Pcpt (cooperation)	.22	.22	.22	.22†	.13	.07	.03	.08
TOTAL PERCENTAGE OF NEUTRAL PERCEPTS	29.94	32.22	30.22	30.80	37.13*	39.07	41.13†	39.11‡
TOTAL UNPLEASANT AFFECT	3.00	29.33	37.33	33.22	37.20	34.73	38.60	36.84

Being more open, members of the nondelinquent group reveal richer underlying symbolic content of both a positive and a negative nature. Among the fathers of the nondelinquent control one particularly notes the significant appearance of more sadomasochistic and oral hostile percepts.

The mothers and sons in the nondelinquent sample show more "competitive" responses than do the mothers and sons in the delinquent sample (suggesting some sublimation of hostility into competitive achievement). The sons in the nondelinquent group also show a greater percentage of indirect hostile responses compared with the sons in the delinquent group. In fact, the sons in the nondelinquent group, in their totals, show a significantly higher overall score of hostile symbolism than their counterparts.

Our findings that the nondelinquent subjects in effect are capable of giving somewhat more hostile symbolism in their records in contrast with the bland type of responses found in the delinquent records raises a number of questions about the meaning of hostile symbolism in Rorschach percepts. The appearance of hostile material in a small proportion of responses in a record is expected. It does not mean that psychologists consider that an individual making such a response is "hostile" in nature, but rather indicates a capacity for the individual to be sufficiently free internally to countenance periodically his own hostile feelings. That is, the individual does not need to repress or deny in himself certain attitudes either directly or indirectly indicative of hostile feelings. In effect, the nondelinquents are less guarded in this respect than are the delinquent subjects, who, we infer, tend either to unconsciously constrict or suppress such material from their responses or to experience hostility without manifest expression. Given the records as a whole, it is my presumption that we are dealing with automatic constrictive mechanisms rather than some deliberate attempt to dissemble and to avoid giving hostile content to an examiner. In previous research with another sample in Japan, we compared the appearance of violent activities on TAT stories in a sample of delinquent and nondelinquent Japanese subjects, contrasting and comparing them with American delinquent and nondelinquent individuals (De Vos and Murakami, 1974). We found that the two groups did not differ in the overall amount of violence in their fantasy. Peculiarly, the delinquents gave periodic expression to themes of aggression on cards that did not evoke such themes from most respondents. Therefore, we concluded that it is the inappropriate appearance of fantasies of violence that characterize delinquent records, rather than the overall quality of violence in their fantasy.

None of the Rorschach inkblots of themselves have particularly high affective stimulus value. The appearance of any affective response, therefore, is much more dependent on the inner state or attitude of the individual than are TAT cards, where the nature of the cards themselves may suggest some type of affective state to many individuals. The Rorschach test is tapping unconscious material sometimes of a nature that may disturb the individual, so that there may be pervasive perceptual repression. We have the impression from the responses of the delinquent sample that there is a greater constriction of all forms of ideation, including hostile content.

In the "anxious" responses we found a higher total for the delinquent sample than for the nondelinquent, but this higher total is an artifact of our scoring system. Card rejection or "evasive" responses are scored under our "anxious" category and thus contribute to the higher total in the delinquents. Evasive responses are such innocuous replies as the mention of maps or islands. The individual, in effect, gives an innocuous response which requires little form definition.

In line with their greater openness, and our previous statements about certain tendencies toward a more "loose" form of maladjustment in the fathers, the nondelinquents produced a number of disphoric or depressive responses, such as clouds, dead trees, and the like.

In the general category of bodily preoccupation responses, the totals did not differentiate between the two groups. However, there was a significantly greater appearance of bone anatomy in the records of both the fathers and the sons in the delinquent sample. This type of anatomical percept is usually regarded as an example of indirect anxiety. A few records in the delinquent sample manifested aberrant responses about disease or decay, which suggest some deeper psychopathology. These responses must be considered clinically significant because they are almost lacking in normative control records. Since they appear in individuals who are otherwise very constricted, they take on an even stronger emphasis in the few records where they appear. The only exceptional material in the mothers of nondelinquents appears in a few referrals to sexual anatomy. We can infer that in some of these mothers there is some preoccupation with their generative functions, which may suggest a tendency toward hypochondriasis.

In the total of percentages of all forms of unpleasant content (hostility, anxiety, and bodily preoccupation) for the two groups, we find no significant difference. The major difference is in the relative lack of positive or dependent content in the delinquent sample. Instead, the proportion of neutral responses is higher, as is the ratio of unpleasant content material to pleasant material. Responses in the dependent categories are significantly lacking for the delinquents, compared with Japanese records generally.

The cultural differences in Rorschach results fit in with differences in Japanese socialization as discussed elsewhere in this volume. Japanese are apt to give dependency responses more frequently than are Americans. As we have seen in chapter 7, the Japanese are freer, characteristically, to take a positive social attitude toward the maintenance of social or personal dependency. We find that this emphasis on dependency in the control group is significant in contrast with the content produced by both the delinquent parents and their children. The nondelinquent sons are more apt to give childishly toned or religious responses and responses that suggest clinging or hanging on, and to perceive various forms of authority symbols. They also periodically give responses of a submissive nature. This is strong evidence that the nondelinquent sons are more apt to favor social dependency and consciously accept it as part of their personalities. Such responses appear only infrequently in the delinquent subjects. Childishly toned responses are also found in the records of the nondelinquent fathers and mothers. Culturally, the period of childhood is positively perceived by Japanese. One can, if permitted by circumstances, indulge oneself by becoming childish; it is not something that one has to repress.

Consistent with other results, it is the nondelinquent parents and children that give "authority" responses. Authority for many Japanese is perceived positively; the individual finds himself identifying with the strength of a group or with an authority symbol. One can submit to authority without conflict. The individual can take a subordinate position in an authority relationship and perceive such a relationship in positive terms. The members of the families of delinquents *do not* symbolize authority in such positive terms.

What is most significant is how the members of both generations of the nondelinquent group give more responses of positive affect on the Rorschach. Those forms most frequently seen by the sons relate to some type of recreational activity, while the parents more characteristically show interest in aesthetic or ornamental objects. In the original study of De Vos (1952), it was noteworthy how many Issei and Nisei Japanese-Americans, despite obvious personality differences of one kind or another, revealed a positive social interest through positively toned symbolic material. In effect, whatever the psychological or social difficulties encountered, many Japanese evidence an optimistic view of their environment or are ready to project positive attributes into it. The fact that we find significant differences in this respect between delinquent and nondelinquent families again suggests that one of the basic differentiators of the type of personal adjustments of various individuals living in the same socioeconomic circumstances is a greater readiness of the families of nondelinquents to take a positive attitude toward life. In effect, these Rorschach results are directly consonant with the results obtained by examining family cohesion by other means, which we have discussed in detail in this book.

In sum, we find that the Rorschach evidence is a striking confirmation of the incremental influence of personality variables in explaining why individuals are socially conforming or socially deviant. But we must quickly reaffirm our conclusion that it is in the expressed *social attitudes* of the individuals and their perception of the meaning of interpersonal relationships, especially within the family, that we find the most significant differentiation between nondelinquents and delinquents. Differences in interpersonal attitudes, not personality per se, explain best why some families have had to become concerned with the deviant behavior of one of their members.

APPENDIX B

Thematic Apperception Test

The version of the Thematic Apperception Test used in our case studies was previously developed in large-scale work initiated at Nagoya in 1953. We have published normative studies of the results (see Muramatsu, 1962).

The test consists of pictures of persons in ambiguous situations designed to elicit in response various stories which are then analyzed for content and tone. A set of such pictures was first developed by Morgan and Murray at Harvard in about 1935. The idea has since been put into a variety of uses, and the picture content of the tests has often been modified for various types of research. We attempted, in adopting the test for use in Japan, to change as little as possible the cards of the third Harvard Edition, which has proved particularly helpful both in clinical and in research work. The Nagoya edition, or Marui–De Vos Japanese Standard TAT, includes 35 cards, not all of which are used with equal frequency in research, since only a limited number may be administered at any one time to any individual. The complete set includes 5 of the original Murray cards without modification, 14 cards from the original series with minor changes of face or background, and 16 new cards on themes potentially valuable for eliciting personality variables or pertinent value attitudes. In our research with the Arakawa families, we used Cards 1, 2, 3, 4, 6M, 7M, 8M, 9, 11, 13, 18, 22, and 27.

As illustrated, Card JM1, a boy with a violin, is used extensively to elicit stories of achievement motivation. Card J2, a farm scene, elicits stories of family interaction, ideas of the future, and stories of ambition or responsibility. Card J3, an original Murray card of a young figure slumped against a couch, elicits a wide variety of stories, as is illustrated in our case history examples. J4 is an interaction between a young man and a woman, often depicted as a marital quarrel. J6M is usually seen as an interaction between an aging mother and an adult son. J7M, an older man and a younger man, is seen as some kind of cooperative or advisory relationship between two men. J8M is a scene with a dreamlike quality, with figures in the background either operating on or attacking a prone figure, and a young boy in the foreground, who could be either dreaming or witnessing what is going on behind. J9 is a family scene indicative of some tension, with a young adult in the foreground and an aging woman in the background, with two observing younger women in between. J13 is another modified card from the original Murray set, of a seminude reclining woman and a distraught male in the foreground. J18, also adopted from the Murray set, is a woman with hands on the throat of another figure.

Cards J11 and J22 were taken from a set developed at Waseda University. J11 depicts what is seen very often as a boy eavesdropping on a older woman, usually a mother. J22 depicts a crying child on a Japanese street, standing between two figures, a man and a woman, who face in opposite directions. J27 is a picture, developed in Nagoya, of teenagers in school uniforms meeting in front of a coffeeshop.

Later De Vos and Murakami published (1974) some of the results of a systematic comparison between the delinquent and the nondelinquent sample.

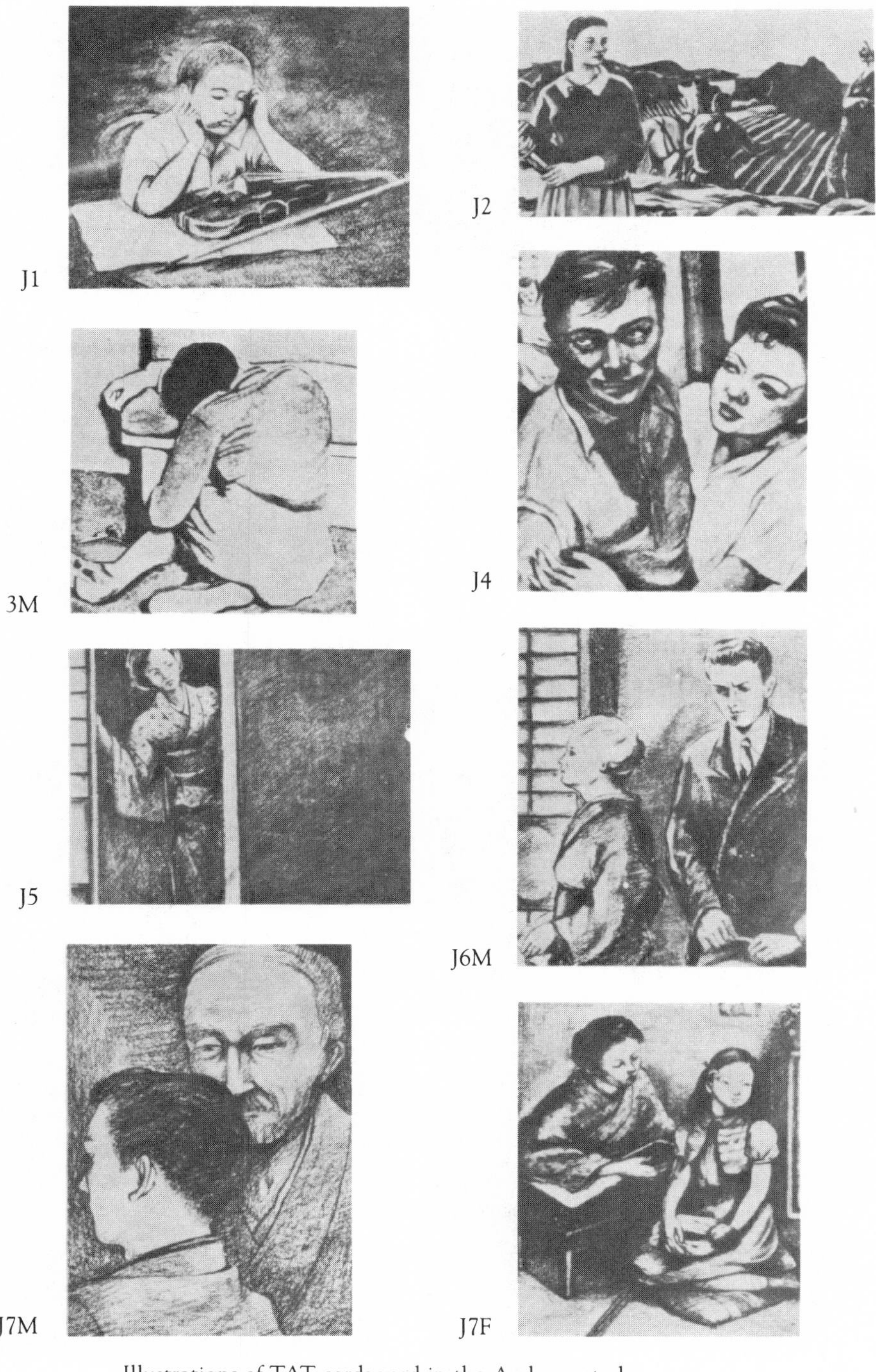

Illustrations of TAT cards used in the Arakawa study.

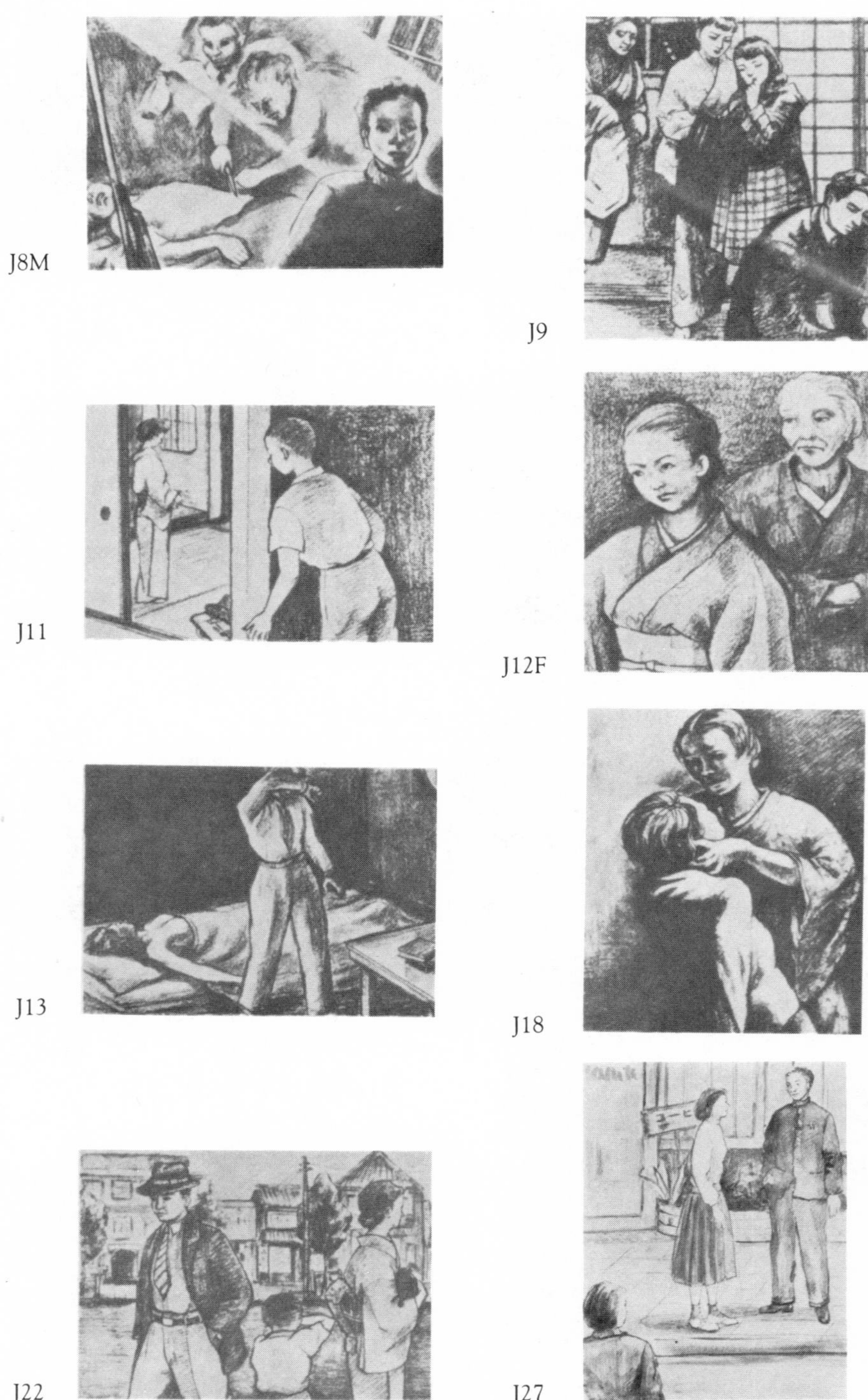

J8M

J9

J11

J12F

J13

J18

J22

J27

APPENDIX C

The Arakawa Cases

(Code Numbers, Pseudonyms, and Citation by Chapter)

NORMALS (19 FAMILIES)			DELINQUENTS (20 FAMILIES)			ISOLATES (11 FAMILIES)		
Code Number	*Name*	*Chapter Cited*	*Code Number*	*Name*	*Chapter Cited*	*Code Number*	*Name*	*Chapter Cited*
N-1	Sakai	11	D-1	Fukui	6	I-1	Iriyama	
N-2	Sakiyama	6	D-2	Fukuyama	12	I-2	Ichitani	7, 8
N-3	Segawa	10	D-3	Furukawa		I-3	Itahashi	6
N-4	Shimizu	8	D-4	Fumita		I-4	Iida	5, 6, 7, 8, 9
N-5	Sonotani	6	D-5	Fuchitani	6	I-5	Ikawa	13
N-6	Sata		D-6	Funahashi	5, 7, 9	I-6	Ikuta	7, 8, 9
N-7	Shoda		D-7	Fudasaka	6, 7, 8	I-7	Ishisaka	6, 7, 9
N-8	Shiratori	7,8	D-8	Fukuhara	5, 6, 7, 8, 9	I-8	Ishino	8
N-9	Saitama	8	D-9	Fuchino	6, 7, 8, 9	I-9	Igayama	8, 9
N-10	Seki	5, 6, 8	D-10	Fukitomi	7, 9	I-10	Imura	6, 7
N-11	Sorai	6, 8	D-11	Tsujioka		I-11	Ihashi	5, 6, 7, 8
N-12	Sayama	5, 6, 7	D-12	Tajima				
N-13	Sumi	8	D-13	Tokuda	8			
N-14	Sakimoto		D-14	Terayama	8			
N-15	Shinojima		D-15	Taruki				
N-16	Sahime		D-16	Tsunada	7, 9			
N-17	Sasagawa		D-17	Torihashi	5, 7, 8, 9			
N-18	Sogi		D-18	Teramoto	8, 9			
N-19	Sanosaka		D-19	Tozori	5, 7, 8			
			D-20	Tayama	5, 6, 7, 8, 9			

Bibliography

Arakawa Ward Office
1963 Arakawa-ku no Seikatsu to Fukushi (Life and Welfare in Arakawa Ward). Tokyo: Arakawa Ward Office.

Banister H., and M. Ravden
1944 The Problem Child and His Environment. British Journal of Psychology, vol. 34, part 2.

Barker, Roger
1968 Ecological Psychology: Concepts and Methods for Studying the Environment of Human Behavior. Stanford: Stanford University Press.

Bayley, David
1976 Forces of Order. Berkeley and Los Angeles: University of California Press.

Beardsley, Richard K., John W. Hall, and R. E. Ward
1959 Village Japan. Chicago: University of Chicago Press.

Bennett, Ivy Lee
1960 Delinquent and Neurotic Children. New York: Basic Books.

Bennett, John W., and Ishino, Iwao
1963 Paternalism in the Japanese Economy. Minneapolis: University of Minnesota Press.

Blood, Robert O., Jr.
1967 Love, Marriage and Arranged Marriage. New York: Free Press.

Bowlby, J.
1947 Forty-four Juvenile Thieves. London: Balliere, Tindall, and Cox.

Breckinridge, S. P., and E. Abbott
1912 The Delinquent Child and the Home. Philadelphia: Fill.

Bruner, Edward
1976 Some Observations on Cultural Change and Psychological Stress in Indonesia. *In* Responses to Change: Society, Culture and Personality. G. A. De Vos, ed. Pp. 234–252. New York: D. Van Nostrand.

Burlingham, D., and A. Freud
1942 Young Children in Wartime: A Year's Work in a Residential War Nursery. London: Allen and Unwin.

Burt, C. L.
1944 The Young Delinquent. 4th ed. Bickley, Kent: University of London Press.

Campbell, M.
1932 The Effect of a Broken Home Upon the Child in the School. Journal of Educational Sociology 5(5):274–281.

Carr-Saunders, A. M., H. Mannheim, and E. F. Rhodes
1942 Young Offenders. Cambridge, England: Cambridge University Press.

Caudill, William
1952 Japanese American Personality and Acculturation. Genetic Psychological Monograph 45:3–102.
1964 Sibling Rank and Style of Life Among Japanese Psychiatric Patients. *In* Proceedings of the Joint Meeting of the Japanese Society of Psychiatry and Neurology and the American Psychiatric Association. Haruo Akimoto, ed. Published as Folio Psychiatrica et Neurologica, Supplement 7. Tokyo. Pp. 35–40.

Caudill, William, and David Plath
1966 Who Sleeps by Whom? Parent-Child Involvement in Urban Japanese Families. Psychiatry 32(3):225–236.

Caudill, William, and Harry A. Scarr
1962 Japanese Value Orientation and Culture Change. Ethnology 1:91–93.

Caudill, William, and Carmi Schooler
1969 Symptom Patterns Among Japanese Psychiatric Patients. *In* Mental Health in Asia and the Pacific. W. Caudill and T. Lin, eds. Pp. 114–147. Honolulu: East-West Center Press.

Caudill, William, and Helen Weinstein
1969 Maternal Care and Infant Behavior in Japan and America. Psychiatry 32(1):12–43.

Craig, Albert M., and Donald H. Shively, eds.
1970 Personality in Japanese History. Berkeley and Los Angeles: University of California Press.

De Vos, George A.
1952 A Quantitative Approach to Affective Symbolism in Rorschach Responses. Journal of Projective Techniques 16(2):133–150.
1954 A Comparison of the Personality Differences in Two Generations of Japanese Americans by Means of the Rorschach Test. Nagoya Journal of Medical Science 17(3):153–265. Reprinted 1966 in University of Hawaii Social Science Research Institute, Reprint 14.
1955 A Quantitative Rorschach Assessment of Maladjustment and Rigidity in Acculturating Japanese Americans. Genetic Psychology Monographs, vol. 52, Pp. 51–87.
1960 The Relations of Guilt Toward Parents to Achievement and Arranged Marriage Among the Japanese. Psychiatry 23(3):301–387.
1961 Symbolic Analysis in the Cross-Cultural Study of Personality. *In* Studying Personality Cross-Culturally. Bert Kaplan, ed. Pp. 599–634. Evanston, Ill.: Row, Peterson.
1973 Socialization for Achievement. Berkeley and Los Angeles: University of California Press.

De Vos, George A., ed.
1976 Responses to Change: Society, Culture, and Personality. New York: D. Van Nostrand.

De Vos, George A., and Orin Borders
1979 A Rorschach Comparison of Delinquent and Nondelinquent Japanese Family Members. Journal of Psychological Anthropology 2(4):425–441.

De Vos, George A., and Horace Miner

1959 Oasis and Casbah: A Study in Acculturative Stress. *In* Culture and Mental Health. Marvin K. Opler, ed., Pp. 333–350. New York: Macmillan.

De Vos, George A., and K. Mizushima

1973 Delinquency and Social Change in Modern Japan. *In* Socialization for Achievement. G. De Vos. Berkeley and Los Angeles: University of California Press.

De Vos, George A., and Eiji Murakami

1974 Violence and Aggression in Fantasy: A Comparison of American and Japanese Lower-Class Youth. *In* Youth, Socialization, and Mental Health. William P. Lebra, ed. Pp. 153–177. Honolulu: University Press of Hawaii.

De Vos, George A., and Hiroshi Wagatsuma

1966 Japan's Invisible Race: Caste in Culture and Personality. Berkeley and Los Angeles: University of California Press.

1970 Status and Role Behavior in Changing Japan. *In* Sex Roles in Changing Society. G. H. Seward and R. C. Williamson, eds. Pp. 334–370. New York: Random House.

Doi, L. Takeo

1962 Amae: A Key Concept for Understanding Japanese Personality Structure. *In* Japanese Culture. R. J. Smith and R. K. Beardsley, eds. Pp. 132–139. New York: Wenner-Gren Foundation for Anthropological Research.

1966 Japanese Psychology, Dependency Need, and Mental Health. Paper presented at the Conference on Mental Health in Asia and the Pacific, East-West Center, Honolulu

1971 Amae no Kōzō (The Anatomy of Dependency). Tokyo: Kobunsho.

Dore, Ronald P.

1958 City Life in Japan. Berkeley and Los Angeles: University of California Press.

Eliot, M.

1928 Delinquent Girls in Pennsylvania. New York: Macmillan.

Falstein, E. I.

1958 The Psychodynamics of Male Adolescent Delinquency. American Journal of Orthopsychiatry 28:613–626.

Fenichel, Otto

1945 The Psychoanalytic Theory of Neurosis. New York: W. W. Norton.

Fisher, S.

1950 Patterns of Personality Rigidity and Some of Their Determinants. Psychological Monographs, vol. 64, no. 1.

Freud, Sigmund

1955 The Economic Problems of Masochism. Collected Papers, vol. 2. New York: Basic Books

Friedlander, K.

1949 Neurosis and Home Background: A Preliminary Report. Psychoanalytic Study of the Child 3(4):424.

Gibney, Frank

1953 Five Gentlemen of Japan: The Portrait of a Nation's Character. New York: Farrar, Straus and Young.

Giffin, M. E., A. M. Johnson, and E. M. Litin
1954 Specific Factors Determining Antisocial Acting Out. American Journal of Orthopsychiatry 24:668–684.
Glueck, S., and E. Glueck
1950 Unravelling Juvenile Delinquency. Cambridge, Mass.: Harvard University Press.
Healy, W., and A. Bronner
1926 Delinquents and Criminals. New York: Macmillan.
Hewitt, L. E., and R. L. Jenkins
1946 Fundamental Patterns of Maladjustment. Springfield, Ill.: State of Illinois.
Higuchi, K.
1953 Sengo ni okeru Hikōshōnen no Seishin-igakuteki Kenkyu (Psychiatric Study of Juvenile Delinquency After the War). Judicial Report, vol. 41, no. 1, entire issue.
Hsu, Francis
1975 Iemoto, the Heart of Japan. New York: Halsted Press.
Inazo, Nitobe
1905 Bushido: The Soul of Japan. New York: Knickerbocker Press.
Inkeles, A.
1976 The Fate of Personal Adjustment in the Process of Urbanization. *In* Responses to Change: Society, Culture, and Personality. G. De Vos, ed. Pp. 214–233. New York: D. Van Nostrand.
Jacobson, E.
1957 Denial and Repression. Journal of the American Psychoanalytic Association 5:61–92.
Johnson, A. M.
1949 Sanctions of Superego Lacunae of Adolescents. *In* Searchlights on Delinquency. K. R. Eisler, ed. New York: International University Press.
Johnson, A. M., and D. B. Robinson
1957 The Sexual Deviant (Sexual Psychopath): Causes, Treatment, Prevention. Journal of the American Medical Association 164:1559–1565.
Johnson, A. M., and S. A. Szurek
1952 The Genesis of Antisocial Acting Out in Children and Adults. Psychoanalytic Quarterly, vol. 21, no. 3.
Karpman, Ben
1948 Milestones in the Advancement of Knowledge in the Psychopathology of Delinquency and Crime. *In* Orthopsychiatry, 1932–1948. E. Lowrey and P. Sloane, eds. Pp. 100–189. Menasha, Wis.: Banta.
Kiefer, Christie W.
1967 Social Change and Personality in a White-Collar Danchi. Ph.D. dissertation, Department of Anthropology, University of California, Berkeley.
Kobayashi, S., et al.
1963 Mondaiji no Kōdō-Shōjō-gun no Bunseki—Haikeibetsu Kōsatsu (Background of Problem Children). Report on Annual Meeting of Japanese Psychological Association. P. 404.
Lanham, Betty B.
1956 Aspects of Child Care in Japan: Preliminary Report. *In* Personal Character

and Cultural Milieu. D. G. Haring, ed. Pp. 565–583. Syracuse: Syracuse University Press.

Lebra, William, ed.

1972 Transcultural Research in Mental Health. Honolulu: University of Hawaii Press.

Lee, Changsoo, and George De Vos

1981 Koreans in Japan: Ethnic Conflict and Accommodation. Berkeley and Los Angeles: University of California Press.

Levy, David

1934 Experiments on the Sucking Reflex and Social Behavior of Dogs. American Journal of Orthopsychiatry 4:203–209.

Lewis, Oscar

1959 Five Families: Mexican Case Studies in the Culture of Poverty. New York: Basic Books.

1966 La Vida: A Puerto Rican Family in the Culture of Poverty. New York: Random House.

Makino, K.

1953 Relation Between Tension of Autonomic Nervous System and Character in Problem Juveniles. Japanese Journal of Corrective Medicine 2:1–11.

McCord, W., and J. McCord

1959 Origins of Crime. New York: Columbia University Press.

Michaels, Joseph C.

1938 The Incidence of Enuresis and Age of Cessation in 100 Delinquents and 100 Sibling Controls. American Journal of Orthopsychiatry. 7:406–411.

1961 Enuresis in Murderous Aggressive Children and Adolescents. Archives of General Psychiatry 5:490–493.

Michaels, Joseph C., and S. E. Goodman

1939 The Incidence of Enuresis and Age of Cessation in 1,000 Neuropsychiatric Patients, with a Discussion on the Relation Between Enuresis and Delinquency. American Journal of Orthopsychiatry 9:59–65.

Mizushima, Keiichi

1956 Hikoshonen no Shakaiteki Yogo ni kansuru Kenkyu (A Study of the Prognosis of Social Adjustment of Delinquents). Japanese Journal of Educational Psychology 3(2):49–58.

1964 Hikōshōnen no Kaimei (Understanding Juvenile Delinquents). Tokyo: Shin Shoken.

Murakami, Eiji

1959 A Normative Study of Japanese Rorschach Responses. Rorschach Kenkyu: Rorschachiana Japanica 2:39–85.

1962 Special Characteristics of Japanese Personality Based on Rorschach Test Results. *In* Nihonjin-Bunka to Pāsonarite no Jisshōteki Kenkyū (The Japanese: An Empirical Study in Culture and Personality). Tsuneo Muramatsu, ed. Pp. 206–235. Tokyo and Nagoya: Reimei Shobō.

Muramatsu, Tsuneo, ed.

1962 Nihonjin-Bunka to Pāsonariti no Jisshōteki Kenkyū (The Japanese: An Empirical Study in Culture and Personality) Tokyo and Nagoya: Reimei Shobō.

Nakane, Chie
1970 Japanese Society. London: Weidenfeld and Nicolson.

Nye, F. I.
1958 Family Relationships and Delinquent Behavior. New York: John Wiley.

Ono, Z.
1958 Hikō-genin ni kansuru Jisshoteki Kenkyu (An Empirical Study of the Causes of Delinquency). Family Court Investigator's Report, vol. 3, entire issue.

Oura, K.
1957 Hikōshōnen to Katei (Delinquent Juveniles and the Family). Family Court Monthly 9:98–132.

Reckless, W. C., and M. Smith
1932 Juvenile Delinquency. New York: McGraw-Hill.

Reik, Theodore
1941 Masochism in Modern Man. M. H. Beigel and G. M. Kurth, trans. New York: Grove Press.

Rexford, E. N., et al.
1957 The Influence of Unresolved Maternal Oral Conflict Upon Impulsive Acting Out in Young Children. American Journal of Orthopsychiatry 27: 75–87.

Reynolds, David
1980 The Quiet Therapies. Honolulu: University of Hawaii Press.

Sasaki, Y.
1962 Hikō ni okeru Katei, Kinrin, Kōdō Keikō no Kanrensei (Relations Between Family, Neighborhood, and Behavior Traits in Delinquency). Choken Kiyo 1(1):83–93.

Satake, R., et al.
1957 Symposium on EEG of Delinquents and Criminals. Journal of Corrective Medicine 6:111–186.

Shaw, C. N., and H. D. McKay
1931 Social Factors in Juvenile Delinquency, vol. 2, no. 13. Washington, D.C.: National Commission on Law Observance and Enforcement.

Slawson, J.
1926 The Delinquent Boy. Boston: R. G. Badger.

Sofue, T.
1976 Postwar Changes in Japanese Urbanization and Related Psychological Problems. *In* Responses to Change: Society, Culture, and Personality, G. De Vos, ed. Pp. 253–268. New York: D. Van Nostrand.

Sōrifu Seishōnen Taisaku Honbu (Prime Minister's Office, Youth Headquarters), ed.
1975 Seishōnen no Rūru Kan-Shakai Kihan Chōsa Hōkoku Sho (Youth's Views of the Rules—A Research Report on Social Norms). Tokyo: The Prime Minister's Office, Government of Japan.

Suzuki, T.
1957 Hikōshōnen to Katei (Delinquent Juveniles and the Family). Family Court Report 50:105–188.

Takemura, H.
1953 Sociological Study of Juvenile Delinquency. Judicial Report 6(4):221.

Tani, T.
1929 Shōnen Hanzai no Seishin-igakuteki Kenkyu (Psychiatric Study of Juvenile Offense). Japanese Journal of Psychiatry and Neurology 31(1):38–50.

Tatezawa, Tokuhiro
1953 The Function of Family Court Probation Officer and Prediction of Juvenile Delinquency. Journal of Case Study, no. 2.

Tsubota, M.
1955 Keibo to Mondai no Seinen (Stepmothers and Problem Adolescents). Japanese Journal of Case Studies 32:36–41.

Ushikubo, H.
1956 Hikōshōnen no Kateiteki Haikei (Family Background of Juvenile Delinquents). Penal Administration 67(11):21–31.

Vogel, Ezra
1965 Japan's New Middle Class: The Salary Man and His Family in Tokyo Suburbs. Berkeley and Los Angeles: University of California Press.

Wagatsuma, Hiroshi
1970 Study of Personality and Behavior in Japanese Society and Culture. *In* Study of Japan in the Behavioral Sciences. E. Norbeck and S. Parman, eds. Rice University Studies 56(4):53–55.

Wagatsuma, Hiroshi, and George A. De Vos
1980 Arakawa Ward: Urban Growth and Modernization. *In* The Cultural Context: Essays in Honor of Edward Norbeck. Rice University Studies 66(1): 201–224.

Warner, W. Lloyd, et al.
1963 Yankee City. Chicago: University of Chicago Press.

Warner, W. Lloyd, and J. C. Abegglen
1955 Occupational Mobility in American Business and Industry. Minneapolis: University of Minnesota Press.

Weeks, H. A.
1940 Male and Female Broken Home Rates by Types of Delinquency. American Sociological Review 5(4):601–609.

Weeks, H. A., and M. D. Smith
1939 Juvenile Delinquency and Broken Homes in Spokane, Washington. Social Forces 18(1):48–55.

Yoshimasu, S.
1952 Hanzai Shinrigaku (Criminal Psychology). Tokyo: Tōyō Shokan.

Young, Kimball
1947 An Outline for Writing a Case History. *In* Personality and Problems of Adjustment. 7th ed. Pp. 819–824. New York: F. S. Crofts.

Index

Designer:	Sandy Drooker
Compositor:	G&S Typesetters, Inc.
Text:	Linotron 202 Goudy Old Style
Display:	Phototypositor Goudy Old Style
Printer:	Braun-Brumfield, Inc.
Binder:	Braun-Brumfield, Inc.